Artificial Intelligence and Government

Stephen Kwamena Aikins ·
Tamara Dimitrijevska-Markoski
Editors

Artificial Intelligence and Government

Examining the Roles and Uses of AI in Enhancing Government Operations

Springer

Editors
Stephen Kwamena Aikins
School of Public Affairs
University of South Florida
Tampa, FL, USA

Tamara Dimitrijevska-Markoski
School of Public Affairs
University of South Florida
Tampa, FL, USA

ISBN 978-3-032-12343-5 ISBN 978-3-032-12344-2 (eBook)
https://doi.org/10.1007/978-3-032-12344-2

This Springer imprint is published by the registered company Springer Nature Switzerland AG
The registered company address is: Gewerbestrasse 11, 6330 Cham, Switzerland

Preface

This book was born from a question that continues to echo across public institutions worldwide: How can governments harness the power of artificial intelligence without compromising the values of public service?

In recent years, the proliferation of AI in the public sector has accelerated. Chatbots handle citizen queries. Predictive analytics inform emergency response and social service delivery. Machine learning algorithms support urban planning, fraud detection, and even policy forecasting. Yet with these advances come serious concerns: What happens when algorithms replicate bias? Who is accountable for automated decisions? Can public agencies maintain transparency in the face of increasingly complex technologies?

Artificial Intelligence and Government was conceived as a response to these tensions. It brings together an international group of scholars and practitioners committed to examining AI's role in transforming governance, while safeguarding public values.

The book is structured in three parts. **Part I** sets the stage by examining frameworks for AI adoption in government, highlighting not just technical readiness but also ethical and institutional considerations. These chapters emphasize that technology alone is insufficient; human-centered design, regulatory foresight, and stakeholder engagement are essential to successful implementation.

Part II explores AI in action. Whether through generative deliberation platforms, AI-enhanced emergency management, or data-driven urban infrastructure, these chapters reveal how governments are innovating with AI while confronting the challenges of inclusion, bias, and trust. Importantly, they highlight the dual nature of AI: as a tool that can democratize access and accelerate services, but also as a system that can entrench inequality if not carefully managed.

Part III offers a philosophical and forward-looking critique. It asks not just how AI should be deployed, but why, where, and for whom. The chapters in this section examine foundational questions about democratic legitimacy, public accountability, and regulatory design, setting the stage for a future-oriented discussion of AI governance.

What unites the chapters in this book is a shared commitment to public values. AI in government is not merely about automation—it is about transformation. But transformation must be guided by ethics, equity, and institutional integrity.

This book is intended for a wide readership. Scholars of public administration and political science will find rich theoretical contributions. Public servants and policymakers will encounter actionable insights and frameworks. Technologists, ethicists, legal experts, and civil society advocates will find arguments that challenge and inform their perspectives.

Above all, we hope this volume contributes to a global conversation—one that puts people at the center of technological governance. If AI is to shape the future of government, let it be a future rooted in justice, inclusivity, and democratic accountability.

Tampa, USA

Stephen Kwamena Aikins
Tamara Dimitrijevska-Markoski

Contents

Editors and Contributors

About the Editors

Dr. Stephen Kwamena Aikins is an Associate Professor and a former Director of the Master of Public Administration program in the School of Public Affairs at the University of South Florida. He has private and public sector experience working in various capacities in management, accounting, and auditing for nearly twenty years, ten of which were spent in the financial services industry. During the 2016/2017 academic year, he served as a Fulbright Scholar in Ghana, where he taught graduate-level courses at the Ghana Institute of Management and Public Administration and co-trained government of Ghana procurement officers on international best practices. His teaching and research interests include government technology, e-government, public budgeting and financial management, government auditing, financial crisis and regulatory governance, and political economy.

He has published in various academic journals, including the*British Journal of Educational Technology, Local Government Studies, International Journal of Public Administration, International Journal of Public Administration in the Digital Age, Public Finance and Management, Journal of Public Budgeting, Accounting and Financial Management, State and Local Government Review, and International Public Management Review*. He is the editor of *Managing E-government Projects: Concepts, Issues and Best Practices* and the co-editor of *Web 2.0 Technologies and Democratic Governance: Politics, Policy and Management Implications*. He holds a B.Sc. degree in accounting from the University of Ghana, as well as an MBA in accounting and finance, an MS in management information systems, and a Ph.D. in public administration from the University of Nebraska. He also holds multiple professional certifications in public accountancy, information systems auditing, risk management, and business management.

Dr. Tamara Dimitrijevska-Markoski earned her Ph.D. in Public Affairs: Governance and Policy Research from the University of Central Florida in 2017 and is now an Assistant Professor of Public Administration in the School of Public Affairs at the University of South Florida. Before joining USF, she was a core MPPA faculty member in the Department of Political Science and Public

Administration at Mississippi State University. Her primary research expertise is in performance measurement and management, local governments, collaborative service delivery, and public management. Her research has been published in *Public Administration Review*, *Administration and Society*, *Public Performance and Management Review*, *Public Administration Quarterly*, *Local Government Studies*, *Public Integrity*, *International Journal of Public Performance Management*, *International Journal of Public Policy*, *Public Organization Review*, and others.

She was Treasurer for the ASPA Section on Public Performance and Management (SPPM) and is an active board member of the section. Most recently, her co-authored article, "Service Delivery During Crises: The Effects of Organizational Capacity, Collaboration, and Public Service Motivation on Organizational Resilience," received the Best Article Award from the ASPA's Section on Professional and Organizational Development and Public Administration Quarterly.

Contributors

Edmund P. Adu Department of Political Science, Arkansas State University, Jonesboro, AR, USA

Stephen Kwamena Aikins School of Public Affairs, University of South Florida, Tampa, FL, USA

Lucas Anastasiou The Open University, Milton Keynes, UK

Jubilee T. Apalowo Department of Political Science and Public Administration, Mississippi State University, Starkville, MS, USA

Alexandra Apostolopoulou Novelcore, Athens, Greece

Annus Azhar School of Public Affairs, Arizona State University, Phoenix, USA

Marcel Becker Chair for Information and Communication Management, German University of Administrative Science Speyer, Speyer, Germany

Elena Cabrio INRIA Centre de Recherche Sophia Antipolis Méditerranée, Université Côte d'Azur, Valbonne, France

Grazia Concilio Department of Architecture and Urban Studies, Politecnico di Milano, Milan, Italy

Claudia Coppola Universita' della Svizzera Italiana, Lugano, Switzerland

Anna De Liddo The Open University, Milton Keynes, UK

Tamara Dimitrijevska-Markoski School of Public Affairs, University of South Florida, Tampa, FL, USA

George Domalis Novelcore, Athens, Greece

Ioannis Efstathiou Novelcore, Athens, Greece

Sofiane Elguendouze INRIA Centre de Recherche Sophia Antipolis Méditerranée, Université Côte d'Azur, Valbonne, France

Kontos Gerasimos University of Aegean, Mitilini, Greece

Sara Greco Universita' della Svizzera Italiana, Lugano, Switzerland

Chiara Jermini Universita' della Svizzera Italiana, Lugano, Switzerland

Nikos Karacapilidis IMIS Lab, University of Patras, Patras, Greece

Nikos Karacapilidis Novelcore, Athens, Greece

Ioannis E. Livieris Novelcore, Athens, Greece;
Department of Business and Organization Administration, University of Peloponnese, Kalamata, Greece

Ilaria Mariani Department of Design, Politecnico di Milano, Milan, Italy

Laura N. Montoya Accel AI Institute, San Francisco, CA, USA

Michael A. O. Ntow Department of Political Science and Public Administration, Mississippi State University, Starkville, MS, USA

Julius A. Nukpezah Department of Political Science and Public Administration, Mississippi State University, Starkville, MS, USA

Ringo Ossewaarde Department of Public Administration, University of Twente, Enschede, The Netherlands

Abraham Ramos-Torres Universidad Central de Venezuela, Accel AI Institute, Caracas, Venezuela

Francesca Rizzo Department of Design, Politecnico di Milano, Milan, Italy

Rodrigo Sandoval-Almazan Autonomous University of the State of Mexico, Toluca, Mexico

Maciej M. Sokołowski Faculty of Policy Management, Keio University Shonan Fujisawa Campus, Fujisawa, Japan;
Carey Law School, University of Pennsylvania, Philadelphia, USA

Ismail Soujaa Albany State University, Albany, USA

Jie Tao Tarleton State University—Fort Worth, Stephenville, USA

Dimitris Tsakalidis Novelcore, Athens, Greece

Serena Villata Novelcore, Athens, Greece;
Center National de la Recherche Scientifique—Délégation Côte D'azur, INRIA Centre de Recherche Sophia Antipolis Méditerranée, Valbonne, France

Bernd W. Wirtz Chair for Information and Communication Management, German University of Administrative Science Speyer, Speyer, Germany

Charalabidis Yannis University of Aegean, Mitilini, Greece

Introduction: Artificial Intelligence and Government

1

Stephen Kwamena Aikins and Tamara Dimitrijevska-Markoski

We are standing at the edge of a profound transformation driven by algorithms and data, where public institutions leverage transformative technologies to meet civic expectations in the digital age. Artificial intelligence (AI) is no longer a futuristic ambition. It is a present-day tool reshaping how governments anticipate problems, design policies, and engage with their citizens. Once confined to the pages of science fiction, AI has emerged as a defining force of our era. Its silent algorithms now orchestrate everyday conveniences, from digital assistants to navigation systems, but its greater impact is yet to unfold: the reshaping of government itself. Across the world, the momentum is building. Countries are drafting national AI strategies, cities are deploying smart infrastructure, and public agencies are experimenting with digital assistants, data analytics, and predictive models. Some view AI as a cost-saving tool; others see it as a gateway to a more inclusive, responsive state. Both are correct, but only if guided by thoughtful design and democratic oversight.

At the intersection of technology and public service lies a historic opportunity and an equally profound challenge. Governments around the world are grappling with the demands of complex societies: aging populations, ballooning budget deficits, climate volatility, economic inequality, and rapid urbanization. Citizens demand not only faster services but fairer systems, transparent processes, and decisions rooted in data rather than inertia. AI offers a new toolkit for governance in the twenty-first century. It presents the possibility of moving from reactive

S. K. Aikins (✉) · T. Dimitrijevska-Markoski
School of Public Affairs, University of South Florida, Tampa, FL, USA
e-mail: saikins@usf.edu

T. Dimitrijevska-Markoski
e-mail: markoski@usf.edu

S. K. Aikins and T. Dimitrijevska-Markoski (eds.), *Artificial Intelligence and Government*, https://doi.org/10.1007/978-3-032-12344-2_1

administration to anticipatory governance, from static rules to adaptive systems. As governments integrate AI into decision-making and service delivery, they do so within a complex web of socio-technical considerations. Imagine a government that not only responds to emergencies but also predicts and prevents them; that not only processes applications but truly understands the needs. That does not just follow laws but evolves with the society it serves.

What if governments could predict traffic before the jam, detect health problems before symptoms appear, or respond to your questions in seconds, day or night? These are no longer dreams. Thanks to AI, they are becoming part of everyday public life. AI is the engine behind smart cities, faster services, and more personalized support. It helps governments work more efficiently, but also more fairly if done right. Whether it is a chatbot that helps you find housing or a program that monitors school attendance to support at-risk students, AI is quietly changing how we interact with public institutions. But the significance of AI in government extends beyond efficiency. It challenges the very notion of public authority. When decisions are informed, or even made, by algorithms, new questions arise. That is, these advances come with legitimate concerns and big questions. Who makes sure the AI is fair? What does accountability look like? Who programs the values into these systems? How do we know our data is safe? How do we ensure equity, privacy, and justice in a world increasingly run by data? The transformative promise of AI and the concerns raised in the above constitute the driving force behind this edited volume. In the following section, we discuss the purpose of *AI and Government* and how it addresses some of the above concerns.

1 The Purpose of AI and Government

The book *Artificial Intelligence and Government* captures an essential, timely discourse at the intersection of public governance and technological innovation. It reflects not only the promise of AI in transforming public administration but also the growing necessity for public institutions to engage critically and responsibly with technological advancements. Governments worldwide are under increasing pressure to modernize their operations, improve service delivery, and address complex societal challenges. AI, as a general-purpose technology, offers unprecedented tools for prediction, automation, and data-driven decision-making that can enhance governmental efficiency and responsiveness. However, this promise comes with risks. The proliferation of AI in government is accompanied by significant concerns about ethics, accountability, and democratic oversight. As noted by Kuziemski and Misuraca (2020), the unchecked use of automated decision-making can erode public trust, particularly in democratic contexts where transparency and citizen participation are paramount. This book, therefore, is not merely about technological adoption but an invocation to examine deeply the philosophical, legal, administrative, and practical implications of AI within the machinery of government.

AI is not just about technology. It is about how we live together, solve problems, and advance the cause of humanity. This edited volume critically examines the expanding interface between AI technologies and public sector operations. Written by experts around the globe, it presents a multifaceted narrative that evaluates AI's potential to transform governance structures, policy processes, and public service delivery mechanisms, while critically examining the challenges of AI adoption in the public sector and proposing solutions to address them. Additionally, it examines AI not just as a technical phenomenon, but as an institutional actor—shaping norms, influencing outcomes, and redefining what it means to govern. As the global momentum builds through national strategies, smart city initiatives, and digital transformation roadmaps, policymakers have a rare window to shape the future of governance. This is not about replacing people with machines. It is about using intelligent systems to enhance human judgment, augment public services, and rebuild trust in institutions. The AI era in governance is not optional. It is inevitable. However, the choice before us is not whether to adopt it, but how to lead with it responsibly and ethically. In the next section, we discuss some of the types of AI used in government, the dilemmas governments face, and some of the national AI strategies and regulatory responses.

2 Understanding Artificial Intelligence

Artificial intelligence refers to the development of computer systems capable of performing tasks that typically require human intelligence. These tasks include learning from data, understanding natural language, visual perception, reasoning, decision-making, and problem-solving. As AI technologies mature, they increasingly permeate sectors from healthcare to transportation, and notably, governance. AI technologies such as machine learning (ML), deep learning, natural language processing (NLP), and predictive analytics have become foundational components of modern digital governance. In this regard, AI is redefining the structures, operations, and accountability frameworks of public institutions worldwide. In recognition of this reality, governments seeking to enhance service delivery, optimize internal processes, and increase responsiveness are increasingly relying on these AI technologies to enhance government operations.

Machine learning, a subset of AI, involves algorithms that improve their performance by learning from data patterns to make predictions or decisions. In public administration, ML has been used in predictive policing, healthcare resource allocation, fraud detection, and transportation planning. For example, the United Kingdom employs ML models in public health forecasting, while USA federal agencies use it for cybersecurity threat detection (Pencheva & Esteve, 2020). Sethi et al. (2025) assert that in addition to urban planning and cybersecurity, ML is increasingly employed in other government applications such as social welfare targeting. Their study emphasizes the need for transparency and explainability in ML systems, given their significant implications for resource distribution and civil liberties (Sethi et al., 2025).

Deep learning, a more advanced form of ML, leverages AI neural networks to analyze unstructured data such as images, audio, or video to recognize complex patterns in large datasets, enabling applications such as image recognition in security or diagnostic tools in public health. It powers applications in disease diagnostics, facial recognition, drone navigation, and disaster response. These systems have shown high utility in smart cities, particularly in automating surveillance and predictive maintenance. Additionally, they have been utilized in diagnosing diseases in the public health domain. For example, Chinese initiatives have leveraged deep learning for analyzing medical images, particularly in diagnosing interstitial lung diseases using lung pattern classification from CT scans. This helps in automating diagnosis and improving treatment planning in public hospitals (Chen et al., 2019). The same infrastructure is also tied to broader smart city health monitoring efforts, including pollution tracking and population health metrics through pattern recognition of visual and environmental sensor data.

Natural Language Processing (NLP) enables computers to interpret and generate human language. As a technology that facilitates machine understanding of human language, NLP underpins chatbots, digital assistants, and legal document automation. In government, it supports automated document processing, sentiment analysis of citizen feedback, and intelligent virtual assistants. Jiang et al. (2023) found that NLP is being deployed in e-government portals and public service chatbots, with notable efficiency gains in handling citizen queries and processing legal documents. As an example, Estonia's e-government framework integrates NLP to support real-time multilingual citizen interactions, improving service delivery and accessibility. Apampa (2024) highlights that NLP facilitates transparency and accountability by analyzing government documents and media content, revealing patterns of corruption or inefficiency. This use of NLP in real-time governance underscores its transformative potential.

Predictive analytics combines statistical models, ML, and data mining to forecast future outcomes. It is extensively used in predictive policing, disaster response, and public health. Governments deploy it in pandemic management, policing, and infrastructure planning. In Finland's AuroraAI program, predictive tools help connect citizens to personalized services, from healthcare to education (Leikas et al., 2022). Mishra et al. (2024) document the impact of predictive analytics in Indian governance, showing its role in optimizing the allocation of emergency services and identifying at-risk populations for proactive interventions. In a similar vein, Ogunleye (2024) describes how predictive analytics enhances responsiveness in urban management, including traffic control and energy distribution. These applications improve not just operational efficiency but also equity by prioritizing services based on need (Ogunleye, 2024). Table 1 summarizes the case studies of AI technology examples used in government.

While the benefits of AI technologies and their roles in improving government operations are widely acknowledged, these technologies also introduce significant ethical, legal, and administrative challenges. For example, algorithms trained on biased data may perpetuate or exacerbate social inequalities. Veale and Brass

Table 1 Case studies of AI technologies examples used in government

Type of AI technology	Functions (tasks performed)	Examples of use in government	References
Machine learning (ML)	Learns from data to make predictions or decisions without explicit programming	UK: Used for public health forecasting USA: Employed by federal agencies for cybersecurity threat detection	Pencheva and Esteve (2020); Sethi et al. (2025)
Deep learning	An advanced form of ML using neural networks to process unstructured data like images, audio, and video; identifies patterns and supports complex recognition tasks	China: Used in analyzing medical images for disease diagnosis, and in pattern recognition for city health monitoring, including pollution tracking	Chen et al. (2019)
Natural language processing (NLP)	Enables machines to understand, interpret, and generate human language	Estonia: Integrated into e-government portals to provide multilingual virtual assistants and improve public service accessibility	Jiang et al. (2023), Apampa (2024)
Predictive analytics	Combines statistics, ML, and data mining to forecast future trends or behaviors	Finland: AuroraAI program delivers personalized services across sectors India: Used to optimize emergency services and target at-risk populations	Leikas et al. (2022), Mishra et al. (2024), Ogunleye (2024)

(2019) argue that many public sector AI applications suffer from a lack of transparency, leading to "administration by algorithm" without adequate oversight. Additionally, the black-box nature of some ML models makes it difficult for public servants and citizens to understand or challenge AI-generated decisions. Pi (2021) notes that the lack of explainability poses a legal and ethical challenge, particularly in areas involving rights and entitlements. Furthermore, governments amassing large datasets for AI analytics raise concerns about surveillance and data misuse. Hodorog et al. (2022) show how social media monitoring, while valuable for event detection in smart cities, risks infringing on privacy rights if left unchecked. Finally, as we have seen in some advanced countries such as the USA, automation threatens public sector jobs, especially in clerical and administrative roles. While some roles evolve to require new skills, others may be lost entirely, necessitating retraining and strategic workforce planning.

In recognition of AI's potential and risks, governments across the globe are increasingly developing national AI strategies and regulatory responses. A cross-national review by Radu (2021) revealed that over 40 countries have published formal strategies, focusing on innovation, ethical deployment, and global competitiveness. For example, the European Union (EU) introduced the Artificial Intelligence Act, a first-of-its-kind regulatory framework categorizing AI systems by risk. It bans systems with "unacceptable risk" (e.g., social scoring), while imposing transparency and accountability on "high risk" systems, such as those used in border control or policing. In Finland, Aurora AI is a national platform integrating AI into life-event-based public service category. By securely analyzing citizen data, it proactively recommends services, thereby minimizing bureaucratic friction. Leikas et al. (2022) argue that such ecosystem-wide designs illustrate a new model of ethical public sector innovation. Canada also mandates the Algorithmic Impact Assessment (AIA) for any federal system that involves AI in decision-making. The assessment evaluates factors like data quality, human oversight, and legal compliance to help reduce adverse impacts of AI adoption. Together, the benefits and risks of AI noted above underscore the need for our edited volume and the chapters therein, each of which presents a unique perspective, empirical analysis, or theoretical framework concerning AI's role in modern governance. In the next section, we provide an overview of the chapters in the book.

3 Chapters Overview

This book is organized into three thematic sections. Part I—Foundations of AI in Government—focuses on AI adoption and foundational strategies for integration. It centers on the strategic adoption, governance, and integration of AI within public sector institutions. The section explores frameworks, challenges, and opportunities involved in embedding AI into government workflows and policy-making. The emphasis is on responsible adoption, public value creation, and institutional preparedness. In Chap. 2, Aikins and Markoski provide an overview of global AI adoption practices. Using comparative case studies, they highlight how countries such as Estonia, Japan, and the UAE integrate AI to improve service delivery and regulatory efficiency. The chapter's core takeaway is that AI can enhance decision-making and service delivery, but only when paired with inclusive, ethical strategies and continuous stakeholder engagement. The authors emphasize capacity building and equitable access as prerequisites for successful implementation.

Focusing on public managers, Sandoval-Almazan introduces in Chap. 3, a framework grounded in sociotechnical theory to guide generative AI (GenAI) adoption. He argues that the urgency for practical principles stems from the rapid technological pace and limited training in public institutions. The chapter's structured approach to evaluating GenAI tools offers a roadmap for thoughtful deployment. The implication is profound: Without strategic guidance, governments risk misapplying powerful AI tools, undermining trust and efficacy. In Chap. 4,

Charalabidis advocates for a hybrid model that combines rule-based AI systems with machine learning in domains such as justice, education, and urban planning. By foregrounding transparency and explainability, the chapter aligns with regulatory trends, such as the EU AI Act. The author stresses that effective AI systems must be auditable and citizen-centric. The implications suggest that the rule-based systems can serve as ethical and operational scaffolds for more complex applications in high-stakes public contexts.

Anastasiou, Elguendouze, Efstathiou, Mariani and others introduce the ORBIS toolkit in Chap. 5, showcasing how AI can scale collective intelligence through modular architecture and key features such as argument clustering and feedback aggregation. ORBIS exemplifies how AI can democratize large-scale deliberations, making public input more manageable and policy-relevant. The innovation lies not just in the technology, but in how it preserves the quality of discourse on a scale. This positions ORBIS as a blueprint for deliberative AI systems in civic technology. Based on a survey of US municipal IT professionals, Aikins and Markoski present in Chap. 6 an empirical study that examines the weight of ethical goals in AI policy decisions. Their findings reveal that transparency, trust, and bias reduction are key drivers of policy adoption, but fiscal and regulatory barriers persist. The insight here is pragmatic: ethical alignment is necessary but insufficient, implying governments must also secure resources and compliance pathways to bring ethical AI visions into practice. In Chap. 7, Ramos-Torres and Montoya explore the global landscape of government-led AI investment, distinguishing between internal modernization and external ecosystem support. Case studies from China, the EU, and the US reveal diverse strategies balancing innovation with civil liberties. The authors conclude that ethical alignment must guide investment to avoid unintended consequences. The message is clear: strategic investment in AI is a geopolitical imperative, but it must be human-centric to be sustainable.

Part II—Applications of AI in Government—delves into AI's functional deployment in specific domains, including emergency management, public deliberation, smart cities, and policymaking. The chapters analyze how AI transforms governments' operational capabilities and citizen interactions. In Chap. 8, Soujaa and Tao depict AI as transformative across disaster management phases—forecasting response, and recovery. Tools like predictive models and generative AI (e.g., chatbots) enable governments to prepare and respond to crises more effectively. The authors present real-world examples from California wildfires and the COVID-19 pandemic, illustrating both the promise and limits of these tools. Importantly, the chapter underscores the ethical stakes of using AI in life-or-death situations, advocating for transparency and equitable deployment. In Chap. 9, Aikins and Markoski explore the socio-political consequences of AI misuse, drawing from global examples. They emphasize that while automation can enhance efficiency, it also poses risks, including job displacement and algorithmic bias. The authors, therefore, call for adaptive policies and inclusive governance to mitigate these effects. The implication here is that responsible AI is not a technical challenge—it is a democratic and social mandate.

Returning to ORBIS, Mariani, Anastasiou, Elguendouze, and others emphasize in Chap. 10 the importance of co-creation and stakeholder involvement in developing AI tools for public discourse. The chapter highlights iterative engagement as a mechanism to align AI functionality with democratic values. The ORBIS case contributes to a growing body of research on participatory AI development, suggesting that legitimacy in AI governance depends as much on process as on outcomes. In Chap. 11, Livieris, Apostolopoulou, Karacapilidis, and others introduce a deep-learning-powered toolkit for deliberation, outlining how AI can transform unstructured feedback into actionable insights. The chapter details components like sentiment clustering and keyphrase extraction. This innovation promises to elevate public input in policy processes, fostering more responsive governance. Additionally, it exemplifies how AI can close the gap between civic participation and decision-making. In Chap. 12, Nukpezah, Ntow, and Adu offer a broad overview of AI in smart urban planning by presenting a historical context, then analyzing current applications in infrastructure, governance, and citizen services. While the promise is immense—greater efficiency, sustainability, and quality of life—the risks are equally pressing. Ethical deployment, data privacy, and infrastructural readiness are recurring concerns, as in other chapters. The authors provide critical policy recommendations to navigate these tensions.

Part III—Challenges, Considerations and Future Trends—reflects on the philosophical, regulatory, and futuristic implications of AI in government. This final section considers AI's long-term implications for bureaucratic systems, legal regimes, and governance philosophies. These chapters challenge assumptions about technology's neutrality and argue for a deeper alignment with democratic values and institutional accountability. In Chap. 13, Ossewaarde provides a philosophical reflection while critiquing the assumption that AI will naturally improve bureaucratic functions. Using the Dutch childcare benefits scandal as a case study, he illustrates how blind reliance on AI can erode accountability. The chapter posits that AI cannot substitute for the judgment and responsibility embedded in public administration. The significance of this chapter lies in its caution against techno-utopianism in governance. Authored by Sokołowski, Chap. 14 adopts a regulatory lens and likens the AI regulator to a day-watchman who is vigilant but non-intrusive. Drawing historical analogies, the chapter analyzes the EU's new AI Office as a modern embodiment of this approach. The author advocates for a balanced regulatory approach that promotes innovation while safeguarding public interests. The day-watchman model offers a promising alternative to both laissez-faire and overly interventionist regimes.

In Chap. 15, Wirtz and Becker categorize and evaluate types of AI-based automation in government. They propose a strategic integration model for embedding robotic systems into public workflows. The authors stress that the success of such initiatives depends on regulatory clarity and thoughtful design. This chapter stands out for its systemic approach, offering actionable frameworks for navigating AI-driven transformation. Authored by Azhar, Chap. 16 concludes the book by scanning the horizon of AI trends in public administration. From hyper-personalized services to predictive governance, the chapter examines emerging technologies and their implications. It issues a call for explainable AI, agile governance, and equitable data infrastructures. Importantly, the author lays out a forward-looking research agenda, anchoring AI's future in ethical, inclusive, and democratic principles.

The chapters in *Artificial Intelligence and Government* are not isolated contributions but interconnected analyses that collectively address a shared question: How can AI enhance government operations without compromising democratic values? Additionally, the chapters converge on a shared realization: AI will not simply optimize government, it will redefine it. But this redefinition must be rooted in public values. From foundational adoption to futuristic projects, the volume demonstrates thematic coherence, intellectual diversity, and practical relevance. Across the case studies, frameworks, and theoretical debates, the book reinforces the need for careful, citizen-centered, and ethically grounded AI integration. The central message across the sections is that AI holds vast potential, but ethics, inclusivity, transparency, and democratic principles must guide its deployment. As we stand at the cusp of a new government era, the lessons within this volume offer not just technical solutions but a vision for human-centric digital transformation. In the next section, we discuss the context of the book in the AI adoption landscape and its contribution to public sector AI literature.

4 Context and Contribution to Public Sector AI Literature

The post-2020 period has seen an exceptional rise in AI experimentation in the public sector, with COVID-19 serving as a catalyst for digital transformation. AI has been deployed in health surveillance, social services, crisis response, and more. At the same time, controversies such as algorithmic bias in welfare algorithms (e.g., the Dutch childcare scandal discussed in Chap. 13) have underscored the risks of unchecked AI deployment. This book explores the delicate equilibrium between innovation and accountability, speed and fairness, efficiency and equity. It serves as a foundational text for navigating the evolving intersection of technology and governance, offering critical insights for a wide array of stakeholders committed to shaping the future of public administration.

Recent literature strongly supports the need for a nuanced, context-sensitive approach to AI in government. For instance, Taeihagh (2021) notes that governments face a "governance paradox" in that they must regulate rapidly evolving AI technologies while also adopting them to meet policy goals. This dual role requires new forms of agile, anticipatory governance. Similarly, Kuziemski and Misuraca (2020) argue that democratic institutions must develop "institutional capacities" to govern algorithmic systems in ways that uphold transparency and citizen rights. This book reflects and contributes to these contemporary debates. Moreover, the regulatory landscape is shifting rapidly. The EU AI Act, enacted in 2024, introduced one of the world's most comprehensive AI governance regimes. In this light, discussions in the book regarding rule-based AI (Chap. 4) and regulatory bodies, such as the AI Office (Chap. 14), become immediately relevant, anchoring the book in current legal and institutional developments.

The book significantly advances the academic and practical literature on AI in government in several ways. First, it offers an integrative framework that links theory (TAM, socio-technical systems), empirical case studies (e.g., Estonia, UAE, and US municipalities), and normative analysis (ethics, democracy, transparency). This interdisciplinary approach is essential for understanding the complexity of AI adoption. Second, it elevates discussions about co-creation and participatory design, themes often neglected in technocratic literature. The ORBIS platform exemplifies how AI can be democratized, a theme supported by recent research from Ben Dhaou et al. (2024), who emphasize that "people-oriented smart cities" must prioritize stakeholder engagement in AI design and implementation.

Third, the book grapples with foundational critiques of digital bureaucracies, as seen in Chap. 13's analysis of AI-induced administrative failure. These critiques align with philosophical and sociological discussions of digital government that caution against dehumanized governance (Almeida et al., 2021). Finally, the book makes a forward-looking contribution by articulating a research and policy agenda in Chap. 16 that addresses explainable AI, equitable data access, and workforce transformation. These issues are top priorities in current global forums on AI governance, including the OECD and World Economic Forum.

The thematic integration across chapters reveals that collectively, they demonstrate how AI is not merely a technical tool, but a catalyst for institutional transformation and reimagination of public service. As stated earlier, Chaps. 2 through 7 form a coherent foundation for understanding how AI adoption is framed within government. These works align with current academic discourse emphasizing the need for adaptive governance, stakeholder engagement, and ethical oversight in AI implementation. For example, the use of theoretical models like TAM and adaptive governance reflects best practices identified by researchers advocating for structured frameworks in AI deployment (Taeihagh, 2021). Chapters 8 through 12, which pivot toward applied scenarios, echo themes in the literature that stress AI's utility in managing urban complexity and public crises, while also warning against algorithmic opacity and inequities (Yigitcanlar et al., 2021; Zhou & Kankanhalli, 2021).

The emphasis on co-creation and participatory AI in ORBIS (Chaps. 5 and 10) reflects contemporary understandings of democratic AI development—systems built not just for the public but with the public (Ben Dhaou et al., 2024). Chapters 13 through 16, which take a philosophical and forward-looking lens, critically examine assumptions of AI's neutrality and efficiency. These align with critical public administration research that highlights the risk of bureaucratic dehumanization through algorithmic decision-making (de Almeida et al., 2021), In this regard, the call for regulatory innovation through models like the "day-watchman" framework in Chap. 14, now manifest in real-world bodies like the EU's AI Office (Bosco et al., 2024).

5 Who Will Benefit from This Book?

This book offers critical insights for multiple audiences, including public administration scholars and students, policymakers and public managers, technologists and civic technology developers, international development agencies, as well as legal and regulatory experts.

Public Administration Scholars and Students: Academics will find the book invaluable for its conceptual clarity and interdisciplinary scope. It contributes to public management, digital governance, and AI ethics discourses, offering a rich source of theory and empirical research. Graduate students, especially in public policy, data science, and governance programs, will benefit from its case studies and analytical frameworks.

Policymakers and Public Managers: Government officials responsible for digital transformation, innovation policy, and public service delivery will gain practical insights from chapters that detail implementation challenges and solutions. For instance, the structured principles in Chap. 3 and strategic models in Chap. 7 offer replicable practices.

Technologists and Civic Tech Developers: Developers working on public sector AI solutions will appreciate the book's attention to ethical design, participatory architecture, and explainability. The ORBIS framework can serve as a prototype for civic technology platforms aiming to facilitate democratic deliberation.

International Development Agencies: Organizations working on governance, transparency, and civic engagement in developing countries can learn from the lessons of the global case studies. The ethical and regulatory considerations addressed in Chaps. 6 and 14 are particularly pertinent to settings with weaker institutional frameworks.

Legal and Regulatory Experts: The analysis of regulatory paradigms and the development of institutions like the AI Office will interest legal scholars and regulators navigating new compliance regimes under legislation like the EU AI Act or similar national laws.

6 Conclusion

This book makes substantial contributions to both academic theory and practical governance. Theoretically, it enriches the literature on digital government and public sector innovation by providing interdisciplinary insights into how AI affects institutional logic, bureaucratic behavior, and democratic accountability. It builds on sociotechnical systems theory and extends it by applying it to contemporary AI contexts. The work also contributes to the field of public administration by framing AI not as a neutral tool, but as a socio-political actor embedded in normative and institutional structures. Practically, the book provides valuable guidance for policymakers, practitioners, and civil servants. It offers frameworks for ethical AI adoption, models for participatory design, and tools for scaling public deliberation. It underscores the importance of aligning AI deployment with core democratic values such as fairness, inclusivity, and transparency.

The book's contributions are critical in a policy environment increasingly characterized by technological uncertainty and regulatory lag. AI technologies such as Machine learning, deep learning, natural language processing, and predictive analytics each offer distinct benefits for governance, from improved service delivery to enhanced policy foresight. Yet, these technologies also introduce significant ethical, legal, and administrative challenges. This implies the need for a balanced approach—one that maximizes AI's utility while preserving the democratic and social values upon which public institutions are built. As governments worldwide prepare to implement and regulate AI technologies, this book arrives at a pivotal moment. It offers not only a map of where we are, but a compass for where we should go. Its insights will inform strategic planning, inspire ethical innovation, and guide the development of inclusive, human-centered governance models that harness AI for the public good.

References

Apampa, O. (2024). Government analytics: Leveraging digital technologies, machine learning, and artificial intelligence for probity and accountability in public service. https://doi.org/10.13140/RG.2.2.19744.39685

Ben Dhaou, S., Isagah, T., Distor, C., & Ruas, I. (2024). *Global Assessment of Responsible Artificial Intelligence in Cities*. UN-Habitat. Retrieved May 2, 2025 from https://collections.unu.edu/view/UNU:9789

Bosco, G., Riccardi, V., & Sciarrone, A. (2024). AI-driven innovation in smart city governance: Achieving human-centric and sustainable outcomes. *Transforming Government: People, Process and Policy*. Retrieved May 2, 2025 from https://www.emerald.com/insight/1750-6166.htm

Chen, Q., Wang, W., Wu, F., De, S., Wang, R., & Zhang, B. (2019). A survey on an emerging area: Deep learning for smart city data,". *IEEE Transactions on Emerging Topics in Computational Intelligence, 3*(5), 392–410. https://doi.org/10.1109/TETCI.2019.2907718

de Almeida, P. G. R., dos Santos, C. D., & Farias, J. S. (2021). Artificial intelligence regulation: A framework for governance. *Ethics and Information Technology, 23*, 505–525. https://doi.org/10.1007/s10676-021-09593-z

Hodorog, A., Petri, I., & Rezgui, Y. (2022). Machine learning and NLP of social media data for event detection in smart cities. *Sustainable Cities and Society, 85*, Article 104026. https://doi.org/10.1016/j.scs.2022.104026

Jiang, Y., Pang, P. C. I., Wong, D., & Kan, H. Y. (2023). Natural language processing adoption in governments. *Applied Sciences, 13*(22), 12346. https://doi.org/10.3390/app132212346

Kuziemski, M., & Misuraca, G. (2020). AI governance in the public sector: Three tales from the frontiers of automated decision-making in democratic settings. *Telecommunications Policy, 44*(6), Article 101976. https://doi.org/10.1016/j.telpol.2020.101976

Leikas, J., Johri, A., Latvanen, M., & Wessberg, N. (2022). Governing ethical AI transformation: A case study of AuroraAI. *Frontiers in Artificial Intelligence*. https://doi.org/10.3389/frai.2022.836557

Mishra, A. K., Tyagi, A. K., & Dananjayan, S. (2024). Revolutionizing government operations. *Wiley Online Library*. https://doi.org/10.1002/9781394200801.ch34

Ogunleye, O. S. (2024). Machine learning and data science techniques for effective government service delivery. *IGI Global*. https://doi.org/10.4018/978-1-6684-9716-6

Pencheva, I., & Esteve, M. (2020). Big data and AI–A transformational shift for government: So, what next for research? *Public Policy and Administration*, 35(4), 451–472. https://journals.sagepub.com/doi/abs/10.1177/0952076718780537

Pi, Y. (2021). Machine learning in governments: Benefits, challenges, and future directions. *JeDEM—eJournal of eDemocracy and Open Government, 13*(2), 141–165. https://doi.org/10.29379/jedem.v13i1.625

Radu, R. (2021). Steering the governance of artificial intelligence: National strategies in perspective. *Policy and Society, 40*(2), 178–193. https://doi.org/10.1080/14494035.2021.1929728

Sethi, I. P. S., Gupta, O. P., Dwivedi, R. K., & Kapoor, M. (2025). Machine learning in government applications: A review. *Procedia Computer Science*. https://doi.org/10.1016/j.procs.2025.04.369

Taeihagh, A. (2021). Governance of artificial intelligence. *Policy and Society, 40*(2), 137–157. https://doi.org/10.1080/14494035.2021.1928377

Veale, M., & Brass, I. (2019). Administration by algorithm? Public management meets public sector machine learning. In K. Yeung & M. Lodge (Eds.), *Algorithmic Regulation* (pp. 121–149). Oxford University Press. https://doi.org/10.1093/oso/9780198838494.003.0006

Yigitcanlar, T., Corchado, J. M., & Mehmood, R. (2021). Responsible urban innovation with local government artificial intelligence (AI): A conceptual framework. *Journal of Open Innovation, 7*(1), 71. https://doi.org/10.3390/joitmc7010071

Zhou, Y., & Kankanhalli, A. (2021). AI regulation for smart cities: Challenges and principles. In E. Estevez, T. A. Pardo & H. J. Scholl (Eds.), *Smart cities and smart governance. Public Administration and Information Technology* (Vol. 37). Springer, Cham. https://doi.org/10.1007/978-3-030-61033-3_5

Part I

Foundations of AI in Government

2 Transforming Government Through AI: Navigating Adoption, Barriers and Solutions

Stephen Kwamena Aikins and Tamara Dimitrijevska-Markoski

1 Introduction

Artificial intelligence (AI) is transforming governance and public administration by enhancing decision-making, improving service delivery, enabling better citizen engagement, and increasing operational efficiency. Governments worldwide are integrating AI into various sectors, including policymaking, public service delivery, and internal management, to address administrative challenges and optimize resource allocation. As governments worldwide seek to leverage the potential of AI, questions about its ethical, technical, and societal implications remain (Medaglia & Gil-Garcia, 2023).

The application of AI in governance is often linked to broader digital transformation efforts, which encompass e-governance, smart cities, and digital public services. For example, nations such as Estonia have demonstrated AI's potential by integrating it into their e-government systems, thereby automating public services such as tax filings and digital identity management. Similarly, Singapore's "Smart Nation" initiative exemplifies the integration of AI across transport, healthcare, and public administration (Van Noordt & Misuraca, 2022).

The primary aim of this chapter is to explore the transformative roles of AI in the public sector and provide samples of case studies from around the world that showcase effective AI use. The study also examines the benefits and challenges of AI adoption and the effective strategies that facilitate overcoming barriers to AI implementation. The chapter is organized as follows: we first provide a brief overview of the theoretical approaches used to understand the varied adoption of

S. K. Aikins (✉) · T. Dimitrijevska-Markoski
University of South Florida, Tampa, USA
e-mail: saikins@usf.edu

S. K. Aikins and T. Dimitrijevska-Markoski (eds.), *Artificial Intelligence and Government*, https://doi.org/10.1007/978-3-032-12344-2_2

AI, followed by an in-depth discussion of how AI is being used to transform government. Next, we discuss AI case studies as well as the lessons learned from AI use and the solutions implemented. The chapter then proceeds to identify common barriers associated with AI adoption (technical, ethical, societal, and regulatory) and presents effective approaches that have been used to address these barriers. The chapter concludes with a discussion and analysis of these AI adoption and implementation barriers and proposes strategies to mitigate these challenges.

2 Theoretical Perspectives on AI in Government

While AI has transformative potential, the adoption of AI in the public sector has not been automatic nor instantaneous. This section aims to understand why some governments have adopted AI, while others still have not. To shed light on the determinants of AI adoption in the public sector, we first explore the theoretical frameworks that explain the key determinants of AI adoption. In the next section, we provide a review of the empirical evidence.

The theoretical exploration of AI in government is informed by frameworks such as technology acceptance models (TAM), socio-technical systems theory, and governance paradigms. Each of these theoretical approaches offers a unique perspective on AI adoption, but they are all consistent in that AI adoption is not linear but is influenced by the interplay of several factors. The TAM framework posits that the adoption of technology in organizations, including government, depends on perceived usefulness and ease of use. Research shows that government employees' willingness to adopt AI is influenced by their perception of its ability to enhance efficiency and decision-making (Ahn & Chen, 2022). For example, AI adoption in tax administration has improved accuracy and reduced fraud in countries such as India and Brazil, driven by a growing belief in AI's effectiveness.

Socio-technical systems theory emphasizes the interplay between technology, people, and organizational structures. In this regard, AI systems in government are not isolated technologies but embedded within socio-technical systems that shape and are shaped by institutional values and societal norms. A study of AI policies in Sweden reveals how socio-technical considerations such as public trust and transparency influence the deployment of AI (Toll et al., 2020).

AI's role in governance aligns with the "governance as a service" paradigm, whereby public services are conceptualized as customer-centric and data-driven. The use of AI to automate administrative tasks, such as chatbots for citizen queries, reflects this paradigm. A notable example is the "AI Singapore" program, which has enhanced public engagement and streamlined service delivery.

Ethics is a critical lens for analyzing AI's role in government. AI systems can perpetuate biases and infringe on privacy, necessitating robust frameworks for ethical AI. Governments have responded with initiatives like the EU's "Ethics Guidelines for Trustworthy AI" and Singapore's "Model AI Governance Framework," which set standards for transparency, accountability, and fairness (Van

Noordt & Misuraca, 2022). In the following section, we dwell on some of the above-mentioned theories to explain the roles and uses of AI in government.

3 Transforming Government with AI—Uses and Benefits

As a pivotal tool in transforming government functions, AI plays critical roles in diverse ways, including enhancing efficiency, improving citizen services, strengthening citizen engagement, enhancing public safety, promoting transparency and accountability, and advancing sustainability and climate action. AI's applications in government extend beyond traditional administrative tasks, playing a crucial role in regulatory oversight, cybersecurity, disaster response, and digital governance. This section provides an in-depth exploration of AI's uses, supplemented with relevant examples.

Enhancing Decision-Making and Policy Development: AI-driven tools provide government officials with sophisticated capabilities to analyze data, model scenarios, and predict policy outcomes. For instance, AI models were instrumental in the United Kingdom's response to COVID-19, where policymakers utilized epidemiological simulations to understand the potential impact of lockdown measures (Straub et al., 2023). By identifying trends and relationships in massive datasets, AI enhances evidence-based policymaking, particularly in areas like public health, education, and transportation. AI's predictive analytics are also utilized in urban planning. In Barcelona, AI systems analyze traffic flow and population density to optimize urban development and reduce congestion. Such applications underscore AI's potential to make complex governance tasks more precise and data-driven (Alshahrani et al., 2024).

Improving Efficiency in Public Services: AI-driven automation and digital assistants have significantly improved the efficiency of public service delivery. AI technologies streamline internal government processes by automating repetitive tasks and improving workflow efficiency. Mishra et al. (2024) note that AI adoption in public administration reduces administrative burdens and increases accuracy in complex decision-making scenarios. Governments worldwide use AI to automate routine administrative tasks, thereby freeing up resources and reducing operational costs. Estonia's "KrattAI" system, for instance, enables automation of over 100 public services, such as tax declarations and pension applications, saving time for citizens and administrators (Medaglia & Gil-Garcia, 2023). AI's application in public procurement is another efficiency-boosting example. Automated procurement platforms use AI algorithms to evaluate contractor bids, ensuring compliance with regulations while minimizing corruption risks. Such systems are in place in countries like Brazil, enhancing transparency and financial operations.

Strengthening Citizen Engagement: AI plays an instrumental role in fostering inclusive and participatory governance. Many government agencies now utilize chatbots and AI-powered virtual assistants to handle citizen inquiries, thereby reducing response times and enhancing accessibility. Ahn and Chen (2022) highlight how AI chatbots in digital government services enhance citizen engagement by providing real-time information and reducing bureaucratic bottlenecks. Through AI-powered chatbots and virtual assistants, governments can respond to citizen queries promptly and ensure accessible and equitable public service delivery. Singapore's "Ask Jamie," an AI chatbot integrated into public agency websites, has handled over 1.5 million interactions and simplified access to government services (Van Noordt & Misuraca, 2022). AI also enhances participatory governance. Tools like "Delib" in the United Kingdom allow citizens to provide feedback on proposed policies, thereby empowering individuals to shape decision-making processes. This technology fosters transparency and trust between government and citizens (Ingrams et al., 2022).

Enhancing Public Safety and Security: AI systems are increasingly used to bolster public safety. Predictive policing tools analyze historical crime data to identify potential hotspots and allocate law enforcement resources effectively. For example, the Los Angeles Police Department employs PredPol, an AI-based crime prediction system, to prevent property crimes and violent offenses (Mikalef et al., 2022). In disaster management, AI systems predict and mitigate risks associated with natural hazards. In Japan, AI tools forecast earthquakes and tsunamis, enabling authorities to issue timely warnings and develop effective evacuation strategies. Additionally, cybersecurity applications of AI, such as anomaly detection in network traffic, protect government systems from cyberattacks (Ahn & Chen, 2022).

Promoting Transparency and Accountability: AI-powered platforms enable real-time monitoring of government performance, fostering accountability. For instance, blockchain-integrated AI systems used in public financial management provide transparent records of transactions. In Brazil, such systems have empowered citizens to track government expenditures, reducing opportunities for corruption. Additionally, the adoption of ethical AI frameworks ensures fairness and accountability automated decision-making. The European Union's " Ethics Guidelines for Trustworthy AI" and Singapore's "Model AI Governance Framework" provide valuable examples of governance structures that prioritize transparency and public accountability (Van Noordt & Misuraca, 2022).

Regulatory Compliance and Fraud Detection: Governments are leveraging AI to enhance regulatory compliance by detecting fraud and ensuring adherence to policies. AI systems can process vast datasets to identify anomalies, reducing financial misconduct in public administration. Zuiderwijk et al. (2021) highlight AI's role in governance, particularly in automating compliance monitoring and detecting fraudulent transactions in social welfare programs. For instance, the U.S. Internal Revenue Service (IRS) uses AI-powered algorithms to detect fraudulent tax returns. Similarly, AI is used in the European Union to monitor financial transactions and prevent money laundering.

Cybersecurity in Government Systems: Public institutions are prime targets for cyber threats due to the sensitive nature of government data. AI enhances cybersecurity by identifying and mitigating cyber threats in real time. Al-Ansi et al. (2024) discuss how AI-driven cybersecurity tools help government agencies proactively prevent data breaches and cyberattacks. For instance, AI-based threat detection systems are used in US federal agencies to monitor network activities and detect potential security threats. AI can analyze vast volumes of data to identify suspicious behavior patterns and prevent unauthorized access.

Disaster Management and Response: AI plays a crucial role in disaster response by predicting natural calamities and improving emergency preparedness. AI models analyze historical data and real-time satellite images to forecast hurricanes, wildfires, and floods. Bullock et al. (2020) emphasize AI's role in automating disaster recovery processes and allocating resources efficiently. For example, AI-powered early warning systems in Japan provide real-time earthquake alerts, helping authorities to implement evacuation procedures promptly. Similarly, AI tools in California help predict wildfire risks and assist in disaster response planning.

Advancing Sustainability and Climate Action: Governments are leveraging AI to address environmental challenges. AI applications in climate modeling help predict the impact of policy interventions on greenhouse gas emissions. For example, the European Space Agency employs AI algorithms to analyze satellite imagery for monitoring deforestation and illegal logging activities (Alhosani & Alhashmi, 2024). AI also optimizes energy consumption in smart cities. Singapore's AI-powered energy grids, which analyze consumption patterns, have helped reduce energy waste and contributed to sustainability goals.

As noted above, AI is revolutionizing government functions by, among others, enhancing decision-making, improving service efficiency, and promoting transparency. Through case studies like Estonia's digital transformation and predictive policing in Los Angeles, this section demonstrates how AI is reshaping public administration. In the following section, we provide detailed case studies from selected countries around the world and state and local governments in the United States to shed more light on the transformative powers of AI.

4 Case Studies of AI Use in Government

In this section, we present global case studies illustrating the application of AI in government operations, supported by examples from various countries and case studies from U.S. state and local governments. AI is transforming governance across the globe, and governments at the national, state, and local levels are leveraging AI to optimize operations and improve outcomes. The diversity of AI use cases shown below highlights its versatility and the opportunities it offers for better governance.

4.1 Global Case Studies

United States: The Los Angeles Police Department (LAPD) employs predictive policing tools such as PredPol, which analyzes historical crime data to predict potential hotspots for criminal activity. This initiative has helped to significantly reduce property crimes. However, its use has sparked debates about fairness and potential biases in AI uses (Yigitcanlar et al., 2024).

Singapore: Through its "Smart Nation" initiative, Singapore has integrated AI into urban management systems. For example, AI monitors public transportation to reduce congestion and improve operational efficiency. AI-powered chatbots like "Ask Jamie" assist citizens with queries related to government services, enhancing user experience.

Sweden: The Swedish government developed an AI governance framework to address ethical considerations in AI use. The initiative applies AI in areas like public health and education, promoting transparency and trust among citizens (Toll et al., 2020).

Estonia: Known for its digital government leadership, Estonia uses AI in its e-Residency program. The Kratt AI system automates over 100 public services, including tax declarations and digital identity management. This program exemplifies the use of AI to create a seamless citizen experience (Alshahrani et al., 2024).

Japan: AI systems in Japan focus on disaster management. Predictive algorithms analyze seismic data to forecast earthquakes, allowing for timely evacuations. These tools have saved countless lives during natural disasters (Ahn & Chen, 2022).

United Arab Emirates: The UAE's "Happiness Meter" initiative uses AI-driven sentiment analysis to gauge citizen satisfaction with public services. Insights from the program help refine service delivery, emphasizing citizen-centric government (Alhosani & Alhashmi, 2024).

Table 1 shows AI initiatives in the selected countries discussed above, and US state and local governments. The contents are categorized by the AI initiatives undertaken, the AI technology used, and the outcome of the initiatives.

4.2 Case Studies from US State and Local Governments

State of California: The Department of Motor Vehicles (DMV) employs AI-powered natural language processing (NLP) chatbots to assist with driver's license renewals and queries. This has significantly reduced wait times and improved customer satisfaction (Ahn & Chen, 2020; Wang et al., 2022).

Table 1 AI initiatives in selected countries and US State and local governments

Country	Initiative	AI technology used	Benefit/outcome
United States	Predictive policing (Los Angeles)	PredPol	Reduced property crimes
Singapore	Smart nation	Smart city infrastructure AI	Improved public service delivery
Sweden	AI governance framework	AI risk assessment systems	Enhanced public trust and transparency
Estonia	e-residency program	KrattAI	Streamlined digital identity management
Japan	Disaster management AI	AI earthquake prediction	Reduced fatalities in natural disasters
UAE	Happiness meter	Sentiment analysis AI	Improved citizen satisfaction
State/city	**Initiative**	**AI technology used**	**Benefit/outcome**
California (State)	AI DMV automation	NLP Chatbots	Reduced wait times for license renewals
Texas (State)	Healthcare fraud detection	Machine learning algorithms	Identified $200 M in fraud savings
Ohio (State)	AI job matching	Resume parsing AI	Increased employment placement rates
New York City	AI traffic management	Traffic flow optimization AI	Reduced congestion by 30%
Chicago (City)	ShotSpotter program	AI gunfire detection	Improved law enforcement response time
Boston (City)	Snowplow optimization	Predictive weather AI	Saved $5 M in annual operational costs

Source Authors' compilation based on the sources in noted in the following narratives

State of Texas: AI-powered fraud detection systems in Medicaid have identified over $200 million in fraudulent claims, ensuring better allocation of public resources (Tangi & Noordt, 2023).

State of Ohio: AI systems for job matching analyze resumes and job listings, thereby helping unemployed individuals find suitable positions faster and more effectively (Yigitcanlar et al., 2024).

New York City: AI traffic management systems optimize signal timings to reduce congestion. A pilot program in Midtown Manhattan achieved a 30% decrease in traffic delays (Yigitcanlar et al., 2024).

City of Chicago: The ShotSpotter program uses AI to detect gunfire incidents in real time. This has improved law enforcement response times and reduced violent crime rates (Preeya, 2022).

City of Boston: Predictive weather AI optimizes snowplow operations during winter storms, thereby saving the city $5 million annually in operations costs (Yigitcanlar et al., 2023).

5 Lessons Learned from AI Use and Solutions Implemented

The implementation of AI in government across various global and local contexts has yielded valuable insights into best practices, challenges, and strategies for optimizing AI adoption. This section explores lessons learned from AI deployments in the USA, Singapore, Sweden, Estonia, Japan, and the UAE, as well as various US state and local governments, and how these lessons were addressed.

AI Requires Clear Objectives and Continual Testing Before Full-Scale Implementation: One of the most significant lessons is that governments must clearly define AI's role before implementation. Many AI projects fail or underperform due to unclear goals or a lack of feasibility assessments. Ramizo Jr. (2021) suggests that before implementing AI, governments should critically assess whether AI is the appropriate solution, and if so, how it should be integrated into existing systems. In line with the needed feasibility assessment, Singapore's Smart Nation initiative conducted pilot projects before full-scale AI implementation, ensuring that AI was truly beneficial for urban management. Their Smart City Infrastructure AI was first tested on a smaller scale in select areas before being deployed citywide (Yigitcanlar et al., 2024).

AI Adoption Requires Phased Implementation Based on Real-World Testing: A key lesson in AI adoption is that AI projects require extensive testing and gradual implementation before full deployment. Early AI projects in Europe and Singapore faced setbacks due to premature implementation without sufficient testing, leading to algorithmic errors and inefficiencies. Van Noordt and Medaglia (2023) emphasize that governments must establish AI pilot programs to evaluate system performance before widespread adoption. The Estonian government, through its KrattAI digital services, conducted phased AI deployment, refining algorithms based on citizen feedback before expanding them across public services. The United Arab Emirates used iterative AI development in its Happiness Meter initiative, adjusting sentiment analysis models on real-world data before broader rollout (Alhosani & Alhashmi, 2024).

Ethical AI Governance and Transparency Are Essential: AI systems must be designed with fairness, accountability, and transparency in mind. In Sweden, AI frameworks were initially criticized for lacking transparency, leading to concerns about algorithmic bias in public service applications. Hickok (2021) highlights the need for AI systems to be explainable and for governments to adopt policies ensuring transparency in AI decision-making. To address the concerns raised, Sweden introduced the AI Governance Framework, requiring all AI models used in public services to undergo explainability testing, ensuring accountability and public trust (Yigitcanlar et al., 2022).

AI Adoption Must Consider Societal Impacts and Equity: AI implementation can sometimes exacerbate inequalities, especially if it is not designed with inclusivity in mind. In the USA, predictive policing tools, including ShotSpotter AI in Chicago, have been criticized for disproportionately targeting minority communities. According to Desouza et al. (2020), governments must conduct impact assessments to prevent bias in AI-based decision-making. As a result of the criticism, Chicago's administration revised its AI strategy by incorporating human oversight in AI decision-making and conducting regular audits to detect biases in ShotStopper's predictive policing system (Santos et al., 2024). This effort aimed to balance crime reduction with civil rights protection.

AI Requires Cross-Sector Collaboration for Effective Implementation: AI systems in governance often require expertise that public agencies may lack. Corrigan (2021) emphasizes that effective AI implementation in Europe depended on collaboration between government agencies, academia, and private sector stakeholders. The United Arab Emirates (UAE) Happiness Meter initiative leveraged AI-driven sentiment analysis but initially lacked sufficient machine learning expertise. The UAE government partnered with AI research institutions and private companies to refine sentiment analysis models, improving accuracy and responsiveness in measuring citizen satisfaction (Corrigan, 2021; Vassilakopoulou et al., 2023). The Swedish government developed co-governance AI frameworks, bringing together technology firms, regulators, and civil society to address biases in AI-driven public services. Similarly, Chicago's ShotStopper AI, initially criticized for accuracy concerns, benefited from an external review by civil rights organizations, leading to transparency enhancements and improved accuracy measures (Santos et al., 2024).

Human Oversight Is Essential in Government AI Systems: While AI enhances efficiency, full automated decision-making without human oversight can result in critical errors and biases. Benedikt et al. (2020) emphasize the importance of "Human-in-the-Loop" AI systems, where human intervention remains a key component in AI-driven decision-making processes. The state of California's DMV AI chatbot initially struggled with misrepresentations of citizen inquiries. A hybrid AI-human response model was introduced, where AI processed initial requests, but human agents intervened in complex cases. In Japan's AI-driven earthquake prediction, officials combined AI forecasts with expert human verification to ensure accuracy before issuing disaster warnings (Benedikt et al., 2020; Dixon, 2023).

AI Adoption in Government Requires Skilled Workforce Training: A major challenge governments face is the lack of skilled personnel to manage AI systems. Estonia's Kratt AI digital government initiative faced initial setbacks due to a lack of AI-literate staff. Santos et al. (2024) found that AI projects often fail because public sector employees do not have the necessary training to operate or interpret AI tools. To address the staffing expertise problem, Estonia invested in AI training programs for civil servants, enabling them to integrate AI with traditional governance structures efficiently. The country also introduced AI literacy as part of its public administration curriculum.

AI Must Be Designed for Citizen Inclusion and Accessibility: AI in government must accommodate all citizens, including marginalized and less tech-savvy populations. Dixon (2023) highlights that AI adoption often overlooks accessibility concerns, resulting in digital exclusion. To address the problem of inclusivity, Ohio's AI-driven job matching system improved accessibility by introducing voice-assisted applications for visually impaired users, thereby increasing job placement success rates among individuals with disabilities. Similarly, Singapore's Smart Nation AI initiatives introduced multilingual chatbot services to accommodate non-English speakers.

AI Policy Frameworks Must Be Continuously Updated: AI policies must evolve alongside technological advancements to ensure ethical compliance and operational efficiency. Hickok (2021) emphasizes the importance of adaptive AI policy frameworks that incorporate ongoing research, public feedback, and global best practices. Boston's AI-powered snowplow optimization system refined its predictive models using real-time data, resulting in a 40% improvement in resource allocation. To address the problem, Japan's AI-driven public safety measures initially faced legal obstacles regarding data privacy. The government revised its data protection laws to align AI deployment with international standards while ensuring civil liberties (Van Noordt & Medaglia, 2023).

Final thoughts on the lessons learned: AI adoption in government presents immense opportunities but also complex challenges. The integration of AI into government services provides numerous benefits, as stated in the prior section, including enhanced efficiency, improved decision-making, and better citizen engagement. However, challenges such as ethical concerns, workforce limitations, transparency issues, and societal impacts must be addressed for AI to be successfully implemented. Key lessons learned from global AI initiatives emphasize the need for gradual deployment, collaborative governance, human oversight, citizen inclusion, and adaptive policies. By adopting clear governance frameworks, fostering cross-sector collaboration, and investing in AI literacy, governments worldwide have refined their AI strategies, making them more effective and equitable. Additionally, by refining AI strategies through continuous testing, cross-sector partnerships, and ethical governance frameworks, governments can harness AI's full potential while mitigating risks. Table 2 shows a summary of the lessons learned from AI implementation in government, including how they were addressed and their corresponding references. In the following section, we discuss the broader challenges of utilizing AI in government and the necessary solutions to address those challenges.

Table 2 Lessons learned from AI implementation in government

AI initiative	Lessons learned	How it was addressed	Source (author and year)
Singapore's smart nation AI	AI must be continuously tested and refined before full-scale implementation	AI was piloted in selected areas before citywide deployment	Yigitcanlar et al. (2024)
Estonia's KrattAI digital services	AI adoption requires phased implementation based on real-world testing	AI services were gradually introduced and refined using citizen feedback	Alhosani and Alhashmi (2024)
Sweden's AI governance framework	Ethical AI governance and transparency are essential	AI models used in public services underwent explainability testing for fairness	Hickok (2021)
Chicago's ShotSpotter AI	AI-driven policing tools must include bias mitigation measures	External audits and transparency enhancements were implemented	Santos et al. (2024)
United Arab Emirates' happiness meter	AI requires cross-sector collaboration for accurate and ethical implementation	Government partnered with research institutions to refine sentiment analysis models	Corrigan (2021)
California DMV AI Chatbot	Human oversight is essential in AI-driven decision-making	A hybrid AI-human response model was introduced for complex inquiries	Benedikt et al. (2020)
Japan's AI-driven earthquake prediction	AI-generated predictions require expert human verification	Government scientists validated AI forecasts before issuing public alerts	Dixon (2023), Benedikt et al. (2020)
Ohio's AI job matching system	AI services must be designed with inclusivity and accessibility in mind	Introduced voice-assisted applications for visually impaired users	Dixon (2023)
Boston's AI-powered snowplow optimization	AI requires real-time data adjustments for accuracy	AI models were refined based on operational data, improving resource allocation	Hickok (2021)
Japan's AI disaster response	AI policies must evolve alongside emerging legal and ethical concerns	Data protection laws were revised to align with AI deployment in emergency planning	Van Noordt and Medaglia (2023)

6 Challenges of AI Adoption in Government

Artificial intelligence offers transformative potential for government operations, yet its adoption and implementation face numerous challenges that hinder equitable and efficient use. These challenges can be broadly categorized into technical, ethical, societal, and policy-related issues. Each presents unique hurdles that governments must overcome to unlock AI's full potential while ensuring accountability, transparency, and fairness. This section discusses these challenges and analyzes how they adversely impact the efficient and equitable use of AI.

6.1 Technical Challenges

Technical barriers are among the most immediate obstacles in AI adoption for governance. These challenges often arise from data-related issues, infrastructure deficits, and the complexity of AI systems. AI systems require vast amounts of clean, unbiased, and high-quality data to function effectively. Governments often struggle with fragmented data silos across departments, inconsistent formats, and a lack of standardized protocols for data sharing. For instance, the Implementation of AI in China's healthcare sector via IBM Watson faced setbacks due to data quality issues and insufficient integration across medical institutions (Sun & Medaglia, 2019).

The lack of robust technological infrastructure further complicates AI implementation, especially in emerging economies. Governments in these countries face limited access to high-performance computing resources and inadequate Internet penetration in rural areas. For example, a study on AI in India's public manufacturing sector highlighted these gaps as significant barriers (Sharma et al., 2022). The integration of AI with existing government IT systems can be complex and costly. Legacy systems in many public agencies are outdated and incompatible with modern AI techniques, leading to delays and inflated budgets during transition (Misra et al., 2023).

6.2 Ethical Challenges

AI's growing influence on government decision-making raises significant ethical concerns. Issues like algorithmic bias, privacy violations, and lack of transparency are particularly pronounced in areas involving surveillance, law enforcement, and public welfare. AI systems can perpetuate and even amplify biases present in training data, leading to discriminatory outcomes. For example, predictive policing tools used in the US have been criticized for disproportionately targeting minority communities, exacerbating racial disparities in the criminal justice system (Fernández, 2023).

AI surveillance systems, such as China's social credit system, have sparked global debates about individual privacy and government overreach. These systems collect and analyze a vast amount of personal data, raising questions about consent, transparency, and misuse (Pi, 2021). Opaque AI algorithms, often described as "black boxes," challenge governments' ability to explain and justify automated decisions. This lack of transparency erodes public trust and undermines accountability, particularly when AI systems are used in welfare eligibility determinations.

6.3 Societal Challenges

AI adoption in governance also encounters societal barriers, including resistance to change, workforce displacement, and the digital divide. Automation-enabled AI threatens to displace workers in public sector jobs, particularly in administrative and operational roles. A report from the United Nations highlights concerns about the long-term implications of job loss due to AI-driven automation in government services (Susar & Aquaro, 2019).

The adoption of AI often encounters resistance from government employees and stakeholders who perceive AI as a threat to their roles or as an overly complex innovation. For instance, studies have shown that public sector employees in India expressed reluctance to embrace AI due to fears of redundancy and inadequate training (Sharma et al., 2020). The unequal distribution of digital infrastructure and skills creates disparities in accessing AI-driven public services. Rural and underprivileged communities are often excluded from the benefits of AI, thereby exacerbating existing inequalities. For example, rural regions in many third-world countries lack the necessary Internet infrastructure to utilize AI-enabled agricultural tools (Chatterjee, 2020).

6.4 Policy and Regulatory Challenges

The rapid development of AI technologies has outpaced the creation of robust regulatory frameworks, creating regulatory gaps, inadequate international cooperation, and ethical concerns that leave governments ill-equipped to address AI-related challenges. Few countries have comprehensive AI regulations that address ethical concerns, data privacy, and algorithmic accountability. The absence of clear guidelines complicates the governance of AI and exposes citizens to risks. A study on public policy challenges in AI adoption emphasized the need for cohesive legal frameworks to safeguard against misuse (Misra et al., 2020).

AI-related challenges, such as cross-border data flows and cybersecurity threats, require international collaboration. However, conflicting national interests and regulatory disparities hinder collective efforts. The AI Sector Deal in the United Kingdom highlights the importance of cross-sector collaboration in addressing these global challenges (Mikhaylov & Esteve, 2018). Governments often struggle to enforce ethical AI standards due to the ambiguity of ethical principles and the absence of global enforcement mechanisms. The European Union's General Data Protection Regulation (GDPR) provides a model for data privacy laws but as of 2021, it had not addressed the broader ethical challenges of AI systems (Pi, 2021). AI's integration into government systems holds immense promise, but as can be seen from the above challenges, it is accompanied by multifaceted barriers that require targeted interventions. In the following section, we discuss the steps for addressing AI challenges.

7 Remediations of AI Adoption Challenges

Addressing the challenges of integrating AI into government requires a structured approach that combines ethical considerations, technical innovation, robust policy frameworks, and global collaboration. Governments must navigate a landscape fraught with risks, such as algorithmic bias, privacy violations, and technological disparities, while ensuring that AI adoption benefits all citizens equitably. In this section, we provide a detailed exploration of actionable steps for addressing these challenges, supported by practical examples.

7.1 Ethical AI Principles and Governance

One of the foundational steps to address challenges in AI development is the establishment of ethical AI principles. Governments must adopt frameworks that prioritize fairness, accountability, and transparency. Notable efforts include the European Union's Ethics Guidelines for Trustworthy AI, which emphasize the importance of human oversight, data governance, and non-discrimination (Van Noordt & Misuraca, 2022). Singapore's Model AI Governance Framework is another example. It provides practical guidance for organizations to implement responsible AI, focusing on transparency in algorithmic decision-making and user-centric designs (Ahhosani & Alhashmi, 2024). Governments can adopt such models and tailor them to their cultural and legal contexts.

Key Actions:

- Mandate human oversight of critical AI systems, particularly in the areas of public safety and criminal justice.
- Require public agencies to audit AI algorithms for potential bias or discrimination.
- Develop public-facing accountability mechanisms, such as AI ethics boards or citizen oversight committees.

7.2 Strengthening Data Governance

Data quality and governance are cornerstones of effective AI implementation. Poor data quality, bias in datasets, and fragmented data repositories undermine the accuracy and fairness of AI models. Governments must invest in robust data infrastructure and adopt policies to ensure data integrity. For instance, Sweden has prioritized data interoperability across public agencies to facilitate AI adoption in governance. Their AI governance frameworks include standardized protocols for data sharing, ensuring high-quality, bias-free datasets (Toll et al., 2020).

Key Actions:

- Standardize data collection and management practices across government departments.
- Implement bias detection tools in datasets used for training AI models.
- Foster partnerships with private organizations to share anonymized datasets while protecting citizen privacy.

7.3 Capacity Building and Workforce Development

Successful AI integration requires a skilled workforce that understands both the technical and ethical dimensions of AI. Training programs for public sector employees can bridge knowledge gaps and foster a culture of innovation. For example, AI Singapore runs initiatives to upskill public sector employees in AI technologies. This program includes workshops on AI ethics, technical training, and case studies of successful deployments (Mikalef et al., 2022).

Key Actions:

- Launch AI literacy programs for government employees at all levels.
- Establish AI centers of excellence within public institutions to provide on-demand training and resources.
- Encourage public–private partnerships to deliver technical and ethical training programs.

7.4 Regulatory Innovations

Governments must craft regulatory frameworks that balance innovation with oversight. Current regulatory gaps hinder the equitable and responsible adoption of AI. Proactive regulations can address issues such as algorithmic accountability, data privacy, and cybersecurity. The General Data Protection Regulation (GDPR) in Europe offers a model for robust data privacy laws. GDPR mandates clear consent for data usage, giving citizens control over their personal data. Similar frameworks can be extended to AI-specific applications, ensuring transparent and ethical use of technology (Ahn & Chen, 2022).

Key Actions:

- Create sector-specific AI regulations (e.g., healthcare, law enforcement) that address unique challenges.
- Enforce mandatory algorithmic impact assessments for public-facing AI systems.
- Develop legislation that protects citizens from AI-enabled discrimination and exploitation.

7.5 Promoting Public Engagement and Trust

Citizens' trust is essential for the successful adoption of AI in government. Governments must engage the public in discussion about AI deployment, ensuring transparency and inclusivity. Participatory governance models, where citizens contribute to policymaking, can help build trust. The United Kingdom's Delib platform exemplifies this approach. Citizens use this AI-powered platform to provide feedback on public policies, fostering a sense of involvement and ownership (Ingrams et al., 2022).

Key Actions:

- Host public consultations and forums on AI adoption and its societal impact.
- Create AI transparency reports that outline how algorithms influence decisions.
- Design AI systems that incorporate citizen feedback and address public concerns.

7.6 Encouraging Global Collaboration

AI challenges are not confined by national borders. Issues such as cross-border data flows, AI ethics, and cybersecurity require international cooperation. Multilateral organizations, such as the OECD (2021) and the United Nations (UN DESA, 2020), have already initiated frameworks to align AI governance globally. Canada and France co-founded the Global Partnership on AI (GPAI), which aims to bridge gaps in AI policy, research, and capacity-building across nations. Such initiatives highlight the value of collective action (Van Noordt & Misuraca, 2022).

Key Actions:

- Participate in international AI governance initiatives and agreements.
- Share best practices and research findings with other nations.
- Harmonize AI standards to facilitate cross-border collaboration.

7.7 Fostering Innovation Through Public–Private Partnerships

Public–private partnerships (PPPs) are critical for accelerating AI innovation. Governments can leverage the expertise and resources of private entities to implement cutting-edge AI solutions. For instance, the US government collaborated with Google and Microsoft (2021) to develop AI systems for COVID-19 contact tracing and vaccine distribution (Tangi & Noordt, 2023).

Key Actions:

- Establish public–private task forces to address specific governance challenges.
- Provide incentives for private companies to collaborate on AI solutions for public services.
- Create regulatory sandboxes that allow companies to test AI technologies in a controlled environment.

7.8 Addressing the Digital Divide

The digital divide poses a significant barrier to equitable AI adoption. Disparities in access to technology and digital literacy can exacerbate existing inequalities, leaving vulnerable populations at a disadvantage. Governments must ensure that AI benefits all citizens, regardless of socio-economic status. India's Digital India initiative aims to bridge this gap by improving Internet access and digital literacy in rural areas (India Digital Ministry, 2021). AI-driven tools have been deployed in agriculture to assist farmers with crop selection and pest management, thereby empowering marginalized communities (Ahn & Chen, 2022).

Key Actions:

- Expand broadband infrastructure to underserved regions.
- Subsidize AI technologies for low-income communities.
- Incorporate digital literacy programs into public education systems.

Addressing the challenges of AI in governance requires a multi-dimensional approach that balances innovation with responsibility. Ethical AI principles, robust data governance, capacity building, regulatory innovation, and global collaboration are the backbone of effective strategies. By prioritizing public engagement and equity, governments can harness AI's potential to create more transparent, efficient, and inclusive systems. As nations continue to grapple with the complexities of AI adoption, these steps offer a roadmap for achieving a fair and sustainable future. In the following section, we analyze the key findings from this study and note their theoretical and practical implications.

8 Discussion and Analysis of Findings

The adoption of AI in government is a multi-faceted process with profound implications for both theoretical frameworks and practical governance. Drawing on global and local case studies, theoretical perspectives, and challenges, this section synthesizes key findings and outlines their significance for the integration of AI in public administration. Our findings from this study suggest that the integration of AI in government has enriched several theoretical frameworks, including the Technological Acceptance Model (TAM), socio-technical systems theory, and governance paradigms. Stenberg and Nilson (2020) assess the readiness of governmental authorities to adopt AI and emphasize that technological infrastructure, organizational culture, and environmental factors collectively influence AI adoption. This collective influence is echoed by socio-technical systems theory, which highlights the interplay between technological systems and social structure.

Zuiderwijk et al. (2021) emphasize that socio-technical systems theory offers a holistic approach to understanding AI's impact on governance structures and citizen engagement. The findings from this study suggest AI adoption in government, as demonstrated in Estonia's KrattAI digital services and Singapore's Smart Nation initiatives, underscores the need for seamless integration of technology with human processes to ensure efficiency and inclusivity. Governance paradigms, particularly adaptive governance theory, advocate for flexible and responsive regulatory frameworks. AI adoption in Japan's disaster management systems and the UAE's sentiment analysis tools highlight the necessity of adaptive policies that evolve alongside technological advancements. This aligns with the work of Misuraca et al. (2024) who assert that adaptive governance is crucial for balancing innovation with ethical considerations and regulatory compliance.

The findings from this study also suggest that the practical implications of AI adoption in government are evident in various domains, including decision-making, public service delivery, citizen engagement, public safety, regulatory compliance, and disaster management. In the area of decision-making and policy formulation, AI's data analytics capabilities enhance evidence-based policymaking. The use of AI in California's DMV chatbot services and Ohio's AI job matching systems demonstrates how AI can optimize resource allocation and improve public service delivery. As highlighted by Madan and Ashok (2023), AI-driven decision support systems enhance accuracy, reduce human error, and expedite administrative processes. On improved public service delivery, the findings reveal that AI-powered virtual assistants and automation tools streamline interactions between citizens and government agencies. Singapore's AI-driven public services exemplify this, with multilingual chatbots enhancing accessibility for diverse populations. This is consistent with the work of Alzebda and Matar (2024), who emphasize that AI adoption in public administration must prioritize user-centric design to ensure inclusivity and efficiency.

Citizen engagement and trust call for AI applications in governance to foster citizen trust through transparency and accountability, which is evidenced in our findings from this study. Sweden's introduction of explainable AI models in public services and Chicago's revised ShotSpotter AI policies, which included external audits, illustrate efforts to enhance public trust. This aligns with the arguments of Schiff et al. (2022), who contend that public value theory necessitates that AI systems in government prioritize fairness, transparency, and citizen well-being. Regarding public safety and security, the findings show that AI's role in public safety, as seen in Japan's AI-driven earthquake prediction systems and Boston's AI-powered snowplow optimization, demonstrates its potential in crisis management and resource optimization. Our findings also suggest that on the issues of regulatory compliance and ethical governance, ethical challenges, including algorithmic bias, data privacy, and transparency, remain significant hurdles. For this reason, the AI governance frameworks in Sweden, Singapore, and Japan emphasize the importance of ethical AI deployment. This is consistent with the findings of Chatterjee (2020), who highlights that AI policies must continuously evolve to address emerging ethical and legal challenges.

The global case studies in this research reveal critical lessons, such as the necessity for phased AI implementation, multi-stakeholder collaboration, human oversight, inclusivity, and adaptive policy frameworks. These lessons highlight that successful AI adoption requires strategic planning, continuous refinement, and robust governance. As emphasized by Yigitcanlar et al. (2024), governments must invest in capacity building, foster cross-sector collaborations, and ensure inclusive AI policies to achieve sustainable AI integration.

9 Conclusion

The adoption of AI in government presents significant opportunities and challenges, with implications for both theoretical and practical dimensions. Technical issues such as data quality and infrastructure deficits, ethical dilemmas like algorithmic bias and privacy concerns, societal challenges including workforce displacement and digital divide, and policy gaps underscore the complexity of AI adoption in government. Addressing these challenges necessitates a holistic approach involving ethical frameworks, capacity-building initiatives, robust regulatory systems, and international collaboration. As governments navigate these hurdles, the emphasis must remain on equity, transparency, and public trust to ensure that AI technologies serve all citizens effectively and responsibly.

Theoretical frameworks such as TAM, socio-technical systems theory, and adaptive governance provide essential insights into AI adoption dynamics. At the same time, practical implications underscore the need for strategic planning, ethical governance, and continuous policy adaptation. Drawing from global and local case studies, it is evident that AI's success in government hinges on balancing innovation with inclusivity, transparency, and public trust. As AI technologies continue to evolve, governments must remain agile, collaborate, and citizen-centric in their AI strategies to realize AI's full potential in enhancing governance and public service delivery.

References

Ahn, M. J., & Chen, Y. C. (2020). Artificial intelligence in government: Potentials, challenges, and the future. In *Proceedings of the 21st Annual International Conference on Digital Government Research* (pp. 352–361). https://doi.org/10.1145/3396956.3398260

Ahn, M. J., & Chen, Y. C. (2022). Digital transformation toward AI-augmented public administration: The perception of government employees and the willingness to use AI in government. *Government Information Quarterly*. Available at: https://www.sciencedirect.com/science/article/pii/S0740624X21001003

Al-Ansi, A. M., Garad, A., Jaboob, M., & Al-Ansi, A. (2024). Elevating e-government: Unleashing the power of AI and IoT for enhanced public services. *Heliyon*. Available at: https://www.cell.com/heliyon/fulltext/S2405-8440(24)16622-4

Alhosani, K., & Alhashmi, S. M. (2024). Opportunities, challenges, and benefits of AI innovation in government services: A review. *Sustainable Development Practices in Public Sector*. Available at: https://link.springer.com/article/10.1007/s44163-024-00111-w

Alshahrani, A., Griva, A., & Dennehy, D. (2024). Artificial intelligence and decision-making in government functions: Opportunities, challenges, and future research. *Transforming Government: People, Process and Policy*. Available at: https://www.emerald.com/insight/content/doi/10.1108/TG-06-2024-0131/full/html

Alzebda, S., & Matar, M. A. I. (2024). Factors affecting citizen intention toward AI acceptance and adoption: The moderating role of government regulations. *Competitiveness Review, 34*(2), 305–322. Available at: https://www.emerald.com/insight/content/doi/10.1108/CR-06-2023-0144/full/html

Benedikt, L., Joshi, C., Nolan, L., & Henstra-Hill, R. (2020). Human-in-the-loop AI in government: A case study. *Proceedings of the ACM International Conference on Human-Computer Interaction*. https://doi.org/10.1145/3377325.3377489

Bullock, J., Young, M. M., & Wang, Y. F. (2020). Artificial intelligence, bureaucratic form, and discretion in public service. *Information Polity*. Available at: https://content.iospress.com/articles/information-polity/ip200223

Chatterjee, S. (2020). AI strategy of India: Policy framework, adoption challenges and actions for government. *Transforming Government: People, Process and Policy, 14*(1), 85–99. Available at: https://www.emerald.com/insight/content/doi/10.1108/TG-05-2019-0031/full/html

Corrigan, C. C. (2021). Lessons learned from co-governance approaches—Developing effective AI policy in Europe. *Springer AI Policy Studies*. Available at: https://link.springer.com/chapter/10.1007/978-3-031-09846-8_3

Desouza, K. C., Dawson, G. S., & Chenok, D. (2020). Designing, developing, and deploying artificial intelligence systems: Lessons from and for the public sector. *Business Horizons, 63*(2), 275–287. https://doi.org/10.1016/j.bushor.2019.09.005

Dixon, R. B. L. (2023). A principled governance for emerging AI regimes: Lessons from China, the European Union, and the United States. *Springer AI & Ethics Journal*. https://doi.org/10.1007/s43681-022-00205-0

European Union. (2019). Ethics Guidelines for Trustworthy AI. *Independent High-Level Expert Group on Artificial Intelligence*. Available at: https://digital-strategy.ec.europa.eu/en/library/ethics-guidelines-trustworthy-ai

Fernández, J. V. (2023). Artificial Intelligence in Government: Risks and Challenges of Algorithmic Governance in the Administrative State. *International Journal of Global Law Studies, 30*(1) Available at: https://heinonline.org/hol-cgi-bin/get_pdf.cgi?handle=hein.journals/ijgls30&section=10

Hickok, M. (2021). Lessons learned from AI ethics principles for future actions. *Springer AI & Society Journal*. https://doi.org/10.1007/s43681-020-00008-1

India Digital Ministry. (2021). Digital India initiative annual report. *Government of India*. Available at: https://digitalindia.gov.in

Ingrams, A., Kaufmann, W., & Jacobs, D. (2022). In AI we trust? Citizen perceptions of AI in government decision making. *Public Performance & Management Review, 45*(2), 345–364. https://doi.org/10.1002/poi3.276

Madan, R., & Ashok, M. (2023). AI adoption and diffusion in public administration: A systematic literature review and future research agenda. *Government Information Quarterly, 40*(1), 101702. Available at: https://www.sciencedirect.com/science/article/pii/S0740624X22001101

Medaglia, R., & Gil-Garcia, J. R. (2023). Artificial intelligence in government: Taking stock and moving forward. *Social Science Computer Review*. https://doi.org/10.1177/08944393211034087

Mikalef, P., Lemmer, K., Schaefer, C., & Ylinen, M. (2022). Enabling AI capabilities in government agencies: A study of determinants for European municipalities. *Government Information Quarterly*. Available at: https://www.sciencedirect.com/science/article/pii/S0740624X21000320

Mikhaylov, S. J., & Esteve, M. (2018). Artificial intelligence for the public sector: Opportunities and challenges of cross-sector collaboration. *Philosophical Transactions of the Royal Society A: Mathematical, Physical and Engineering Sciences, 376*(2128). https://doi.org/10.1098/rsta.2017.0357

Mishra, D., Mishra, R. K., & Agarwal, R. (2024). *Impacts of artificial intelligence on society*. Retrieved March 18, 2025, from https://www.researchgate.net/publication/389938529_Impacts_of_artificial_intelligence_on_society

Misra, S. K., Sharma, S. K., Gupta, S., & Das, S. (2020). Public policy and regulatory challenges of artificial intelligence (AI). *Springer AI Policy Handbook*, 143–159. Available at: https://link.springer.com/chapter/10.1007/978-3-030-64849-7_10

Misra, S. K., Sharma, S. K., Gupta, S., & Das, S. (2023). A framework to overcome challenges to the adoption of artificial intelligence in Indian Government Organizations. *Technological Forecasting & Social Change*. Available at: https://www.sciencedirect.com/science/article/pii/S0040162523004067

Misuraca, G., Rossel, P., & Sibal, P. (2024). AI adoption as a high-value challenge for governments worldwide. In *Handbook of Digital Public Administration* (pp. 180–210). Springer. Available at: https://books.google.com/books?hl=en&lr=&id=6442EQAAQBAJ&oi=fnd&pg=RA2-PT180

OECD (Organization for Economic Co-operation and Development). (2021). Framework for the Governance of Artificial Intelligence. *AI Policy Observatory*. Available at: https://www.oecd.ai

Pi, Y. (2021). Machine learning in governments: Benefits, challenges and future directions. *Journal of E-Democracy and Open Government, 13*(1), 45–60. Available at: https://www.jedem.org/index.php/jedem/article/view/625/515

Preeya, P. (2022). The costs of technology: An analysis of the community concerns about the use of ShotSpotter in Chicago. *University of Chicago Knowledge Repository*. Available at: https://knowledge.uchicago.edu/record/5830

Ramizo Jr, G. (2021). Practical Lessons for Government AI Projects. *SSRN Working Paper*. Available at: https://papers.ssrn.com/sol3/papers.cfm?abstract_id=3840398

Santos, R., Brandão, A., & Veloso, B. (2024). The use of AI in government and its risks: Lessons from the private sector. *Emerald Insight*. https://doi.org/10.1108/TG-02-2024-0038

Schiff, D. S., Schiff, K. J., & Pierson, P. (2022). Assessing public value failure in government adoption of artificial intelligence. *Public Administration, 100*(3), 507–521. https://doi.org/10.1111/padm.12742

Sharma, G. D., Yadav, A., & Chopra, R. (2020). Artificial intelligence and effective governance: A review, critique and research agenda. *AI and Ethics*. Available at: https://www.sciencedirect.com/science/article/pii/S2666188819300048

Sharma, M., Luthra, S., Joshi, S., & Kumar, A. (2022). Implementing challenges of artificial intelligence: Evidence from public manufacturing sector of an emerging economy. *Government Information Quarterly*. Available at: https://www.sciencedirect.com/science/article/pii/S0740624X21000605

Singapore Government. (2020). Model AI governance framework. *Infocomm Media Development Authority*. Available at: https://www.imda.gov.sg

Stenberg, L., & Nilsson, S. (2020). Factors influencing readiness of adopting AI: A qualitative study of how the TOE framework applies to AI adoption in governmental authorities. *DIVA Portal* (pp. 1–84). Available at: https://www.diva-portal.org/smash/get/diva2:1460888/FULLTEXT01.pdf

Straub, V. J., Morgan, D., Bright, J., & Margetts, H. (2023). Artificial intelligence in government: Concepts, standards, and a unified framework. *Social Science Computer Review*. Available at: https://www.sciencedirect.com/science/article/pii/S0740624X23000813

Sun, T. Q., & Medaglia, R. (2019). Mapping the challenges of artificial intelligence in the public sector: Evidence from public healthcare. *Government Information Quarterly, 36*(2), 368–383. Available at: https://www.sciencedirect.com/science/article/pii/S0740624X17304781

Susar, D., & Aquaro, V. (2019). Artificial intelligence: Opportunities and challenges for the public sector. In *Proceedings of the 20th Annual International Conference on Digital Government Research* (pp. 420–425). https://doi.org/10.1145/3326365.3326420

Tangi, L., & Van Noordt, C. (2023). The challenges of AI implementation in the public sector: An in-depth case studies analysis. *Proceedings of the ACM International Digital Government Research Conference*. https://doi.org/10.1145/3598469.3598516

Toll, D., Lindgren, I., Melin, U., & Madsen, C. Ø. (2020). Values, benefits, considerations and risks of AI in government: A study of AI policies in Sweden. *Journal of e-Democracy and Open Government, 12*(1), 40–60. Available at: https://jedem.org/index.php/jedem/article/view/59

UN DESA. (2020). E-Government Survey: Digital government in the decade of action for sustainable development. *United Nations Department of Economic and Social Affairs*. Available at: https://publicadministration.un.org/egovkb/en-us/Reports/UN-E-Government-Survey-2020

Van Noordt, C., & Medaglia, R. (2023). Policy initiatives for Artificial intelligence-enabled government: An analysis of national strategies in Europe. *SAGE Public Policy Journal*. https://doi.org/10.1177/09520767231198411

Van Noordt, C., & Misuraca, G. (2022). Artificial intelligence for the public sector: Results of landscaping the use of AI in government across the European Union. *Government Information Quarterly*. Available at: https://www.sciencedirect.com/science/article/pii/S0740624X22000478

Vassilakopoulou, P., Haug, A., & Salvesen, L. M. (2023). Developing human/AI interactions for chat-based customer services: Lessons learned from the Norwegian government. *Information Systems Journal, 32*(4), 1–18. https://doi.org/10.1080/0960085X.2022.2096490

Wang, Y., Zhang, N., & Zhao, X. (2022). Understanding the determinants in the different government AI adoption stages: Evidence of local government chatbots in China. *Social Science Computer Review, 40*(2), 148–163. https://doi.org/10.1177/0894439320980132

Yigitcanlar, T., Agdas, D., & Degirmenci, K. (2023). Artificial intelligence in local governments: Perceptions of city managers on prospects, constraints, and choices. *AI & Society*. https://doi.org/10.1007/s00146-022-01450-x

Yigitcanlar, T., David, A., Li, W., Fookes, C., Bibri, S. E., & Ye, X. (2024). Unlocking artificial intelligence adoption in local governments: Best practice lessons from real-world implementations. *Smart Cities, 7*(4), 64–80. https://doi.org/10.3390/smartcities7040064

Yigitcanlar, T., Li, R. Y. M., Inkinen, T., & Paz, A. (2022). Public perceptions on application areas and adoption challenges of AI in urban services. *Emerging Science Journal, 6*(6), 1199–1236. https://doi.org/10.28991/ESJ-2022-06-06-01

Zuiderwijk, A., Chen, Y. C., & Salem, F. (2021). Implications of the use of artificial intelligence in public governance: A systematic literature review and a research agenda. *Government Information Quarterly*. Available at: https://www.sciencedirect.com/science/article/pii/S0740624X21000137

From Theory to Practice: Constructing AI Principles for Effective Public Service

3

Rodrigo Sandoval-Almazan

1 Introduction

Artificial intelligence (AI) applications in the public sector trace back to early innovations such as MYCIN,[1] an expert system for medical diagnosis (Buchanan & Shortliffe, 1984). Another notable project, DENDRAL, a collaborative effort between NASA and Stanford, sought to automate the analysis of organic compounds in soil samples for NASA's space program. This demonstrated the potential for AI to support government-led scientific initiatives (Lindsay et al., 1993). However, the first "AI winter" of the 1970s halted significant progress in the field until renewed interest in the twenty-first century. The emergence of the internet in the 1980s, rapid advancements in microchip technology, and the widespread adoption of personal computers in the 1990s, coupled with the expansion of the information technology (IT) industry, created a fertile environment for a resurgence in AI development.

In recent years, applications such as the Metaverse in the public sector (Kshetri et al., 2024) and generative AI tools like ChatGPT have faced considerable challenges. Davenport and Ronanki (2018) emphasized that one of the primary barriers to successful AI initiatives is the difficulty of integrating AI projects into existing organizational processes and systems. Similarly, Mikalef et al. (2019) highlighted that ineffective integration of systems and data, along with poor data quality,

[1] The name "MYCIN" was chosen as a **reference to antibiotics**, many of which end in **"-mycin"** (like **erythromycin**, **streptomycin**, **gentamicin**, etc.), which are used to treat **bacterial infections** (Buchanan & Shortliffe, 1984).

R. Sandoval-Almazan (✉)
Autonomous University of the State of Mexico, Toluca, Mexico
e-mail: rsandovala@uaemex.mx

S. K. Aikins and T. Dimitrijevska-Markoski (eds.), *Artificial Intelligence and Government*, https://doi.org/10.1007/978-3-032-12344-2_3

hampers AI progress. Further, Wirtz et al. (2020) examined the breadth of AI applications in the public sector and underscored the accompanying implementation challenges.

The post-2022 era marked a significant shift in AI's integration within the public sector, particularly with the public release of ChatGPT. This milestone has prompted systematic analysis of the benefits and challenges related to the design, management, adoption, and implementation of AI in government contexts, building on earlier research focused on risk and benefit mapping (Medaglia & Tangi, 2022).

Generative AI presents distinctive challenges for the public sector. Although empirical documentation of AI implementation in governmental bureaucracies remains limited, significant cases have emerged. These include applications within the U.S. Postal Service (Bracken, 2023), educational institutions in the United Kingdom (Tobin, 2023; Weston, 2023), and survey data on public administrators in Mexico (Criado et al., 2021). Microsoft has developed specialized AI systems for U.S. intelligence agencies, including the CIA, under the designation "Project Guardian" (Chappell, 2024). Additionally, a new e-government model utilizing ChatGPT technologies, known as ChatGPT Gov, has been introduced (APAC, 2025).

Research by Bright et al. (2025) examining GenAI usage among UK public administrators surveyed more than 900 participants, revealing that 45% incorporate this technology into their daily operations. Despite the limited availability of comprehensive research, the evidence indicates that public administrators, officials, and bureaucrats globally are adopting generative AI for various personal and professional applications, often without adequate preparation or cautionary guidance. The central question guiding this research is: To what extent can evidence-based practical principles be developed to guide public servants in the implementation and operational governance of generative AI technologies, given the current state of technological development and public sector constraints?

This chapter intends to answer this question on the strategic introduction of GenAI in the public sector. Adopting a socio-technical framework, it proposes several guiding principles for the effective implementation of generative AI in government operations.

The chapter is structured into four sections. Following this introduction, the second section presents a literature review, outlining socio-technical theory and AI concepts, along with case studies of current AI applications and the proposed ten principles framework. The third section introduces proposed principles for AI use in bureaucratic contexts as an implementation example. Finally, the conclusion discusses future research directions and offers practical insights for public sector practitioners.

2 Literature Review

This section is divided into fourth main subsections. The first addresses the theoretical background and key concepts of sociotechnology; second section gathers recent research on GenAI in different government areas and countries. While the third section reviews similar frameworks on principles for AI in the public sector. The fourth section proposes the principles for GenAI in public managers with their theoretical support.

2.1 Sociotechnology and AI

The sociotechnology theoretical framework encompasses diverse approaches and interpretations (Trist & Bamforth, 1951). Coined by Mario Bunge, sociotechnology emerged in the 1950s and 1960s as a response to the limitations of purely technological or social paradigms in explaining technological advancements and organizational transformation. Researchers at the Tavistock Institute in the UK further refined the theory. Central to this framework is the concept of sociotechnical systems, which posits that technologies and organizations are inherently linked, with social and technical components requiring integration to design effective systems holistically (Trist & Bamforth, 1951). Technology is built in collaboration with society.

The sociotechnical framework, first established by Trist and Bamforth (1951) in their seminal study of coal mining operations, demonstrates that technological implementations must consider social dynamics to achieve optimal outcomes. This theoretical foundation proves particularly relevant for AI integration in public administration.

Another foundational principle related to this research is joint optimization, emphasizing that social and technical systems should be co-designed to achieve optimal outcomes (Trist, 1981). This idea aligns with the concept of participatory design, which involves engaging end-users and workers in implementing new technologies and organizational systems (Mumford, 1983). Furthermore, the contingency approach asserts that the optimal design of sociotechnical systems depends on the organization's specific context and requirements, rejecting a one-size-fits-all solution (Lawrence & Lorsch, 1967).

In sum, the key sociotechnical concepts that integrates this investigation are: (a) sociotechnical systems; (b) Joint optimization; (c) Contingency approach and, (d) monitoring and cognitive capital.

Incorporating these concepts into Artificial Intelligence (AI) research has spurred new developments. For instance, Makarius et al. (2020) emphasize that successful integration of AI requires fostering cognitive, relational, and structural capital to ensure effective collaboration and value creation. Asatiani et al. (2021) argue that AI systems can become inscrutable unless organizations establish interaction boundaries, curate training data, and manage input/output processes. These measures are essential for balancing the potential benefits of AI, such as generative AI, while ensuring accountability in deployment.

A complementary perspective is the Collective Human–Machine Intelligence (COHUMAIN) approach, which promotes human-AI collaboration. Gupta et al. (2023) integrate instance-based learning theories to design AI agents that collaborate effectively with humans. In another direction, Weidinger et al. (2023) utilize sociotechnology to evaluate safety regulations for AI systems. Gabriel (2021) further extends these principles, arguing that AI systems must protect citizens' rights and adhere to public justification standards that prioritize disadvantaged members of society.

These studies highlight the interplay between AI systems and sociotechnological principles. However, more research is required to fully understand the evolving relationship between humans and technology in this domain.

2.2 Generative AI on Government

The emerging role of Generative AI in government has gained significant traction worldwide, particularly in smart city initiatives where it helps manage medical emergencies in urban environments (Sowmitha et al., 2022). In the Republic of China, Li et al. (2023) document how local governance has leveraged technological infrastructure to enhance service delivery, dramatically improving the agility of public service provision. Complementing this research, Lin (2023) examines the nuanced differences between large language models and chatbots in Chinese local government applications, revealing distinct implementation patterns and outcomes. Meanwhile, recent analysis of the Global Partnership on Artificial Intelligence (GPAI) by Keith (2024) identifies several concerning barriers to equitable participation—notably imbalanced global representation, overly restrictive membership processes, and limited translation services—that particularly disadvantage Southeast Asian stakeholders.

These developments collectively illustrate both the transformative potential and persistent challenges in governmental AI adoption across different regions.

2.3 Frameworks for AI Principles

The formulation of guiding principles has long been a cornerstone within public administration and the evolution of e-government initiatives. Historical frameworks, such as those proposed by Sandoval-Almazán et al. (2017) for e-government, the OECD's guidelines on public sector digitalization (2022), and principles of public governance as elaborated by Manoharan et al. (2023), have provided structured paths to manage technological transitions within governmental contexts. Recently, however, the advent of Generative AI (GenAI) has prompted a shift towards crafting principles specifically attuned to the distinct opportunities and challenges of these technologies.

Among contemporary frameworks, the UK government's Generative AI Framework for Public Managers (Gov.UK, 2024) outlines ten foundational principles, intended to foster responsible and effective adoption. Central to this approach is a balanced emphasis on understanding the technology's capabilities and limitations, ethical and lawful utilization, security assurance, human oversight, and the full lifecycle management of AI tools. Additionally, it encourages appropriate tool selection, openness, early engagement with private-sector partners, skills development, and integration with existing organizational policies. While commendable for promoting constructive engagement and cross-sector collaboration, three critical points emerge upon analysis: first, the framework tends to presume a uniform capacity across governmental agencies, which overlooks disparities in resources and expertise; second, it underestimates the potential complexities arising from rapid technological advancements that can quickly render guidelines obsolete; and third, it lacks specificity on how precisely ethical oversight and human involvement are operationalized within diverse governmental contexts.

Complementing this practical guidance, Richter's (2024) report for the IBM Center for the Business of Government takes a more structural perspective, highlighting key challenges such as a lack of cohesive AI strategy, insufficient literacy among public managers, inadequate foundational data sets, ethical and compliance issues, communication difficulties, cultural resistance, and pervasive trust deficits. In response, Richter proposes strategic pathways that include principles such as: enhanced public engagement, stronger ethical oversight, improved data management infrastructure, and workforce development to foster innovation. While the report effectively underscores systemic challenges often ignored by more operational guidelines, it nonetheless exhibits critical limitations: firstly, it inadequately addresses how to practically overcome cultural resistance within entrenched bureaucracies; secondly, it places insufficient emphasis on the urgent necessity for adaptability and flexibility within organizational structures; and thirdly, it fails to provide concrete mechanisms for fostering long-term trust among stakeholders and the public at large. And most important it does not propose how to foster literacy on public managers using these technologies.

Another proposal of GenAI principles is the OECD-G7 Toolkit for Artificial Intelligence (AI) in the Public Sector (OECD/UNESCO, 2024) outlines several core principles and guidelines aimed at ensuring the ethical, safe, secure, and trustworthy deployment of AI systems. Among these principles, emphasis is placed on service improvement, transparency and accountability, inclusivity, privacy and security, and skills development. Specifically, the toolkit underscores the importance of employing AI to automate repetitive tasks to enhance public services, advocating for transparency to enable informed decision-making, and emphasizing inclusivity to prevent discrimination. It further insists on rigorous privacy and security standards and promotes continuous skills development within public administrations to effectively manage AI technologies. Moreover, the proposal suggests the necessity for comprehensive standards and sustainability considerations to minimize environmental impacts associated with AI systems.

Lastly, the AGI principles proposed by Morris et al. (2023), although initially targeted at Artificial General Intelligence rather than specifically at GenAI, offer a compelling conceptual foundation relevant to the current discourse. This framework emphasizes the importance of evaluating capabilities over processes, prioritizing generality and performance, focusing on cognitive and metacognitive abilities, assessing potential rather than deployed instances, ensuring ecological validity of evaluation metrics, and understanding AGI as a progressive development path. While offering valuable insights into assessing complex AI systems, critical reflection reveals two primary shortcomings: firstly, the principles' abstraction makes them challenging to operationalize concretely within specific government functions; secondly, the framework does not sufficiently account for the socio-political dynamics unique to public sector decision-making, potentially limiting its immediate applicability within government contexts.

These principles represent a significant contribution to this research on generative artificial intelligence by providing a structured framework for evaluating and classifying AI systems' progress toward GenAI. The authors argue that this principled approach enables more nuanced discussions about AI capabilities, risks, and development trajectories while avoiding some of the limitations of previous definitions that focused on single criteria or end states. The idea of these principles provides some inputs for developing the principles for public managers.

The principles for GenAI use in government organizations represent a critical step toward leveraging this transformative technology responsibly. By focusing on awareness, collaboration, and ethical oversight, these frameworks provide a roadmap for public managers.

These four theoretical models demonstrate how public administrators are seeking ways to utilize generative AI. The four cases share common ground in their pursuit of cybersecurity policies to appropriately use GenAI technologies, as well as in their similar quest to develop capabilities and skills to better leverage the technology. Where they differ is in how they use the technology with others; for example, the British case lacks a proposal for external interaction; the IBM case (Richter, 2024) focuses heavily on internal development: skills and strengths, data and infrastructure improvement, without emphasizing outcomes for citizens or stakeholders from other government agencies. The OECD-G7 Toolkit stands out for its use of tools that improve public service, but its principles remain very general and insufficiently specific for application. These lessons enable the development of the principled approach proposed by this research.

2.4 Proposed GenAI Principles for Public Managers

The overlap of sociotechnological theory and government functions which uses AI are show on Fig. 1. Description of any principle will be done in the following paragraphs.

Public managers must balance innovation with responsibility as they integrate Generative AI (GenAI) into government operations. This framework elaborates on

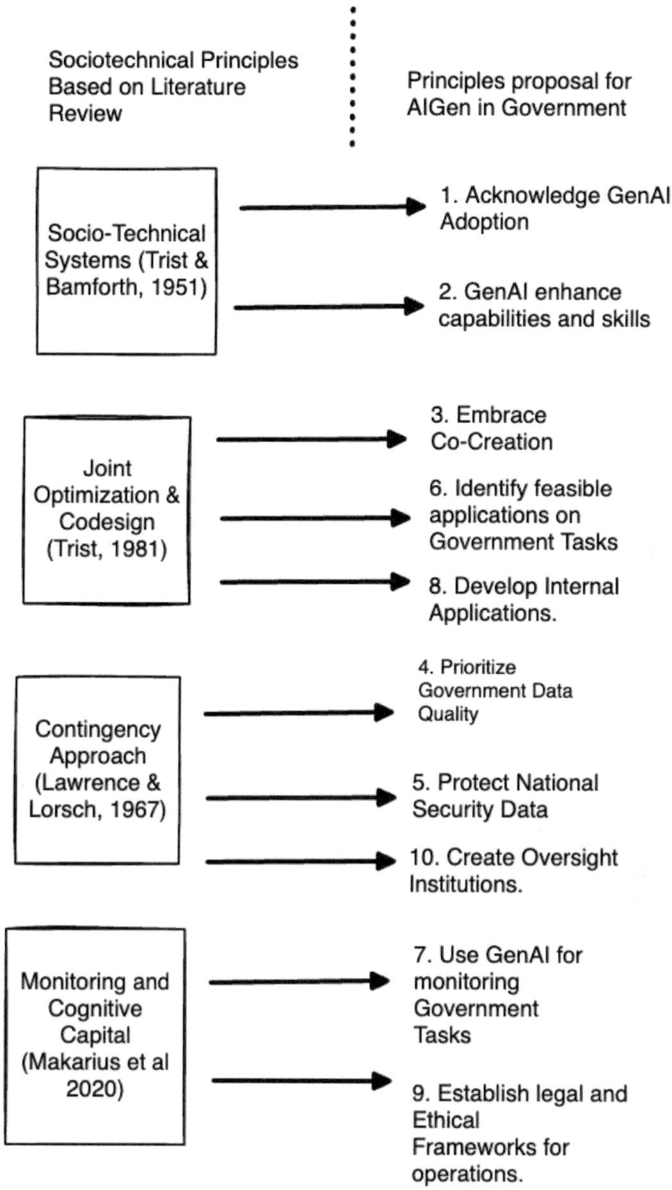

Fig. 1 Sociotechnological key concepts and proposed framework. *Source* Author own elaboration

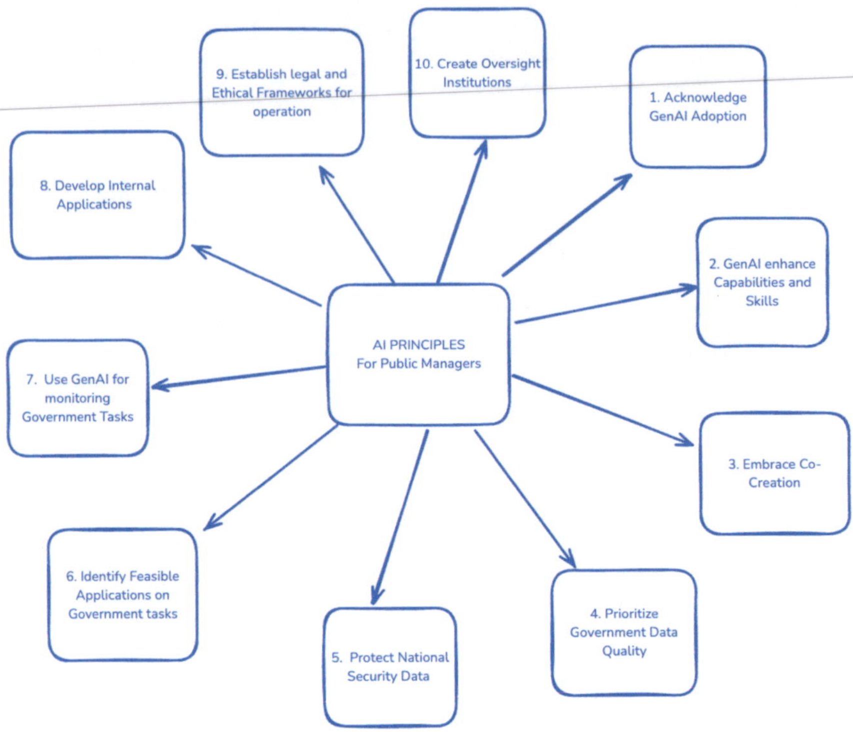

Fig. 2 Principles for GenAI and public managers. *Source* Author own elaboration

the key principles that guide the adoption and application of GenAI in the public sector, (see Fig. 2):

1. Acknowledge GenAI Adoption.
2. GenAI enhance Capabilities and Skills
3. Embrace Co-Creation
4. Prioritize Government Data Quality
5. Protect National Security Data
6. Identify Feasible Applications on Government tasks
7. Use GenAI for monitoring Government Tasks
8. Develop Internal Applications
9. Establish legal and Ethical Frameworks for government operation
10. Create Oversight Institutions

By elaborating on these principles, public managers can gain a deeper understanding of how to navigate the complexities of GenAI integration. This approach ensures that they are not only leveraging the technology's benefits but also maintaining public trust, safeguarding sensitive information, and aligning AI usage with the broader goals of public service.

1. Acknowledge GenAI Adoption

Public managers are already experimenting with and integrating Generative AI (GenAI) in various capacities—ranging from personal use to testing its potential for public service tasks. This early, informal adoption underscores the importance of recognizing GenAI as a growing influence in public administration. Sociotechnological is implicit on this principle because a key statement of this theory is to consider innovation as a social process (Rogers, 2003), to build technology in integrated perspective (Trist, 1981).

2. GenAI enhance Capabilities and Skills

GenAI can amplify government efficiency by automating repetitive tasks, analyzing large datasets, and generating insights that might be missed by traditional methods. For instance, it can support drafting reports, improving citizen services, and predicting policy outcomes. Public managers must foster a culture of continuous learning to enhance the workforce's ability to collaborate effectively with AI systems, thus creating a synergy between human expertise and machine intelligence. This principal statement comes from the idea of user-design centered, as a participatory design from sociotechnological theoretical framework (Mumford, 1983). Also relates to the principle of Focus on Capabilities, not Processes from Morris et al. (2023).

3. Embrace Co-Creation

GenAI is a work-in-progress, and its integration into government systems will require iterative development. Public managers should actively engage in co-creating solutions alongside AI developers, stakeholders, and end-users. By remaining flexible and adaptive, managers can tailor GenAI applications to address specific public needs while learning how to improve it. This idea of co-creation is supported by sociotechnological concepts such as building technical skill with social (Pinch & Bijker, 1984), and innovation as part of a social process (Rogers, 2003).

4. Prioritize Government Data Quality

The effectiveness of GenAI depends heavily on the quality of the data it processes. Public managers must ensure that government data is accurate, complete, and free from biases. Establishing stringent data governance practices, conducting regular audits, and implementing data-cleaning protocols are essential steps to maintain the integrity of AI-generated outcomes. Data quality is related with the technological impact of the AI technology (Coates, 1976), both are interrelated as input and output of the process.

5. Protect National Security Data

Not all data is suitable for use in GenAI systems. National security information and other highly sensitive datasets must remain isolated from AI tools to prevent potential vulnerabilities. Public managers should develop clear policies and safeguards, such as data encryption, access controls, and strict compliance standards, to ensure that sensitive information is protected. A researcher from the sociotechnological, Feenberg (2017) argues that technology is a factor of power, key data as national security must be considered like that.

6. Identify Feasible Applications on Government tasks

Not all government tasks are equally suitable for GenAI integration. Public managers should focus on areas where AI can deliver measurable benefits with minimal risk, such as automating administrative workflows, streamlining public service delivery, or enhancing communication with citizens. Conducting a comprehensive risk assessment and feasibility study is critical to identifying appropriate use cases while avoiding tasks where the risks outweigh the benefits. Government tasks relate with society and this to become interdependent on technology uses, this idea also from sociotechnological (Bijker, 1997) supports this principle to interact along with GenAI. Also complementary from Morris et al. (2023) principle of Focus on Cognitive and Metacognitive Tasks.

7. Use GenAI for monitoring Government Tasks

Government tasks are multidimensional, with many variables, contexts and levels of applications. The correct use of GenAI to analyze, diagnose and monitor tasks will provide and extra value for decision making and provide alternatives for wicked problems, this principle is supported by the idea of relationship with society and technology (Bijker, 1997), and the impact of the use of technology as a factor power (Feenberg, 2017).

8. Develop Internal GenAI Applications

Governments should prioritize the development of proprietary GenAI applications tailored to their specific needs and challenges. Building in-house tools ensures data sovereignty and minimizes dependence on external vendors, thereby mitigating potential security and privacy risks. Moreover, internal applications can be designed to align with core public sector values such as transparency, equity, and accountability. This approach aligns with the concept of citizen-centered design (Mumford, 1983) and the sociotechnical framework emphasizing the co-construction of knowledge and technology through user-centered design (Trist, 1981).

9. Establish Legal and Ethical Frameworks for Government Operation

Comprehensive legal frameworks are essential to safeguard personal data, address algorithmic biases, and ensure accountability in GenAI system deployment. Public managers should implement oversight mechanisms, including review boards or independent audits, to monitor AI system performance and assess their societal impact. This includes detecting unintended consequences, ensuring compliance with legal and ethical standards, and updating policies to address emerging risks. This principle aligns with Feenberg's (2017) notion of technology as a factor of power and Makarius et al.'s (2020) assertion that AI reshapes organizational structures.

10. Create Oversight Institutions

Establishing dedicated institutions to oversee GenAI applications is critical for ensuring transparency, accountability, and regulatory compliance. These bodies should monitor the algorithms, outcomes, and impacts of GenAI systems while fostering collaboration between technical experts and social stakeholders. This principle is supported by Pinch and Bijker's (1984) emphasis on aligning technical systems with societal needs and Feenberg's (2017) insights into the distribution of power through technology.

3 Discussion. Applications of GenAI Principles for Public Managers

The purpose of this section is twofold. On one side to provide some examples of the AI principles in the public sector. On the other side, to present a discussion about some key points of GenAI and the present debate. The first part describes the examples in the same order of the principles.

1. Acknowledge GenAI Adoption

The United Kingdom's public sector has seen widespread adoption of GenAI tools, with a survey revealing that 45% of public service professionals are aware of GenAI usage in their work areas, and 22% actively use these systems (Bright et al. (2024). This is also supported by Criado et al. (2021) survey of Mexico's CIOs perception about AI, and Ruvalcaba-Gómez and Cifuentes-Faura (2023). These examples demonstrate the informal and growing integration of GenAI in public administration, underscoring the necessity to recognize its expanding influence.

More research is needed to show the presence on government operations and data management using this technology.

2. Enhance Capabilities and Skills

The U.S. Department of Homeland Security (DHS) is piloting AI to train officers reviewing refugee applications, aiming to simulate various applicant scenarios and improve interviewing skills. This initiative exemplifies how GenAI can augment government efficiency by automating training processes and enhancing workforce capabilities (Spetalnick (2024). Another example of this principle is the CIA AI-powered chatbot capable of simulating interactions with foreign leaders, marking a significant advancement in the use of Artificial intelligence for strategic decision-making and Intelligence analysis (Barnes, 2025).

3. Embrace Co-Creation with GenAI

The main objective of this principle is to promote collaboration, co-production as an activity of human co-creation along different agencies, government levels to produce better systems of GenAI, correct mistakes, and iterate for developing better platforms. The most recent example is the Tokyo Metropolitan Government collaborated with AI developers and stakeholders to implement GenAI tools for urban planning and disaster response, ensuring solutions are tailored to specific public needs. This case highlights the importance of iterative development and active collaboration in integrating GenAI into government systems (Apolitical (2024).

4. Prioritize Government Data Quality

The aim of this principle is to foster data quality on government agencies to produce good outcomes from GenAI. The example of the Brazilian government partnered with OpenAI to process and analyze numerous lawsuits, emphasizing the need for accurate and comprehensive data to ensure effective AI-generated outcomes. This partnership underscores the critical role of high-quality data in the successful application of GenAI in public administration, specially because it is referred to the judiciary system on Brazil (Ayres & Caram, 2024); data quality is crucial to produce high quality outputs.

5. Protect National Security Data

There are different purposes on this principle: to select datasets, create policies to safeguard highly sensitive data before use for GenAI and put at risk some decision-making or information. A preliminary example is the U.S. intelligence community is cautiously integrating GenAI, focusing on unclassified data to avoid compromising sensitive information, and implementing robust safeguards (Bajak, 2024). Another example is the Guardian Project, from the CIA was building its own internal ChatGPT-style tool to sift through public data for clues (Mauran, 2024). Also Meta is letting the US military and defense contractors use its Llama AI model for national security purposes (Roth, 2024). These examples support the necessity to separate government data and create isolated platforms for different purposes. Not all GenAI is for all government agencies.

6. Identify Feasible Applications in Government Tasks

The aim of this principle is that public managers should find areas for GenAI deliver benefits. An example of automating administrative workflows is the One-Service Chatbot from the Municipal Services Office (MSO) from streamlining public service delivery or enhancing communication with citizens (GovTech Singapore, 2021). This initiative demonstrates a strategic focus on applying GenAI to tasks with measurable benefits and minimal risk.

7. Use GenAI for Monitoring Government Tasks.

The best example is in California, USA. four state departments will test generative AI: The Department of Tax and Fee Administration, the California Department of Transportation, the Department of Public Health, and the Health and Human Services Department, all of them monitor different government task in different levels (Nguyen, 2024) Most of these agencies does not allow access to the public this GenAI efforts are more for internal use.

8. Develop Internal GenAI Applications

Estonia's e-government system employs proprietary AI applications to automate services like registering births, ensuring greater control over sensitive data and reducing dependency on external vendors. In the Health sector, AI algorithms analyze patient data to identify trends, predict potential health issues, and recommend preventive measure. In transportation, the AI systems utilize data from sensors and cameras to analyze traffic patterns, adjust traffic signals in real-time, and provide timely information to commuters. Also, the introduction of AI chatbots to improve citizen engagement and streamline communication between citizens and government agencies (Hammer, 2024). Also de C.I.A. developed mentioned on principle 2, and ChatGPT Gov developed by OpenAI for the US government (APAC, 2025) are two clear examples of inside development for GenAI tools.

9. Establish Legal and Ethical Frameworks for Government Operations

A notable example of this principle is the Victorian Supreme Court in Australia, which issued guidelines requiring legal practitioners to disclose the use of AI in preparing legal arguments or drafting documents. This directive addresses concerns related to data privacy, algorithmic bias, and transparency. Lawyers and litigants involved in legal proceedings must inform the court and opposing parties about AI tools used and the nature of their assistance (So, 2024). Self-represented litigants are also encouraged to disclose AI involvement in document preparation, enabling judicial officers to better interpret submissions (Supreme Court of Victoria, 2024).

The Victorian Supreme Court highlights the ethical implications of AI usage, emphasizing the need to mitigate algorithmic biases and ensure transparency in legal processes (Legal Find, 2024). Other examples are the European Commission (2024) is the most recent and authoritative legal resource for Europe. In the U.S. the Executive Order on the safe, secure, and trustworthy development and use of artificial intelligence, was published on 2023 (The White House, 2023). Other efforts like de OECD Recommendation of the Council on Artificial Intelligence (OECD, 2019) and UNESCO (2021). Recommendation on the ethics of artificial intelligence, support this efforts on the legal domain.

Australia's approach represents a pioneering effort to define the boundaries of GenAI applications within the legal domain. While legal frameworks may vary by country due to cultural and institutional contexts, establishing clear ethical and legal guidelines is essential to govern the integration of GenAI into public sector operations effectively.

10. Create Oversight Institutions

Several international examples demonstrate the application of this principle within federal governments. For instance, the U.S. Patent and Trademark Office (USPTO) has established policies to monitor and regulate the use of generative AI (GenAI) tools within the agency, promoting transparency and accountability (Wired, 2024). Similarly, Canada has implemented policies ensuring that GenAI use in decision-making complies with established directives for transparency, accountability, and fairness. The Canadian government has also published a guide on generative AI, addressing challenges, opportunities, and best practices for responsible implementation (Canada Government, 2024).

These initiatives illustrate the creation of dedicated oversight institutions aimed at aligning GenAI applications with societal needs and regulatory frameworks.

While these examples are not comprehensive, they provide a preliminary view of how these principles can be applied by public managers. Table 1 summarizes these examples, highlighting two key trends. First, GenAI implementation and reporting are more prevalent in North America and parts of Asia, with fewer documented cases in Europe and Latin America. This reflects an emerging but uneven global adoption. Second, most examples represent early-stage initiatives rather than fully mature systems, underscoring both the novelty of GenAI and the potential for countries to measure its impact and expand its use.

Table 1 Principles and examples of GenAI for public managers in 2024–2025

Principle	Example	Source	Country-Region
1. Acknowledge GenAI adoption	UK Survey reports 45% public managers use AI	Bright et al. (2024)	UK-Europe
2. Enhance capabilities and skills	U.S. Department of Homeland Security (DHS) train migration officers using AI and CIA chatbot	Spetalnick (2024), Barnes (2025)	U.S. North America
3. Embrace co-creation with GenAi	Tokyo Metropolitan Government for Emergency response	Apolitical (2024)	Japan, Asia
4. Prioritize government data quality	GenAI in the judiciary system on Brazil	Ayres and Caram (2024)	Brazil, Latin America
5. Protect national security data	U.S. Intelligence Community. "Guardian Project"	Bajak (2024), Mauran (2024)	U.S. North America
6. Identify feasible applications in government tasks	One Service Chat Bot	GovTech Singapore (2021)	Singapore, Asia
7. Use GenAI for monitoring government tasks	California, USA, four state departments	Nguyen (2024)	U.S. North America
8. Develop internal GenAI applications	Estonia's e-government system employs proprietary AI. ChatGPT Gov	Hammer, (2024) APAC (2025)	Estonia. Europe, US
9. Establish legal and ethical frameworks for government operation	Victorian Supreme Court in Australia issued guidelines requiring lawyers to disclose the use of AI	So (2024), Supreme Court of Victoria (2024), OECD (2019) European Commission (2024)	Australia European Commission UNESCO OECD U.S
10. Create oversight institutions	U.S. Patent and Trademark Office and Canada's Government	Wired (2024), Canada Government (2024)	U.S. & Canada North America

4 Conclusions

The objective of this chapter was to develop a strategic framework for implementing artificial intelligence in the public sector, addressing the research question: To what extent can evidence-based practical principles be developed to guide public servants in the implementation and operational governance of generative AI technologies, given the current state of technological development and public sector constraints? The answer for this question is through the lens of sociotechnical theory, this research proposes ten principles for AI adoption in governmental contexts.

The first conclusion establishes that generative AI adoption for the public sector represents an inevitable reality that requires proactive engagement. Public organizations must create conducive conditions to support public managers in their administrative functions and address citizens' needs utilizing this technology. This aligns with the socio-technical systems framework, which informs two key principles: (1) acknowledging generative AI adoption and (2) recognizing how generative AI enhances capabilities and skills. These principles serve as mechanisms to facilitate social participation in the ongoing development of governmental AI initiatives.

The second conclusion posits that responsible AI implementation (whether generative AI or other forms) is optimally achieved through joint optimization processes. This iterative approach should integrate technological capabilities with human interaction to improve machine learning outcomes. Three principles of the framework support this position: (3) embracing co-creation methodologies; (6) identifying feasible applications for governmental tasks; and (8) developing internal applications. These principles require empirical testing within public administration contexts to generate evidence regarding their potential impact on public sector operations.

The third conclusion recognizes that artificial intelligence development must account for organizational context, background, and legacy systems. While large language models are trained on extensive datasets, the public sector consistently experiences learning curves that affect implementation. Therefore, the sociotechnical concept of contingency approach must accommodate changes, updates, and new conditions within the system. Three principles address this requirement: (4) prioritizing government data quality to mitigate bias and comprehension issues; (5) protecting national security data within contextual boundaries; and (10) creating oversight institutions to ensure accountability and continuous improvement independent of political fluctuations.

The fourth conclusion emphasizes that the ten principles for adopting generative AI in the public sector constitute an integrated toolkit. This holistic approach encompasses social awareness of technological applications, quality data inputs, task-specific implementations, safeguards for sensitive information, and ethical frameworks with oversight institutions that promote responsible technology use. The principles are designed as an integrated system rather than discrete or exclusive elements, allowing for simultaneous application across diverse contexts, scenarios, and management situations.

The fifth conclusion connects principles (7) using generative AI for monitoring governmental tasks, and (9) establishing legal and ethical frameworks for operations. These principles align with the sociotechnical approach of monitoring cognitive capital proposed by Makarius et al. (2020). Continuous assessment of AI evolution is essential for establishing boundaries on governmental operations and restricting certain AI functionalities that may affect citizens. These principles are interdependent—the monitoring of governmental tasks must be governed by legal and ethical frameworks to ensure data protection, privacy, and legitimacy. Given AI's rapid evolution, these principles must facilitate ongoing adaptive processes.

The research agenda emerging from this analysis encompasses several critical domains. Primary among these is the empirical validation of individual principles through rigorous testing in public sector environments. This research stream should focus particularly on practical elements such as co-creation processes and AI capability development, examining their implementation efficacy and impact on public service delivery.

A second research avenue involves investigating GenAI's role in governmental decision-making processes and governance structures. While the current analysis focuses primarily on operational implementation, future research must address the strategic implications of AI integration in policy formation and executive decision-making processes. This investigation should examine how GenAI influences governmental oversight, regulatory frameworks, and institutional accountability mechanisms.

The third research direction should focus on developing practical frameworks for government technology leaders. Chief Information Officers (CIOs) and Chief Technology Officers (CTOs) require evidence-based guidelines for technology adoption, security protocol implementation, and regulatory compliance. This research stream should emphasize the development of actionable frameworks that facilitate informed decision-making while protecting governmental data integrity and citizen privacy.

This research aims to address one of the current gaps in how generative AI is used in the public sector. At the very least, it hopes to spark a conversation that encourages new ideas in this area—ideas that can help build a more effective government: one that makes fewer mistakes, works more efficiently, and stays closely connected to its citizens.

References

APAC Business Headlines. (2025, January 31). ChatGPT for Government: New Era in Public Sector. *APAC Business Headlines*. https://apacbusinessheadlines.com/chatgpt-for-government-new-era-in-public/

Apolitical. (2024). Transforming Public Sector Services Using Generative AI: Global Case Studies. *Microsoft*. https://wwps.microsoft.com/blog/services-AI-apolitical

Asatiani, A., Malo, P., Nagbøl, P., Penttinen, E., Rinta-Kahila, T., & Salovaara, A. (2021). Sociotechnical envelopment of artificial intelligence: An approach to organizational deployment of inscrutable artificial intelligence systems. *Journal of the Association for Information Systems, 22*, 8. https://doi.org/10.17705/1JAIS.00664

Ayres, M., & Caram, B. (2024, June 11). Brazil hires OpenAI to cut costs of court battles. *Reuters*.

Barnes, J. (2025, 18 de enero). CIA's chatbot stands in for world leaders. *The New York Times*. https://www.nytimes.com/2025/01/18/us/politics/cia-chatbot-technology.html

Bajak, F. (2024). US intelligence agencies' embrace of generative AI is at once wary and urgent. *AP News*. https://apnews.com/article/us-intelligence-services-ai-models-9471e8c5703306eb29f6c971b6923187

Bright, J., Enock, F., Esnaashari, S., Francis, J., Hashem, Y., & Morgan, D. (2025). Generative AI is already widespread in the public sector: Evidence from a survey of UK public sector professionals. *Digital Government: Research and Practice, 6*(1), 1–13. https://doi.org/10.1145/3700140

Bijker, W. E. (1997). *Of bicycles, bakelites, and bulbs: Toward a theory of sociotechnical change* (p. 274). MIT Press.

Bracken, M. (2023). The Postal Service is leaning into AI for better shipping experiences. *FedScoop*. https://fedscoop.com/ai-postal-service-shipping-delivery/

Bright, J., Enock, F. E., Esnaashari, S., Francis, J., Hashem, Y., & Morgan, D. (2024). Generative AI is already widespread in the public sector [Preprint]. arXiv. https://arxiv.org/abs/2401.01291

Buchanan, B. G., & Shortliffe, E. H. (1984). *Rule-based expert systems: The MYCIN experiments of the Stanford Heuristic Programming Project*. Addison-Wesley.

Chappell, W. (2024, 7 de mayo). Microsoft reveals AI that lives away from the internet for spies and top-secret info: 'It is now deployed, it's live, it's answering questions, it will write code'. *Fortune*. https://fortune.com/2024/05/07/microsoft-ai-for-spies-divorced-from-internet-top-secret-intelligence/

Coates, J. F. (1976). Technology assessment—A tool kit. *ChemTech, 6*(6), 372–383.

Criado, J. I., Sandoval-Almazán, R., Valle-Cruz, D., & Ruvalcaba-Gómez, E. A. (2021). Chief information officers' perceptions about artificial intelligence: A comparative study of implications and challenges for the public sector. *First Monday, 26*(1).

Davenport, T. H., & Ronanki, R. (2018). Artificial intelligence for the real world. *Harvard Business Review, 96*(1), 108–116.

European Commission. (2024, January 24). Commission Decision of 24 January 2024 establishing the European Artificial Intelligence Office (C / 2024 / 390 final). Official Journal of the European Union C / 2024 / 1459. Retrieved from https://eur-lex.europa.eu/eli/C/2024/1459/oj

Feenberg, A. (2017). *Technosystem: The social life of reason*. Harvard University Press.

Gabriel, I. (2021). Toward a theory of justice for artificial intelligence. *Daedalus, 151*, 218–231. https://doi.org/10.1162/daed_a_01911

Government of Canada. (2024). *Guide on the use of generative artificial intelligence*. https://www.canada.ca/en/government/system/digital-government/digital-government-innovations/responsible-use-ai/guide-use-generative-ai.html

GOV.UK. (2024). Generative AI framework for HMG. https://www.gov.uk/government/publications/generative-ai-framework-for-hmg/generative-ai-framework-for-hmg-html

GovTech Singapore. (2021). Developing the OneService chatbot to improve municipal services. https://www.tech.gov.sg/media/technews/developing-the-one-service-chatbot/

Gupta, P., Nguyen, T. N., Gonzalez, C., & Woolley, A. W. (2023). Fostering collective intelligence in human–AI collaboration: Laying the groundwork for COHUMAIN [E-pub ahead of print]. *Topics in Cognitive Science*. https://doi.org/10.1111/tops.12679

Hammer, C. (2024). Case study: AI implementation in the Government of Estonia. Public Sector Network. https://publicsectornetwork.com/insight/case-study-ai-implementation-in-the-government-of-estonia

Keith, A. J. (2024). Governance of artificial intelligence in Southeast Asia. *Global Policy, 15*(5), 937–954. https://doi.org/10.1111/1758-5899.13458

Kshetri, N., Dwivedi, Y. K., & Janssen, M. (2024). Metaverse for advancing government: Prospects, challenges and a research agenda. *Government Information Quarterly, 41*(2), Article 101931. https://doi.org/10.1016/j.giq.2024.101931

Lawrence, P. R., & Lorsch, J. W. (1967). *Organization and environment: Managing differentiation and integration*. Harvard University Press.

Legal Find. (2024). AI in law: Victoria's Supreme Court sets new guidelines. https://legalfinda.com.au/blog/ai-in-law-victorias-supreme-court-sets-new-guidelines

Li, Y., Fan, Y., & Nie, L. (2023). Making governance agile: Exploring the role of artificial intelligence in China's local governance. *Public policy & administration.* Advance online publication. https://doi.org/10.1177/09520767231188229

Lindsay, R. K., Buchanan, B. G., Feigenbaum, E. A., & Lederberg, J. (1993). DENDRAL: A case study of the first expert system for scientific hypothesis formation. *Artificial Intelligence, 61*(2), 209–261.

Lin, Z. (2023). How Generative-AI can be Effectively used in Government Chatbots. arXiv preprint arXiv:2312.02181. https://doi.org/10.48550/arXiv.2312.02181

Makarius, E., Mukherjee, D., Fox, J., & Fox, A. (2020). Rising with the machines: A sociotechnical framework for bringing artificial intelligence into the organization. *Organizations & Markets: Policies & Processes eJournal.* https://doi.org/10.1016/j.jbusres.2020.07.045

Manoharan, A. P., Melitski, J., & Holzer, M. (2023). Digital governance: An assessment of performance and best practices. *Public Organization Review, 23*(1), 265–283. https://doi.org/10.1007/s11115-021-00584-8

Mauran, C. (2024). Microsoft launched a new 'air-gapped' AI model—But none of you can use it. *Mashable.* https://mashable.com/article/microsoft-launched-air-gapped-ai-model-us-intelligence-agencies

Medaglia, R., & Tangi, L. (2022). The adoption of artificial intelligence in the public sector in Europe: Drivers, features, and impacts. In *proceedings of the 15th international conference on theory and practice of electronic governance* (pp. 10–18). https://doi.org/10.1145/3560107.3560110

Mikalef, P., Fjørtoft, S. O., & Torvatn, H. Y. (2019). Artificial intelligence in the public sector: A study of challenges and opportunities for Norwegian municipalities. In *Digital Transformation for a Sustainable Society in the 21st Century: 18th IFIP WG 6.11 Conference on e-Business, e-Services, and e-Society*, I3E 2019 (pp. 267–277). Springer International Publishing.

Morris, M., Sohl-Dickstein, J., Fiedel, N., Warkentin, T., Dafoe, A., & Faust, A. (2023). *Levels of AGI for operationalizing progress on the path to AGI.* arXiv. https://arxiv.org/abs/2311.02462

Mumford, E. (1983). *Designing human systems for new technology: The ETHICS method.* Manchester Business School.

Nguyen, S. (2024, 23 de mayo). California is testing new generative AI tools. Here's what to know. *AP News.* https://apnews.com/article/0d6b3827138d744b1a40a4057dba8634

OECD/UNESCO. (2024). *G7 Toolkit for Artificial Intelligence in the Public Sector.* OECD Publishing. https://doi.org/10.1787/421c1244-en

Organisation for Economic Co-operation and Development (OECD) (2019). Recommendation of the Council on Artificial Intelligence (OECD/LEGAL/0449). https://legalinstruments.oecd.org/en/instruments/OECD-LEGAL-0449

Pinch, T. J., & Bijker, W. E. (1984). The social construction of facts and artefacts: Or how the sociology of science and the sociology of technology might benefit each other. *Social Studies of Science, 14*(3), 399–431.

Richter, A. (2024). *Navigating generative AI in government.* IBM Center for the Business of Government. https://www.businessofgovernment.org/report/navigating-generative-ai-government

Rogers, E. M. (2003). *Diffusion of innovations* (5th ed.). Free Press.

Roth, E. (2024, 4 de noviembre). Meta AI is ready for war. *The Verge.* https://www.theverge.com/2024/11/4/24287951/meta-ai-llama-war-us-government-national-security

Ruvalcaba-Gómez, E. A., & Cifuentes-Faura, J. (2023). Analysis of the perception of digital government and artificial intelligence in the public sector in Jalisco, Mexico. *International Review of Administrative Sciences, 89*(4), 1203–1222. https://doi.org/10.1177/00208523231164587

Sandoval-Almazán, R., Luna-Reyes, L. F., Luna-Reyes, D. E., Gil-García, J. R., Puron-Cid, G., & Picazo-Vela, S. (2017). Building digital government strategies. In *Public Administration and Information Technology* (Vol. 16). https://doi.org/10.1007/978-3-319-60348-3

So, J. (2024). Victorian, Queensland Supreme Courts publish guidelines for AI use. *Australasian Lawyer.* https://www.thelawyermag.com/au/news/general/victorian-queensland-supreme-courts-publish-guidelines-for-ai-use/490557

Sowmitha, R., Shanmuga Raju, S., Harshini, R., Arjuna, S., & Ram Kumar, C. (2022). Artificial Intelligence in smart cities and healthcare. *EAI Endorsed Transactions on Smart Cities, 2*(6). https://doi.org/10.4108/eetsc.v6i3.2275

Spetalnick, M. (2024). U.S. explores AI to train immigration officers on talking to refugees. *Reuters.* https://www.reuters.com/world/us/us-explores-ai-train-immigration-officers-talking-refugees-2024-05-08/

Supreme Court of Victoria. (2024). Guidelines for litigants: Responsible use of artificial intelligence in litigation. https://www.supremecourt.vic.gov.au/forms-fees-and-services/forms-templates-and-guidelines/guideline-responsible-use-of-ai-in-litigation

Tobin, C. (2023). Educational technology: Digital innovation and AI in schools. *House of Lords Library.* https://lordslibrary.parliament.uk/educational-technology-digital-innovation-and-ai-in-schools/

Trist, E. L. (1981). The evolution of socio-technical systems: A conceptual framework and an action research program. Ontario Quality of Working Life Centre. https://www.lmmiller.com/blog/wp-content/uploads/2013/06/The-Evolution-of-Socio-Technical-Systems-Trist.pdf

Trist, E. L., & Bamforth, K. W. (1951). Some social and psychological consequences of the longwall method of coal-getting. *Human Relations, 4*(1), 3–38.

UNESCO. (2021, November 23). Recommendation on the Ethics of Artificial Intelligence. Retrieved from https://unesdoc.unesco.org/ark:/48223/pf0000381130

Weidinger, L., Rauh, M., Marchal, N., Manzini, A., Hendricks, L., Mateos-Garcia, J., Bergman, S., Kay, J., Griffin, C., Bariach, B., Gabriel, I., Rieser, V., & Isaac, W. (2023). Sociotechnical safety evaluation of generative AI systems. arXiv, abs/2310.11986. https://doi.org/10.48550/arXiv.2310.11986

Weston, T. (2023). The dawn of AI in UK schools: A new term, a new challenge. Teacher Development Trust. https://tdtrust.org/2023/09/08/press-release-the-dawn-of-ai-in-uk-schools-a-new-term-a-new-challenge/

Wired. (2024). The US Patent and Trademark Office banned staff from using generative AI. https://www.wired.com/story/us-patent-trademark-office-internally-banned-generative-ai/

Wirtz, B. W., Weyerer, J. C., & Sturm, B. J. (2020). The dark sides of artificial intelligence: An integrated AI governance framework for public administration. *International Journal of Public Administration, 43*(9), 818–829.

White House. (2023, October 30). Executive Order on the Safe, Secure, and Trustworthy Development and Use of Artificial Intelligence (E.O. 14110). Retrieved from https://bidenwhitehouse.archives.gov/briefing-room/presidential-actions/2023/10/30/executive-order-on-the-safe-secure-and-trustworthy-development-and-use-of-artificial-intelligence/

Rule Based AI Systems for Public Governance. A Framework for Smarter, Transparent and Citizen-Centered Governance

4

Charalabidis Yannis and Kontos Gerasimos

1 Introduction

Governments worldwide are entering a pivotal phase in their digital transformation journeys, with Artificial Intelligence (AI) emerging as a cornerstone of future-ready public administration. As the scope and scale of AI applications expand across domains such as service delivery, policy formulation, and regulatory oversight, strategic planning becomes essential for ensuring that these technologies reinforce, rather than compromise, democratic principles and institutional legitimacy (Zhou, 2020).

While the potential benefits of AI adoption in the public sector are substantial—including improved efficiency, predictive analytics, and adaptive service models—several critical governance challenges must be proactively addressed. These include the opacity and limited explainability of many AI systems, which can undermine transparency and public accountability (Oleksy et al., 2022); the persistence of algorithmic bias, which risks reproducing existing societal inequities (Jain et al., 2021); and rising concerns about surveillance, autonomy, and the erosion of civil liberties, especially in the absence of robust oversight mechanisms (Al-Besher & Kumar, 2021). Furthermore, the lack of harmonized regulatory frameworks impedes interoperability and hinders the development of scalable, cross-sectoral AI strategies.

In response, this chapter examines rule-based AI systems as a strategic governance model that offers legal clarity, operational predictability, and ethical

C. Yannis (✉) · K. Gerasimos
University of Aegean, Mitilini, Greece
e-mail: yannisx@aegean.gr

K. Gerasimos
e-mail: gerasimosk@aegean.gr

S. K. Aikins and T. Dimitrijevska-Markoski (eds.), *Artificial Intelligence and Government*, https://doi.org/10.1007/978-3-032-12344-2_4

alignment. Unlike opaque machine learning models, rule-based systems provide explainable and auditable decision logic, making them especially well-suited for high-stakes public sector applications. The chapter proposes a conceptual framework grounded in three foundational governance pillars—transparency, fairness, and security—and elaborates a multi-layered implementation roadmap that addresses foundational readiness, adoption strategies, and long-term acceleration. This layered approach aims to support policymakers in designing AI governance models that are both resilient and responsive to shifting technological, institutional, and societal dynamics.

The final sections present strategic policy recommendations and explore emerging trends such as human-centered AI, explainable systems, and anticipatory governance. In doing so, this chapter contributes to the broader discourse on AI in the public sector by offering a normative and operational pathway that aligns AI innovation with the enduring values of democratic governance, civic trust, and institutional legitimacy.

The remainder of the chapter is structured as follows: Sect. 2 (Framework and Methodology for AI-Driven Public Governance) outlines the research design, including a chronological review of smart and AI-enabled governance developments, and identifies key public sector applications. Section 3 (Challenges and Ethical Considerations) examines core barriers to AI adoption, such as algorithmic bias, privacy risks, accountability gaps, and regulatory uncertainty. Section 4 (Rule-Based AI Systems for Transparent and Fair Public Governance) presents rule-based AI as a strategic enabler of transparent, explainable, and legally coherent decision-making. Section 5 (Policy Recommendations and AI Governance Implementation Roadmap) introduces a multi-layered roadmap to support secure, inclusive, and adaptive AI governance models. Finally, Sect. 6 (Future Directions, Limitations, and Concluding Reflections) synthesizes findings, discusses conceptual limitations, and proposes expanded pillars and future research directions to support adaptive, equitable, and ethically robust AI governance. The remainder of this chapter is structured as follows:

2 Framework and Methodology for AI-Driven Public Governance

The aim of this section is to outline the research methodology, including the chronological evolution of AI in public governance as well as a review of existing AI—Based government applications.

2.1 Methodological Framework for Research on AI-Driven Public Governance

This study employs a systematic literature review (SLR) methodology to investigate the role of AI—particularly rule-based systems—in enhancing transparency, fairness, and accountability in public governance. The research process was designed to ensure methodological rigor and thematic relevance across multiple disciplines, including public administration, ethics, AI policy, and digital transformation. The SLR approach was selected due to its rigorous, transparent, and replicable process, which allows for a comprehensive synthesis of existing knowledge on the topic. Following established guidelines such as those proposed by Kitchenham and Charters (2007) and the PRISMA framework (Preferred Reporting Items for Systematic Reviews and Meta-Analyses), the review involved a structured process of identifying, selecting, evaluating, and synthesizing relevant scholarly sources. This method ensured the inclusion of high-quality and pertinent studies, enabling a robust understanding of current research trends, gaps, and theoretical advancements within the field.

The systematic literature review was conducted in several distinct phases: planning, execution, and analysis. In the planning phase, clear research questions were formulated to guide the review process. During execution, multiple academic databases such as Scopus, Web of Science, and Google Scholar were systematically searched using predefined keywords and Boolean operators. Inclusion and exclusion criteria were applied to ensure relevance and quality. Selected studies were then critically appraised using standard quality assessment tools. Finally, data from the studies were extracted, categorized, and analyzed to identify recurring themes, theoretical models, and research gaps.

A structured search strategy was applied across major academic databases (e.g., Scopus, Web of Science, and IEEE Xplore), focusing on peer-reviewed articles published between 2010 and 2023. Keywords included combinations of: "artificial intelligence", "public governance", "rule-based systems", "transparency", "fairness", "accountability", "AI ethics", and "government innovation". The search was supplemented with grey literature, policy papers, and reports from organizations such as the OECD, UNESCO, and the European Commission to capture real-world implementations and policy developments.

The inclusion criteria were: (a) relevance to AI use in public governance contexts; (b) explicit discussion of ethical, legal, or procedural concerns; and (c) applicability to rule-based or explainable AI systems. Selected publications were thematically analyzed to identify key trends, ethical dilemmas, and governance challenges. This analysis forms the basis for the conceptual framework proposed in the subsequent sections.

The subsequent subsections present the principal findings derived from the systematic literature review undertaken in this study. Section 2.2 offers a chronological account of the evolution of smart public governance, tracing the integration of digital technologies within public administration. Section 2.3 examines the parallel development of AI-specific governance frameworks, highlighting regulatory milestones and ethical considerations. Finally, Sect. 2.4 synthesizes key AI applications in public governance, as identified in the literature, to illustrate current practices and emergent trends. Collectively, these analyses provide a conceptual foundation for understanding the evolving intersection of AI and public governance.

2.2 Chronological Overview of Smart Public Governance

The concept of smart governance has evolved over several decades as a response to the growing influence of information and communication technologies (ICTs) in the public sector. Its origins can be traced back to the 1990s, during the early stages of e-government initiatives, when governments began leveraging the internet and basic digital systems to enhance administrative efficiency and citizen access to services. These early efforts were largely transactional—focused on digitizing existing services rather than transforming governance structures. The emphasis at this stage was on automation, online portals, and improving service delivery (Heeks, 2006; Layne & Lee, 2001). This era was characterized by a top-down approach, where ICTs were primarily tools for automation and internal optimization rather than public engagement or policy transformation.

The 2000s marked a significant turning point with the proliferation of broadband networks, mobile technologies, and open data. This period saw a shift from simple digitalization to more interactive and participatory forms of governance. Concepts such as digital democracy, open government, and citizen-centric services began to emerge, reflecting a move toward transparency, collaboration, and civic engagement (Janssen et al., 2012). Governments began experimenting with data-driven decision-making and real-time public service management, enabled by the increasing availability of digital infrastructure and sensor networks. This period also saw the rise of Web 2.0 technologies, allowing for interactive public interfaces, crowd-sourced data, and the participatory design of public services. Digital platforms began to serve not just administrative functions but also deliberative and collaborative governance roles.

The term "smart governance" gained prominence in the 2010s, particularly as part of the smart cities movement. Unlike earlier phases of e-government, smart governance emphasized the integration of real-time data, advanced analytics, and cross-sector collaboration to enable evidence-based, adaptive, and networked decision-making. This period was defined by the use of sensor networks, urban dashboards, AI algorithms, and data-sharing ecosystems to support governance processes across domains such as traffic management, waste collection, emergency response, and environmental monitoring (Mergel et al., 2019; Nam & Pardo, 2011; Scholl & Alawadhi, 2016). Governance models also shifted from hierarchical structures toward platform-based ecosystems, where governments acted as facilitators or orchestrators of digital services in partnership with the private sector and civil society (Kitchin, 2014).

From the late 2010s into the 2020s, smart governance has matured into a strategic governance paradigm, increasingly aligned with values of resilience, equity, sustainability, and digital sovereignty. New technological capabilities, such as artificial intelligence (AI), blockchain, and machine learning, have been integrated into policy-making and administrative systems to support real-time decision-making, automate public services, and personalize citizen engagement. However, these developments have also brought new challenges, including concerns over surveillance, algorithmic bias, and the centralization of digital power (Zouridis et al.,

2020). As a result, ethics, accountability, and digital rights have become critical dimensions of smart governance, prompting national and international frameworks aimed at ensuring that smart technologies are deployed in ways that are transparent, inclusive, and democratically legitimate (European Commission, 2020; UN-Habitat, 2020).

In summary, the history of smart governance reflects a shift from technology-as-efficiency to technology-as-enabler of participatory, data-driven, and anticipatory governance. It represents an evolving interplay between digital innovation and institutional transformation, where the focus has broadened from operational improvements to achieving societal goals through networked, responsive, and participatory forms of governing. On the other side, these promising opportunities create also ethical and societal considerations including transparency and accountability which necessitate the need for effective governance frameworks, for AI—Driven Governance.

In the present day, Smart governance development has been accelerated by advancements in technologies like Internet of Things (IoT), artificial intelligence (AI), big data analytics, blockchain, cryptography, and networking infrastructure—Around the world, several pilot initiatives and practical applications have been carried out, with a focus on issues including smart transportation, energy management, public safety, and citizen involvement (Wirtz et al., 2019).

The historical development of smart governance across time may be considered to be a continuous process, from early attempts at integrating technology into public administration to the all-encompassing, integrated strategies used today. Figure 1 above, briefly portrays this evolution. The following section presents the foundamental concepts for AI Driven Public Governance.

2.3 Chronological Overview of AI Driven Public Governance

The evolution of AI public governance reflects a growing global recognition of the transformative—and potentially disruptive—impact of artificial intelligence on society, democracy, and public administration. Initially, governance responses were limited and fragmented, often treating AI under the umbrella of broader digital or data-related regulatory frameworks. Up to the early 2010s, AI systems were relatively nascent in public sector deployment, and concerns surrounding them were largely subsumed under existing legal categories such as data protection (e.g., the EU's Data Protection Directive of 1995) and digital infrastructure regulation.

The first significant shift occurred in the mid-2010s, when the increasing integration of AI into public services—such as welfare allocation, predictive policing, and health diagnostics—began to raise ethical, legal, and accountability concerns. Governments and international organizations started formulating national and regional AI strategies. Canada became the first country to launch a national AI strategy in 2017, followed closely by countries such as France, Germany, and

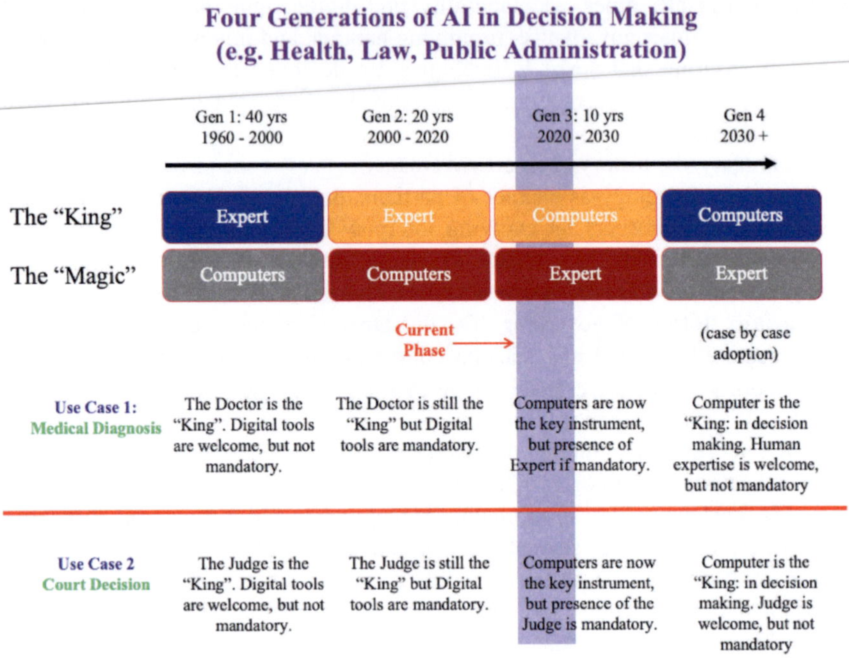

Fig. 1 Four generations of AI in decision making (e.g. Health, Law, Public Administration)

China, each articulating their own visions for ethical and competitive AI development (Government of Canada, 2017; State Council of China, 2017; Villani, 2018).

A major milestone in AI governance came in 2019, when the European Commission's High-Level Expert Group on Artificial Intelligence released the Ethics Guidelines for Trustworthy AI. This document emphasized seven key requirements for ethical AI, including human agency and oversight, transparency, non-discrimination, and accountability (European Commission, 2019). In the same year, the Organisation for Economic Co-operation and Development (OECD) adopted the OECD AI Principles, marking the first intergovernmental agreement on AI ethics and governance. These principles were later endorsed by the G20, signaling a growing consensus on the need for shared norms (OECD, 2019a, 2019b). Since 2020, Brazil's Supreme Federal Court has used Victor, an AI system designed to analyze judicial documents and prioritize cases. It assists in identifying cases related to constitutional matters or previous rulings, with Brazil's supreme court to credit enhanced judicial efficiency and transparency.

Concurrently, the United Nations Educational, Scientific and Cultural Organization (UNESCO) began leading discussions on global standards for AI. In 2021, UNESCO adopted the Recommendation on the Ethics of Artificial Intelligence, the first global normative instrument of its kind, which emphasized the importance of protecting human rights, promoting inclusive development, and ensuring sustainability (UNESCO, 2021a, 2021b). That same year, the European Commission proposed the Artificial Intelligence Act (EU AI Act), a comprehensive legal framework designed to regulate AI systems based on their risk level. The Act proposes strict obligations for high-risk AI applications—particularly those used in public domains—setting a precedent for enforceable, legally binding governance mechanisms (European Commission, 2021).

Recent years have also seen the rise of multilateral initiatives aimed at coordinating global governance efforts. The G7's Hiroshima Process on Generative AI (2023) and the Bletchley Declaration (UK AI Safety Summit, 2023) reflect the geopolitical urgency to align governance frameworks across democratic states. These developments suggest a paradigm shift from voluntary ethical guidelines to regulatory convergence, especially in high-risk public sector applications such as biometric surveillance, automated decision-making in public benefits, and criminal justice.

In sum, the governance of AI in the public domain has evolved from reactive and principles-based approaches to increasingly proactive and regulatory models. The current trajectory points toward multi-level governance that blends ethical principles, legal instruments, and institutional innovation to safeguard public interest and democratic values in an AI-driven world.

Despite the undisputable benefits of AI Driven Public Governance, there are still concerns about AI uses, especially regarding ethical considerations, bias and fainess as well as transparency and accountability. It is the role of the following section, (i.e. Section 3), to highlight and briefly discuss these considerations, while Sect. 4, that follows after, proposes a rule-based AI system as a solution for improving accountability, explainability, and public trust in AI-driven governance.

2.4 Major Applications of AI Driven Public Governance

Table 1 presents the major applications for AI Driven Public Governance as these were identified from the literature review. The applications were selected based on the frequency of occurrence in the scientific literature to ensure that they represent commonly discussed and well-documented applications of artificial intelligence in various areas of public governance. We deliberately provide also a brief description in order to reflect the most prevalent and impactful use cases. This approach helps to highlight trends, emerging technologies, and successful strategies that have gained recognition and traction within the research community, contributing to a more robust understanding of the potential benefits and challenges associated with AI in a public governance context.

However, while these AI—Driven technologies offer unprecedented opportunities for efficiency, innovation, and personalization, their deployment also raises critical questions around transparency, fairness, accountability, and public trust. These questions will now be discussed in the following section.

Table 1 Major applications for AI driven public governance

Applications	Description
AI Chatbots for Citizen Services	Implementing AI-powered chatbots to provide instant responses to citizens' queries, streamline information dissemination, and enhance accessibility to government services
AI-Based Decision Support Systems	Deploying decision support systems that leverage AI to assist government officials in making informed and data-driven decisions, improving overall governance processes
Fraud Detection in Public Policy	Utilizing AI for fraud detection and prevention in public services, such as welfare programs, to enhance accountability and ensure resources are allocated efficiently
AI-enhanced Civic Engagement Platforms	Developing platforms that leverage AI to analyze citizen feedback, preferences, and concerns, facilitating better policymaking and fostering active civic participation
Automated Document Processing	Implementing AI for automated processing of documents, reducing administrative burdens, minimizing errors, and enhancing the efficiency of government workflows
Facial Recognition for Security	Using AI-powered facial recognition systems for enhanced security and identity verification in public spaces or government facilities to ensure public safety
AI in Urban Planning	Integrating AI in urban planning processes to analyze data, predict future trends, and optimize city development, leading to more efficient and sustainable urban environments
Smart Traffic Management Systems	Implementing AI-driven traffic management systems to optimize traffic flow, reduce congestion, and enhance overall transportation efficiency within smart cities
AI-enabled Disaster Response	Utilizing AI for efficient disaster response by analyzing real-time data, predicting disaster impacts, and coordinating timely and effective emergency services

3 Challenges and Ethical Considerations of AI-Driven Public Governance

The aim of this section is to explore privacy risks, algorithmic bias, ethical dilemmas, and regulatory challenges affecting AI adoption in governance.

As artificial intelligence becomes increasingly embedded in public governance systems, ethical concerns surrounding bias, fairness, accountability, and transparency have become central to academic and policy debates. Unlike private-sector applications, AI systems in the public domain often deal with high-stakes decisions—such as welfare allocation, criminal justice, immigration, and healthcare—where errors or discriminatory outcomes can directly infringe upon fundamental rights and public trust. These risks underscore the ethical responsibility of governments to ensure that AI systems uphold democratic values, equity, and justice (Cowls & Floridi, 2018; Eubanks, 2018).

3.1 Algorithmic Bias and Fairness

One of the most pressing issues is algorithmic bias, which can emerge from historical data, model design, or structural inequalities embedded in institutional systems. For instance, predictive policing tools have been criticized for reinforcing racial profiling by relying on biased crime data, while risk assessment algorithms in social services may inadvertently penalize marginalized groups based on socioeconomic indicators (Angwin et al., 2016; Obermeyer et al., 2019). Because many AI systems operate as "black boxes," the opacity of decision-making processes further exacerbates concerns over due process, contestability, and explainability in public decision-making. Such outcomes not only replicate but institutionalize discrimination, turning ethical failings into systemic governance problems.

Fairness in AI-driven governance is not a purely technical problem—it is also a normative and contextual one. What counts as "fair" may differ across jurisdictions and public domains, requiring deliberative processes and legal scrutiny. Efforts to promote fairness often involve bias auditing, human-in-the-loop systems, and ex-ante impact assessments, especially in high-risk applications such as biometric surveillance or eligibility screening (Barocas et al., 2019). Several governance frameworks, such as the EU's proposed Artificial Intelligence Act and UNESCO's Ethics of AI Recommendation, mandate fairness as a core requirement and call for institutional mechanisms to monitor and mitigate potential harms (European Commission, 2021; UNESCO, 2021a, 2021b).

3.2 Transparency

A major barrier to ethical AI in governance is the opacity of many algorithmic systems. Popularly referred to as "black box" algorithms, these systems often lack interpretability, making it difficult for decision-makers, auditors, or the public to understand how outcomes are produced. This lack of algorithmic transparency undermines key principles of administrative law, such as the right to an explanation and the ability to challenge a decision. In critical domains—such as immigration, criminal justice, or health eligibility—this can severely erode procedural fairness and due process (Pasquale, 2015).

Efforts to improve transparency include thBre use of explainable AI (XAI), algorithmic impact assessments, and open-source governance tools, but their effectiveness depends on institutional capacity and legal mandates. Some governments, such as Canada and the Netherlands, have adopted algorithmic registries to improve transparency and allow citizens to view how algorithms are used in public decision-making. However, global standards remain inconsistent, and many jurisdictions still lack the infrastructure or expertise to implement transparent AI systems at scale (Wagner, 2019).

3.3 Accountability

The introduction of AI into governance challenges traditional notions of accountability. In conventional public administration, responsibility is typically ascribed to identifiable human actors or institutions. However, with AI systems, decision-making is often distributed among multiple actors: data scientists, software developers, vendors, and public officials. This diffusion creates an accountability vacuum, where no single actor is clearly responsible for adverse outcomes (Zouridis et al., 2020).

To address this, scholars and policymakers have emphasized the need for algorithmic accountability frameworks, which include robust audit trails, third-party assessments, appeals mechanisms, and clearly defined liability structures. Legal frameworks such as the EU's Artificial Intelligence Act (2021) explicitly require public authorities using high-risk AI systems to maintain human oversight, ensure traceability, and provide mechanisms for recourse. Additionally, initiatives such as UNESCO's Recommendation on the Ethics of AI stress the importance of institutional checks and balances, impact evaluations, and inclusive governance to safeguard public interest (European Commission, 2021; UNESCO, 2021a, 2021b).

3.4 Privacy Risks and Ethical Considerations

The use of AI in public governance raises significant privacy risks due to its reliance on sensitive personal, behavioral, and biometric data. Government systems increasingly process data from health records, geolocation, facial recognition, and social services—exposing citizens to risks such as data breaches, surveillance overreach, and the misuse of information without informed consent (Cath, 2018; Wachter et al., 2017). These risks are amplified when data is repurposed across agencies without robust safeguards (Veale & Brass, 2019).

Beyond data misuse, privacy concerns are rooted in the power asymmetry between citizens and the state. Individuals often lack control over how their data is collected, used, or shared—raising ethical questions about autonomy, consent, and discrimination, especially for vulnerable communities subjected to profiling or predictive targeting (Eubanks, 2018).

Legal instruments such as the EU General Data Protection Regulation (GDPR) and UNESCO's Ethics of AI Recommendation assert privacy as a non-negotiable right, reinforcing the need for privacy-by-design principles in digital governance systems. Ensuring data governance, fairness, and ethical safeguards is not only a technical requirement but a political and institutional obligation.

In this context, rule-based AI systems—which operate using explicit logic, regulatory constraints, and predefined rules—offer a compelling alternative to opaque machine-learning models. Their auditable and explainable structure supports transparency, legal compliance, and procedural fairness, especially in high-stakes domains (Wachter et al., 2017). Unlike adaptive models, rule-based systems limit unintended behavior, support ex-ante control, and enhance institutional accountability.

While less flexible than data-driven approaches, rule-based systems promote democratic values by embedding ethical safeguards into their architecture—offering a reliable foundation for transparent, fair, and rights-respecting public governance.

The preceding analysis highlights critical limitations in current AI deployments, particularly in relation to opacity, bias propagation, and regulatory ambiguity. These challenges underscore the necessity for architectures that support procedural traceability, logic-based reasoning, and normative compliance. The next section proposes rule-based AI systems as a technically robust alternative to black-box models—offering greater explainability, verifiability, and alignment with legal and ethical standards essential for public governance (Bryson, 2018).

4 Rule Based AI Systems for Transparent and Fair Public Governance

The aim of this section is to propose a rule-based AI system as a solution for improving accountability, explainability, and public trust for AI-driven governance.

Rule-Based Artificial Intelligence systems offer a promising pathway to modernizing public governance with transparency, efficiency, and fairness. Their ability to simplify complex processes and provide explainable decisions makes them a valuable tool for fostering transparency and fairness in governance. By thoughtfully integrating Rule-Based AI systems into governance, governments can pave the way for a more accountable and citizen-focused future.

4.1 Understanding Rule-Based AI Systems

Rule-based AI (RBAI) systems are a class of artificial intelligence built on explicit "if–then" logic defined by domain experts. Unlike machine learning models that rely on statistical inference from large datasets, RBAI systems operate deterministically, offering high transparency, consistency, and traceability in decision-making.

For instance, a typical rule in public governance might state: If an individual's income falls below a defined threshold, then they are eligible for financial aid. Such rules are well suited to domains where decision criteria can be clearly codified, particularly in contexts requiring accountability, fairness, and legal compliance.

Key characteristics of rule-based systems include:

- Structure: Rules are developed by experts based on policies, laws, or guidelines.
- Transparency: Every output is directly traceable to a specific rule, supporting explainability.
- Adaptability: Rules can be updated to reflect changing regulations or institutional priorities.

Compared to machine learning models, rule-based systems offer several advantages:

- Transparency and Explainability: Decisions are fully auditable and understandable, reinforcing public trust.
- Predictability and Consistency: Deterministic logic ensures uniform application of rules across cases.
- Ease of Deployment: No need for large datasets or complex training, making RBAI systems more accessible and cost-effective.
- Legal and Ethical Alignment: Since rules are crafted and validated by human experts, they naturally align with institutional and regulatory frameworks.

These features make RBAI particularly compelling for high-stakes public governance applications where interpretability and procedural fairness are paramount.

4.2 Real World Examples of Rule Based AI in Public Governance

Rule-based systems are already making a mark in areas where predictability, transparency, and accountability are critical. Here are some existing key applications in public governance worldwide:

Estonia—KrattAI Virtual Assistants for Government Services

Estonia has long been recognized as a digital governance pioneer, and its KrattAI framework exemplifies the application of rule-based AI to improve public service delivery. KrattAI is a network of interoperable virtual assistants integrated across various government agencies to facilitate citizen access to administrative services such as tax filing, business registration, and social welfare. The system is designed with a rule-based decision engine that ensures responses and actions comply with Estonia's legal, societal and administrative rules (Estonian Ministry of Economic Affairs & Communications, 2020).

Canada—Rule-Based AI in Immigration Case Management (Chinook System)
Canada's Immigration, Refugees and Citizenship Canada (IRCC) department has implemented rule-based AI tools to support visa processing and immigration case management. The Chinook tool is a spreadsheet-based system that applies predefined rules and filters to triage and assess visa applications, helping human officers identify straightforward cases while flagging complex ones for further review. Chinook remains largely rules-driven, relying on structured, transparent logic to support decisions. The system improves operational efficiency while retaining human oversight and explainability, essential in a legal context where decisions must be justified and appealable (Molnar & Gill, 2021).

Brazil—Victor AI in the Judiciary
The Supreme Federal Court of Brazil (STF) has implemented Victor, an AI system that supports the prioritization and classification of judicial cases. Although some components involve natural language processing, Victor largely operates as a rule-based system, identifying whether new cases meet specific criteria aligned with established constitutional jurisprudence. The goal is not to make legal rulings, but to expedite case triaging by surfacing those that warrant attention based on procedural rules and past precedent (CNJ, 2021).

While a comprehensive analysis of additional real-world applications of rule-based AI systems falls beyond the scope of this study, it can be reasonably concluded that such systems represent a highly suitable—if not essential—solution for specific domains of public governance including but not limited to:

1. **Regulatory Compliance and Monitoring**—Governments can implement rule-based systems to ensure businesses and individuals comply with regulations. For instance, tax compliance systems can automatically flag anomalies based on predefined rules such as income thresholds or suspicious transactions.
2. **Social Welfare Distribution**—Rule-based systems simplify the process of determining eligibility for welfare programs. By encoding eligibility criteria, these systems ensure that benefits reach those who qualify without delays or biases
3. **Public Service Automation**—Many governments are using Rule Based Systems to automate routine administrative tasks such as license renewals, application processing, or permit approvals, reducing bureaucracy and enhancing service delivery.
4. **Crisis Response—**In disaster management, Rule Based systems can quickly assess the severity of an incident and recommend immediate actions based on established protocols. For example: In the unlike event of an earthquake, if magnitude exceeds 6.0, then activate emergency response teams.

4.3 Theoretical Foundations for Rule Based AI Systems for Transparent and Fair Public Governance

A primary advantage of rule-based AI is its inherent explainability. Unlike statistical or neural network models, which often yield accurate but opaque outputs, rule-based systems can justify decisions through explicit references to legal or policy rules. This capability is critical in public governance contexts—such as eligibility determination, regulatory enforcement, or benefits administration—where individuals have a legal and ethical right to understand how decisions are made (Pasquale, 2015; Veale & Brass, 2019). Traceable logic supports appeals processes, judicial oversight, and protection against arbitrary or discriminatory outcomes. It also enables non-technical personnel to maintain and revise systems in alignment with evolving public policy.

These systems also enhance institutional accountability. Their deterministic structure, governed by codified procedures, facilitates external audits, impact assessments, and compliance monitoring (Bovens, 2007; European Commission, 2021). Unlike complex, vendor-developed models with unclear boundaries of responsibility, rule-based AI provides a clear chain of attribution, allowing for transparent governance and more effective risk management.

Crucially, rule-based AI systems can foster public trust. In governance, trust derives not only from efficiency but from perceptions of fairness, transparency, and procedural justice (Bovens, 2007). When citizens perceive AI as a "black box," trust erodes. Rule-based systems, by contrast, offer predictability and visibility, allowing individuals to understand how their data is used, how decisions are made, and how they can seek redress—essential features of legitimate and trustworthy digital governance (Zouridis et al., 2020).

However, rule-based systems are not without limitations. They may be rigid, struggle with contextual nuance, and require extensive manual upkeep, particularly in complex domains with evolving rulesets. Maintaining a coherent rule base at scale can be challenging, and expert input is not always readily available.

Despite these constraints, the normative alignment, transparency, and legal auditability of rule-based AI make it well suited for high-stakes decision-making in the public sector—contexts where ethical and legal safeguards must take precedence over raw predictive performance. In many cases, hybrid models—combining the explainability of rule-based logic with the adaptive learning capabilities of data-driven AI—may offer the most balanced solution. Such systems must be designed with robust human oversight to guard against automation bias, ensure accountability, and uphold procedural fairness.

Ultimately, the choice of AI architecture should be determined not solely by technical sophistication, but by its ability to meet the ethical, legal, and institutional demands of the governance context in which it operates.

4.4 Towards a Framework for Rule—Based AI for Public Governance

The integration of artificial intelligence and emerging technologies into public governance represents a transformative development in how governments deliver services, make decisions, and interact with citizens. These technologies offer considerable promise for improving the efficiency, responsiveness, and accessibility of public services. However, their deployment also introduces complex ethical, legal, and institutional challenges—particularly around issues of transparency, fairness, and public accountability.

In this evolving landscape, it is essential for policymakers and public institutions to develop clear, principled frameworks that guide the design and implementation of AI systems in ways that reinforce democratic values and protect the public interest. Effective governance of AI requires more than technical competence; it demands alignment between technological capabilities and normative commitments, ensuring that these systems serve as instruments of social equity, legitimacy, and public trust. Achieving such alignment necessitates collaborative engagement among a broad spectrum of stakeholders—including governments, technology developers, civil society organizations, academic experts, and affected communities.

In response to this need, we propose a conceptual framework built around three fundamental pillars that serve as the normative and operational baseline for the development of rule-based AI systems in public governance:

- **Pillar 1: Transparency in Public Governance**—ensuring visibility, explainability, and traceability in algorithmic processes and decision-making.
- **Pillar 2: Fairness in Public Governance**—promoting equitable treatment, nondiscrimination, and inclusive outcomes across diverse social groups.
- **Pillar 3: Security in Public Governance**—safeguarding the integrity, reliability, and resilience of AI systems, while protecting data privacy and institutional trust.

These pillars are not isolated principles but interdependent components of an integrated approach to ethical AI deployment. Together, they provide a structured foundation for balancing innovation with accountability, enabling governments to harness AI's potential while upholding the rule of law, social justice, and democratic oversight. The following sections examine each pillar in depth, outlining its significance, challenges, and implications for the future of AI-driven public governance. Figure 2 below, graphically portrays the proposed framework.

Pillar 1: Transparency in Public Governance

Transparency is a cornerstone of democratic governance and is equally critical in the deployment of AI systems in the public sector. In AI-driven governance, transparency refers not only to open access to information but also to the interpretability, explainability, and traceability of algorithmic decisions. Rule-based AI

Fig. 2 Three pillars for rule based AI in public governance

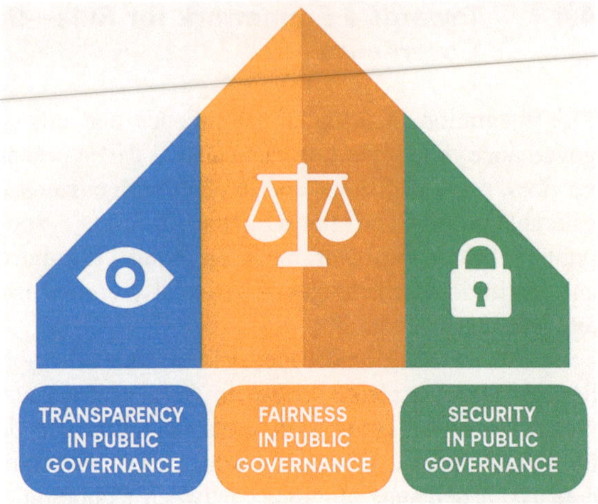

systems are particularly advantageous in this context, as their decision logic is explicitly defined, auditable, and easier to communicate to stakeholders compared to more opaque, data-driven models such as deep learning.

For public institutions, ensuring transparency entails clear documentation of how AI systems operate, what data is being used, what rules or criteria underpin decisions, and how outputs can be interpreted and challenged. It also involves the public disclosure of algorithmic tools, such as through algorithmic registries or impact assessments. This openness is crucial for maintaining public trust, enabling accountability, and supporting the right to contest automated decisions—a legal and ethical requirement in many jurisdictions.

Moreover, transparency fosters institutional learning and external oversight, allowing civil society, regulators, and academia to evaluate the fairness, legality, and effectiveness of AI implementations. As such, it is not simply a technical feature but a governance imperative, central to upholding procedural justice and democratic legitimacy.

Pillar 2: Fairness in Public Governance

Fairness in AI-driven public governance is about ensuring that automated systems do not perpetuate or exacerbate existing social inequalities, and that all individuals are treated with equity and dignity. This includes preventing discrimination based on race, gender, socio-economic status, or other protected attributes, as well as addressing systemic biases embedded in both institutional practices and datasets.

Rule-based AI systems offer a structured pathway to fairness by allowing developers and policymakers to embed explicit ethical constraints and legal norms into system design. Unlike machine learning models that may reflect hidden biases in training data, rule-based systems operate under predefined criteria that can be reviewed, modified, and aligned with human rights principles and public policy goals.

Operationalizing fairness requires ongoing evaluation and engagement. This includes bias audits, stakeholder consultation, and inclusive design processes that involve marginalized communities. Fairness also intersects with accessibility, ensuring that AI-enabled services are usable and beneficial to all citizens, regardless of digital literacy or geographic location. Ultimately, fairness must be treated not only as a compliance requirement but as a moral commitment to equitable public service.

Pillar 3: Security in Public Governance

Security in the context of AI-enabled public governance refers to the protection of systems, data, and decision-making processes from misuse, manipulation, and unintended harm. As governments increasingly rely on automated tools to manage sensitive operations—ranging from social welfare to public safety—the stakes for ensuring robust, secure, and resilient AI systems are extremely high.

Rule-based AI systems contribute to security by offering deterministic behavior, which reduces the unpredictability and emergent risks often associated with adaptive algorithms. This predictability allows for more effective threat modeling, error handling, and system validation. Additionally, rule-based systems can be more easily configured to comply with data protection regulations, such as the General Data Protection Regulation (GDPR), through principles like data minimization and purpose limitation.

Given that rule-based AI systems operate on predefined logic, their responses to security breaches or external threats can be predictable. Governments can easily design security protocols and responses for these systems, knowing that they will always adhere to the established—predetermined rules. For example, if a security breach is detected in a rule-based system that handles citizens' data, a set of predefined security protocols can be activated to limit damage and prevent unauthorized access. In addition, rule-based systems are often easier to align with existing security and regulatory frameworks, ensuring that governance processes adhere to national and international security standards. This is particularly relevant in sectors like finance or defense, where compliance with strict security regulations is critical.

Beyond technical safeguards, security in public governance includes institutional and procedural dimensions. This involves regular audits, cyber risk assessments, staff training, and crisis response protocols. It also encompasses the protection of citizens' privacy and digital rights, particularly as public sector databases become more interconnected and susceptible to breaches or surveillance overreach.

Having written the above, the proposed three-pillar framework should be seen not as a fixed structure, but as a living model—one that can evolve through interdisciplinary collaboration, empirical evaluation, and continuous engagement with public values. Future research and practice may benefit from expanding it to include additional pillars that address emerging challenges and dimensions of ethical AI governance. In the final Section, we will highlight some further dimensions that merit particular attention.

5 Policy Recommendations and AI Governance Implementation Roadmap

The aim of this section is to present a set of policy recommendations as well as a roadmap for policymakers on how to develop secure, fair, and regulatory-compliant AI models for governance.

The advancement of artificial intelligence in public governance presents both unprecedented opportunities and serious normative challenges. While AI systems can enhance administrative efficiency, responsiveness, and service quality, their deployment in public contexts—especially without adequate safeguards—can risk eroding public trust, entrenching bias, and undermining democratic accountability. To address these dual realities, this section offers policy recommendations and a governance implementation roadmap that provide structured guidance for the development of secure, fair, and ethically compliant AI models in public administration.

5.1 Policy Recommendations for Ethical AI Governance

This section outlines a set of actionable policy recommendations and a governance roadmap to support the development of secure, fair, and regulatory-compliant AI systems in public administration. As AI becomes increasingly embedded in public governance, its deployment presents both unprecedented opportunities and critical normative challenges. While AI can enhance efficiency, responsiveness, and service quality, insufficient safeguards may risk entrenching bias, eroding public trust, and weakening democratic accountability.

To address these complexities, we propose the following recommendations, grounded in the foundational pillars of transparency, fairness, and security, aimed at helping policymakers, city planners, and institutional leaders design a future-ready, responsible, and citizen-centered public sector.

1. **Strengthen Data Infrastructure and Analytics for Transparent Decision-Making**

Investing in robust, interoperable data ecosystems is essential for enabling evidence-based governance. These systems allow AI models to optimize resource allocation, streamline administrative processes, and foster cross-sector innovation. High-quality data infrastructures also reinforce transparency by making decision-making processes auditable, measurable, and accessible.

2. **Enhance Citizen Participation through AI-Enabled Engagement Tools**

AI can facilitate inclusive public participation by powering tools such as chatbots, sentiment analysis, and interactive platforms. Governments should adopt secure and transparent digital channels that encourage two-way communication, empower marginalized voices, and promote co-created policy-making—thus fostering civic trust and ownership in governance processes.

3. **Implement Comprehensive Cybersecurity, Privacy, and Compliance Frameworks**

Governments must institutionalize cybersecurity-by-design principles, ensure compliance with data protection regulations (e.g., GDPR), and conduct regular audits of AI systems. These safeguards are particularly vital in sensitive domains such as healthcare, welfare, and law enforcement, where algorithmic decisions carry direct societal impacts.

4. **Promote Interoperability Across AI and Emerging Technologies**

Smart governance requires the integration of AI with complementary technologies such as IoT and blockchain to enable real-time data processing, auditability, and system resilience. Policymakers should support cross-technology collaboration to create adaptive, holistic solutions for complex urban and administrative challenges.

5. **Design Inclusive and Accessible AI Solutions**

AI systems must serve all segments of society, including those with limited digital access or specific needs. Governments should fund AI literacy programs, promote universal design, and engage communities—especially vulnerable populations—in co-designing technologies. This ensures inclusivity and reduces the risk of digital exclusion.

6. **Institutionalize Rule-Based AI for Legally Grounded Governance**

Rule-based AI systems are well-suited for domains where legal traceability, policy alignment, and public scrutiny are essential. Policymakers should prioritize their deployment in high-stakes contexts and ensure that embedded rules are transparent, regularly updated, and accessible to the public.

7. **Establish Evaluation Metrics and Standards for Rule-Based AI**

To ensure quality, accountability, and scalability, public institutions should develop standardized frameworks for evaluating explainability, consistency, and legal alignment of rule-based AI systems. This includes promoting open-data libraries, interoperable architectures, and auditable system design protocols.

5.2 Toward an Implementation Roadmap for Rule Based AI Governance

As outlined earlier, rule-based AI systems hold transformative potential across sectors such as healthcare, education, transportation, finance, and public administration. When responsibly developed and deployed, these systems can drive economic growth, enhance service quality, and improve societal outcomes. However, to fully realize these benefits, a comprehensive implementation roadmap—grounded in ethical, legal, and institutional principles—is essential.

Our research emphasizes that such a roadmap must extend beyond technical development to encompass the governance, investment, regulatory, and operational dimensions of AI adoption. This includes ensuring that AI systems are ethically aligned, secure by design, and socially beneficial, with clear mechanisms for accountability and oversight embedded throughout their lifecycle.

To navigate the inherent complexities of AI governance, we propose a multi-layered approach consisting of three interdependent layers: **the Foundational Layer**, **the Adoption Layer**, and **the Acceleration Layer**. Each layer targets distinct but interconnected priorities, forming a holistic model for ethical AI integration. This layered model calls for the collaborative engagement of key stakeholders, including policymakers, public institutions, private sector leaders, academic researchers, and civil society actors. Together, these actors must work toward a shared vision of AI governance that fosters innovation while upholding democratic values, individual rights, and societal equity. Figure 3 below, presents the three interdependent layers for the implementation roadmap.

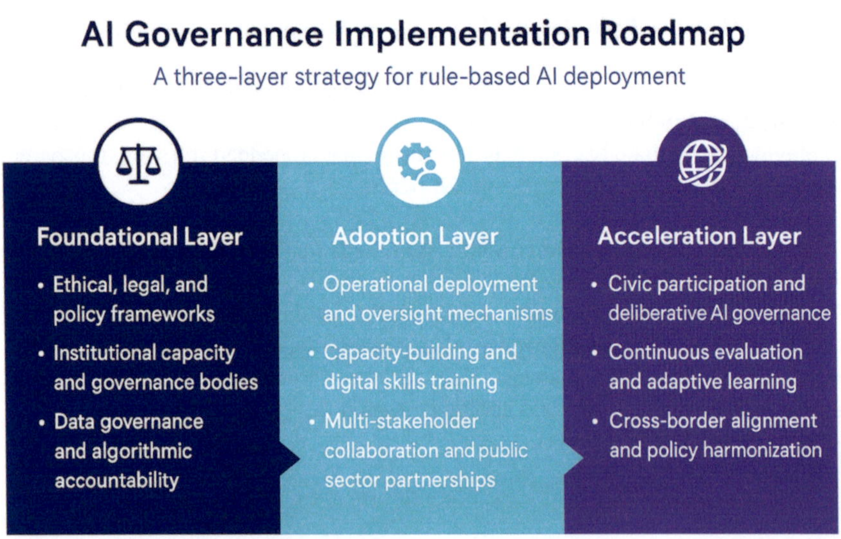

Fig. 3 Three interdependent layers for the implementation roadmap

Foundational Layer

The Foundational Layer serves as the structural bedrock of responsible AI deployment in public governance. It encompasses the core institutional and normative components, including policy and legal frameworks, governance structures, and data management protocols. This layer provides the essential regulatory, ethical, and organizational infrastructure required to guide AI adoption in a manner that is transparent, accountable, and aligned with public values. By establishing clear rules, oversight mechanisms, and data governance standards, the foundational layer ensures that AI systems are embedded within a robust framework that safeguards rights, promotes trust, and supports long-term institutional resilience.

Ethical, Legal, and Policy Frameworks

The establishment and continual refinement of ethical, legal, and regulatory frameworks are essential to guide the development and deployment of AI in a manner that aligns with national priorities, democratic values, and global ethical standards. These frameworks must comprehensively address key concerns such as data privacy, cybersecurity, accountability, algorithmic transparency, and online safety. Moreover, the development of technical standards and interoperability protocols is critical to ensuring that AI systems are not only safe and reliable but also consistent with international norms and cross-border regulatory expectations.

In parallel, governments should formulate and regularly update a national AI strategy that articulates a long-term vision for responsible AI adoption, one that is integrally connected to broader national development goals, including social inclusion, economic sustainability, and innovation-led growth. Such strategic alignment ensures that AI technologies are not developed in isolation but embedded within a larger socio-political and economic context. Collectively, these frameworks constitute the institutional backbone of AI governance, offering policymakers and stakeholders clear, enforceable guidelines for the ethical and effective use of AI across sectors.

Institutional Capacity and Governance Structures

Building robust institutional capacity is fundamental to the ethical and effective governance of AI. This involves the establishment of dedicated agencies, regulatory bodies, and cross-sectoral coordination mechanisms equipped to oversee the lifecycle of AI systems—from design and deployment to monitoring and evaluation. Institutions must be empowered with technical expertise, legal authority, and sufficient resources to enforce compliance, conduct audits, and respond to evolving technological risks.

Strengthening institutional capacity also requires investing in human capital development, ensuring that public officials and policymakers are equipped with the necessary skills in AI literacy, data governance, and ethical decision-making. In addition, governments should encourage inter-agency collaboration and establish multidisciplinary advisory boards—comprising experts from academia, civil society, and industry—to provide independent oversight and policy guidance.

Data Governance and Algorithmic Accountability
Effective data governance is a cornerstone of ethical, secure, and trustworthy AI deployment in the public sector. It encompasses not only the technical management of data but also the legal, ethical, and procedural safeguards necessary to protect individual rights and promote responsible innovation. Central to this effort is the establishment of comprehensive data privacy laws that clearly define how personal data may be collected, stored, processed, shared, and deleted.

Equally important is the implementation of robust data security protocols to ensure that sensitive information is protected from unauthorized access and misuse. This includes encryption standards, access controls, regular audits, and well-defined incident response mechanisms. These technical safeguards must be integrated with clear accountability structures to ensure enforcement and transparency.

Finally, open data initiatives can support public sector innovation and foster civic engagement by making non-sensitive datasets accessible to researchers, developers, and the general public. When designed with appropriate safeguards, these initiatives contribute to government transparency, data-driven policymaking, and a more inclusive digital ecosystem.

Adoption Layer
The Adoption Layer builds upon the foundational infrastructure by focusing on the ethical integration, capacity development, and strategic collaboration required for the practical deployment of AI systems. This phase emphasizes the importance of embedding ethical principles—such as fairness, accountability, and transparency—into AI implementation processes. It also involves the promotion of AI literacy and education, ensuring that both public servants and the wider society are equipped to understand, use, and critically engage with AI technologies. Furthermore, the adoption layer fosters cross-sector partnerships between government, industry, academia, and civil society, enabling shared innovation, resource pooling, and co-governance. Together, these efforts ensure that AI adoption is not only technically effective but also socially responsible and democratically legitimate.

Operational deployment and oversight mechanisms
To ensure AI technologies are developed and used in a manner that is ethical, transparent, and accountable, nations must implement robust mechanisms that build public trust and promote fairness. This involves establishing ethical guidelines that address issues such as bias, fairness, and the societal impact of AI, ensuring that the technology is used for the greater good. To promote transparency, AI developers should be encouraged to disclose how algorithms work, including the data sources, decision-making processes, and underlying logic that will help identify potential biases. Transparency also enables external audits and reviews, fostering an environment where AI development is open and accountable to oversight. Nations should require comprehensive impact assessments for AI projects, evaluating their social, economic, and environmental effects along with

appropriate accountability mechanisms, including guidelines and protocols for AI development, deployment, and use.

Capacity-building and digital skills training
Implementing educational programmes to improve AI literacy among the general public, policymakers, and business leaders will be key to ensuring the necessary cultural shift to propel AI adoption across all levels. Nations should also develop training and reskilling programmes specifically targeted at building a skilled workforce capable of developing and managing AI technologies. Industry-academia partnerships should be promoted to advance AI research and integrate AI-related courses into educational curricula.

Multi-stakeholder collaboration and public sector partnerships
Collaboration between the public and private sectors, as well as with international partners, is key to advancing AI adoption. Ample support should be provided to public–private partnerships to promote collaborative R&D initiatives to drive AI innovation and address societal challenges. Finally, promoting open data initiatives and policies will be crucial to enable access to high-quality datasets for AI research and development.

Acceleration Layer
The Acceleration Layer represents the apex of the AI governance framework, focusing on the scaling, optimization, and global alignment of AI technologies. This layer emphasizes the importance of public engagement and awareness-building, ensuring that citizens are informed, consulted, and empowered to shape AI-driven transformations. It also prioritizes ongoing monitoring and evaluation to assess the societal impacts of AI systems, measure effectiveness, and facilitate iterative improvement. Furthermore, the acceleration layer fosters international cooperation and policy harmonization, recognizing the global nature of AI innovation and governance challenges. By integrating these elements, the layer ensures that AI adoption is not only widespread and innovative but also continually refined to reflect evolving ethical norms, societal expectations, and global standards.

Civic participation and deliberative AI governance
Public engagement fosters transparency and trust, which are essential for the successful adoption of AI technologies. Governments should organise public consultations and open forums to gather diverse perspectives on AI governance. These forums should be inclusive, welcoming input from various stakeholders, including citizens, experts, industry representatives, and civil society organisations. Conducting awareness campaigns is also necessary to inform citizens about the benefits and risks of AI technologies. Additionally, governments should publish regular transparency reports on AI policies, initiatives, and regulatory actions detailing the progress of AI projects, the outcomes of public consultations, and any changes to AI regulations.

Cross-border alignment and policy harmonization
Nations must work together to establish common standards, share knowledge, and address cross-border challenges, ensuring that AI development benefits all. Harmonising national AI regulations with international standards will facilitate cross-border collaboration and trade. This can help create a level playing field for businesses and ensure that AI systems are safe and reliable worldwide. It is equally important to collaborate with other countries to address cross-border challenges related to AI, such as cybersecurity and data privacy. Joint efforts can include sharing threat intelligence, developing common security protocols, and coordinating responses to cyber incidents. Engaging in knowledge-sharing initiatives with other nations will help to diffuse learnings from best practices and advancements in AI governance. Sharing expertise and resources to support capacity-building efforts in developing countries can promote global AI development that is inclusive and ethical.

Continuous evaluation and adaptive learning
Continuous monitoring and adaptive learning are essential components of effective AI governance, ensuring that regulatory frameworks remain relevant, adaptive, and responsive to emerging technological, social, and environmental challenges. Monitoring efforts should adopt a holistic approach, assessing not only the technical performance and economic impact of AI systems but also their broader societal, ethical, and ecological implications. This comprehensive perspective enables policymakers to make more informed decisions grounded in an understanding of AI's full impact across sectors.

To this end, the implementation of real-time monitoring systems is recommended to track the deployment, functionality, and unintended consequences of AI applications. These systems can facilitate the early detection of performance anomalies or risks, helping to ensure that AI technologies operate safely and as intended. In parallel, the development of structured evaluation frameworks—incorporating quantitative and qualitative metrics—will be critical to assess the effectiveness of AI-related policies and regulatory interventions.

Furthermore, the use of pilot programs is strongly encouraged to test new AI governance models and policy instruments in controlled environments before broader implementation. This approach allows for experimentation, iterative refinement, and evidence-based scaling, ultimately supporting the creation of policies that are both practical and ethically sound.

These governance layers are not discrete or sequential; rather, they are interdependent and dynamic, operating through continuous feedback loops that enable adaptation, learning, and iterative improvement. Depending on the maturity and context of a nation's AI ecosystem, policymakers may prioritize different layers at different times, while ensuring that all three remain mutually reinforcing and responsive to evolving technological and societal needs. This structured, layered approach provides a flexible yet coherent roadmap for developing a resilient, inclusive, and forward-looking AI governance framework—one capable of effectively navigating the complex challenges and transformative opportunities presented by artificial intelligence in public governance.

6 Future Directions, Limitations and Conclusion

The aim of this section is to present a concluding summary, highlight our research limitations and connect these limitations with meaningful avenues for further research.

6.1 Concluding Comments

The strategic integration of Artificial Intelligence into public governance marks a pivotal moment in the evolution of the modern state. As governments confront increasingly complex societal challenges—ranging from demographic shifts to climate resilience and digital inclusion—AI offers a suite of tools capable of transforming how public institutions deliver services, design policies, and engage citizens. However, the long-term success of this transformation depends not only on technological capability but on the strategic foresight and institutional design that guide its implementation.

This chapter has argued that rule-based AI systems, when anchored in the pillars of transparency, fairness, and security, present a compelling model for ethically sound and strategically aligned governance. These systems offer a level of explainability, legal traceability, and normative coherence that is essential for sustaining public trust and democratic legitimacy in high-stakes administrative contexts.

As AI applications proliferate—particularly in sectors such as healthcare, welfare, transportation, and environmental management—governments must adopt a strategic governance lens. This includes embedding AI within broader frameworks of national development, public sector modernization, and societal well-being. Moreover, emerging technologies such as IoT, blockchain, and geospatial analytics amplify both the opportunities and risks associated with AI, underscoring the need for integrated governance architectures that are anticipatory, adaptive, and ethically robust.

The call for human-centered AI remains central to this strategic agenda. It requires that algorithmic systems prioritize human agency, dignity, and inclusivity—ensuring that technology supports, rather than substitutes, democratic participation and civic empowerment. Achieving this vision entails sustained multi-stakeholder collaboration, cross-disciplinary policy design, and ongoing capacity-building within public institutions.

The three-layer implementation roadmap introduced in this chapter—comprising Foundational, Adoption, and Acceleration layers—offers a practical yet forward-looking model for strategic AI deployment. It enables governments to tailor their approach based on institutional maturity, technological readiness, and societal context, while ensuring alignment with democratic values and public expectations.

In conclusion, the future of AI in public governance must be defined not merely by efficiency or automation, but by a deliberate and principled commitment to responsible innovation. The challenge before us is not just to govern AI, but to strategically embed it within the ethical, legal, and institutional fabric of democratic societies. Doing so will require more than digital infrastructure—it will require a shared vision of AI as a public good, and a governance model that places human dignity, public value, and democratic accountability at its core.

6.2 Limitations and Future Research Directions

While this paper presents a comprehensive conceptual framework for rule-based AI governance grounded in the foundational pillars of transparency, fairness, and security, several limitations merit acknowledgment and open pathways for future research and refinement.

First, the study adopts a conceptual and policy-oriented approach, focusing on high-level frameworks rather than empirical validation. This limits its ability to capture context-specific variations, such as legal capacity, institutional maturity, or cultural values across different governance systems. Future research should incorporate comparative case studies and field-based evaluations to assess the real-world implementation of rule-based AI systems in varied socio-political environments.

Second, the framework's emphasis on rule-based AI—while justified by its advantages in explainability and legal compliance—does not fully address the potential of machine learning and hybrid AI models, which are increasingly deployed in predictive analytics and dynamic decision-making. Comparative studies examining the trade-offs between transparency and predictive performance would provide valuable insights for refining governance strategies.

Third, the framework would benefit from a deeper exploration of stakeholder perspectives, particularly those of civil society, marginalized communities, and frontline public administrators. Future work should involve participatory methods, such as co-design workshops, stakeholder interviews, and deliberative consultations, to ensure the framework is both inclusive and contextually grounded.

Finally, the rapid evolution of AI and emerging technologies presents a challenge to the long-term applicability of static governance models. To enhance resilience and future-proof the framework, ongoing empirical research and real time testing and refinement will be essential.

Expanding our Conceptual Framework: Toward a Multi-Pillar Governance Model for AI Driven Public Administrations

In recognition of these limitations and the growing complexity of AI governance, we propose an expansion of the original three-pillar model to incorporate four additional pillars that reflect emerging ethical and strategic priorities:

- Inclusiveness: Ensuring that AI systems are co-designed with diverse and underrepresented communities, enabling governance models that are reflective, equitable, and socially embedded.
- Sustainability: Integrating environmental impact assessments and long-term societal outcomes into the lifecycle of AI systems, particularly in areas such as infrastructure, energy, and urban planning.
- Adaptability and Resilience: Embedding mechanisms within governance structures that allow for real-time responsiveness to technological innovation, regulatory shifts, and sociopolitical changes.
- Ethical Oversight and Governance Capacity: Developing institutional infrastructures—such as independent AI ethics boards, public sector regulatory sandboxes, and cross-sectoral oversight bodies—to monitor, enforce, and continuously evaluate responsible AI implementation.

These additional pillars not only complement the core values of transparency, fairness, and security, but also provide the flexibility and normative depth required to support adaptive, inclusive, and ethically robust AI governance over time.

References

Albino, V., Berardi, U., & Dangelico, R. M. (2015). Smart cities: Definitions, dimensions, performance, and initiatives. *Journal of Urban Technology, 22*(1), 3–21. https://doi.org/10.1080/10630732.2014.942092

Al-Besher, N., & Kumar, R. (2021). Privacy preservation of Internet of Things–integrated social networks: A comprehensive review. *Pervasive and Mobile Computing, 79*, 101531.

Angwin, J., Larson, J., Mattu, S., & Kirchner, L. (2016). *Machine Bias*. ProPublica. https://www.propublica.org/article/machine-bias-risk-assessments-in-criminal-sentencing

Barocas, S., Hardt, M., & Narayanan, A. (2019). *Fairness and Machine Learning: Limitations and Opportunities*. fairmlbook.org

Binns, R. (2018). Fairness in machine learning: Lessons from political philosophy. In *Proceedings of the 2018 Conference on Fairness, Accountability and Transparency (FAT*)* (pp. 149–159).

Bovens, M. (2007). Analysing and assessing accountability: A conceptual framework. *European Law Journal, 13*(4), 447–468. https://doi.org/10.1111/j.1468-0386.2007.00378.x

Bryson, J. J. (2018). Patiency is not a virtue: The design of intelligent systems and systems of ethics. *Ethics and Information Technology, 20*, 15–26. https://doi.org/10.1007/s10676-018-9448-6

Cath, C. (2018). Governing artificial intelligence: Ethical, legal and technical opportunities and challenges. *Philosophical Transactions of the Royal Society A, 376*(2133). https://doi.org/10.1098/rsta.2018.0080

Chourabi, H., Nam, T., Walker, S., Gil-Garcia, J. R., Mellouli, S., Nahon, K., Pardo, T. A., & Scholl, H. J. (2012). Understanding smart cities: An integrative framework. In *Proceedings of the 45th Hawaii International Conference on System Sciences* (pp. 2289–2297). https://doi.org/10.1109/HICSS.2012.615

CNJ—Conselho Nacional de Justiça. (2021). *Inteligência Artificial no Poder Judiciário Brasileiro*. https://www.cnj.jus.br

Cowls, J., & Floridi, L. (2018). Prolegomena to a white paper on an ethical framework for a good AI society. *Minds and Machines, 28*(4), 689–707.

Crawford, K. (2021). *Atlas of AI: Power, Politics, and the Planetary Costs of Artificial Intelligence*. Yale University Press.

Department for Science, Innovation and Technology. (2023). The Bletchley Declaration by countries attending the AI Safety Summit, 1-2 November 2023. GOV.UK. Available from https://www.gov.uk/government/publications/ai-safety-summit-2023-the-bletchley-declaration/the-bletchleydeclaration-by-countries-attending-the-ai-safety-summit-1-2-november-2023

Doshi-Velez, F., & Kim, B. (2017). Towards a rigorous science of interpretable machine learning. arXiv preprint arXiv:1702.08608

Engin, Z., & Treleaven, P. (2019). Algorithmic government: Automating public services and supporting civil servants in using data science technologies. *The Computer Journal, 62*(3), 448–460. https://doi.org/10.1093/comjnl/bxy082

Estonian Ministry of Economic Affairs and Communications. (2020). *KrattAI Strategy Document*.

Eubanks, V. (2018). *Automating Inequality: How High-Tech Tools Profile, Police, and Punish the Poor*. St. Martin's Press.

European Commission. (2019). High-level expert group on artificial intelligence. *Ethics Guidelines for Trustworthy AI*. https://ec.europa.eu/digital-strategy/news/ethics-guidelines-trustworthy-ai_en

European Commission. (2020). Digital Government Benchmark 2020. https://digital-strategy.ec.europa.eu/en/library/digital-government-benchmark-2020

European Commission. (2021). *Proposal for a Regulation Laying Down Harmonised Rules on Artificial Intelligence*. Artificial Intelligence Act. https://eur-lex.europa.eu/legal-content/EN/TXT/?uri=CELEX%3A52021PC0206

Floridi, L., Cowls, J., Beltrametti, M., et al. (2018). AI4People—An ethical framework for a good AI society: Opportunities, risks, principles, and recommendations. *Minds and Machines, 28*(4), 689–707. https://doi.org/10.1007/s11023-018-9482-5

Gil-Garcia, J. R., Dawes, S. S., & Pardo, T. A. (2018). Digital government and public management research: Finding the crossroads. *Public Management Review, 20*(5), 633–646. https://doi.org/10.1080/14719037.2017.1327186

Government of Canada. (2017). *Pan-Canadian Artificial Intelligence Strategy*. https://ised-isde.canada.ca/site/innovation/en/artificial-intelligence

Heeks, R. (2006). Implementing and Managing eGovernment: An International Text. SAGE Publications.

Jain, B., Huber, M., & Elmasri, R. (2021). Increasing fairness in predictions using bias parity score based loss function regularization. In 2021 IEEE International Conference on Big Data (Big Data) (pp. 3704–3713). IEEE.

Janssen, M., Charalabidis, Y., & Zuiderwijk, A. (2012). Benefits, adoption barriers and myths of open data and open government. *Information Systems Management, 29*(4), 258–268. https://doi.org/10.1080/10580530.2012.716740

Kitchenham, B., & Charters, S. (2007). Guidelines for performing systematic literature reviews in software engineering (Technical Report No. EBSE-2007-01). Keele University and University of Durham. Available from https://www.elsevier.com/__data/promis_misc/525444systematicreviewsguide.pdf

Kitchin, R. (2014). The real-time city? Big data and smart urbanism. *GeoJournal, 79*(1), 1–14. https://doi.org/10.1007/s10708-013-9516-8

Layne, K., & Lee, J. (2001). Developing fully functional e-government: A four stage model. *Government Information Quarterly, 18*(2), 122–136. https://doi.org/10.1016/S0740-624X(01)00066-1

Meijer, A., Curtin, D., & Hillebrandt, M. (2012). Open government: Connecting vision and voice. *International Review of Administrative Sciences, 78*(1), 10–29. https://doi.org/10.1177/0020852311429533

Mergel, I., Edelmann, N., & Haug, N. (2019). Defining digital transformation: Results from expert interviews. *Government Information Quarterly, 36*(4), Article 101385. https://doi.org/10.1016/j.giq.2019.06.002

Molnar, P., & Gill, L. (2021). *Bots at the Gate: A Human Rights Analysis of Automated Decision-Making in Canada's Immigration System*. Citizen Lab.

Morley, J., Floridi, L., Kinsey, L., & Elhalal, A. (2021). From what to how: An overview of AI ethics tools, methods and research to translate principles into practices. *AI & Society, 36*, 939–962. https://doi.org/10.1007/s00146-020-00920-w

Nam, T., & Pardo, T. A. (2011). Smart city as urban innovation: Focusing on management, policy, and context. In *Proceedings of the 5th International Conference on Theory and Practice of Electronic Governance* (pp. 185–194). https://doi.org/10.1145/2072069.2072100

Obermeyer, Z., Powers, B., Vogeli, C., & Mullainathan, S. (2019). Dissecting racial bias in an algorithm used to manage the health of populations. *Science, 366*(6464), 447–453. https://doi.org/10.1126/science.aax2342

OECD. (2019a). *OECD Principles on Artificial Intelligence.* https://www.oecd.org/going-digital/ai/principles/

OECD. (2019b). *Recommendation of the Council on Artificial Intelligence.* OECD Publishing. https://legalinstruments.oecd.org/en/instruments/OECD-LEGAL-0449

Oleksy, T., Wnuk, A., Maison, D., & Łysiak, T. (2022). Artificial intelligence in public services: The role of explainability and transparency in building trust and public accountability. *Human-Technology Interaction, 18*(1), 45–62.

Pasquale, F. (2015). *The Black Box Society: The Secret Algorithms That Control Money and Information.* Harvard University Press.

Scholl, H. J., & Alawadhi, S. (2016). Smart governance: A roadmap for research and practice. In *Proceedings of the 17th Annual International Conference on Digital Government Research* (pp. 574–575).

State Council of China. (2017). *A Next Generation Artificial Intelligence Development Plan.* (Unofficial translation) https://www.newamerica.org/cybersecurity-initiative/digichina/blog/full-translation-chinas-new-generation-artificial-intelligence-development-plan-2017/

UNESCO. (2021a). *Recommendation on the Ethics of Artificial Intelligence.* https://unesdoc.unesco.org/ark:/48223/pf0000381137

UNESCO. (2021b). *Recommendation on the Ethics of Artificial Intelligence.* https://unesdoc.unesco.org/ark:/48223/pf0000380455

UN-Habitat. (2020). *People-centered smart cities: A call to action.* https://unhabitat.org/people-centered-smart-cities-a-call-to-action

Veale, M., & Brass, I. (2019). Administration by algorithm? Public management meets public sector machine learning. In *Proceedings of the 17th Annual International Conference on Digital Government Research* (pp. 574–575).

Villani, C. (2018). *For a Meaningful Artificial Intelligence: Towards a French and European Strategy.* https://www.aiforhumanity.fr/pdfs/MissionVillani_Report_ENG-VF.pdf

Wachter, S., Mittelstadt, B., & Floridi, L. (2017). Why a right to explanation of automated decision-making does not exist in the General Data Protection Regulation. *International Data Privacy Law, 7*(2), 76–99. https://doi.org/10.1093/idpl/ipx005

Wachter, S., Mittelstadt, B., & Russell, C. (2018). Counterfactual explanations without opening the black box: Automated decisions and the GDPR. *Harvard Journal of Law & Technology, 31*(2), 841–887.

Wagner, B. (2019). Algorithms and transparency in the EU: An analysis of the emerging legal framework. *Philosophical Transactions of the Royal Society A, 376*(2128). https://doi.org/10.1098/rsta.2018.0086

Wirtz, B. W., Weyerer, J. C., & Geyer, C. (2019). Artificial intelligence and the public sector—Applications and challenges. *International Journal of Public Administration, 42*(7), 596–615. https://doi.org/10.1080/01900692.2018.1498103

Zhou, N. (2020). Artificial intelligence in the public sector: Strategic planning for a future-ready public administration. *OECD Publishing*

Zouridis, S., Van Eck, M., & Bovens, M. (2020). Automated discretion. *Public Administration Review, 80*(5), 831–837. https://doi.org/10.1111/puar.13292

ORBIS: An AI-Enabled Architecture for Scaling Online Deliberation

5

Lucas Anastasiou, Sofiane Elguendouze, Ioannis Efstathiou, Ilaria Mariani, Elena Cabrio, Serena Villata, Nikos Karacapilidis, Grazia Concilio, Francesca Rizzo, Sara Greco, Chiara Jermini, Claudia Coppola, Alexandra Apostolopoulou, George Domalis, Dimitris Tsakalidis, and Anna De Liddo

L. Anastasiou (✉) · A. De Liddo
The Open University, Milton Keynes, UK
e-mail: lucas.anastasiou@open.ac.uk

A. De Liddo
e-mail: anna.deliddo@open.ac.uk

S. Elguendouze · E. Cabrio
Université Côte d'Azur, INRIA Centre de Recherche Sophia Antipolis Méditerranée, Valbonne, France
e-mail: sofiane.elguendouze@univ-cotedazur.fr

E. Cabrio
e-mail: elena.cabrio@univ-cotedazur.fr

I. Efstathiou · S. Villata · N. Karacapilidis · A. Apostolopoulou · G. Domalis · D. Tsakalidis
Novelcore, Athens, Greece
e-mail: efstathiou@novelcore.eu

S. Villata
e-mail: serena.villata@cnrs.fr

N. Karacapilidis
e-mail: karacap@upatras.gr

A. Apostolopoulou
e-mail: apostolopoulou@novelcore.eu

G. Domalis
e-mail: domalis@novelcore.eu

D. Tsakalidis
e-mail: tsakalidis@novelcore.eu

S. Villata
Center National De La Recherche Scientifique—Déllégation Côte D'azur, INRIA Centre de Recherche Sophia Antipolis Méditerranée, Valbonne, France

S. K. Aikins and T. Dimitrijevska-Markoski (eds.), *Artificial Intelligence and Government*, https://doi.org/10.1007/978-3-032-12344-2_5

1 Introduction

1.1 Background and Motivation

The digital transformation of democratic processes presents both opportunities and challenges for civic participation (Androutsopoulou et al., 2019) and collective decision-making (Borge et al., 2022; Esau et al., 2017). While digital technologies have expanded the potential reach of public deliberation and consultation, effectively scaling deliberative practices while maintaining quality discourse remains a significant challenge (Manosevitch, 2014). The growing disconnect be-tween citizens and policy-making institutions, combined with declining trust in democratic institutions, calls for innovative approaches to large-scale civic engagement managed or facilitated by public institutions (Aström et al., 2017).

The ORBIS project presents a systematic attempt to address these challenges through an integrated socio-technical approach that combines artificial intelligence (AI), argumentation theory, and deliberative democratic practices. This chapter presents the architecture developed within ORBIS for scaling and enhancing the capacity of governments and public bodies to conduct large-scale online deliberation while maintaining discourse quality, inclusiveness, and transparency.

1.2 Challenges in Large-Scale Online Deliberation

Current online deliberation platforms face several key challenges that ORBIS aims to address. First, existing solutions struggle to effectively structure and aggregate

I. Mariani · F. Rizzo
Department of Design, Politecnico di Milano, Milan, Italy
e-mail: ilaria1.mariani@polimi.it

F. Rizzo
e-mail: francesca.rizzo@polimi.it

G. Concilio
Department of Architecture and Urban Studies, Politecnico di Milano, Milan, Italy

S. Greco · C. Jermini · C. Coppola
Universita‘ della Svizzera Italiana, Lugano, Switzerland
e-mail: sara.greco@usi.ch

C. Jermini
e-mail: chiara.jermini@usi.ch

C. Coppola
e-mail: claudia.coppola@usi.ch

arguments[1] in a way that provides clear, synthesised insights for policy analysis when discussions scale to hundreds or thousands of participants (Aitamurto, 2016). Second, maintaining deliberation quality becomes increasingly difficult at scale, with issues of information overload, echo chambers, and toxic behaviour emerging in larger online discussions (Anastasiou & Liddo, 2023; Friess & Eilders, 2015). Third, current platforms provide limited support for evidence-based reasoning and struggle to enhance participants' understanding of complex policy issues (Dryzek et al., 2019; Esau et al., 2017).

Additionally, ensuring inclusivity while scaling presents particular challenges, as marginalised groups often face barriers to meaningful participation in digital deliberation (Karpowitz & Raphael, 2016; Velikanov, 2017). The architecture must therefore balance between accessibility and capabilities of the underlying technology.

1.3 The Role of AI in Collective Intelligence

AI plays a crucial role in addressing these scaling challenges faced by public administrations by augmenting human capabilities rather than replacing them. The ORBIS architecture leverages AI in several key ways. First, it employs argumentation mining and natural language processing to automatically detect and structure arguments from large-scale discussions, making citizen contributions more manageable and navigable for policy analysts (Lawrence & Reed, 2017; Palau & Moens, 2009). Second, machine learning pipelines help identify patterns and aggregate similar arguments, reducing redundancy while preserving diverse perspectives. Third, AI-powered explanation generation helps make complex deliberations more transparent and comprehensible to participants.

Importantly, ORBIS adopts a "Human on the Loop" (HOTL) approach where AI augments rather than automates deliberative processes (Enarsson et al., 2022). This ensures that human judgment remains central while leveraging computational capabilities to handle scale.

[1] By argumentation within this context, we mean the "verbal, social and rational activity aimed at convincing a reasonable critic of the acceptability of a standpoint by putting forward a constellation of propositions justifying or refuting the proposition expressed in the standpoint" as proposed in the Pragma-dialectical model by van Eemeren and Grootendorst (2004). Throughout this chapter, the term "argument" is used with two distinct meanings: (1) as a complete argumentative unit consisting of premises and a conclusion, and (2) more narrowly as a synonym for"premise"—a statement supporting a position or conclusion. This terminological variation reflects different analytical approaches across sections.

2 Related Work

2.1 Online Deliberation Platforms

Online deliberation platforms have evolved significantly over the past decades, with early efforts focusing primarily on basic discussion forums and voting mechanisms. Klein (2015) identified five main types of deliberation technologies: time-centric, topic-centric, question-centric, debate-centric, and argument-centric approaches. The latter are recognised as particularly significant for ORBIS for the following reasons: First, argument-centric platforms enable a more structured capturing of the reasoning of the participants while those also dialogically inter-act with peers in the same space (creating what Iandoli describes as "socially augmented argumentation" (Iandoli et al., 2014). This structured approach enables processing and analysis of complex policy discussions by keeping track of the logical connections between different positions and their supporting evidence. Secondly, this approach aligns with ORBIS' core objective of fostering evidence-based deliberation. Promoting participants to engage in dialogical interaction by explicitly representing their positions, claims, premises and the relationship between them, not only assists them to evaluate the quality of their arguments but also makes it clear to identify key areas of agreement and disagreement. This is particularly important in policy-making contexts where decisions need to be supported with hard evidence and with clear transparent reasoning.

Early platforms like MIT's Collaboratorium (Klein, 2007) and Deliberatorium (Klein, 2011) attempted to address limitations of traditional online forums by supporting large-scale argumentation. These systems aimed to reduce redundancy and enable systematic exploration of complex problems. However, research has shown that current platforms still struggle with balancing structured argumentation and natural conversation flow, particularly when scaling to hundreds or thousands of participants (Mahyar et al., 2019).

Recent platforms like Decidim[2] (Aragón et al., 2017), Consul[3] (Arana-Catania et al., 2021), and Loomio[4] (Jackson & Kuehn, 2016) among others, have demonstrated success in supporting participatory democracy processes. While platforms like Decidim and Consul excel in areas like participatory budgeting or proposal management, ORBIS differentiates itself through its deep integration of AI, particularly for automated argument mining, structuring, summarization, and policy recommendation generation from unstructured text at scale. This focus aims to support more complex, in-depth policy deliberations where understanding the nuances and relationships between arguments is critical for governmental decision-making, complementing rather than replacing the functionalities of these other valuable platforms (Aragón et al., 2017).

[2] https://decidim.org/
[3] https://consuldemocracy.org/
[4] https://www.loomio.com/

2.2 AI in Collective Decision Making

The integration of AI in collective decision-making processes represents a growing field of research and practice. Recent advances in natural language processing (NLP) and machine learning (ML) have enabled new approaches to aggregating and analysing large-scale deliberations. However, as Landemore (Brennan & Landemore, 2021) notes, the challenge lies not just in processing more input, but in maintaining the quality and legitimacy of deliberative processes. Current state-of-the-art approaches focus on several key areas:

Automatic summarisation of complex debates: The field has moved be-yond simple extractive summarisation towards more abstractive approaches. Examples include (Bar-Haim et al., 2020) where arguments are summarised to identify a small set of key points that cover the majority of arguments, Duan et al. (2019) summarisation of multi-role debate dialogues by focusing on the controversy or even (Anastasiou & Liddo, 2021) that proposes a blend of hybrid templated and abstractive argumentative way to summarise long online discussions.

Recommendation systems: Recent work has focused on context-aware recommendation systems that suggest relevant precedents, arguments and evidence. This may be recommendation of relevant scientific references (citation recommendation), e.g. Liu et al., (2015), suggesting discussion posts using implicit ratings and semantic similarity (Riyahi & Sohrabi, 2020) or suggesting feedback in argumentative writing (Noroozi et al., 2023).

Natural language processing for argument mining Argument Mining (AM) (Cabrio & Villata, 2018) focuses on the automatic extraction of argumentative components such as premises and claims, and classifying the relationships between them (support, attack etc.). This process aims to reveal the underlying structure of argumentation within a text. AM models have seen numerous approaches typically relying on hand-crafted syntactic and lexical features (Stab & Gurevych, 2014), pre-trained language models (Agarwal et al., 2022) or both (Rago et al., 2020). One of the early learning-based approaches for AM in the context of political debates consisted of using multi-class Support Vector Machine classifiers (Menini et al., 2018) which achieved good results on the relation classification stage of the AM pipeline. Most recent works leverage supervised approaches with autoencoding transformer architectures like BERT (Kenton & Toutanova, 2019), due to their capabilities in understanding the surrounding context and long-term dependencies of arguments. Habernal et al. (2024) applied argument mining to decisions from the European Court of Human Rights (ECHR). They built models based on pre-trained BERT and RoBERTa, and achieved comparable results. Chen et al. (2024) explored the use of Large Language Models (LLMs) in computational argumentation, specifically focusing on "counter speech generation".

However, significant challenges remain in ensuring these AI systems support rather than supplant human deliberation. This has led to increased attention on hybrid approaches that combine human judgment with computational capabilities (Buhmann & Fieseler, 2021).

2.3 Hybrid Human-AI Systems

The development of hybrid Human-AI systems represents a crucial direction in online deliberation research. These systems aim to combine the scalability and processing capabilities of AI with human judgment and ethical considerations. There are two different approaches in the interaction between humans and AI systems that are particularly relevant in the development of AI-enhanced tools supporting deliberative democracy: Human in the Loop (HITL) and Human on the Loop (HOTL) (Varga et al., 2024). In the HITL (Mosqueira-Rey et al., 2023), human input is integral to the operation of the AI system, with persons actively participating in decision-making processes through the provision of real-time feedback and by making critical decisions, thus ensuring that AI-supported decisions are constantly overseen and validated by humans in a symbiotic relationship where AI supports but does not replace human judgment. The HOTL approach involves a more supervisory role of humans, who are in charge of monitoring the overall system operation rather than being involved in every decision (Li et al., 2020). In this case, humans are expected to intervene only when the system behaves unexpectedly or a decision requires ethical or contextual judgment from a person.

Both approaches align with what (Dignum, 2017) describes as 'responsible artificial intelligence' (RAI) where AI systems are designed to enhance rather than replace human capabilities in democratic processes, as they incorporate human oversight into AI operations, ensuring that the technology is used ethically and effectively. The challenge lies in creating systems that can effectively scale while maintaining the essential human elements of deliberation.

The literature reveals a clear need for integrated approaches that can effectively combine these different elements—online deliberation platforms, AI capabilities, argument mining, and hybrid human-AI interaction—into coherent systems that can support large-scale deliberation while maintaining quality and legitimacy. The ORBIS architecture, presented in subsequent sections, represents an attempt to address this need through a comprehensive socio-technical approach.

3 ORBIS Architecture Overview

This section discusses the back-end infrastructure required for the operation of the ORBIS knowledge graph, together with mechanisms to capture the evolution and dynamics of a large-scale deliberation. The Data management services module is composed of two separate sub-modules. The first sub-module is dedicated to support the data management services of the Feedback aggregator (FA thereafter) and Policy Recommendation (PR thereafter) components, while the second sub-module supports the operations of the Argumentation Mining (AM thereafter) and Explanation Generator (EG thereafter) components.

In the context of the ORBIS toolkit, third party services are correlated with the deliberation data providers. Data coming from the associating deliberation

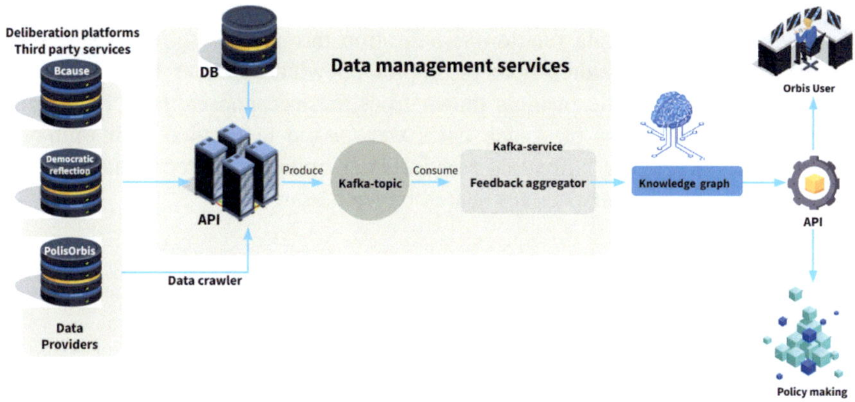

Fig. 1 The overview of the data management services architecture for feedback aggregator and policy recommendation components

platforms are crawled by the ORBIS toolkit components in order to perform processing and analysis of the raw deliberation data. To crawl the raw data from the deliberation platforms, ORBIS toolkit utilises the data management services—an abstracted ontology, which describes the process of retrieving, cleaning, structuring the raw deliberation data from the third party services. These processes are represented by a templated data crawler, capable of crawling raw deliberation data from the third party services. Those data are filtered, transformed, structured and persisted on an S3 bucket (Minio 6[5]) as a source of truth. Furthermore, that data is produced to an internal message bus to be analysed by software modules. Figure 1 provides a high-level description of the data pipeline used for feeding the knowledge base and the operations executed for the deliberation structuring services. The data crawler is served in the form of an API to provide the crawling of deliberation topics from data providers as a service. Once a crawling request is received and the contents of the topic are successfully produced, the analysis pipeline is triggered.

The analysis pipeline is facilitated by the FA service, which takes over to perform the data analysis tasks. The FA service performs several operations on the deliberation data and more analytically feedback clustering, keyword extraction for each generated cluster, title generation for each generated cluster and summarization based on the feedback of each cluster. More information on each individual analysis step will be provided in Sect. 4.3.

Subsequently, the persistence stage ensures the generated analysis reports alongside their metadata are stored in a Neo4j[6] database, which serves as the knowledge base. This system is designed to maintain vectorised relationships be-tween data

[5] https://min.io/
[6] https://neo4j.com/

points, enabling efficient querying and facilitating in-depth analysis. Figure 2 showcases a complex data relation visualisation through Neo4j. In this visualisation, the structure captures both the topics on which citizens have expressed feedback and the specific insights drawn from these responses. Pink nodes represent the general topics on which users were asked to provide their opinions. Orange nodes denote the individual user feedback opinions related to these topics, preserving the unique perspectives shared by each user.

Fig. 2 An instance of the visualisation of the knowledge graph

For deeper analysis and enhanced explainability, we process the feedback text and extract meaningful triplets from each response, which are then incorporated into the graph. Each triplet is represented by distinct nodes and edges, structured as 'Subject → Verb → Object'. This structure enables the extraction of actionable insights by breaking down feedback into core elements, which help in understanding relationships and recurring themes.

For example, a citizen's feedback might state: "I strongly support the suggestions made by the European Commission. New genomic techniques in the breeding of plants need to be allowed on a broad scale in Europe. Furthermore, I support EFSA's scientific opinion on glyphosate and urge the Commission to end the efforts to ban glyphosate as a so-called 'carcinogen'." From this feedback, we can extract multiple triplets, such as:

('I' → 'support' → 'European Commission's suggestions')
('New genomic techniques' → 'need to be' → 'allowed')
('I' → 'support' → 'EFSA's scientific opinion').

Additionally, green nodes highlight Wiki entities identified within these triplets. For instance, "EFSA" (European Food Safety Authority) would be recognised as a Wiki entity. This entity is then linked to relevant nodes in the graph, adding external context and background. Such enrichment enhances the graph's utility for analysis within Neo4j, providing users with a more comprehensive under-standing of the interconnected feedback landscape.

The composition of the raw deliberation data stored in S3 (Minio) and the enhanced analytics alongside metadata stored in Neo4j combined represent the overall Knowledge Base of this component. Finally, the data is made accessible to authorised stakeholders via an API interface which is connected to the enhanced knowledge base. The interface controls access to the analysed topics based on user authorization levels, ensuring that only properly authorised individuals can retrieve the information. Tools supporting this pipeline include Kafka[7] for data injection and text analysis processes, Minio for cloud storage, Neo4j for maintaining data relationships, and Python with FastAPI to construct the API service.

The data pipeline is supported by a range of advanced technologies and tools, each serving distinct purposes to ensure efficient and seamless operation. Kafka is utilised for message queuing and event streaming, playing a critical role in injecting raw topics and triggering the text analysis pipelines. Minio provides an S3-compatible object storage solution, offering reliable cloud storage for both raw and processed data. Neo4j serves as a graph database, which stores vectorised relations between data points, thereby enabling complex queries and facilitating comprehensive data traversal. The primary programming language employed is

[7] https://kafka.apache.org/

Python, which is pivotal in implementing data processing, executing analysis algorithms, and managing the logic for the API. Additionally, FastAPI[8] is the web framework chosen for building the API services, enabling the construction of a RESTful API that facilitates data access and component interaction efficiently. The data pipeline's key features include Scalability for efficient processing of large data volumes, flexibility to handle diverse data sources, real-time ingestion and processing via Kafka, advanced analytics using clustering and summarisation, graph-based knowledge representation through Neo4j, and API-driven architecture for seamless integration. These features enable effective handling of deliberation data from crawling to analysis, informing policy-making within ORBIS.

Additionally, ORBIS ensures data protection through decentralised storage across partner-controlled servers, with API-regulated access following data minimisation and security principles.

4 ORBIS Components

4.1 Argument Mining (AM)

The Argument Mining (AM) component within ORBIS serves as a crucial mechanism for automatically analysing argumentation structures across deliberative discussions. Operating at the intersection of Natural Language Processing and Computational Models of arguments, this component identifies argumentative components (e.g., Premises, Claims) and predicts their relations (e.g., Attack, Support) within deliberative texts.

Architecture and Implementation: The AM component follows a twofold mindset, each consisting of a modular pipeline architecture with two primary modules. The main reason behind this twofold mindset resides in the structure of the data we are dealing with within ORBIS.

The first one is the classical AM which handles argumentative component detection, identifying claims and evidence within the text, and relation classification, determining the relationships between these components (Cabrio and Villata, 2018). This fashion is well adapted to discussions that occur in a flow of discourse as raw text. To better accommodate structured data like the one from BCause, where statements are segmented into short sentences typically expressing a single position or piece of evidence, the classical AM pipeline has been adjusted to focus on what we now refer to as 'statement-level' AM. Similar to traditional AM, the process is carried out in two key steps: Statement Classification, where pre-segmented statements are classified into positions (stances on argumentative topics) and arguments (supporting or opposing these positions). Statement Relation Classification first determining whether a statement represents a position or

[8] https://fastapi.tiangolo.com/

an argument (supporting/attacking), then identifying which position the arguments relate to.

Technical Implementation: The system utilises DeBERTa-v3 models for all argument mining sub-tasks, trained on publicly available datasets from various online platforms, such as the Touche23-ValueEval data (Mirzakhmedova et al., 2023), political debates from Disputool (Haddadan et al., 2019), and exchanges from the BCause platform.

Data Processing: The component processes various data formats, with input and output handled in JSON format for standardization. Data preprocessing includes anonymization, transcription, and cleaning steps to ensure quality and privacy compliance. The system currently focuses on intra-participant argument relations, analysing relationships between statements made by the same participant.

Integration and Scalability The AM component seamlessly integrates into the broader ORBIS ecosystem via a standardised API, ensuring smooth inter-action with other modules. This integration allows for real-time argumentation analysis during ongoing deliberations, enabling the AM system to process and classify user contributions automatically. By detecting and categorising arguments as claims, premises, supports, or attacks, the AM component outputs structured data that can be utilised by computational models, aiding in informed decision-making. Furthermore, this system is designed to support various deliberation platforms.

This design allows the system to handle large-scale deliberative processes while maintaining processing efficiency and accuracy. The component's modular architecture facilitates future enhancements and adaptations to specific use case requirements.

The AM component represents a crucial advancement in automated deliberation analysis, providing structured understanding of argumentative dialogue that supports higher-level decision-making and policy formation processes. Its integration within the ORBIS framework demonstrates the practical application of computational argumentation techniques in supporting large-scale democratic deliberation.

4.2 Explanation Generator

The Explanation Generator (EG) component of ORBIS aims to enhance the toolkit's overall interpretability and transparency by providing clear insights into how deliberative decisions are made. This component is essential for several reasons. First, as AI systems become increasingly complex, their lack of interpretability creates barriers to user understanding and trust. Second, in the context of deliberative democracy, where informed participation is crucial, stake-holders need to comprehend how information is processed and interpreted by the system. Third, transparency in decision-making processes is fundamental for building trust and ensuring accountability in democratic deliberations.

Several implementation approaches exist in the explainable AI (XAI) literature. These can be broadly categorised into intrinsic and post-hoc methods (Adadi &

Berrada, 2018). Intrinsic methods focus on building inherently interpretable models, such as decision trees, while post-hoc approaches generate explanations after model development. Notable techniques include Local Interpretable Model-Agnostic Explanations (LIME) (Ribeiro et al., 2016), Shapely Additive Explanations (SHAP) (Ribeiro et al., 2016), and Counterfactual Explanations (Wachter et al., 2017).

For ORBIS's EG, the implementation strategy focuses on two main approaches. First, attention mechanisms will be utilised to highlight which words the model emphasises when making decisions, in particular for the AM component, providing intuitive visual explanations for human users. This builds on work by Mensonides et al. (2019) in argument component detection. Second, natural language explanations will be generated following the framework established by Camburu et al. (2018), which al-lows for more comprehensive and user-friendly explanations of system decisions. The implementation will involve prompt construction, free-text generation, few-shot learning, and fine-tuning to generate both predictions and explanations.

The EG integrates with other ORBIS components by providing explanatory layers to the AM, FA, and PR components. This integration ensures that users can understand not just the final outputs but also the reasoning process be-hind the system's decisions. By exposing potential gaps, biases, or weaknesses in reasoning, the EG contributes to deeper reflection and more informed consensus-building within the deliberative process. This transparency helps transform what might otherwise be perceived as "black box" decisions into rational, traceable processes that users can understand and trust.

4.3 Feedback Aggregation

Machine Learning (ML) models are broadly used for various knowledge discovery issues, due to their ability to analyse, automatically identify, and correlate data, even when dealing with massive datasets. Techniques such as clustering (Saxena et al., 2017), classification (Sen et al., 2020), and dimensionality reduction (Jia et al., 2022) assist in identifying meaningful entities and their relationships. Recently, the integration of Large Language Models (LLMs) further enhances the aforementioned processes (Zhang et al., 2024), providing sophisticated understanding, context, and predictions from complex data, allowing for more accurate and dynamic knowledge discovery. Text clustering, title generation, summarization (Chang et al., 2024), and keyword/keyphrase extraction (Giarelis & Karacapilidis, 2024) are core tasks in NLP, aiding the organisation, identification, condensation, and understanding of large volumes of text data, respectively.

In ORBIS, to facilitate Knowledge Graph discovery and effectively address the critical tasks of clustering, summarisation, keyphrase extraction, and title generation, we have developed the FA component (see Fig. 5). Clustering and summarisation are both performed on arguments. For the BCause platform, arguments (premises in this context) are categorised into 'in favour' and 'against' groups, expressing the users' support and opposition to the corresponding topic, respectively. We have also implemented a method (called Opinion Classification) that performs the above categorisation (classification) for feedback that is not already characterised as 'in favour' or 'against'. In this method, we used LLMs to analyse the provided feedback, and decide whether this is 'in favour' or 'against' the corresponding topic. In more detail, we experimented with multiple prompts and prompting techniques, based on the literature (Sahoo et al., 2024). GPT-3.5 Turbo was initially explored for its strong general summarization capabilities and API availability. Kunoichi, utilized via Hugging Face, demonstrated superior performance in handling nuanced or potentially ironic comments often found in public discourse, which is crucial for accurate sentiment classification in favour/against arguments. The choice reflects a balance between performance on specific deliberative text characteristics and accessibility. Given the rapid pace of LLM development, ongoing evaluation and potential fine-tuning or model replacement are anticipated to maintain state-of-the-art performance. The FA component can handle data from all three deliberative platforms (BCause, PolisOrbis and Democratic Reflection) used in the project. The ORBIS project uses K-Means Clustering to partition embeddings derived from deliberative feedback. After UMAP dimensionality reduction, optimal cluster numbers are determined via Silhouette score. GPT 3.5 Turbo generates cluster summaries through abstractive summarization, while Kunoichi creates cluster titles. LMRank (Giarelis & Karacapilidis, 2023) extracts keyphrases from cluster text. These processes (clustering for link prediction, summarization for feature enrichment, and keyphrase/title extraction) form the FA component.

The cleaned data (with removed noise, duplicates, stopwords, and special characters) passes through the Transformer, generating normalised embeddings via pooling. UMAP then reduces dimensionality while preserving data structure.

Arguments then are clustered by 'in favour' and 'against' positions (Fig. 3), with optimal cluster numbers determined through tuning. Each cluster receives a summary of its deliberative content, a generated title reflecting its theme, and extracted keyphrases highlighting key concepts.

Below we provide some argument processing examples demonstrating the results of the previously described functionalities.

Knowledge Graph enrichment Knowledge Graphs (KGs) are advanced representations of information that have evolved significantly from traditional graph and non-graph-based visualizations. They are structured using a triplet-based framework (e.g., node-relationship-node), where entities (nodes) are connected via semantic (Fensel et al., 2020). Additionally, the semantic layer embedded in KGs facilitates contextual understanding, which is critical for tasks like natural language processing (NLP) and machine reasoning (Schneider et al., 2022). KG semantic enrichment (Ozcan et al., 2021) is the process of enhancing the knowledge graph with semantic information in order to increase its interpretability. This typically means adding more nodes (entities), edges (relationships) and corresponding properties to its original composition, which bear semantic context. The ultimate goal is to increase the performance of ML-related applications that utilise it, such

Fig. 3 Data ontology after clustering in the feedback aggregator component

as recommender systems, search engines, AI agents, NLP etc. Key features of KG semantic enrichment involve entity linking, where the nodes (entities) of the knowledge graph are connected to external resources, such as Wikidata, in order to provide definitions. State-of-the-art semantic enrichment of knowledge graphs often leverages deep learning models (Tian et al., 2022) for entity linking, which connects textual data with corresponding entities in the knowledge graph through contextual embeddings. Techniques like zero-shot and few-shot learning (Patil & Gudivada, 2024), where models are provided with one or a few examples, are widely employed to identify and fill in missing links and other components within the knowledge graph (Fig. 4).

With the use of NLP methods (such as Named Entity Recognition), the knowledge graphs originate from large text corpora, as Large Language Models are capable of inferring those accurately. Furthermore, these models are capable of providing annotations for the graph's entities and relationships, increasing its interpretation. Enrichment can be performed either asynchronously or in real time, depending on the system's needs. In ORBIS, data are on deliberative dialogues, originating from nodes, relationships and their corresponding properties (annotations) where the answers are illustrated. Initially we designed the ontology where the GDB schema and subsequently the KG is built upon, see Fig. 5. According to that, a 'subject' has a position, either 'in favor' or 'against'. They both relate with a 'cluster' which in turn has at least one 'keyphrase'. The afore-mentioned 'in favour' and 'against' positions both relate with an 'entity' which may relate

Field	Value
Text (input)	I agree that if governments are not willing to inform the public and stop manipulating us by placing chemical in the air for solar engineering then how do they expect individuals to comply
Cluster ID (output)	-M_1_CenQ3BU_yRhblhX_argument_for_0
Cluster title (output)	Challenges of Climate Change Feedback Loops and Industry Influence
Keyphrases (output)	feedback loops, solar engineering, overshoot, governments, industry
Summary (output)	The concern revolves around whether policymakers are too influenced by industrial interests to acknowledge the growing risks of overshoot and other climate challenges. Any eventual action may come too late, rendering it impossible to stop self-reinforcing feedback loops. Moreover, if governments continue withholding information and manipulating the public with controversial practices like solar geoengineering, it's unreasonable to expect individuals to comply with necessary climate initiatives. Clear communication and transparent actions are essential for fostering public trust and cooperation in addressing climate change.

Fig. 4 Argument processing example

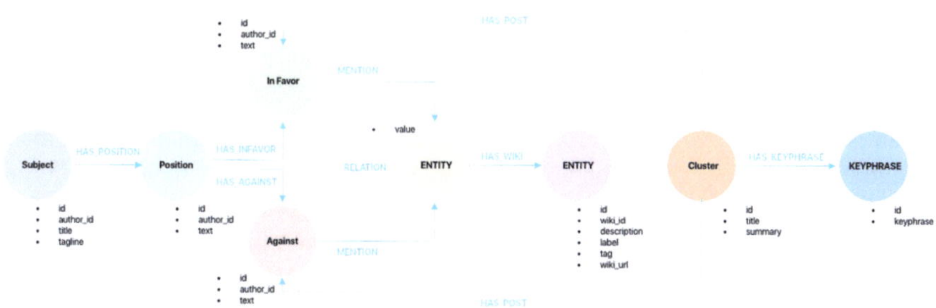

Fig. 5 The KG ontological schema

to another one through a 'has wiki' relationship. This is where the wiki data information is provided, in the form of node properties for the completion of the KG enrichment part (known as 'Entity Linking System'). For the construction of the knowledge graph, we use a LLM to extract triplets from the text, in a node-relationship-node fashion, according to the ontology (known as 'Triplet Extraction System'). We experimented with various LLMs. Kunoichi-iGPTQ proved to be the most accurate as it was more precise and preserved the original text's meaning.

For the 'Entity Linking System', we experimented with three different approaches: Spacy and wikiData API, GPT3.5 Turbo and wikiData API as well as ReFinED. GPT3.5 Turbo and wikiData API extracted very accurate entities, linked effectively to their corresponding wikiData information. The processing times overall were decent. The end result after creating and enriching the KG is shown in Fig. 6, where on the left part the creation and enrichment run in parallel, and the resulting KG is depicted on the right part. The main challenge was pronoun resolution in texts. While Crosslingual Coreference struggled with multiple pronouns, Kunoichi-GPTQ automatically replaced pronouns with their contextual references during triplet extraction, requiring no additional processing.

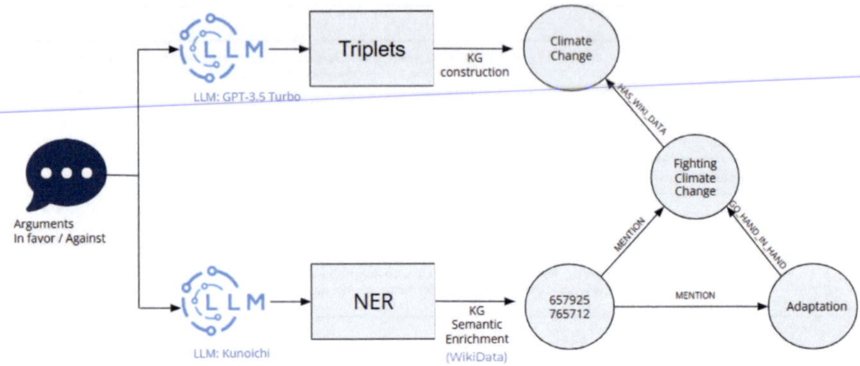

Fig. 6 Creation and enrichment of the KG

4.4 Conflict Detection Framework

When people communicate with each other on complex social topics such as those potentially addressed in deliberative democracy, it is inevitable to have different perspectives on an issue. In argumentation studies, disagreement is not negative: in fact, it is not the endpoint of an argumentative discussion but its origin (Eemeren, 2018; Perret-Clermont et al., 2019). Well constructed argumentative discussions ideally include a critical exchange of reasons and listening to the other parties' reasons, which is an alternative to an escalation of disagreement into overt conflict (Greco, 2018; Morasso, 2011).

However, argumentative dialogue often does not happen 'spontaneously', especially when the discussion involves many people with strong opinions on complex topics. Taking this into account, it is necessary to devote time to the construction of a dialogue space (Greco, 2018; Morasso, 2020). In the context of the ORBIS technological solution, we propose to consider human moderators, as well as generative AI interventions based on a careful understanding and reproduction of the discursive tools used by conflict resolution professionals such as dispute mediators.

To that end, ORBIS designed a Conflict Detection Framework employing a three-steps qualitative approach that includes both an inductive and a deductive dimension (inspired by Bingham, 2023). We first analysed datasets derived from previous research on discourse and argumentation in conflict resolution to retrieve discursive tools for conflict prevention and resolution (inductive part). Then we compared them with datasets of discussions around deliberative democracy topics collected within ORBIS (deductive part) to identify recurrent 'dysfunctional' patterns and we matched them with possible discursive tools to avoid conflict escalation. Eventually, we identified three main areas in which an AI moderator (if need be, assisted by a human moderator) could intervene. The first is the silence of one or more participants, which could be addressed by explicit prompts asking questions to the silent participants, phrased learning from formulation of explorative questions by mediators (e.g. "Would you like to add something on this matter?"). The second area is the presence of speech acts of accusation, which could be detected based on specific linguistic indicators; in the presence of an accusation (e.g. "X does not listen"), the AI moderator could be trained to intervene by means of a reframing (Greco & Jermini-Martinez Soria, 2021) that goes from the individual to the system (e.g. "In this type of discussion, it is normal to hold different opinions") or a circular question (Morasso, 2020). For example, if someone writes "Participant X never helped us in achieving our goal", a question might be "Could you please explain to participant X what s/he could do to assist you in achieving your common goal?". The third area is the sharp expression of positions by participants, which can be addressed by interventions comprising shifts that bring attention to the discussion as a whole, to common interests or to concrete examples. For example, if someone writes "I want this", an intervention might be "Do you think that there is something that is important to you both?".

The ORBIS Conflict Detection Framework ensures that while the rich tapestry of differing perspectives is preserved, the interactions remain constructive and do not devolve into hostility or exclusion. Importantly, these measures are neither intended to suppress any individual's expression of viewpoints nor to silence dis agreement. Instead, they aim to support moderators in fostering an environment where all participants can express their opinions freely yet respectfully. The objective is not to limit the variety of positions presented but to ensure that these positions are expressed in a manner conducive to productive and respectful dialogue, regardless of the divergent views held by participants. In a word, these argumentation-based linguistic instruments are meant to help parties keep their disagreement manageable through reasonable argumentation without compromising personal relationships and bringing discussions to an impasse.

4.5 Policy Recommendation (PR) System

Policy-making nowadays is increasingly leveraging AI to transform participatory and deliberative democracy into adaptive, evidence-driven processes. Participatory democracy enables direct citizen contribution to decision-making, ensuring inclusivity and diverse representation. Deliberative democracy focuses on structured discussions within smaller, representative groups, characterised by fairness and mutual respect. The goal is to integrate competing perspectives into cohesive, evidence-based policy outcomes. State-of-the-art AI methodologies revolutionise these democratic approaches by addressing challenges such as information overload, bias, and inefficiencies in processing large volumes of public input. AI-driven tools like argumentation mining extract claims, counterclaims, and reasoning from vast public inputs, enabling policymakers to analyse not just what citizens think, but why, by understanding the underlying arguments (Fergadis et al., 2021). NLP techniques, such as abstractive summarisation, synthesise complex discussions into coherent summaries, highlighting areas of consensus and contention crucial for policy analysis. Additionally, stance classification models sort arguments into "pro", "con", or neutral categories, enriching the understanding of public sentiment regarding specific policy options (Bar-Haim et al., 2017). This structured analysis provides a deeper insight than simple keyword counts or basic sentiment analysis.

AI-enabled deliberative platforms combine real-time sentiment analysis with knowledge graph visualizations to track debate dynamics, ensuring transparent, inclusive decision-making. Metrics like the Discourse Quality Index (DQI) (Steenbergen et al., 2003) evaluate the quality of deliberations, assessing respect for diverse views, evidence-backed reasoning, and collaborative outcomes. Hybrid search engines, powered by neural and symbolic AI (Colelough & Regli, 2024), further aid in filtering and organising policy-relevant data. Collective intelligence methodologies, enhanced by AI, emphasise collaborative sensing and ideation among stakeholders. Tools like ML-enhanced clustering and topic modelling identify key themes and unintended consequences, driving evidence-based deliberative outputs (Sia et al., 2020). These innovations ensure that participatory and deliberative frameworks remain human-centric and adaptable, aligning outputs with practical policy applications to address complex societal challenges effectively. This convergence of AI with democratic principles marks a transformative shift toward governance that is inclusive, transparent, and responsive to diverse public needs.

Our applied process below provides a structured framework for generating actionable policy recommendations by combining citizen feedback, clustering methodologies, and Large Language Models (LLMs). To support effective policy-making, this methodology begins by analysing citizen feedback on a specific topic. The first step is opinion classification, where arguments are categorised into "in favour" and "against" based on their sentiment towards the topic. For example, public feedback on "mutated food" would include arguments supporting its potential benefits and opposing views highlighting its dangers. Following this, the arguments in each category are clustered to group similar themes, revealing the structure of public opinion around distinct viewpoints. For instance, "dangers of mutated food in the human brain" might form one cluster in the "against" category, while "improved crop yields" could be a cluster in the "in favour" category. Once clusters are formed, abstractive summarization is per-formed on each group to distill their core arguments into concise summaries. Crucially, this approach moves beyond simple topic identification; it focuses on capturing the argumentative substance and relationships within the discourse. These summaries highlight the key themes and concerns within the feedback, such as summarising a cluster on health concerns about mutated food into a statement such as: "Concerns raised about potential neurological impacts of consuming genetically modified organisms."

As described previously (Sect. 4.3 and Fig. 7), the process identifies relevant policy or guideline documents and performs abstractive summarization on them. For instance, if a policy on "mutated food safety" exists, its summary might include regulatory guidelines, safety measures, and scientific findings. The core step involves feeding the feedback cluster summaries and the policy summary into an LLM. By analysing these inputs together, the LLM generates tailored recommendations for policy decisions. The output aims explicitly to help policymakers understand the structure of public arguments, identify the key points of agreement and disagreement, recognize the trade-offs citizens perceive, and clearly see how different lines of public reasoning align or conflict with existing or proposed policy goals. For example, if the "against" cluster is about health risks and the policy summary highlights existing safety guidelines, the LLM may suggest enhancing research on long-term neurological effects of increasing transparency in public communication about the safety of mutated foods. To further refine this process, keywords and generated titles can be extracted from the clusters and included in the input to the LLM. This step enriches the information provided and ensures the LLM captures the most critical elements of the feedback and policy context. This systematic approach ensures that citizen feedback is meaningfully integrated into policy decisions, promoting transparency, inclusivity, and evidence-based governance. By leveraging modern NLP techniques and clustering algorithms focused on argumentative content, the PR system provides policymakers with structured, actionable insights—moving beyond raw data or simple themes to deliver intelligence tailored for the complexities of public sentiment analysis and policy formulation.

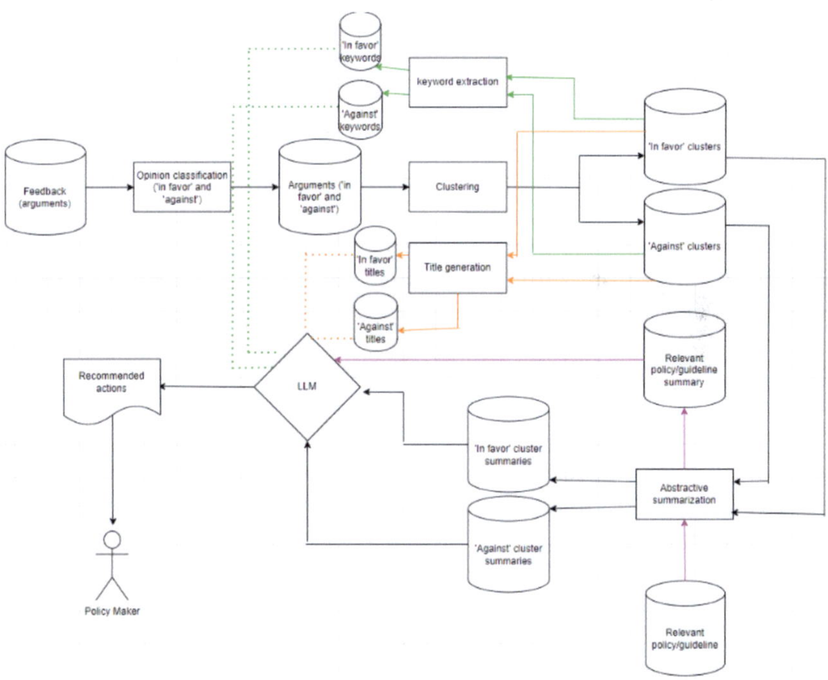

Fig. 7 Policy recommendation module—feedback aggregation

4.6 User Interface Layer

This layer serves as the primary point of interaction between users and the OR-BIS toolkit, implemented through integration with three distinct deliberation platforms. The rationale behind this approach is to ensure accessibility and us-ability for people with different abilities and backgrounds while maintaining a clear and transparent deliberation process.

Deliberation Interface Components

BCause:[9] provides a structured platform specifically designed for privacy-sensitive discussions. It implements a layered argumentative approach where discussions are organised around clearly defined positions. Users can contribute with supporting (pro) and opposing (con) arguments, which are visualised through both a time-ordered timeline and an argument tree. To enhance collective understanding, BCause incorporates synoptical summaries and identifies "Sense-making nuggets"—key contributions that advance the deliberation.

Democratic Reflection:[10] this platform transforms passive content consumption into active engagement by overlaying an interactive reflective layer onto live or recorded events. It presents users with digital reflection cards containing carefully crafted statements that serve as cognitive nudges. The platform captures engagement patterns and generates personalised analytics visualising users' reflection journeys, creating a full cycle from initial viewing through guided reflection to meta-analysis.

PolisOrbis:[11] Built upon the open-source Pol.is[12] engine, PolisOrbis is designed for scalable participation with thousands of simultaneous users. It employs advanced AI algorithms to provide real-time analysis of discussion patterns, automatically identifying and visualising opinion clusters as they form. The platform maintains GDPR compliance while enabling coherent discussion flows at scale.

User Experience Design We outline below some examples of services data interchange among user-facing services and ORBIS toolkit analysis services

Exploration of key concepts and arguments in a structured discussion ORBIS facilitates deep exploration of deliberative content through an analysis pipeline that begins when a BCause discussion is processed by the AM services, which generates an aggregated key argument graph representing the discussion's logical structure. This graph becomes accessible through BCause's analytics view, where ORBIS users can explore a synthesised representation of complex issues based on the main arguments while maintaining the ability to seamlessly navigate back to the source data for detailed context. The analysis is further enriched by the Feedback Aggregation component, which identifies and clusters main concepts

[9] https://bcause.app/

[10] https://democratic-reflection.web.app/

[11] https://polisorbis.eu/

[12] https://pol.is/

from the discussion. These concept clusters are visually rendered alongside the argument graph (see Fig. 8).

Argument-Aware reply assistance ORBIS enhances reply interfaces by integrating real-time AM and EG feedback. As users draft responses, the system analyses text to identify claims and premises while providing guidance on argument structure. For example, when a user drafts a response to a given position in BCause, ORBIS toolkit is utilised in the following ways:

1. Use of AM component to identify and visually highlight claims and premises
2. Use of EG to provide tooltips why certain phrases are identified as claims or premises and also
3. Highlight key tokens that contribute to the argumentative strength, helping users to understand what keywords make their argument effective.

This creates a learning loop where users see how their contributions map to argumentative structures in real-time, encouraging stronger argumentation while maintaining engagement. The approach aligns with ORBIS's goal of transparent, evidence-based deliberation (Fig. 9).

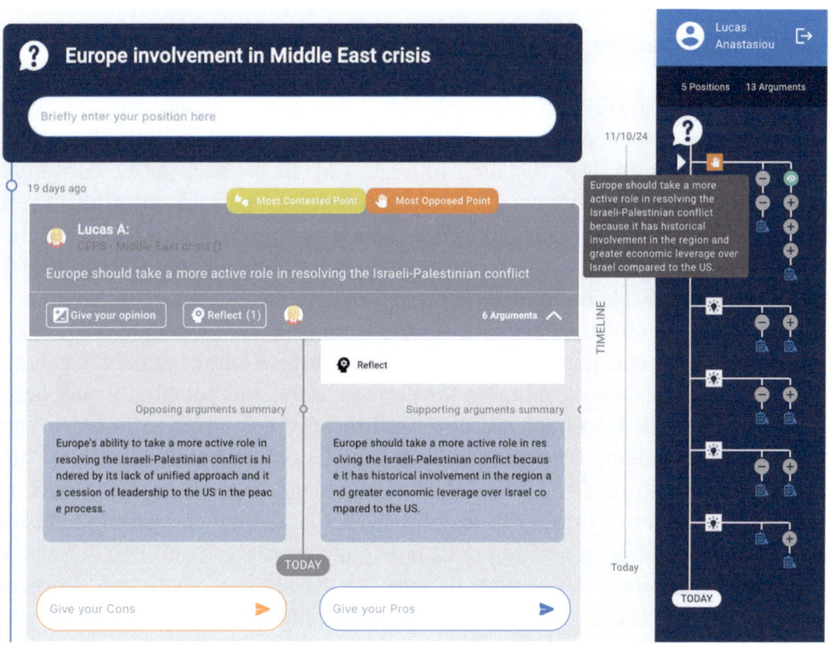

Fig. 8 Argument clusters summaries rendered in BCause main view and argument tree

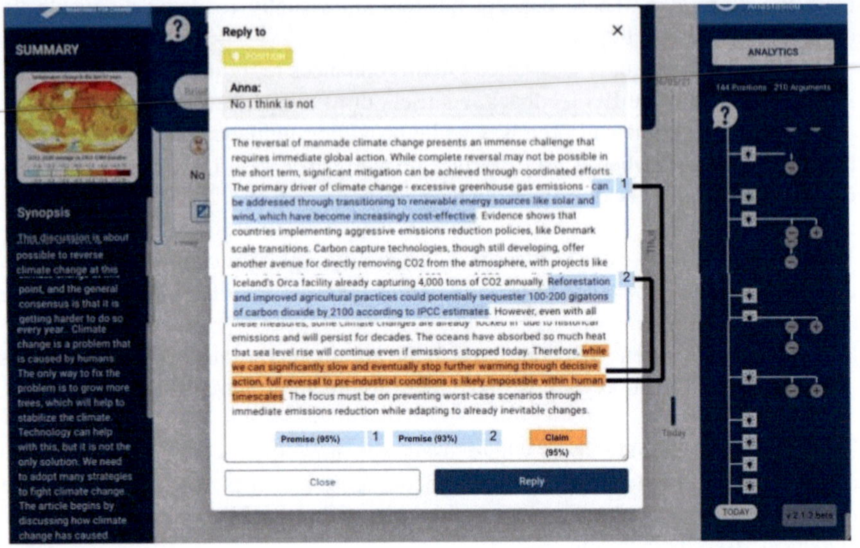

Fig. 9 Reply assistant—highlight of argumentative components via the use of AM component

4.7 Illustrative Application in Public Policy

To illustrate how the ORBIS components function synergistically within a governmental context, consider a municipal government utilizing an ORBIS-integrated platform, such as BCause (detailed in Sect. 4.6), to conduct public consultation on a proposed climate action plan. Citizens submit feedback regarding specific proposals, like new bike lanes or waste reduction targets. The Argument Mining (AM) component (Sect. 4.1) processes this textual input, automatically identifying argumentative claims and their supporting premises related to these policy actions. Subsequently, the Feedback Aggregation (FA) component (Sect. 4.3) clusters related arguments (e.g., grouping pro- and con-bike lane arguments), generates concise summaries and keyphrases for these clusters, and potentially enriches the underlying Knowledge Graph (as discussed in Sect. 4.3 under Knowledge Graph enrichment) by linking concepts like'bike lanes' to related entities such as "trafic congestion" or "air quality". The Policy Recommendation (PR) system (Sect. 4.5) then leverages these synthesized insights from FA. It may compare the clustered public sentiment against existing draft policy documents (as outlined in Sect. 4.5) and generate actionable recommendations for the relevant municipal department (e.g., Planning). These recommendations would highlight areas of strong public consensus or contention, identify key concerns raised, and point towards potential evidence gaps noted in the deliberation. Furthermore, the Explanation Generator (EG) (Sect. 4.2) could potentially provide rationale to policymakers regarding why a particular theme (like bike lanes) emerged as highly salient or contentious, perhaps based on the volume and polarity of arguments identified by AM and FA.

This integrated workflow demonstrates how ORBIS aims to transform raw citizen input into structured, analysed insights suitable for informing evidence-based policy-making within public administration.

5 Discussion

The ORBIS toolkit represents a significant advancement in augmented deliberative democracy, offering a comprehensive solution to the challenges of scaling online deliberation while maintaining quality discourse. One of its most relevant implications is its ability to empower individuals to engage in democratic processes more actively and knowledgeably. Integrating different AI supports within deliberations is indeed a way to enhance participants' abilities to understand a broad spectrum of opinions and arguments, thereby fostering a more informed and diverse public discourse. As such, through its innovative integration of AI components and human oversight, ORBIS demonstrates how technology can enhance rather than replace human deliberation processes—aligned with the words of early visioner Douglas Engelbart (2021) that AI shall augment human intelligence, rather than to replace it.

5.1 Key Innovations and Components

The primary innovation of ORBIS lies in its scalable, modular architecture that successfully combines multiple AI-powered components to augment deliberative processes. A key innovation distinguishing ORBIS from many existing participation platforms is its sophisticated AI pipeline designed to analyse and synthesize the substance of deliberation at scale. Particularly noteworthy is the system's capacity to provide insights to both participants and policymakers, facilitating more informed and structured discussions.

The toolkit's components work together to enhance deliberative processes. The AM system effectively structures and visualizes complex discussions, making them more navigable and comprehensible; directly addressing the governmental challenge of processing high volumes of qualitative citizen input. The feedback aggregation component successfully clusters and summarizes arguments, reducing information overload while preserving diverse perspectives. The explanation generator promotes transparency by making AI-driven decisions interpretable, while the PA system helps bridge the gap between public deliberation and pol-icy formation, offering policymakers synthesized insights grounded in citizen discourse. At the moment, the toolkit is successfully integrated into three deliberation platforms, while it remains open and interoperable to be integrated further to other services. Being based on a flexible API and providing outputs that can be easily integrated, the ORBIS toolkit constitutes a relevant innovation with significant scalability potentiality. Its approach allows it to adapt to various plat-forms and services, expanding its potential impact across different domains of deliberative engagement.

Moreover, the potential impact of ORBIS on deliberation processes could be transformative. Its capacity to identify patterns and cluster similar arguments while surfacing minority viewpoints could help break down traditional barriers to participation. This may foster more evidence-based discussions, potentially leading to better-informed policy outcomes. This could mark a shift from sporadic public consultations to continuous, meaningful civic engagement integrated into policy cycles within democratic processes.

5.2 Ethical Considerations and Limitations

We acknowledge some limitations currently in the ORBIS toolkit. First, the system relies on high quality training data for training the underlying algorithms or building the internal knowledge graph. This could be limiting when switching to new unexplored domains and societal contexts. We anticipate that effective pipelines can be devised, which are able to handle societal context switch successfully. Moreover, the toolkit currently only supports text-only deliberation; this could be potentially limiting for users that prefer multi-modes of communication.

A human-in-the-loop (HITL) approach has been consistently adopted to ensure that AI components operate within the bounds of ethical guidelines, addressing concerns such as data privacy, bias mitigation, and the integrity of AI-generated content. In ORBIS, a specific commitment concerns data privacy and the responsible deployment of ML. This regards, on the one side, the adoption of a data minimisation approach to ensure sensitive information is protected from unauthorised access and breaches, and on the other, the use of anonymised or pseudonymised data from dialogue for model training. The integration of ethical considerations within the ORBIS toolkit is rooted in a secure and trust-worthy environment for participants, enhanced through a co-creation approach and continuous engagement with multiple stakeholders. This ongoing interaction ensures that feedback is by-design incorporated, maintaining the relevance and enhancing the desirability of the solutions to support large-scale deliberative activities.

Algorithmic Bias & Fairness: Beyond data privacy, responsible deployment in government contexts requires attention to potential algorithmic bias. Clustering or summarization might inadvertently overweight dominant viewpoints or misinterpret arguments from specific demographics. While the HITL approach provides oversight, ongoing research within ORBIS aims to incorporate fairness metrics and bias detection techniques into the FA and PR components to ensure equitable representation of diverse citizen voices.

Manipulation & Information Quality: The open nature of deliberation carries risks of manipulation or the spread of misinformation, which AI might inadvertently amplify. The Conflict Detection framework (Sect. 4.4) and human moderation layers are crucial safeguards. Future work may involve integrating

AI-based misinformation detection or source credibility indicators, although these present their own challenges.

Transparency for Accountability: While the EG component (Sect. 4.2) aims to improve interpretability, ensuring sufficient transparency for government accountability when using AI-generated policy inputs remains a challenge. Clear documentation of the AI pipeline and its limitations is essential for public trust.

6 Conclusions

The ORBIS system opens several promising research directions for enhancing technology-mediated governance and public administration. First, investigating the long-term impact of AI-supported deliberation on participant engagement and the quality of policy inputs could provide valuable insights for democratic innovation. ORBIS already serves as a testbed for evaluating the impact of AI on deliberation, with pilots acting as subjects for assessing immediate impacts. As these pilot organizations conduct deliberative activities beyond the scope of ORBIS, they also present opportunities for longitudinal studies to examine the long-term impacts of such interventions.

Moreover, exploring the potential of advanced NLP techniques to improve argument quality assessment and feedback generation presents an important avenue for research. Finally, studying the effectiveness of different sensemaking support features, such as summarisations and insightful visualisations could inform future developments in explainable AI for deliberative democracy.

Implementation Challenges in Public Administration: Successfully deploying ORBIS within public administration faces practical hurdles beyond the technology itself. Governments must consider integration with existing civic tech ecosystems, invest in staff capacity building to interpret AI outputs, and over-come institutional inertia. Ensuring digital inclusion for citizens, managing costs, and navigating procurement add complexity. Crucially, effective adoption demands not only technical integration but also significant organizational adaptation to fully leverage AI-augmented deliberation for enhanced governance.

Overall, ORBIS not only demonstrates that AI can effectively augment human deliberation while maintaining democratic values and discourse quality, but it also measures the extent of this augmentation to inform future enhancements and refinements. In ORBIS, the combination of collective intelligence with artificial intelligence undergoes interdisciplinary investigation and contribution, aiming at systematic implementation across various fields including human–computer interaction, computer science, and design, as well as incorporating broader socio-political and philosophical perspectives. Indeed, AI is introduced within a framework of socio-technical innovation and is intentionally designed as such. In doing so, ORBIS comes as an experiment to innovate democratic deliberation at scale, making it more inclusive, eficient, and effective, thus establishing a foundational model for future advancements. As democratic institutions continue to evolve in the digital age, the insights and innovations developed through ORBIS ultimately provide valuable guidance for future developments in technology-enhanced public administration and deliberative governance.

7 Fundings

The work presented in this document is funded through the project ORBIS. Augmenting participation, co-creation, trust and transparency in Deliberative Democracy at all scales'. This project has received funding from the European Union's Horizon Europe Programme under Grant Agreement No. 101094765. However, the opinions expressed herewith are solely of the authors and do not necessarily reflect the point of view of any EU institution.

References

Adadi, A., & Berrada, M. (2018). Peeking inside the black-box: A survey on explainable artificial intelligence (XAI). *IEEE Access, 6*, 52138–52160.

Agarwal, C., Johnson, N., Pawelczyk, M., Krishna, S., Saxena, E., Zitnik, M., & Lakkaraju, H. (2022). Rethinking stability for attribution-based explanations. https://doi.org/10.48550/arXiv.2203.06877. arXiv:2203.06877

Aitamurto, T. (2016). Crowdsourced democratic deliberation in open policymaking: Definition, promises, challenges. In: *Crowdsourced democratic deliberation in open policymaking: Definition, promises, challenges. International Reports on Socio-Informatics (IRSI), Proceedings of the CSCW 2016–Workshop: Toward a Typology of Participation in Crowdwork* (Vol. 13, pp. 67–78).

Anastasiou, L., & De Liddo, A. (2021). Making sense of online discussions: Can automated reports help? In *Extended Abstracts of the 2021 CHI Conference on Human Factors in Computing Systems* (pp. 1–7). ACM. https://doi.org/10.1145/3411763.3451815

Anastasiou, L., & De Liddo, A. (2023). BCause: Reducing group bias and promoting cohesive discussion in online deliberation processes through a simple and engaging online deliberation tool. In *Proceedings of the Annual Meeting of the Association for Computational Linguistics* (pp. 39–49).

Androutsopoulou, A., Karacapilidis, N., Loukis, E., & Charalabidis, Y. (2019). Transforming the communication between citizens and government through AI-guided chatbots. *Government Information Quarterly, 36*(2), 358–367.

Aragón, P., Kaltenbrunner, A., Calleja-López, A., Pereira, A., Monterde, A., Barandiaran, X. E., & Go´mez, V. (2017). Deliberative platform design: The case study of the online discussions in decidim barcelona. In *Social Informatics: 9th International Conference, SocInfo 2017, Oxford, UK, September 13–15, 2017, Proceedings, Part II 9* (pp. 277–287). Springer.

Arana-Catania, M., Lier, F.A.V., Procter, R., Tkachenko, N., He, Y., Zubiaga, A., & Liakata, M. (2021). Citizen participation and machine learning for a better democracy. *Digital Government: Research and Practice, 2*(3), 1–22. https://doi.org/10.1145/3452118

Aström, J., Jonsson, M. E., & Karlsson, M. (2017). Democratic innovations: Reinforcing or changing perceptions of trust? *International Journal of Public Administration, 40*(7), 575–587.

Bar-Haim, R., Bhattacharya, I., Dinuzzo, F., Saha, A., & Slonim, N. (2017). Stance classification of context-dependent claims. In *Proceedings of the 15th Conference of the European Chapter of the Association for Computational Linguistics: Volume 1, Long Papers* (pp. 251–261).

Bar-Haim, R., Eden, L., Friedman, R., Kantor, Y., Lahav, D., & Slonim, N. (2020). From arguments to key points: Towards automatic argument summarization. https://doi.org/10.48550/arXiv.2005.01619. arXiv:2005.01619

Bingham, A. J. (2023). From data management to actionable findings: A five-phase process of qualitative data analysis. *International Journal of Qualitative Methods, 22*, 16094069231183620. https://doi.org/10.1177/16094069231183620

Borge, R., Brugué, J., & Duenas-Cid, D. (2022). Technology and democracy: The who and how in decision-making. The cases of Estonia and Catalonia. *Profesional de la Información, 31*(3).

Brennan, J., & Landemore, H. (2021). *Debating democracy: Do we need more or less?* (1 ed.). Oxford University Press. https://doi.org/10.1093/oso/9780197540817.001.0001

Buhmann, A., & Fieseler, C. (2021). Towards a deliberative framework for responsible innovation in artificial intelligence. *Technology in Society, 64*, Article 101475. https://doi.org/10.1016/j.techsoc.2020.101475

Cabrio, E., & Villata, S. (2018). Five years of argument mining: A data-driven analysis. In *IJCAI* (Vol. 18, pp. 5427–5433).

Camburu, O. M., Rockta¨schel, T., Lukasiewicz, T., & Blunsom, P. (2018). e-snli. (2018). Natural language inference with natural language explanations. *Advances in Neural Information Processing Systems, 31*.

Chang, Y., Wang, X., Wang, J., Wu, Y., Yang, L., Zhu, K., Chen, H., Yi, X., Wang, C., Wang, Y., Ye, W., Zhang, Y., Chang, Y., Yu, P. S., Yang, Q., & Xie, X. (2024). A survey on evaluation of large language models. *ACM Transactions on Intelligent Systems and Technolgy, 15*(3), 1–45. https://doi.org/10.1145/3641289

Chen, G., Cheng, L., Tuan, L. A., & Bing, L. (2024). Exploring the potential of large language models in computational argumentation. https://doi.org/10.48550/arXiv.2311.09022. arXiv: 2311.09022

Colelough, B. C., & Regli, W. (2022). Neuro-symbolic AI in 2024: A systematic review.

Dignum, V. (2017). Responsible artificial intelligence: Designing AI for human values.

Dryzek, J. S., Bächtiger, A., Chambers, S., Cohen, J., Druckman, J. N., Felicetti, A., Fishkin, J. S., Farrell, D. M., Fung, A., Gutmann, A., Landemore, H., Mansbridge, J., Marien, S., Neblo, M. A., Niemeyer, S., Setälä, M., Slothuus, R., Suiter, J., Thompson, D., & Warren, M. E. (2019). The crisis of democracy and the science of deliberation. *Science, 363*(6432), 1144–1146. https://doi.org/10.1126/science.aaw2694

Duan, X., Zhang, Y., Yuan, L., Zhou, X., Liu, X., Wang, T., Wang, R., Zhang, Q., Sun, C., & Wu, F. (2019). Legal summarization for multi-role debate dialogue via controversy focus mining and multi-task learning. In *Proceedings of the 28th ACM International Conference on Information and Knowledge Management* (pp. 1361–1370). ACM. https://doi.org/10.1145/3357384.3357940

Van Eemeren, F. H. (2004). *A systematic theory of argumentation: The pragma-dialectical approach.* Cambridge University Press.

Van Eemeren, F. H. (2018). *Argumentation theory: A pragma-dialectical perspective, argumentation library* (Vol. 33). Springer International Publishing. https://doi.org/10.1007/978-3-319-95381-6

Enarsson, T., Enqvist, L., & Naarttija¨rvi, M. (2022). Approaching the human in the loop—Legal perspectives on hybrid human/algorithmic decision-making in three contexts. *Information & Communications Technology Law, 31*(1), 123–153. https://doi.org/10.1080/13600834.2021.1958860

Engelbart, D. C. (2021). Augmenting human intellect: A conceptual framework (1962).

Esau, K., Friess, D., & Eilders, C. (2017). Design matters! An empirical analysis of online deliberation on different news platforms. *Policy & Internet, 9*(3), 321–342. https://doi.org/10.1002/poi3.154

Fensel, D., Şimşek, U., Angele, K., Huaman, E., Kärle, E., Panasiuk, O., Toma, I., Umbrich, J., & Wahler, A. (2020). Introduction: What is a knowledge graph? In D. Fensel, U. Şimşek, K. Angele, E. Huaman, E. Kärle, O. Panasiuk, I. Toma, J. Umbrich, & A. Wahler (Eds.), *Knowledge graphs: Methodology, tools and selected use cases* (pp. 1–10). Springer International Publishing.

Fergadis, A., Pappas, D., Karamolegkou, A., & Papageorgiou, H. (2021). Argumentation mining in scientific literature for sustainable development. In *Proceedings of the 8th Workshop on Argument Mining* (pp. 100–111).

Friess, D., & Eilders, C. (2015). A systematic review of online deliberation research: A review of online deliberation research. *Policy & Internet, 7*(3), 319–339. https://doi.org/10.1002/poi3.95

Giarelis, N., & Karacapilidis, N. (2023). LMRank: Utilizing pre-trained language models and dependency parsing for keyphrase extraction. *IEEE Access.*

Giarelis, N., & Karacapilidis, N. (2024). Deep learning and embeddings-based approaches for keyphrase extraction: A literature review. *Knowledge and Information Systems, 66*(11), 6493–6526. https://doi.org/10.1007/s10115-024-02164-w

Greco, S. (2018). Designing dialogue: Argumentation as conflict management in social interaction. *Travaux NeuchâTelois De Linguistique, 68*, 7–15.

Greco, S., & Jermini-Martinez Soria, C. (2021). Mediators' reframing as a constitutive element of a reconciliatory argumentative style. *JAIC, 10*(1), 73–96. https://doi.org/10.1075/jaic.20019.gre

Habernal, I., Faber, D., Recchia, N., Bretthauer, S., Gurevych, I., Spiecker Genannt Döhmann, I., & Burchard, C. (2024). Mining legal arguments in court decisions. *Artificial Intelligence and Law, 32*(3), 1–38. https://doi.org/10.1007/s10506-023-09361-y

Haddadan, S., Cabrio, E., & Villata, S. (2019). Yes, we can! mining arguments in 50 years of US presidential campaign debates. In *ACL 2019–57th Annual Meeting of the Association for Computational Linguistics* (pp. 4684–4690).

Iandoli, L., Quinto, I., De Liddo, A., & Shum, S. B. (2014). Socially augmented argumentation tools: Rationale, design and evaluation of a debate dashboard. *International Journal of Human-Computer Studies, 72*(3), 298–319.

Jackson, S. K., & Kuehn, K. M. (2016). Open source, social activism and "Necessary Trade-offs" in the digital enclosure: A case study of platform co-operative, Loomio. org. tripleC: Communication, capitalism and critique. *Open Access Journal for a Global Sustainable Information Society, 14*(2), 413–427.

Jia, W., Sun, M., Lian, J., & Hou, S. (2022). Feature dimensionality reduction: A review. *Complex & Intelligent Systems, 8*(3), 2663–2693. https://doi.org/10.1007/s40747-021-00637-x

Karpowitz, C. F., & Raphael, C. (2016). Ideals of inclusion in deliberation. *Journal of Deliberative Democracy, 12*(2).

Kenton, J. D. M. W. C., & Toutanova, L. K. (2019). Bert: Pre-training of deep bidirectional transformers for language understanding. In *Proceedings of naacL-HLT* (Vol. 1, p. 2). Minneapolis, Minnesota.

Klein, M. (2007). *The MIT collaboratorium: Enabling effective large-scale deliberation for complex problems.* MIT Sloan Research Paper (2007)

Klein, M. (2011). The MIT deliberatorium: Enabling large-scale deliberation about complex systemic problems. In *2011 International Conference on Collaboration Technologies and Systems (CTS)* (pp. 161–161). IEEE.

Klein, M. (2015). *A critical review of crowd-scale online deliberation technologies.* MIT Sloan Research Paper.

Lawrence, J., & Reed, C. (2017). Using complex argumentative interactions to reconstruct the argumentative structure of large-scale debates. In *Proceedings of the 4th Workshop on Argument Mining* (pp. 108–117).

Li, N., Adepu, S., Kang, E., & Garlan, D. (2020). Explanations for human-on-the-loop: A probabilistic model checking approach. In *Proceedings of the IEEE/ACM 15th International Symposium on Software Engineering for Adaptive and Self-Managing Systems* (pp. 181–187). ACM. https://doi.org/10.1145/3387939.3391592

Liu, H., Kong, X., Bai, X., Wang, W., Bekele, T. M., & Xia, F. (2015). Context-based collaborative filtering for citation recommendation. *IEEE Access, 3*, 1695–1703.

Mahyar, N., Nguyen, D. V., Chan, M., Zheng, J., & Dow, S. P. (2019). The civic data deluge: Understanding the challenges of analyzing large-scale community input. In *Proceedings of the 2019 on Designing Interactive Systems Conference* (pp. 1171–1181). ACM. https://doi.org/10.1145/3322276.3322354

Manosevitch, I. (2014). The design of online deliberation: Implications for practice, theory and democratic citizenship. *Journal of Deliberative Democracy, 10*.

Menini, S., Cabrio, E., Tonelli, S., & Villata, S. (2018). Never retreat, never retract: Argumentation analysis for political speeches. In *Proceedings of the AAAI Conference on Artificial Intelligence* (Vol. 32, No. 1).

Mensonides, J. C., Harispe, S., Montmain, J., & Thireau, V. (2019). Automatic detection and classification of argument components using multi-task deep neural network. In *3rd International Conference on Natural Language and Speech Processing*.

Mirzakhmedova, N., Kiesel, J., Alshomary, M., Heinrich, M., Handke, N., Cai, X., Valentin, B., Dastgheib, D., Ghahroodi, O., Sadraei, M. A., Asgari, E., Kawaletz, L., Wachsmuth, H., & Stein, B. (2023). The Touch´e23-valueeval dataset for identifying human values behind arguments. https://doi.org/10.48550/arXiv.2301.13771. arXiv:2301.13771

Morasso, S. G. (2011). *Argumentation in dispute mediation: A reasonable way to handle conflict* (Vol. 3). John Benjamins Publishing.

Morasso, S. G. (2020). *Dal conflitto al dialogo: Un approccio comunicativo alla mediazione*. Apogeo Education.

Mosqueira-Rey, E., Herna´ndez-Pereira, E., Alonso-R´ıos, D., Bobes-Bascaran, J., & Fernandez-Leal, A. (2023). Human-in-the-loop machine learning: A state of the art. *Artificial Intelligence Review, 56*(4), 3005–3054. https://doi.org/10.1007/s10462-022-10246-w

Noroozi, O., Banihashem, S. K., Biemans, H. J. A., Smits, M., Vervoort, M. T., & Verbaan, C. L. (2023). Design, implementation, and evaluation of an online supported peer feedback module to enhance students' argumentative essay quality. *Education and Information Technologies, 28*(10), 12757–12784. https://doi.org/10.1007/s10639-023-11683-y

Ozcan, F., Lei, C., Quamar, A., & Efthymiou, V. (2021). Semantic enrichment of data for AI applications. In *Proceedings of the Fifth Workshop on Data Management for End-To-End Machine Learning* (pp. 1–7). ACM. https://doi.org/10.1145/3462462.3468881

Palau, R. M., & Moens, M. F. (2009). Argumentation mining: The detection, classification and structure of arguments in text. In *Proceedings of the 12th International Conference on Artificial Intelligence and Law* (pp. 98–107). ACM. https://doi.org/10.1145/1568234.1568246

Patil, R., & Gudivada, V. (2024). A review of current trends, techniques, and challenges in large language models (LLMS). *Applied Sciences, 14*(5), 2074.

Perret-Clermont, A. N., Schär, R., Greco, S., Convertini, J., Iannaccone, A., & Rocci, A. (2019). Shifting from a monological to a dialogical perspective on children's argumentation. In *Argumentation in actual practice: Topical studies about argumentative discourse in context 17*. John Benjamins Publishing Company.

Rago, A., Cocarascu, O., Bechlivanidis, C., & Toni, F. (2020). Argumentation as a frame-work for interactive explanations for recommendations. In *Proceedings of the International Conference on Principles of Knowledge Representation and Reasoning* (Vol. 17, No. 1, pp. 805–815).

Ribeiro, M. T., Singh, S., & Guestrin, C. (2016). Why Should I Trust You?: Explaining the predictions of any classifier. In *Proceedings of the 22nd ACM SIGKDD International Conference on Knowledge Discovery and Data Mining* (pp. 1135–1144). ACM. https://doi.org/10.1145/2939672.2939778

Riyahi, M., & Sohrabi, M. K. (2020) Providing effective recommendations in discussion groups using a new hybrid recommender system based on implicit ratings and semantic similarity. *Electronic Commerce Research and Applications, 40*, 100938.

Sahoo, P., Singh, A. K., Saha, S., Jain, V., Mondal, S., & Chadha, A. (2024). A systematic survey of prompt engineering in large language models: techniques and applications. https://doi.org/10.48550/arXiv.2402.07927

Saxena, A., Prasad, M., Gupta, A., Bharill, N., Patel, O. P., Tiwari, A., Er, M. J., Ding, W., & Lin, C. T. (2017). A review of clustering techniques and developments. *Neuro-Computing, 267*, 664–681.

Schneider, P., Schopf, T., Vladika, J., Galkin, M., Simperl, E., & Matthes, F. (2022). A decade of knowledge graphs in natural language processing: A survey. https://doi.org/10.48550/arXiv.2210.00105, arXiv:2210.00105

Sen, P. C., Hajra, M., & Ghosh, M. (2020). Supervised classification algorithms in machine Learning: A survey and review. In J. K. Mandal, & D. Bhattacharya (Eds.), *Emerging technology in modelling and graphics. Advances in Intelligent Systems and Computing* (Vol. 937, pp. 99–111). Springer.

Sia, S., Dalmia, A., & Mielke, S. J. (2020). Tired of topic models? Clusters of pre-trained word embeddings make for fast and good topics too! https://doi.org/10.48550/arXiv.2004.14914, arXiv:2004.14914

Stab, C., & Gurevych, I. (2014). Identifying argumentative discourse structures in persuasive essays. In *Proceedings of the 2014 Conference on Empirical Methods in Natural Language Processing (EMNLP)* (pp. 46–56).

Steenbergen, M. R., Bächtiger, A., Spörndli, M., & Steiner, J. (2003). Measuring political deliberation: A discourse quality index. *Comparative European Politics, 1*(1), 21–48. https://doi.org/10.1057/palgrave.cep.6110002

Tian, L., Zhou, X., Wu, Y. P., Zhou, W. T., Zhang, J. H., & Zhang, T. S. (2022). Knowledge graph and knowledge reasoning: A systematic review. *Journal of Electronic Science and Technology, 20*(2), Article 100159. https://doi.org/10.1016/j.jnlest.2022.100159

Varga, B., Flemisch, F., & Hohmann, S. (2024). Human in the loop. *At—Automatisierung-stechnik, 72*(12), 1109–1111. https://doi.org/10.1515/auto-2024-0148

Velikanov, C. (2017). Can deliberative governance become inclusive? In *Proceedings of the 18th Annual International Conference on Digital Government Research* (pp. 531–540). ACM. https://doi.org/10.1145/3085228.3085237

Wachter, S., Mittelstadt, B., & Russell, C. (2017). Counterfactual explanations without opening the black box: Automated decisions and the GDPR. *Harvard Journal of Law & Techology, 31*, 841.

Zhang, H., Yu, P. S., & Zhang, J. (2024). A systematic survey of text summarization: From statistical methods to large language models. https://doi.org/10.48550/arXiv.2406.11289

An Investigation of the Impacts of Ethical Goals on Government AI Policy Adoption

6

Stephen Kwamena Aikins and Tamara Dimitrijevska-Markoski

1 Introduction

This study investigates the impacts of ethical goals on local government adoption of artificial intelligence (AI) policy in the United States. The adoption of AI policies has emerged as a crucial aspect of ethical integration of AI technologies into society. The rapid advancement of AI brings significant benefits such as efficiency, innovation, and data-driven decision-making capabilities. Despite these benefits, AI adoption also introduces ethical challenges, including issues related to transparency, accountability, bias, and public trust. These challenges necessitate a comprehensive understanding of how ethical considerations shape AI policy adoption to balance innovation with societal values and norms. For the purpose of this study, ethical considerations refer to the following ethical goals to the extent they are considered important in AI policy adoption decisions: enhanced transparency, improved accountability, ethical AI deployment, reduced bias in AI applications, and improved public trust.

AI systems influence various aspects of human life, ranging from healthcare and education to governance and public safety. As these systems become increasingly integrated into decision-making processes, their ethical implications cannot be ignored. According to Gianni et al. (2022), governance frameworks that prioritize ethical considerations are essential to mitigating risks and ensuring AI technologies serve societal interests. Ethical challenges such as algorithmic bias and lack of transparency not only hinder the equitable deployment of AI but also

S. K. Aikins (✉) · T. Dimitrijevska-Markoski
School of Public Affairs, University of South Florida, Tampa, USA
e-mail: saikins@usf.edu

S. K. Aikins and T. Dimitrijevska-Markoski (eds.), *Artificial Intelligence and Government*, https://doi.org/10.1007/978-3-032-12344-2_6

erode public trust—a critical factor for policy adoption. Consequently, understanding how the consideration of these ethical challenges influences policy adoption is imperative in fostering effective AI policy implementation.

Some scholars have studied propositions on the co-dependence of AI and AI ethical framework adoption (Bansal & Heath, 2023), ethical considerations and implications of AI governance for social responsibility (Camilleri, 2024), and a theoretical framework to guide AI ethical decision-making (Ferrell et al., 2024). Others have studied ethical considerations in AI adoption (Olabiyi, 2024), mapping ethical AI policy landscape (Saheb & Saheb, 2024), and the role and limits of principles in AI ethics (Whittlestone et al., 2021). Additionally, other scholars have examined the global landscape of AI ethics guidelines, bias, and fairness in machine learning (Mehrabi et al., 2021), and the role of fairness, accountability, and transparency in AI decision-making processes.

While the above-mentioned studies have made significant contributions to the literature on AI adoption, the effects of ethical considerations on government AI policy adoption in local governments have gained little attention in public administration and AI adoption research. In particular, there are unanswered questions regarding the extent to which local government goals to enhance transparency, improve accountability, ethical deployment of AI, reduce AI bias in application, and improve public trust, influence the adoption of AI governance policy in municipal governments. Our study fills this research gap by examining institutional theory, the literature on AI, and the adoption of ethical AI to establish a theoretical foundation for empirically explaining how the aforementioned goals can impact AI policy adoption.

Investigating the impacts of ethical considerations on AI policy adoption in local governments is significant because of the potential of the findings to provide evidence-based guidance to address the challenges posed by the rapid advancement of AI technologies in government. By understanding how ethical considerations influence policy adoption, scholars, policymakers and practitioners can develop governance frameworks that align innovation with societal values. Additionally, such ethical governance frameworks can enhance the legitimacy and credibility of AI policies, thereby fostering public confidence and facilitating sustainable adoption. Furthermore, this study could contribute to the broader discourse on responsible AI use in government by ensuring that AI technologies serve as a force for good while minimizing risks and unintended consequences.

2 Theoretical Framework

The ethical impacts of government AI policy adoptions represent a critical area of scholarly inquiry that addresses the challenges and opportunities presented by AI technologies. Examining the role of transparency, accountability, ethical deployment, bias reduction, and public trust can aid in the development of AI governance frameworks that balance innovation and societal values. Costa et al. (2024) emphasize that transparency is a cornerstone of democratizing AI governance, enabling inclusivity and fostering public trust. Bansal and Heath (2023) argue that ethical practices in AI deployment are critical to fostering trust and ensuring long-term sustainability. Saheb and Saheb (2024) emphasize the importance of reducing bias through diverse training datasets, rigorous testing, and inclusive practices to help enhance confidence and public trust in AI systems.

Institutional theory would be a good guiding framework for explaining how ethical considerations could impact government AI policy adoption. The theory examines how institutional structures, norms, and practices influence organizational behaviors, including policy adoption. It argues that organizations adopt policies not only to improve efficiency but also to gain legitimacy within a social or institutional context. Key proponents of institutional theory include DiMaggio and Powell (1983), who introduced the concepts of isomorphism (coercive, mimetic, and normative forces) that influence policy adoption.

The concept of coercive isomorphism argues that external pressures from regulatory bodies, governments, and public advocacy groups compel organizations to adopt ethical policies (DiMaggio & Powell, 1983). The normative isomorphism asserts that professional norms and values, such as ethical guidelines and societal expectations for technology usage, drive organizations to adopt the relevant policies. Mimetic isomorphism posits that organizations emulate the practices of industry leaders who adopt ethical policies to remain competitive and socially legitimate (DiMaggio & Powell, 1983). Additionally, the adoption of ethical policies signals organizational legitimacy to stakeholders, improving public trust and accountability. This implies that institutional theory is particularly relevant for analyzing AI policy adoption because it explains how ethical considerations, public trust, and regulatory expectations shape organizational behavior in AI governance. Over the years, the applicability of institutional theory has appeared in various aspects of ethical studies (Fjeld et al., 2020; Floridi et al., 2020; Mehrabi et al., 2021; Whittlestone et al., 2021; Zuboff, 2020).

The goal of having enhanced transparency in AI systems may be a key determinant of local government adoption of AI policy. Transparency in AI systems is crucial for fostering trust and accountability in AI policy adoption. Transparency allows stakeholders, including policymakers, organizations, and the public, to understand how AI systems operate, their decision-making processes, and potential implications. Institutional theory emphasizes that organizations adopt transparency practices due to coercive pressures from regulators and mimetic pressures from industry peers. Zuboff (2020) argues that transparency aligns with coercive isomorphism as regulators demand clear explanations of AI systems. Additionally, mimetic forces drive transparency as organizations emulate peers to maintain legitimacy. The governance of responsible AI requires transparent systems to mitigate risks associated with algorithmic bias and misuse (Floridi et al., 2020; Gianni et al., 2022). Transparent practices, such as disclosing AI system algorithms and decision-making processes, empower stakeholders to hold organizations accountable, thereby increasing policy adoption rates. A study by Raji et al. (2021) demonstrated that organizations with transparent AI systems reported higher rates of policy adoption due to improved regulatory compliance. Based on the foregoing, we posit that municipal governments aiming to enhance transparency are more likely to adopt AI policies. We therefore hypothesize that:

H1: There is a positive relationship between the goal to enhance transparency and municipal government adoption of AI Policy.

The goal of having improved accountability is also likely to influence local government adoption of AI policy. Accountability in AI governance reflects the institutional theory concept of normative isomorphism, as professional standards and societal expectations dictate ethical conduct. Theoretical frameworks from Whittlestone et al. (2021) argue that accountability measures reinforce legitimacy. Floridi and Cowls (2019) also argue that accountability ensures adherence to ethical principles, thereby making organizations more willing to adopt and comply with policies. Accountability mechanisms, such as audit trails, oversight committees, and responsibility assignments, play a critical role in AI policy adoption. Such mechanisms ensure that organizations and individuals deploying AI systems can be held responsible for their actions and decisions. Camilleri (2024) argues that ethical AI governance necessitates frameworks that establish clear accountability structures, ensuring compliance with ethical principles. Improved accountability not only reduces the risks of misuse but also builds trust among stakeholders. Olabiyi (2024) highlights that organizations with robust accountability measures are more likely to gain public and regulatory approval, thereby facilitating the adoption of AI policies. Based on the foregoing, we argue that municipal governments aiming for improved accountability are more likely to implement formalized AI policies. Consequently, we posit that:

H2: There is a positive relationship between the goal to improve accountability and municipal government adoption of AI Policy.

Ethical AI deployment, another key goal of many governments, may be a key determinant of municipal government adoption of AI policy. Ethical deployment of AI involves integrating fairness, equity, and human-centric principles into AI design and operation, with a profound impact on policy adoption. From the perspective of institutional theory, ethical AI deployment exemplifies the concept of normative and mimetic isomorphism, where societal norms and industry leaders drive adoption. A study by Fjeld et al. (2020) found that normative pressures from ethics boards drove policy adoption. Jobin et al. (2019) emphasize that ethical AI deployment aligns organizational goals with societal values, thereby reducing resistance to AI policy implementation. Similarly, Bansal and Heath (2023) emphasize that ethical AI deployment is a cornerstone of responsible AI adoption, as it addresses societal concerns regarding fairness, privacy, and equity. Organizations that prioritize ethical considerations in AI deployment are more likely to receive support from regulators and the public. Rahman (2024) discusses how cultivating awareness of ethical AI practices can alleviate fears and promote acceptance, ultimately driving policy adoption. Additionally, ethical deployment also minimizes risks of unintended consequences and ensures sustainable integration of AI technologies into societal systems. Based on the foregoing, we argue that local governments that aim at ethical AI deployment are more likely to adopt AI policy. Therefore, we hypothesize that:

H3: There is a positive relationship between ethical AI deployment and municipal government adoption of AI policy.

Reduced AI bias in applications may also influence local government adoption of AI policy. Mitigating biases in AI applications may directly influence policy adoption by addressing societal concerns and regulatory pressures. Efforts to mitigate AI bias align with the institutional theory concept of coercive and normative isomorphism, due to the regulatory and societal pressures organizations face. Mehrabi et al. (2021) argue that organizations adopt bias mitigation practices to comply with legal and societal expectations. AI systems perceived as unbiased face fewer public and regulatory challenges. On the contrary, biases in AI systems can lead to discriminatory outcomes, erode public trust, and hinder policy adoption. Saheb and Saheb (2024) highlight the importance of addressing algorithmic bias to ensure equitable outcomes and maintain stakeholder confidence. Efforts to reduce bias, such as diverse training datasets and rigorous testing enhance the fairness and reliability of AI systems. Mehrabi et al. (2021) argue organizations that prioritize fairness are more willing to institutionalize policies to address these concerns (Mehrabi et al., 2021). Similarly, Ferrell et al. (2024) argue organizations that proactively address AI bias are better positioned to gain regulatory approval and public support, paving the way for successful policy adoption. Additionally, reducing bias aligns with ethical principles, thereby reinforcing the legitimacy of AI governance frameworks. This implies that local governments that aim to reduce AI bias in applications are more likely to adopt AI policy. Therefore, we posit that:

H4: There is a positive relationship between the goal to reduce AI bias in applications and municipal government adoption of AI policy.

The need for improved public trust, a key factor that ensures legitimacy, may also be an important determinant of local government adoption of AI policy. Public trust is foundational for AI policy adoption as organizations depend on societal acceptance to deploy AI systems. It reflects the legitimacy organizations seek to establish through ethical AI governance, which institutional theory underscores. Trust improves the perceived legitimacy of AI policies and reduces resistance to their adoption. Trustworthy AI systems that demonstrate transparency, accountability, and fairness are more likely to gain widespread acceptance. Costa et al. (2024) highlight that public perception and understanding of AI significantly influence its adoption. Initiatives to educate and engage the public, such as awareness campaigns and stakeholder consultations, can enhance trust and facilitate policy adoption. Additionally, Rahman (2024) emphasizes that addressing fears and concerns related to AI technologies is crucial in building trust and fostering acceptance. It can therefore be argued that organizations that prioritize public trust through ethical practices and transparent communication are more likely to succeed in implementing AI policies. Consequently, we contend that local governments that aim at improved public trust are more likely to adopt AI policies. Based on this reasoning, we posit that:

H5: There is a positive relationship between the goal to improve public trust and municipal government adoption of AI policies.

2.1 Control Variables

In addition to the above-mentioned factors, other factors such as regulatory compliance requirements, inadequate funding for AI, the need for enhanced cybersecurity, improved accessibility of government services, and enhanced citizen engagement are also likely to influence local government adoption of AI policy. Consequently, these factors were included as control variables.

Regulatory compliance requirements significantly impact the adoption of AI technologies in government settings. Veale and Borgesius (2021) note that organizations frequently perceive compliance as a costly and time-consuming process, which discourages policy adoption. Compliance with data protection laws, such as the General Data Protection Regulation (GDPR) in Europe, imposes constraints on the design and deployment of AI systems. Adhering to these regulations often requires substantial investments in data governance frameworks and operational changes, which can deter adoption (Carayannis et al., 2024) with a profound negative impact on the formulation and implementation of AI policy. Additionally, inconsistencies in regulatory frameworks across regions create challenges for governments attempting to deploy AI systems. The need for interoperability between various AI systems and adherence to global standards can also complicate implementations, especially for multinational projects (Yang et al., 2019).

Funding plays a pivotal role in the adoption and scalability of AI technologies. Inadequate funding is a major hurdle for organizations seeking to integrate AI technologies and adopt related policies (Brynjolfsson & McAfee, 2019). Similarly, organizations with limited resources often struggle to invest in accountability mechanisms, bias mitigation tools, and ethical AI practices (Kumar & Patel, 2023). Additionally, governments with constrained budgets often fail to prioritize AI adoption, which leads to fragmented and subpar implementations (Bokhari & Myeong, 2023). Such failure to prioritize AI adoption is more likely to have a negative impact on AI policy implementation, which justifies the inclusion of inadequate funding as a control variable. Moreover, inadequate funding affects the ability to recruit and retain skilled professionals required to design and manage AI systems. Furthermore, the absence of carefully crafted AI policy stemming from inadequate funding limits investment in critical areas like cybersecurity, further exposing governments to risks (Yang et al., 2019).

Cybersecurity is a cornerstone of AI adoption in government systems, which requires a good governance framework in the form of AI policy. AI technologies, while beneficial, can expose governments to new cyber threats if not adequately protected (Yigitcanlar et al., 2024). Therefore, the integration of AI into e-government services requires robust cybersecurity measures to safeguard sensitive data and maintain public trust (Hossain et al., 2024). Research (e.g. Chatfield &

Reddick, 2019) underscores the importance of embedding cybersecurity principles—confidentiality, integrity, and availability—into AI systems from the design stage. This implies municipal governments that aim for enhanced cybersecurity are more likely to adopt AI policy that incorporates cybersecurity to help provide guidance for AI implementation.

Improved accessibility to government services through AI adoption enables governments to provide more efficient, inclusive, and responsive public services. Local governments using AI to modernize their IT systems experience increased efficiency in service provision and user satisfaction (Papel et al., 2024). For instance, AI-powered platforms streamline administrative tasks, reducing the waiting time for public service access and enabling tailored responses to citizen needs. This transformation is evident in e-government initiatives where AI is used to enhance service delivery and reduce inequalities in access (Al-Anis et al., 2024). For AI-powered platforms to enable accessible, efficient, and responsive services, an effective AI policy needs to be in place to help provide the necessary user guidelines. Therefore, governments that aim for improved accessibility to government services through AI adoption are more likely to adopt AI policy.

Citizen engagement is critical for the successful implementation of AI in governance. AI can facilitate participatory governance by enabling platforms that incorporate public opinions into decision-making processes. Tools like AI-driven sentiment analysis on social media data allow governments to gauge public sentiment and adjust policies accordingly (Duberry, 2022). For this to happen effectively, a good AI governance framework is needed. AI systems also enhance citizen engagement by improving transparency and accountability. For example, e-government systems leveraging open data and AI analytics foster trust by allowing citizens to monitor government activities. Enhanced engagement also involves creating AI systems that are adaptive and responsive to user needs, leading to more inclusive governance (Chatfield & Reddick, 2019). Based on the foregoing, it can be argued that the existence of AI governance framework such as policy guidelines could be an enabler that facilitates the adaptation and responsiveness of AI systems to user needs. Therefore, we contend that local governments that aim for AI-powered citizen engagement and responsiveness are more likely to adopt AI policy.

3 Methodology

This research is a survey-based project. An online survey was sent to 1200 municipal information technology officers, and 141 of them returned the survey. Government information technology officers were selected as the unit of analysis due to their valuable insights regarding the management and implementation of government technology, including e-government, as well as the needs of their respective governments pertaining to AI policy adoption. Additionally, they play key roles in acting on behalf of the government when it comes to researching, vetting, and hiring AI technology vendors. The survey was conducted from June through September 2024.

Survey responses represented municipalities from 38 U.S. states. Among the 38 states, 24 percent are in the Northeast region of the United States, 26 percent are in the Southeast, 29 percent are in the Midwest, 8 percent are in the Southwest, and 13 percent are in the West. Additionally, 19 percent of the survey respondents work for municipalities in the Northeast region of the United States, 29 percent work for municipalities in the Southeast, 26 percent work for municipalities in the Midwest, 4 percent work for municipalities in the Southwest, and 22 percent work for municipalities in the West.

3.1 Variable Measurement

Our dependent variable of interest is AI policy adoption. This variable was measured by asking respondents to check Yes or No whether their municipal government has an AI use policy in place.

Our independent variables of interest are the following five goals pertaining to ethical considerations in AI policy adoption: Enhanced Transparency, Improved Accountability, Ethical AI Deployment, Reduced Bias in AI Applications and Improved Public Trust. These variables were measured on a five-point Likert scale by asking respondents to select from the following options the extent of the importance of each goal in their government's decision to adopt AI policy: 1 = Not At All Important; 2 = Slightly Important; 3 = Moderately Important; 4 = Very Important; and 5 = Extremely Important.

Our Control variables are Improved Accessibility; Enhanced Citizen Engagement; Inadequate AI Funding, Regulatory Compliance; and Enhanced Cybersecurity. These variables were measured on a five-point Likert Scale by asking respondents to select, based on their perceived needs, from the following options the extent to which each of them is important in their governments' decision-making to adopt AI policy: 1 = Not At All Important; 2 = Slightly Important; 3 = Moderately Important; 4 = Very Important; and 5 = Extremely Important.

3.2 Research Model

Descriptive statistics was used to analyze AI policy adoption, and the degree of importance of Enhanced Transparency, Improved Accountability, Ethical AI Deployment, Reduced AI Bias in Application, and Improved Public Trust in AI policy adoption decisions. Logit regression was used to analyze the effects of our independent variables on the dependent variable. The following details the logit regression model of our empirical prediction of the effects of ethical considerations on AI policy Adoption.

$$Y = \left[\exp(a + b_1X_1 + b_2X_2 \cdots b_nX_n)\right] / \left[1 + \exp(a + b_1X_1 + b_2X_2 \cdots b_nX_n)\right]$$

where

Y	the dependent variable
exp	the base of the algorithm exponential function
a	constant (or intercept) of the model
b_i	the parameters (or coefficients of the predictors) of the model, and
X_i	the predictors of the model.

4 Research Findings

4.1 Importance of Ethical Considerations in AI Policy Adoption Decisions

Table 1 shows the descriptive statistics of the variables used in our study. As can be seen in Table 1, the mean value of having AI Use Policy in Place is 0.23, which means slightly less than a quarter of the governments whose officials responded to the survey have adopted AI policy, with three-quarters of them not having an AI policy. Table 1 also shows that the mean value of how long the AI Use Policy has been in place is 1.32 years. The means the adoption of AI Use Policy by the municipal governments is relatively recent.

With regard to the degree of importance of each of the independent variables in AI policy adoption decisions, Table 1 shows the mean value of Enhanced Transparency is 3.55, and the mean value of Improved Accountability is 3.77. This implies that in their ethical considerations regarding AI policy adoption, the

Table 1 Descriptive statistics—AI use policy and importance of ethical considerations

Variables	N	Minimum	Maximum	Mean	Std. deviation
AI use policy	141	0	1	0.23	0.361
How long AI use policy has been in place	141	1	4	1.32	0.479
Enhanced transparency	141	1	5	3.55	1.159
Improved accountability	141	1	5	3.77	1.174
Ethical AI deployment	141	1	5	3.73	1.273
Reduced bias in AI applications	141	1	5	3.49	1.334
Improved public trust	141	1	5	3.89	1.200
Improved accessibility to e-government services	141	1	5	3.53	1.160
Enhanced citizen engagement	141	1	5	3.42	1.068
Inadequate funding for AI adoption	141	1	4	3.91	0.949
Ensure regulatory compliance	141	1	4	3.86	0.842
Enhanced cybersecurity	141	1	5	3.66	1.274

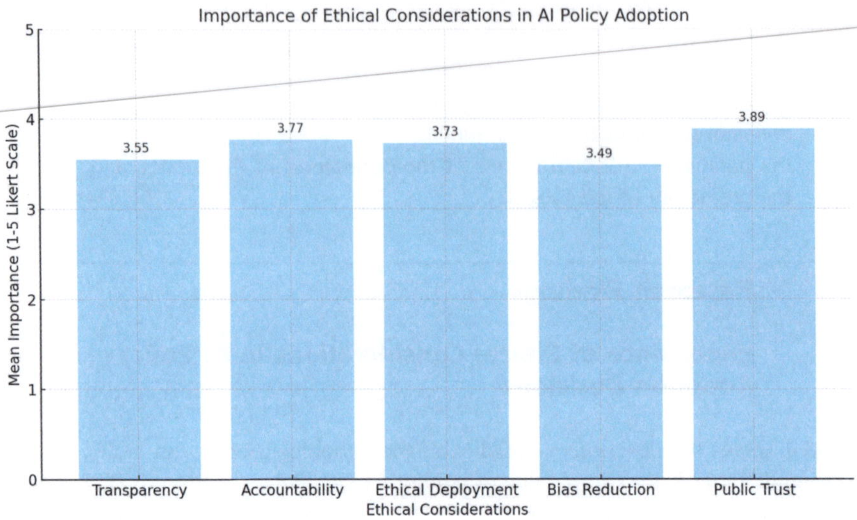

Fig. 1 Importance of ethical considerations in AI policy adoption

municipal governments that responded to the survey view both goals of Enhanced Transparency and Improved Accountability as very important, with much premium placed on Improved Accountability. Similarly, the mean value of Ethical AI Deployment is 3.73, and that of Reduced Bias in AI Application is 3.49. This means while the municipalities consider the goal of Reduced Bias in AI Applications as important, they view the Ethical Deployment of AI as more important. Table 1 also reveals that Improved Public Trust has the highest mean value (3.89) among all the independent variables, implying this is the most important ethical consideration of municipal governments when it comes to AI Policy adoption. Table 1 also shows among all the control variables, Inadequate Funding for AI Adoption has the highest mean value of 3.91, followed by Regulatory Compliance and Enhanced Cybersecurity with mean values of 3.86 and 3.66, respectively.

Figure 1 illustrates the average importance rating (on a 5-point Likert scale) of five ethical goals considered in the adoption of AI policy by municipalities.

4.2 Multicollinearity Test

Table 2 shows the results of the multicollinearity test we conducted for our independent variables of interest. Multicollinearity occurs when independent variables in a regression model are highly correlated with each other, which could mask the individual effect of each predictor on the dependent variable, and potentially obscure the true relationships in data, leading to misleading conclusions if not corrected.

Table 2 Correlation matrix among independent variables

		1	2	3	4	5	6	7	8	9	10
1	Enhance transparency	1									
2	Improve accountability	0.142*	1								
3	Ethical AI deployment	0.251*	0.268**	1							
4	Reduce bias in AI applications	0.173	0.113*	0.128	1						
5	Improve public trust	0.121***	0.205*	0.131*	0.167*	1					
6	Improved accessibility	0.213**	0.127	0.226*	0.113	0.213*	1				
7	Enhanced citizen engagement	0.032	0.041	0.053	0.119	− 0.117*	− 0.110	1			
8	Inadequate funding for AI adoption	− 0.127**	0.038	0.048	0.142*	− 0.121	− 0.216*	− 0.223	1		
9	Regulatory compliance	−.0329*	− 0.152	0.139	− 0.116	0.159	− 0.137*	0.119*	0.211	1	
10	Enhanced cybersecurity	0.018	0.096	0.114	0.017	0.113	0.124	0.082	0.183	0.098	1

Note ** = Significant at 0.05; *** = Significant at 0.001

Typically, a correlation greater than 0.80 or less than -0.80 is considered strong and indicates the presence of multicollinearity. As can be seen in Table 2, although enhanced transparency has statistically significant relationships with improved accountability, ethical AI deployment, improved public trust and three of our control variables, the correlation in each instance is markedly less than 0.80. Similarly, the correlations among all the rest of the independent variables is less than 0.80 which indicates there is no presence of multicollinearity.

4.3 Effects of Ethical Considerations on AI Policy Adoption

With regard to the degree of importance of the ethical considerations in AI policy adoption decisions, we have noted in Table 1 that the municipal ethical goals to have enhanced transparency, improved accountability, ethical deployment of AI, and improved public trust are all considered very important in AI policy adoption decisions. The question then becomes how statistically significant are the impacts of these goals on municipals' decision to adopt AI policy?

Table 3 shows the results of the logistic regression model to determine the effects of ethical considerations on AI Policy Adoption. The values in bold shown in Table 3 denote results that are statistically significant at the $p < 0.05$ level. The analysis reveals there is a statistically significant positive relationship between Improved Accountability and AI Policy Adoption ($P = 0.29$). Additionally, AI Policy Adoption is statistically and significantly related to Ethical AI Deployment ($P = 0.15$).

Furthermore, Reduced Bias in AI Applications and Improved Public Trust were also found to have statistically significant and positive relationships with AI Policy Adoption [($P = 0.049$) and ($P = 0.011$)] respectively. An important revelation in Table 3 is that two of our control variables—Inadequate funding for AI Adoption, and Regulatory Compliance—have statistically significant relationships with AI Policy Adoption [($P = 0.031$) and ($P = 0.50$)], respectively. These findings are not surprising, as both inadequate funding and the need for regulatory compliance adversely impact AI adoption which, in all likelihood, tends to have a demotivating effect on AI Policy Adoption. The Cox and Snell R Square and the Nagelkerke R Square values shown in Table 3 are 0.678 and 0.759 respectively. This means at least 68 percent of the variation in AI Policy Adoption is explained by the need to have Improved Accountability, Ethical AI deployment, Reduced Biased in AI Adoption, and Improved Public Trust.

5 Discussion

Our analysis of the survey results shows that almost a quarter of the surveyed municipalities have AI governance policies in place, and on average, these policies have been in existence for slightly over a year, indicating that the adoption of AI policies is a relatively recent phenomenon. This finding is consistent with prior

Table 3 Logistic regression model: ethical determinants of government AI policy adoption, dependent variable: government AI policy adoption

Variables	B	S.E	Wald	df	Sig. (*P*)
Enhanced transparency	0.987	1.393	0.468	1	0.533
Improved accountability	0.365	0.625	4.775	1	**0.029**
Ethical AI deployment	1.036	0.822	6.106	1	**0.015**
Reduced bias in AI applications	2.359	1.344	3.792	1	**0.049**
Improved public trust	1.046	0.413	6.423	1	**0.011**
Improved accessibility to e-government services	0.735	0.488	2.273	1	0.132
Enhanced citizen engagement	− 0.462	0.637	2.318	1	0.158
Inadequate funding for AI adoption	− 2.539	1.739	4.352	1	**0.031**
Ensure regulatory compliance	− 3.283	1.390	3.527	1	**0.050**
Enhanced cybersecurity	0.441	0.610	0.676	1	0.374
Constant	2.465	0.849	6.012	1	0.016
Omnibus test of model	Model Chi-Square = 18.678 DF = 10 *P* = 0.026				
Hosmer & Lemeshow test	Chi-Square = 10.564 DF = 10 *P* = 0.047				
− 2 Log likelihood	89.820				
Cox and Snell R Square	0.678				
NagelKerke R Square	0.759				

studies indicating the slow adoption of AI governance frameworks, particularly at the local government level. This finding is also consistent with the work of Costa et al. (2024), which shows that the adoption of AI policies is often hindered by a combination of financial constraints, a lack of expertise, and concerns over ethical implications. The relatively low adoption rate observed in this study reflects these challenges, and underscores the need for targeted interventions to support municipalities in developing and implementing AI governance frameworks.

The finding that these AI policies are relatively new not only highlights the nascent stage of AI governance at the municipal level but also corroborates the work of Gianni et al. (2022) who argue that the early stages of AI policy implementation often involve a steep learning curve as governments adapt to rapidly evolving technologies and ethical considerations. The short duration of these policies therefore, underscores the need for ongoing support and capacity building to ensure their effectiveness and sustainability over time.

Further analysis using logistic regression reveals that four ethical goals—improved accountability, ethical AI deployment, reduced bias in AI applications, and improved public trust—are among the key drivers of AI policy adoption.

Accountability is a crucial enabler for organizations to align AI practices with ethical and regulatory frameworks. The statistically significant positive relationship between improved accountability and AI policy adoption highlights the importance of embedding accountability into organizational practices to ensure compliance with ethical principles and mitigate risks associated with AI implementation. Additionally, this result is consistent with prior research emphasizing the importance of accountability mechanisms in fostering responsible AI governance. As noted by Camilleri (2024), clear accountability mechanisms such as audit trails and oversight committees are pivotal in enhancing public trust and organizational credibility. Our finding corroborates his findings by demonstrating that organizations with robust accountability measures are more likely to adopt AI policies successfully.

Ethical AI deployment's positive relationship with AI policy adoption reflects municipalities' growing recognition of aligning AI use with societal norms and values. This finding underscores the importance of ethical deployment for maintaining public trust and meeting regulatory demands. In practice, ethical deployment can ensure that municipal AI systems operate within the boundaries of fairness and non-discrimination to help reduce legal and reputational risks for municipalities. By prioritizing ethical considerations, municipalities can address societal concerns regarding fairness, privacy, and equity, thereby facilitating policy adoption. Our finding aligns with the work of Bansal and Heath (2023), who emphasized that ethical practices in AI deployment foster trust among stakeholders and promote regulatory approval. The finding contributes to the existing literature by providing empirical evidence of the positive impact of ethical AI deployment on policy adoption and highlights the need for municipalities to align AI systems with societal values and norms. From a practical perspective, the finding suggests that municipalities integrating ethical AI principles into their systems, such as fairness and inclusivity, are better positioned to implement policies that align with societal expectations.

The statistically significant relationship noted between the municipal goal to reduce bias in AI applications and AI policy adoption highlights the need for ethical frameworks that institutionalize practices to monitor and address bias to help ensure equitable outcomes for all stakeholders. Reduced bias not only enhances the fairness and equity of AI systems but also reduces legal challenges and public criticism. This implies that addressing bias lays a foundation for responsible AI use and enables smoother policy implementation. Our finding is consistent with previous studies that underscore the detrimental effects of algorithmic bias on public trust and policy implementation. As emphasized by Saheb and Saheb (2024), addressing bias through diverse training datasets and inclusive design practices is critical to ensure equitable outcomes. Our finding reinforces the above argument by demonstrating that efforts to mitigate bias enhance the reliability and fairness of AI systems, thereby facilitating policy adoption.

The importance of the statistically significant relationship noted between the municipal goal of improving public trust and AI policy adoption lies in the finding's implications for municipalities seeking to enhance their AI governance framework. Public trust serves as both an enabler and a catalyst for the adoption of municipal AI policies, as it influences the willingness of stakeholders to accept and support these policies. Transparent communication and inclusive decision-making processes foster trust among stakeholders, thereby creating a supportive environment for implementing AI policies. Our finding also underscores the importance of aligning municipal goals with societal values to foster public trust and facilitate AI governance. By integrating trust-building initiatives into their policy frameworks, municipalities can lay a foundation for long-term success in AI adoption. The finding also aligns with prior research emphasizing the critical role of public trust in driving AI governance. As noted by Rahman (2024), initiatives aimed at building public awareness and addressing fears associated with AI technologies significantly influence policy adoption. Additionally, our finding corroborates those of Costa et al. (2024), who note that public trust is not only a product of ethical practices but also a determinant of successful policy implementation.

An important revelation in our findings is that two key control variables—inadequate funding for AI adoption, and regulatory compliance—have inverse relationships with AI policy adoption. The significant negative relationship between inadequate funding and AI policy adoption reflects the critical role of financial resources in implementing AI policies. Financial constraints often result in limited access to advanced technologies, inadequate training for personnel, and insufficient resources for ethical oversight, all of which impede the adoption of AI policies. The finding therefore, underscores the importance of addressing funding gaps to ensure the successful implementation of AI governance frameworks. In this regard, the finding is consistent with the work of Costa et al. (2024), who noted that insufficient funding hinders the development and deployment of AI systems, thereby limiting policy adoption.

To address the funding shortfalls, municipalities can explore public–private partnerships (PPPs). These arrangements allow local governments to collaborate with technology vendors, academic institutions, and nonprofits to co-develop AI solutions and share resource burdens. For instance, the *AI4 Public Policy* initiative, a Horizon 2020 project, enabled five European cities to pilot AI tools through EU co-funding. As noted by Kalliontzi et al. (2024), the project emphasized stakeholder engagement, technological readiness, and legal compliance as foundational pillars, illustrating how coordinated funding models can reduce municipal risk exposure. Municipalities can also tap into federal grants and digital innovation funds. Programs like the US Digital Service or AI-specific NSF grants provide seed funding for civic technology projects. These resources can defray upfront costs associated with infrastructure, procurement, and training.

The negative relationship between regulatory compliance and AI policy adoption also highlights the critical challenge of AI governance, namely the need for regulatory frameworks that strike a balance between enforcement and support for organizations. While regulations are essential for ensuring ethical AI deployment, overly restrictive compliance requirements can deter municipalities from adopting AI policies. Consequently, simplifying compliance processes and providing resources for implementation could alleviate these barriers. This finding is therefore consistent with Olabiyi (2024), who noted that complex regulatory frameworks often create barriers to innovation and policy adoption. Overall, the finding suggests the need for balanced regulatory approaches that promote ethical AI governance while minimizing administrative burdens on municipalities.

A study on financial AI compliance frameworks emphasized the value of embedded regulatory toolkits that perform automated risk assessments and align algorithmic operations with jurisdiction-specific rules (Deshpande, 2024). A promising solution is adopting modular compliance frameworks that integrate Explainable AI (XAI) tools. These allow governments to maintain transparency and traceability, which are often demanded by law. Case studies from cities like Amsterdam show how tools like algorithm registers—public databases of algorithms used by the government—improve both internal governance and public trust. Additionally, sandbox environments—policy labs where municipalities can test AI tools under relaxed compliance—allow experimentation without full-scale regulatory liability. This is particularly beneficial for small or mid-sized municipalities lacking legal teams or compliance infrastructure.

6 International Case Studies and Comparative Analysis

Table 4 shows the summary of key findings from our study. As reiterated in Table 4, the results of our US-based survey research reveal that while improved accountability, ethical AI deployment, bias reduction, and the goal of enhancing public trust drive municipal AI policy adoption, significant barriers remain in the form of funding constraints and complex regulatory compliance. To contextualize these findings and provide deeper comparative insights, we examine five international case studies that explore municipal or national-level adoption of ethical AI.

Global Smart Cities—Transparency and Trust: A comprehensive global assessment by Ben Dhaou et al. (2024) for UN-Habitat examined AI deployment across multiple urban centers globally. The study emphasized the importance of embedding ethical AI frameworks that prioritize transparency, accountability, and public participation. Cities that successfully adopted AI policies, such as Seoul and Singapore, developed robust ethical charters and public engagement mechanisms. The global cities report aligns with our finding that trust, bias mitigation, and accountability are core to adoption, while also highlighting that cities in the Global South are particularly hindered by funding and infrastructure limitations.

Amsterdam, Netherlands—Algorithmic Transparency in Practice: In the Netherlands, Barrientos (2024) analyzed Amsterdam's AI policy landscape, where municipal efforts have been focused on enhancing algorithmic transparency. The city developed tools such as the Algorithm Register, a public-facing documentation platform designed to improve public trust and institutional accountability. While Amsterdam benefited from national-level funding and supportive regulation, the case study underscores the need for clear communication strategies and

Table 4 Summary of key findings

Variable	Coefficient (B)	*p*-value	Significance	Direction	Interpretation
Enhanced transparency	0.987	0.533	Not significant	–	Less influential
Improved accountability	0.365	0.029	Significant	Positive	Drives adoption
Ethical AI deployment	1.036	0.015	Significant	Positive	Drives adoption
Reduced bias in AI applications	2.359	0.049	Significant	Positive	Drives adoption
Improved public trust	1.046	0.011	Significant	Positive	Drives adoption
Inadequate funding	– 2.539	0.031	Significant	Negative	Barrier to adoption
Regulatory compliance	– 3.283	0.050	Significant	Negative	Barrier to adoption

robust compliance frameworks to mitigate public skepticism, paralleling the US municipalities' struggle with regulatory clarity and underfunded initiatives.

Canada, Finland, and UK—Governance in Democratic Societies: Kuziemski and Misuraca (2020) studied AI governance in three democratic countries, focusing on public trust in automated decision-making systems. Their findings demonstrate that despite high-level frameworks, transparency lapses and a lack of clear redress mechanisms undermine public trust. Canada and the UK, for example, have invested in ethical audits and impact assessments, which have been effective where implementation is consistent. These cases echo the US municipalities' challenges in sustaining public trust amid limited oversight mechanisms and fiscal constraints.

Finland and Norway—Nordic Ethical Frameworks in Local Services: Kinder et al. (2023) explored how municipalities in Finland and Norway have integrated ethical AI principles into local public services. These municipalities focus on co-creation with citizens, bias detection mechanisms, and transparency audits. Interestingly, the study identifies organizational culture and leadership commitment as critical success factors, dimensions not directly captured in our US survey but potentially significant in future work. Furthermore, while Nordic models excel in inclusive deployment, they too report funding and technical knowledge as limiting factors in smaller jurisdictions.

Australia—Responsible Innovation through Ethical AI: Yigitcanlar et al. (2024) documented ethical AI adoption across local governments in Australia, emphasizing design thinking, public consultation, and ethical risk assessment. This bottom-up approach—driven by both national strategy and localized trust-building—proved especially effective in smaller councils, which relied on tailored guidelines rather than universal mandates. Australian municipalities prioritized inclusivity and algorithmic fairness as foundational to ethical deployment, similar to the emphasis seen in our US findings. However, Australian governments benefited from federal funding and strong academic-public partnerships, addressing barriers that US municipalities reported around resources and compliance navigation.

Taken together, these five international case studies validate and expand upon our research findings. There is a global consensus that ethical considerations, notably improved accountability, bias reduction, and public trust, are critical to the successful adoption of AI in public administration. Where US municipalities report statistically significant impacts from these drivers, international case studies provide contextual nuance by illustrating implementation strategies such as algorithm registers, co-creation platforms, and citizen engagement protocols.

Our finding on the negative impact of regulatory complexity is echoed in Amsterdam and the UK, where well-intended guidelines can inadvertently create friction if not harmonized with operational realities. Similarly, the role of funding as a barrier is reported across the Global South, Nordic municipalities, and in the US context, underscoring the universal need for resource alignment to match ethical ambition.

Significantly, international cases emphasize cultural and structural readiness for AI policy integration. In general, municipalities that exhibit leadership buy-in, ethical literacy, and public engagement infrastructures tend to perform better in aligning AI use with ethical governance objectives. These elements present opportunities for future research and policy development in the US, where variables may further elucidate disparities in adoption rates and policy maturity.

The results of the above international comparison imply that supplementing our US survey with global case analysis not only validates our core findings but also provides a strategic road map. Municipalities must develop ethical governance frameworks that integrate funding, regulatory pragmatism, and public trust to achieve sustainable AI policy adoption.

6.1 Limitations and Significance of the Study

This study is limited in a number of ways. First, the study focuses on a limited set of variables that may not capture the full range of factors influencing AI policy adoption. Future research could explore additional variables such as cultural and organizational factors to provide a more comprehensive understanding of the determinants of AI policy adoption. Second, the study is cross-sectional, which, compared to longitudinal studies, could limit its ability to establish causal relationships between variables. Longitudinal studies could provide deeper insights into the dynamic interplay between ethical considerations and AI policy adoption over time. Finally, the findings are based on a sample of municipal governments, which may limit their generalizability to other contexts or regions. Future research could examine the relationships between ethical considerations and AI policy adoption in diverse settings to enhance the generalizability of the results.

Despite the above-mentioned limitations, the findings of this study are useful in that the investigation of the effects of ethical goals on municipal governments' adoption of AI policy has gained little attention in public administration and AI adoption research. Additionally, the significance of the findings lies in the fact that they provide empirical evidence of the critical role of ethical considerations in shaping AI policy adoption in municipal settings, contributing to the growing body of literature on responsible AI governance. By demonstrating the positive impact of accountability, ethical deployment, bias reduction, and public trust on policy adoption, this study highlights the importance of aligning AI systems with societal values and ethical principles. Finally, the findings underscore the need for policymakers and municipalities to address funding constraints and streamline regulatory requirements to facilitate the adoption of AI policies. By identifying these barriers, the study provides actionable insights for enhancing the implementation of AI governance frameworks.

7 Conclusion

This study examined the effects of ethical goals on municipal AI policy adoption. The findings reveal that not only about a quarter of the municipalities that contributed to the survey have adopted AI policies, but also these policies have recently been put in place. Further analysis reveals that, although the municipalities are driven by the goal to achieve accountability, ethical deployments, bias reduction, and public trust when deciding on AI adoption, funding constraints and regulatory compliance act as barriers to adoption. The study provides valuable insights into the critical role of ethical considerations in shaping AI policy adoption.

By demonstrating the positive and negative impacts of the drivers and barriers of adoption, the study highlights the importance of aligning AI systems with societal values and addressing barriers to policy adoption. The findings contribute to the growing body of literature on responsible AI governance and provide actionable insights for policymakers and municipalities seeking to implement ethical AI policies. Additionally, the findings have practical implications for local governments seeking to adopt AI policies. By prioritizing ethical considerations and addressing funding and regulatory challenges, local governments can enhance public trust, gain regulatory approval, and ensure the sustainable integration of AI systems into governmental frameworks.

References

Al-Anis, A. M., Garad, A., Jaboob, M., & Al-Ansi, A. (2024). Elevating e-government. Unleashing the power of AI and IoT for enhanced public services. *Heliyon, 10*(23), e40591. https://doi.org/10.1016/j.heliyon.2024.e40591

Bansal, G., & Heath, D. (2023). Ten propositions on co-dependence of AI and AI ethical framework adoption: View from industry and academia. *Journal of Technology Ethics, 32*(3), 200–220. https://doi.org/10.1080/15228053.2023.2194106

Barrientos, M. L. (2024). *Governance in local governments: Case study on the city of Amsterdam: Context, enablers and barriers for implementing algorithmic transparency*. Tallinn University of Technology. https://digikogu.taltech.ee/en/Download/13240561-7b9e-4196-8df3-e96653c4e92d

Ben Dhaou, S., Isagah, T., Distor, C., & Ruas, I. (2024). *Global assessment of responsible artificial intelligence in cities: Research and recommendations to leverage AI for people-centred smart cities*. United Nations University. https://collections.unu.edu/view/UNU:9789

Brynjolfsson, E., & McAfee, A. (2019). The business of artificial intelligence: What it can—and cannot—do for your organization. *Harvard Business Review, 87*(4), 67–78.

Bokhari, S. A. A., & Myeong, S. (2023). The Influence of artificial intelligence on e-governance and cybersecurity in smart cities: A stakeholder's perspective. *IEEE Access, 11*, 69783–69797. https://doi.org/10.1109/ACCESS.2023.3293480

Camilleri, M. A. (2024). Artificial intelligence governance: Ethical considerations and implications for social responsibility. *Expert Systems, 41*(1), 15–30.

Carayannis, E. G., Askounis, D., Andoutropoulou, M., & Zotas, N. (2024). Leveraging AI for enhanced e-government: Optimizing the use of open governmental data. *The Journal of Knowledge Economy*. https://doi.org/10.1007/s13132-024-02317-w

Chatfield, A. T., & Reddick, G. G. (2019). A framework for internet of things-enabled smart government: A case of IoT cybersecurity policies and use cases in US federal government. *Government Information Quarterly, 36*(2), 346–357. https://doi.org/10.1016/j.giq.2018.09.007

Costa, C. J., Aparicio, M., & Aparicio, S. (2024). The democratization of artificial intelligence: Theoretical framework. *Applied Sciences, 14*(18), 8236.

Deshpande, A. (2024). Regulatory compliance and AI: Navigating the legal and regulatory challenges of AI in finance. In *International conference on knowledge engineering and communication systems (ICKECS), Chikkaballapur, India* (pp. 1–5). https://doi.org/10.1109/ICKECS61492.2024.10616752

DiMaggio, P. J., & Powell, W. W. (1983). The iron cage revisited: Institutional isomorphism and collective reality in organizational fields. *American Sociological Review, 48*(2), 147–160.

Duberry, J. (2022). *Artificial intelligence and democracy: Risks and promises of AI-mediated citizen-government relations*. Edward Elgar Publishing. https://doi.org/10.4337/9781788977319

Ferrell, O. C., Harrison, D. E., Ferrell, L. K., & Ajjan, H. (2024). A theoretical framework to guide AI ethical decision making. *Journal of Business Ethics, 167*(4), 401–420. https://doi.org/10.1007/s13162-024-00275-9

Floridi, L., & Cowls, J. (2019). A unified framework of five principles for AI in society. Available at SSRN: https://ssrn.com/abstract=3831321

Floridi, L., Cowls, J., King, T. C., & Taddeo, M. (2020). How to design AI for social good: Seven essential factors. *Science and Engineering Ethics, 26*, 1771–1796. https://doi.org/10.1007/s11948-020-00213-5

Fjeld, J., Achten, N., Hilligoss, H., Nagy, A. C., & Srikumar, M. (2020). Principled artificial intelligence: Mapping consensus in ethical and rights-based approaches to principles for AI. Available at SSRN: https://ssrn.com/abstract=3518482

Gianni, R., Lehtinen, S., & Nieminen, M. (2022). Governance of responsible AI: From ethical guidelines to cooperative policies. *Frontiers in Computer Science, 4*, Article 873437.

Hossain, S. T., Yigitcanlar, T., Nguyen, K., & Xu, Y. (2024). Local government cybersecurity landscape: A systematic review and conceptual framework. *Applied Sciences, 14*(13), 5501. https://doi.org/10.3390/app14135501

Jobin, A., Ienca, M., & Vayena, E. (2019). The global landscape of AI ethics guidelines. *Nature Machine Intelligence, 1*(9), 389–399.

Kinder, T., Stenvall, J., Koskimies, E., & Webb, H. (2023). Local public services and the ethical deployment of artificial intelligence. *Government Information Quarterly, 40*(4), Article 101781. https://doi.org/10.1016/j.giq.2023.101865

Kalliontzi, V., Voulgarakis, V., & Delinavelli, G. (2024). Data-driven policy development of municipalities: Preparation steps for integrating AI tools in policymaking. *The International Archives of the Photogrammetry, Remote Sensing and Spatial Information Sciences, XLVIII-4/W10*, 85–92. https://doi.org/10.5194/isprs-archives-xlviii-4-w10-2024-85-2024

Kumar, R., & Patel, S. (2023). Ethical AI deployment: A comparative study. *International Journal of AI Governance, 5*(1), 45–60. https://doi.org/10.1016/j.ijag.2023.03.001

Kuziemski, M., & Misuraca, G. (2020). AI governance in the public sector: Three tales from the frontiers of automated decision-making in democratic settings. *Telecommunications Policy, 44*(6), Article 101847. https://doi.org/10.1016/j.telpol.2020.101976

Mehrabi, N., Morstatter, F., Saxena, N., Lerman, K., & Galstyan, A. (2021). A Survey on bias and fairness in machine learning. *ACM Computing Surveys, 54*(6), 1–35.

Olabiyi, W. (2024). Ethical considerations in AI adoption: Balancing innovation with societal impact and corporate responsibility. *Journal of Digital Ethics, 11*(2), 150–170.

Papel, M. S. I., Mridha, A. B. M. A., Rahman, A., & Ashrafuzzaman, M. (2024). Enhancing government IT infrastructure: Develop frameworks for modernizing government IT systems to improve security, efficiency, and citizen engagement. *Frontiers in Applied Engineering and Technology, 1*(1), 157–174. https://doi.org/10.70937/faet.v1i01.31

Raji, I. D., Bender, E. M., & Mitchell, M. (2021). AI ethics discourse: Moving from principles to practices. *Nature Machine Intelligence, 3*(3), 245–252.

Rahman, M. (2024). Unraveling fear, cultivating awareness: A research proposal for alleviating AI concerns and guiding ethical adoption. *IEEE Transactions on Technology Management, 15*(1), 120–135.

Saheb, T., & Saheb, T. (2024). Mapping ethical artificial intelligence policy landscape: A mixed method analysis. *Springer Journal of Ethics, 18*(2), 95–110.

Veale, M., & Borgesius, F. Z. (2021). Demystifying the draft EU artificial intelligence act. *Computer Law & Security Review, 43*, Article 105567. https://doi.org/10.1016/j.clsr.2021.105567

Whittlestone, J., Nyrup, R., Alexandrova, A., & Cave, S. (2021). The Role and limits of principles in AI ethics: Towards a focus on tensions. *AI & Society, 36*(1), 59–72.

Yang, et al. (2019). Privacy and security aspects of e-government in smart cities. In D. B. Rawat, & K. Z. Ghafoor (Eds.), *Smart cities cybersecurity and privacy* (pp. 89–102).

Yigitcanlar, T., David, A., Li, W., Fookes, C., Bibri, S., & Ye, X. (2024). Unlocking artificial intelligence adoption in local governments: Best practice lessons from real-world implementations. *Smart Cities, 7*(4), 64–82. https://doi.org/10.3390/smartcities7040064

Zuboff, S. (2020). *The age of surveillance capitalism: The fight for a human future at the new frontier of power* (Revised Edition). Public Affairs.

Government AI Investment: Fostering Innovation, Collaboration, and Global Leadership

7

Abraham Ramos-Torres and Laura N. Montoya

1 Introduction

Artificial intelligence is rapidly remaking the topography of governance. On the plus side, it offers an opportunity not only for better delivery of public services but also for better processes leading to decision-making and taking up critical challenges in society. A large number of governments in times of fast technological change recognize that investment in AI is fundamental for any government that desires to spur innovation and achieve the core goals of economic growth, national security, and social equity. This chapter explores crucial dimensions of government investments in artificial intelligence, underlining the transformative potential of the technology while invoking concurrent studies of challenges and responsibilities associated with the diffusion of AI technologies worldwide.

In enhancing the operational frameworks, artificial intelligence has become indispensable in the optimization of resource allocation and improving services provided. AI-driven predictive analytics allow for proactive intervention against emergencies in public health, natural calamity management, or infrastructure repairs. In addition, automation is used in easing administrative processes to reduce costs and inefficiencies, hence freeing resources for more value-enhancing activities.

However, these events have far more wide-reaching implications than that of effective functioning. Today, Artificial Intelligence is also a strategic asset in the

A. Ramos-Torres (✉)
Universidad Central de Venezuela, Accel AI Institute, Caracas, Venezuela
e-mail: abraham@accel.ai

L. N. Montoya
Accel AI Institute, San Francisco, CA, USA
e-mail: laura@accel.ai

S. K. Aikins and T. Dimitrijevska-Markoski (eds.), *Artificial Intelligence and Government*, https://doi.org/10.1007/978-3-032-12344-2_7

framework of international competition, with several countries competing to be the leading players in its development and use. This is not done to improve their economic position but to seek a geopolitical advantage. This competition is often referred to as the 'AI race', which involves not only powers such as the U.S., China, and the EU, but also emerging economies such as Colombia and Argentina, who play an increasingly important role, in investing in AI to address local challenges, drive economic growth, and potentially gain geopolitical influence (Ramos & Montoya, 2024).

In harnessing artificial intelligence, it will be important that governmental bodies outline the key principles and priorities while focusing highly on long-term benefits to society, including ethical and collaborative approaches. Besides transparency, accountability, equity, and elements of ethical protection, it will be important that strong structures assure effectiveness and stability in AI systems. The relevant frameworks should address issues like algorithmic bias, data privacy, and accountability for the actions of the artificial intelligence system, especially when operating in areas where society is most vulnerable, such as criminal justice, welfare, and health. By instituting these principles in AI systems, governments have a unique opportunity to build public trust and show their commitment to ensuring fair governance.

This chapter examines a range of funding models and strategies adopted by governments to incentivize AI innovation with investment. These strategies range from direct funding in research and infrastructure to cooperation between public and private sectors, including international cooperation, reflecting an increasing recognition of the potential that AI has to deal with complex societal challenges. It is important to note that government investment strategies in artificial intelligence have evolved significantly between 2010 and 2023. For instance, OECD countries have focused their investments on healthcare and research and development (R&D). A study examining 10 OECD countries found that most of them are at the "Emerging" stage of AI maturity in the healthcare sector (Castonguay et al., 2023).

Innovation funds and grants may advance the development of AI technologies, especially for startups and research institutions. Subsidies and tax incentives can be used to encourage smaller businesses to adopt AI so that AI benefits would be distributed more proportionally across an economy. Other examples of such efforts might be reinforced through and advanced by international cooperation across borders, including multilateral programs like the Global Partnership on AI (GPAI, 2021).

However, the investment in artificial intelligence does face some serious ethical and legal challenges. In this respect, every government is facing its dilemma: how to encourage innovation on one hand and create all the possible safeguards for the responsible use of AI technologies on the other. Fairness and accountability issues go in the direction of demanding transparency at all levels, audits of the highest order, and regulatory mechanisms. This chapter therefore presents how this has been pursued by leading countries in the establishment and implementation of safeguards, and thus provides useful lessons for those attempting to create ethical governance systems for artificial intelligence.

The global setting for investing in artificial intelligence presents a two-pronged-strategy paradigm-one of competition-cum-collaboration. While the countries are trying to be at the top in AI, they are expected to come together over common inhibiting factors and evolve one standard. It is this competitive spirit that breeds creativity and innovation, while collaboration will ensure that such innovations meet the benchmarks of global ethical standards and serve the interests of humanity. However, the nature of this effort, as shown by the OECD AI Principles (OECD, nd) and the AI for Good Global Summit (AI For Good, n.d.-a), is a much-needed successful international partnership toward a more cohesive and cooperative artificial intelligence ecosystem.

New technologies are likely to intervene and change the course of governments investing in artificial intelligence. Recent breakthroughs are capable of furthering the scope of AI applications, offering very unique opportunities to bring in sea changes in the approach toward good governance. Therefore, policy frameworks must capture the ethical, social, and economic implications of such technological innovation. It will be equally important to foster inclusiveness in the development of AI as governments work to reduce the gap between developed and developing nations to ensure equity in AI resources and benefits.

This chapter invites the reader to consider some of the most significant consequences of embedding artificial intelligence in the domain of government. Putting AI into the heart of governmental functions is not simply a technological advance but a deep cultural change; it can totally reshape the relationship between individuals and the state. With these principles, strategies, and challenges in mind, the chapter suggests how governments can deploy artificial intelligence responsibly and inclusively, ensuring that the benefits of this technology are shared by all.

This chapter is a source of foundational knowledge and a call to action. It encourages all the actors of policymaking, research, and practice to commit to a prospect where artificial intelligence is a meaningful driver for social welfare and international collaboration.

Additionally, this analysis of government investments in AI will be conducted within the global context of growing competition among nations for leadership in this technology. In addition to analyzing funding models and investment strategies, this chapter will address fundamental ethical and legal considerations such as transparency, equity, accountability, and privacy, recognizing their crucial role in the responsible deployment of AI. Emphasis will be placed on how these investments seek to address pressing social and economic challenges, improving the efficiency of public services and fostering innovation. At the same time, it will examine the challenges inherent in AI adoption in government, including the handling of sensitive data and the need for international collaboration to establish standards and mitigate risks.

2 The Strategic Importance of AI Investments in Governance

Government investments in artificial intelligence (AI) are fundamentally transforming the conceptualization, delivery, and administration of public services. The adjustments bring substantial benefits to the policy cycle: innovative business and performance frameworks, continuous real-time assessment, improved policy evaluation, service delivery, decision-making mechanisms, fraud prevention, cost reductions, and efficiency increases. Moreover, the changes are conducive to better accountability and transparency, more legitimacy, joint efforts, and higher accuracy, effectiveness, and speed (Berryhill et al., 2019; Hornjak, 2024). However, the use of artificial intelligence in public administration faces challenges in the form of privacy issues, cost considerations, and a lack of expertise in the field (Kaushik & Rathore, 2020). Another significant consideration pertains to the ethicality and the upholding of the trust of the public (Hamirul et al., 2023). Accordingly, the right allocation of financial resources to artificial intelligence projects should be incorporated into the strategic plans of governments in order for them to reap the aforementioned benefits while, at the same time, ensuring ethical standards and building governmental trust and transparency.

The use of artificial intelligence has the potential to enhance efficiency and support modernization by automating routine activities, which helps in simplifying public service delivery. Some sectors, such as energy, public health, and transportation, show promise for efficiency improvement through AI implementation (Surdej, 2021). AI applications encompass automated decision-making, chatbots for information and advice, and public safety tools. These applications can identify complex patterns that may elude human detection, such as correlations between multiple DNA segments and diseases (Henman, 2020). Pattern recognition can also provide the means by which predictive models are developed to accurately forecast future events, including economic contractions and crises. Research also shows that in public services, AI-driven chatbots increase operational efficiency, reduce response times, and enhance user experience by automating routine administrative tasks, such as answering regular questions, providing procedural information, and handling simple application processes (Ma'rup et al., 2024). Appropriate investments in the field of artificial intelligence will ensure competitiveness in the economy and strengthen national security.

Nations that dedicate resources to the development of artificial intelligence and position themselves as leaders in this domain are expected to experience significant benefits. Consequently, investments in artificial intelligence are regarded as essential for enhancing competitiveness. For example, Australia currently needs strategies that actively aim to achieve a leading position in the emerging field of artificial intelligence, which is expected to bring significant productivity improvement and drive inclusive economic growth, instead of depending upon importing innovations and technologies from existing AI leaders and therefore getting marginalized (Williams, 2019).

As AI capabilities grow, there's a need for a comprehensive national strategy that balances competition with collaboration in areas of mutual interest, while addressing security concerns and preserving leadership advantages (Schmidt, 2022). Governments are increasingly implementing AI to improve public services and build trust. This deployment has, however, special challenges. For example, a citizen survey in Finland demonstrated that citizens demand transparency from government AI services. This transparency involves provisions like recognizing the intended goals, revealing the sources of data used in AI services, being able to understand how it works, controlling the use of personal data, and merging human involvement in AI services (Drobotowicz et al., 2021).

By observing these requirements, governmental institutions can employ capabilities from artificial intelligence to bring convenience and transparency in public service delivery for the benefit of improving the trust of the public. The possibilities regarding the influence of artificial intelligence on public services are immense and varied. With increased technological development, more avenues are opened for enhanced efficiency and effectiveness in the use of AI in public service delivery.

2.1 The Role of International Organizations in AI Government Investments

International organizations play a crucial role in the governance of artificial intelligence (AI), particularly in the allocation of funds for AI investments. These organizations provide frameworks, guidelines, reports, and platforms that address the global nature of AI development and its implications. They also help ensure that AI governance is developed through a multi-stakeholder approach.

The United Nations (UN) has produced various reports highlighting the significant impact of artificial intelligence and promoting a global governance framework for this technology. One notable report is "Governing AI for Humanity," which was launched in September 2024 by the UN Secretary-General's High-level Advisory Body on Artificial Intelligence (United Nations, 2024b). This report underscores the necessity of establishing a global governance framework for AI. It identifies gaps in AI governance and provides recommendations for addressing ethical risks while enhancing global cooperation.

A key point of the report is its emphasis on the "global governance deficit" in artificial intelligence (AI). It highlights several gaps in the existing rules and organizations that are intended to regulate AI usage, including representation, coordination, and implementation. The report also points out the disparity among countries involved in AI governance discussions, particularly regarding developing nations. This discrepancy poses a challenge for ensuring equitable access to advanced AI resources worldwide, as many developing countries lack high-performance computing clusters. Additionally, it raises the risk of creating disconnected and incompatible AI governance systems, which may fail to address the diverse needs and specific contexts of all nations. The report also stresses the importance is aligning AI governance with Sustainable Development

Goals (SDGs), implying that strategic AI investments should be directed towards achieving these global objectives (Global Partners Digital, 2024).

To address these critical gaps and foster a global approach, the UN report suggests several recommendations aimed at enhancing international cooperation. One important proposal is the establishment of an AI standards exchange, which can serve as a platform bringing together representatives from various standard-setting organizations, technology companies, and civil society to develop a register of definitions and applicable standards for measuring and evaluating AI systems, while also identifying areas where new standards are urgently required. To address the disparities in access to AI resources and expertise, the UN report also suggests creating an AI capacity development network, allowing smaller countries and marginalized groups to connect to AI training centers worldwide. To further support equitable access to AI resources, the UN also suggests the creation of a Global Fund for AI, whose mission would be to provide access to compute resources, models, and data through all nations for them to participate in the global AI ecosystem. To ensure a coherent and coordinated UN response to the multifaceted challenges of AI governance, the report also suggests establishing a light and agile AI Office within the UN Secretariat, which will oversee global AI governance initiatives (Meyer, 2024; United Nations, 2024b).

The World Bank also emphasized the crucial role of government AI investments in its reports, particularly in "Global Trends in AI Governance: Evolving Country Approaches" (Appaya & Ng, 2025). The authors acknowledged the AI's potential to revolutionize sectors like education, healthcare, and public services, but also cautioned about the risks of misuse and bias. The World Bank stresses the need for effective AI governance frameworks, which require strategic government investments in regulatory mechanisms and ethical guidelines.

The authors' analysis emphasizes the importance of foundational elements for thriving AI ecosystems, including investments in digital infrastructure such as high-performance computing (HPC) and local cloud services, underscoring the critical need for local investments. It also highlights the significance of research and development (R&D), suggesting the promotion of private sector investment alongside partnerships with academic institutions and public–private partnerships (PPP). Furthermore, a stable power supply is essential to support AI initiatives, as are supportive digital development policies that enable growth within the ecosystem. Finally, investing in local AI talent is vital for nurturing a robust AI landscape.

The World Bank Group has several initiatives that explore and leverage artificial intelligence (AI) to improve governance and development outcomes. These initiatives include the GovTech Innovation Lab, which addresses governance challenges at both national and global levels, intending to promote equitable and effective government and public administration practices (Okahashi & Blanco, 2024). Additionally, the Development Impact Group's Artificial Intelligence Team (DIME AI) utilizes AI and machine learning (ML) to develop impactful solutions for development challenges while adhering to rigorous standards (World Bank, n.d.).

Furthermore, the World Bank is actively involved in other publicly disclosed projects that utilize AI, underscoring the importance of government investment in these areas. Some of these projects focus on solving specific problems in various countries, including: "Transmitting AI Training: Evidence from Policymakers in Pakistan," the "Croatia Business Environment Reform with applied AI," and "Croatia Innovation and Digital Economy" (AI for Good, n.d.-b).

The International Telecommunication Union (ITU), as well as the prior international organizations mentioned, plays an important role in promoting a global understanding and governance of AI, focusing on fostering its development through strategic investments. The ITU's AI for Good platform aims to identify practical AI applications for advancing the UN Sustainable Development Goals and scaling these solutions globally (International Telecommunication Union, n.d.-b). This initiative requires significant investment in research, development, and infrastructure to translate AI's potential into real-world impact.

2.2 National AI Strategies in Developed and Developing Countries: Focus and Investment Priorities

Developed countries have been leading the way in AI regulation and policy formulation since 2017. By 2024, the number of national initiatives related to AI has increased compared to previous years, reflecting a global recognition of AI's strategic importance. North America, particularly the United States and Canada, along with Europe, has emerged as a leader in this field. These regions are characterized by strong government support, established technology companies, and significant financial investments in research and development (R&D) (UNESCO, 2025). Early adopters like Canada and Finland, which launched their national AI strategies in 2017, are focusing on funding innovation and positioning themselves as centers for AI research and development (Galindo et al., 2021; Papyshev & Yarime, 2023).

The development of AI strategies is not exclusive to developed countries; developing countries have also seen an increase in the implementation of these strategies. However, the initiatives in these regions have not been as strong as those in developed countries. For instance, in Latin America and the Caribbean, only 19% of countries have established a National AI Policy and Strategy (NAIS). In the Middle East and North Africa, this figure is 30%, while in Sub-Saharan Africa, it drops to just 4%. In Central Asia, only two countries have developed an NAIS. In comparison, North American countries and 65% of countries in Europe have established such strategies (UNESCO, 2025).

As shown in Table 1, the strategies for implementing AI technology differ between developing and developed countries. For example, developed nations like Japan focus on integrating AI technologies into real-world industries. The European Union emphasizes ethical and regulatory considerations in its approach. In contrast, countries like the United States and the United Kingdom prioritize policies that encourage AI adoption and innovation within the private sector. Nordic countries such as Finland highlight business competitiveness through efficient data utilization, while Sweden concentrates on societal and economic benefits derived from education and the ethical use of AI (NordForsk, 2024; Papyshev & Yarime, 2023).

Meanwhile, developing countries often align their priorities with the United Nations' Sustainable Development Goals (SDGs). For instance, Mauritius's AI strategy aims to address social and financial challenges while revitalizing the traditional economic sector (Teleanu & Kurbalija, 2022). The African Union's

Table 1 Comparative analysis of national AI strategy focus and priorities

Country	Strategic focus	Key investment areas	Noteworthy outcomes/Reported effectiveness
Canada	Research & Development	Funding innovation, establishing research excellence clusters	Early mover advantage in AI research and talent acquisition; positioned as a research and development center
Japan	Industry Integration	Integrating AI into real industries, solving social problems	Aiming for economic growth and solutions to societal issues through AI adoption in various sectors
European Union	Regulation & Ethics	Developing ethical guidelines, promoting human-centric AI	Established comprehensive regulatory frameworks (e.g., EU AI Act) aiming to set global standards for responsible AI development and deployment
United Kingdom	Promotion & Private Sector	Supporting private sector innovation, intricate governance	Focus on fostering AI growth within the private sector; actively tracking AI maturity and readiness through national matrices
India	Social Good & Development	Healthcare, agriculture, education, and digital infrastructure	Leveraging AI for addressing social challenges and advancing SDGs; emphasis on building secure data infrastructure to support AI innovations
Kenya	Infrastructure & Skills	Investment in African Information and Communications Technology (ICT) infrastructure, and AI skills development	Emerged as a top investment destination for global tech giants, increasing focus on AI capacity and regulation
African Union	Regional Approach & Ethics	Addressing data scarcity, algorithmic bias, and African values	Developing a continental vision for AI governance and use, emphasizing ethical principles and addressing challenges specific to the African context

Analysis of the different approaches from various developed and developing countries regarding their AI national strategies. Sources were taken from: Galindo et al. (2021), Papyshev and Yarime (2023), NordForsk (2024), UNESCO (2025), Ogenga and Stanley (2024), Musoni (2024)

Continental Strategy on AI emphasizes the need for an "African Approach to AI" that tackles the scarcity of African datasets and the risk of algorithmic biases, while also promoting African cultures and values (Musoni, 2024).

Developing countries face unique challenges, such as limited financial resources, inadequate infrastructure, and a shortage of AI-skilled talent (Alania & Kong, 2024; Melkamu, 2025).

3 Government AI Funding Strategies and Models

National strategies and initiatives to promote AI innovation and its application in public services have been developed by governments around the world (Stanford University, 2024). In general, ethics-oriented approaches are preferred over rule-based systems, and functional indetermination is favored in AI governance (Radu, 2021). Government AI projects can be categorized into different types according to their importance to government functions and organizational resources available, each requiring specific risk management strategies in order to be executed properly (Ramizo, 2021).

AI technologies require substantial financial investments in R&D, infrastructure, human capital, and regulatory frameworks. In this context, in order to fully harness the potential of AI, several funding models should be assessed: direct investments, public–private partnerships (PPPs), innovation funds, and international collaborations that develop funding mechanisms that specifically allow for the effective implementation of AI strategies that ensure both innovation and sustainability. This section analyzes the main funding models employed by governments to support AI initiatives.

One of the funding models is direct government investment. Under this approach, public sector institutions make available certain financial resources to artificial intelligence programs for the development of competencies in areas related to cybersecurity, healthcare, and public safety. This model can be implemented in three different ways.

The first strategy involves a dedicated budget for AI initiatives; in this case, the government could allocate a specified amount of funds to initiatives that can drive innovation to its territory. Such investments can be in core areas like artificial intelligence health systems, self-driving public transportation vehicles, and similar areas. For example, in 2021, the National Security Commission on Artificial Intelligence NSCAI published an extensive 750-page report calling for the strengthening of artificial intelligence capabilities in the United States. It also makes a recommendation for the United States to double its annual spending on non-defense research and development for AI every year until it reaches $32 billion by 2026 (Peterson, 2021).

For example, the U.S. government, through the National AI Initiative Act of 2020, has provided billions of dollars towards AI research, education, and workforce development, including authorizing the National Science Foundation to receive $868 million in fiscal year 2021, $911 million in fiscal year 2022,

$957 million in fiscal year 2023, $1.005 billion in fiscal year 2024, and $1.055 billion in fiscal year 2025 to carry out AI research, education, and workforce development activities (National Artificial Intelligence Initiative Act of 2020, 2020).

Another major approach is the creation of artificial intelligence research labs and centers. This second strategy focuses on investments that will either create standalone organizations or strengthen academic institutions to enable and increase innovation. An example is how the UK government financed the Alan Turing Institute, which is a body charged with the leadership of interdisciplinary research in AI and Data Science aimed at problems of benefit to people in the UK (The Alan Turing Institute, n.d.).

A third strategy focuses on public service-related activities that are powered by artificial intelligence and involve direct investment in specific activities. Effective artificial intelligence projects in the public sector can be categorized based on their importance to government operations and the resources available within the entity. Each type calls for a different strategy (Ramizo, 2021). For instance, in 2014, Singapore launched the Smart Nation Programme Office to lead the national effort to transform Singapore into a Smart Nation. This program focuses on AI projects designed to leverage the power of technology in bringing transformation to health, transport, urban living, government services, and businesses (Smart Nation Singapore, 2024).

The Public–Private Partnerships (PPPs) model has been one of the most imperative mechanisms through which governmental entities can construct infrastructure and deliver services (Sciulli, 2010). In such collaborations, both sectors—public and private—can share resources, knowledge, and risks in a way that improves operational efficiency, refines decision-making processes, and tackles key challenges (Murad et al., 2023). The Public–Private Partnership model in India, for instance, has been particularly effective in the infrastructure development sector in terms of highway construction projects (Prasad et al., 2024). Seamless incorporation of Artificial Intelligence into PPPs would, however, require industrial-level standards to be established on issues of data sharing, transparency, and cybersecurity (Bhatia, 2020). Three strategies can be pursued for successful development and investment in this model.

The first strategy is co-funding for R&D and infrastructure. The main idea is that the government and private companies should share both the risks and the benefits of AI R&D projects in partnerships. For instance, the EU's Horizon 2020 program, which ran from 2014 to 2020 with a budget of nearly 80 billion euros, supported projects such as AI4EU (European Commission, n.d.).

AI4EU aimed to create the first European Artificial Intelligence On-Demand Platform and Ecosystem to help European countries foster the AI ecosystem, perform research and development actions around five tightly connected scientific AI areas, and implement industry-driven pilot projects through the AI4EU platform. This project allowed many beneficiaries to be part of it, such as the Fondazione Bruno Kessler and will develop an NLP-based application for mapping job descriptions and competencies to the ESCO ontology—the European reference framework for Skills, Competencies, Qualifications, and Occupations (Carraro, 2021). The AI4EU project is therefore a symbol of the cooperation and high relevance of Horizon 2020 in making this kind of initiative possible.

The second strategy involves the joint deployment of AI in public services. In this regard, a government can collaborate with AI companies in the application of AI solutions to domains in public service. For instance, in 2019, the United States Department of Veterans Affairs and DeepMind formed a partnership, resulting in a major medical technology breakthrough. The two developed a system that could predict a critical kidney disease up to two days before its occurrence. In this case, researchers from VA and DeepMind collaborated in the deployment of this solution. According to them, the model predicted 56% of all in-patient episodes of AKI and 90% of the most severe cases where the patient later required renal dialysis. The VA-DeepMind partnership allowed DeepMind to analyze patterns from over 700,000 VA health records in order to develop algorithms able to pinpoint risk factors for patient deterioration and predict their progress (Richman, 2019).

Data sharing between governments and private firms constitutes the third strategy. Governments generate and own huge amounts of data through different mechanisms, such as sensors, recording devices, and other sources (Charalabidis et al., 2018; Watson & Ryan, 2020). The data has the potential to benefit the public sector by working in coordination with private entities to establish innovative solutions. For example, PPPs enable the sharing of compounds and information within the drug discovery process, hence allowing science to advance while addressing health needs within the public domain (Davis et al., 2021). However, these data-sharing methods face challenges such as potential privacy breaches, data sensitivity and security, embargo period, organizational changes, benefits obtained by others other than the government, and other negative consequences (Charalabidis et al., 2018). Moreover, it is not always possible for organizations to share data directly in order to construct the models.

To tackle this problem, innovations such as privacy-preserving machine learning have been developed; these allow the training of models collaboratively without direct sharing of sensitive information. Various techniques have been advanced toward this end. One involves cryptographic and randomization methods, especially distributed big data systems (Xu et al., 2015).

Another method is through autoencoder latent space embeddings, autoencoders compress sensitive data into abstract "latent embeddings," sharing only these lower-dimensional representations, which enable collaborative data sharing without directly sharing the original data. These privacy-preserving data representations can be shared between organizations to improve the performance of machine learning models in collaborative scenarios with multiple data sources while keeping the privacy of sensitive data of the original users (Quintero-Ossa et al., 2022). One example of this strategy is the IMI2 project, Machine Learning Ledger Orchestration for Drug Discovery (MELLODDY). Launched in 2019, it aims at improving predictive machine learning models using decentralized data from 10 pharmaceutical companies and 7 public partners—without exposing proprietary information (Davis et al., 2021; Melloddy, n.d.).

In an effort to encourage the development of artificial intelligence and its innovation, most government agencies come up with different funds and grants that are essentially meant to provide financial support to startups, research organizations, and corporations focused on developing AI solutions relevant to public sector needs. The impact created by government grants and patents filed by government agencies has been significant during the early stage of AI development mainly (Iori et al., 2021). This funding model lends itself to three different strategies.

The first strategy involves the government's creation of AI-focused innovation funds. These funds are provided to support early-stage AI companies, academic research, and R&D in the private sector, as developing AI is a costly and risky endeavor. Their use results in many positive outcomes such as boosting economic growth and improving public services (Brandusescu, 2021). A good example is the Pan-Canadian Artificial Intelligence Strategy—a big investment by the government to encourage the adoption of artificial intelligence in the economic and social fabric of the country. The three pillars on which this initiative rests are commercialization, standards, talent, and research. The Canadian government has the objective of translating AI research into commercial applications, advancing the development and adoption of AI-related standards, retaining and developing academic research talent, and providing dedicated computing capacity for AI researchers across Canada. More than CAD 440 million will be invested in those areas over the period between 2021 and 2030 (Government of Canada, 2022).

A second strategy includes providing grants for AI applications in the public sector. The government provides financial grants to institutions and startups so that they can develop technological solutions for specific problems identified in the public sector. Normally, this is coupled with requirements specifying that the awardees' projects will be certain tools that will better governance, health, transportation, or other services within the public sector. The sources of funding for artificial intelligence in education and research projects have dramatically improved, particularly from institutions such as the National Science Foundation (NSF), the Australian Research Council, the European Union's FP7 and H2020 projects, and the National Natural Science Foundation of China. Funding for these projects facilitates conferences, publications in journals, and the production of software applications (Ahn & Chen, 2020).

The third strategy involves using competitions and prizes to drive the rapid development of various technologies. Prize competitions have a long history of producing innovation in AI, especially for public sector and national security applications. More recently, governments have increasingly used prize competitions to test the operational effectiveness of AI technologies before procurement in an effort to drive progress on key issues in AI safety, security, and trust. Successful prize competitions have led to breakthroughs and significant technological advances dating back to the eighteenth century. NASA's research indicates that the most productive competitions of this sort include factors such as the following: simplicity, a fitting level of difficulty, near-term economic possibility, activity by potential sponsors and participants, as well as public interest (Crawford & Wulkan, 2021; Davidian, 2005).

A good example is the America's Seed Fund from the National Science Foundation, which seeks to 'translate' scientific and engineering discoveries into commercially viable products and services with the potential to produce societal benefits. The program has awarded over $200 million in R&D funding to nearly 400 startups located in the U.S. Each startup under this program can attract up to $2 million in funding and can be in almost all areas of technology, from manufacturing to artificial intelligence. Application entails a project pitch submission, followed by a proposal submission, and finally a proposal review and a final decision. This entire process is about 7 months long, and corporations such as "Cruz Foam, Inc", "Tetramer Technologies, L.L.C.", and "GridBridge, Inc." have received over USD 1.6 million under this program (National Science Foundation, n.d.).

International cooperation and multilateral funding are other funding models for government AI investments. Various international organizations may play critical governance functions, including enabling consensus among professionals, setting safety and other standards, and increasing access to leading-edge AI (Ho et al., 2023). This approach is thus linked to two different strategies.

The first strategy focuses on collaborative AI research projects that involve multiple countries, allowing governments to leverage global expertise and resources in tackling shared challenges.

A related example is the Global Partnership on Artificial Intelligence (GPAI), an international and multistakeholder effort toward the responsible development and use of artificial intelligence. Its founding members include Australia, Canada, France, Germany, India, Italy, Japan, Mexico, New Zealand, the Republic of Korea, Singapore, Slovenia, the United Kingdom, the United States of America, and the European Union (GPAI, 2021).

The second strategy involves multilateral AI funding programs. In this scenario, various global organizations join together to finance governments engaged in the development of AI. An example is the program "AI for Development," initiated by the World Bank. Its principal objective is to build the capacities of policymakers through workshops and training programs (Krishnaswami, 2023).

The latest funding model that harnesses AI from governments involves tax incentives and subsidies related to AI. Empirical research also depicts that subsidies can have a positive impact on investment along with economic growth in developing countries (Erick, 2023). This type of model can be analyzed using the deployment of two different approaches.

R&D tax credits are among the most important tools for organizations engaged in the innovation of technology. Most governments extend tax credits to such organizations, thereby making the region more attractive to potential investors. The government of the United Kingdom encourages R&D activities by extending tax relief to companies that engage in innovative projects in the science and technology arena. These small and medium enterprises (SMEs) can especially benefit as they are entitled to an extra deduction of 86% of their qualifying expenditure (HM Revenue & Customs, 2024).

The second approach is providing financial support for the adoption of artificial intelligence in SMEs. SMEs usually face the challenge of finding resources to invest in AI due to budget constraints. To curb this challenge, government institutions can provide various forms of subsidies to promote the adoption of AI in SMEs. For instance, the United Kingdom has a fund that the government specifically created to aid in boosting AI adoption in SMEs. £7 million has been set aside for this project, and the aim is to support innovative artificial intelligence projects focused on business problems facing several industries (Belderbos, 2024).

3.1 Analysis of the Impact of Government Investments in AI

While the potential of AI to boost various sectors of the economy is significant, obtaining precise empirical data directly linked to government funding for AI is complex. Reports like the Stanford AI Index primarily track overall AI advancements, research outputs, and investment trends, with much of the investment coming from the private sector (Stanford University, 2024). These reports offer valuable context regarding the general state of AI development globally and highlight which nations are leading in this field. However, they do not specifically address the isolated impact of government AI funding across different sectors.

There are, however, projections from organizations such as the World Economic Forum, which estimates that 170 million AI-related jobs will be created by 2030 (Tews, 2025). Additionally, PwC projects that AI could contribute $15.7 trillion to the global economy by 2030 (Rao & Verweij, 2017). A study by the McKinsey Global Institute suggests that approximately half of the activities performed in the workplace could potentially be automated. However, only about 5% of these activities can be fully automated. This discrepancy is influenced by several factors, including the costs associated with developing and implementing automation, as well as labor market dynamics. As a result, the impact of this technology varies across different countries (Manyika et al., 2024). This indicates that government AI investment strategies must consider the evolving skills needed in the future workplace and prioritize funding for education and training programs to equip workers with the skills required for emerging roles.

Concrete examples of quantifiable improvements include the New York MTA's use of Google AI, which identified 92% of subway track defects during a pilot program, signaling significant potential for enhancing transportation safety and efficiency (Mitchell, 2025). Furthermore, the US federal government has tripled the number of AI use cases between 2023 and 2024, indicating a growing adoption of AI technologies across various agencies (Gopisetty, 2025).

4 What Are the Ethical and Legal Considerations in Government AI Investments?

As AI is revolutionizing industries globally and becoming more integrated into governmental operations, the ethical and legal aspects surrounding its use need to be carefully taken into account, particularly regarding fairness, transparency, accountability, and privacy. These principles are crucial for developing responsible AI in government services and decision-making processes (Ontario, 2021). International cooperation and the involvement of various stakeholders, including governments, industry, and civil society, are essential for establishing effective AI governance. Ongoing research and debate are necessary to address the evolving challenges posed by AI in high-risk areas and to ensure its responsible use in society (Cath, 2018; Ontario, 2021).

Ethical AI development remains one of those core considerations within government AI investments. This remains a key point because, while they must tap into the power of AI, they are also required to ensure that the implementation and use of AI are within the set principles for fairness, transparency, accountability, and privacy.

Fairness in AI is a complex concept that requires an interdisciplinary understanding, as it is influenced by various factors such as race, gender, class, economic status, country, and life experiences (Sarra, 2013). There are numerous definitions of fairness, each with its own rationale and implications for different contexts. These varying definitions can shape people's perceptions of fairness, with some interpretations being viewed as less fair than others (Dodge et al., 2019; Verma & Rubin, 2018). To achieve responsible and trustworthy AI decision-making, it is crucial to consider the relationship between explainability and fairness while addressing challenges in both areas (Zhou et al., 2022). In other words, fairness in AI development involves the creation and implementation of AI systems in a way that any element of discrimination or bias is avoided, so that deployed AI technologies do not disadvantage people for reasons such as race, gender, or socio-economic status.

Transparency in government AI investments is a crucial ethical and legal factor that has to be carefully considered. The EU's General Data Protection Regulation emphasizes transparency through information provision and explanation. However, contextual factors can influence the effectiveness of transparency measures, suggesting a relational approach to transparency that considers trustworthiness (Felzmann et al., 2019).

In this context, two definitions are relevant to the discussion: "black box" and "glass box." The term "black box" refers to systems with opaque decision-making processes, whereas the "glass box" concept emphasizes transparency and interpretability (Franzoni, 2023). Black box models raise concerns about fairness and accountability (Lee et al., 2023) because their internal workings are not easily understood or interpretable by humans. The reason for this lack of transparency has to do with the complex nonlinear relationships formed by deep neural networks and deep learning algorithms. Black box models also provide conclusions without explaining the decision-making process, hence making it difficult to detect any biases and mistakes within the system. How can someone trust a decision if the rationale is unclear? This uncertainty calls for "glass box" models. These models are transparent about how they come to conclusions since humans can understand the factors that have influenced the decision-making process (McGrail, 2023). The government must commit to ensuring that AI government investments are transparent, but also the technology that they are investing in. To achieve this, it is essential to prioritize investments that can convert "black box" AI models into more open "glass box" systems. This transformation will help guarantee that AI is ethically sound and aligned with human values (Franzoni, 2023).

Accountability in AI investments is equally important: it involves answerability, the recognition of authority, scrutiny, and the limitation of power (Novelli et al., 2022). Accountability ensures that when the AI systems fail, mechanisms are in place through which responsibility for the design, implementation, or maintenance of the systems is traced back to individuals or organizations. This principle acts to safeguard the citizens as well as assist governments in adhering to various ethical standards.

The importance of privacy in AI government investments is critical as governments increasingly deploy AI for collective intelligence and security (Saura et al., 2022). Data plays an important role in AI development, particularly in training and improving machine learning algorithms (Bessen et al., 2020). Privacy concerns are one of the major issues, considering how the data used to train AI is handled, and can be used to ensure the security and privacy of personal information. In this respect, regulations on privacy can help in finding a balance between the benefits brought by AI development and the risks imposed on the privacy of individuals. A major example of such regulations is the General Data Protection Regulation (GDPR) in the EU. This strong privacy law protects the personal data that organizations obtain from individuals in EU member states. In contrast, there is no all-encompassing privacy law that applies comprehensively to all sectors within the US. The US takes a sectoral approach to data protection legislation: only a few sectors fall under the regulations. The difference in approach does indeed suggest the varying level of privacy protection between the two regions and can be evidenced in internet privacy protection and policies rankings, whereby two of the top ten countries are located in the EU (Estonia and Germany) and the US is located in the fifteenth position (ElBaih, 2023; Stevens Institute of Technology, 2023).

These considerations need to be carefully weighed to ensure that government investments in AI are successful and support ethical and legal standards related to the public good. It requires substantial governmental effort to ensure such technologies are used responsibly and in an equitable manner. This responsibility can help in building citizen trust, which will, in turn, result in solid public support for AI-driven initiatives and close coordination between government entities and the communities they serve.

When there is trust in government, transparency in AI processes, and human oversight in citizens, they are more likely to engage with and benefit from AI-enhanced public services (Schmager et al., 2024). This creates a positive feedback loop: as trust and transparency increase, the public's willingness to accept and adapt to AI-driven changes in governance also grows, facilitating smoother and more effective integration of the technology.

Building this trust can also encourage innovation through public–private partnerships, collaborative research, and better societal outcomes, as a result of economic development and an improved quality of life.

4.1 Integrating Ethical and Legal Considerations into Government AI Investment Strategies

It's important to highlight the ethical and legal aspects surrounding AI, especially the issue of bias. Many AI systems can end up perpetuating discrimination due to biased or incomplete training data, which can further marginalize already underrepresented groups (World Bank, 2021). To tackle this, governments should direct funds towards the research and development of techniques that detect and mitigate bias while also creating strong guidelines for fair and equitable AI use (Galindo et al., 2021).

Another major concern is the potential for AI-driven automation to disrupt the workforce (Fan & Qiang, 2024). Governments need to anticipate these changes and invest in education and retraining programs, as well as social safety nets, to support workers who may be affected (Joshi, 2021). Additionally, the persistence of the digital divide is another important aspect to take into account when it comes to ethical and legal considerations. It is important to make concerted efforts to ensure equitable access to AI technologies and improve digital literacy; otherwise, the advantages of AI could end up amplifying existing inequalities, both between nations and within them (United Nations, 2024b).

Some regions, like Ontario in Canada, are making strides by implementing frameworks that focus on transparency, fairness, and accountability in AI deployment. One key principle of their framework is "No AI in Secret," which emphasizes the importance of informing citizens about AI usage in government, including the investments made in this area (Darcy, 2024). This approach could serve as a useful model for other governments looking to navigate these challenges.

Addressing ethical and legal issues goes beyond simple compliance; it is essential for building public trust and ensuring that AI investments contribute to a more equitable society.

5 The Global Competition and Collaboration in Government AI Investments

The rapid development and adoption of artificial intelligence (AI) have ignited a global competition among governments, often referred to as the "AI race". In this race, countries strive to reach the highest levels of development and implementation of AI, capitalizing on the substantial dividends AI can provide to the public sector. Simultaneously, collaborative efforts emerge with the view to ensuring the responsible, ethical, and inclusive deployment of this technology.

The interconnected relationship between competition in the AI race and the necessity for global collaboration highlights the importance of balancing national interests with international cooperation in AI research, policy-making, and regulation. This balance is essential to address the AI divide between developed and developing nations and to better serve citizens worldwide.

In this context, geopolitical rivalry demands explicit recognition that the landscape of AI is mainly dominated by global powers such as China, the United States, the European Union, India, Russia, Singapore, and other nations eager to capitalize on the enormous potential of artificial intelligence. However, this concentration of power creates a substantial challenge for developing economies seeking to participate in and benefit from the AI revolution, potentially exacerbating existing global inequalities.

These power economies are targeting various strategies toward economic competitiveness, enabling them to benefit from all the advantages this technology offers in various sectors like cybersecurity, healthcare, education, and many more. Mainly, this race or competition is driven by the recognition that AI leadership is crucial for strategic dominance (Grochmalski, 2020). However, this technology is also transforming military capabilities, enhancing existing security threats, and potentially destabilizing international relations, transforming not only global commercial and economic competition but also the international security environment (Schmidt, 2022). This shows the importance of becoming a major competitor in the field of AI.

In developing economies, there is an increasing recognition of the strategic importance of artificial intelligence (AI). Governments are proactively creating national and regional strategies to utilize this technology to meet their specific development needs. One example is the African Union's Continental Strategy on AI, which aims to establish a unified framework for tackling the unique challenges and opportunities in Africa. This includes addressing the limited availability of local datasets and ensuring that African cultural values are integrated into AI governance (Musoni, 2024).

To bridge the AI divide, developing economies are focusing on several key strategies: strengthening data governance, building domestic AI talent pipelines, and encouraging multistakeholder engagement (Alania & Kong, 2024). A vital aspect of these strategies is seeking international collaboration and partnerships with developed countries, international organizations, and the private sector. Such partnerships provide access to expertise, financial resources, and technological infrastructure, as explained in Sect. 3.

By strategically investing in specialized areas, fostering regional collaboration, and prioritizing AI applications that address their unique challenges, developing nations have the potential to leapfrog traditional development stages and create new competitive advantages in the global AI landscape.

Competitiveness in AI has been pursued through numerous approaches by governments. For example, the US has taken different funding and operational methods. The EU has adopted a very strong legal framework to make trustworthy AI possible. China invests in education and research to bring new ideas to AI. Meanwhile, Singapore has pushed forward high-quality projects to transform itself into a smart nation, together with cooperation from educational institutions and the private sector in order to reach its goals. In response to competitive pressures like these, various collaborative efforts have been developed in an effort to harmonize and standardize the ethical use of AI, in order to incentivize the development and deployment of this technology in line with human rights, promoting inclusivity, and aligning with global values.

In 2019, the OECD came forward for the first time with an intergovernmental standard on AI, innovation, trustworthy AI, and democratic values. The standard comprises five values-based principles: inclusive growth, sustainable development, and well-being; human rights and democratic values, including fairness and privacy; transparency and explainability; robustness, security, and safety; and accountability. The standards also have recommendations for policy-makers, such as investment in AI R&D (OECD, n.d.).

The Global Partnership on Artificial Intelligence, GPAI, was launched in June 2020. The aim of GPAI is to bridge the gap between theory and practice in AI through both research and practical applications. It has a number of working groups that deal with scientific, technical, and socio-economic information regarding understanding the impacts of AI. This also allows for the pursuit of responsible development and exploring adaptive options as countermeasures to potential challenges that might come with AI (GPAI, n.d.). On this, GPAI, together with the OECD, in June 2024, announced an integrated partnership in advance of an ambitious implementation agenda for human-centric, safe, secure, and trustworthy AI as embodied in the principles of the OECD Recommendation on AI. This integration brought together OECD Members and GPAI countries, including a total of 44 countries across six continents, reflecting a broad commitment to the responsible stewardship of AI (OECD, 2024).

The United Nations (UN) has launched several programs to promote global collaboration in the field of artificial intelligence (AI). One of these initiatives is the AI for Good Global Summit, organized annually by the International Telecommunication Union (ITU). The summit brings to light how AI can help solve global challenges such as poverty, healthcare, and environmental sustainability (International Telecommunication Union, n.d.). Other initiatives include the High-Level

Advisory Body on Artificial Intelligence, HLAB-AI, which advises on AI governance to ensure that AI technologies are developed and used responsibly and ethically (United Nations, 2024a).

In examining the dynamics of competition and collaboration in the race for government AI development, it is essential to strike a balance between these two factors. Governments must recognize that the ethical, legal, and societal implications of AI cannot be addressed by a single government alone; rather, they require collaboration between multiple governments. Effectively balancing competition and collaboration to promote responsible AI development poses challenges, particularly in reconciling resource competition with cooperation across various industries (Shao et al., 2020).

Among them, one big challenge is the trade-off between national security and international norms. Applications of AI to this domain are very sensitive, and often classified, and hence, an easy consensus on regulatory standards that promote cooperation is hard to come by. The absence of cooperation in this area may lead to an AI arms race with possible destabilizing consequences. Therefore, a collaborative effort toward forging transparent AI arms control agreements is necessary in order to handle this issue.

Other challenges involve data handling. Data is one of the important resources for strategic purposes, just like national security. The information handled by governments is very sensitive; for example, governments in the EU have strict restrictions with respect to data sovereignty, which can limit collaborative opportunities with other countries. Such regulations need to be worked out by nations to create collaboration in the AI sector.

Ethical and cultural differences also present significant challenges for government collaboration. Moral judgments and behaviors can vary substantially both between and within cultures due to cultural factors like religion, social ecology, and social institutions (Graham et al., 2016). This can create substantial gaps between governments concerning the ethical use of AI and their priorities. However, collaboration can still be achieved through ongoing dialogue and mutual respect for cultural differences.

6 Policy Recommendations for AI Funding Priorities

Based on the analysis presented in the prior sections, several concrete recommendations can be formulated in order for governments to optimize their AI investments.

In this context, Fig. 1 highlights several important recommendations, including funding priorities, regulatory safeguards, and public–private collaboration.

Under the funding priorities, as the first recommendation, governments must prioritize alignment with their national strategic goals, whether they pertain to societal well-being, private security, public sector efficiency, or other areas. This alignment requires a robust national AI strategy that clearly articulates these priorities.

Fig. 1 Summary of policy recommendations for AI funding priorities, regulatory safeguards, and public–private collaboration

The second recommendation emphasizes the importance of foundational research by advocating for a substantial allocation of the AI strategy budget to both basic and applied AI research. This investment can stimulate innovation and yield valuable discoveries that contribute to long-term progress and benefits. Additionally, an important aspect is the interdisciplinary research that examines both the technical and societal dimensions of AI.

The third recommendation pertains to infrastructure development, emphasizing the necessity of allocating resources towards the creation of a comprehensive national AI infrastructure. This includes the establishment of high-performance computing (HPC) facilities, secure data repositories, and high-speed digital networks. Access to such an infrastructure is essential for facilitating both research and the effective deployment of AI solutions.

The fourth recommendation under this section is equitable access. Governments should prioritize initiatives that promote equitable access to AI technologies and digital skills, addressing the digital divide within and between nations. This may involve targeted funding for underserved communities and developing countries.

In addressing regulatory safeguards, it is essential for governments to consider a number of key recommendations. Primarily, the establishment and enhancement of an adaptive framework is crucial. This framework should comprehensively address ethical concerns, safety and security risks, as well as potential societal impacts associated with artificial intelligence. Furthermore, these frameworks must possess the flexibility to evolve in conjunction with the dynamic advancements in AI technology.

The second recommendation is to establish sector-specific guidelines and standards for the development and deployment of AI in high-impact sectors such as healthcare, finance, and law, ensuring transparency, human oversight, and accountability.

The third recommendation is the international harmonization of AI standards and regulations to facilitate cross-border collaboration and prevent a "race to the bottom" on safety and ethical considerations.

Lastly, we must focus on public–private collaborations as a key priority. I recommend building robust partnerships among government agencies, industry leaders, and academic institutions. By combining their unique expertise and resources, we can drive AI innovation and development more effectively. Establishing platforms for ongoing dialogue and consultation will help align our goals and tackle emerging challenges together.

The second recommendation under this key point is to support the development of AI innovation ecosystems through incubators, accelerators, and funding programs that encourage startups and SMEs to develop AI solutions for public good and economic growth.

The third and final recommendation on this list is to promote data-sharing initiatives. Governments need to encourage responsible data sharing between the public and private sectors while ensuring data privacy and security. Doing so can facilitate the development of high-quality AI models and applications.

By strategically prioritizing these funding recommendations and creating a strong and adaptable framework, government investments in AI will not only have economic and technological benefits but also play a crucial role in shaping the future of nations and the global economy. This chapter highlights the transformative potential of AI to drive innovation, foster collaboration, and establish global leadership while adhering to ethical and legal standards.

7 What is the Future of AI Investments in Governance?

Governments' interest in AI is continuously on the rise, making investment in AI important from a global perspective. Future investment in government AI will occur around the adoption of advanced emerging technologies, the landscape of collaboration, and legal frameworks.

In analyzing the various approaches that governments are adopting toward AI investment, it has become clear that a robust framework is necessary, one that transcends mere financial quantification. This framework should be built around three key aspects: strategic intent, investment instruments, and governance modalities.

The strategic intent dimension categorizes investments based on their primary overarching goals. As previously discussed, governments can tailor their strategies based on different objectives. For example, the U.S. focuses on boosting GDP, the EU aims to enhance citizens' private security, and Singapore is converting its territory into a smart city to promote societal well-being, among other goals.

The investment instrument dimension analyzes the manner in which governments allocate their investments. It enables governments to clearly identify the specific areas in which they are funding their strategic initiatives. For example, a government may predominantly provide direct funding for research and development, infrastructure, talent cultivation, or industry adoption, among other priorities. The critical objective is to achieve a harmonious balance and establish guidelines that align with the overarching strategic intent.

The governance modality dimension focuses on how to guide and oversee AI investments. Governments need to assess whether they have a centralized national AI strategy or a decentralized approach for managing AI initiatives. A centralized strategy can simplify decision-making and resource allocation, promoting cohesive national objectives and standards. In contrast, a decentralized approach may foster innovation and flexibility at local levels, allowing regions or sectors to address specific needs more effectively.

It is important that governments state their guiding principles and priorities concerning benefits derived from investments in artificial intelligence, while undertaking to assume ethical and cooperative approaches. For them to do this, they must come up with policies focusing on AI investment in the service of society. This calls for the making of sophisticated AI frameworks embedding ethics, transparency, fairness, and accountability.

It is essential to guarantee that investments in artificial intelligence yield advantages for all sectors of society while upholding ethical principles, as this is vital for cultivating international collaboration among nations possessing substantial AI resources and those experiencing restricted access to such technologies. The objective ought to be to enhance the inclusivity of AI investments to facilitate equitable advantages.

Eventually, the future of AI investments in governance will also relate to enhancing the collaboration landscape, while balancing the competition in the so-called 'AI race'. While AI government investments are continuously changing, their focus shall move from pure technological advantage toward these investments being able to reshape policy frameworks, decision-making processes, and collaborative practices so as to make full use of AI's potential for the common good and global cooperation.

As great as the views surrounding investments in artificial intelligence may be, it is these aspects touched on in this chapter that need deep consideration if the potential is to be realized. Innovation, inclusiveness, collaboration, competition, and ethical foresight will be balanced in the successful attainment of that.

References

Ahn, M. J., & Chen, Y. (2020). Artificial intelligence in government. In *The 21st Annual International Conference on Digital Government Research* (pp. 243–252). https://doi.org/10.1145/3396956.3398260

AI for Good. (n.d.-a). AI for Good Global Summit. https://aiforgood.itu.int/summit24/

AI for Good. (n.d.-b). World Bank Group (WBG)—AI for good. AI For Good. https://aiforgood.itu.int/about-us/un-ai-actions/wbg/

Alania, A., & Kong, B. (2024, December). *Four ways developing countries can build safe, effective AI policies.* Asian Development Blog. https://blogs.adb.org/blog/four-ways-developing-countries-can-build-safe-effective-ai-policies

Appaya, S., & Ng, J. (2025, February). *Global trends in AI governance: Evolving country approaches.* World Bank. http://documents.worldbank.org/curated/en/099120224205026271

Belderbos, H. (2024, April 26). *UK government allocates £7 million funding for SMEs to drive AI innovation.* Open Access Government. https://www.openaccessgovernment.org/uk-government-allocates-7-million-funding-for-smes-to-drive-ai-innovation/176695/#:~:text=The%20United%20Kingdom%20has%20revealed%20a%20funding%20initiative,projects%20that%20address%20business%20challenges%20across%20diverse%20industries

Berryhill, J., Heang, K. K., Clogher, R., & McBride, K. (2019). *Hello, world.* OECD Working Papers on Public Governance. https://doi.org/10.1787/726fd39d-en

Bessen, J. E., Impink, S. M., Reichensperger, L., & Seamans, R. (2020). GDPR and the importance of data to AI startups. *SSRN Electronic Journal*. https://doi.org/10.2139/ssrn.3576714

Bhatia, S. (2020). Driving PPP projects through AI standards: A review. *Journal of Economics Management and Trade,* 47–58.https://doi.org/10.9734/jemt/2020/v26i330237

Brandusescu, A. (2021). Artificial intelligence policy and funding in Canada: Public investments, private interests. *SSRN Electronic Journal*. https://doi.org/10.2139/ssrn.4089932

Carraro, T. (2021). AI4EU|DKM|FBK. https://dkm.fbk.eu/ai4eu/

Castonguay, A., Wagner, G., Motulsky, A., & Paré, G. (2023). AI maturity in health care: An overview of 10 OECD countries. *Health Policy, 140*, Article 104938. https://doi.org/10.1016/j.healthpol.2023.104938

Cath, C. (2018). Governing artificial intelligence: Ethical, legal and technical opportunities and challenges. *Philosophical Transactions of the Royal Society a Mathematical Physical and Engineering Sciences, 376*(2133), 20180080. https://doi.org/10.1098/rsta.2018.0080

Charalabidis, Y., Zuiderwijk, A., Alexopoulos, C., Janssen, M., Lampoltshammer, T., & Ferro, E. (2018). Organizational issues: How to open up government data? In *Public administration and information technology* (pp. 57–73). https://doi.org/10.1007/978-3-319-90850-2_4

Crawford, A., & Wulkan, I. (2021). Federal prize competitions: Using competitions to promote innovation in artificial intelligence. https://doi.org/10.51593/2021ca002

Customs, H. R. (2024, May 1). *Claiming Research and Development (R&D) tax relief*. GOV.UK. https://www.gov.uk/government/collections/research-and-development-rd-tax-relief#r&d-tax-relief-for-small-and-medium-sized-enterprises-(smes)

Darcy, M. (2024, October 18). *The impact of AI on government technology and strategic pathways forward*. Public Sector Network. https://publicsectornetwork.com/insight/the-impact-of-ai-on-government-technology-and-strategic-pathways-forward

Davidian, K. (2005). Prize competitions and NASA's Centennial Challenges program. https://www.semanticscholar.org/paper/Prize-Competitions-and-NASA's-Centennial-Challenges-Davidian/e729322c0ce78b328b99b3444e8cd74d68855c63

Davis, A. M., Engkvist, O., Fairclough, R. J., Feierberg, I., Freeman, A., & Iyer, P. (2021). Public-Private partnerships: Compound and data sharing in drug discovery and development. *SLAS Discovery, 26*(5), 604–619. https://doi.org/10.1177/2472555220982268

Dodge, J., Liao, Q. V., Zhang, Y., Bellamy, R. K. E., & Dugan, C. (2019). Explaining models. In *Proceedings of the 24th International Conference on Intelligent User Interfaces*. https://doi.org/10.1145/3301275.3302310

Drobotowicz, K., Kauppinen, M., & Kujala, S. (2021). Trustworthy AI services in the public sector: What are citizens saying about it? In *Lecture notes in computer science* (pp. 99–115). https://doi.org/10.1007/978-3-030-73128-1_7

ElBaih, M. (2023). The role of privacy regulations in AI development (A discussion of the ways in which privacy regulations can shape the development of AI). *SSRN Electronic Journal*. https://doi.org/10.2139/ssrn.4589207

Erick, O. (2023). Effects of tax incentives and subsidies on economic growth in developing economies. *International Journal of Research and Innovation in Social Science, VII*(VII), 567–581. https://doi.org/10.47772/ijriss.2023.70744

European Union. (n.d.). Horizon 2020. Research and Innovation. Retrieved November 29, 2024, from https://research-and-innovation.ec.europa.eu/funding/funding-opportunities/funding-programmes-and-open-calls/horizon-2020_en

Fan, Q., & Qiang, C. Z. (2024, June). *Tipping the scales: AI's dual impact on developing nations*. World Bank Blogs. https://blogs.worldbank.org/en/digital-development/tipping-the-scales--ai-s-dual-impact-on-developing-nations

Felzmann, H., Villaronga, E. F., Lutz, C., & Tamò-Larrieux, A. (2019). Transparency you can trust: Transparency requirements for artificial intelligence between legal norms and contextual concerns. *Big Data & Society, 6*(1), 205395171986054. https://doi.org/10.1177/2053951719860542

Franzoni, V. (2023). From black box to glass box: Advancing transparency in artificial intelligence systems for ethical and trustworthy AI. In *Lecture notes in computer science* (pp. 118–130). https://doi.org/10.1007/978-3-031-37114-1_9

Galindo, L., Perset, K., & Sheeka, F. (2021). An overview of national AI strategies and policies. Going Digital Toolkit, No. 14. https://goingdigital.oecd.org/data/notes/No14_ToolkitNote_AIStrategies.pdf

Global Partners Digital. (2024, September). *The final report of HLAB-AI: Our analysis and thoughts*. Global Partners Digital. https://www.gp-digital.org/news/the-final-report-of-hlab-ai-our-analysis-and-thoughts/

Gopisetty, L. (2025, March 7). *The beneficial impact of AI in public services*. RTInsights. https://www.rtinsights.com/the-beneficial-impact-of-ai-in-public-services/

Government of Canada. (2022). Pan-Canadian artificial intelligence strategy. https://ised-isde.canada.ca/site/ai-strategy/en#pillar1

GPAI. (n.d.). About GPAI. https://gpai.ai/about/

GPAI. (2021, November). Frequently asked questions. https://www.gpai.ai/about/gpai-faq.pdf#:~:text=The%20Global%20Partnership%20on%20Artificial%20Intelligence%20or%20GPAI,as%20reflected%20in%20the%20OECD%20Recommendation%20on%20AI.

Graham, J., Meindl, P., Beall, E., Johnson, K. M., & Zhang, L. (2016). Cultural differences in moral judgment and behavior, across and within societies. *Current Opinion in Psychology, 8*, 125–130. https://doi.org/10.1016/j.copsyc.2015.09.007

Grochmalski, P. (2020). US-China rivalry for strategic domination in the area of artificial intelligence and the new AI geopolitics. *Kwartalnik Bellona, 701*(2), 5–25. https://doi.org/10.5604/01.3001.0014.3837

Hamirul, N., Darmawanto, N., Elsyra, N. N., & Syahwami, N. (2023). The Role of Artificial Intelligence in Government Services: A Systematic Literature review. *Open Access Indonesia Journal of Social Sciences, 6*(3), 998–1003. https://doi.org/10.37275/oaijss.v6i3.163

Henman, P. (2020). Improving public services using artificial intelligence: Possibilities, pitfalls, governance. *Asia Pacific Journal of Public Administration, 42*(4), 209–221. https://doi.org/10.1080/23276665.2020.1816188

Ho, L., Barnhart, J., Trager, R., Bengio, Y., Brundage, M., Carnegie, A., Chowdhury, R., Dafoe, A., Hadfield, G., Levi, M., & Snidal, D. (2023, July 10). International institutions for advanced AI. arXiv.org. https://arxiv.org/abs/2307.04699

Hornjak, A. (2024). The impact of artificial intelligence on the efficiency of E-government: Student paper. In *2024 23rd International Symposium INFOTEH-JAHORINA (INFOTEH)* (pp. 1–6). https://doi.org/10.1109/infoteh60418.2024.10495946

International Telecommunication Union. (n.d.-a). *AI for good—All year always online*. AI For Good. https://aiforgood.itu.int/

International Telecommunication Union. (n.d.-b). *Artificial intelligence*. ITU. https://www.itu.int/en/action/ai/Pages/default.aspx

Iori, M., Martinelli, A., & Mina, A. (2021). The direction of technical change in AI and the trajectory effects of government funding. In Sant'Anna School of Advanced Studies. Retrieved November 29, 2024, from https://iri.jrc.ec.europa.eu/sites/default/files/inline-files/Mina_et%20al_CONCORDi2021_0.pdf

Joshi, N. (2021, April). Why countries need a national AI strategy. https://www.allerin.com/blog/why-countries-need-a-national-ai-strategy

Kaushik, P., & Rathore, S. P. S. (2020). Impact and usage of AI in public sector. *International Journal of Engineering in Computer Science, 2*(1), 38–43. https://doi.org/10.33545/26633582.2020.v2.i1a.99

Krishnaswami, S. (2023, October 14). How the World Bank leverages AI to help low-income families. *The Borgen Project*. Retrieved November 29, 2024, from https://borgenproject.org/how-the-world-bank-leverages-ai/#:~:text=The%20World%20Bank%20leverages%20AI%20to%20address%20the,of%20AI%20delivering%20financial%20services%20to%20the%20poorest.

Lee, T., Natalwala, J., Chapple, V., & Liu, Y. (2023). A brief history of artificial intelligence embryo selection: From black-box to glass-box. *Human Reproduction, 39*(2), 285–292. https://doi.org/10.1093/humrep/dead254

Manyika, J., Lund, S., Chui, M., Bughin, J., Woetzel, L., Batra, P., Ko, R., & Sanghvi, S. (2024, July 16). *Jobs lost, jobs gained: What the future of work will mean for jobs, skills, and wages.* McKinsey & Company. https://www.mckinsey.com/featured-insights/future-of-work/jobs-lost-jobs-gained-what-the-future-of-work-will-mean-for-jobs-skills-and-wages

Ma'rup, M., Tobirin, N., & Rokhman, N. A. (2024). Utilization of artificial intelligence (AI) chatbots in improving public services: A Meta-Analysis study. *Open Access Indonesia Journal of Social Sciences, 7*(4), 1610–1618. https://doi.org/10.37275/oaijss.v7i4.255

McGrail, S. (2023, June 1). *What is white box (Glass Box) versus black box AI?* TalentSelect.ai. https://www.talentselect.ai/resources/what-is-white-box-glass-box-vs-black-box

Melkamu, M. (2025). Artificial intelligence implementation challenges in industries: Developing countries prospective. *Deleted Journal, 2*(1). https://doi.org/10.61552/jai.2025.01.004

Melloddy. (n.d.). Melloddy. https://melloddy.eu

Meyer, S. (2024, September). *Key takeaways from the UN report: 'Governing AI for Humanity.'* FENWICK. https://www.fenwick.com/insights/publications/key-takeaways-from-the-un-report-governing-ai-for-humanity

Mitchell, B. (2025, February 28). Gen AI for government: Google public sector live & labs takeaways. *Google Cloud Blog.* https://cloud.google.com/blog/topics/public-sector/investing-in-ai-collaboration-and-the-next-generation-of-leaders

Murad, T., Azərbaycan, R., Prezidenti, Y., Dövlət, İ., & Akademiyası, A. (2023). Dövlət-Özəl Sektor Tərəfdaşliği Sahəsində Süni İntellektin Tətbiqi. *Journal of Science and Innovative Technologies.* https://doi.org/10.30546/2616-4418.28.2023.42

Musoni, M. (2024, January). Envisioning Africa's AI governance landscape in 2024. *ECDPM.* https://ecdpm.org/work/envisioning-africas-ai-governance-landscape-2024

NordForsk. (2024). A Nordic initiative for research and innovation on responsible and ethical use of artificial intelligence. https://norden.diva-portal.org/smash/get/diva2:1856812/FULLTEXT02

National Artificial Intelligence Initiative Act of 2020. (2020). Division E—National artificial intelligence initiative act of 2020. https://www.aip.org/sites/default/files/aipcorp/images/fyi/pdf/national-ai-initiative-act-final.pdf

National Science Foundation. (n.d.). How it works—Get started|NSF SBIR. https://seedfund.nsf.gov/apply/get-started/

Novelli, C., Taddeo, M., & Floridi, L. (2022). Accountability in artificial intelligence: What it is and how it works. *SSRN Electronic Journal.* https://doi.org/10.2139/ssrn.4180366

OECD. (n.d.). AI principles. https://www.oecd.org/en/topics/ai-principles.html

OECD. (2024). GPAI and OECD unite to advance coordinated international efforts for trustworthy AI. https://www.oecd.org/en/about/news/speech-statements/2024/07/GPAI-and-OECD-unite-to-advance-coordinated-international-efforts-for-trustworthy-AI.html

Ogenga, F., & Stanley, A. (2024, September 18). *Regulating artificial intelligence in Africa: Strategies and insights from Kenya, Ghana, and the African Union.* Wilson Center. https://www.wilsoncenter.org/blog-post/regulating-artificial-intelligence-africa-strategies-and-insights-kenya-ghana-and-african

Okahashi, A., & Blanco, C. (2024, March). *How is the World Bank using AI and machine learning for better governance?* World Bank Blogs. https://blogs.worldbank.org/en/governance/how-world-bank-using-ai-and-machine-learning-better-governance

Ontario, L. C. O. (2021). Legal issues and government AI development. *SSRN Electronic Journal.* https://doi.org/10.2139/ssrn.3853229

Papyshev, G., & Yarime, M. (2023). The state's role in governing artificial intelligence: Development, control, and promotion through national strategies. *Policy Design and Practice, 6*(1), 79–102. https://doi.org/10.1080/25741292.2022.2162252

Peterson, A. (2021, March 5). *AI advocates seek vast expansion of new national initiative.* AIP.ORG. AIP. https://ww2.aip.org/fyi/2021/ai-advocates-seek-vast-expansion-new-national-initiative

Prasad, K. R., Karanam, S. R., Ganesh, D., Liyakat, K. K. S., Talasila, V., & Purushotham, P. (2024). AI in public-private partnership for IT infrastructure development. *The Journal of High Technology Management Research, 35*(1), Article 100496. https://doi.org/10.1016/j.hitech.2024.100496

Quintero-Ossa, A. M., Solano, J., Jarcía, H., Zarruk, D., Bahnsen, A. C., & Valencia, C. (2022, November 10). Privacy-preserving machine learning for collaborative data sharing via auto-encoder latent space embeddings. arXiv.org. https://arxiv.org/abs/2211.05717

Radu, R. (2021). Steering the governance of artificial intelligence: National strategies in perspective. *Policy and Society, 40*(2), 178–193. https://doi.org/10.1080/14494035.2021.1929728

Ramizo, G. J. (2021). Practical lessons for government AI projects. *SSRN Electronic Journal.* https://doi.org/10.2139/ssrn.3840398

Ramos-Torres, A., & Montoya, L. N. (2024, September 17). Evaluating investment risks in LATAM AI startups: Ranking of investment potential and framework for valuation. arXiv.org. https://arxiv.org/abs/2410.03552

Rao, A., & Verweij, G. (2017). *PwC's global artificial intelligence study: Sizing the prize.* PwC. https://www.pwc.com/gx/en/issues/artificial-intelligence/publications/artificial-intelligence-study.html

Richman, M. (2019, August 20). *VA-DeepMind partnership reports on technology for early detection of life-threatening kidney condition.* U.S. Department of Veteran Affairs. Retrieved November 29, 2024, from https://www.research.va.gov/currents/0819-VA-DeepMind-partnership-reports-on-technology-for-early-detection-of-kidney-condition.cfm

Sarra, J. P. (2013). *An exploration of fairness: Interdisciplinary inquiries in law, science and the humanities.* Thomson Carswell.

Saura, J. R., Ribeiro-Soriano, D., & Palacios-Marqués, D. (2022). Assessing behavioral data science privacy issues in government artificial intelligence deployment. *Government Information Quarterly, 39*(4), Article 101679. https://doi.org/10.1016/j.giq.2022.101679

Schmager, S., Grøder, C. H., Parmiggiani, E., Pappas, I., & Vassilakopoulou, P. (2024). Exploring citizens' stances on AI in public services: A social contract perspective. *Data & Policy, 6*.https://doi.org/10.1017/dap.2024.13

Schmidt, E. (2022). AI, great power competition and national security. *Daedalus, 151*(2), 288–298. https://doi.org/10.1162/daed_a_01916

Sciulli, N. (2010). Building a framework for public private partnerships research. *International Review of Business Research Papers, 6*(1), 367–381. ISSN 1837-5685 (Print) 1832-9543 (Online). https://vuir.vu.edu.au/7311/

Shao, Z., Yuan, S., & Wang, Y. (2020). Institutional collaboration and competition in artificial intelligence. *IEEE Access, 8*, 69734–69741. https://doi.org/10.1109/access.2020.2986383

Smart Nation Singapore. (2024). A Smart Nation that we can trust. https://www.smartnation.gov.sg/

Stanford University. (2024). Artificial intelligence index report 2024. https://aiindex.stanford.edu/wp-content/uploads/2024/05/HAI_AI-Index-Report-2024.pdf

Stevens Institute of Technology. (2023, May 12). *Countries ranked by internet privacy.* Stevens Online. https://online.stevens.edu/info/countries-ranked-by-internet-privacy/

Surdej, A. (2021). AI solutions and productivity of public services: Insights from Poland. In *Springer proceedings in complexity* (pp. 375–387). https://doi.org/10.1007/978-3-030-62066-0_28

Teleanu, S., & Kurbalija, J. (2022). Stronger digital voices from Africa: Building African digital foreign policy and diplomacy. https://www.diplomacy.edu/wp-content/uploads/2023/01/African-digital-foreign-policy_En.pdf

Tews, S. (2025, February). *The critical role of administration officials in America's AI future.* American Enterprise Institute—AEI. https://www.aei.org/technology-and-innovation/the-critical-role-of-administration-officials-in-americas-ai-future/

The Alan Turing Institute. (n.d.). The Alan Turing Institute. Retrieved November 29, 2024, from https://www.turing.ac.uk/about-us

UNESCO. (2025, March). Shaping the future: Higher education's impact on national AI policies. https://www.iesalc.unesco.org/en/articles/shaping-future-higher-educations-impact-national-ai-policies

United Nations. (2024a). *UN secretary-general's high-level advisory body on artificial intelligence releases proposals for global governance of AI*. Welcome to the United Nations. Retrieved November 29, 2024, from https://www.un.org/sites/un2.un.org/files/governing_ai_for_humanity_press_release.pdf

United Nations. (2024b). Governing AI for humanity. https://doi.org/10.18356/9789211067873

Verma, S., & Rubin, J. (2018). Fairness definitions explained. In *Proceedings of the International Workshop on Software Fairness* (pp. 1–7).https://doi.org/10.1145/3194770.3194776

Watson, R. B., & Ryan, P. J. (2020). Big data analytics in Australian local government. *Smart Cities, 3*(3), 657–675. https://doi.org/10.3390/smartcities3030034

Williams, M. (2019). The AI race: Will Australia lead or lose? *Journal and Proceedings of the Royal Society of New South Wales, 152*(1), 105–114. https://doi.org/10.5962/p.361856

World Bank. (n.d.). DIME artificial intelligence. https://www.worldbank.org/en/about/unit/unit-dec/impactevaluation/ai

World Bank. (2021). *Harnessing artificial intelligence for development in the post-Covid-19 ERA A review of national AI strategies and policies*. World Bank. https://documents1.worldbank.org/curated/en/487931621237422984/pdf/Harnessing-Artificial-Intelligence-for-Development-on-the-Post-COVID-19-Era-A-Review-of-National-AI-Strategies-and-Policies.pdf

Xu, K., Yue, H., Guo, L., Guo, Y., & Fang, Y. (2015). Privacy-preserving machine learning algorithms for big data systems. In *IEEE 35th International Conference on Distributed Computing Systems* (pp. 318–327). https://doi.org/10.1109/icdcs.2015.40

Zhou, J., Chen, F., & Holzinger, A. (2022). Towards explainability for AI fairness. In *Lecture notes in computer science* (pp. 375–386). https://doi.org/10.1007/978-3-031-04083-2_18

Part II

Applications of AI in Government

AI in Emergency Management 8

Ismail Soujaa and Jie Tao

1 Introduction

Artificial Intelligence (AI) has emerged as a transformative tool in disaster management, driven by the increasing demand for real-time data and intelligence. Across all four phases—preparedness, response, mitigation, and recovery, AI technologies, particularly predictive and generative models offer significant capabilities. These include improved forecasting, coordinated response efforts, risk reduction strategies, and accelerated recovery. For instance, AI enhances early warning systems by analyzing historical and environmental data to model future risks (Robertson, 2020), supports real-time response coordination through satellite and communication data (Hawley, 2025), and aids in recovery logistics by reducing administrative burdens (Hasanuzzaman et al., 2023). In mitigation, AI helps identify vulnerable zones and simulate hazards to guide early interventions (Dineva, 2023), while in recovery, it facilitates infrastructure assessment and long-term resilience planning (Clement, 2024).

Building on these capabilities, the growing utility of AI has laid the groundwork for broader institutional adoption in disaster management. As the value of AI becomes more evident in real-time response, its integration has expanded into long-term planning and mitigation efforts through strategic partnerships. Notably, public–private collaborations have emerged as a driving force behind the development and deployment of advanced AI solutions tailored to the evolving needs of

I. Soujaa (✉)
Albany State University, Albany, USA
e-mail: ismail.soujaa@asurams.edu

J. Tao
Tarleton State University—Fort Worth, Stephenville, USA
e-mail: jtao@tarleton.edu

S. K. Aikins and T. Dimitrijevska-Markoski (eds.), *Artificial Intelligence and Government*, https://doi.org/10.1007/978-3-032-12344-2_8

disaster risk management (Clement, 2024; Engima Advisory, 2025). These initiatives not only boost the technological sophistication of emergency systems but also ensure that innovations are grounded in practical realities (Hasanuzzaman et al., 2023).

Extending the reach of AI integration, Generative AI technologies including ChatGPT and disaster-specific chatbots are also playing an emerging role in communication and community engagement. These tools support preparedness by delivering accurate, real-time information, countering misinformation, and answering public queries during crises (Jakaza et al., 2024; Robertson, 2020). Internally, AI helps disaster agencies reduce routine administrative burdens, while externally, it reduces the informational burden on affected populations, enabling more targeted and equitable service delivery (Hanwacker, 2025). However, as the role of AI in disaster management grows, so too do ethical concerns around data privacy, surveillance, algorithmic bias, and accountability. Responsible implementation requires clear ethical frameworks and governance structures to ensure transparency, fairness, and public trust (Velev et al., 2023). Drawing on real-world examples such as California wildfire management and COVID-19 pandemic, this chapter provides a critical examination of how AI technologies are reshaping disaster management in areas of wildfire management and COVID- 19-pandmeic response.

This chapter is structured around five core sections. First, it begins by reviewing the role of AI in disaster management and emphasizes the importance of collaboration. Second, it then explores the integrated adoption and application in emergency management including predictive analytics and generative AI. Third, it focuses on AI impact on both administrative operations and public service delivery. Fourth, it addresses key ethical considerations in AI implementation. Finally, the chapter presents two real-world case studies of AI in California wildfire management and the COVID-19 pandemic response to assess practical outcomes and lessons learned.

2 Adoption of AI in Emergency Management

2.1 Overview

Artificial Intelligence (AI) stands at the forefront of transforming emergency management phases for which it creates opportunities and unprecedented capabilities in disaster preparedness, response, mitigation and recovery (Visave, 2025). AI applications are viewed as potential solutions that can be used to resolve disaster preparedness, response, mitigation and recovery challenges. AI-powered tools including generative AI, predictive analytics, machine learning algorithms, and real-time data processing systems are helping emergency agencies better anticipate disasters, allocate resources efficiently, and respond more effectively to evolving crises. These technologies enhance situational awareness by analyzing vast and diverse datasets, including satellite imagery (Domínguez & Beltran, 2025); infrastructure data, (Şengöz, 2024) and even social media activity (Abid & Sulaiman, 2025); therefore, providing rapid insights into emerging threats.

To understand how AI achieves these outcomes, it is useful draw on theoretical frameworks that explain how complex systems functions in changing environment. One such framework is Complex Adaptive Systems Theory (CAS) which views emergency management as a network of interdependent agents including governments, responders and communities that interact and adapt to various threats (Yu et al., 2024). From this perspective, AI functions as a catalyst agent that enhance system-wide adaptability by processing real-time data, generating predictive insights, and enabling decentralized coordination. AI-driven models contribute to systemic resilience by improving feedback loops, enabling rapid reconfiguration of strategies, and supporting emergent behavior across subsystems Drawing on frameworks of Complex Adaptive Systems Theory and Socio-technical Systems Theory, Al Marzooqi (2024) note that AI not only is a technical tool but an integrative system that interact with human decision makers, institutional structures and data ecosystems. Al Marzooqi emphasizes that AI-driven models particularly machine learning models, predictive analytics, and real-time surveillance technologies enable more timely and accurate situational awareness during disasters.

In summary, the adoption of AI predictive analytics and generative AI are reshaping emergency management systems by making it more anticipatory, adaptive, and data-driven. while significant challenges remain, including concerns about data privacy and algorithmic bias, the strategic use and integration of AI have the potential to substantially enhance disaster preparedness and response, mitigation and recovery capabilities. For example, during the California wildfires, AI-driven models were used to predict fire spread in real time by analyzing satellite imagery, wind patterns, and vegetation density, enabling faster evacuations and more efficient deployment of firefighting resources. Similarly, during the COVID-19 pandemic, AI systems supported outbreak forecasting, resource allocation, and contact tracing, helping public health agencies respond more effectively under rapidly changing conditions. These case studies illustrate how AI can improve outcomes in complex emergencies. Additionally, AI adoption in disaster management require the alignment of efforts among stakeholders including the effectiveness of prediction analytics which depends on Human-AI collaboration (Yin et al., 2022).

2.2 AI Adoption Through Collaboration

Public sector organizations are showing growing interest in leveraging data science and artificial intelligence (AI) to enhance policy implementation and improve efficiency, especially in uncertain and complex environments operations (Hosseini et al., 2021; Mikhaylov et al., 2018). The sustained success of AI and data science in the public domain depends on their effective integration into policy delivery mechanisms. However, governments alone cannot achieve this integration; collaboration with external partners and stakeholders is essential for embedding AI into public service operations (Mikhaylov et al., 2018). AI can be used to streamline communication, information sharing among various agencies involved in disaster response. Therefore, the integration of AI tools into emergency response systems not only improve and enhance operational efficiency but also enables more effective collaboration and coordination among various stakeholders and organizations which increase the level of collective action in response and recovery (Cate, 2022). Collaborative education setting such as interdisciplinary training initiatives and simulation powered by AI which promote the exchange of knowledge among technology experts, policy makers and emergency management professionals (Hosseini et al., 2021).

Despite these advanced, meaningful collaboration in AI implementation remains limited. In many cases, AI-based algorithmic projects conducted within academic settings are also constrained in scope. Once an AI-driven emergency management project is completed, the findings are often shared only through scientific conferences, specialized committees, or peer-reviewed publications, rarely reaching stakeholders and end users (Kuglitsch et al., 2022). While AI systems have introduced both challenges and opportunities, they have also fostered new forms of collaboration across various fields such as technology (information processing) (Meyrowitsch et al., 2023) business (decision-making and AI-enabled automation) (Hermann & Puntoni, 2024); education (intelligent tutoring and personalized learning), Wickramasinghe et al. (2024); healthcare (smart health systems and AI-assisted diagnostics) (Delgado et al., 2022); the arts and humanities (human-centered design and cultural engagement) (Chun & Elkins, 2023). In short, the key to fully harnessing these benefits lies in fostering strong AI-human collaboration (Yin et al., 2022).

Disaster management relies on smooth coordination and effective collaboration among several stakeholders including government agencies, non-profit organizations and local communities. AI-driven systems support the process by employing centralization platforms that streamline information sharing and coordination. These systems can automate routine tasks such as issuing alerts and updating progress reports, allowing personnel to concentrate on more urgent responsibilities. Moreover, AI tools can examine communication trends and social media activity to gauge public sentiment and assess real-time needs, helping ensure that response strategies are both focused and effective (Markezinis, 2024).

2.3 Integrated Adoption and Application in Emergency Management

Artificial Intelligence has emerged as a transformative force across all phases of emergency management including preparedness, response, mitigation, and recovery. In these cycles of emergency management, AI-powered systems introduce innovative capabilities that improve responsiveness and effectiveness of disaster management systems. These systems include AI-driven predictive Analytics and generative AI.

In the preparedness phase, disaster planning ensures that both responders and the public are equipped to handle the impacts of disasters (Saravi et al., 2019). AI-enabled systems play a pivotal role in disaster preparedness. In establishing early warning systems, the use of AI-enhanced systems enable action through interpretable predictions from real-time data. In flooding events, AI can analyze data on river levels, rainfall and soil saturation to make prediction on the likelihood of flooding or cascading events (Robertson, 2020). In preparedness phase, AI-enabled systems assist with fire wildfire management by determining population density, infrastructure damage and access routes to make distribution for relief center more feasible and smoother. In addition, AI-powered systems play a pivotal role in efficiently managing resources, optimizing logistics for effective distribution and coordinated approach to emergency services. This includes developing response approach that is both timely and effective, enhancing the ability to address the effects and impacts of disasters on affected areas.

In preparedness phase, predictive analytics and models are used predict hazard risks and simulate possible disaster scenarios. For example, supervised learning algorithms can detect early signs of wildfire spread or impending storm surges, giving emergency managers more lead time to act (Sun et al., 2020). For example, AI has been effective in enhancing disaster preparedness and warning systems that enable real time data from remote sensing, satellite-based technology that predict natural disasters. Through predictive analytics, AI-driven systems can anticipate disasters by analyzing patterns and integrating real-time data from satellite imagery, meteorological sources, sensor networks, and historical disaster records to forecast events such as floods, hurricanes, wildfires, and earthquakes (Domínguez & Beltran, 2025). During the response phase, AI and optimization tools are used to allocate resources such as rescue teams, medical units, and emergency supplies efficiently especially in environments where time and resources are limited (Sun et al., 2020). Despite AI challenges, Velev et al., (2023) note that the benefits of AI are too great to ignore. They refer to AI potential success in transforming disaster risk management, improving speed of disaster prediction and warning systems. For example, image recognition and classification enabled by deep learning assist in real-time damage assessment, sign identification and aerial drone imagery (Velev & Zlateva, 2023).

In response phase, emergency response systems are viewed as approaches that lead and manage crisis effectively, yet, in recent years, these systems are enhanced by the AI tools and predictive analytics: AI includes a range of methods that allow machines to replicate human cognitive functions such as learning, reasoning, and problem-solving (Hanwacker, 2025). Meanwhile, predictive analytics leverage statistical algorithms and machine learning to detect patterns in past data and forecast future events (Agoro & Adams, 2025), and ensure real time situational awareness and optimized resource allocation (Rehan, 2022). In disaster response, monitoring, and damage assessment, AI models can be used to obtain real-time satellite imagery and remote sensing data to track natural disasters. For instance, AI-driven machine learning can analyze and assess the extent of damage, predict disaster impacts, and assist with resource allocation and response strategies for effective disaster management (Chew et al., 2025). AI-powered post-disaster management systems have revolutionized disaster response by integrating real-time data, mobile technologies, and GIS-based tools to strengthen coordination and operational efficiency (Vyas et al., 2025). As a result, AI-systems help reduce response times, optimize resource distribution, and enhance overall disaster management strategies.

In disaster mitigation, AI is used to process large datasets for calculations, forecasting, and predicting natural disasters, helping to reduce risks and avoid hazardous situations. The value of AI in mitigation efforts is evident through its wide-ranging benefits across multiple applications (Dineva, 2023). Key applications include: (1) AI-assisted prediction models for climate change mitigation; (2) the use of machine vision in climate informatics and forecasting; (3) emerging AI trends aimed at reducing carbon footprints to support environmental sustainability; (4) AI applications in managing earth-related hazards; (5) AI technologies that promote eco-friendly energy production and consumption; (6) AI-supported expert systems for predicting and assessing climate change risks; (7) advanced AI techniques for climate change prediction and mitigation; and (8) the use of AI in minimizing the impacts of global warming. These targeted AI methods demonstrate significant potential in mitigating the adverse effects of natural disasters.

In mitigation phase, Rehan (2022) explores the application of AI in enhancing disaster mitigation strategies. some of these mitigation strategies are the use of AI-enhanced GIS platforms that integrate satellite imagery and topographical data and real time sensor feeds to generate dynamic risk maps. Mitigation strategies include the use of internet of things sensor data using advanced detection that mitigate infrastructure risks during natural disasters. In dissimilar vein, Cheye et al. (2024) analyze both historical projected climate data and evaluate the effectiveness of AI technologies in predicting managing-related changes. Their research focus on how AI supports advanced climate modeling by enhancing the accuracy of simulations that predict long-term shifts in temperature, rainfall, and sea-level rise. These models are critical for coastal cities planning flood defense systems or drought-prone regions developing water conservation strategies (Cheye et al., 2024).

Furthermore, AI-driven mitigation strategies also leverage vast datasets from satellite imagery and weather sensors to social media to detect patterns and predict potential hazards before they materialize (Jakaza et al., 2024). This predictive capability empowers communities to take preventive actions and reduce disaster impacts. For instance, machine learning algorithms can enhance flood mapping by analyzing topography, hydrology, and land-use patterns. In wildfire mitigation, AI-based systems integrate sensor data, satellite imaging, and weather forecasts to enable real-time fire detection and automated alerts for rapid response.

Advancing beyond mitigation, AI has emerged as a promising solution to recovery challenges. Technologies such as predictive analytics, machine learning, and automated response systems are reshaping post-disaster management by improving forecasting, resource allocation, and communication (Vyas et al., 2025). AI-powered predictive analytics has significantly improved disaster recovery through the use of early warning systems. AI has enabled effective weather analysis for patterns, satellite imagery with exceptional precisions (Lakum, 2024). This assist with rapid damage through satellite and drone imagery. For instance, Models like DahiTra utilizes high-resolution satellite images to classify destruction levels and building critical data. However, when resources are limited, AI algorithms can analyze various trends including impact, accessibility and population density. AI-powered chatbots further enhance recovery efforts by providing real-time information on evacuation zones and relief operations, improving communication between responders and the public.

In the recovery cycle, traditional disaster recovery strategies have been transformed by AI-driven solutions in disaster management (Lakum, 2024). The potential of AI in disaster recovery efforts is enormous (Rehan, 2022). In recovery, Natural Language Processing techniques (NLP) facilitate rapid information extraction from media organizations and news reports, providing emergency managers with real-time insights into affected areas (Rehan, 2022). In addition, AI-driven drones equipped with computer vision capabilities assist in damage assessment and surveying. In some cases, some use of AI in the recovery process include AI-powered techniques such as predictive analytics, anomaly detection, automated failover that enhance organizational resilience and develop human skills and technical capabilities (Lakum, 2024).

In short, as AI adoption expands across all four phases of emergency management preparedness, response, mitigation, and recovery, its practical applications are strengthening capabilities at each stage. Predictive analytics and generative AI are at the forefront, enhancing the efficiency and effectiveness of disaster management systems.

2.4 Predictive AI: AI-Driven Predictive Analytics

As emergencies grow in scale and severity, AI attempts to improve and increase the efficiency of disaster management process. AI has become crucial in providing the tools that accelerate human decision-making. AI-driven tools such as sensors assist with disaster by allowing for the exchange of information through ontologies, relaying information to different factors and employing multi-agent platforms for simulated scenarios and real time support (Abid et al., 2021). In an era driven by big data and AI, emergency management teams can enhance their crisis response by utilizing AI applications and tools to make more informed decisions (Ortiz et al., 2020). AI advancement in technology provides the ability to analyze enormous volume of complex data, recognize patterns and optimize decision making processes. In this regard, AI applications include early warning systems, automated response mechanism and predictive analytics that enhance and improve emergency management effectiveness (Şengöz, 2024).

Sun et al. (2020) review the current state of AI applications in disaster management by classifying AI methods into six categories: (1) supervised models, (2) unsupervised models, (3) deep learning, (4) reinforcement learning, (5) deep reinforcement learning, and (6) optimization.

1. **Supervised models** are trained on labeled datasets annotated by humans and have been widely used for tasks such as information extraction, pattern recognition, and speech recognition.
2. **Unsupervised models** use statistical techniques to identify hidden structures in data and to detect anomalies without predefined labels.
3. **Deep learning** involves neural networks with multiple layers that extract complex features from input data. This method has broad applications, including damage assessment, motion detection, facial recognition, and natural language processing to support disaster management.
4. **Reinforcement learning** focuses on learning optimal actions through trial and error, guided by rewards, and is useful for optimizing disaster response strategies, resource allocation, and real-time decision-making.
5. **Deep reinforcement learning** combines deep learning with reinforcement learning to develop effective long-term policies and is increasingly applied to complex disaster management scenarios.
6. **Optimization** techniques enhance decision making and improve the efficiency of resource allocation during disaster events particularly where resources are constrained. In such cases, optimization can be used to allocate rescue teams, medical personnel, and emergency vehicles effectively.

In AI-driven practice, machine learning is regarded as a subset of artificial intelligence that involves computer programs automatically learning from and adapting to new data without explicit human intervention. By integrating artificial intelligence and machine learning with data analytics technologies, disaster management systems can operate more efficiently. This combination enables image recognition and classification techniques that support damage assessment, image analysis, and the identification of damaged buildings, flooded areas, and blocked roads (Velev & Zlateva, 2023). By predicting disasters, AI-driven predictive analytics enable better resource allocation, early warning systems, evacuation planning and mitigation strategies. In disaster management, AI-predictive analytics can be used in many ways: (1) early warning systems, (2) risk assessment, (3) resource optimization (4) impact prediction. However, effective AI utilization requires leveraging diverse data sources to build predictive models and forecast disasters. These datasets may include real-time data, satellite imagery, sensor networks, historical records, as well as social media and other publicly available data (Clement, 2024). Table 1 reviews and presents AI techniques and their impacts on disaster preparedness and response. It also contextualizes their applications in disaster areas.

Traditionally, the use of historical data in disaster management models has been limited in both scope and adaptability. However, the integration of AI and

Table 1 Examples of predictive AI techniques and their disaster management applications

AI-techniques	Description	Disaster management application	Preparedness and response impact
Cluster analysis	Groups data into clusters with similar characteristics	Segmentation of affected populations or vulnerable regions	Improves allocation of relief and emergency services
Time-series forecasting	Uses historical data trends to predict future events	Forecasting hurricanes, floods, or disease outbreaks	Enables timely alerts and strategic planning
Deep learning	Utilize artificial neural networks to interpret complex data such imagery data	Identify and locating structures and fire areas using drone imagery	Better damage assessment and rapid mapping
Classification models	Assigning data into categories based on input	Predicting high and low risk of a disaster	Improves risk assessment, alert levels and preparedness measures

predictive analytics have helped overcome these limitations, enhancing the effectiveness and responsiveness of disaster response systems. For example, Domínguez and Beltran (2025) demonstrate how AI-enhanced models enable more dynamic and real-time decision-making during disaster events. They find that integrating real time sensor data, machine learning algorithms and GIS significantly improves emergency response effectiveness, yet the success of AI-based analytics is premised on developing holistic approaches when integrating AI into disaster preparedness plans. Furthermore, recent advances have allowed many new models to be built using AI from the start, improving the accuracy and speed of forecasting (Şengöz, 2024). Machine learning and data analytics are two data techniques that are incorporated in disaster management systems to improve forecasting, risk assessment and response planning. Khan et al. (2023) highlight how these techniques process vast amount of historical and real time data such as rainfall patterns, river levels and metrological conditions, trends and flooding conditions. More broadly, AI driven predictive analytics leverage real time data, machine learning models, neural networks and deep learning algorithms as foundational tools for disaster detection, prediction and simulation.

The integration of AI and predictive analytics in data management enables processing of vast, complex datasets to identify patterns, forecast disasters, and inform preparedness. Recently, AI has been used to predict earthquakes and manage hurricanes by analyzing historical and meteorological data. As such, advanced neural networks process real-time and historical remote sensor data to improve the accuracy of hurricane and flood predictions (Hasanuzzaman et al., 2023). Therefore, AI-enabled analytics enable emergency managers to make informed decisions and coordinate response efforts more effectively. Examples of the predictive analytics are developed accordingly,

- **PAIRS Geoscope** (AI-driven tech tool that analyses geo-special data, examining rainfall and temperature too predict flooding).
- **DesInventar** (Describes Disaster Information Management System for assessing disaster trends over time, historical disaster database, risk trend analytics).
- **ClimateSERV** (Provides climate and weather data for food security and disaster resilience; the application is used in drought early warning, agricultural monitoring).
- **DisasterAWARE** (Incorporates all-hazard risk assessment and early warning platform with AI-driven alert capabilities, real-time global disaster monitoring and alerts).
- **AlertHub/CAP Collector** (Includes open source tool that uses Common Alerting Protocol (CAP) and AI filters for emergency communications; automated public alerts, early warning distribution).
- **AI4Earth (Microsoft)** (Includes grants and tools for AI applications in environmental and disaster response; climate modeling, wildfire detection, biodiversity impacts).

AI driven disaster prediction models rely on several key elements including techniques, analysis, estimation and detection. These AI-powered predictive models are data driven, it allows the system to analyze and learn from data as such real time data (weather station, seismic sensors, satellite monitoring); satellite imagery (weather patterns, land movement, terrain and warning sign detection; sensor networks (seismic sensors for earthquakes, temperature sensors for wildfires); social media and public data (Twitter, Facebook and public databases) (Clement, 2024).

2.5 Generative AI in Emergency Communication

The use of generative artificial intelligence (AI) models like Chat GPT marks a major step forward in helping societies adapt to and succeed in the face of different challenges (Paramesha et al., 2024). In disaster response and preparedness, Chat GPT assist with communication, support policy development and provides data analysis that enhance decision making and preparedness. In addition, Chat GPT offers solutions for risk assessment, ongoing learning in every phase of emergency management cycle, and therefore, enhancing organizational capabilities in threat detection and incident management. In fact, integrating generative AI models, particularly Chat GPT in disaster management is critically important on how community may adapt and survive the aftermath of disasters. These Chat GPT applications such as tracking, mapping, geospatial analysis, remote sensing techniques, robotics, drone technology, learning and environmental impact analysis that drive the outcomes in disaster management (Abid & Sulaiman, 2025).

These AI-driven applications help communities adapt more effectively and recover more quickly from disasters. For example, Rane et al. (2024) demonstrate how ChatGPT can analyze vast datasets related to climate change, supporting environmental risk assessment and planning. Rane and his colleagues note that

AI-driven strategies play pivotal role in developing robust infrastructure, improving disaster response and promoting climate resilience. AI-driven models also can also process extensive climate data to detect patterns and forecast climate scenarios for extreme weather events such as hurricanes, floods and droughts. Building on this, Xue et al. (2023) highlight ChatGPT's ability to interpret complex information and assist in developing accurate climate models including tools that are essential for scientists and policymakers engaged in mitigation strategy design. In this regard, Xue et al. (2023) state that Chat GPT can provide a wealth of information about natural hazards where users can interact with Chat GPT to obtain the necessary knowledge, understanding disasters' causes, characteristics, impacts and response measures.

ChatGPT can facilitate this by generating interactive and user-friendly interfaces tailored to stakeholders, policymakers, and the general public. Chat GPT can provide instant responses to users queries even without internet coverage. In disasters, users using Chat GPT can swiftly access relevant disaster knowledge and guidance. In addition, Chat GPT can help users provide information on natural disaster early warning systems and monitoring technologies (Xue et al., 2023).

The use of AI-powered chatbots in disaster management has gained increasing attention for their ability to bridge communication gaps and enable rapid information dissemination, particularly in high-risk regions prone to natural hazards (Wickramasinghe et al., 2024). These chatbots provide a streamlined and accessible platform for delivering critical updates and guidance to the public, enhancing situational awareness and supporting key functions in disaster preparedness, response, and mitigation and recovery. By offering real-time, user-friendly interactions, Chabots serve as valuable tools in improving public engagement and institutional coordination during emergencies. AI-driven chatbots powered by natural language processing facilitate real-time communication between disaster-affected individuals and emergency responders, providing timely assistance and disseminating critical information (Rehan, 2022).

For instance, Chatbots enable users to communicate and interact with software applications that use AI-based tools (Almalki & Azeez, 2020). These applications can be accessed via a website or social media messaging platforms such as What's App and Facebook. In Covid-19 response, Chatbot are used to exchange knowledge, disseminate news and findings and converse with people with different language via voice or text. For example, California's Ask CAL FIRE chatbot provides quick, reliable answers to frequently asked questions by drawing from information already available on the CAL FIRE website. It also guides users to relevant resources and delivers real-time updates in multiple languages, helping connect Californians with essential information during emergencies (News, 2025).

3 Impact of AI Application in Emergency Management

3.1 Internal Impact of AI: Reducing Administrative Burden

AI-based chatbot can assist with easing the burden incurred on tribal citizens and emergency managers in documenting and reporting damages through effective communication and real-time data storage. (Tsai et al., 2023). AI-chatbot application can assist with image storing and information; while it leads emergency managers to file reports and prioritize work based on needs, it also unable people to report damage through text and document events with photos rather calling. In hazard mitigation efforts, FEMA develops AI-powered chatbot that utilizes Natural language Processing (NLP) to reduce burdens in accessing and processing vast amounts of information related to application and grants. The use of AI-chatbot assists with new hire onboarding, reducing time to full productivity, reducing errors, enhancing decision mailing by providing real time data and improving program outcomes (FEMA, 2024).

In public health emergency, AI chatbots has two folds to reduce burden overload; (1) It serves a frontline communication platform offering real time answers to citizens questions about symptoms, preventive measures and state and local health laws. (2) it alleviates public anxiety and promote adherence to health protocols that help curb the spread of infectious diseases (Branda et al., 2025). Additionally, AI-chatbot serve the purpose of sorting requests and proving initial guidance, reduce the burdens on health providers, and help with data collection and analysis when resources are limited in the health system.

- **Clara Chatbot** as developed by the Red cross, uses Natural Language Processing (NLP) to process language data and answer questions about local shelter, financial assistance, volunteering.
- **The Hazard Mitigation Assistance (HMA)** chatbot is used for internal stakeholders navigating HMA grant applications with Benefits-Cost Analysis) assistance, project scooping and feasibility support.
- **OMDENA Chatbot** used as an AI-driven disaster relief chatbot that provides real time, accurate information to disaster- affected persons. It includes data gathering, Natural Language Processing (NLP), AI integration, testing and validation.

AI-powered system through early warning systems allows for the timely dissemination of emergency alerts, facilitating prompt evaluation and resource mobilization, thereby reducing human and economic losses that incurred on people (Hasanuzzaman et al., 2023). During disaster events, integrating AI into resilience planning strengthens an organization's ability to endure disruptions and maintain performance. The AI-powered technology also helps maintain psychological interventions that are crucial for sustaining mental health and enable people to navigate stress, hardship, and trauma effectively.

By analyzing behavioral patterns related to stress and mental health issues, AI-driven systems can detect early signs of emotional distress, offer tailored guidance, and help users access suitable mental health resources. In this emergency, AI also assists professionals by generating insights, handling administrative duties, and supporting telehealth services. Moreover, AI-powered applications encourage self-care routines mindfulness practices, and stress reduction, thereby reinforcing individual mental well-being and resilience (Rane et al., 2024).

3.2 External Impact of AI: Reducing Burden on Affected Populations

In various natural disasters, effective delivery of messages and data collection is enhanced through AI-driven techniques such natural Language Processing (NLP) and AI-chatbot and other automated messaging systems that answer frequently asked questions and provide information to disasters victims and provide relief on human responders (Skillfloor, 2023). In disaster management, the emergence of AI-chat bots presents opportunities that help disaster victims to file for public assistance from the Federal Emergency Management Agency), and assist with easing paperwork and documentation (Tsai et al., 2023). For example, in California wildfire, Chat bot allows first responders to integrate inputs from multiple sources. This data input allows responders to share information to residents and aids decision to reduce the noise of irrelevant information.

AI chatbots play a vital role in disseminating critical information by providing real-time updates and detailed guidance during emergencies. This capability ensures that the public remains informed about rapidly evolving situations. During the COVID-19 pandemic, AI chatbots proved particularly valuable by delivering accurate information, addressing frequently asked questions, and significantly reducing the burden on healthcare and communication teams. By streamlining communication, these systems enable the efficient distribution of verified emergency information while allowing human responders to focus on more complex and high-priority tasks (Sandeep, 2024). For instance, California debuts AI chatbot to deliver information on several languages. This new Chabot enable to deliver real time information and critical wildfire information around the clock (Jose, 2025).

4 AI-Based Challenges and Ethical Consideration

Despite substantial benefits, AI implementation faces significant challenges (Hanwacker, 2025). These challenges include ethical considerations surrounding privacy and decision-making, technical limitations that may affect the reliability and effectiveness of AI systems (Engima Advisory, 2025). Despite notable advancements, the application of AI in disaster management continues to face several persistent challenges. These include inconsistent data formats, algorithmic bias, and ethical concerns related to data privacy and the equitable distribution of resources. Hasanuzzaman et al. (2023) emphasize that addressing these issues requires a multidisciplinary approach, incorporating insights from computer science, environmental science, and emergency management to guide responsible AI integration.

A major challenge in applying AI to disaster management is the limited quality and quantity of data, which hampers model training and accurate predictions (Ozyer et al., 2019). Despite significant advances, AI implementation still faces issues such as inconsistent data formats, algorithmic biases, and ethical concerns around privacy and equitable resource distribution (Hasanuzzaman et al., 2023). Addressing these challenges requires a multidisciplinary approach that combines computer science, environmental science, and emergency management expertise. Persistent obstacles include poor data quality, low transparency of AI models, inherent biases, and ethical dilemmas, underscoring the need for a workforce skilled in responsible AI use (Hosseini et al., 2021). Additional concerns involve overreliance on historical data, unpredictable human responses to AI interventions, cybersecurity risks, unintended negative impacts, and difficulties in evaluating AI effectiveness (Nishant et al., 2020).

AI-powered systems offer significant potential to improve disaster risk management by enhancing forecasting and streamlining response strategies. However, their implementation is challenged by the need for high-quality, diverse data and seamless integration with existing technologies. Velev and Zlateva (2023) highlight the technical and infrastructural hurdles that impede effective deployment, while Visave (2024) emphasizes the ethical complexities such as ensuring equitable resource distribution, protecting data privacy, and promoting transparent, accountable decision-making. Addressing these challenges requires sustained innovation, cross-sector collaboration, and the development of ethical frameworks that guide responsible AI use in crisis settings. Although challenges persist, the advantages of using AI in disaster risk management are substantial and cannot be overlooked. Addressing these obstacles will require dedicated investment in research, technological innovation, and strong collaboration among key stakeholders to fully harness AI's capabilities in enhancing disaster preparedness and response (Velev & Zlateva, 2023).

5 Case Studies

5.1 AI Application in California Wildfire Management

In recent years, the frequency and intensity of wildfires have been growing across the United States. Additionally, fire-related threat is increasing as more people live near forests, grasslands and other natural areas. According to the National Oceanic and Atmospheric Administration (NOAA), from 1980 to 2023, the United States experienced 22 wildfire events that each caused over $1 billion in damages, with 18 of those occurring after 2000. In recent decades, the U.S. has consistently spent more than $1 billion annually on wildfire suppression, reaching $3.5 billion in 2022 alone (EPA, 2025). Moreover, the growing intensity and recurrence of wildfires present serious risks to natural ecosystems, human safety, and infrastructure. Accurately forecasting wildfire behavior is now crucial for developing effective prevention and response strategies (Calderer, 2024). There is an urgent demand for innovative wildfire forecasting and alert systems that can support more effective fire control, risk reduction, and evacuation planning (Huot et al., 2022).

In recent years, the growing frequency and severity of wildfires has underscored the urgent need to integrate artificial intelligence (AI) into disaster management. AI technologies now play a critical role in assessing post-wildfire damage and enhancing early detection and response efforts (Galanis et al., 2021). Since the 1990s, AI has been applied in wildfire science, initially through neural networks and expert systems (Jain et al., 2020). Contemporary wildfire management research focuses on three key areas: (1) image and video-based detection, (2) wildfire behavior forecasting, and (3) susceptibility assessment (Jain et al., 2020; Walters, 2022). These AI models leverage data from weather conditions, vegetation, satellite imagery, and historical fire patterns. Common techniques include Support Vector Machines (SVM), Basic Neural Networks (BNN), Recurrent Neural Networks (RNN), Long Short-Term Memory (LSTM) networks, and Convolutional Neural Networks (CNN) (Walters, 2022).

Artificial intelligence has transformed wildfire prediction by facilitating real-time, data-driven risk assessments. Through machine learning algorithms, AI-based predictive analytics can process large volumes of meteorological, topographic, and vegetation data to generate more precise and timely forecasts. Unlike conventional models, AI systems continuously improve by incorporating real-time satellite images, climate indicators, and historical fire data to identify potential wildfire threats before they intensify (George & Ayiku, 2024). Therefore, incorporating artificial intelligence into fire risk indices greatly improves their precision and flexibility, supporting more informed decision-making in wildfire management. For instance, AI-generative application enables researchers collected historical wildfire data using high-resolution satellite imagery to analyze how wildfires start, spread, and are eventually contained. Their detailed examination uncovered key patterns shaped by variables such as weather conditions, available fuel (like trees and brush), and the landscape. To model these dynamics, they trained a generative AI system called a conditional Wasserstein Generative Adversarial Network (cWGAN). This model learned to simulate wildfire progression by identifying visual patterns in satellite images that correspond to real-world fire behavior (Raffio, 2024).

In sum, AI technologies are revolutionizing wildfire management by harnessing data from drones, satellites, sensors, and weather models (Third Eye, 2025). These advanced systems enhance early detection, response, and prevention through several key capabilities:

- **Predictive Analytics**: AI analyzes weather, vegetation, and historical fire data to forecast high-risk zones.

- **Computer Vision**: Drone and satellite imagery help detect hazards like downed power lines or overgrown vegetation.
- **Real-Time Monitoring**: IoT sensors track temperature, smoke, and fire outbreaks to enable rapid response.

A variety of artificial intelligence (AI) and machine learning (ML) models have been developed and trained to detect and predict wildfires by analyzing key factors such as weather conditions, vegetation, and topography. AI-driven tools offer early warning capabilities that help facilitate timely evacuations and efficient allocation of resources, thereby, lessening the effects of wildfires on communities and natural environments. As AI technology evolves, its contribution to wildfire prediction is expected to play an increasingly critical role in addressing the rising danger of uncontrolled fires (George & Ayiku, 2024).

Various AI and machine learning models have been developed to detect and predict wildfires using different approaches. First, wildfire occurrence prediction relies on analyzing weather signals and thermal data such as temperature, humidity, and air pressure differentials to estimate fire likelihood (Mani, 2024). Tools like the Visible Infrared Imaging Radiometer Suite (VIIRS) and the Moderate Resolution Imaging Spectroradiometer (MODIS) support these predictions. VIIRS captures both visible and infrared data on aerosols, fire, smoke plumes, and chlorophyll, aiding fire detection and pollution monitoring. MODIS identifies biomass burning and tracks aerosol properties linked to dust storms and fire activity. Second, wildfire detection involves AI-enabled camera systems that examine imagery for visual signs like smoke and heat shimmer, while remote sensors detect heat, smoke, humidity, and gases trained to distinguish wildfires from sources such as campfires or construction dust. Third, wildfire mapping uses AI-driven satellite data to model the trajectory, speed, and spread of ongoing fires. Generative AI models are trained to recognize the fire triangle and detect behavioral patterns in satellite images, enhancing the accuracy of fire forecasting (Mani, 2024).

In California, AI-powered chatbots are being used to enhance public access to emergency information and resources. The California Department of Forestry and Fire Protection (CAL FIRE) has launched *Ask CAL FIRE*, a multilingual chatbot that delivers real-time fire prevention guidance and emergency support in over 70 languages (Hughes, 2025). Drawing from the CAL FIRE website, the chatbot provides quick, reliable answers to frequently asked questions and directs users to relevant resources for more detailed information. Additionally, it serves as a two-way communication tool, offering CAL FIRE valuable insights into the public's most pressing concerns during emergencies (News, 2025).

6 Does AI Live up to Its Potential? AI Applications in the COVID-19 Pandemic

A novel coronavirus (COVID-19) disrupted the world in early 2019, triggering a major public health crisis due to its high transmissibility and extended incubation period. The impact of the pandemic has been profound, with over 770 million confirmed cases and approximately 7.8 million deaths worldwide (World Health Organization, 2025). In response, policymakers and governments implemented population-level interventions such as travel bans, mask mandates, school and business closures, and stay-at-home orders (Syrowatka et al., 2021). Concurrently, unprecedented global data-sharing efforts enabled the use of artificial intelligence (AI) as a vital tool in managing the crisis, ranging from early detection in at-risk patients to virtual support via AI-powered chatbots (Srivastava, 2021).

While no universally accepted definition exists, this chapter adopts the OECD's (2019) definition of AI as "a machine-based system that can, for a given set of human-defined objectives, make predictions, recommendations, or decisions influencing real or virtual environments." During the COVID-19 pandemic, AI applications broadly fell into two categories: (1) predictive models to support decision-making and (2) generative models such as transformers and diffusion models and also for producing text, images, audio, or video (Hermann & Puntoni, 2024). AI significantly reshaped healthcare delivery, improved response coordination, and enhanced public communication (Ding et al., 2025). By mid-2020, China had integrated AI into diagnostic imaging, patient monitoring, data systems, and predictive analytics. Notably, Alibaba and Baidu employed machine learning, computer vision, and thermal imaging to streamline CT-scan interpretation and fever detection in public spaces (Ding et al., 2025). Globally, the most widespread use of predictive AI involved triaging and diagnosing symptomatic individuals. Studies demonstrated how convolutional neural networks (CNNs) were applied to open-access chest imaging for classifying COVID-19, distinguishing it from other infections, and estimating severity (Syrowatka et al., 2021).

On the generative AI front, the unprecedented surges in online inquiries and service requests from citizens facilitate the staggered rollout of AI-powered chatbots, capable of delivering automated, human-like support in a 24/7 environment (Glasscock, 2020; Srivastava, 2021). During the height of the pandemic, the Texas Workforce Commission (TWC) received up to 98,000 online unemployment claims in a single day, equivalent to three and a half years' worth of claims processed in just 56 days. The deployment of "Larry the Chatbot" on TWC's website enabled the rapid handling of 4.8 million queries from 1.2 million users within four days, vastly outpacing traditional staffing and call-center capacities (Glasscock, 2020).

6.1 Challenges and Limitations of COVID-19 AI Solutions

Despite widespread deployment of predictive AI algorithms in clinical settings, their validity and accuracy remain questionable. Delgado et al. (2022), in a systematic review of 20 studies, further identified four principal sources of bias in AI algorithms used for triage and digital contact tracing (DCT): (1) racial disparities, (2) biased data, (3) socioeconomic disparities, and (4) unequal accessibility. Indeed, racial disparities introduce bias because Black and Latinx communities experienced disproportionately severe COVID-19 outcomes, driven by historic health inequities, environmental exposures, and front-line occupations (Smith & Rustagi, 2020). AI systems trained on large datasets often inherit social and cultural biases: marginalized groups may be under-represented or misrepresented, resulting in inaccurate predictions and reinforcement of stereotypes (Smith & Rustagi, 2020). In the context of DCT, the efficacy of exposure notifications depends heavily on individuals' financial capacity to self-quarantine, thereby exacerbating socioeconomic inequities (Moss & Metcalf, 2020). Moreover, AI-based solutions require broad public access; "digital deserts" or regions of data poverty undermine voluntary adoption and systematic use of DCT applications (Roche, 2020).

The rollout of generative-AI chatbots and online symptom checkers has also drawn criticism for implicit biases, privacy infringements, safety risks, abusive language, and the spread of misinformation (Meyrowitsch et al., 2023; Ross, 2020). Perhaps, most concerning is the inconsistency of medical advice. Ross (2020) queried eight different chatbots about common symptoms such as fever, sore throat, runny nose and received widely divergent recommendations, ranging from immediate home isolation for high COVID-19 risk to assessments of medium or low risk. For instance, the Centers for Disease Control's own chatbot advised contacting a healthcare provider within 24 h and beginning immediate self-isolation, whereas the Cleveland Clinic's chatbot, allegedly based on the same CDC guidelines, assessed the symptoms as medium risk. Buoy Health's symptom checker then contradicted both by suggesting a low risk of infection. Such variability and the challenge of validating chatbot outputs raises serious concerns about their clinical efficacy and suggests that some government agencies may have outpaced the technology's readiness in an effort to deploy AI tools rapidly during the pandemic.

7 Recommendations for Ethical and Effective AI Integration

The use of AI in pandemic response holds great promise but also presents significant risks. To ensure ethical and effective integration, leaders across sectors must be deliberate at every stage—design, development, deployment, maintenance, and regulation. Key recommendations include:

1. **Build AI systems on a more comprehensive datasets**

The accuracy and fairness of AI systems rely on diverse, representative datasets. Global data-sharing initiatives that include traditional health records and non-traditional sources like smartphone mobility data can help mitigate bias (Delgado et al., 2022).

2. **Promote Transparency in AI**

Open-source AI models and transparent reporting are essential for public trust. Regulatory frameworks should require disclosure of algorithms, data sources, and performance metrics to identify hidden biases and improve reliability (Smith & Rustagi, 2020).

3. **Foster Cross-Sector Collaboration**

Ethical AI deployment depends on coordination among researchers, clinicians, policymakers, and communities. Each group brings critical insights to align AI tools with ethical standards and public needs (Smith & Rustagi, 2020).

4. **Develop Clear Regulatory guidance**

Policymakers must define guidelines throughout the AI lifecycle. For example, frameworks like Chatbot RESET can help ensure privacy, safety, and fairness in the deployment of healthcare chatbots (Srivastava, 2021).

7.1 Discussion and Analysis

The examination of AI applications during California wildfire management and COVID-19 pandemic reveal both the promise and limitations of AI in complex in crisis response particularly in improving decision-making, situational awareness, and response efficiency. In the COVID-19 Context, AI supported outbreak prediction, contact tracing, and resource allocation, yet its impact was limited by data quality issues, lack of transparency, and poor integration with public health systems. Ethical concerns around privacy and equity further hindered widespread adoption, underscoring the need for trust, transparency, and robust data governance (Srivastava, 2021). Additionally, in rapidly evolving situations such as those involving mutating viruses like COVID-19, the data used to train AI models can become outdated quickly, diminishing their effectiveness (Balasubramanian et al., 2025). To address this, it is essential to develop robust, pre-trained, and cross-validated models that can maintain accuracy and adaptability over time.

Insights from both contexts suggest that AI delivers the greatest value when embedded within collaborative frameworks that amplify human expertise rather than replace it (Yin et al., 2022). However, this also requires sustained investment in technological development, cross-sector coordination, and capacity-building efforts. For example, in the pandemic context, Majeed and Hwang (2021) argue for the expansion of AI applications beyond real-time outbreak management to include broader functions across the data lifecycle such as data collection, pre-processing, storage, archiving, and deletion as well as roles in drug discovery, vaccine development, and epidemic containment strategies. In the context of California wildfire, AI presents a promising solution by continuously monitoring expansive areas, analyzing real-time data for early indicators of fire, and notifying human operators when a threat is identified. This approach not only accelerates response efforts but also utilizes historical data to improve both accuracy and dependability. While the advantages of using AI for wildfire detection are clear, it is crucial to deploy these technologies under proper oversight. Achieving transparency, accountability, and effectiveness in AI systems demands a well-structured framework that strikes a balance between encouraging innovation and enforcing responsible regulation (Griffin, 2024).

Equally important, the AI application in disaster management demonstrates a high degree of generalizability beyond its current use in Southern California. AI use can be extended far beyond California Wildfires to be applicable to forecasting, hurricane tracking, and earthquake response by analyzing varied environmental data.

8 Conclusion

As the frequency, scale, and complexity of disasters continue to rise, the integration of Artificial Intelligence (AI) across all phases of disaster management has emerged as both a practical necessity and a transformative opportunity. The inclusion of AI-capabilities such predictive analytics and generative AI can enhance disaster preparedness and response efforts (Sun et al., 2020). Additionally, AI-driven technologies such as machine learning and natural language processing offer essential tools for hazard detection, risk mapping, and rapid damage assessment (Velev & Zlateva, 2023). As a result, capabilities like predictive analytics, machine learning, and natural language processing are no longer supplementary, they are becoming core components of the emergency management cycle, including preparedness, response, mitigation, and recovery (Sun et al., 2020). Despite AI's technical potential in disaster management, its effectiveness relies on more than advanced algorithms, ethical concerns such as data privacy, accountability, transparency, and algorithmic bias must be carefully addressed. These challenges are further exacerbated by unequal access to AI-generated insights among stakeholders (Yin et al., 2022). Therefore, AI development and deployment should occur within collaborative frameworks that actively involve emergency responders, government agencies, and other key actors.

The cases of California wildfire management and the COVID-19 pandemic highlight both the practical benefits and persistent challenges of implementing AI in disaster response. AI-driven tools such as satellite imagery, environmental sensors, and real-time data streams have improved wildfire detection and monitoring.

During the COVID-19 pandemic, AI enhanced public assistance and decision-making through predictive analytics and data integration. Overall, AI-assisted analysis and chatbot-powered systems provided scalable solutions to healthcare demands and emergency response.

References

Abid, S. K., Sulaiman, N., Chan, S. W., Nazir, U., Abid, M., Han, H., & Vega-Muñoz, A. (2021). Toward an integrated disaster management approach: How artificial intelligence can boost disaster management. *Sustainability, 13*(22), 12560.

Abid, S. K., & Sulaiman, N. (2025). Revolutionizing the future: unleashing the potential of generative AI ChatGPT in disaster management. *Environmental Science and Pollution Research*, 1–16.

Agoro, H., & Adams, P. (2025). Enhancing emergency response systems with AI and predictive analytics.

Almalki, M., & Azeez, F. (2020). Health chatbots for fighting COVID-19: A scoping review. *Acta Informatica Medica, 28*(4), 241.

Al Marzooqi, M. (2024). The contribution of artificial intelligence (AI) to disaster response and management. Anglia Ruskin Research Online (ARRO).

Balasubramanian, S., Shukla, V., Islam, N., Upadhyay, A., & Duong, L. (2025). Applying artificial intelligence in healthcare: Lessons from the COVID-19 pandemic. *International Journal of Production Research, 63*(2), 594–627.

Branda, F., Stella, M., Ceccarelli, C., Cabitza, F., Ceccarelli, G., Maruotti, A., & Scarpa, F. (2025). The role of AI-based Chatbots in public health emergencies: A narrative review. *Future Internet, 17*(4), 145.

Calderer, P. I. (2024). *Predicting California wildfire spread with time-series and spatial-temporal models* [Master's thesis, Universitat Politècnica de Catalunya].

Cate, M. (2022). *AI applications in emergency response coordination.*

Chew, Y. J., Ooi, S. Y., & Pang, Y. H. (2025). AI in disaster monitoring and early warning systems. In *The smart life revolution: Embracing AI and IoT in society* (p. 83).

Cheye, S., Adewale, A. A., & Ademola, O. M. (2024). Harnessing Artificial Intelligence for climate resilience: Analyzing the impact of climate change on sea level rise and precipitation patterns. *International Journal of Research Publication and Reviews.*

Chun, J., & Elkins, K. (2023). The crisis of artificial intelligence: A new digital humanity curriculum for human-Centered AI. *International Journal of Humanities and Arts Computing, 17*(2), 147–167.

Clement, M. (2024). AI-driven predictive analytics in disaster management: Advancements and challenges.

Delgado, J., de Manuel, A., Parra, I., Moyano, C., Rueda, J., Guersenzvaig, A., & Puyol, A. (2022). Bias in algorithms of AI systems developed for COVID-19: A scoping review. *Journal of Bioethical Inquiry, 19*(3), 407–419.

Dineva, S. (2023). Applying artificial intelligence (AI) for mitigation climate change consequences of the natural disasters. *Research Journal of Ecology and Environmental Sciences, 3*(1), 1–8. https://www.scipublications.com/journal/index.php/rjees/article/view/343

Ding, X., Shang, B., Xie, C., Xin, J., & Yu, F. (2025). Artificial intelligence in the COVID-19 pandemic: Balancing benefits and ethical challenges in China's response. *Humanities and Social Sciences Communications, 12*(1), 1–19. https://doi.org/10.1057/s41599-025-04564-x

Domínguez, C., & Beltran, M. (2025). AI-powered predictive analytics for disaster response in smart cities. *International Journal of Emerging Trends and Innovation (IJETI), 1*(1), 10–21.

Engima Advisory. (2025). *From chaos to control: How AI is revolutionizing emergency response.* https://enigma-advisory.com/the-role-of-ai-in-disaster-management/

EPA. (2025). Climate change indicators: Wildfires. *EPA*. https://www.epa.gov/climate-indicators/climate-change-indicators-wildfires#ref6

FEMA. (2024). Federal Emergency Management Agency—AI use cases. Homeland Security.

Jakaza, E., Mangeya, H., & Mhute, I. (Eds.). (2024). *The Palgrave handbook of language and crisis communication in sub-Saharan Africa*. Springer Nature.

Jain, P., Coogan, S. C., Subramanian, S. G., Crowley, M., Taylor, S., & Flannigan, M. D. (2020). A review of machine learning applications in wildfire science and management. *Environmental Reviews, 28*(4), 478–505.

Jose, J. (2025). New AI Chatbot helps Californian access wildfire information effortlessly. https://keyt.com/cnn-regional/2025/05/16/new-ai-chatbot-helps-californians-access-wildfire-information-effortlessly/

Hanwacker, L. S. (2025). The role of artificial intelligence in disaster recovery. *Journal of Business Continuity & Emergency Planning, 18*(2), 167–179.

Hasanuzzaman, M., Hossain, S., & Shil, S. K. (2023). Enhancing disaster management through AI-driven predictive analytics: Improving preparedness and response. *International Journal of Advanced Engineering Technologies and Innovations, 1*(1), 533–562.

Hawley, E. O. (2025). How U.S. military AI can mitigate California's wildfire crisis. *Defense opinion.* https://defenseopinion.com/how-u-s-military-ai-can-mitigate-californias-wildfire-crisis/809/

Hermann, E., & Puntoni, S. (2024). Artificial intelligence and consumer behavior: From predictive to generative AI. *Journal of Business Research, 180*, Article 114720. https://doi.org/10.1016/j.jbusres.2024.114720

Hosseini, S. H., Khodabin, M., Soroori Sarabi, A., & Sharifipour Bgheshmi, M. S. (2021). Artificial intelligence and disaster risk management: A need for continuous education. *Socio-Spatial Studies, 5*(1), 13–29.

Hughes, L. (2025). AI Chatbot launched to help residents during California wildfires. *AI Business.* https://aibusiness.com/nlp/ai-chatbot-launched-to-help-residents-during-california-wildfires#close-modal

Huot, F., Hu, R. L., Goyal, N., Sankar, T., Ihme, M., & Chen, Y. F. (2022). Next day wildfire spread: A machine learning dataset to predict wildfire spreading from remote-sensing data. *IEEE Transactions on Geoscience and Remote Sensing, 60*, 1–13.

Galanis, M., Rao, K., Yao, X., Tsai, Y. L., Ventura, J., & Fricker, G. A. (2021). Damage Map: A post-wildfire damaged buildings classifier. *International Journal of Disaster Risk Reduction, 65*, Article 102540.

Glasscock, A. (2020, June 24). Chat with us: How states are using Chatbots to respond to the demands of COVID-19. *NASCIO*. https://www.nascio.org/resource-center/resources/chat-with-us-how-states-are-using-chatbots-to-respond-to-the-demands-of-covid-19

George, M. B., & Ayiku, E. O. (2024). AI-driven fire risk indices integrating climate, fuel, and terrain for wildfire prediction and management. *International Journal of Engineering Technology Research and Management, 8*(2), 67.

Griffin, S. (2024). Artificial Intelligence can be our first line of defense in limiting the effects of wildfires. Mountain Sates Policy Center.

Khan, S. M., Shafi, I., Butt, W. H., Diez, I. D. L. T., Flores, M. A. L., Galán, J. C., & Ashraf, I. (2023). A systematic review of disaster management systems: Approaches, challenges, and future directions. *Land, 12*(8), 1514.

Kuglitsch, M. M., Pelivan, I., Ceola, S., Menon, M., & Xoplaki, E. (2022). Facilitating adoption of AI in natural disaster management through collaboration. *Nature Communications, 13*, 1579.

Lakum, S. (2024). AI-enhanced disaster recovery: A collaborative approach. *International Journal of Research in Computer Applications and Information Technology, 7*(2), 2419–2429.

Majeed, A., & Hwang, S. O. (2021). Data-driven analytics leveraging artificial intelligence in the era of COVID-19: An insightful review of recent developments. *Symmetry, 14*(1), 16.

Mani, E. (2024). The role of AI in wildfire risk prediction, mitigation, and management. *HTR.* https://harvardtechnologyreview.com/2024/09/15/the-role-of-ai-in-wildfire-risk-prediction-mitigation-and-management/

Markezinis, G. (2024). AI in disaster management: Transforming crisis response and resilience. *Eco skills*. https://ecoskills.academy/ai-in-disaster-managementtransforming-resilience/
Meyrowitsch, D. W., Jensen, A. K., Sørensen, J. B., & Varga, T. V. (2023). AI chatbots and (mis)information in public health: Impact on vulnerable communities. *Frontiers in Public Health, 11*, 1226776. https://doi.org/10.3389/fpubh.2023.1226776
Mikhaylov, S. J., Esteve, M., & Campion, A. (2018). Artificial intelligence for the public sector: Opportunities and challenges of cross-sector collaboration. *Philosophical Transactions of the Royal Society a: Mathematical, Physical and Engineering Sciences, 376*(2128), 20170357.
Moss, E., & Metcalf, J. (2020). High tech, high risk: Tech ethics lessons for the COVID-19 pandemic response. *Patterns, 1*(7). https://www.cell.com/patterns/fulltext/S2666-3899(20)30136-7
News. (2025). California launches new AI-powered chatbot that provides wildfire resources in 70 languages. https://www.gov.ca.gov/2025/05/09/california-launches-new-ai-powered-chatbot-that-provides-wildfire-resources-in-70-languages/
Nishant, R., Kennedy, M., & Corbett, J. (2020). Artificial intelligence for sustainability: Challenges, opportunities, and a research agenda. *International Journal of Information Management, 53*, Article 102104.
OECD. (2019). Recommendation of the council on Artificial Intelligence. https://legalinstruments.oecd.org/en/instruments/OECD-LEGAL-044
Ortiz, B., Kahn, L., Bosch, M., Bogden, P., Pavon-Harr, V., Savas, O., & McCulloh, I. (2020). Improving community resiliency and emergency response with artificial intelligence. arXiv preprint arXiv:2005.14212
Ozyer, T., Bakshi, S., & Alhajj. R. (Eds.). (2019). *Social networks and surveillance for society*. Springer.
Paramesha, M., Rane, N., & Rane, J. (2024). Enhancing resilience through generative artificial intelligence such as ChatGPT. Available at SSRN 4832533.
Roche, S. (2020). Smile, you're being traced! Some thoughts about the ethical issues of digital contact tracing applications. *Journal of Location Based Services, 14*(2), 71–91. https://doi.org/10.1080/17489725.2020.1811409
Robertson, T. V. (2020). Applying Artificial Intelligence to emergency and disaster management. In *Proceedings of the TIEMS annual conference.*
Rehan, H. (2022). Enhancing disaster response systems: Predicting and mitigating the impact of natural disasters using AI. *Journal of Artificial Intelligence Research, 2*(1), 501.
Rane, N., Choudhary, S., & Rane, J. (2024). Artificial intelligence for enhancing resilience. *Journal of Applied Artificial Intelligence, 5*(2), 1–33.
Raffio, N. (2024). USC scientists use AI to predict a wildfire's next move, Science/Technology. https://today.usc.edu/using-ai-to-predict-wildfires/
Ross, C. (2020). I asked eight chatbots whether I had Covid-19. The answers ranged from "low" risk to "start home isolation." *STAT*. https://www.statnews.com/2020/03/23/coronavirus-i-asked-eight-chatbots-whether-i-had-covid-19/
Sandeep. (2024). How AI can assist in emergency communication. https://fastbots.ai/blog/how-ai-can-assist-in-emergency-communication
Saravi, S., Kalawsky, R., Joannou, D., Rivas Casado, M., Fu, G., & Meng, F. (2019). Use of artificial intelligence to improve resilience and preparedness against adverse flood events. *Water, 11*(5), 973.
Şengöz, M. (2024). Harnessing Artificial Intelligence and Big Data for proactive disaster management: Strategies, challenges, and future directions. *Haliç Üniversitesi Fen Bilimleri Dergisi, 7*(2), 57–91.
Skillfloor. (2023). The role of AI in disaster management and human aid, medium. https://skillfloor.medium.com/the-role-of-ai-in-disaster-management-and-humanitarian-aid-30fd52c57f15
Smith, G., & Rustagi, I. (2020). The problem with COVID-19 artificial intelligence solutions and how to fix them. https://ssir.org/articles/entry/the_problem_with_covid_19_artificial_intelligence_solutions_and_how_to_fix_them

Srivastava, B. (2021). Did chatbots miss their "Apollo Moment"? Potential, gaps, and lessons from using collaboration assistants during COVID-19. *Patterns, 2*(8), Article 100308. https://doi.org/10.1016/j.patter.2021.100308

Syrowatka, A., Kuznetsova, M., Alsubai, A., Beckman, A. L., Bain, P. A., Craig, K. J. T., Hu, J., Jackson, G. P., Rhee, K., & Bates, D. W. (2021). Leveraging artificial intelligence for pandemic preparedness and response: A scoping review to identify key use cases. *NPJ Digital Medicine, 4*(1), 1–14. https://doi.org/10.1038/s41746-021-00459-8

Sun, W., Bocchini, P., & Davison, B. D. (2020). Applications of artificial intelligence for disaster management. *Natural Hazards, 103*(3), 2631–2689.

Third Eye. (2025). The growing threat of wildfires. https://thirdeyedata.ai/how-ai-can-prevent-devastation-like-the-recent-Los-Angeles-wildfires/

Tsai, C. H., Rayi, P., Kadire, S., Khan, Y. F., Krafka, S., Zendejas, E., & Chen, Y. C. (2023). Co-design disaster management Chatbot with indigenous communities. In *20th international conference on information systems for crisis response and management* (vol. 1).

Velev, D., & Zlateva, P. (2023). Challenges of artificial intelligence application for disaster risk management. *The International Archives of the Photogrammetry, Remote Sensing and Spatial Information Sciences, 48*, 387–394.

Vyas, R., Agrawal, V., Verma, D. R., & Patel, P. (2025). AI to the rescue: Revolutionizing post-disaster recovery systems. In *Proceedings of international conference on artificial intelligence for innovations in healthcare industries* (pp. 190, 235). *Springer Nature*

Visave, J. (2024). AI in emergency management: Ethical considerations and challenges. *Journal of Emergency Management and Disaster Communications, 5*, 165–183.

Visave, J. (2025). Transparency in AI for emergency management: Building trust and accountability. *AI and Ethics*, 1–14.

Walters, M. (2022). Predicting the likelihood and scale of wildfires in California using meteorological and vegetation data. University of Arkansas.

Wickramasinghe, P., Akalanka, H. M. N., Jayaprakash, S., Chathuranga, U. D. S., & Munasinghe, D. S. (2024). Chatbot-assisted disaster preparedness: A tool for educating the public on landslide-resilient building practices. *National Building Research Organization, 14*, 978–624.

World Health Organization. (2025). COVID-19 cases | WHO COVID-19 dashboard. Datadot. https://data.who.int/dashboards/covid19/cases.

Xue, Z., Xu, C., & Xu, X. (2023). Application of ChatGPT in natural disaster prevention and reduction. *Natural Hazards Research, 3*(3), 556–562.

Yin, Y., Siau, K., Wen, X., & Yan, S. (2022). Smart health: Intelligent healthcare systems in the metaverse, artificial intelligence, and data science era. *Journal of Organizational and End User Computing, 34*(1), 1–14. https://doi.org/10.4018/JOEUC.308814

Yu, J., Ma, H., & Li, Y. (2024). The mechanisms of artificial intelligence impacting on the transformation of family systems: A perspective of complex adaptive systems theory. In *International conference on edge computing* (pp. 59–73). Springer Nature Switzerland.

Balancing AI Innovation and Integrity: Responsible Artificial Intelligence in Government and Its Implications

9

Stephen Kwamena Aikins and Tamara Dimitrijevska-Markoski

1 Introduction

Artificial intelligence (AI) is rapidly transforming public sector operations and governance frameworks across the globe. Governments are increasingly embracing AI technologies to enhance decision-making, streamline administrative processes, and deliver more efficient public services. However, this technological shift is not without significant implications, particularly concerning employment within the public sector. The rapid adoption of AI technologies presents numerous ethical challenges pertaining to accountability, transparency, and fairness. As AI systems become increasingly sophisticated, there is a growing concern about the displacement of human workers, raising critical questions about the responsible adoption of AI and effective workforce management.

The purpose of this chapter is to examine the responsible integration of AI in governmental settings and its implications, focusing on the ethical dimensions and global case studies, as well as the economic, social, and policy impacts. While AI has the potential to revolutionize governance through increased efficiency and data-driven decision-making, it simultaneously poses risks related to job displacement and ethical dilemmas. Governments worldwide are grappling with how to responsibly leverage AI while safeguarding human rights and maintaining public trust. Therefore, understanding how to balance innovation with responsible use is essential to ensuring that technological advancements do not come at the cost of public sector livelihoods.

S. K. Aikins (✉) · T. Dimitrijevska-Markoski
School of Public Affairs, University of South Florida, Tampa, FL, USA
e-mail: saikins@usf.edu

S. K. Aikins and T. Dimitrijevska-Markoski (eds.), *Artificial Intelligence and Government*, https://doi.org/10.1007/978-3-032-12344-2_9

The adoption of AI in public administration is reshaping governance structures and operational paradigms worldwide. From automating routine tasks to augmenting human decision-making, the integration of AI systems offers unprecedented efficiency. However, this transformation also necessitates careful consideration of ethical standards and societal, economic, and policy implications. Governments must not only leverage AI for operational enhancement but also ensure that its implementation aligns with public trust, transparency, and social equity.

This chapter argues that responsible AI adoption in government requires a comprehensive approach that addresses ethical, social, economic, and workforce-related impacts. Striking a balance between technological innovation and the preservation of public sector jobs is critical to maintaining societal stability and public confidence. Through a critical examination of current practices, policies, and frameworks, this chapter aims to provide insights into how governments can navigate the complex landscape of AI implementation while implementing evidence-based and inclusive policymaking that upholds public trust and ethical standards.

2 Ethical Dimensions of Responsible AI Use in Government

Responsible AI is a multi-dimensional concept that emphasizes the ethical and accountable application of AI technologies. The concept of responsible AI has evolved as AI technologies began playing significant roles in public decision-making, prompting concerns over potential biases, discrimination, and adverse societal impacts. To this end, responsible AI in governance implies leveraging technology in a manner that aligns with ethical standards, social justice, and human rights protection. The concept prioritizes aligning AI systems with societal values, fairness, and governance standards. Therefore, the core principles of responsible AI include transparency, accountability, fairness, and human oversight. This is because, despite its potential benefits, AI can exacerbate social inequalities and introduce biases if not appropriately managed. Based on the foregoing, the primary challenge lies in designing AI systems that are fair, transparent, and accountable.

Jobin et al. (2019) define responsible AI as the pursuit of integrating ethical considerations throughout the AI lifecycle, including data collection, algorithm design, deployment, and monitoring. They argue that responsible AI should be designed with fairness, transparency, and accountability as core tenets, to prevent unintended harm and to uphold public trust (Jobin et al., 2019). Binns (2018) also highlights that fairness in machine learning is a critical aspect of responsible AI, focusing on the need to prevent discrimination and promote justice.

One significant study by Jana et al. (2024) discusses the importance of embedding ethics and accountability within AI development. Their work highlights that the fundamental aspects of responsible AI governance involve creating transparent models and frameworks that stakeholders can scrutinize and understand. Ensuring accountability requires clear attribution of responsibility when algorithms malfunction or produce biased outcomes. The study further emphasizes integrating human oversight as a critical element to mitigate risks (Jana et al., 2024). In another seminal work, Onebunne and Alade (2024) address the issue of bias and fairness in AI models, particularly in machine learning applications within governance. Their research reveals that biases can emerge from training data that inherently reflect social inequalities. They propose techniques such as algorithmic auditing and bias correction methods to enhance fairness and accountability (Onebunne & Alade, 2024).

The utilization of AI in governance is not entirely new, but recent advancements have amplified its relevance, especially when it comes to ethics and accountability. Governments worldwide are increasingly adopting AI for predictive analytics, resource management, public service delivery, and policy-making. However, the lack of robust ethical frameworks often leads to discriminatory practices and loss of public trust. Raza (2024) explores the relationship between data ethics and human rights in AI governance. The study emphasizes the importance of designing governance structures that protect individual rights and ensure fairness. Raza warns that government's reliance on automated decision-making without human oversight can result in unfair treatment and discrimination. He advocates for integrating algorithmic governance frameworks that include human rights assessments (Raza, 2024). Gladwin (2024) further contributes to this discourse by examining the role of algorithmic governance in maintaining fairness and accountability. He posits that the use of automated systems in public administration should be accompanied by stringent regulatory measures to avoid human rights violations. Gladwin's analysis calls for the standardization of AI governance practices across countries to ensure uniform ethical approach (Gladwin, 2024).

One of the most pressing concerns in AI governance is maintaining accountability for decisions made by automated systems. Accountability in AI governance is crucial to maintaining public trust. As AI systems make more autonomous decisions, it becomes increasingly challenging to determine liability when errors occur. The lack of clear accountability mechanisms can undermine the credibility of public administration and lead to widespread skepticism about AI adoption. This is partly because public sector applications often involve high-stakes decisions, such as welfare allocation, criminal justice, public health interventions, and government employment. Consequently, as AI becomes more integrated, the public demands higher standards of transparency and fairness. Given this reality, integrating responsible AI into governance requires a balanced approach that promotes innovation while safeguarding public values and ethical practice. One major challenge is developing cross-sector collaborations to harmonize technological capabilities with ethical imperatives. This implies the need for establishing regulatory frameworks that adapt to the evolving nature of AI while ensuring equity and justice. As noted by the above-referenced studies, responsible AI adoption calls for clear policy guidelines, training for public administrators, and engagement with civil society organizations to reflect diverse perspectives. Integrating public consultations into AI governance can further align technologies with democratic values and reduce the risk of societal harm.

As stated earlier, the adoption of AI in government and the public sector is both an opportunity and a challenge. Responsible AI in the public sector is not only a matter of technological optimization but also of ethical and governance alignment. While AI technologies can enhance efficiency and optimize resource allocation, they also raise concerns regarding ethics, fairness, and accountability. The literature demonstrates the path forward requires a robust ethical framework that ensures responsible AI deployment, combined with consistent oversight and public engagement. By embedding principles of accountability, fairness, and transparency into AI systems, governments, and institutions can safeguard public interests while leveraging AI's potential to improve administrative efficiency. Additionally, by adopting comprehensive policies and maintaining human oversight, public sector applications of AI can become more equitable and trustworthy. The role of continuous monitoring and stakeholder involvement remains pivotal to ensuring that AI applications align with public sector values and societal expectations. This implies governments must remain vigilant about algorithmic biases and actively work to mitigate potential harms by promoting transparency and accountability and avoiding policy failure. In the next section, we discuss some of the success stories of responsible AI adoption as well as pitfalls and policy failures.

3 Global Case Studies of AI Use: Success Stories and Policy Failures

AI is transforming governance worldwide through efficiency enhancements and data-driven decision-making. Yet, while some governments have achieved considerable success in integrating AI, others have faced substantial challenges, including algorithmic bias and privacy breaches. This section evaluates empirical evidence of AI use in government, focusing on global case studies, including success stories, failures, and key lessons learned from these implementations. The strategic integration of AI into public administration and governance has yielded transformative outcomes in countries such as Singapore, Estonia, Finland, and South Korea. These nations provide compelling case studies of successful AI implementation in enhancing public sector performance, citizen engagement, and administrative efficiency. Table 1 shows the examples of global success stories.

Singapore: Singapore stands out as a global leader through its *Smart Nation Initiative*, which embeds AI across various domains including healthcare, transportation, and education. For example, AI has been integrated into urban planning and traffic management, reducing congestion and improving commuter experiences. Notable in the Smart Nation initiative is the SkillsFuture program that leverages AI to deliver personalized adult education pathways, thereby improving employability and workforce adaptability. According to Pak (2021), this initiative has significantly improved citizen satisfaction and learning outcomes, setting a benchmark for human-centric AI deployment in skills development.

Table 1 Examples of global case studies of AI use—success stories

Country name	AI initiative	Success story	Source (References)
Singapore	Smart nation initiative/ SkillsFuture	Leveraged AI to deliver personalized adult education pathways, improving workforce adaptability and lifelong learning outcomes	Pak (2021)
Estonia	KrattAI framework	Developed a decentralized digital assistant ecosystem for real-time citizen interaction with government services, enhancing transparency and trust	Wibowo (2025)
Finland	AuroraAI project	AI-enabled life-event-based service delivery increased efficiency and inclusivity in public service access, supported by high ethical oversight	Leikas et al. (2022)
South Korea	Smart city platforms (AI-based traffic and safety systems)	Applied real-time analytics to urban management, reducing traffic congestion and improving emergency response, earning strong public support	Santonen and Kaivo-Oja (2024)

Estonia: Known for its digital governance model and one of the most cited success stories, Estonia has implemented over 70 AI solutions in government services. The country has leveraged its AI-enabled e-government platforms and streamlined public services, reduced bureaucratic inefficiencies, and enhanced citizen satisfaction. Its *Kratt AI framework* exemplifies a decentralized digital assistant ecosystem that facilitates real-time citizen interaction with government services. Wibowo (2025) highlights that Estonia's emphasis on interoperability and transparency has enhanced administrative responsiveness and citizen trust.

Finland: Finland has successfully integrated AI in areas such as taxation and social services. Its *AuroraAI* project aims to deliver predictive and proactive public services based on life events, thereby improving efficiency and inclusiveness. Leikas et al. (2022) note that Finland's success in aligning AI initiatives with high public trust levels and ethical oversight has led to one of the highest AI adoption rates in Europe.

South Korea: This nation has pioneered AI use in *traffic optimization* and urban *safety systems*. Leveraging real-time data analytics, its Smart City platforms have reduced congestion and improved emergency response. According to Santonen and Kaivo-Oja (2024), public support for AI in urban management reflects successful communication and integration strategies.

These case studies demonstrate that successful AI adoption in the public sector hinges on transparent governance, citizen-centered design, and alignment with societal values. These countries provide replicable frameworks for others aiming to responsibly deploy AI for administrative transformation.

Table 2 Examples of global case studies of AI use—pitfalls and controversies

Country name	AI initiative	Pitfalls and controversies	Source (References)
United States	Predictive policing/ welfare fraud detection	Predictive policing tools like *PredPol* led to racial profiling, while welfare fraud detection systems falsely accused thousands, resulting in lawsuits and erosion of public trust	Kempeneer and Ranchordas (2024)
United Kingdom	Algorithmic welfare decision-making	Algorithmic systems used in welfare determinations lacked transparency and explainability, causing wrongful denials and public backlash	Mikhaylov and Esteve (2018)
Netherlands	SyRI (System risk indication) welfare detection	SyRI was declared discriminatory and unlawful due to targeting of low-income immigrant populations; led to legal bans and dismantling of the system	Van Noordt and Misuraca (2022)
Australia	Robodebt (Automated debt recovery scheme)	Robodebt wrongly issued debt notices to over 400,000 citizens, causing widespread psychological and financial harm; ultimately, it was terminated	Yigitcanlar et al. (2024)

Despite its potential, the increasing use of AI in public administration has not been without significant challenges and pitfalls. Across several countries, poorly implemented AI systems have led to adverse outcomes, including bias, loss of public trust, and legal consequences. Examples of some policy challenges in this regard can be found in the United States, United Kingdom, the Netherlands, and Australia (Table 2).

United States: A prominent and one of the most cited pitfall in the United States entails predictive policing systems like PredPol, which were intended to predict crime hotspots but have led to apparent racial profiling, discrimination, and disproportionately targeted minority communities. The AI system was heavily criticized for a lack of transparency, biased training data, and inadequate oversight. Kempeneer and Ranchordas (2024) report that biased data inputs led to systemic racial profiling, undermining public confidence and raising constitutional concerns. This case, which later incorporated auditing to ensure fairness, is a testament to the fact that incorporating ethics frameworks and continuous auditing can mitigate bias.

United Kingdom: The UK's deployment of algorithmic decision-making in welfare benefits systems drew criticism after numerous citizens were unjustly denied support. As noted by Mikhaylov and Esteve (2018), the lack of transparency and explainability in algorithmic processes created accountability gaps and sparked political controversy. Another notable case of a pitfall is the United Kingdom's A-Level Grading Scandal (2020). In this case, an AI algorithm used to determine student grades during the COVID-19 pandemic disproportionately downgraded students from underprivileged backgrounds. The deployment of the system faced criticism for lack of stakeholder consultation and insufficient testing.

Netherlands: Another prominent failure occurred in the Netherlands, where an algorithm designed to detect welfare fraud disproportionately targeted minority groups, leading to accusations of racial profiling and social unrest. The infamous SyRI (System Risk Indication) algorithm, used to detect welfare fraud, was declared unlawful in 2020 due to its discriminatory impact. Van Noordt and Misuraca (2022) explain that the system's lack of transparency and disproportionate targeting of low-income, immigrant communities led to legal interventions and policy rollbacks.

Australia: The *Robodebt* scheme, which used automated debt recovery algorithms to match tax and welfare records, was a stark example of irresponsible AI use. It wrongly accused over 400,000 citizens of debt, causing financial hardship and mental health issues. Yigitcanlar et al. (2024) note that the program's design lacked adequate human oversight, leading to its eventual termination and public apology.

4 Lessons Learned from the Global Case Studies of AI Adoption in Government

AI adoption in government presents a dual-edged sword of potential benefits and significant risks. The contrast between successful and failed implementation offers invaluable insights into the complexities of integrating advanced technologies into public administration. Analyzing both success stories and failures reveals critical lessons that governments and policymakers must heed to maximize positive outcomes while minimizing ethical and practical challenges. This section discusses lessons learned from both successes and failures, beginning with success stories.

4.1 Lessons Learned from Success Stories

Comprehensive Regulatory Frameworks Foster Trust: One of the most consistent themes in successful AI implementation is the presence of robust legal and ethical frameworks. In Estonia, the development of e-government platforms was accompanied by strong data governance laws, such as the Digital Identity Act, ensuring data integrity and cybersecurity (Alshahrani et al., 2024). Similarly, Singapore's Smart Nation initiative emphasized data protection and established stringent guidelines for AI applications in public services. Governments must proactively draft and enforce regulations that address privacy, data protection, and transparency to build public trust.

Public Engagement and Transparency are Critical: Countries that engage citizens in the design and implementation of AI systems tend to experience more sustainable outcomes. In Singapore, transparent communication about how AI would improve public services garnered public support (Pak, 2021). Estonia's transparent digital governance efforts fostered widespread public approval, partly due to public awareness campaigns about data security. Transparency not only builds public confidence but also helps mitigate resistance to change (Wibowo, 2025).

Interdisciplinary Collaboration Enhances Effectiveness: Governments that integrate expertise from various fields, including data science, ethics, sociology, and law, tend to create more resilient AI systems. Singapore's urban planning AI projects were guided by urban planners, data scientists, and policymakers working collaboratively, ensuring holistic approaches. Interdisciplinary approaches ensure that AI systems are not only technically sound but also socially responsible (Pak, 2021).

Flexibility and Adaptability are Essential: Governments that implement AI with an adaptive mindset can better address unforeseen challenges. The UK's use of AI in healthcare during the COVID-19 pandemic demonstrated flexibility, as healthcare policies were continuously adapted based on algorithmic outputs and real-time data. Flexibility in AI implementation allows governments to respond to unexpected developments without undermining public service quality.

4.2 Lessons Learned from Pitfalls and Controversies

Algorithmic Bias Undermines Public Confidence: A major lesson from the failures of predictive policing in the United States is the detrimental impact of algorithmic bias. Algorithms that inadvertently reinforce racial or socioeconomic disparities, such as those identified in predictive policing systems, can erode public trust and fuel societal division (Yigitcanlar et al., 2024). Governments must conduct thorough bias audits and engage diverse stakeholders during model training to detect and mitigate potential discrimination.

Lack of Stakeholder Involvement Leads to Policy Backlash: When stakeholders are not involved in the development and testing phases, unintended consequences become more likely, and public resistance intensifies. Inclusive policymaking practices are crucial to gaining stakeholder buy-in and ensuring fair implementation. Hickok (2021) highlights the need for AI systems to be explainable and for governments to adopt policies ensuring transparency in AI decision-making.

Absence of Accountability Mechanisms Promote Irresponsibility: One of the most common pitfalls in failed AI implementation is the lack of clear accountability frameworks. For instance, in the Netherlands' welfare fraud detection case, the absence of accountability measures lead to unjustified profiling and loss of public confidence (Van Noordt & Misuraca, 2022). To prevent such occurrences, governments must define responsibility at every level of AI deployment, from developers to policymakers.

Insufficient Testing and Evaluation Compromise Effectiveness: When AI systems are rushed into deployment without rigorous testing, they are prone to errors and biases. A case in point is the predictive policing saga mentioned above. As a best practice, Singapore's Smart Nation initiative conducted pilot projects before full-scale AI implementation, ensuring that AI was truly beneficial for urban management (Yigitcanlar et al., 2024). Governments must prioritize extensive testing, peer reviews, and pilot studies before widespread implementation.

As noted in the lessons learned above, the successes and failures of AI adoption in government demonstrate that responsible integration requires a delicate balance between innovation and caution. Successful initiatives are grounded in transparency, interdisciplinary collaboration, and robust governance, while failures often stem from hasty implementation, lack of stakeholder involvement, and inadequate accountability. By internalizing these lessons, governments can better navigate the complexities of AI adoption and ensure that public services are both innovative and ethically sound.

5 AI and Government Efficiency: International Comparison and Implications

As noted in the previous section, governments have been actively integrating AI to enhance efficiency, streamline processes, reduce bureaucracy, improve decision-making and enhance citizen engagement. However, ill-thought-out adoption of AI could result in colossal failure with profound implications. While AI has the potential to create new job opportunities, it also poses risks to existing roles, particularly those that are routine and manual. One of the most impacted areas is public sector employment, where automation and workforce transformation are reshaping how services are delivered. This section explores the effects of AI adoption on government efficiency and public sector employment, focusing on automation and job displacement, skill gaps, and workforce transformation, as well as economic, social, and policy implications.

Automation and Job Displacement: As AI technologies are increasingly integrated into government operations, concerns are rising about job displacement. According to Wirtz et al. (2019), the adoption of AI in public administration could significantly affect job structures, particularly in routine-based roles. For instance, in countries like Estonia and the United Arab Emirates, automation has streamlined tasks such as data processing and administrative documentation, reducing the need for human intervention. Similarly, Du (2024) discusses the potential of AI to replace human workers in various government functions, particularly those involving data entry and analysis. While some jobs are displaced, new roles requiring digital proficiency and oversight emerge, emphasizing the need for reskilling.

Skill Gaps and Workforce Transformation: The adoption of AI demands a transformation in workforce capabilities. As discussed by Medaglia and Tangi

(2022), employees with low digital literacy face challenges adapting to AI systems. Therefore, public sector organizations must invest in training programs to enhance AI literacy and technical skills. Additionally, governments need to invest significantly in training programs to bridge the skills gap, ensure smooth workforce transition, and minimize socio-economic impact of AI adoption. Recognizing this challenge, countries like Canada and Finland have initiated comprehensive training schemes for public employees to bridge the digital skills gap. Moreover, the European Union has been active in assessing the public sector's readiness to adopt AI technologies, highlighting that skills related to data analytics, ethics, and policy integration are essential for modern government functions (Van Noordt & Misuraca, 2022).

5.1 International Comparison and Perspectives

United States: Efficiency at a Cost: In 2025, the US federal government established the Department of Government Efficiency (DOGE) with the aim of streamlining federal operations by adopting cutting-edge technologies such as AI and automation. The primary goal was to reduce redundancy, enhance processing speed, and modernize federal services while trimming the cost of federal government operations. The establishment of DOGE marks a pivotal moment in the intersection of AI and public administration. The rationale behind the department was rooted in long-standing criticisms of federal bureaucracy being sluggish, costly, and outdated.

The creation of DOGE marks a shift toward data-driven automation and modernization. The drive to modernize federal operations through automation has had profound implications for public sector employment and administrative practices. Proponents argued that AI-driven restructuring could eliminate redundancies, streamline processes, and enhance decision-making accuracy. However, critics have raised concerns about the lack of stakeholder engagement and transparency during the department's formation.

One of the most notable impacts of DOGE has been the implementation of widespread layoffs across federal agencies. In a recent article, Stein et al. (2025) state that federal health agencies such as the CDC and NIH were among the first to experience mass layoffs, particularly targeting middle management and administrative positions. The aim was to minimize operational costs while promoting a more efficient and data-driven approach to government services. However, this move was met with significant backlash from labor unions and civil rights groups who argued that layoffs disproportionately affected lower and mid-level employees.

While DOGE's implementation of AI technologies has undeniably increased operational efficiency, it has also led to substantial human costs. In particular, social services and public health offices have seen significant cuts, with social security services being heavily affected (Carter, 2025). AI-driven data analytics have enabled faster processing and more accurate aggregation, reducing bureaucratic backlogs. However, the introduction of these systems has resulted in a steep learning curve for existing employees, many of whom lacked the technical expertise to transition to new roles.

Bejarano-Murillo (2025) notes that the US approach has emphasized technological implementation over workforce integration, leading to public sector morale issues and diminished trust. The US experience shows that while governments pursue efficiency and innovation, challenges related to automation, employment, and ethical governance could persist if not carefully managed. To put the impact of DOGE in perspective, we provide comparisons with more balanced international public sector technology-driven strategies in Estonia, Singapore, Canada, and Sweden.

Estonia: Digital Governance with Inclusive Training: Estonia, known for its advanced digital governance, serves as an interesting counterpoint to the US approach. Instead of mass layoffs, Estonia's e-government initiatives have focused on upskilling public employees and integrating digital literacy into civil service training. The country's e-government model emphasizes citizen access and digital literacy across the civil service. Unlike the US, Estonia has focused on preparing public employees for digital transformation through national training initiatives. According to Tamm and Leis (2020), Estonia's approach has resulted in increased public satisfaction without drastic workforce reductions. Similarly, Khanra (2024) also notes that Estonia's strategy has enhanced service delivery and employee satisfaction without large-scale layoffs.

Singapore: Workforce Repositioning through Smart Nation Strategy: Singapore has also leveraged AI and smart technologies to enhance public sector efficiency. The smart nation initiative demonstrates strategic redeployment rather than displacement. AI tools are used to automate services and monitor urban systems, but public servants are retrained and reassigned to manage and interpret these systems. Unlike the U.S. model, which led to significant job cuts, Singapore's strategy involved repositioning employees within new technology-driven roles rather than outright dismissals. Tan et al. (2021) report that this has maintained employment stability despite rapid technological changes, attributing success to strong institutional coordination and continuous professional development.

Canada: Balancing Automation with Human Oversight: Canada has adopted a more balanced approach to public sector automation, prioritizing hybrid models where AI assists human decision-makers rather than replacing them outright. This approach emphasizes a hybrid model where AI supports but does not replace human decision-makers. For example, the Canada Revenue Agency (CRA) employs AI to detect tax fraud patterns but requires human analysts to validate flagged cases. That is, although AI flags suspicious tax behavior, human analysts make final determinations. As noted by Susar and Aquaro (2019), this model has preserved employment while enhancing public service efficiency, thereby supporting trust and transparency in decision-making processes.

Sweden: Ethical Automation and Workforce Protections: Sweden's automation strategy within its public sector is shaped by strong ethical guidelines that prioritize worker protection. The country's AI integration not only reflects strong ethical commitments but also focuses on worker upskilling and social responsibility. Trade unions and government bodies co-develop automation strategies to protect employment. Policies mandate retraining programs and require that any new technology must demonstrate clear social benefits before implementation. Voss and Rego (2019) highlight Sweden's requirements for demonstrable social benefit prior to deployment and a mandatory retraining program for affected employees. As a result, Sweden has not only preserved jobs but also improved job quality through upskilling initiatives. Sweden's model aligns with Scandinavian welfare principles and ensures minimal disruption.

5.2 Analytical Perspective

The stark contrast between the US and international models highlights the need for nuanced policy frameworks that integrate efficiency with human considerations. While DOGE's model prioritizes rapid technological adoption, international cases emphasize both innovation and worker adaptability. Technocratic governance risks alienating vulnerable populations, as the focus on metrics and efficiency can overlook the social functions that public servants often fulfill (Bejarano-Murillo, 2025). The erosion of public trust has been a major unintended consequence of DOGE's operations and may undermine government effectiveness.

DOGE has fundamentally altered how federal agencies operate, with both promising advancements in efficiency and detrimental impacts on employment stability. The DOGE model exemplifies the risks of prioritizing technological adoption without adequately considering social and ethical ramifications. The dampened public employee morale and mistrust may hinder the effectiveness of future government modernization efforts, suggesting a need for transparent and inclusive decision-making. International cases from Estonia, Singapore, Canada, and Sweden demonstrate that a more balanced approach is possible, one that leverages AI while protecting human employment and ensuring social justice.

The cross-international review reveals significant differences in how governments integrate AI into the public sector. The US strategy, rooted in efficiency metrics, often sacrifices employment continuity and trust. In contrast, Estonia's inclusive training frameworks, Singapore's adaptive retraining, Canada's hybrid approach, and Sweden's ethical safeguards offer models that balance technological innovation with employment stability. The above comparative insights underscore the potential for crafting balanced policies that safeguard both efficiency and employment. To mitigate adverse outcomes, policymakers must develop frameworks that balance efficiency with job security, ethical oversight, and public engagement.

From a public administration perspective, these findings suggest that the theory and practice of AI governance must be reoriented toward stakeholder inclusion, continuous learning, and preparatory policy design. The US could benefit from adopting international best practices that emphasize human oversight and long-term workforce investment. In the following section, we discuss the broader implications of the adverse effects of AI use in government.

5.3 Economic, Social, and Policy Implications of AI Use in Government

While AI offers numerous benefits, its adverse effects on employment and the ramifications of its irresponsible use in government necessitate a comprehensive examination. A comprehensive study on the long-term societal and ethical impact of automation highlights how AI-driven technologies are transforming the work environment by replacing repetitive and manual tasks (Khogali & Mekid, 2023). Zhao and Gómez Fariñas (2023) argue that despite potential benefits, the irresponsible development of AI software leaves communities vulnerable to economic destabilization and social exclusion. This section delves into the economic, social and policy implications of AI-induced employment disruptions and the consequences of negligent AI deployment in governmental operations.

Economic Implications: The economic consequences of AI-induced job displacement are profound. As AI systems become more sophisticated, the demand for high-skilled workers increases, while low-skilled workers face rising unemployment rates. Economically, AI-induced job displacement has profound effects on consumer spending and overall economic growth. As automation replaces human labor, displaced workers experience income reductions, leading to decreased purchasing power and dampened demand for goods and services. This cycle not only stifles economic growth but also leads to recessionary pressures. Additionally, the benefits of AI-driven productivity gains are often concentrated among a few technology companies, exacerbating income inequality. The challenge of governing AI in economic contexts has been addressed by Wirtz et al. (2022), who advocate for comprehensive policies that address economic risks while fostering technological innovation.

Economically, the irresponsible deployment of AI in government functions can lead to inefficiencies and increased public expenditure. For instance, flawed AI systems used to detect fraud in unemployment insurance programs have resulted in wrongful accusations against thousands of individuals, leading to financial hardships and costly legal battles. An article by Dyson (2023) revealed that in Michigan, an algorithm deployed by the state's unemployment insurance agency wrongly flagged around 40,000 people as committing unemployment fraud, which resulted in fines, denied benefits, and bankruptcy. Such errors not only impose direct financial costs on affected individuals but also erode public trust in governmental institutions, potentially leading to decreased compliance with public programs and increased administrative costs. Furthermore, the reliance on AI systems without adequate human oversight can result in costly mistakes, such as the misallocation of resources for failure to identify critical issues, ultimately leading to economic inefficiencies and wastage of public funds.

Social Implications: The integration of AI into the workforce has led to significant social transformations, particularly concerning employment patterns. AI-driven automation has displaced numerous low-skilled and routine jobs, exacerbating unemployment rates and widening socioeconomic disparities. For instance, in many governmental settings, administrative tasks previously performed by humans are now performed by chatbots leading to job losses. Similarly, AI algorithms in the retail industry have automated inventory management and customer service roles, reducing the need for human intervention. These shifts not only result in immediate job displacement but also contribute to long-term social challenges, such as increased poverty levels and reduced social mobility.

Although the deployment of AI in government operations holds the potential to enhance efficiency and decision-making processes, irresponsible or poorly regulated use of AI can lead to significant social repercussions. For example, the use of AI algorithms in welfare systems to detect fraud has been criticized for disproportionately targeting marginalized communities, leading to unjust penalties and exacerbating existing social inequalities. In France, legal challenges have been mounted against the government's use of algorithms for identifying welfare payment errors, with claims that these discriminate against disabled individuals and single mothers (Meaker, 2024). Similarly, the United Kingdom's automated welfare decision systems faced increased public criticism over perceived injustice and social exclusion (Williamson et al., 2023). Additionally, the use of AI in law enforcement in the United States, such as Chicago's predictive policing algorithms, has raised concerns and led to protests over unjust profiling, particularly among minority communities (Stark et al., 2021). Such instances highlight the potential for AI to reinforce societal biases if not implemented with adequate oversight and ethical considerations.

Policy Implications: The rapid advancement of AI poses significant challenges for policymakers tasked with mitigating its adverse effects on employment and society. Traditional labor laws and social safety nets may be inadequate to address the unique challenges posed by AI-driven automation. Policymakers must consider implementing comprehensive strategies that include reskilling and upskilling programs to equip workers with competencies relevant to the evolving job market. Additionally, social safety nets, such as universal basic income (UBI), have been proposed as potential solutions to provide financial stability to individuals affected by AI-induced job displacement. However, the implementation of UBI remains a topic of debate among economists and policymakers, with concerns about its feasibility and potential impact on labor market dynamics. Furthermore, regulatory frameworks must be updated to address the ethical and fairness concerns associated with AI in recruitment and employment practices, ensuring that AI-driven decisions do not perpetuate existing biases.

The challenges associated with the irresponsible use of AI in government necessitate the development of robust policy frameworks that ensure ethical and effective deployment. That is, the integration of AI into economic systems requires thoughtful governance to mitigate risks. Truby (2020) emphasizes the importance of embedding ethical considerations and robust governance frameworks to ensure AI developments benefit sustainable goals without compromising socioeconomic stability. This implies policymakers must establish clear guidelines for the use of AI, emphasizing transparency, accountability and fairness. This includes implementing measures for regular auditing of AI systems, ensuring that algorithms are free from biases, and maintaining human oversight in decision-making processes. Additionally, there is a need for comprehensive data protection laws to safeguard citizens' privacy and prevent misuse of personal information.

Ethical Considerations: The establishment of independent regulatory bodies to oversee AI development in government can further enhance accountability and public trust. When AI is employed irresponsibly within governance structures, the consequences can be severe, including surveillance abuses and violations of civil liberties. Sætra (2021) warns that weaponizing AI for government control is inherently dangerous and calls for more responsible integration aligned with the Sustainable Development Goals. Additionally, Helbing (2019) points out that open government initiatives utilizing AI can lead to harmful societal consequences when misapplied or driven by profit-oriented motives. To this end, engaging with diverse stakeholders, including civil society organizations and the communities affected by AI policies, is crucial to ensure that the implementation of AI technologies aligns with societal values and ethical standards. The ethical landscape of responsible AI governance is complex, encompassing the following key principles that aim to address potential risks associated with AI adoptions:

- Privacy: Protecting individuals' data from unauthorized access while maintaining transparency regarding how data is utilized;
- Accountability: Defining clear responsibility when AI-driven decisions result in negative outcomes or unintended biases;
- Transparency: Developing AI systems whose inner workings and decision pathways are interpretable and comprehensible to stakeholder; and
- Fairness: Ensuring that AI algorithms do not replicate or reinforce social biases and inequalities.

Floridi et al. (2018) highlight that integrating ethical frameworks into AI design and implementation is crucial for mitigating harm and fostering public trust in AI-driven governance. As noted above, the societal, economic, and policy implications of AI use in government are far-reaching, especially when considering its effects on efficiency and employment. Developing comprehensive governance frameworks that emphasize ethical AI deployment is essential for mitigating these risks and promoting societal well-being. Tables 3 and 4 summarize the social, economic and policy implications of global success stories as well as pitfalls and controversies of AI deployment. These implications make the need for AI governance crucial.

Table 3 Implications of AI use in government—global success stories

Country name	AI use (Initiative)	Social implication	Economic implications	Policy implications	Source (Reference)
Estonia	e-residency program	Enhanced digital inclusion and international engagement	Increased revenue from business registrations and innovation investments	Developed robust digital identity governance frameworks to ensure cybersecurity and data privacy	Attard-Frost and Lyons (2024)
China	Social credit system	Social surveillance and loss of individual freedoms	Improved credit management and risk mitigation for businesses	Implementation of rigorous data governance policies to handle social scoring systems	Mike (2024)
India	Aadhaar biometric ID system	Improved access to services for many but concerns over privacy violations	Economic inclusion through streamlined welfare distribution	Enactment of the Aadhaar Act to provide legal backing and address privacy challenges	Camilleri (2023)
Finland	Automated tax filing system	Simplified and accurate tax reporting, reducing administrative burden for citizens	Improved efficiency and cost savings from automated processes	Introduced data privacy regulations to protect citizens' financial information	Ivanov et al. (2025)

6 Critical Perspectives on AI Governance

Given the above economic, social and policy implication of AI deployment in government, AI governance is increasingly becoming a focal point of public discourse as AI technologies permeate various sectors, including governance itself. As public sector entities consider integrating AI into decision-making processes, a critical debate emerges: Is it practical or ethical to replace policymakers and public servants with AI systems? In this section, we delve into the multifaceted perspectives on AI governance, examining the debate over AI-led government, expert opinions from thought leaders, as well as public perception and trust.

Regarding AI-led Government, the potential for AI to govern autonomously raises significant ethical and practical concerns. Proponents argue that AI systems, unburdened by human biases, can make more efficient and data-driven decisions. However, critics caution against the loss of human accountability and the risks associated with algorithmic bias and lack of transparency. While some researchers and opinion leaders have argued that replacing human policymakers

Table 4 Implications of AI use in government—pitfalls and controversies

Country name	AI use (Initiative)	Social implication	Economic implications	Policy implications	Source (Reference)
United States	Predictive policing systems (e.g., PredPol)	Increased community distrust and protests over algorithmic racial bias	High costs related to litigation and public backlash	Heightened demand for transparency and accountability measures in policing algorithms	Stark et al. (2021)
United Kingdom	Automated welfare decision systems	Increased public criticism over perceived injustice and social exclusion	Cost savings from reduced human involvement but increased costs from legal challenges	Revisions in data protection regulations and demands for human oversight in automated decisions	Williamson et al. (2023)
Canada	AI-based immigration assessment	Social backlash due to perceived bias against marginalized groups	Cost savings in processing applications but reputational damage and legal costs from advocacy groups	Adoption of human rights impact assessments in AI-based decision-making processes	Oliveira (2024)
South Africa	Smart policing with facial recognition technology	Public fear of constant surveillance, disproportionately affecting low-income communities	Reduced crime rates but increased legal disputes and public distrust	Calls for regulations on biometric data usage and improved public consultation processes	Ulnicane et al. (2021)

with AI could lead to unintended societal disruptions, others have suggested that AI can complement, rather than replace, human decision-making, especially in areas requiring complex ethical reasoning. Recent scholarship (e.g., Bogucka et al., 2024) emphasizes the need for robust ethical frameworks to assess the implications of delegating governance tasks to AI.

A decolonial approach to AI governance emphasizes the need to challenge Eurocentric and hegemonic paradigms that dominate current frameworks. Oliveira (2024) critically examines how moral alignment and egalitarian principles can be reconceptualized within the scope of AI ethics, drawing from hermeneutic traditions and intersectional perspectives (Oliveira, 2024). The evolution of AI governance reflects divergent global perspectives. Mike (2024) contends that international coordination, transparency, and inclusive stakeholder engagement are fundamental in establishing robust governance protocols. Similarly, Camilleri (2024) focuses on the ethical considerations essential for socially responsible governance, integrating both theoretical and applied approaches. This implies understanding AI governance as a system is vital in comprehending its multifaceted nature. Attard-Frost and Lyons (2024) propose a multi-scale analysis framework, offering empirical findings that contextualize governance within strategic and operational levels.

The role of civil society and education in AI governance is also critical. LePere-Schloop and Zook (2023) advocate for the critical engagement of civil society in governance frameworks. They argue that incorporating diverse societal perspectives enhances inclusivity and equity within governance processes. Williamson, Eynon, and Knox (2023) explore the impact of AI in education, focusing on political economy, discrimination, and commercialization. Their analysis underscores the complex interplay between technological innovation and governance strategies. Stark, Green, and Hoffmann (2021) provide a critical evaluation of proposed governance mechanisms for AI and machine learning systems, stressing the need for ethically grounded and practical solutions. This calls for policy framing that helps to shape public perception about AI governance.

Public trust in AI governance remains low, with surveys indicating that a majority of citizens express skepticism toward AI-led decision-making processes. Recent studies indicated that fostering transparency and accountability is crucial to building public confidence (Miller, 2023). Public perception is shaped by high-profile failures and the lack of clear accountability mechanisms, emphasizing the need for policies that prioritize human oversight. The ongoing debate on AI governance therefore, underscores the necessity of balancing technological advancement with ethical and social considerations. The diverse perspectives from thought leaders and public sentiment highlight the complexities of integrating AI into governance structures. The critical perspectives on AI governance reveal the importance of embedding ethical considerations and inclusivity at the core of policy frameworks to enhance public trust. Addressing both decolonial and systemic approaches while balancing public perception and ethical imperatives remains crucial in fostering responsible AI governance. Moving forward, interdisciplinary collaboration and continuous public engagement will be vital in shaping responsible AI governance frameworks.

7 Framework for Responsible AI Implementation

The implementation of responsible AI is grounded in the foundational principles of fairness, accountability, inclusivity, and transparency. These principles are essential to mitigate biases, enhance stakeholder trust, and promote ethical AI use. According to Tripathi and Kumar (2025), businesses should embrace ethical practices that uphold individual rights while promoting societal fairness. They emphasize the importance of integrating social-cognitive frameworks into AI systems to foster explainability and fairness. Similarly, Bogucka et al. (2024) propose the AI Design Framework, which focuses on impact assessment as a critical component of responsible AI practices. Furthermore, Shamsuddin et al. (2025) discuss how integrating explainability with responsible AI systems strengthens transparency and accountability. Their proposed blueprint emphasizes that fairness should not only be conceptual but practically embedded during AI development and deployment stages.

7.1 Policy Recommendations

Balancing Automation and Human Oversight: Effective policy recommendations for responsible AI focuses on balancing automation with human oversight to maintain accountability. To balance automation and human oversight, responsible AI frameworks must include comprehensive policies that outline human-in-the-loop mechanisms. Bogucka et al. (2024) advocate for frameworks that facilitate impact assessment reports, allowing stakeholders to evaluate AI system implications to full-scale implementation.

Vyhmeister et al. (2023) suggest contextualizing responsible AI frameworks by considering environmental and social conditions throughout AI system deployment. They emphasize a flexible, adaptable approach that maintains human accountability even when automation is integrated. Additionally, Walsh et al. (2023) suggest that AI education and training should be central to policy initiatives to maintain human oversight while fostering innovation. Barletta et al. (2023) conducted a rapid review of existing responsible AI frameworks, advocating for guidelines that enhance ethical AI development through stakeholder engagement. Furthermore, Tjondronegoro et al. (2022) emphasize a human-centered approach that integrates innovation while safeguarding individual rights.

Involving Stakeholders in Decision-Making and Oversight: Collaborative governance in AI implementation requires the involvement of diverse stakeholders in decision-making and oversight processes. Stakeholders from diverse backgrounds help to achieve inclusive and transparent decision-making. Sanderson et al. (2022) highlight the significance of participatory governance models to embed ethical considerations at each stage of AI implementation. Barletta et al. (2023) propose a multi-stakeholder approach that ensures ethical AI practices while balancing technical and non-technical perspectives. Additionally, Peters et al. (2020) discuss how stakeholder involvement helps to develop structured frameworks for ethical impact analysis, supporting long-term responsible AI practices. Furthermore, Asif et al. (2023) introduce the blockchain-based governance framework to facilitate decentralized oversight of AI systems, highlighting how leveraging distributed technologies enhances transparency and fosters collaborative management.

Based on the foregoing, implementing responsible AI requires adherence to guiding principles of fairness, accountability, inclusivity, and transparency, along with robust policy frameworks that balance automation and human oversight. Continuous stakeholder involvement and ongoing policy evaluation are crucial for the development of sustainable and ethical AI. Collaborative governance is vital, ensuring that stakeholders actively participate in decision-making and monitoring processes. As the field evolves, continuous updates to these frameworks will be necessary to align with emerging ethical and social challenges.

8 Discussion

The rise of AI has transformed the public sector by enhancing decision-making processes, improving efficiency and offering innovative solutions to long-standing challenges. However, the use of AI in government also raises important questions about ethical implementation, public trust, and employment dynamics. Responsible AI implementation aims to balance efficiency with ethical considerations, yet it poses challenges related to workforce displacement and skill matches. As AI-driven automation replaces routine tasks, the public sector must address potential job losses and retrain affected workers. As evidenced by government efficiency initiatives in the United States, automation in the public sector could lead to significant disruptions in employment, necessitating a proactive approach to workforce development. This aligns with prior studies (e.g. Barletta et al., 2023), which suggest that job displacement is particularly significant in data-driven administrative roles, prompting concerns about workforce skill gaps and social inequality. Government must address these risks through proactive training programs and robust social safety nets to maintain workforce resilience.

Responsible AI implementation in the public sector is crucial to preserving social equity and public trust. Successful case studies from countries like Canada, Singapore, the United Kingdom, and Estonia illustrate how AI-driven initiatives can enhance service delivery and administrative efficiency without undermining human oversight. However, cautionary tales from the United States and the Netherlands demonstrate how biased algorithms and insufficient transparency can erode public confidence and result in socio-economic disparities. These cautionary tales notwithstanding, responsible AI practices can promote transparency and fairness in decision-making. For example, algorithmic impact assessments (AIAs) have been proposed as instruments to evaluate the societal implications of AI applications before their deployment. Such frameworks mitigate the risk of biased algorithms undermining public trust and help ensure that AI adoption aligns with democratic values.

The integration of AI in government requires a robust policy framework to guide its responsible use. Socio-economic implications like exacerbation of disparities due to irresponsible AI use such as bias in decision-making in law enforcement and social welfare systems, call for more rigorous oversight and governance frameworks. In light of this, the global debate on AI governance emphasizes the need for transparency, ethical, and accountable implementation practices, underscoring the balance between technological innovation and human rights preservation. Policy measures must consider ethical standards, privacy concerns, and the need for inclusive practices to prevent the marginalization of vulnerable populations. As noted by Kumar and Dadhich (2024), it is important to build frameworks that align with societal norms and regulatory standards, fostering equitable and trustworthy AI systems.

Moving forward, it is imperative for policymakers to develop comprehensive frameworks that foster the responsible adoption of AI. Responsible AI governance needs to incorporate strategic approaches that bridge technology and human-centered values. This entails prioritizing human-centric approaches to governance that include stakeholder engagement and public consultation. Moreover, integrating collaborative governance models that involve multidisciplinary experts can enhance the robustness of AI governance. AI technology will inevitably continue to evolve, posing both opportunities and challenges. This implies governments must strive to strike a balance between leveraging AI's potential and mitigating its adverse impacts. By promoting transparency, inclusivity, and fairness in AI implementation, policymakers can better align technological progress with societal values.

The findings in this study have implications for public administration theory and practice. The growing reliance on AI challenges traditional theories of public administration by necessitating new governance models that are adaptive and resilient. This calls for policymakers to integrate algorithmic accountability into public management theories to accommodate AI-driven transformation. As stated earlier, implementing responsible AI in public administration involves navigating practical challenges, including training public employees to work alongside AI systems and integrating human oversight into automated processes. Additionally, public managers must develop competency frameworks that encompass both technical and ethical dimensions, as emphasized by Anagnostou et al. (2022), who discuss how responsible AI systems must account for societal impact and ethical considerations. In addition to training, legal frameworks must address liability and accountability in the event of AI errors.

The evidence in this study reveals that to achieve responsible AI integration in the public sector, there must be an unwavering commitment to evidence-based policymaking. Governments and institutions must proactively monitor the socio-economic effects of AI adoption and prioritize public engagement. This calls for concerted efforts to develop adaptive policy frameworks that are both context-specific and globally informed. Ultimately, responsible AI use is not just a technical issue but a fundamental societal challenge that requires collaboration across sectors and disciplines. Government must therefore invest in capacity building and public awareness to navigate the complexities of AI-driven transformations while upholding ethical standards and public trust.

9 Conclusion

The adoption of AI in government is both an opportunity and a challenge. AI use in the public sector has significant economic, social, and ethical impacts, requiring thoughtful balancing of innovation and integrity regarding policy interventions and robust governance frameworks. While AI technologies can enhance efficiency and optimize resource allocation, they also raise concerns regarding ethics, fairness, and accountability. As AI adoption accelerates, public administrators must develop adaptive strategies that ensure transparency, equity, inclusivity, and accountability. Addressing these challenges will facilitate a sustainable transition to AI-enhanced governance, aligning technological progress with public values while upholding ethical standards. This implies that, ultimately, implementing responsible AI requires robust policy frameworks that balance automation and human oversight.

References

Alshahrani, A., Griva, A., & Dennehy, D. (2024). Artificial intelligence and decision-making in government functions: Opportunities, challenges, and future research. *Transforming Government: People, Process and Policy, 8*(4), 678–698. https://doi.org/10.1108/TG-06-2024-0131

Asif, R., Hassan, S. R., & Parr, G. (2023). Integrating a blockchain-based governance framework for responsible AI. *MDPI Future Internet*. https://doi.org/10.3390/fi15030097

Attard-Frost, B., & Lyons, K. (2024). AI governance systems: A multi-scale analysis framework, empirical findings, and future directions. *AI and Ethics, 5*, 2557–2604. https://doi.org/10.1007/s43681-024-00569-5

Anagnostou, M., Karvounidou, O., Katritzidaki, C., et al. (2022). Characteristics and challenges in the industries towards responsible AI: a systematic literature review. *Ethics Information Technology, 24*(37). https://doi.org/10.1007/s10676-022-09634-1

Barletta, V. S., Caivano, D., & Gigante, D. (2023). A rapid review of responsible AI frameworks: How to guide the development of ethical AI. *ACM Digital Library*. https://doi.org/10.1145/3593434.3593478

Bejarano-Murillo, E. (2025). *Digital governance across continents: Cases from diverse national strategies* (Chap. 1, pp. 1–25). IGI Global. https://doi.org/10.4018/979-8-3693-6945-6.ch001

Binns, R. (2018). Fairness in machine learning: Lessons from political philosophy. *Ethics and Information Technology, 20*(1), 1–13. https://doi.org/10.1007/s10676-018-9448-7

Bogucka, E., Constantinides, M., Šćepanović, S., & Quercia, D. (2024). AI Design: A responsible artificial intelligence framework for prefilling impact assessment reports. *IEEE Internet Computing, 28*(5), 37–45. https://doi.org/10.1109/MIC.2024.3451351

Camilleri, M. (2023). Artificial intelligence governance: Ethical considerations and implications for social responsibility. https://doi.org/10.1111/exsy.13406

Camilleri, M. A. (2024). Artificial intelligence governance: Ethical considerations and implications for social responsibility. *Expert Systems, 41*(1), 15–30. https://doi.org/10.1111/exsy.13406

Carter, J. (2025). Closing social security offices: Harming access to services. Retrieved April 2, 2025, from https://www.medicarerights.org/medicare-watch/2025/03/13/trump-administration-and-elon-musks-doge-closing-social-security-offices-harming-access-to-services

Du, J. (2024). The impact of artificial intelligence adoption on employee unemployment: A multifaceted relationship. *International Journal of Social Sciences and Public Administration, 2*(3). https://doi.org/10.62051/ijsspa.v2n3.45

Dyson, I. (2023). How AI threatens civil rights and economic opportunities. Retrieved April 2, 2025, from https://www.brennancenter.org/our-work/analysis-opinion/how-ai-threatens-civil-rights-and-economic-opportunities?utm_source=chatgpt.com

Floridi, L., Cowls, J., Beltrametti, M., Chatila, R., Chazerand, P., Dignum, V., Luetge, C., Madelin, R., Pagallo, U., Rossi, F., Schafer, B., Valcke, P., & Vayena, E. (2018). AI4People—an ethical framework for a good AI society: Opportunities, risks, principles, and recommendations. *Minds and Machines, 28*, 689–707.

Gladwin, O. (2024). Human rights in the age of AI: Establishing fairness and accountability through algorithmic governance. Retrieved March 28, 2025, from https://www.researchgate.net/publication/384967187

Helbing, D. (2019). Societal, economic, ethical, and legal challenges of the digital revolution: From big data to deep learning, artificial intelligence, and manipulative technologies. In D. Helbing (Eds.), *towards digital enlightenment*. Springer. https://doi.org/10.1007/978-3-319-90869-4_6

Hickok, M. (2021). Lessons learned from AI ethics principles for future actions. *Springer AI & Society Journal*. https://doi.org/10.1007/s43681-020-00008-1

Ivanov, M. I., Ghercă, A. M., & Gafencu, L. N. (2025). Artificial intelligence and sustainable development: Reducing food waste, building resilient organisations, and enhancing public financial administration. *BRAIN – Broad Research in Artificial Intelligence and Neuroscience, 16*(1). https://edusoft.ro/brain/index.php/brain/article/view/1673

Jana, S., Sekh, R., Oladele, S., & Das, A. (2024). Responsible AI development: Prioritizing ethics and accountability. Retrieved April 11, 2025, from https://www.researchgate.net/publication/387428590

Jobin, A., Ienca, M., & Vayena, E. (2019). The global landscape of AI ethics guidelines. *Nature Machine Intelligence, 1*, 389–399. https://doi.org/10.1038/s42256-019-0088-2

Kempeneer, S., & Ranchordas, S. (2024). AI failure, AI success, and AI power dynamics in the public sector. Retrieved April 9, 2025, from https://papers.ssrn.com/sol3/papers.cfm?abstract_id=4983622

Khanra, S. (2024). Evaluating AI in public sector operations: Estonia's strategic model. In *Operations management on the new frontier* (pp. 123–134). Retrieved May 5, 2025 from https://sbm.nmims.edu/docs/2024/Operations-Management-on-the-New-Frontier_compressed.pdf#page=123

Khogali, A., & Mekid, S. (2023). The blended future of automation and AI: Examining some long-term societal and ethical impact features. *Technology in Society, 73*, Article 102232. https://doi.org/10.1016/j.techsoc.2023.102232

Kumar, A., & Dadhich, H. (2024). Regulatory frameworks for artificial intelligence in law: Ensuring accountability and fairness. *NUJS Journal of Regulatory Studies,* 9, 13–25.

Leikas, J., Johri, A., Latvanen, M., Wessberg, N., & Hahto, A. (2022). Governing ethical AI transformation: A case study of AuroraAI. *Frontiers in Artificial Intelligence, 5*, 1–13. Article 836557. https://doi.org/10.3389/frai.2022.836557/full

LePere-Schloop, M., & Zook, S. (2023). AI governance and civil society: the need for critical engagement. In S. Lindgren (Ed.), *Handbook of critical studies of artificial intelligence*. Edward Elgar Publishing. Retrieved June 4, 2025, from https://doi.org/10.4337/9781803928562.00087

Meaker, M. (2024). Algorithms policed welfare for years: Now, they're under fire for bias. Retrieved April 3, 2025, from https://www.wired.com/story/algorithms-policed-welfare-systems-for-years-now-theyre-under-fire-for-bias/?utm_source=chatgpt.com

Medaglia, R., & Tangi, L. (2022). The adoption of artificial intelligence in the public sector in Europe: drivers, features, and impacts. In *ICEGOV'22: Proceedings of the 15th international conference on theory and practice of electronic governance*. Guimarães Portugal. Retrieved February 27, 2025, from https://doi.org/10.1145/3560107

Mike, N. (2024). Global perspectives on AI governance: A comparative overview. Retrieved March 21, 2025, from https://unipub.lib.uni-corvinus.hu/10648/1/paper4-2.pdf

Mikhaylov, S. J., & Esteve, M. (2018). Artificial intelligence for the public sector: Opportunities and challenges of cross-sector Collaboration. *Philosophical Transactions of the Royal Society A, 376*(2128). https://doi.org/10.1098/rsta.2017.0357

Miller, C. L. (2023). Critical evaluation of AI in the workplace and recommendations for governance roles and policies to mitigate risks. Wilmington University (Delaware).

Oliveira, N. H. (2024). A decolonial critical theory of artificial intelligence. Retrieved April 27, 2025 from https://app.scholarai.io/paper?paper_id=DOI:10.4013/fsu.2024.251.14

Onebunne, A. P., & Alade, B. (2024). Bias and fairness in AI models: Addressing disparities in machine learning applications. Retrieved April 11, 2025, from https://www.researchgate.net/publication/384367427

Pak, M. (2021). Promoting the diffusion of technology to boost productivity and well-being in Korea. In *OECD economics department working papers*, No. 1674 (pp. 1–45). OECD Publishing. https://search.proquest.com/openview/de568b9a2e5278756e446ee7877d3608

Peters, D., Vold, K., Robinson, D., & Calvo, R. A. (2020). Responsible AI—Two frameworks for ethical design practice. *IEEE Transactions on Technology and Society, 1*(1), 34–47. https://doi.org/10.1109/TTS.2020.2974991

Raza, H. (2024). Data ethics and human rights: Designing robust governance structures for AI systems. Retrieved March 28, 2025, from https://www.researchgate.net/publication/385001789

Sætra, H. S. (2021). AI in context and the Sustainable Development Goals: Factoring in the unsustainability of the sociotechnical system. *Sustainability, 13*, 1738. https://doi.org/10.3390/su13041738

Sanderson, C., Lu, Q., Douglas, D., Xu, X., Zhu, L., & Whittle, J. (2022). Towards implementing responsible AI. In *2022 IEEE international conference on Big Data (Big Data), Osaka, Japan* (pp. 5076–5081). https://doi.org/10.1109/BigData55660.2022.10021121

Santonen, T., & Kaivo-Oja, J. (2024). Global interest in artificial intelligence: A big data study. *Theseus—Laurea University of Applied Sciences Publications* (pp. 12–28). Retrieved March 28, 2025, from https://www.theseus.fi/handle/10024/864754

Shamsuddin, R., Tabrizi, H. B., & Gottimukkula, P. R. (2025). Towards responsible AI: An implementable blueprint for integrating explainability and social-cognitive frameworks in AI systems. *AI Perspective and Advances, 7*(1). https://doi.org/10.1186/s42467-024-00016-5

Stark, L., Greene, D., & Hoffmann, A. L. (2021). Critical perspectives on governance mechanisms for AI/ML systems. In J. Roberge, & M. Castelle (Eds.), *The cultural life of machine learning*. Palgrave Macmillan. https://doi.org/10.1007/978-3-030-56286-1_9

Stein, R., Lupkin, S., Simmon-Duffin, S., Shapiro, J., Roth, C., & Noguchi, Y. (2025). Widespread firings start at federal health agencies including many in leadership. Retrieved April 2, 2025, from NPR https://www.npr.org/sections/shots-health-news/2025/04/01/g-s1-57485/hhs-fda-layoffs-doge-cdc-nih

Susar, D., Aquaro, V. (2019). Artificial Intelligence: Opportunities and challenges for the public sector. In *ICEGOV'19: In proceedings of the 12th international conference on theory and practice of electronic governance* (pp. 418–426). https://doi.org/10.1145/3326365.3326420

Tamm, R., & Leis, J. (2020). Digital governance in Estonia. *European Journal of Digital Governance, 22*(3), 89–101.

Tan, S., Ng, R., & Chua, Y. (2021). AI and urban planning in Singapore. *Asian Governance Quarterly, 17*(4), 45–60.

Tjondronegoro, D., Yuwono, E., & Richards, B. (2022). Responsible AI implementation: A human-centered framework for accelerating the innovation process. *arXiv*. https://doi.org/10.48550/arXiv.2209.07076

Tripathi, A., & Kumar, V. (2025). Ethical practices of artificial intelligence: A management framework for responsible AI deployment in businesses. *AI and Ethics*. https://doi.org/10.1007/s43681-025-00670-3

Truby, J. (2020). Governing artificial intelligence to benefit the UN sustainable development goals. *Sustainable Development*. https://doi.org/10.1002/sd.2048

Ulnicane, I., Knight, W., Leach, T., Stahl, B. C., & Wanjiku, W. (2021). Framing governance for a contested emerging technology: Insights from AI policy. *Policy and Society, 40*(2), 158–177. https://doi.org/10.1080/14494035.2020.1855800

Van Noordt, C., & Misuraca, G. (2022). Artificial intelligence for the public sector: Results of landscaping the use of AI in government across the European Union. *Government Information Quarterly, 39*(3). Retrieved April 11, 2025 from https://www.sciencedirect.com/science/article/pii/S0740624X22000478

Voss, E., & Rego, R. (2019). *Digitalization and public services: A labor perspective* (pp. 1–30). University of Lisbon. Retrieved May 6, 2025, from https://repositorio.ulisboa.pt/bitstream/10451/40088/1/ICS_RRego_Digitalization.pdf

Vyhmeister, E., Castane, G., Östberg, P. O., & Thevenin, S. (2023). A responsible AI framework: Pipeline contextualisation. *AI and Ethics, 3*, 175–197. https://doi.org/10.1007/s43681-022-00154-8

Wibowo, A. (2025). Redefining governance in Indonesia through Blockchain-integrated AI. In *Proceedings of the 4th international conference on governance, ethics, and management in technology (ICoGEMT-4)* (pp. 79–85). Retrieved February 23, 2025 from http://conference.loupiasconference.org/index.php/ICoGEMT-4/article/view/567

Williamson, B., Eynon, R., Knox, J., & Davies, H. (2023). Critical perspectives on AI in education: Political economy, discrimination, commercialization, governance and ethics. In B. du Boulay, A. Mitrovic, & K. Yacef (Eds.), *Handbook of artificial intelligence in education*. Edward Elgar Publishing. Retrieved June 4, 2025, from https://doi.org/10.4337/9781800375413.00037

Wirtz, B. W., Weyerer, J. C., & Geyer, C. (2019). Artificial intelligence and the public sector—Applications and challenges. *Journal of Public Administration, 42*(7), 596–615.

Wirtz, B. W., Weyerer, J. C., & Kehl, K. (2022). Governance of artificial intelligence: A risk and guideline-based integrative framework. *Government Information Quarterly, 39*(4), Article 101685. https://doi.org/10.1016/j.giq.2022.101685

Yigitcanlar, T., David, A., Li, W., Fookes, C., Bibri, S. E., & Ye, X. (2024). Unlocking artificial intelligence adoption in local governments: Best practice lessons from real-world implementations. *Smart Cities, 7*(4), 64. https://doi.org/10.3390/smartcities7040064

Zhao, J., & Gómez Fariñas, B. (2023). Artificial intelligence and sustainable decisions. *European Business Organization Law Review, 24*, 1–39. https://doi.org/10.1007/s40804-022-00262-2

Walsh, G., Stogiannos, N., Van de Venter, R., Rainey, C., Tam, W., McFadden, S.,... & Malamateniou, C. (2023). Responsible AI practice and AI education are central to AI implementation: A rapid review for all medical imaging professionals in Europe. *BJR| open, 5*(1), 20230033.

Enhancing Democratic Deliberations with AI: Insights from the ORBIS Co-creation Journey

10

Ilaria Mariani, Lucas Anastasiou, Sofiane Elguendouze, Francesca Rizzo, Grazia Concilio, Elena Cabrio, Serena Villata, Ioannis Efstathiou, George Domalis, and Anna De Liddo

I. Mariani (✉) · F. Rizzo
Department of Design, Politecnico di Milano, Milan, Italy
e-mail: ilaria1.mariani@polimi.it

F. Rizzo
e-mail: francesca.rizzo@polimi.it

G. Concilio
Department of Architecture and Urban Studies, Politecnico di Milano, Milan, Italy
e-mail: grazia.concilio@polimi.it

L. Anastasiou · A. De Liddo
The Open University, Milton Keynes, UK
e-mail: lucas.anastasiou@open.ac.uk

A. De Liddo
e-mail: anna.deliddo@open.ac.uk

S. Elguendouze · E. Cabrio
INRIA Centre de Recherche Sophia Antipolis Méditerranée, Université Côte d'Azur, Valbonne, France
e-mail: sofiane.elguendouze@inria.fr

E. Cabrio
e-mail: elena.cabrio@inria.fr

S. Villata
Center National de la Recherche Scientifique—Délégation Côte D'azur, INRIA Centre de Recherche Sophia Antipolis Méditerranée, Valbonne, France
e-mail: serena.villata@inria.fr

I. Efstathiou · G. Domalis
Novelcore, Athens, Greece
e-mail: efstathiou@novelcore.eu

S. K. Aikins and T. Dimitrijevska-Markoski (eds.), *Artificial Intelligence and Government*, https://doi.org/10.1007/978-3-032-12344-2_10

1 AI and the Democratic Discourse

1.1 AI's Role in Public Deliberation

The integration of AI into public deliberation processes has introduced a paradigm shift in citizen engagement, promising enhanced efficiency, inclusivity, and responsiveness in democratic governance (Sieber et al., 2024). It acts as a catalyst for participatory democracy, from offering new pathways for public interaction with government to effectively increasing civic input through advanced data collection and processing tools—exploring techniques such as NLP and sensor networks (Ghahramani et al., 2021). Moreover, by implementing tools like automated translation, key point identification, monitoring of public sentiment, and policy feedback analysis—just to mention a few—it can enhance citizen-government relations and empower public engagement (Fernández-Martínez et al., 2018; Galais et al., 2021). Acknowledging that AI systems can be leveraged to support more informed and plural decision-making, it is worth exploring how greater citizen engagement could lead to improved design and UX in AI applications (Leslie et al., 2021; Straub et al., 2023).

These advancements are bringing specific challenges, including a lack of transparency and accountability (Manias et al., 2023), as well as concerns over algorithmic bias, fairness, and the protection of individual rights (Buhmann & Fieseler, 2023). These issues are particularly relevant and impactful in public decision-making processes where AI systems can inadvertently perpetuate inequalities and representation issues, or lack the explicability required to gain public trust, thereby complicating their role in democratic deliberation. Moreover, the opacity of AI poses risks in bridging knowledge divides between experts and citizens, challenging inclusive governance (Sachdeva et al., 2015; Sieber et al., 2024).

Buhmann and Fieseler (2023) emphasise 'responsible AI innovation' as central in this discourse, requiring a 'deep democratic' debate that involves stakeholders from public sectors (government and academia), private sectors, and civil society—the quadruple helix model (Carayannis & Campbell, 2010; Schütz et al., 2019)—in critically assessing AI's goals and impacts. Responsible AI innovation refers to a governance approach that addresses operational and technological aspects of AI while prioritising its ethical implications, thus ensuring that AI systems are developed and deployed in a way that is transparent, accountable, and equitable. This meta-level governance responsibility involves scrutinising and tracing AI systems to effectively manage potential harms and maximise opportunities for beneficial outcomes, while favouring performance and innovation potential (Goodman & Flaxman, 2017; Herrmann, 2023; Voegtlin & Scherer, 2017).

G. Domalis
e-mail: domalis@novelcore.eu

In this regard, active and collaborative engagement is specifically recognised as central for fostering responsible innovation and public trust, yet the technical opacity of AI systems often prevents citizens from fully engaging in or scrutinising these processes. The authors highlight the need to critically examine the power dynamics among various stakeholders, particularly the knowledge gaps and epistemic inequalities between AI specialists and the broader public. It also raises questions about the potentially ambiguous role of the AI industry in controlling and shaping access to these initiatives, thus arguing for a multi-dimensional approach to AI innovation and governance, targeting challenges related to data quality, biassed outcomes, and epistemic concerns (Buhmann & Fieseler, 2023).

AI systems can serve as both the catalyst for and means of public participation. AI technologies might be the reason for participation, as when their deployment in sensitive areas—such as determining welfare eligibility or assessing child protection risks—sparks public interest and debate. Additionally, AI can enhance how the public interacts with government processes (de Sousa et al., 2019). For instance, AI-driven systems can be used to elaborate and make sense of citizens' inputs (Romberg & Escher, 2024), use citizens' data to inform decision-making for instance monitoring environmental conditions like air quality through data analysis from sensors and public inputs (Represa et al., 2020), or it can enhance interaction via apps or websites, reporting issues, and receiving updates and advisories. Moreover, AI can streamline interactions between citizens and governments (Kuziemski & Misuraca, 2020), such as through chatbots that facilitate access to public services or collect feedback efficiently (Aoki, 2020). Nevertheless, the integration of AI into deliberation processes calls for a deeper engagement of civil society in the design and decision-making stages of AI systems, ensuring that their implementation is attentive to public needs and concerns and guards against manipulative or biased practices. In this regard, Sieber and colleagues (2024) emphasise the necessity of a multi-disciplinary approach to integrating AI into deliberative processes, advocating for an inclusive framework that engages citizens not only in the deliberative practices themselves (Ekman & Amnå, 2012) but also in designing the AI tools and platforms that support these activities, extending beyond traditional civic participation. They argue that this approach must extend beyond traditional technical and governance domains to incorporate ethical, social, and policy-oriented perspectives. A cross-disciplinary framework can serve to facilitate meaningful civic engagement, addressing complex ethical considerations inherent in AI deployment (Prabhakaran et al., 2022).

1.2 Background and State of the Art

AI is currently applied to enhance civic engagement across multiple government functions, from public administration to healthcare (de Sousa et al., 2019). This shift marks a transition from traditional technology solutions that often require manual intervention and processing, to more dynamic, AI-powered solutions able to automate complex tasks, enhance accuracy, and provide real-time analytics. In the area of AI for deliberation, citizen engagement is evidently departing from lower tiers of participation, such as consultative and informative roles (Arnstein, 1969). This transition to the upper tiers is feasible by leveraging the capabilities of AI to enhance participation, towards more dynamic, interactive forms that transform passive participants into active co-creators, enhancing their capacity to influence decisions and monitor their implementation continuously, and pointing at a future characterised by full citizen control and partnership. Studies on AI initiatives for government digitalisation show a growing usage of such technologies to engage citizens more directly, particularly in the co-production and sharing of information (Reis et al., 2019; Simonofski et al., 2017; Wilson, 2022). This is specifically discussed in the literature stream on Civic Tech, especially in the role of AI in processing large datasets to amplify citizens' voices (Skaržauskienė & Mačiulienė, 2020).

This evolution reflects, on the one hand, a shift towards leveraging AI to enhance the collaborative aspects of public services, policy-making, and governance (Duberry, 2022; Zuiderwijk et al., 2021)—for instance relying on AI to turn social media into hubs of collective intelligence (Ghahramani et al., 2021), thus emphasising the role of technology in facilitating citizen participation as co-producers and informed users (Gilman, 2017). On the other hand, it is moving towards multi-stakeholder dialogues and the inclusion of diverse perspectives in the design and monitoring of AI (Cath et al., 2018; de Sousa et al., 2019).

Complementarily, Simonofski and colleagues (2017) delineate various roles citizens can assume in smart cities—ranging from democratic participants and value co-producers to system users—, thus highlighting how digital technologies are restructuring traditional civic roles, aiming to rectify the shortcomings of previous governance models through enhanced collaborative processes. Nevertheless, despite the recognised importance of involving citizens and multi-stakeholder groups in designing AI solutions to enhance deliberation practices, there is scant literature on the subject, particularly regarding how such engagement is operationalised to shape AI solutions (Zuiderwijk et al., 2021).

1.3 Current Challenges and Research Gaps

In exploring the interplay between AI and civic participation, particularly within the context of democratic deliberation, Sieber and colleagues (2024) outline how it can offer both new pathways and unique barriers to engagement. AI's opacity, or its 'black-box' nature, often emerges as a limit to public comprehension and oversight, making it difficult for non-experts to understand or engage in meaningful dialogue about its functions and implications.

By examining civic participation in AI across a range of disciplines, current reviews often remain confined to specific disciplines—especially urban planning—posing less attention to the role that software engineers and computer scientists play in setting the AI governance ecosystem, especially when AI development is frequently outsourced by municipalities, potentially sidelining the diverse perspectives necessary for comprehensive governance strategies (Wan & Sieber, 2023). This lack of transparency affects how citizens use AI as end-users, often with limited awareness of how it operates, and also impacts their ability to participate effectively in AI-enhanced processes and AI-related discussions, including shaping AI applications for supporting deliberation.

In addition to the well-documented challenges of explainability in AI-enhanced deliberations (Coussement et al., 2024; Siachos & Karacapilidis, 2024), establishing sound ethical foundations, and embedding principles of trustworthy AI by design, there is the need for a more multidisciplinary approach to effectively enact the participatory turn (Delgado et al., 2021), thus ensuring a broad range of insights into how AI technologies are designed, implemented, and governed (Duberry, 2022; Wilson, 2022).

In this regard, continuous stakeholder engagement and co-creation could be adopted to enhance alignment of AI-tools for deliberation with societal needs (Mariani et al., 2025). Still, the various reviews on the use of AI in enhancing civic participation and deliberative democracy (Reis et al., 2019; Savaget et al., 2019; Sieber et al., 2024; Zuiderwijk et al., 2021) reveals a gap on citizen and stakeholder engagement for the development of AI solutions for public services and democratic deliberation. The literature on co-creating AI for deliberative democracy is still in its formative stages, suggesting an emerging field that intertwines technology with participatory governance. Duerinckx and colleagues (2024) highlight the paucity of comprehensive studies focused specifically on this intersection. While there is extensive discourse on public participation in technology development and the implications of AI in societal contexts, focused discussions on how co-creation processes can directly enhance deliberative democracy through AI are less frequent and sparse.

In this landscape, the approach taken by ORBIS offers a privilege setting to address this gap, demonstrating how inclusive and participatory methodologies can significantly enrich AI development for enhancing democratic deliberation and subsequent governance. This chapter specifically explores how the co-creation journey has informed the development of AI tools designed to foster democratic processes, deriving knowledge from two years of on-field experimentation. Nevertheless, as more empirical evaluation of ORBIS pilots and the effectiveness of these AI tools in real-world policymaking are underway, these are beyond the current scope of this chapter.

2 The ORBIS Project

2.1 Integrating AI with Democratic Processes in ORBIS

This chapter presents insights from the Horizon Europe project ORBIS (GA: 101094765),[1] situated at the intersection of AI and democratic processes. At its core, ORBIS develops and integrates AI-enhanced tools that are designed to enhance the accessibility, understandability, and overall quality of deliberation processes, allowing for broader participation and a deeper comprehension of public positions and opinions across various policy issues. Four AI tools are identified to address the persistent challenges within the deliberative domain, such as the need to effectively summarise extensive discussions, process large volumes of data, identify central discussion topics, capture diverse perspectives, and transition towards generating actionable inputs for decision-making and policy formulation.

The four tools are: Argument Mining (AM), which extracts and structures arguments from text; Feedback Aggregator (FA), which organises and summarises discussion content; Explanation Generator (EG), which provides transparent explanations of AI processes; and Policy Recommendation (PR), which generates actionable insights for policy-making. Each tool plays a specific role in transforming the raw data of public discourse into more graspable, structured, insightful, and strategically actionable information. Overall, their integration streamlines the deliberation process while ensuring that the outcomes are directly applicable to policy-making and governance, thereby supporting more informed and inclusive decision-making frameworks.

The tools use advanced data analytics, NLP, and algorithmic models to distil vast public input—from structured arguments and position statements to open discussions and real-time feedback—into actionable insights. All together they constitute the ORBIS toolkit, which runs within a sub-set of deliberative platforms related to the project (Fig. 1):

- **BCause** (bcause.app) focuses on structured discussions, organised into pro and con positions, visualised through timelines and argument trees; it also generates summaries and identifies key insights that advance discussions.
- **PolisOrbis** (polisorbis.eu) is built on the open-source Pol.is engine, and is designed for large-scale participation and visualises emerging opinion clusters in real-time.
- **Democratic Reflection** (democratic-reflection.web.app) is a collective intelligence platform to harness real-time audience feedback over live or video recorded events, using visual analytics technology to provide insights on the audience position against the ongoing discussion.

[1] ORBIS (2023–2026) aims to bridge the gap between citizens and policy-making institutions by creating innovative socio-technical solutions for fostering a more inclusive, transparent, trustworthy and trust-based deliberative democracy in Europe through AI-enhanced tools.

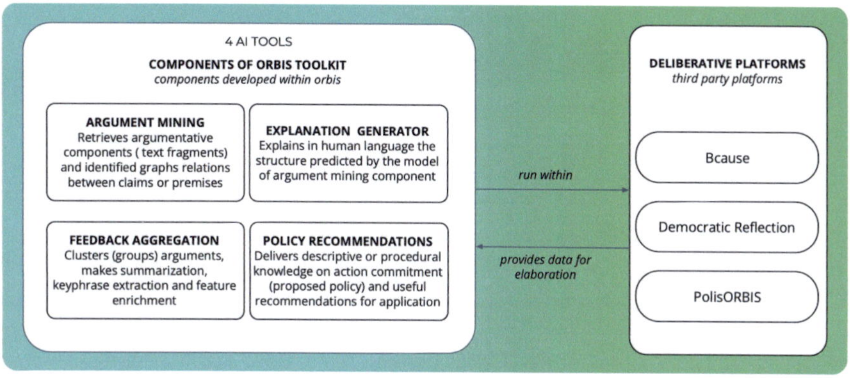

Fig. 1 AI components in the ORBIS toolkit, their description, and interaction with a subset of third-party deliberative platforms

In different ways, each platform can significantly benefit from the further integration of AI to analyse and visualise data, providing debate moderators with essential support for managing discussions. AI can support both moderators and participants in gathering insights from extensive discussions and comprehend the variety of contributions, enhancing the overall effectiveness and inclusivity of the debate. Therefore, through its toolkit, ORBIS is contributing to advancing AI-enhanced democratic and inclusive deliberations by exploring how co-creation can inform and steer the development of more desirable AI tools. The entire experimentation is rooted in principles of ethical AI system development (Kop, 2021), which in the domain of AI-based tools for deliberative democracy refers to the intentional development of AI systems that embody principles of transparency, fairness, accountability, and ethical alignment with democratic values from the outset, ORBIS engages multiple stakeholders into the design of AI-based tools through co-creation and co-design, thus ensuring socially desirability and ethically robustness.

2.2 ORBIS Pilots as Settings for Driving Innovation

ORBIS stands out for a continuous approach to stakeholder engagement for informing its AI solutions, incorporating a structured co-creation and co-design methodology that actively involves diverse participants throughout the analysis, design, development, and testing. This approach strongly relied upon the ORBIS six pilots, aiming at aligning strategies and tools with the multifaceted needs of the communities they aim to serve. As such, pilots are intended as specific, real-world applications where the project's methodologies and technologies are implemented and tested. ORBIS involves pilots initiated by civil society organizations and think tanks, which were identified as relevant real-life scenarios for exploring the multi-level intricacies of deliberative practices across different scales.

	P1 REIMAGINING THE BUILDING BLOCKS OF DEMOCRACY	P2 TEENS FOR DEMOCRACY	P3 YOUNG THINKERS AND EU DECISION-MAKERS	P4 FUTURE4CITIZENS	P5 TRANSITION MECHANISMS FOR A DEMOCRATIC CITY	P6 ALLIANCE FOR ENTREPRENEURSHIP AND DEVELOPMENT IN WESTERN GREECE
Org.	Democracy and Culture Foundation	Democracy and Culture Foundation	Center for European Policy Studies	Re-Imagine Europa	Rob De Matt	Perifereia Dytiki Ellada
Scale	International	Initially European, to scale out to a global level	European	Initially national, to scale out to a European level	Initially local, to scale out to national and EU level	Initially regional, to scale out to the national level
Objective	Proposing policy recommendations to enhance democratic resilience, initiating global debates via DCF community and Athens Democracy Forum.	Engages teenagers (aged 13-17) in policy design through municipal councils in five cities. Aims to bridge the intergenerational gap.	Provide a platform for young minds to express innovative ideas and perspectives on the policy scene.	Enhance dialogue between citizens and policymakers to foster inclusive, transparent, and trustful deliberative democracy in Europe.	Collect diverse voices in Milan to foster democratic processes and participation in urban planning and policy-making.	Acts as a network to facilitate the principles of the Small Business Act, promoting economic and social development.
Team	2 persons from pilot	2 persons from pilot	4 to 5 persons from pilot	4 persons from pilot	3 persons from pilot	2 persons from pilot
Method	Employs citizen assemblies, structured workshops, and policy advocacy sessions. Integrates top-down and bottom-up approaches..	Annual Teens' Athens Democracy Forum, preparatory meetings, and collaborative sessions with policymakers.	Workshops, online webinars, in-person sessions, and Ideas Lab sessions for public events.	Listen-Reframe-Act methodology integrated with ORBIS platform functionalities.	Structured dialogues, co-design workshops, and public consultations facilitated by RDM in collaboration with associations.	Regional policy recommendation development, collaborative networks of entrepreneurs, and thematic assemblies.

Fig. 2 ORBIS's six pilots (P) described per organisation, scale, democratic objectives, team from each pilot, and deliberative method

These pilots feature a diverse range of methodologies, participants, and deliberative objectives, aiming to enhance the efficacy of deliberation within democratic systems. All together, these real-world settings provide a valuable opportunity to assess to what extent the AI tools and deliberative models perform across different demographic, cultural, and organisational settings. Each pilot presents a specific and complementary form of deliberation, serving as a unique setting to examine how various deliberative approaches, community interactions, and technological innovations interact and influence one another.

The primary objective of these pilots is to advance deliberative practices that support democratic transformations, positioning them as essential contributors to the responsible and informed development of technological solutions. However, they are not only settings for testing and refining AI-based tools; they serve as innovative experiments in their own right, designed to generate, validate, and refine insights that drive democratic enhancement through technology. As such, they are central for developing AI tools that genuinely align with and promote the principles of effective and inclusive deliberation. Figure 2 details the specific features and characteristics of each pilot, highlighting their unique contributions to the project's overarching goals. As such, they contribute to bridging the gap between theoretical research and practical application.

2.3 Co-creation and Co-design in ORBIS. The Study Methodology

Relying on its pilots, the ORBIS project adopts an iterative co-creation approach, engaging stakeholders through multiple phases to continuously refine and improve project outcomes. The data gathering methodology for the ORBIS pilots involves a structured co-design process, initiated with a series of exploratory workshops

(Fig. 3). Six online workshops were held in July 2023, involving the organisers responsible for running the deliberative experiments into pilots (two to three for pilot), alongside community members ranging from 3 to 10 individuals per session, and one to two stakeholders from their broader ecosystem. Focused on deliberative democracy principles and practices, these workshops engaged a total of 35 participants and were instrumental in shaping initial user scenarios. This groundwork laid the foundation for subsequent user and technical requirements.[2] In October 2023, a follow-up collaborative in-person workshop in Milan involved 26 persons as representatives from all consortium partners. This session focused on matching technological capabilities with real community needs identified by the pilots. These discussions helped shape the development of requirements for deliberation platforms and AI tools, ensuring they would effectively serve each pilot's unique goal.

A second series of online workshops with 10 participants each delved deeper into past and planned activities of each pilot, mapping out their deliberative purposes and interactions with their ecosystems. This activity resulted in the identification of specific technological needs, expectations, and potential scaling directions. The series includes a follow-up of three additional workshops focused on exploring technological possibilities, further shaping the design of pilot activities and ensuring that technology development was closely aligned with their operational and democratic objectives.

3 Co-creation's Role in Shaping AI-Enhanced Tools

The iterative development process of ORBIS's technological components was fundamentally shaped through a structured co-creation journey with six organisations in charge of running deliberative experiments in pilot settings (pilot organisers from now on), which included two series of co-design workshops—see par. 2.2. Following a value-driven methodology (Friedman & Hendry, 2019), each development iteration incorporated direct feedback from pilot communities through dedicated co-design workshops and testing sessions. These sessions, conducted in regular periodic time instances since the early stages of the project, enabled real-time adjustments to component functionalities, particularly in areas of argument mining and feedback aggregation, ensuring alignment with actual deliberative needs.

The process employed a five-phase process, which incorporated co-design activities (Fig. 4). (i) 1-on-1 co-design workshops allowed the identification of points of struggle, challenges and aspirations, shaping the design of (ii) initial scenarios prototyping, which were (iii) analysed and reworked to reach consensus on

[2] This is detailed in ORBIS deliverable "D2.2 Technical and operational specifications and reference architecture".

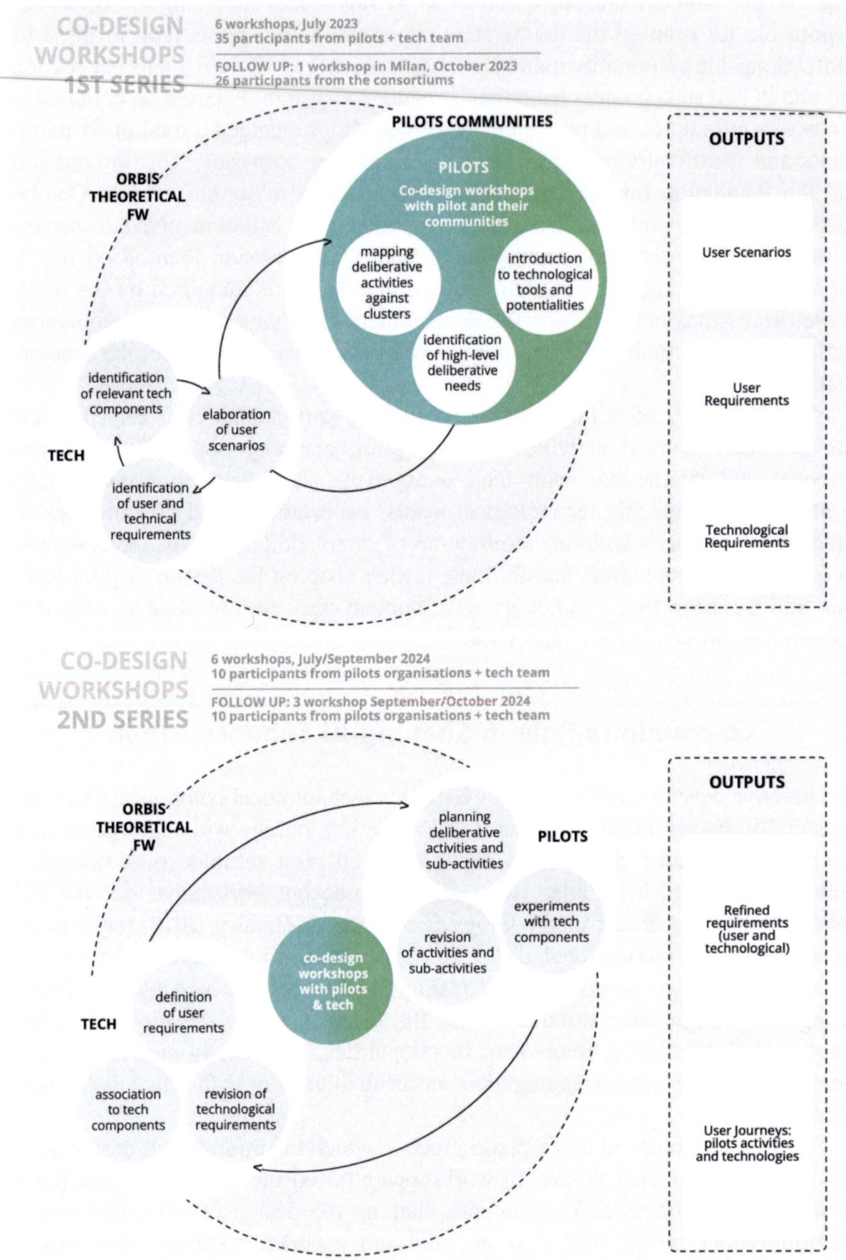

Fig. 3 The structure of the first and second series of co-design workshops, highlighting iterations and interplays between the tech team, the project six pilots, and their communities

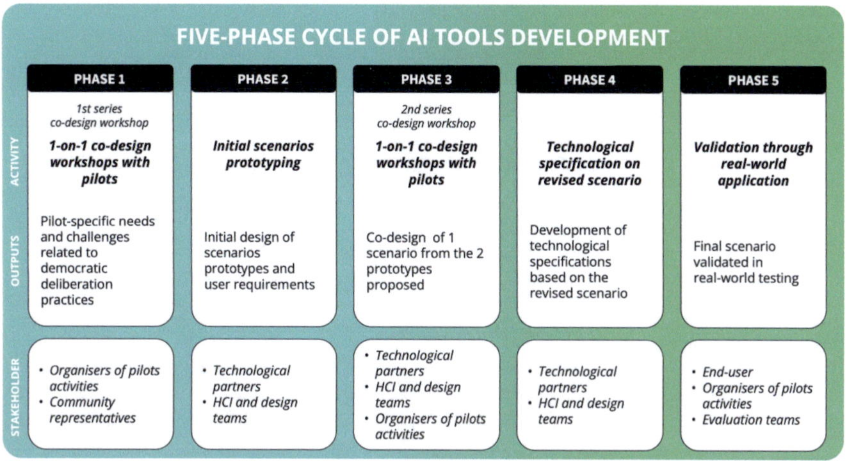

Fig. 4 Five-phase of the development process, detailing activities, the tangible outputs generated, and the stakeholders involved at each phase

one revised scenario per pilot. (iv) The detailed feedback from pilots organisations guided the development of technical specifications, which are ultimately (v) validated through real-world application.

3.1 Insights from ORBIS's Pilot Organisers and Communities

The multi-phase co-design process facilitated a continuous generation of data, ensuring insights and requirements were consistently captured to inform the design and development of AI-enhanced tools and their integration into the deliberation platforms. User requirements were mainly gathered from the first series of co-design workshops, where those responsible for organising deliberative experiments in the pilot settings engaged with representatives from their communities and provided insights based on their deliberative experiences. Each pilot has contributed to a deeper understanding of how technology can be tailored to enhance democratic deliberation, spotting several key areas where AI functionalities can be exploited to better serve democratic objectives. The high-level user requirements elaborated from these inputs are summarised in Table 1, further elaborating their relevance to specific deliberative objectives and how the ORBIS toolkit components meet these needs with distinct functionalities.

The insights in Table 1 highlight how the use of AI to analyse large volumes of public input is particularly relevant for distilling complex data, ranging from summarising long discussions and identifying key points and emerging themes, thereby making public deliberations more accessible and understandable, up to producing actionable insights able to support policy-making. Overall, the user requirements

Table 1 AI functionalities for democratic objectives

User requirements from pilots	Support towards deliberative objectives	AI functionalities
Efficient brainstorming and idea management	Facilitated brainstorming sessions, with functionalities for automatically identifying, clustering, and prioritising ideas to maintain focus and momentum during discussions	FA extracts and clusters key ideas from discussions and displays results in BCause; AM analyses the various topics and provides interconnections among different participants' points of view within the same topic
Enhanced discussion management	Automated identification and organisation of opinions and discussion threads to effectively manage complex debates. Includes clustering discussions by positions (pro-against) and topics to enhance rational engagement	BCause structures discussions in threads; AM and FA work together to extract, cluster and summarise discussions, enhancing better understanding of complex debates
Real-time data analysis	Analysis of ongoing discussions to enhance understanding of arguments, track discussion directions, diversify contributions, and identify potential polarisations	BCause organises real-time inputs from discussion within threads; FA and AM provides inputs for visualisation of directions and diversity of discourse
Asynchronous and synchronous interaction support	Capturing inputs from both in-person and online discussions consistently, accommodating real-time and delayed interactions to maintain continuity across various communication modes	BCause supports real-time discussion and provision of inputs; Implementation of asynchronous interactions via upload of transcript, then structured in threads with main topics and positions
Integration of visual inputs	Integration of visual aids into platforms to help participants quickly comprehend complex data, thereby facilitating informed decision-making during discussions	Visualisations are provided in BCause and PolisOrbis upon toolkit inputs—they are not provided real-time but upon moderator's approval, to ensure human verification before release of unsupervised elaborations
Facilitation and moderation support	Enhancing discussion effectiveness by preventing dominance by few participants or groups and ensuring balanced, inclusive dialogue, identify potential sources of conflict early	BCause has an in-platform feature that invites to share interest against positions, providing a comprehensive visualisation; FA supports clustering from discourses, showing diversity of positions

(continued)

Table 1 (continued)

User requirements from pilots	Support towards deliberative objectives	AI functionalities
Transparent and trustworthy AI processes	Implements transparent mechanisms that clearly explain the generation and use of information, particularly when AI is involved, ensuring that all stakeholders understand and trust how their inputs are processed and integrated into decision-making processes	EG clarifies how AI processes data into actionable information like argument relation identification, clustering and summarization, enhancing transparency and trust in the system
Multi-linguality	Enhances participation and inclusivity by accommodating a broader segment of the population, allowing non-English speakers to engage meaningfully in AI-enhanced deliberations	Beyond the current scope of ORBIS for developing specific features; however, experiments are being conducted to exploit automatic translation, enabling inputs in non-English languages to be processed by the ORBIS toolkit
Reporting and summarising	Summarise discussions, distil key-points, establish common grounds for consensus, and provide context-sensitive decision-making support; support for breaking down decisions into smaller, manageable parts to achieve more effective and inclusive outcomes	FA summarises discourses and clusters topics outputting accurate and fine-grained summaries which are topic-specific, enhancing understanding and consensus-building
Policy conversion and actionable outputs	Translation of discussion outcomes into actionable policies, ensuring that deliberations are productive and lead to tangible policy changes	FA clusters are built upon structured discussions provided by AM, and PR extracts data for building actionable and non-generic recommendations, shown in BCause

AM Argument mining; *FA* Feedback aggregator; *EG* Explanation generator; *PR* Policy recommendation

indicate the need of AI functionalities that contribute to the creation of more dynamic, inclusive, and effective democratic conditions in environments where decisions need to be made based on broad community input, as it ensures that diverse voices are heard and considered in the decision-making process. Moreover, they also highlight the importance of aligning with ethical considerations which are inherent in democratic governance, suggesting the development of AI functionalities that are technically proficient and robust in terms of ethical integrity.

Below the components are shortly presented and discussed against the democratic objectives they support, showing how they meet user requirements emerged from pilots.

1. **Argument Mining (AM)**. AM focuses on automatically extracting and structuring argumentative components from texts. It aims to analyse how arguments are constructed, helping to understand and map the reasoning within various types of discourse, such as debates, legal documents, or online discussions. In the classical AM pipeline, the argumentative components are categorised into Premises (Evidences) and Claims (Positions, Opinions, etc.), and the relationships between them are either Support or Attack (Cabrio & Villata, 2018). These components along with their relationships are typically organised into logical graph structures, revealing the reasoning behind public policy discussions and showing how conclusions are reached by representing argument interactions which enhances the structural understanding of discussions.
2. **Feedback Aggregation (FA)**. FA clusters and summarises discussions, extracting key phrases and enriching the data with relevant features to provide concise and meaningful insights. This component processes the vast amounts of input generated during discussions to highlight prevalent themes, sentiment trends, and emerging consensus, which supports organisers and participants in focusing on critical issues and streamlining decision-making processes.
3. **Explanation Generator (EG)**. This component generates human-readable explanations of the data processed by AI components, aiming at enhancing users' (both citizens and institutions) understanding of how deliberative conclusions were derived, outlining the AI's process in a transparent manner, thereby increasing trust in decision-making processes within ORBIS. When the system relies on interpretable AI models, EG outlines the computational steps behind clustering, summarisation, or sentiment detection to make the reasoning process transparent and traceable. However, when large language models (LLMs) are used—whose inner workings cannot be fully explained due to their black-box nature—explainability is achieved through complementary design strategies: data visualisations, narrative summaries, and contextual cues that communicate how the model has interpreted and rephrased content.
4. **Policy Recommendation (PR)**. PR analyses inputs provided by FA to support policy formation and collective decision-making. It elaborates insights from the structured arguments and summarised feedback, shaping them into potential policy recommendations, which are aligned with the articulated preferences and concerns of the discussion participants.

AM and FA work in tandem to manage and refine the discourse within these platforms; AM structures and identifies key elements of the debate, while FA clusters and summarises this information to make discussions more accessible and actionable. EG enhances transparency by providing clear, understandable explanations of how data is processed and presented, building trust among users by ensuring the AI's decision-making process is visible and comprehensible. PR leverages inputs from FA to formulate informed, pragmatic policies that reflect collective discussions. Together, these components exploit AI's capabilities to boost interactions in an environment where different voices are empowered to contribute to shaping democratic processes.

3.2 Component-Specific Co-creation

All the components of the ORBIS toolkit have been shaped to varying extents by insights from pilot organisers, benefiting from ongoing interactions with those overseeing deliberative activities across the pilots. These interactions have brought a deep understanding of specific needs and challenges into the development phases. Each component was designed in response to the diverse requirements gathered during the interaction with the pilots. The iterative co-design and feedback sessions significantly informed the outcomes of all components—from refining their structure and visual outputs to integrating them into the deliberation platforms in ways that are meaningful and supportive for democratic deliberation purposes. Among these, the argument mining component in particular underwent substantial refinements that enhanced its structure and closely tailored it to the democratic needs of pilots.

Below, the different components are discussed, highlighting how the overall co-creation journey, and the specific co-design with pilots affected their development and refinement.

Argumentation Mining (AM)
In the context of ORBIS, AM holds significant potential to support AI-enhanced democratic deliberation and decision-making, particularly for the responsible deployment of AI in a wider range of contexts where such practices occur, such as non-governmental organisations, community groups, and other public or private sectors involved in policymaking and civic engagement. Following initial discussions with pilots, the primary focus was on adapting AM theory to meet the needs of participatory democracy by designing AM methods capable of extracting argumentative structures from pilot data (raw text). A key challenge concerned the lack of sufficient pilot data to effectively train AM models, which became evident when the project was in its early phases, and required action before the starting of experimentation with real participants in the pilot settings. The use of BCause platform implies a specific approach to AM, since discourses are structured. BCause data presents indeed a distinct format, where discussions are organised at the statement level. Each statement (i.e., an argumentative sentence articulated by a participant) is either a position (a stance taken on a particular argumentative topic) or an argument that either supports or attacks a given position. This data limitation and the contextual features of BCause prompted a shift towards refining AM models for both argument component detection and relation classification. As a consequence, existing pseudonymised datasets of discussions available in the BCause platform were used to drive the implementation.

Given the availability of such structured statement-level data, the classical AM pipeline has been adjusted to focus on what we now refer to as 'statement-level' argumentation mining. This initial modification was introduced to better align the AM model with the type of discourse occurring within the BCause platform, which is one of the platforms used by participants during pilot deliberative experiments. Furthermore, this adjustment ensures that the AM component is compatible with the actual deliberative interactions within the BCause platform, making it a valuable and relevant adaptation for the project's objectives. Similar to traditional AM, the process is carried out in two key steps: (1) Statement Classification, where each statement is categorised as either a position, a supporting argument, or an attacking argument, and (2) Statement Relation Classification, where the specific positions targeted by specific supporting or attacking arguments are identified and linked to each other. Further enhancement and refinement of relation classification is achieved through iterative testing within pilot settings, and feedback from both pilot organisations and participants to their deliberative experiments as end-users.

However, as initial data from preliminary pilot experiments became available, it was evident that the argumentation pipeline required further refinement to better accommodate discussions that occur in a flow of discourse, rather than as structured data. Unlike the BCause data, where statements are segmented into short sentences typically expressing a single position or piece of evidence, the pilot data lacked this predefined structure. While the first modification effectively processed data from the BCause platform, the unstructured and continuous nature of discussions in certain deliberative settings introduced complexities not previously accounted for. To answer this need, a return to a more classical AM approach has been experimented, revising the model to handle the formats of deliberative discourse. The challenge then was to extend and refine the AM component to process the pilot data effectively, enabling the automatic detection and retrieval of argumentation components directly from raw text, which could be not or weakly annotated, depending on the pilot—e.g. audio transcripts of discussions. Participants data and interaction with pilot organisers allowed the identification of specific issues with the AM model when applied to unstructured data, prompting a shift back towards a more classical approach that could handle a broader range of discourse types without the need for pre-segmentation.

As a consequence, in the current version of the component both the classical approach and the newer statement-level approach are coexisting, addressing the complementary needs that have emerged from the experimentation with the pilots. Therefore, the innovation brought during the project is twofold: the first is optimised for environments that inherently support structured argumentation, while the second extends the technology's applicability to more traditional, free-form deliberative texts, ensuring comprehensive coverage and functionality across varied settings. Table 2 outlines how each innovation caters to different data conditions within ORBIS, showing the flexibility and adaptability introduced in the AM model to handle various deliberative data formats.

Further iterative testing with pilots, aimed at improving the relation identification between argumentative components, revealed valuable insights for further

Table 2 Innovations in argument mining within ORBIS project

AM innovation type	Application setting	Description of AM application	AI functionalities
AM in structured discussions	Discussions in BCause	AM techniques are applied to discussions that are already pre-structured into discrete statements, each classified as a position, support, or attack, facilitating systematic mapping of argument relationships. AM is also applied to uncover implicit interactions between arguments across multiple discussions	– Direct processing of structured statements – Systematic relationship mapping between argumentative components – Inter-discussion relationship identification
AM in unstructured transcripts	Uploaded transcripts	AM adapts to handle raw text transcripts from deliberations not originally conducted on BCause. This approach processes continuous discourse to identify and classify argumentative components	– Capability to process raw, unstructured text – Classification of arguments without predefined segmentation

refinements of the AM component. One of the most promising directions pointed out was to support cross-discussion argument linkage, or inter-discussion argumentation. This means that the system is able to automatically identify relationships between arguments not just within a single discussion, but across multiple discussions centered around the same topic. This new feature is particularly useful in scenarios where discussions originate from different groups or communities—represented, in this case, by different pilots. The automatic identification of such cross-discussion relations allows the system to forecast argument linkages between diverse conversations, providing a more comprehensive view of the discourse landscape and offering further insights into overarching trends and patterns of reasoning within topics. For instance, users can be informed if their idea supports or attacks another idea from a separate discussion, even if that discussion is happening in a different thread, engaging a diverse community or group (i.e. reinforcing/challenging statements that span different discussions). This can significantly enhance user participation by stimulating interaction between discussions, encouraging participants to respond to or build on ideas outside their immediate discussion space. Bringing these links to light enriches the deliberative process beyond stimulating in-depth reflection. It facilitates deeper and more inclusive participation, by enabling a wider exchange of perspectives, thus resulting in more comprehensive, multifaceted, and deliberations which helps break down silos that can often form in deliberative settings, while being responsive to evolutions across different discussions. In turn, this could lead to more robust and well-rounded deliberation, as users gain insight into how their arguments resonate across different groups, potentially bridging gaps and building consensus on complex issues. Recent experimentation within ORBIS has also explored the integration of LLMs into AM (Elguendouze et al., 2025). This hybrid approach has yielded initial results indicating improved detection and connection of arguments across complex and lengthy discussions, thereby strengthening cross-discussion reasoning and interpretation. By combining LLMs with traditional AM techniques, these ongoing developments are enhancing the overall understanding of deliberative exchanges and offering richer, more transparent insights into public discourse dynamics.

Feedback Aggregator (FA)
FA summarises discussions for establishing a foundation for consensus and sensitive decision-making by clustering topics, and breaks down complex decisions into manageable parts. Its development involved integrating clustering and opinion analysis capabilities tailored to aggregate and synthesise the variety and diversity of opinions provided in deliberative settings effectively—a primary requirement identified by the pilot organiser and their communities of users.

FA performs multiple data analysis tasks, including feedback clustering, keyword extraction, title generation, and summarisation, based on the feedback of each cluster. Each of these tasks contributes to processing and presenting the feedback to participants in the deliberative discourse:

1. **Clustering**. FA groups feedback into coherent themes using an unsupervised machine learning algorithm, tailored to the specific discussion styles observed in the pilot settings. This operation categorises the data while integrating Wiki metadata to enrich the contextual understanding of the feedback. This approach leverages the extensive knowledge and insights contributed by a global community, informing the process with comprehensive and widely recognised information sources.
2. **Summarisation and title generation**. Employing advanced NLP techniques, FA generates titles and summaries for each cluster. These summaries are created through an abstractive summarisation approach that paraphrases large volumes of text constituting the content of the discussions, providing contextually rich insights. This method serves to distil complex discussions into concise overviews, which are representative of the different perspectives emerging across them, while enhancing the digestibility and relevance of the information. As such, it improves the accessibility and actionability of deliberative content, favouring a better understanding of the substance of debates without losing the specificity and depth that reflect the nuances of the discourse. Finally, concise and informative titles are generated to headline each cluster.
3. **Keyphrase extraction**. This function extracts and deduplicates the most relevant phrases from each cluster's text, highlighting significant themes and

facilitating quick insights into the clustered data. This feature aims at highlighting significant themes for facilitating quick insights into the clustered data.

Policy Recommendations (PR)

PR has been designed to translate outcomes of deliberative discourse into actionable insights for supporting policy formulation and collective decision-making, being recognised as especially relevant for pilot organisers who are actively seeking to bridge the gap between public discourse and policy action. By deriving descriptive or procedural knowledge from discussions, the tool suggests recommendations for policymakers that can be considered to inform policy adjustments or the creation of new initiatives. To enhance the utility of these recommendations, the component has been developed with the capability to link deliberations to existing policies. This functionality allows the tool to compare outcomes of ORBIS discussions with current policy frameworks, assessing how well public sentiments and recommendations are reflected in existing regulations. Its underlying LLM processes the discourse to determine whether points raised by participants are already addressed by current policies or if they represent novel considerations.

If participants introduce a novel perspective or recommendation not covered by existing policies, the tool suggests actions that could be taken to incorporate these new insights. This feature not only ensures that policies remain responsive to the evolving public opinion but also empowers participants by making their contributions potentially impactful on policy decisions. Thus, PR acts as a bridge for translating civic insights into policy actions, potentially playing a crucial role in enabling public discussions to inform policy development and reform.

The design of PR outcomes is a result of ongoing co-creation involving various experts from the consortium, aiming at integrating comprehensive insights from different fields. Current considerations regard the inclusion of functions to improve transparency and relevance of policy recommendations against the discussion and its constitutive elements. One of the features identified as relevant within co-creation sessions includes the reference to the volume of discussion posts that support a specific recommendation. This function would highlight the level of consensus or interest among participants while showing the weight of support behind certain ideas which are emerging from the discourse. This approach is also relevant for deliberation management purposes, especially during discussions unfolding through time. Moderators can leverage this feature to spot potential policy areas that have not yet been addressed by current policies, and would eventually benefit from additional exploration. By showing how many posts support a particular recommendation, moderators can encourage participants to further elaborate on these topics, thus contributing to making the discussions focused and productive.

The development of PR features is currently ongoing and it is drawing on the expertise of pilot organisers as well as of consortium members with different scientific backgrounds. This co-creation process is aimed at going beyond meeting the functional requirements identified in early stages (1st series of co-design workshop). Additional functionalities are currently being explored to further refine the tool's capability in enhancing policy deliberations, making each recommendation more actionable and backed by a significant body of participant input.

Explanation Generator (EG)

The role of the EG is that of translating complex decision-making processes into clearer, human-friendly insights,, revealing the structure, evolution, and dynamics of deliberation over time and in different contexts, as well as how such insights were reached, in a XAI perspective (Coussement et al., 2024; Karacapilidis et al., 2023; Rai, 2020; Siachos & Karacapilidis, 2024). As such, it answers a shared need of having a more transparent view of how decisions are shaped, allowing both citizens and institutions to better understand the mechanisms at play within AI-supported deliberation processes and thus build trust. To support this goal, a suite of functionalities aligned with the trust requirements identified by pilots, and summarised in Table 1, is being developed. One of the first steps was to generate explanations behind AM decisions. For instance, 'attention exploration' is a technique that highlights the parts of the text the model focuses on, assigning weights to each word based on its relevance to the task of argumentation. This allows users to intuitively understand which parts of the text influenced the model's decision most.

Further collaboration with pilot teams has led to the design of explanation strategies based on real-world usability feedback. One key direction is the development of explanations that reflect the model's confidence in classifying argumentative components, such as Premises and Claims, and the relationships between them (e.g., support or attack). This would not only enhance trust in the system's predictions but also complement AM by providing argument recommendations that enrich deliberations. These recommendations could be driven by explanation scores, helping users identify the strongest or weakest premises related to a claim, for instance. Such knowledge could stimulate ongoing discussions and deepen engagement between participants. However, careful moderation is necessary to manage the frequency and volume of recommendations, ensuring they add value without overwhelming users. This balance can be tailored on deliberative platforms like BCause to ensure the recommendations are well-integrated into the platform's workflow and user experience.

Integration of explanations for other components using their outputs has then been considered, and is currently ongoing, especially the ones from FA. Summaries, keyphrases, titles and clusters provide a rich layer of data that can be analysed to generate argumentative-style explanations to create a more holistic and interconnected understanding of the deliberative process. For instance, by examining the arguments within the same cluster, the EG can highlight patterns of agreement or disagreement around specific topics or policies. The goal is to move beyond just classifying arguments and their relations, clustering them or summarising them towards generating explanations that can inform policy making. For example, based on these explanations, the system could recommend which clusters of opinions to address, or where to seek further evidence or engagement. This would enable navigating complex issues more effectively, ensuring a wide range of perspectives is considered and offering participants a clearer understanding of how their contributions fit into the broader discussion. For instance, users could receive feedback on how their arguments align with or challenge those within the same cluster, encouraging more thoughtful and targeted contributions. This, in turn, could promote a more dynamic and productive deliberative process, where the quality and depth of debate are continuously improved through these insights.

3.3 How It Works in BCause. A Practical Example

This paragraph presents a more concrete example of how the ORBIS toolkit and its tools function, using the BCause platform as a practical case study. BCause is one of the three third-party platforms associated with ORBIS, and it shows the operational dynamics of the toolkit in enhancing deliberative processes through AI support.

The integration of the ORBIS toolkit in BCause is activated by accessing the 'Analytics' section (top right of Fig. 5), where the AI-enchanted tools consistently display their elaborations. Figure 6 is a synthesis of the interactions among the four tools, when they contribute to policy recommendations extraction. It illustrates the clusters generated from the discussion data (AM and FA), identifies the contributions to these clusters (EG), and highlights policy recommendations that provide actionable guidance (PR). A more detailed explanation of this process is provided below.

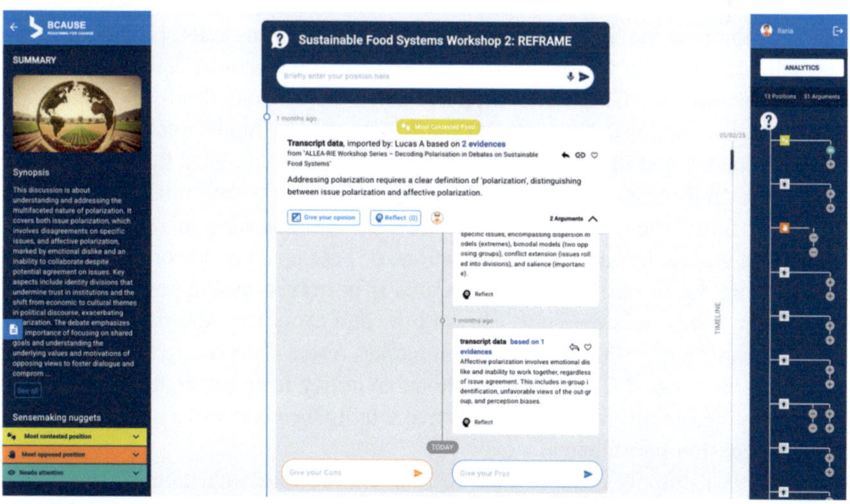

Fig. 5 Example of thread in BCause platform and how the discussion articulates

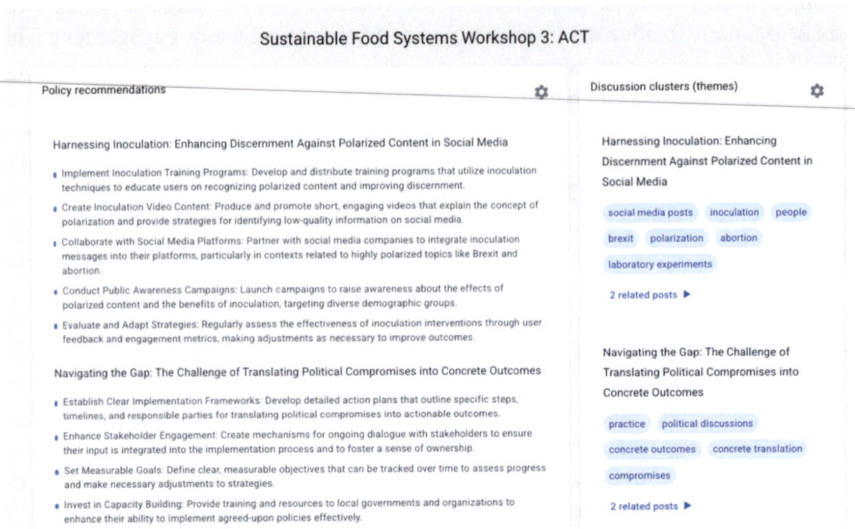

Fig. 6 The example of policy recommendations (PR) and clustering (FA) in BCause

In BCause, when a discussion is ongoing, FA enters the loop to extract key ideas from the discussion and cluster them, helping in clearly displaying these clusters within the BCause interface. This allows moderators and also participants to easily navigate through major discussion themes and insights. Meanwhile, AM analyses the content of the discussion, identifying different viewpoints and establishing connections between participants' opinions on similar topics. This analysis helps in structuring the discussions into coherent threads, making it easier for users to follow complex debates and understand the diversity of perspectives. As such, FA and AM contribute to the visual representation of these discussions, providing inputs that help visualise the various themes emerged in the discourse and the variety of positions within it. BCause also supports both synchronous (real-time) and asynchronous contributions. For asynchronous interactions, inputs such as transcripts can be uploaded and then structured by FA and AM into threads that highlight the main topics and positions, thus maintaining the continuity and integrity of discussions over time. Then, the EG clarifies how the AI processes this data, providing transparent and understandable explanations of how conclusions or summaries are derived from the discussions. In Fig. 6, this is portrayed by the posts contributing to a cluster, where it is explicitly shown how and to what extent each post and its elements contribute to it. Lastly, FA summarises discussions to highlight prevailing themes and supports PR to propose actionable policy recommendations, which are specifically tailored to reflect the collective intelligence and variety of perspectives of the discussion participants.

The toolkit outputs unsupervised results. Before releasing them to the public, they undergo a check by the moderator to provide human oversight before becoming publicly accessible. This step ensures the results represent the discourse and prevents misinterpretation of AI-generated outputs, before being shared. Beyond publication, the moderator has the discretion to use these insights to inform the next steps of the discussion, choosing either to keep them undisclosed for strategic purposes, rather than making them available to participants.

This use case shows how the synergic work of these tools contribute to facilitating a more informed, efficient, and responsive decision-making process, thereby directly informing policy-making with granular, community-driven insights.

4 ORBIS as a Model for Integrating AI into Democratic Practices

4.1 Iterative Development Process and Technical Requirements Alignment

Across the co-creation journey, significant effort has been dedicated to identifying the optimal settings, conditions, and methodologies for effectively engaging with pilots and their communities, and gathering actionable guidance and insights that would shape the development of the ORBIS digital solution—which includes the interplay between ORBIS toolkit and the deliberative platforms— to meet the needs and feedback of the pilots. Concurrently, this collaborative process informed the design and refinement of deliberative experiments across the six ORBIS pilots, capitalising on the technological advancements they helped foster.

The collaborative approach adopted proved particularly effective in identifying and addressing gaps between theoretical capabilities and practical requirements, as evidenced in the development of the EG component where pilot feedback significantly influenced the implementation of transparency mechanisms (Carstens & Friess, 2024). Regular integration of pilot feedback also helped refine the balance between automated processing and human oversight, ensuring that AI augmentation enhanced rather than replaced human deliberation capabilities (De Liddo et al., 2023).

Building on the technical requirements outlined in the initial scenario prototyping, the alignment process between pilot needs and technical specifications followed a structured methodology that prioritised both functionality and implementation feasibility. A continuous interaction with pilots has been informing and driving the translation of pilot-specific requirements into actionable technical specifications, resulting in distinct high-level system requirements that spanned from user interaction mechanisms to multi-phase deliberation capabilities (Anastasiou et al., 2023). This systematic approach ensured that essential features like argument-based retrieval, feedback mechanisms, and data visualisation were developed to meet pilot' specific contexts and constraints.

The technical alignment process particularly emphasised the need for transparency and scalability requirements as identified through pilot engagement, while respecting privacy and ethical requirements. For instance, the implementation of GDPR-compliant data handling protocols was directly informed by pilot's needs for secure deliberation spaces, while scalability solutions were developed based on projected usage patterns from pilot testing. This on top of how, by design, ORBIS inherently aligns with key regulatory developments, such as the EU AI Act (2023), which mandates stringent compliance for AI applications within public governance, and the OECD AI Principles, which advocate for transparency and fairness in government AI implementations (Buhmann & Fieseler, 2023).[3] The resulting technical framework incorporated both standardised components for cross-pilot compatibility and customisable elements to address pilot-specific requirements, such as specialised authentication mechanisms and tailored data processing pipelines. This balanced approach to technical requirements alignment has proven crucial in ensuring that the ORBIS toolkit remains both technically robust and practically applicable across diverse deliberative contexts (De Liddo et al., 2023).

4.2 Aligning AI Tools with Public Values

The six diverse ORBIS pilots, representing as many complementary instances of deliberations, have actively participated in developing and refining innovations for enhancing deliberative democracy, steering the alignment of AI-based tools with public values by design. The co-creation process with pilots served as a basis for gathering requirements and tailoring AI tools to specific deliberative needs, while contributing to a sense of legitimacy and acceptance—thus underscoring a commitment to open and responsible AI development (Buhmann & Fieseler, 2023). The presence of six different pilots and the engagement of diverse stakeholders throughout the development phase bridges the gap between technological capabilities, societal expectations, and public acceptability (Cath et al., 2018). These real-life applications bring into the development fundamental needs such as the importance of identifying key discussion points, managing group dynamics, and understanding diverse viewpoints. They point out the need to support the collection and analysis of large and complex volumes of data generated from community-led deliberations; they demand that all voices are captured and adequately represented once data is processed, and that remains relevant; they stress the relevance of maintaining continuity in the discourse across multiple sessions, building upon previous discussions to develop a cohesive and cumulative understanding of the topic at hand, keeping engagement and relevance.

The requirements gathered through co-design activities indicate that democratic deliberations would benefit from AI functionalities that support various aspects of the deliberative process, up to the policy-making. For instance, translating complex data into visualisations that enable participants to quickly understand the essence of the discourse, data patterns, and the range of positions presented, enhancing

[3] EU AI Act: https://digital-strategy.ec.europa.eu/en/policies/regulatory-framework-ai; OECD AI Principles: https://oecd.ai/en/ai-principles.

user experience—as suggested by Leslie et al. (2021). AI tools should also break down decisions into smaller, manageable components to enhance comprehension. Additionally, they should synthesise opinions and arguments to reflect the collective intelligence of the participants, producing outcomes that are comprehensive and representative of the group's viewpoints, rather than being dominated by a few vocal individuals (Prabhakaran et al., 2022). Inclusivity constitutes a central topic also in terms of reducing barriers to participation. This can be addressed on the one hand by providing access to a variety of event formats that leverage AI, on the other supporting participants' understanding of the discussion's dynamics and the spectrum of opinions present. Particularly noteworthy is the engagement with youth in two pilots, which underscores the societal need to integrate younger populations into participatory models of deliberation and policy-making enhancing their participation skills. AI-enhanced platforms and tools can ease this, contributing to raise youth voices into institutional frameworks and forming new generations towards more active citizenship (Simonofski et al., 2017).

Socio-technical innovation related to digitally enhanced deliberation should be designed and implemented to enhance community cohesion and foster a collaborative environment where diverse groups work together towards common goals. In this framework, platforms where AI-based tools support activities should offer a space where to explore and value diversity, and develop consensus-building without flattening the diversity of viewpoints, but easing the accessibility to deliberation, to empower participants to engage in meaningful discussions and contribute to collective decision-making processes. From local to international scales, they should support meaningful and constructive interaction among diverse stakeholders not only to discuss and deliberate on relevant challenges, but also to reach the level of co-creating evidence-based policies, thus moving towards more responsive and comprehensive governance strategies (Zuiderwijk et al., 2021).

4.3 From Deliberation to Policymaking and Broader Strategy Information

Building upon a foundation of socio-technical innovation for digitally enhanced deliberation, the ORBIS project aims to strengthen democratic processes to then enhance the quality of policymaking. AI-driven tools are supporting a nuanced analysis, interpretation, and synthesis of public opinions, enabling a direct integration of these insights into policy formation processes. This ensures that emerging policies are comprehensive and responsive to public needs and perspectives. The experimentation within the ORBIS pilots is currently exploring how the outcomes of deliberative processes can provide policymakers with contextualized and actionable knowledge, informing decision-making and for integrating citizens' voices into the public policy arena. These insights help policymakers understand public priorities and the underlying reasons, identify potential conflicts, and discern areas where consensus may be achievable. Especially PR efficiently uses deliberative data to propose specific policy actions aligned with the articulated preferences and concerns of participants. It effectively identifies key topics and themes, providing policymakers with actionable insights. This capability facilitates a shift from simply understanding public sentiments to actively implementing policies that reflect these sentiments, thus enhancing the responsiveness and legitimacy of governance systems. ORBIS equips policymakers with crucial tools to seamlessly transition from public deliberation to policy action, fostering more dynamic, responsive, and democratically legitimate governance frameworks.

Overall, the four tools demonstrate advancements in AI-driven governance aimed at tackling complex societal challenges across various scales—from local to international—ensuring contribution to policy development that is both evidence-based and inclusive of various perspectives. This approach not only supports the immediate goals of enhancing democratic deliberation but also lays the groundwork for broader strategic applications in governance, demonstrating the potential of AI to significantly impact policy-making and public administration.

4.4 ORBIS Contribution to the AI-Enhanced Deliberation Landscape

The current integration of AI in democratic contexts showcases an evolving landscape, with a diverse range of applications aimed at enhancing transparency, public engagement, and efficiency. Various well-known platforms are leveraging AI. This is exemplified, among the other, by the array of use cases in the 'Digital Participation Tools Ratings 2025' by People Powered.[4] Of the 30 cases mapped, 12 explicitly report AI uses. For instance, Your Priorities and Loomio adopt AI to enhance user engagement through moderated, constructive discussions, employing basic NLP tools for content moderation and idea generation support. Beyond using AI for automatic translation and accessibility support for broader participation, Decidim uses specific algorithms for automatic spam moderation, thus focusing on maintaining content quality and accessibility but not necessarily on extracting structured argumentative insights. Meanwhile, Pol.is and Adhocracy + apply AI techniques to analyze participant feedback and detect disinformation, safeguarding the integrity of the participatory process while aiding decision-makers by clarifying public opinion patterns. Finally, LiquidFeedback uses XAI to support procedural transparency, explaining how decisions are processed and concluded within the platform.

Unlike the often fragmented approaches observed in other platforms, the ORBIS toolkit proposes a more integrated and consistent approach. This is the result of a co-creation journey that started from the identification of diverse user needs, leading to well-defined requirements rigorously included in the tools developed. This process resulted in deliberation-focused application of AI that not only gathers and

[4] https://www.peoplepowered.org/platform-ratings;
https://airtable.com/app2hbVSkewDqkDqF/shrUTAsTXBDdXrDjt.

analyses data but also interprets it to suggest actionable outcomes in the form of policy recommendations. While other platforms tend to focus on specific aspects of participation like moderation, translation, or feedback analysis without necessarily connecting these elements to policy-making processes, the ORBIS toolkit proposes an integrated and deliberation-focused application of AI, supporting the full flow from data collection to policy formulation. This makes ORBIS a significant example in the landscape of AI-driven democratic engagement, offering tools that go beyond enhancing participation, informing and influencing policy-making through their analysis of deliberative content.

4.5 Limitations and Challenges

Although ORBIS is bringing significant contribution, it still comes with limitations. Its co-creation journey to inform AI tools development was conducted within pilots that functioned as niche environments where socio-technical innovations could be safely tested and refined. These settings provide controlled, secure conditions that welcomed early failures as opportunities for innovation and learning, fostering an atmosphere where iterative development was encouraged to drive advancements in deliberative democracy. Despite these ideal conditions, challenges inevitably arose, nurtured by the complexity of the innovation addressed. The co-creation engaged participants from diverse domains and backgrounds, which feature distinct vocabularies and perspectives that sometimes required extended efforts to align, reach consensus, and therefore advance in the process. Pilot organisers responsible for designing and implementing AI-enhanced deliberative activities often lacked the necessary familiarity with and literacy in emerging technologies, struggling to include in their deliberative activities the breadth of options available and their potential impacts. Conversely, those with a technology background found it challenging to share the capabilities of AI tools in accessible language, affecting the creation of a common ground on the full range of support these tools could offer. This situation necessitated significant efforts to deeply understand the real needs and subtle requirements of pilot organisers at all levels of deliberative practices. It often required the adoption of additional co-design methods to trigger the understanding of relevant contributions brought by the different parties involved, and build upon diversity. The insights gained underscore the importance of enhancing technological literacy among all participants and improving communication between technologists and non-technologists to fully realise the potential of AI in enhancing democratic processes.

4.6 Next Steps and Future Directions

Despite these challenges, the scalability of this co-creation model holds significant promise for future applications. It suggests that such participatory approaches can be adapted to various contexts and sectors, enhancing the impact and relevance of AI tools across different public domains. As the project progresses, the ongoing revision and fine-tuning of AI tools based on pilot feedback continues to improve their capabilities and contribution to deliberative democracy, demonstrating the critical role of co-creation and iterative testing in developing AI solutions that are both technologically robust and democratically legitimate. In these terms, efforts are currently focused on gathering empirical evidence as the project enters its third year. Both qualitative and quantitative data for comprehensive evaluation are being collected through ongoing deliberative experiments across the pilot sites, with early results already showing promise. As these experiments in pilots progress, attention is increasingly directed toward evaluating how AI tools affect the quality of decision-making, enhance civic engagement rates, and support policy development. However, limited evidence regarding effective implementation will be gathered during the current project timeframe. The visibility of impacts, which are expected to emerge in the medium to long term, will become clearer as the project progresses beyond its initial phases.

Overall, this chapter has provided a thorough exploration of ORBIS's co-creative approach to AI tool development in deliberative democracy settings, pointing at how it can serve as a model for future technological integrations in deliberative processes and governance. Future directions include further aligning diverse stakeholder interests and integrating more policymakers to effectively incorporate and address their needs. Looking ahead, the potential integration of these tools into broader policy frameworks offers a transformative opportunity for public deliberation and policy formation, potentially leading to governance systems that are more inclusive and dynamically responsive. The potential of co-created AI tools to enhance policy-making lies in providing decision-makers with sophisticated technologies that can parse complex public inputs effectively, ensuring that policies are not only informed by a broad spectrum of opinions but also reflective of collective intelligence, thereby enhancing democratic governance.

Acknowledgements The authors of this chapter, representing partners who have actively contributed to this publication, also recognise and appreciate the foundational work carried out by other consortium activities. These efforts have provided the knowledge and insights upon which this article is built, contributing significantly to the advancements discussed herein. Consequently, deep thanks go to all members of the ORBIS consortium for their collaborative efforts throughout the project.

Fundings The work presented in this document is funded through the project 'ORBIS. Augmenting participation, co-creation, trust and transparency in Deliberative Democracy at all scales'. This project has received funding from the European Union's Horizon Europe Programme under Grant Agreement No. 101094765. The opinions expressed herewith are solely of the authors and do not necessarily reflect the point of view of any EU institution.

References

Anastasiou, L., De Moor, A., Brayshay, B., & De Liddo, A. (2023). A tale of struggles: An evaluation framework for transitioning from individually usable to community-useful online deliberation tools. pp. 144–155.

Aoki, N. (2020). An experimental study of public trust in AI chatbots in the public sector. *Government Information Quarterly, 37*, Article 101490. https://doi.org/10.1016/j.giq.2020.101490

Arnstein, S. R. (1969). A ladder of citizen participation. *Journal of the American Institute of Planners, 35*, 216–224. https://doi.org/10.1080/01944366908977225

Buhmann, A., & Fieseler, C. (2023). Deep learning meets deep democracy: Deliberative governance and responsible innovation in artificial intelligence. *Business Ethics Quarterly, 33*, 146–179. https://doi.org/10.1017/beq.2021.42

Cabrio, E., & Villata, S. (2018). Five years of argument mining: A data-driven analysis. In *Proceedings of the twenty-seventh international joint conference on artificial intelligence, IJCAI-18* (pp. 5427–5433). International Joint Conferences on Artificial Intelligence Organization.

Carayannis, E. G., & Campbell, D. F. J. (2010). Triple helix, quadruple helix and quintuple helix and how do knowledge, innovation and the environment relate to each other? A proposed framework for a trans-disciplinary analysis of sustainable development and social ecology. *International Journal of Social Ecology and Sustainable Development (IJSESD), 1*, 41–69.

Carstens, J. A., & Friess, D. (2024). AI within online discussions: Rational, civil, privileged? *Minds and Machines, 34*, 10. https://doi.org/10.1007/s11023-024-09658-0

Cath, C., Wachter, S., Mittelstadt, B., et al. (2018). Artificial Intelligence and the 'Good Society': The US, EU, and UK approach. *Science and Engineering Ethics, 24*, 505–528. https://doi.org/10.1007/s11948-017-9901-7

Coussement, K., Abedin, M. Z., Kraus, M., et al. (2024). Explainable AI for enhanced decision-making. *Decision Support Systems, 184*, Article 114276. https://doi.org/10.1016/j.dss.2024.114276

De Liddo, A., Concilio, G., Rizzo, F., & Siemon, D. (2023). Critical deliberative democracy tech: Questions, tensions, norms and directions for working with institutions, communities and technologies to scale up democratic innovations. In *C&T '23: The international conference on communities and technologies* (pp. 255–257). ACM.

de Sousa, W. G., de Melo, E. R. P., Bermejo, P. H. D. S., et al. (2019). How and where is artificial intelligence in the public sector going? A literature review and research agenda. *Government Information Quarterly, 36*, Article 101392. https://doi.org/10.1016/j.giq.2019.07.004

Delgado, F., Yang, S., Madaio, M., & Yang, Q. (2021). Stakeholder participation in AI: Beyond "add diverse stakeholders and stir".

Duberry, J. (2022). *AI and civic tech: Engaging citizens in decision-making processes but not without risks* (pp. 195–224). Edward Elgar Publishing.

Duerinckx, A., Veeckman, C., Verstraelen, K., et al. (2024). Co-creating artificial intelligence: Designing and enhancing democratic AI solutions through citizen science. *Citizen Science: Theory and Practice*. https://doi.org/10.5334/cstp.732

Ekman, J., & Amnå, E. (2012). Political participation and civic engagement: Towards a new typology. *22*, 283–300. https://doi.org/10.2478/s13374-012-0024-1

Elguendouze, S., Anastasiou, L., Hain, E., Cabrio, E., De Liddo, A., Villata, S. (2025). AM4DSP: Argumentation mining in structured decentralized discussion platforms for deliberative democracy. In I. Habernal, P. Schulam, J. Tiedemann (Eds.), *Proceedings of the 2025 conference on empirical methods in natural language processing: System demonstrations* (pp. 796–805). Association for Computational Linguistics. https://aclanthology.org/2025.emnlp-demos.61/

Fernández-Martínez, J. L., Lopez-Sanchez, M., Aguilar, J. A. R., et al. (2018). Co-designing participatory tools for a New Age: A proposal for combining collective and artificial intelligences. *International Journal of Public Administration in the Digital Age (IJPADA), 5*, 1–17. https://doi.org/10.4018/IJPADA.2018100101

Friedman, B., & Hendry, D. G. (2019). *Value sensitive design: Shaping technology with moral imagination.* The MIT Press.

Galais, C., Fernández-Martínez, J. L., Font, J., & Smith, G. (2021). Testing the input-process-output model of public participation. *European Journal of Political Research, 60*, 807–828. https://doi.org/10.1111/1475-6765.12427

Ghahramani, M., Galle, N. J., Ratti, C., & Pilla, F. (2021). Tales of a city: Sentiment analysis of urban green space in Dublin. *Cities, 119*, Article 103395. https://doi.org/10.1016/j.cities.2021.103395

Gilman, H. R. (2017). Civic tech for urban collaborative governance. *PS: Political Science & Politics, 50*, 744–750. https://doi.org/10.1017/S1049096517000531

Goodman, B., & Flaxman, S. (2017). European Union regulations on algorithmic decision-making and a "right to explanation." *Aimag, 38*, 50–57. https://doi.org/10.1609/aimag.v38i3.2741

Herrmann, H. (2023). What's next for responsible artificial intelligence: A way forward through responsible innovation. *Heliyon.* https://doi.org/10.1016/j.heliyon.2023.e14379

Karacapilidis, N., Tsakalidis, D., & Domalis, G. (2023). An AI-enhanced solution for large-scale deliberation mapping and explainable reasoning. In M. Papadaki, P. Rupino da Cunha, M. Themistocleous, & K. Christodoulou (Eds.), *Information systems* (pp. 305–316). Springer Nature Switzerland.

Kop, M. (2021). EU artificial intelligence act: The European approach to AI. In *Stanford-Vienna transatlantic technology law forum, transatlantic antitrust developments.* Stanford University.

Kuziemski, M., & Misuraca, G. (2020). AI governance in the public sector: Three tales from the frontiers of automated decision-making in democratic settings. *Telecommunications Policy, 44*, Article 101976. https://doi.org/10.1016/j.telpol.2020.101976

Leslie, D., Burr, C., Aitken, M., et al. (2021). Artificial intelligence, human rights, democracy, and the rule of law: A primer. Zenodo.

Manias, G., Apostolopoulos, D., Athanassopoulos, S., et al. (2023) AI4Gov: Trusted AI for transparent public governance fostering democratic values. In *2023 19th International conference on distributed computing in smart systems and the Internet of Things (DCOSS-IoT)* (pp. 548–555).

Mariani, I., Mortati, M., Rizzo, F., & Deserti, A. (2025). *Design thinking as a strategic approach to e-participation. From current barriers to opportunities.* Springer Nature Switzerland.

Prabhakaran, V., Mitchell, M., Gebru, T., & Gabriel, I. (2022). A human rights-based approach to responsible AI.

Rai, A. (2020). Explainable AI: From black box to glass box. *Journal of the Academy of Marketing Science, 48*, 137–141. https://doi.org/10.1007/s11747-019-00710-5

Reis, J., Santo, P. E., & Melão, N. (2019). Artificial intelligence in government services: A systematic literature review. In Á. Rocha, H. Adeli, L. P. Reis, & S. Costanzo (Eds.), *New knowledge in information systems and technologies* (pp. 241–252). Springer International Publishing.

Represa, N. S., Fernández-Sarría, A., Porta, A., & Palomar-Vázquez, J. (2020). Data mining paradigm in the study of air quality. *Environmental Processes, 7*, 1–21. https://doi.org/10.1007/s40710-019-00407-5

Romberg, J., & Escher, T. (2024). Making sense of citizens' input through artificial intelligence: A review of methods for computational text analysis to support the evaluation of contributions in public participation. *Digital Government: Research and Practice.* https://doi.org/10.1145/3603254

Sachdeva, N., Tuikka, A.-M., Kimppa, K. K., & Suomi, R. (2015). Digital disability divide in information society. *Journal of Information, Communication and Ethics in Society, 13*, 283–298. https://doi.org/10.1108/JICES-10-2014-0050

Savaget, P., Chiarini, T., & Evans, S. (2019). Empowering political participation through artificial intelligence. *Science and Public Policy, 46*, 369–380. https://doi.org/10.1093/scipol/scy064

Schütz, F., Heidingsfelder, M. L., & Schraudner, M. (2019). Co-shaping the future in quadruple helix innovation systems: Uncovering public preferences toward participatory research and innovation. *She Ji: THe Journal of Design, Economics, and Innovation, 5*, 128–146. https://doi.org/10.1016/j.sheji.2019.04.002

Siachos, I., & Karacapilidis, N. (2024). Explainable artificial intelligence methods to enhance transparency and trust in digital deliberation settings. *Future Internet*. https://doi.org/10.3390/fi16070241

Sieber, R., Brandusescu, A., Sangiambut, S., & Adu-Daako, A. (2024). What is civic participation in artificial intelligence? *Environment and Planning B: Urban Analytics and City Science*. https://doi.org/10.1177/23998083241296200

Simonofski, A., Asensio, E. S., De Smedt, J., & Snoeck, M. (2017). Citizen participation in smart cities: Evaluation framework proposal. In *2017 IEEE 19th conference on business informatics (CBI)* (pp. 227–236).

Skaržauskienė, A., & Mačiulienė, M. (2020). Mapping international civic technologies platforms. *Informatics*. https://doi.org/10.3390/informatics7040046

Straub, V. J., Morgan, D., Bright, J., & Margetts, H. (2023). Artificial intelligence in government: Concepts, standards, and a unified framework. *Government Information Quarterly, 40*, Article 101881. https://doi.org/10.1016/j.giq.2023.101881

Voegtlin, C., & Scherer, A. G. (2017). Responsible innovation and the innovation of responsibility: Governing sustainable development in a globalized world. *Journal of Business Ethics, 143*, 227–243. https://doi.org/10.1007/s10551-015-2769-z

Wan, S., & Sieber, R. (2023) Artificial intelligence (AI) adoption in Canadian municipalities: In-house development versus outsourcing. In *The 18th international conference on computational urban planning and urban management.*

Wilson, C. (2022). Public engagement and AI: A values analysis of national strategies. *Government Information Quarterly, 39*, Article 101652. https://doi.org/10.1016/j.giq.2021.101652

Zuiderwijk, A., Chen, Y.-C., & Salem, F. (2021). Implications of the use of artificial intelligence in public governance: A systematic literature review and a research agenda. *Government Information Quarterly, 38*, Article 101577. https://doi.org/10.1016/j.giq.2021.101577

Leveraging AI Techniques to Augment Actionable Knowledge Discovery and Informed Policy Making in Public Deliberation

11

Ioannis E. Livieris, Alexandra Apostolopoulou, Dimitris Tsakalidis, George Domalis, and Nikos Karacapilidis

1 Introduction

Deliberation is a systematic process of discussion and reasoning, which brings together diverse stakeholders to collaboratively explore, debate and assess ideas for tackling complex challenges (Fishkin, 2018; Moshman, 2020). It covers a wide range of fields, from public governance and policy-making to organizational decision-making, aiming to balance diverse perspectives and foster inclusive participation (Roberts, 2004, 2015). By encouraging meaningful dialogue, deliberation enhances transparency and accountability, while reducing biases and polarization that may arise from one-sided approaches (Karacapilidis & Papadias, 1998). Its major benefits include the generation of actionable insights, consensus building and the enhancement of trust among participants. In the realm of

I. E. Livieris (✉) · A. Apostolopoulou · D. Tsakalidis · G. Domalis
Novelcore, Athens, Greece
e-mail: livieris@novelcore.eu; livieris@unipi.gr

A. Apostolopoulou
e-mail: apostolopoulou@novelcore.eu

D. Tsakalidis
e-mail: tsakalidis@novelcore.eu

G. Domalis
e-mail: domalis@novelcore.eu

I. E. Livieris
Department of Business and Organization Administration, University of Peloponnese, Kalamata, Greece

N. Karacapilidis
IMIS Lab, University of Patras, Patras, Greece
e-mail: karacap@upatras.gr

S. K. Aikins and T. Dimitrijevska-Markoski (eds.), *Artificial Intelligence and Government*, https://doi.org/10.1007/978-3-032-12344-2_11

public policy, deliberation can play a vital role as a foundation for developing well-informed, sustainable and broadly accepted solutions to societal issues (Nabatchi, 2010).

As manifested in recent studies (Androutsopoulou et al., 2019), Artificial Intelligence (AI) has become a powerful tool to enhance deliberation processes, enabling discussions, which are more efficient, inclusive and insightful. Advanced AI techniques such as Natural Language Processing (NLP), Large Language Models (LLMs), and sentiment analysis are increasingly used to analyze and summarize participant input, uncover discourse patterns, and highlight areas of consensus or disagreement. Knowledge Graphs and Machine Learning (ML) models further aid in organizing complex arguments, making large volumes of information more accessible and actionable for stakeholders. While AI brings many benefits, including scalability, objectivity and the ability to process multilingual and multimodal data, it is not without challenges. In detail, these include biases in AI systems, concerns related to transparency and accountability and the risk of over-relying on technology at the expense of human judgment. Nonetheless, the integration of AI into deliberative processes holds great promise for enhancing actionable knowledge discovery and supporting informed policy-making in increasingly complex societal contexts.

Although AI techniques are increasingly applied in deliberation, they still face several limitations, which impact their effectiveness. Current solutions often fall short in capturing the context-specific aspects of human deliberation, such as cultural nuances, ethical considerations and emotional tones. Additionally, the complexity of advanced AI models, particularly those based on deep learning, poses challenges in interpretability, raising concerns about the transparency and reliability of AI-generated insights. Another key challenge lies in integrating AI-driven insights into the practical decision-making processes of policymakers and stakeholders, where human judgment and values remain essential. Addressing these challenges requires ongoing research and innovation to enhance the robustness and contextual awareness of AI tools and associated techniques in deliberative environments (El Helou et al., 2008).

Adopting a joint discourse-level and information-seeking perspective, while simultaneously paying attention to data aggregation mechanisms for the context under consideration, this chapter presents an innovative software toolkit, which leverages a series of AI techniques to address the issues of actionable knowledge discovery and informed policy making in public deliberation (Karacapilidis et al., 2004). Our specific contribution lies in the meaningful integration of advanced deep learning and NLP techniques, which articulate the structure and content of a deliberation to develop a semantically-rich pool of actionable knowledge. The proposed toolkit is based on a intelligent modular multi-stage system, named Feedback Aggregator, which is designed to handle, organize and structure feedback data from deliberative discussions and it is composed by four main components: (i) a pre-processsing component, which cleans the participants' feedback and incorporates a polarity detection mechanism, for assigning each feedback into a sentiment group; (ii) a clustering component, which groups the participants' feedback according to its content and stance to the issue under discussion; (iii) a summarization component, which provides an informative summary of the content of each generated cluster; (iv) and a keyphrase extraction component, which identifies the most influential phrases from the feedback of each cluster.

The remainder of this chapter is organized as follows: Sect. 2 reports on prominent related works addressing deliberation issues such as text clustering, summarization and keyword extraction; Sect. 3 presents in detail the proposed toolkit and its constituent components; Sect. 4 demonstrates the functionality and applicability of the proposed solution through a use case concerning a real deliberation setting; Sect. 5 presents a preliminary evaluation by different types of users; finally, Sect. 6 presents the advantages of the proposed approach for enhancing policy making and government effectiveness, while Sect. 6 outlines concluding remarks and recommends future work directions.

2 Related Work

In recent years, the employment of NLP and ML techniques to deliberative discussions has grown significantly, motivated by the need to extract actionable insights from complex, often unstructured dialogues (Karacapilidis, 2014). The primary aim is to enable the systematic organization of deliberations' content, the clustering of participants' feedback according to topical relevance and stance and the distillation of core ideas and summaries, which reflect the collective insight of participants. In this section, we present a series of state-of-the-art approaches to text clustering, summarization and keyphrase extraction, which serve as foundational techniques for transforming, semantically enriching and structuring deliberative discussions, the ultimate aim being to support decision and policy making.

Ravi and Kulkarni (2023) used several embedding techniques on tweets of popular news channels, aiming at clustering the tweets using k-means algorithm. Specifi-cally, the employed Term Frequency-Inverse Document Frequency (TF-IDF), GloVe, Word2Vec and Bidirectional Encoder Representations from Transformers (BERT) for generating the tweet embeddings, which were used by k-means for providing the clusters. Their experiments reported that BERT achieved the highest accuracy rate, outperforming all other embedding techniques.

Petukhova et al. (2024) compared the performance of four of the most widely used clustering algorithms (Spectral, Agglomerative, k-means and Fuzzy k-means) in text clustering based on embeddings provided by state-of-the-art LLM models (BERT, GPT-3.5-turbo, Llama 2 and Falcon). The major scope of their research was to evaluate the influence of clustering algorithms and text embeddings in the clustering process. Based on their experiments, the authors stated that LLM are able to provide higher quality embeddings in terms of capturing details in structured language. In addition, GPT-3.5-turbo model reported the best results in three out of five metrics in most cases. Finally, the authors highlighted that the exponential increase in cost through obtaining text embeddings from LLMs such as Llama

2 and Falcon compared to a BERT-type model do not guarantee an increase in clustering performance.

Mihalcea and Tarau (2004) introduced TextRank, an unsupervised graph-based algorithm for text summarization, which was inspired by Google's PageRank algorithm (Langville & Meyer, 2006). TextRank focuses on constructing a graph where sentences (or phrases) are nodes and edges between them are weights based on lexical or semantic similarity. Next, TextRank determines the importance of each node based on its connections within the graph through the application of a ranking algorithm. A considerable advantage of this algorithm is that it requires no training data, making it widely applicable across different domains and languages. The competitive perfor-mance of TextRank was demonstrated in a variety of datasets, proving its effectiveness in generating coherent summaries.

Basyal and Sanghvi (2023) conducted a comparative study of three generative models (MPT-7b-instruct, Falcon-7b-instruct and OpenAI Chat-GPT) for text summarization. Their primary goal was to provide a concise assessment of how LLMs address the challenges of text summarization by evaluating the performance of advanced generative AI solutions. The numerical experiments was based on two widely used datasets: CNN/Daily Mail 3.0.0 and Extreme Summarization. The comprehensive experimental analysis revealed that OpenAI's Chat-GPT reported the best perfor-mance, outperforming both MPT and Falcon models. Nevertheless, a considerable limitation of this approach is that this extractive-based approach cannot to be applied for summarizing large texts.

Nadim et al. (2023) conducted a comprehensive review for keyword and keyphrase extraction, providing special attention to the challenges rising in this problem. Specifically, the authors presented the challenges in this NLP problem and also highlighted the reliability of evaluation techniques and their flaws examination as the major problems in keyphrase extraction. Additionally, they evaluated the performance of twelve of the most efficient and effective unsupervised keyphrase extraction algorithms in four challenging datasets. Their broad experimental analysis revealed that KeyBERT (Grootendorst, 2020) reported the best overall performance while KPminer (El-Beltagy & Rafea, 2009) and YAKE (Campos et al., 2020) exhibited the best scores for different text lengths and the lower computational time, respectively.

Giarelis and Karacapilidis (2023) proposed a new algorithm for keyword extraction, named LMRank, which effectively exploits sentence embeddings together with dependency parsing. The key idea behind LMRank is to improve the ranking process for extracting the most appropriate keyphrases. In detail, LMRank utilizes syntactic dependency parsing for extracting keyphrases and then it exploits a sentence transformer model for capturing the semantic similarity between the candidate keyphrases and the document. The proposed algorithm was evaluated against state-of-the-art keyphrase extraction approaches (KeyBERT, TextRank, Key3Vec, …) in eight datasets. The reported comparative evaluation revealed that LMRank considerably outperform all SoA approaches in terms of accuracy and time performance.

3 The Proposed Solution: Feedback Aggregator

In this section, we present Feedback Aggregator, a modular multi-stage system designed to process and structure feedback data from deliberative discussions. The proposed aggregator retrieves a deliberation discussion, namely a deliberation title and its description as well as the participants' feedback, from a third-party service and process, organize and structure the retrieved data into a structured format suitable for deeper analysis and visualization in a dashboard (Fig. 1).

Figure 2 present a high-level description of Feedback aggregator module which is composed by five main components: (i) Pre-processing component, which filters and cleans the retrieved feedback, ensuring that sentiment-labeled data is passed forward; (ii) Clustering component, which groups the participants' feedback based on semantic and contextual similarity; (iii) Summarization component, which generates concise summaries of each generated cluster (iv) Keyphrase Extraction component, which identifies and highlights the most important concepts within the feedback; (v) Title Generation Component, which generates contextually relevant titles for each set of feedback. Next, a detailed description of these components is presented.

Pre-processing Component is responsible for filtering feedback data for further analysis, ensuring that only relevant and structured information is passed on to sub-sequent components. It takes as input the raw feedback and performs two procedures: (i) Clean the participants' feedback by removing any special characters, urls, emails as well as emotionally charged language (emojis and emoticons), which may skew analysis (ii) incorporate a polarity detection mechanism, leveraging an LLM to classify each piece of feedback into one of two sentiment groups:

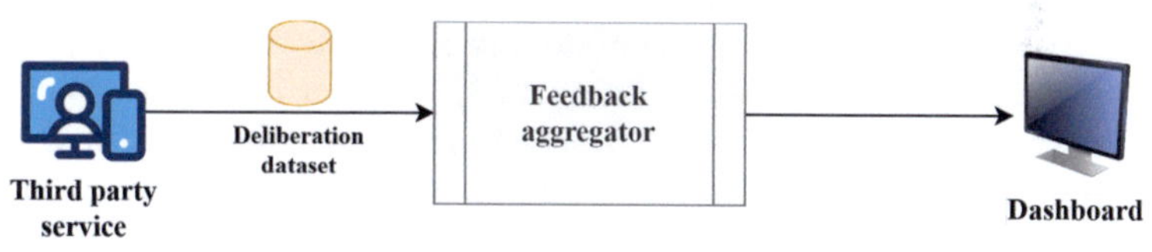

Fig. 1 The process flow of feedback aggregator from input to visualization

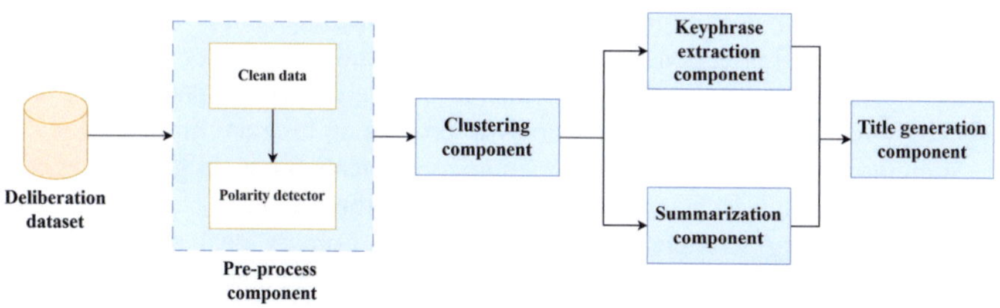

Fig. 2 High-level description of feedback aggregator

"In favor" and "Against", based on the feedback's stance relative to the discussion topic, which is provided through its title and description. The motivation behind this mechanism is to facilitate a balanced analysis of differing viewpoints, enabling a clearer understanding of the strengths and weaknesses of each position. Summarizing, the "Pre-processing" component ensures that the retrieved feedback data is cleaned and accurately categorized by sentiment, providing a refined dataset for further processing and analysis.

Clustering component aims at providing a structured representation of the feedback within each polarity group ("In favor", "Against") employing a clustering-based methodology. Each group is segmented into distinct clusters, which reflect feedback with similar contextual or semantic characteristics. These clusters offer deeper insights into the subgroups of opinions within each polarity category, enabling a more detailed analysis of the feedback.

Initially, the embeddings of the feedback of each polarity group are calculated using a transformer model composing two embeddings datasets. Then, the dimension of each embeddings dataset is reduced using Uniform Manifold Approximation and Projection (UMAP) (McInnes et al., 2018) for improved clustering performance by preserving the essential structure of the data, reducing noise and highlighting meaningful relationships between text embeddings (Eklund et al., 2023).

For clustering the feedback of each polarity group, k-means (Wierzchon´ & Klopotek, 2018) was employed on the calculated embeddings, which constitutes one of the most effective clustering algorithms. By using k-means, it is possible to partition the embeddings into distinct clusters by assigning each data point to the nearest centroid; hence, creating a clear separation of clusters based on the inherent structure of the data. Although k-means is probably one of the simplest algorithms, it is highly efficient and usually performs well in capturing the general structure of the data, especially when clusters are relatively well-separated and unimodal in nature (Pintelas & Livieris, 2023; Wang et al., 2019). Notice that in each case, k-means is optimized by maximizing Silhouette score, aiming at achieving well-separated clusters and assessing both the cohesion and separation of clusters simultaneously.

In general, a notable advantage of k-means is its computational efficiency and scalability, making it suitable for large datasets. Additionally, by maximizing the Silhouette score, we ensure that the clustering not only reflects tight and well-defined groups but also minimizes the risk of misassigning data points to incorrect clusters. This dual attention on cohesion and separation improves the robustness of the clustering results, making k-means a reliable choice for partitioning data, especially when computational resources or processing time are limited.

Summarization & Keyphrase Extraction components focus on generating concise summaries as well as extracting key phrases from the each cluster generated by the "Clustering" component, respectively. The primary goal is to provide a clear and comprehensive overview of the most important points, allowing an easier interpretation and understanding of the underlying opinions, trends and viewpoints within each polarity group.

"Summarization" component iteratively provides a summary of the feedbacks com-posing each generated cluster based on the following two-step process: Firstly, an abstractive summarization is generated by applying the TextRank algorithm (Mihalcea & Tarau, 2004) on the collective text composed of all feedbacks of the cluster. TextRank identifies and ranks key sentences from the text based on the structural relationships within the feedback, creating a concise and coherent summary, which captures the main ideas. In the second step, this abstractive summary is further refined using an extractive summarization approach employing a Large Language Model (LLM), which enhances the quality of the summary by offering deeper insights and more nuanced interpretations of the feedback, ensuring that the final output is both precise and contextually rich. It is worth mentioning that abstractive-only approaches may struggle to generate concise and coherent summaries from large datasets, while extractive-only approaches are not able to be applied to large text. In contrast, the advantage of the proposed approach over both traditional approaches, lies on its ability to handle large volumes of text more efficiently while maintaining a high-quality summary.

In addition to summarization, the "Keyphrase Extraction" component is independently applied on the text composed by the feedbacks of each dataset for extracting the most relevant and informative keyphrases. This component is based on the application of LMRank algorithm (Giarelis & Karacapilidis, 2023), which identifies the most relevant and informative phrases from the feedback in each cluster. LMRank utilizes language models to rank candidate phrases based on their importance and relevance, enabling the extraction of key phrases that succinctly capture the essence of the feed-back. Finally, it is worth mentioning that the scope of this component is to further enhance interpretability, offered by summarization component, by providing a quick overview of the most important keyphrases and themes discussed within each cluster.

Title generation component is utilized for providing a title on each set of feedback, aiming at reflecting the core themes of each cluster of participants' feedback, capturing the essence of the content in an informative manner. Specifically, the generated summary and keyphrases of each cluster produced by "Summarization" & "Keyphrase extraction" components, respectively are exploited by an LLM for generating a contextually relevant title for each set of feedback. Notice that the generated summary provides a concise representation of the key ideas discussed, while the extracted keyphrases highlight the most important topics and concepts.

4 Use Case Scenarios

In this section, we present two use-case scenarios to demonstrate the functionality and applicability of the proposed feedback aggregator module. Along this line, we retrieved data from Pol.is platform,[1] facilitates public input on policies and

[1] https://pol.is/home.

legislative developments, serving as a crucial channel for stakeholder engagement for policy assessments.

In the "Clustering" component, the text embeddings were calculated using the transformer model: jina-embeddings-v2-base-en[2] while the implementation code as well as the prompt for polarity detection, summarization title generation can be found in https://github.com/novelcore/EUORBIS.

4.1 First Use-Case Scenario

In the first scenario, the data concern 68 citizens' feedback from the consultation entitled "Is the concussion crisis and Chronic Traumatic Encephalopathy (CTE) the end of the NFL?" from a time period between Jan-11, 2015 to Dec-27, 2018.[3] From our analysis, we excluded irrelevant feedback such as: "...", "I am bored", etc. A visual interpretation of use case scenario 1 is presented in Fig. 3.

The feedback assigned to the "In favor" sentiment group defines 2 clusters:

- Cluster 1
  - Title: Balancing Tradition and Safety: Addressing Concussions in Tackle Football—Summary: Football will remain a significant part of American culture despite ongoing safety concerns. While the sport is beautiful and has a compelling narrative, issues like concussions need to be addressed. Suggestions include banning tackle football for children under 14 and implementing reforms to ensure player safety. The NFL is taking steps to tackle these issues, but independent oversight is necessary. Despite the risks, many will continue to enjoy watching football, emphasizing the need for a balanced approach to safety without losing the essence of the game.
  - Summary: Football will remain a significant part of American culture despite ongoing safety concerns. While the sport is beautiful and has a compelling narrative, issues like concussions need to be addressed. Suggestions include banning tackle football for children under 14 and implementing reforms to ensure player safety. The NFL is taking steps to tackle these issues, but independent oversight is necessary. Despite the risks, many will continue to enjoy watching football, emphasizing the need for a balanced approach to safety without losing the essence of the game.
  - Keywords: "tackle football", "safety", "head injuries", "coaches", "boxing", "kids", "league", "brain damage", "willing players", "tribal enthusiasm".
- Cluster 2
  - Title: Empowering Choices: The Role of Helmets and Personal Responsibility in Football Safety.

[2] https://huggingface.co/jinaai/jina-embeddings-v2-base-en.

[3] https://github.com/compdemocracy/opendata/blob/master/football-concussions/.

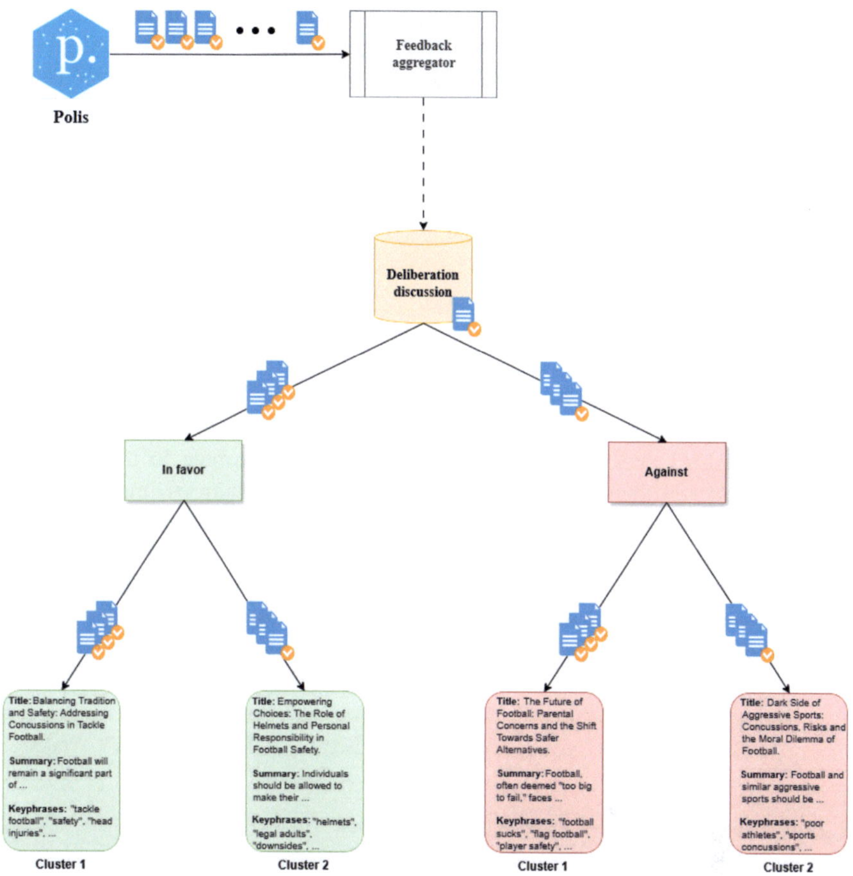

Fig. 3 Visual interpretation of use case scenario 1

  - Summary: Individuals should be allowed to make their own decisions regarding safety, provided they understand the consequences. Softening helmet exteriors could prevent their use as weapons, while larger, more padded helmets could enhance protection. Legal adults passionate about their sport value their choices and may resist having those choices taken away, even if others believe they know better.
  - Keywords: "helmets", "legal adults", "downsides", "things".

The feedback assigned to the "Against" sentiment group also defines 2 clusters:

- Cluster 1
  - Title: The Future of Football: Parental Concerns and the Shift Towards Safer Alternatives.
  - Summary: Football, often deemed "too big to fail," faces growing scrutiny as parents increasingly refuse to let their children participate due to safety

concerns. While the sport remains popular, its future is uncertain, with a potential recruiting problem looming. Many believe tackle football should not be a school-sponsored activity, as future generations may view it as a barbaric pastime. Despite ongoing support for the sport, the current rules do not prioritize player safety, leading to a shift in parental attitudes.
  - Keywords: "football sucks", "flag football", "player safety", "unenlightened pastime", "future generations", "banks", "fellow parents", "heads".
- Cluster 2
  - Title: The Dark Side of Aggressive Sports: Concussions, Risks and the Moral Dilemma of Football.
  - Summary: Football and similar aggressive sports should be replaced with those emphasizing cooperation and social skills. The allure of football, driven by socioeconomic factors, often leads poorer individuals to take risks for fame and money, despite the known dangers. The moral implications of watching such sports are troubling, as they contribute to a culture that neglects well-being and exposes players to severe injuries, including concussions. While some argue for the sport's value, the reality is that the risks are significant, akin to the dangers of smoking. The ongoing popularity of football persists despite these risks, with many children entering the sport unaware of the potential consequences. The revelation of chronic traumatic encephalopathy (CTE) highlights the severe impact of football on health, raising questions about the normalization of such risks in society.
  - Keywords: "poor athletes", "sports concussions", "pro football", "aggressive sports", "injuries", "youth hockey", "gladwell", "QBs", "players", "risks".

4.2 Second Use-Case Scenario

Regarding the second scenario, the data concern 29 citizens' feedback from the consultation entitled "How do you think the new minimum wage law will affect Seattle? Will it be for the better or for the worse? Why?" from a time period between Jun-18, 2014 to Sep-28, 2014.[4] A visual interpretation of use case scenario 2 is presented in Fig. 4.

The feedback assigned to the "In favor" sentiment group defines the following 3 clusters:

- Cluster 1
  - Title: Addressing Income Inequality: The Impact of Minimum Wage on Seattle's Low-Income Families.
  - Summary: Businesses, regardless of size, should pay workers a livable wage to avoid subsidizing those that rely on inadequate compensation. With rising inflation, workers must advocate for fair wages, as current minimum wages are insufficient for basic living expenses. Revisiting wage laws is essential

[4] https://github.com/compdemocracy/opendata/tree/master/15-per-hour-seattle/.

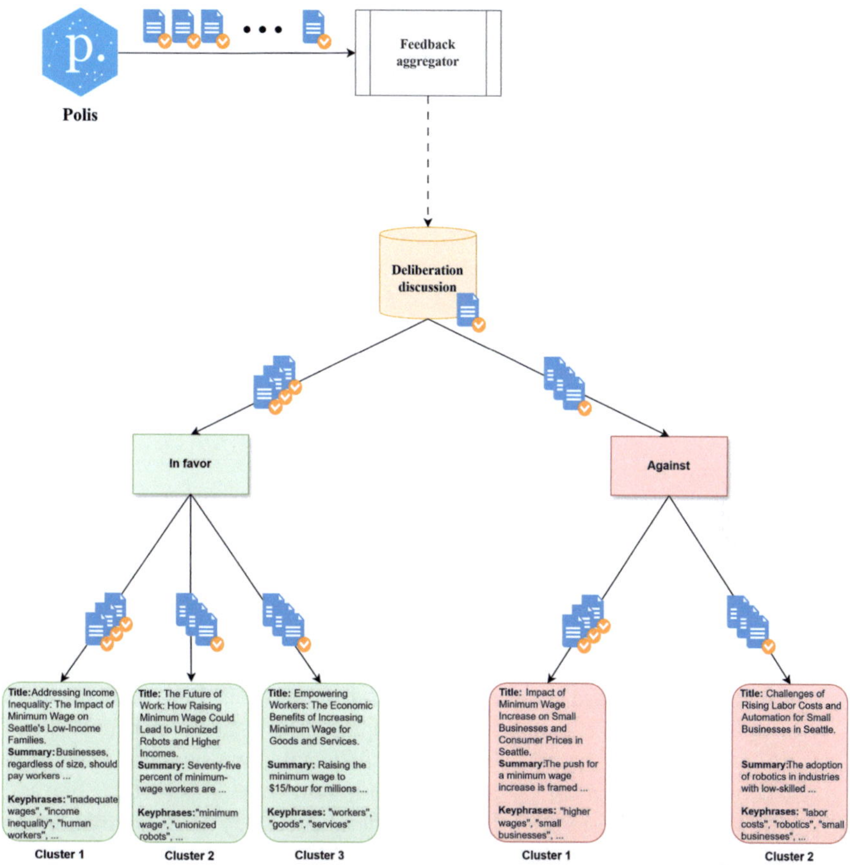

Fig. 4 Visual interpretation of use case scenario 2

  to ensure the economy supports low-income families. Addressing income inequality is crucial, and establishing a living wage is a necessary step toward a future where basic income may become essential as job availability declines.
- Keywords: "inadequate wages", "income inequality", "human workers", "poor families", "inflation", "businesses", "good move", "rent", "bills", "populace".

- Cluster 2
  - Title: The Future of Work: How Raising Minimum Wage Could Lead to Unionized Robots and Higher Incomes.
  - Summary: Seventy-five percent of minimum-wage workers are 20 or older, and raising their incomes is essential. Companies are unlikely to raise prices to stay competitive, which may result in lower profits, a trade-off that is

  acceptable. Increasing the minimum wage to $25 per hour could lead to unionized robots, which is seen as a positive outcome.
  - Keywords: "minimum wage", "unionized robots", "higher incomes", "less profits", "robots", "prices", "people", "companies", "hour".
- Cluster 3
  - Title: Empowering Workers: The Economic Benefits of Increasing Minimum Wage for Goods and Services.
  - Summary: Raising the minimum wage to $15/hour for millions of workers will enhance their spending power, significantly benefiting the economy. A suggestion is made to increase it further to $20/hour to better support families.
  - Keywords: "workers", "goods", "services".

Finally, the feedback assigned to the "Against" sentiment group defines 2 groups:

- Cluster 1
  - Title: Impact of Minimum Wage Increase on Small Businesses and Consumer Prices in Seattle.
  - Summary: The push for a minimum wage increase is framed as a fight against corporate greed, yet larger companies are better equipped to handle the change, leaving small businesses at a disadvantage. This could lead to innovative cost-cutting measures, like self-service in restaurants. The potential consequences are complex, and customers may face higher prices, which could reduce their spending. The assumption that business owners will simply pay employees more overlooks the financial strain on small businesses, where owners often earn less than the proposed wage. Alternatives like subsidies could be more effective, as the new wage may lead to inflation and reduced benefits for employees, raising questions about fairness.
  - Keywords: "higher wages", "small businesses", "wages", "restaurant veterans", "business owners", "higher income population", "anti corporate greed", "customers", "inflation", "subsidies".
- Cluster 2
  - Title: Challenges of Rising Labor Costs and Automation for Small Businesses in Seattle.
  - Summary: The adoption of robotics in industries with low-skilled workers is accelerating, but this approach merely addresses symptoms of a systemic issue. While it may not be entirely negative, only resilient small businesses will endure, as rising labor costs threaten their survival. Consequently, many small enterprises, like local coffee shops, may face closure, leading to job losses and increased poverty.
  - Keywords: "labor costs", "robotics", "small businesses", "reactionary liberal trash", "industries", "poverty", "effect", "only owners", "disappear".

5 Preliminary Evaluation

The proposed toolkit has already been evaluated by different types of users, including citizens expected to use the overall solution for deliberation purposes, moderators responsible for guiding discussions and curating content, policy makers and institutional stakeholders who intend to use the results of the toolkit for informed decisions, and representatives of NGOs or special interest groups. This evaluation was conducted through an online questionnaire, using a five-point Likert scale (1 = strongly disagree, ..., 5 = strongly agree). The questionnaire was designed to assess four dimensions of the toolkit's performance, namely: usability ("Is the toolkit intuitive for participants of various digital literacy levels?"), deliberation structure ("Does the toolkit promote reasoned argumentation, balanced discussion, and informed decision-making?"), transparency ("Can users track how their input is used or what impact it has?"), and overall effectiveness ("How effective the proposed toolkit is in facilitating deliberation?").

Users were actively involved in the evaluation process to ensure that the assessment reflected real-world usage and diverse perspectives. Feedback was collected from 34 users, covering a representative sample of the key stakeholder groups mentioned above. They interacted with the toolkit in realistic scenarios and subsequently completed the online questionnaire to report their experiences. This user-centered approach ensured that the evaluation results were grounded in practical use and addressed the needs of various types of users.

The results obtained were highly promising across all dimensions elaborated. The participants rated the usability of the toolkit favorably (at an average of 4.1), indicating that it was intuitive and accessible even for users with varying levels of digital literacy. The dimension assessing the deliberation structure received particularly strong scores (at an average of 4.5), suggesting that the toolkit effectively fostered reasoned dialogue and balanced participation. Similarly, the transparency of the platform was well-regarded (at an average of 4.2), with users affirming that they could easily understand how their contributions were utilized in the deliberative process. Finally, the overall effectiveness of the toolkit in facilitating meaningful deliberations received high scores (at an average of 4.3), confirming its potential to support inclusive and informed decision making. These results underscore the capacity of the toolkit to serve as a robust and user-friendly digital deliberation solution.

6 Discussion

6.1 From Feedback Aggregator to Policy Making

The meaningful integration of the four main components of the proposed AI-powered toolkit provides a robust and holistic solution to improve policy making processes. By addressing the inherent complexities of processing and interpreting extensive deliberative feedback, the proposed solution can empower policy makers to extract meaningful insights with precision and efficiency, enabling them to derive actionable insights and make informed decisions.

Specifically, the pre-processing component provides valuable support for understanding public sentiment by systematically categorizing feedback into distinct sentiment groups. This classification offers policymakers a clear and immediate sense of the emotional tone and overall public attitude about the issue under consideration. By providing these insights, the particular component enables decision makers to assess the level of public support, identify disputed issues, and craft policies that effectively address the concerns and priorities of stakeholders.

The clustering component organizes feedback by content similarity and stance, creating clusters that are thematically and contextually relevant. These clusters enable policy makers to discern key themes, shared viewpoints, and diverse opinions within the deliberative process. The underlying mechanisms ensure a thorough representation of public sentiment and help prioritize critical issues that require action or further investigation, thus facilitating targeted and effective policy responses.

The summarization component delivers a clear and concise overview of the content of each cluster, enabling policy makers to efficiently and quickly grasp the essential points of long deliberative input. By distilling complex discussions into manageable summaries, this feature alleviates cognitive overload and ensures that critical perspectives are not overlooked. The particular component facilitates evidence-based policy design by streamlining the analysis of diverse feedback, enabling decision-makers to focus their efforts on addressing high-priority issues with precision.

Finally, the keyphrase extraction component identifies the most impactful phrases and ideas within each cluster, bringing attention to critical concerns and commonly emphasized priorities. These keyphrases can act as focal points that trigger policy discussions, providing decision-makers with a clear pathway to engage deeply with the most significant aspects of public deliberations.

By integrating the outputs of these four components, the proposed solution can transform unstructured, large-scale deliberations into a semantically rich repository of actionable knowledge and empower policymakers to effectively elaborate complex societal challenges. The overall solution facilitates data-driven decision-making by providing evidence-based insights that enable an objective evaluation of public input, ensuring a balanced representation of stakeholder views; it enhances transparency and trust by demonstrating how public contributions are analyzed and incorporated into decision-making processes; additionally, it addresses polarization by systematically organizing and summarizing differing viewpoints, helping policymakers develop inclusive solutions that bridge divides. Its automated analysis and summarization capabilities also improve responsiveness, accelerating the feedback loop and enabling prompt action on public concerns.

6.2 Enhancement of Government Effectiveness

The ability to efficiently process public feedback is a critical determinant of government effectiveness. Governments must not only create sound policies but also implement them effectively, ensuring that they are responsive to public concerns and carried out in a transparent and inclusive manner. In this context, the proposed toolkit contributes significantly to improving the overall quality of governance. By transforming unstructured deliberative input into semantically-rich, actionable knowledge, it facilitates evidence-based decisions that are well-informed and contextually sensitive, directly impacting the effectiveness of governmental decision-making.

Based on this foundation, we identify two specific pathways through which the Feedback Aggregator can enhance government effectiveness:

- Strengthening participatory policy design through structured citizen input: Governments often struggle to integrate large-scale citizen feedback into formal policy processes due to the sheer volume, fragmentation and unstructured nature of public contributions. The proposed toolkit addresses this issue by trans-forming raw feedback into structured thematic clusters, annotated with summary narratives and key concepts. This structured output enables public institutions to incorporate the "voice of the people" into the early stages of policy formulation in a systematic and scalable manner.
- Operationalizing evidence-based governance through real-time deliberation analytics: The Feedback Aggregator also supports real-time monitoring of public sentiment and issue salience; thereby, enabling adaptive governance. By embedding the proposed toolkit into ongoing deliberative platforms (e.g., civic forums, e-participation platforms, online consultations), governments can access up-to-date insights into how public preferences and concerns evolve in response to new policies or emerging crises.
- Improving responsiveness in public policy formation: The toolkit has the notable ability to handle large volumes of citizen feedback into coherent thematic clusters and provide summaries, which enables policymakers to rapidly identify the core concerns and priorities of various stakeholder groups. This ability reduces the latency between public expression and institutional response, allowing governments to formulate policies, which are both timely and closely aligned with societal needs. By integrating sentiment analysis and stance detection, the toolkit further allows for the differentiation between supportive and critical feedback, enabling more targeted and calibrated policy interventions.
- Strengthening participatory governance through scalable deliberation: Traditional methods of civic engagement and public consultation often struggle to scale efficiently, especially when confronted with large volumes of heterogeneous input. The Feedback Aggregator automates and augments this process, making it feasible for governments to incorporate extensive and diverse deliberative input without compromising analytical depth. By ensuring that even

marginal voices are systematically captured and represented in decision-making processes, the toolkit fosters inclusivity and legitimacy in governance practices.
- Enhancing transparency and accountability in decision-making: The structured outputs of the Feedback Aggregator, including sentiment-grouped clusters, informative summaries, and distilled keyphrases, can be published as part of participatory audit trails. These outputs provide a clear rationale for policy decisions, rooted in citizen input, and can be used to demonstrate how public feedback influenced final outcomes. This not only enhances transparency but also builds institutional trust and accountability, two pillars essential for effective governance in democratic contexts.

Summarizing, the proposed approach not only contributes to deliberative theory and computational frameworks but also provides concrete mechanisms to operationalize government effectiveness. By integrating diverse citizen input into formal policy channels and enabling responsive, evidence-based governance, the toolkit addresses a fundamental gap in contemporary public administration, namely the need for scalable, intelligent systems that mediate between civic discourse and institutional action.

6.3 Toward Responsible AI: Addressing Methodological Gaps and Ethical Implications in Deliberative Technologies

The primary aim of the proposed approach is to address several limitations of current AI approaches in processing deliberation discussions by offering enhanced contextual understanding and interpretability. Traditional AI applications in public deliberation often struggle to grasp the depth, diversity, and dynamic nature of human discourse. They tend to rely on surface-level text analysis that inadequately represents the under-lying sentiments, contextual nuances, and evolving stances that characterize public feedback. As a result, these systems risk oversimplifying complex arguments, ignoring minority viewpoints, or misclassifying sentiment and intent ultimately leading to biased or incomplete outputs that undermine the deliberative process.

To overcome these limitations, the proposed Feedback Aggregator integrates a suite of advanced natural language processing (NLP) techniques within a modular architecture tailored specifically for public deliberation contexts. The pre-processing component categorizes feedback into sentiment groups, providing an initial emotional mapping of public opinion. Clustering and stance detection components then group feedback not only by thematic similarity but also by attitudinal orientation, ensuring that both content and perspective are captured. The summarization module dis-tills detailed discussions into concise, representative overviews, while the keyphrase extraction mechanism highlights influential ideas with semantic clarity. These features collectively enhance the contextual richness and transparency of AI-generated insights, enabling decision-makers to engage with deliberative content in a more accurate, inclusive, and meaningful way.

Despite the growing integration of AI tools into civic and policy-making processes, current AI applications in public deliberation face several critical limitations. One major constraint lies in their limited ability to grasp the nuanced, context-dependent nature of human discourse. Many existing systems rely heavily on surface-level key-word matching or sentiment scoring without accounting for the deliberative intent, tone, or stance embedded within the feedback. As a result, they often produce reductive interpretations that overlook minority viewpoints, misclassify subtle opinions, or fail to recognize the dynamic interplay between competing arguments. Additionally, most AI systems used in this domain lack transparency and interpretability, making it difficult for policymakers to understand how conclusions are derived or to justify AI-informed decisions in a democratic context.

The proposed Feedback Aggregator addresses these limitations through a modular architecture that integrates advanced natural language processing techniques specifically tailored to the demands of public deliberation. It goes beyond simplistic categorization by incorporating sentiment and stance detection to distinguish supportive, neutral, or opposing positions within complex debates. The clustering component groups feedback based on thematic and attitudinal similarity, while the summarization and keyphrase extraction modules generate concise, interpretable outputs that highlight the most relevant arguments and concerns. This pipeline not only captures a broader and more accurate picture of stakeholder input but also enhances transparency and interpretability, allowing policymakers to trace the analytic logic behind each out-put. Moreover, the system's modularity enables its adaptation to various deliberative contexts and linguistic domains, ensuring both scalability and contextual sensitivity.

By leveraging polarity detection and thematic clustering, the toolkit offers a more nuanced depiction of stakeholder positions, moving beyond surface-level text analytics. The inclusion of interpretable summaries and keyphrases further supports the transparency of outputs, ensuring that decision-makers are not merely presented with abstract metrics but with semantically-rich representations of public input. These capabilities help bridge the gap between the granularity of deliberative discourse and the need for actionable, comprehensible insights in policymaking.

However, the integration of AI in public deliberation processes also raises important ethical considerations. Chief among these is the risk of algorithmic bias, which can emerge from training data, model design, or deployment contexts. To mitigate such risks, the proposed system advocates for transparency in algorithmic decisions and traceability in its analytic processes. Each output, from sentiment categorization to summarization, is designed to be explainable and auditable, allowing policymakers and analysts to verify the rationale behind system-generated insights.

Furthermore, bias mitigation strategies should be embedded at multiple stages of the pipeline, including the selection of training data that is representative of diverse social groups, the continuous evaluation of clustering and sentiment models for fair-ness, and the application of human oversight during interpretation. Importantly, the system's modularity allows for the integration of additional fairness-aware algorithms or domain-specific adjustments, depending on the policy area or cultural context in which it is deployed.

In conclusion, the Feedback Aggregator not only advances the technical frontier of AI-supported deliberation platforms but also actively contributes to responsible and ethical AI practices. Its emphasis on contextual sensitivity, interpretability, and bias mitigation ensures that it remains aligned with democratic values and public trust, enabling the reliable integration of AI into critical governance functions.

7 Conclusion

In this chapter, we proposed an innovative software toolkit, which leverages deep learning and NLP techniques techniques for addressing the issues of actionable knowledge discovery and informed policy making in public deliberation. The proposed toolkit is based on a modular system, named Feedback Aggregator, which is designed to organize and structure users' feedback data from deliberative discussions, aiming at developing a semantically-rich pool of actionable knowledge. It is comprised of four main components: (i) pre-processing component, which refines participants' feedback by removing noise and employs a polarity detection mechanism to categorize feedback into sentiment groups; (ii) clustering component, which organizes feedback into groups based on its thematic content and stance toward the discussion topic; (iii) summarization component, which generates concise summaries encapsulating the core content of each cluster; and (iv) keyphrase extraction component, which identifies the most impactful phrases from the feedback within each cluster.

It is worth mentioning that the transformation of unstructured feedback into actionable knowledge by Feedback Aggregator, considerably enhances policy-making and decision-making processes. In detail, clustering and summarization components synthesize diverse viewpoints, ensuring that decision-makers have access to well-organized and concise representations of public opinion while The extraction of key phrases highlights critical issues and influential ideas, helping policymakers prioritize and address the most pressing concerns. This systematic processing of deliberative discussions not only facilitates evidence-based decision-making but also ensures that diverse stakeholder perspectives are effectively incorporated. By providing a transparent, scalable, and data-driven approach, the toolkit empowers policymakers to make informed, equitable, and contextually sensitive decisions, ultimately improving the quality and inclusiveness of governance.

Despite the promising feedback obtained through preliminary evaluation of the proposed toolkit, its effectiveness has yet to be validated in large-scale real-world environments. Real-world testing would illuminate practical challenges such as scalability issues, the adaptability of the system to diverse cultural contexts and the accuracy of sentiment and stance detection within complex, nuanced feedback.

The input of end users would provide valuable information on the usability and effectiveness of the proposed approach in real deliberative processes, potentially uncovering unforeseen limitations and areas for improvement. Comprehensive field testing remains a necessary step to ensure the toolkit's applicability and efficacy in real decision-making and policy-formulation scenarios and it is certainly a future work direction.

Another future work direction concerns the development of pipelines for retrieving data from other deliberation platforms such as "Conference on the Future of Europe" (Kotanidis, 2021) and "BCause" (Anastasiou & De Liddo, 2023). Expanding the toolkit's compatibility with additional platforms will enable a broader application across diverse deliberative environments. Another idea for future research is to enhance the toolkit's capabilities by incorporating more advanced sentiment and stance detection techniques as well as multilingual NLP models, which account for cultural nuances and contextual subtleties. Finally, we plan to integrate real-time feedback analysis and visualization features to support dynamic deliberation sessions, empowering policymakers to gain immediate insights and foster interactive and responsive decision-making processes.

Acknowledgements This work received funding from the Horizon Europe research and innovation programme under Grant Agreement No. 101094765, project ORBIS (Augmenting participation, co-creation, trust and transparency in Deliberative Democracy at all scales).

References

Anastasiou, L., & De Liddo, A. (2023). Bcause: Reducing group bias and promoting cohesive discussion in online deliberation processes through a simple and engaging online deliberation tool. In *Proceedings of the annual meeting of the association for computational linguistics* (pp. 39–49).

Androutsopoulou, A., Karacapilidis, N., Loukis, E., & Charalabidis, Y. (2019). Trans-forming the communication between citizens and government through AI-guided chatbots. *Government Information Quarterly, 36*(2), 358–367.

Basyal, L., & Sanghvi, M. (2023). Text summarization using large language models: a comparative study of MPT-7B-instruct, Falcon-7b-instruct, and OpenAI Chat-GPT models. arXiv preprint arXiv:2310.10449

Campos, R., Mangaravite, V., Pasquali, A., Jorge, A., Nunes, C., & Jatowt, A. (2020). YAKE! Keyword extraction from single documents using multiple local features. *Information Sciences, 509*, 257–289.

Eklund, A., Forsman, M., & Drewes, F. (2023). An empirical configuration study of a common document clustering pipeline. *Northern European Journal of Language Technology (NEJLT), 9*(1).

El-Beltagy, S. R., & Rafea, A. (2009). KP-Miner: A keyphrase extraction system for English and Arabic documents. *Information Systems, 34*(1), 132–144.

El Helou, S., Tzagarakis, M., Gillet, D., Karacapilidis, N., & Yu, C. M. (2008, May). Symposium 6: Participatory design for awareness features: Enhancing interaction in communities of practice. In *Proceedings of the international conference on networked learning* (6, pp. 523–530). https://doi.org/10.54337/nlc.v6.9370. https://journals.aau.dk/index.php/nlc/article/view/9370

Fishkin, J. S. (2018). *Democracy when the people are thinking: Revitalizing our politics through public deliberation.* Oxford University Press.

Giarelis, N., & Karacapilidis, N. (2023). LMRank: Utilizing pre-trained language models and dependency parsing for keyphrase extraction. *IEEE Access*.

Grootendorst, M. (2020). KeyBERT: Minimal keyword extraction with BERT. Zenodo.

Karacapılıdıs, N. (2014). Mastering data-intensive collaboration and decision-making: Cutting edge research and practical applications in the dicode project. *Studies in Big Data Series, 5*.

Karacapilidis, N., Loukis, E., & Dimopoulos, S. (2004). A web-based system for sup-porting structured collaboration in the public sector. In *International conference on electronic government* (pp. 218–225).

Karacapilidis, N., & Papadias, D. (1998). A computational approach for argumentative discourse in multi-agent decision making environments. *AI Communications, 11*(1), 21–33. https://doi.org/10.3233/EAI-1998-142

Kotanidis, S. (2021). Conference on the future of Europe. Briefing–European Parliament.

Langville, A. N., & Meyer, C. D. (2006). *Google's PageRank and beyond: The science of search engine rankings*. Princeton University Press.

McInnes, L., Healy, J., & Melville, J. (2018). Umap: Uniform manifold approximation and projection for dimension reduction. arXiv preprint arXiv:1802.03426

Mihalcea, R., & Tarau, P. (2004). Textrank: Bringing order into text. In *Proceedings of the 2004 conference on empirical methods in natural language processing* (pp. 404–411).

Moshman, D. (2020). *Reasoning, argumentation, and deliberative democracy*. Routledge.

Nabatchi, T. (2010). Addressing the citizenship and democratic deficits: The potential of deliberative democracy for public administration. *The American Review of Public Administration, 40*(4), 376–399.

Nadim, M., Akopian, D., & Matamoros, A. (2023). A comparative assessment of unsupervised keyword extraction tools. *IEEE Access*.

Petukhova, A., Matos-Carvalho, J. P., & Fachada, N. (2024). Text clustering with LLM embeddings. arXiv preprint arXiv:2403.15112

Pintelas, E., & Livieris, I. E. (2023). XSC - an explainable image segmentation and classification framework: A case study on skin cancer. *Electronics, 12*(17), 3551.

Ravi, J., & Kulkarni, S. (2023). Text embedding techniques for eficient clustering of twitter data. *Evolutionary Intelligence, 16*(5), 1667–1677.

Roberts, N. (2004). Public deliberation in an age of direct citizen participation. *The American Review of Public Administration, 34*(4), 315–353.

Roberts, N. (2015). *Public deliberation: An alternative approach to crafting policy and setting direction. The age of direct citizen participation* (pp. 212–225). Routledge.

Wang, Z., Da Cunha, C., Ritou, M., & Furet, B. (2019). Comparison of k-means and GMM methods for contextual clustering in HSM. *Procedia Manufacturing, 28*, 154–159.

Wierzchon´, S. T., & Klopotek, M. A. (2018). *Modern algorithms of cluster analysis* (Vol. 34). Springer.

The Transformative Potential of Artificial Intelligence in Smart Cities

12

Julius A. Nukpezah, Michael A. O. Ntow, Edmund P. Adu, and Jubilee T. Apalowo

1 Introduction

The rapid pace of urbanization in the twenty-first century has presented cities with unprecedented challenges, including transportation, technological, environmental, societal, economic, governance, and calls for more efficient public services (Nukpezah et al., 2025). In response, smart cities have emerged as a transformative model for urban development, leveraging advanced technologies to enhance the quality of life for residents while promoting sustainability and economic growth (Abutabenjeh et al., 2022, 2024; Nukpezah et al., 2025). Among these technologies, artificial intelligence (AI) stands out as a critical enabler, offering powerful tools for data analysis, automation, and decision-making (Mitchell, 2019). Integrating AI into smart city infrastructure is not merely a technological evolution but a paradigm shift in how cities are designed, managed, and experienced (Kankanhalli et al., 2019; Nukpezah et al., 2025; Rjab et al., 2023; Valle-Cruz et al., 2022).

J. A. Nukpezah (✉) · M. A. O. Ntow · J. T. Apalowo
Department of Political Science and Public Administration, Mississippi State University, Starkville, MS, USA
e-mail: jan214@msstate.edu

M. A. O. Ntow
e-mail: man351@msstate.edu

J. T. Apalowo
e-mail: jta313@msstate.edu

E. P. Adu
Department of Political Science, Arkansas State University, Jonesboro, AR, USA
e-mail: eadu@astate.edu

S. K. Aikins and T. Dimitrijevska-Markoski (eds.), *Artificial Intelligence and Government*, https://doi.org/10.1007/978-3-032-12344-2_12

AI encompasses a broad range of computational techniques that enable machines to perform tasks typically requiring human intelligence, such as learning, reasoning, and problem-solving (Goertzel, 2014; Turing, 2009; Von Neumann, 1956). These capabilities are made possible through the convergence of AI with other digital technologies, including the Internet of Things (IoT), big data analytics, and cloud computing. Collectively, these form the backbone of smart cities—urban ecosystems that are responsive, adaptive, and data-driven (Abutabenjeh et al., 2022; Nukpezah et al., 2022).

The significance of AI in smart cities lies in its potential to address complex urban issues through predictive and prescriptive analytics. For instance, AI algorithms can analyze traffic patterns in real time to reduce congestion and emissions, or detect anomalies in utility networks to prevent service disruptions (Abduljabba et al., 2019; Wang et al., 2016). Moreover, AI-powered platforms can facilitate more inclusive governance by enabling data-informed policy decisions and improving citizen engagement through digital interfaces (He & Chen, 2024; Luusua et al., 2023). These applications not only improve operational efficiency but also contribute to more equitable and resilient urban systems (Rjab et al., 2023; Valle-Cruz et al., 2022).

Despite its promise, integrating AI into smart cities raises critical ethical, social, and technical challenges (Ruschemeier & Hondrich, 2024). Concerns about data privacy, algorithmic bias, and the digital divide must be addressed to ensure that AI-driven urban development is inclusive and just (Ahmad et al., 2020Blanco et al., 2009; Zhou & Kankanhalli, 2021). Furthermore, deploying AI technologies requires robust infrastructure, skilled human capital, and supportive regulatory frameworks (Díaz-Rodríguez et al., 2023; Wang et al., 2021). As such, the successful implementation of AI in smart cities depends on a holistic approach that balances innovation with governance and public trust.

This chapter examines the multifaceted relationship between AI and smart cities, tracing the historical evolution of both concepts and examining the technologies that underpin their integration. It explores the practical applications of AI in urban infrastructure and governance, presents real-world examples, and examines the benefits and risks associated with adopting AI. Ultimately, it provides valuable insights into future trends and offers policy recommendations to guide the ethical and effective use of AI in shaping tomorrow's cities. By understanding the transformative potential of AI in smart cities, stakeholders can better navigate the opportunities and challenges of urban innovation in the digital age.

2 Historical Background

2.1 Evolution of AI Technology

Artificial Intelligence (AI) has evolved since the 1950s, when the concept was first introduced in the tech sector; it gained momentum and was propelled by advancements in computing (Mitchell, 2019). The term conveys the idea that there are parallels between computation and the human brain (Turing, 2009; Von Neumann, 1956). John McCarthy formalized the term in 1956 during the Dartmouth Workshop to describe the phenomenon of machines mimicking humans (Mitchell, 2019). This led to research on symbolic AI and sub-symbolic AI. While symbolic AI uses logic and rules to represent knowledge and solve problems, sub-symbolic AI[1] uses neural networks, statistical models, and pattern recognition to process information and learn from data (Nilsson, 1998, p. 7).

Symbolic AI dominated the 1950s, while sub-symbolic AI had a quieter start. Advances in AI were scant in the 1960s, partly due to reduced resources resulting from unstable economic conditions, including two economic recessions. Because of criticisms leveled at neural networks[2] (Minsky & Papert, 1969), research about the phenomenon was slow (Mycielski, 1972). After notable research gains in the 1970s, AI rebounded as multilayer neural networks, aided by the back-propagation training algorithm in the 1980s (Mitchell, 2019). The breakthrough came in 1985 when David Rumelhart, Geoffrey Hinton, and Ronald Williams published their seminal article, *Learning representations by back-propagating errors*, which demonstrated the back-propagation algorithm's effectiveness in training deep networks (Rumelhart et al., 1985). Yann LeCun's convolutional networks advanced image recognition, while machine learning methods gained traction (LeCun & Bengio, 1995). Powered by this technology, IBM's Deep Blue beat chess champion Garry Kasparov in 1997, marking a milestone for AI.

AI entered a golden era in the early 2000s, driven by advances in big data, computer hardware, and improved algorithms, particularly neural networks. Advances in neural networks facilitated a deep learning revolution (Mitchell, 2019). Deep learning is a subset of machine learning that utilizes deep neural networks—networks with multiple hidden layers. Deep learning models can automatically extract features from raw data, making them highly effective for complex tasks like image recognition and natural language processing (Bongo-Awah, 2024). Milestones included IBM Watson's 2011 Jeopardy! victory, the 2012 breakthrough of AlexNet in image recognition, and DeepMind's AlphaGo defeating a Go champion in 2016, powered by neural networks (Mitchell, 2019). In 2024, Geoffrey Hinton, *the Godfather of AI* and the pioneer in the development of neural networks, was recognized with a Nobel Prize in Physics (Nobel Prize Outreach, 2025).

The current neural networks power various technologies, including but not limited to speech and image recognition, natural language processing, and translation. Almost all major technology companies, including Meta and Google, have invested billions of dollars in AI products since the success of OpenAI's popular natural language processing tool, ChatGPT. However, challenges remain; AI lacks common sense, struggles with bias, and faces ethical concerns (Ruschemeier & Hondrich, 2024). Therefore, the quest for Artificial General Intelligence (AGI) continues.

[1] Also known as connectionist AI.

[2] Inspired by the human brain, neural networks are statistical models that learn from data and adjust their connections to improve performance (LeCun et al., 1989).

Artificial General Intelligence (AGI) refers to AI systems that can perform any intellectual task a human can, demonstrating reasoning, learning, and adaptability across multiple domains without task-specific programming (Goertzel, 2014). Unlike narrow AI, which excels at specific tasks (such as image recognition or language translation), AGI would possess general intelligence, enabling it to transfer knowledge across fields and solve novel problems.

2.2 Development of Smart Cities

One area that has benefited from AI applications is smart cities (Nukpezah et al., 2025; Rjab et al., 2023), which the next section discusses. The development of smart cities is multifaceted, characterized by historical precedents, competing visions, technological advancements, and significant challenges (Townsend, 2013). The concept of smart environments dates back to early building automation systems, such as the *Crystal Palace's ventilation system* (1851), and later conceptual works, including *Cedric Price's Generator* (1970s), which envisioned adaptive, reconfigurable spaces (Townsend, 2013). The 1990s saw the emergence of terms like digital city (e.g., Amsterdam Digital City) and intelligent city, often focused on e-governance, online communities, or attracting high-tech industries to foster economic development (Halegoua, 2020). These were precursors but differed from the later smart city emphasis on pervasive data collection and real-time optimization of all urban systems.

From a historical perspective, the evolution of smart cities reflects the ongoing debates in urban planning. The early vision of smart cities from the perspective of Ebenezer Howard's *Garden Cities* (early 20th c.) and GM's *Futurama* (1939) represent grand, often technologically driven, master-planned visions, like some corporate smart city proposals today (e.g., Songdo[3]). On the other hand, Patrick Geddes' emphasis on civics, regional surveys, and citizen participation, and Jane Jacobs's championing of existing urban fabric and grassroots order, find echoes in the *civic hacker* and open-source smart city movements (Townsend, 2013).

Until the 2010s, the smart city concept gained prominence, primarily driven by major technology corporations, such as IBM, with its *Smarter Cities* campaign, Cisco, and Siemens (Halegoua, 2020). The period was characterized by the aggressive championing of e-government through the implementation of Information and Communication Technologies (ICTs), including sensors, networks, big data analytics, and the Internet of Things (IoT), to monitor, manage, and optimize urban infrastructures, such as transportation, energy, waste, and public safety. The goals were primarily efficiency, sustainability, economic competitiveness, and improved quality of life, often framed through a lens of technological solutions to "urban

[3] Songdo is a smart city in South Korea. Songdo is a high-tech urban development built on reclaimed land near Incheon, designed to integrate cutting-edge technology into daily life (Overstreet, 2021).

problems" like congestion and pollution (Kankanhalli et al., 2019; Nukpezah et al., 2025; Rjab et al., 2023; Valle-Cruz et al., 2022).

Starting in the 2020s, the traditional perspectives on smart cities were challenged. For instance, Ben Green critiqued the traditional smart city model, arguing that cities should not blindly embrace technology as a solution to all urban challenges (Green, 2019). Instead of optimizing cities solely through algorithms, automation, and surveillance, Green advocated for a "smart enough" approach—where technology is used thoughtfully in conjunction with social and political reforms to promote democracy, equity, and livability. This represents a shift in focus from technology as the driver to sociality, placemaking, and citizen agency. It emphasizes bottom-up approaches, participatory culture, collective intelligence, and do it yourself (DIY) ethics. Citizens are seen as *producers* of the city, co-creating solutions using technology to address their own needs (Halegoua, 2020). Examples include open data initiatives driven by community needs (beyond just government portals), citizen-led data collection (e.g., LocalData,[4] Ushahidi[5]), community-owned networks, and platforms for genuine deliberation (e.g., Better Reykjavik[6]).

Given the criticism of the smart cities concept, some smart city project executives have renounced the term based on its negative connotation (Halegoua, 2020). For instance, "Rohit Aggarwala, director of urban policy implementation at Sidewalk Labs, rejected "smart city" as a descriptor for Google's Toronto megaproject" (Halegoua, 2020, p. 107). Halegoua (2020) demonstrates that the smart city concept has evolved from a largely uncritical, corporate-led, technology-first approach to a more critical, human-centered, and participatory model. While the techno-centric vision remains influential, there is a growing understanding that true *smartness* lies in how technology can be leveraged to empower citizens, foster equity, and enhance the social fabric of urban life, rather than just optimizing systems. The next section examines the nexus between smart cities and developments in AI, discussing some early attempts to integrate recent AI technology in self-proclaimed smart cities.

---

[4] LocalData is a tool designed for urban planning and community engagement, allowing users to collect and analyze location-based data. It helps cities, nonprofits, and researchers map local issues like housing, infrastructure, and environmental concerns.

[5] Ushahidi is an open-source crowdsourcing platform used for crisis response, human rights reporting, and election monitoring. It was originally developed in Kenya to track violence after the 2007 elections and has since been used globally for disaster relief, conflict mapping, and civic engagement.

[6] Better Reykjavik is an online platform designed to crowdsource solutions to urban challenges in Reykjavik, Iceland. Launched in May 2010, it allows citizens to submit, debate, and prioritize policy ideas, fostering direct democratic engagement.

2.3 Key Milestones in AI and Smart City Integration

The nexus between AI and smart city development has evolved from parallel conceptual growth to increasingly intricate integration, marking several key milestones. These milestones are summarized in Table 1 and further explained in the subsequent sections.

2.3.1 Nascent Stages and Conceptual Parallels (Late 20th Century)

During the latter half of the twentieth century, AI, initially dominated by symbolic approaches and early urban smart concepts, such as building automation (e.g., Crystal Palace's ventilation in 1851 and Cedric Price's "Generator" in the 1970s), largely developed independently. While AI research explored logic and rules, early smart infrastructure focused on isolated mechanical or electronic controls. Direct, large-scale integration was limited, as AI was not yet geared towards urban-scale data processing, and comprehensive smart city visions were still in their embryonic stages.

2.3.2 The Data-Driven Convergence (Early 2000s–2010s)

The turn of the millennium witnessed AI entering a *golden era*, significantly propelled by the increasing availability of big data and advancements in computing power and algorithms (Mitchell, 2019). This period coincided with the emergence of smart cities, which gained prominence in the 2010s, often driven by major technology corporations (Halegoua, 2020; Townsend, 2013). Initial integrations revolved around data analytics. As cities began deploying Information and Communication Technologies (ICTs)—sensors, networks—they generated unprecedented volumes of urban data. Early AI, especially machine learning techniques, provided the initial tools to analyze this data, primarily to optimize urban infrastructures like transportation and energy systems, aligning with efficiency and economic competitiveness goals that characterized early smart city initiatives.

2.3.3 Deep Learning and Enhanced Integration (Mid-2010s–Present)

The deep learning revolution, exemplified by breakthroughs such as AlexNet in 2012, has dramatically expanded AI's capabilities in complex tasks, including image recognition, natural language processing, and advanced pattern detection. This unlocked new and more sophisticated avenues for AI integration in smart cities. Beyond basic analytics, AI began to be applied to:

- Real-time adaptive traffic management systems (Snow, 2017).
- Intelligent surveillance for public safety (though accompanied by ongoing ethical discussions) (McCray, 2024).
- Predictive maintenance algorithms for critical city infrastructure, reducing downtime and costs (Hjaltalin & Sigurdarson, 2024; Snow, 2017).

Table 1 Milestones in AI and smart city development

Era/Period	AI development status	Smart city development status	Integration level	Key characteristics and impact
Late 20th century	Dominated by symbolic AI (logic, rules)	Early urban concepts, such as building automation (e.g., Crystal Palace, 1851, and Cedric Price's Generator, 1970s)	Highly limited and independent development. AI was not geared for urban-scale data processing	Concepts were developed in parallel with little direct integration. Smart city visions were embryonic
Early 2000s–2010s	AI entered a "golden era" propelled by big data, computing power, and improved algorithms	Gained prominence, often driven by major technology corporations (e.g., IBM's Smarter Cities campaign). Focused on ICTs (sensors, networks) generating urban data	Initial integrations centered on data analytics, with early AI/ML models used to analyze urban data and optimize infrastructure (e.g., transportation, energy)	Focus on efficiency and economic competitiveness. Laid the groundwork for data-driven urban management
Mid-2010s–Present	Deep learning revolution (e.g., AlexNet 2012) expanded AI capabilities in complex tasks (image recognition, NLP, pattern detection)	Broader vision for smart cities, shifting towards more human-centric and participatory models, though tech-first remained influential	Applied AI beyond basic analytics to Real-time adaptive traffic management, Intelligent surveillance, predictive maintenance for infrastructure, and Personalized citizen services via chatbots	Sophisticated AI applications unlocked new avenues for urban optimization. Growing awareness of ethical considerations (surveillance) alongside continued technological advancement
Early 2020s onwards	Emergence and rapid advancement of Generative AI (e.g., Large Language Models like ChatGPT)	Growing emphasis on "smart enough" approaches, prioritizing equity, citizen empowerment, and livability	Burgeoning interest in leveraging GenAI for intuitive and dynamic citizen interactions (advanced chatbots), sophisticated urban planning simulations, policy analysis, and co-creating urban solutions	A new phase of integration seeking more dynamic and intuitive urban solutions. Stronger focus on addressing inherent AI challenges (e.g., bias, ethics, and governance) and balancing innovation with public trust and inclusive development

- Personalized citizen services through AI-driven platforms like chatbots (Aoki, 2020).

The vision for smart cities has started to broaden, with some discourse shifting beyond purely techno-centric optimization toward more human-centric and participatory models (Green, 2019; Halegoua, 2020), although the technology-first approach remains influential.

2.3.4 The Generative AI Era and Future Prospects (Early 2020s Onwards)

The recent emergence and rapid advancement of generative AI, including Large Language Models (LLMs), such as the technology behind OpenAI's ChatGPT, signal a new integration phase. There is burgeoning interest in leveraging these AI capabilities for more intuitive and dynamic citizen interactions (e.g., highly capable chatbots for city services), sophisticated urban planning simulations, policy analysis, and even co-creating urban solutions. Continued substantial investments by technology giants into AI products are poised to further accelerate the development and deployment of advanced AI solutions in smart cities. This progress occurs alongside a growing emphasis on addressing the inherent challenges of AI, such as bias, ethical considerations, and the need for robust governance frameworks, as well as a stronger push for *smart enough* approaches that prioritize equity, citizen empowerment, and livability (Green, 2019). The subsequent section discusses recent applications of AI technology in smart cities.

3 Applications and Benefits of AI in Smart Cities

Over the past several decades, local governments have employed various appropriate technologies, including AI in smart city operations. These technologies have contributed to smart governance, smart economies, smart mobility, smart environment, smart living, and smart people (Wolniak & Stecuła, 2024). The following sections discuss the applications and benefits of AI in smart cities.

3.1 AI and Smart Mobility

AI has significantly contributed to smart mobility in global cities by developing effective and efficient traffic management and transportation systems. Beginning with planning, AI contributes to identifying the community's needs and selecting the most effective strategy to meet them, while considering the social, environmental, and economic impacts on transportation (Abduljabba et al., 2019). For example, the Network Design Problem (NDP) involves designing an optimal road network for transport planning (Bagloee et al., 2017). The legacy system's inherent barrier in smart cities (Nukpezah et al., 2025) also makes planning imperative. When the capacity of the current transport infrastructure (i.e., the extension of lane width, median, and shoulder area) changes or when additional infrastructure is added, incompatibility difficulties arise. However, by drawing on sophisticated AI techniques such as machine learning, Deep Learning, and predictive modeling, city planners can analyze past and current data to optimize transportation efficiency.

AI-powered Intelligent Transport Systems (ITS) utilize various technologies and communication networks to enable better traffic prediction, reduce congestion, and improve commute times (Abduljabba et al., 2019). ITS is also used to manage intersection traffic signals (Wang et al., 2016) and enhance driving experience. Using AI-assisted historical road sensor data to create intelligent predictive systems for real-time, short-term, and long-term forecasts (Mahamuni, 2018) has contributed to status monitoring for predicting the likelihood of accidents and injuries on heavily populated routes (Doğan & Akgüngör, 2013), benefitting not only commuters but also pedestrians. AI-assisted technologies also make parking more efficient (Iqbal et al., 2019).

The micro-mobility and sharing economy concepts, where users pay for shared assets such as vehicles or bicycles, are becoming a key element in the smart urban mobility ecosystem, where they can even be customized for individual and family short-distance transport and urban parcel delivery (Abduljabbar et al., 2021). AVs are transforming global transportation systems, despite concerns about their safety and reliability (Abduljabba et al., 2019; Bagloee et al., 2016), they are being used in areas including freight and supply chain logistics. In-vehicle electronic devices, Inter-vehicle networking, and vehicular network applications have become the standard for innovative capabilities, such as electronic fuel injection, adaptive cruise control, electronic stability control, autonomous driving, parking assistance systems, lane-keeping assistance, and ultimately, traffic management, safety, and energy efficiency (Dibaei et al., 2021).

Ultrasonic sensors provide real-time vehicle speed information, thereby improving traffic flow (Jagatheesaperumal et al., 2024). Alcohol sensors such as MQ3 and Arduino controller monitor the driver's alcohol levels to address road safety concerns, utilizing GPS and GSM technologies, which autonomously restrict the vehicle's speed and provide alerts for immediate action (Jagatheesaperumal et al., 2024). An eyeblink sensor detects possible threats quickly, alerting drivers and boosting smart city road safety (Jagatheesaperumal et al., 2024).

Examples where these tools are used include Indian smart cities, where dynamic displays direct drivers to available parking slots, as all information is monitored online, addressing inadequate parking spaces and associated accidents (Agarwal et al., 2015). Many cities in the USA, China, and the EU commonly adopt shared vehicles, bicycles, and e-scooters for short trips instead of private cars (Abduljabbar et al., 2021). San Francisco has introduced a dockless electric bike-sharing system, in addition to its existing station-based regional bike-sharing system (Lazarus et al., 2020). In Chicago and Indianapolis, AI and data analytics enable data collected from shared schemes to be used to assess the daily trip frequencies of bike-sharing systems as well as identifying the spatio-temporal patterns and reallocation of bike quantities, which help to understand people's behavior, the impact of usage and possible solutions to rising challenges (Abduljabbar et al., 2021). AI-powered autonomous vehicles (AVs) that can operate without a driver, enabling the car to learn and drive safely with lane discipline and control, have been introduced in the City of Singapore, Singapore, Shenzhen, China, San Francisco, US, Dubai, UAE, and Tokyo, Japan. Additionally, Automatic Vehicle Location (AVL) systems are widely used to improve operational efficiency of public transport in large cities, including New York, U.S., London, UK, Toronto, Canada, and Seoul, South Korea. These manage operational control and enhance bus service dependability, prioritizing bus traffic signals and informing passengers of bus schedules at bus stops (Barabino et al., 2015; Tilocca et al., 2017).

3.2 AI and Smart Environment

AI has also contributed to advances in energy efficiency and sustainability in smart cities. AI-assisted tools ensure efficient energy usage, reduce water, air, noise pollution, congestion, and other externalities (Yigitcanlar et al., 2020), identify environmental concerns, and enable timely responses to minimize and manage them (Dos Santos et al., 2024). AI in waste management optimizes waste collection routes, reduces overflow incidents, and improves recycling processes, thus decreasing landfill utilization and promoting recycling efforts (Lakhouit, 2025).

AI-enabled smart grids optimize energy use and power systems and plan and manage electric car charging, public lights, and data (Yigitcanlar et al., 2020). AI can also help distribute renewable electricity from non-traditional sources, such as body heat. By enhancing resource management, monitoring energy consumption, and planning, cities can utilize resources more efficiently and meet their renewable energy targets (Yigitcanlar et al., 2020). For instance, Singapore invested in an AI-enhanced thermostat to regulate office temperatures.

Moreover, cities utilize AI to comprehend climate change, make predictions, and recommend suitable solutions, thereby facilitating proactive preparations and adaptation (Cowls et al., 2023). Deep-learning tools such as the Convolutional Neural Network (CNN model) produce skillful ENSO forecasts to enhance climate predictions and modeling, energy production, CO_2 removal, solar geo-engineering, and financial applications (Ham et al., 2019). These innovations enable the development of more energy-efficient buildings, low-carbon materials, deforestation monitoring, and greener transportation (Rolnick et al., 2022).

Integrating AI into smart cities is an essential tool for achieving sustainability objectives. AI-based tools and big urban data can significantly influence the formulation of urban policies to facilitate urban transformation. Applying AI-related tools in city planning often provides a more nuanced understanding of a city's functional and spatial structure, thereby enhancing urban change management. This results from the capacity of AI-based tools to conduct more accurate analyses of urban dynamics (Kamrowska-Załuska, 2021).

AI systems can facilitate knowledge-based decision-making in the context of complex environmental issues and substantial data volumes, aiming to reconcile the environmental outcomes of urban areas with the social and economic welfare of residents (Cortès et al., 2000). These optimize resource utilization, improve environmental monitoring, encourage citizen participation, promote the development of efficient, eco-friendly urban environments while prioritizing resilience and sustainability in cities (Dos Santos et al., 2024). AI can also enhance disaster prevention and management through improved early warning systems and more effective disaster response (Singh & Manoharan, 2025). This contributes to reduced environmental impacts of disasters and increased resilience in smart cities.

Global cities are leveraging AI effectively to advance the smart environment concept. For example, the Barcelona Supercomputing Center uses AI models for hazard prediction, earthquake monitoring, and climate forecasting (Booth & Pillay, November 4, 2024). Tallahassee, US uses AI traffic sensor placement algorithms for Hurricane response and traffic management during inclement weather (Booth & Pillay, November 4, 2024). Adıyaman, Turkey, and Quelimane, Mozambique, use Google's ML models to analyze satellite and aerial imagery for post-disaster damage assessment (Booth & Pillay, November 4, 2024). Singapore uses AI in the Smart Nation Initiative, urban heat island mitigation, and waste and water management to advance city sustainability and environmental monitoring. Amsterdam, Netherlands, uses AI for energy demand prediction and digital twin models for climate adaptation, including smart grids and flood prevention. San Francisco, California, USA uses AI to analyze and track carbon footprint (Gadwal, Sep 23, 2024). Copenhagen, Denmark, uses AI for traffic and energy optimization to achieve carbon neutrality. Tokyo, Japan, uses AI seismic activity prediction for earthquake early warning and energy efficiency. Cape Town, South Africa, is improving waste management through sensors, data analytics, and drones that monitor bin levels in real time to ensure timely collection and minimize overflow and littering (Das, 2025).

3.3 AI and Smart Living

Cities are leveraging AI to enhance the quality of life through improved healthcare, education, safety, and public services, utilizing AI-enabled IoT, Digital Twins, Computer Vision, and Natural Language Processing (NLP) tools. AI is being utilized in public safety face detection cameras. AI-enabled surveillance drones detect threats or attacks (Alam & Khan, 2022) and predict fire danger (Maraveas et al., 2021; Su et al., 2021). AI in smart cities enhances urban livability by mitigating the challenges of population growth and the ripple effects. Advanced AI surveillance technologies, utilizing motion detection, predictive analytics, drones, and other autonomous devices, are capable of monitoring urban areas and identifying threats, including crime, fraud, accidents, and fires (Alam & Khan, 2022; Maraveas et al., 2021; Su et al., 2021).

Notable examples around the world include Vienna, Austria, which is using data analytics and Large Language Models (LLMs), exemplified by initiatives such as the FIWARE-based IoT platform to develop a digital twin for optimizing urban services (Wirtz et al., 2020). The health department in Las Vegas, U.S., utilizes AI-assisted apps, such as the nEmesis app in detecting eateries with food safety issues and identifying unauthorized restaurants (Yigitcanlar et al., 2020). Durham Constabulary in the UK is employing the Harm Assessment Risk Tool (HART) to identify recidivism patterns among offenders (BBC, 2020). Singapore uses smart health monitoring in public housing to help elderly residents with predictive alerts (Negi, January 16, 2025). London, UK, uses AI-enhanced air quality sensors to provide real-time pollution data and suggest mitigation actions. San Francisco, U.S., uses AI-enabled Gunshot detection systems that alert law enforcement in real time of threats (Flynn, March 12, 2025). Amsterdam uses smart water management systems to predict flooding and manage canal levels, and NLP to analyze public sentiments and guide policy (Flynn, March 12, 2025). Dubai uses AI-powered smart grids to balance energy loads and reduce waste.

3.4 AI and Smart Economy

AI contributes to and enhances the productivity and innovation of smart cities. AI is crucial in developing robust entrepreneurial ecosystems within smart cities by promoting enhanced green investments and creating job opportunities (Ergasheva et al., 2025). It is an effective tool for the rapid and precise management and analysis of extensive datasets, facilitating informed business decision-making (Yigitcanlar & Cugurullo, 2020). AI also has the potential to enhance productivity by automating data management processes, thereby eliminating the need for intermediaries and repetitive business tasks (Wolniak & Stecuła, 2024). AI data management capacity supports customer service, projecting demand while boosting supply and increasing profitability. AI lowers costs and allows for the reallocation of resources to more productive or innovative areas (Wolniak & Stecuła, 2024; Yigitcanlar & Cugurullo, 2020). Because AI can automate processes and perform statistical analyses that exceed what humans can manage, this greatly eliminates economic uncertainty, reduces the likelihood of errors, and enhances the operational efficiency of businesses and industries (Yigitcanlar & Cugurullo, 2020). Although rapid technological changes are likely to result in an unstable job market, AI introduces new skill requirements across various sectors, requiring the education sector to adequately prepare students for future job markets (Yigitcanlar & Cugurullo, 2020). Governments that meet these requirements reap the benefits.

For example, India's shift to digital payment by adopting the Unified Payments Interface (UPI) has revolutionized financial transactions by facilitating efficient digital payments, particularly in metropolitan regions, while mitigating fraud and decreasing corruption (Ojha, 2023). Singapore uses AI tools in logistics, finance, and urban planning to streamline operations and attract tech investment (North,

July 24, 2024). Through the Smart Dubai initiative, Dubai, UAE, uses AI in tourism, finance, and logistics to diversify the economy. London, UK, has boosted its fintech, real estate, and public sector efficiency with predictive analytics for infrastructure and smart mobility. Shanghai, China, is driving industrial automation and smart port logistics with AI-powered port operations and smart city infrastructure.

3.5 AI and Smart Governance

AI is also used to enhance citizen engagement and provide efficient public services to residents. AI is pivotal to the growth of various smart city applications and ensures the optimal delivery of services to citizens across multiple sectors. AI fosters collaborative innovation processes that enhance opportunities for citizen engagement and involvement of other stakeholders, such as the private sector, in policy decisions. This includes citizen participation in policy development through crowdsourcing and the implementation of online services like electronic voting and smart contracts (Criado & Gil-Garcia, 2019; He & Chen, 2024; Luusua et al., 2023). Tools such as chatbots and intelligent assistants for public engagement, robo-advisors to assist civil servants, real-time management of national infrastructure utilizing IoT and blockchain, automated compliance and regulation, securely stored public records in blockchain distributed ledgers, online judicial and dispute resolution systems, and laws and statutes encoded as blockchain smart contracts, are all potentials that can positively transform governance (Engin & Treleaven, 2019).

Cities around the globe are adopting AI and integrating it into the core of urban governance, improving efficiency, transparency, and citizen engagement. A notable example is Singapore, which has introduced over 100 generative AI solutions, including a digital twin of the city and multilingual chatbots for public services (North, July 24, 2024). Buenos Aires, Argentina, launched the *Boti*, a government chatbot in 2019, which provided COVID-19 response, bike-sharing information, social care, and public service access to residents (North, July 24, 2024). London, UK, uses AI in predictive policing and digital citizen engagement platforms, providing real-time information to residents (Negi, January 16, 2025). Estonia's e-Estonia program provides every individual with a digital identity, digital signature, and personal record, while almost all government services are accessible online (e-estonia, April 9, 2018). Additionally, Estonia's e-Residency allows residents to apply for and get access to a platform founded on inclusivity, validity, and transparency. E-residents also gain access to the EU economic ecosystem and can utilize public e-services via their digital identity (e-estonia, April 9, 2018; Lufkin, October 19, 2017).

3.6 AI and Smart People

Since a smart city can be assessed by the aggregate intelligence of its residents (Nukpezah et al., 2025), the goal of smart people is to prioritize initiatives that equip residents with the necessary skills, knowledge, and resources to actively participate in and gain from urban developments (Wolniak & Stecuła, 2024). AI aids the implementation of a human-centric smart city initiative and contribute to the education of its residents.

For instance, as one of the top AI innovation hubs in the European Union, Barcelona, Spain instituted sophisticated technologies like large learning models (LLMs) to enhance access to municipal services and facilitate contact with its inhabitants. These systems manage hundreds of daily interactions via digital channels and are engineered to accommodate many languages to acknowledge the city's multicultural and global status to promote inclusion, civic involvement, and administrative efficiency. Additionally, Copenhagen, Denmark uses LLMs to solicit public feedback through a sophisticated natural language processing pipeline that handles inputs from various sources, including formal public consultations to social media discussions (Salierno et al., 2025). Another attempt to communicate with and empower citizens includes Civic Lab which operated as a co-working place in Chicago, U.S. for over two years as a gathering venue, and a learning center for residents (Engin & Treleaven, 2019).

4 Challenges and Risks of AI in Smart Cities

4.1 Privacy and Data Security Concerns

Incorporating AI into smart cities has enhanced government efficiency (Herath & Mittal, 2022). However, it has also prompted apprehensions about data management and societal implications (Szpilko et al., 2023). Smart cities collect a vast quantity of data regarding the daily activities, movements, and preferences of residents using a diverse array of Internet of Things (IoT) devices, sensors, and cameras (Minoli & Occhiogrosso, 2018; Talari et al, 2017). This could result in privacy violations, as individuals may not be fully informed about the data they share and their intended use (Kshetri, 2014). There are significant security and privacy challenges due to vulnerabilities resulting from data intrusions, cyberattacks, and the misuse of personal information (Silva et al., 2018; Wolniak & Stecula, 2024). Sensitive data from various sources, including healthcare, transportation, and energy systems (Zhang et al., 2017), are prompting academics and practitioners to underscore the necessity of privacy-aware frameworks, standardized regulations, and comprehensive security measures to resolve these concerns (Kibriya et al., 2024; Williamson & Prybutok, 2024).

While conventional data collection models provide informed consent regarding the collection and intended use of personal information, these are frequently obscured by the complexity and opacity of AI systems in smart cities (Eckhoff & Wagner, 2017). This lack of transparency raises ethical concerns regarding informed consent, as individuals may unknowingly consent to terms that permit the extensive surveillance or exploitation of their personal information (De Hert & Gutwirth, 2006). The interconnectedness of smart city systems generates numerous vulnerabilities that cybercriminals can exploit (Kitchin & Dodge, 2020). A vulnerability in a single area could compromise the entire network, as multiple devices collect and transmit sensitive information, posing significant risks to both public safety and individual privacy (Elmaghraby & Losavio, 2014; Morrow, 2012).

Another concern among practitioners and researchers is the bias in AI algorithms used in smart cities, which affects various domains, including urban planning (Kontokosta & Hong, 2021), autonomous vehicles (Lim & Taeihagh, 2019), and ride-sharing services (Pandey & Caliskan, 2021). These biases have the potential to propagate discrimination and introduce new safety hazards, which are particularly detrimental to marginalized communities (Samala et al., 2025). Skewed training data, societal influences, and the inherent limitations of machine learning models in managing nuance and outliers are all sources of bias (Schwartz et al., 2022). To address these concerns, strategies such as algorithmic transparency, fairness-aware learning, and participatory AI practices are recommended (Falco, 2019; Samala et al., 2025).

Furthermore, the utilization of social media data for decision-making in urban settings raises concerns regarding inclusivity and impartiality (Mashhadi et al., 2021). As AI systems are only as effective as the data on which they are trained (Ntoutsi et al., 2020), biases present in training datasets can lead to discriminatory outcomes. These include unjust treatments based on race, socioeconomic status, and other factors in resource allocation decisions and law enforcement practices (Brauneis & Goodman, 2018; Kontokosta & Hong, 2021), thereby exacerbating existing social inequalities.

4.2 Legal and Ethical Concerns

Incorporating AI into smart cities also raises ethical concerns regarding the moral and legal appropriateness of its use. The ethical dilemmas associated with privacy invasion, algorithmic bias, data management, and security issues (Ahmad et al., 2020; Zhou & Kankanhalli, 2021) are among the concerns practitioners have expressed. Reducing hazards associated with autonomous and intelligent systems primarily depends on addressing ethical issues (Jedličková, 2024). Applications such as digital payments, waste management, and law enforcement (Desouza & Bhagwatwar, 2012; Sharma & Safa, 2022) raise significant ethical concerns such as privacy and data protection, surveillance and civil liberties, algorithmic models and discrimination, transparency, accountability, informed consent, security, and cyber risk.

A primary ethical dilemma in smart cities is the widespread acquisition and utilization of data (Chang, 2021). Smart cities collect extensive data on individuals, encompassing their activities, behaviors, interactions, and health information (Pramanik et al., 2017), to comprehend urban dynamics and facilitate AI applications (Nissenbaum, 2020), which raises potential concerns regarding the exploitation of sensitive personal data (Nissenbaum, 2004). The dependence on data, encompassing location-based information, public service utilization, and personal details, engenders considerable privacy issues (Zhou, 2011). The ethical management, dissemination, and anonymization of urban and personal data are crucial to prevent monitoring or misuse (Ahmad et al., 2022). A significant ethical consideration is the possibility of bias in AI systems (Prem, 2023).

One of the ethical concerns is that algorithms may inherit biases in their training data, thereby perpetuating historical prejudices and societal inequities (Turner Lee, 2018). Using biased algorithms for resource allocation, public service delivery, or predictive policing can perpetuate and exacerbate existing imbalances, disproportionately impacting underprivileged communities (Birhane, 2021), raising social justice concerns. Bias extends beyond technical considerations to encompass social and cultural elements, emerging when data collection methodologies and algorithms overlook the diverse cultural nuances, practices, and values of distinct societies (Birhane, 2021; Gupta et al., 2022). This may provide results that are misaligned with the culture and specific demographic groups, thus leading to discriminatory actions and diminished trust (Smith, 2010). Moreover, there are ethical concerns with predictive models for evaluating property values or identifying development zones that may overlook low-income or minority neighborhoods, potentially leading to displacement or exacerbating existing inequities in housing and infrastructure if not developed with inclusivity in mind (Blanco et al., 2009).

4.3 Technology and Infrastructure Concerns

Key barriers associated with adopting AI in smart cities include insufficient infrastructure, funding limitations, and cybersecurity risks (Wang et al., 2021). These barriers are critical as they directly impact the efficiency, scalability, and sustainability of AI-driven solutions in urban environments. IT infrastructure is considered a critical yet important element in implementing AI in smart cities. This IT infrastructure consists of solar-based electrical systems, data collection systems, data management frameworks, cloud and edge computing, cybersecurity systems, capabilities of artificial intelligence (e.g., e-health smart grids and intelligence transport systems) (Batty, 2018; Nukpezah et al., 2025). Additionally, the technological challenges and risks associated with using AI in smart cities are multifaceted and substantial, including data infrastructure challenges as cities struggle with fragmented data systems, inadequate data standardization, and a lack of a robust data governance framework. Other concerns include the need for state-of-the-art technology, a shortage of technical expertise, and high-speed internet issues such as interoperability concerns (Nukpezah et al., 2025).

The AI and smart cities environment often comprise a fragmented ecosystem assembled from various stakeholders, vendors, and technologies (Bibri et al., 2023;

Yigitcanlar & Cugurullo, 2020). This fragmentation can hinder the infrastructure's ability to effectively align with planned municipal services or construction efforts, support new technologies, or meet demands as the initiative expands (Wang et al., 2021). Misalignment between departments in implementing AI or digital infrastructure can lead to duplication of efforts, wasted resources, and delayed public services due to a lack of interdepartmental communication (Mikhaylov et al., 2018).

Moreover, the physical infrastructure of many cities is not inherently equipped to support large-scale smart cities initiatives, necessitating substantial and potentially disruptive modifications (Bibri et al., 2023). Consequently, the seamless integration of sensors, applications, and services is contingent upon establishing a robust IT infrastructure, which includes a common network that adheres to industry-proven open standards. However, this can be challenging due to technical expertise and the cost of implementation (Dennedy et al., 2014). Additionally, smart cities' IT infrastructure must be agile, adaptable, and scalable to ensure they remain useful as smart cities evolve (Yigitcanlar & Cugurullo, 2020). Moreover, the infrastructure must be able to expand in response to the growing volume of data produced by connected devices and systems.

As the efficacy of smart cities is directly related to their ability to process data, the capacity to acquire, store, and analyze the growing volume of IoT data generated by smart cities is crucial for accelerating the benefits (Gharaibeh et al., 2017). To ensure the uninterrupted provision of mission-critical services, it is crucial to prioritize the most critical or beneficial data for real-time processing and analysis (Petrov et al., 2018). It is imperative to automate data prioritization, as connectivity becomes irrelevant without this capability. Intelligent infrastructure that can scale, manage the data burden, and support accurate analytic tools for rapid and responsible reactions is necessary for smart cities initiatives.

5 AI Policy and Regulations

Addressing concerns about incorporating AI in smart cities requires a comprehensive state, local, and national AI policy and regulatory framework. To ensure effective security measures and privacy protection policies, collaboration among governments, the private sector, and residents is necessary (Braun et al., 2018). Government initiatives and policies for AI in smart cities are to establish frameworks that guarantee the responsible, ethical, and effective utilization of AI technologies (Díaz-Rodríguez et al., 2023). These policies would enhance urban living by mitigating potential risks associated with AI deployment and improving services, safety, sustainability, and efficiency (Braun et al., 2018).

5.1 Government Initiatives and Policies

Governments are recognizing the importance of organized frameworks to govern the use of AI technologies in urban environments (De Almeida et al., 2021). Consequently, governments are creating a Trustworthy Artificial Intelligence (AI) Framework, which outlines guidelines for the safe and ethical use of AI across government initiatives (Díaz-Rodríguez et al., 2023). Government initiatives to regulate AI use focus on openness, accountability, and public trust in AI applications by forcing departments to engage in risk management when installing AI systems (De Almeida et al., 2021; Radu, 2021).

5.1.1 US Government Initiatives

The US government has prepared and implemented several initiatives and policies aimed at supporting AI in smart cities. For example, Executive Order 14,179, titled, "Removing Barriers to American Leadership in Artificial Intelligence," was signed by President Donald Trump on January 23, 2025. It provides the blueprint for an AI Bill of Rights, envisions AI as a transformative potential to improve American lives, and intends to support the development of policies and practices that protect civil rights and promote democratic values in the building, deployment, and governance of automated systems. The 2025 Executive Order was built on previous orders, where the government sought to promote AI innovation while ensuring public trust and national security. It encourages federal agencies to utilize AI to enhance services such as traffic management, energy efficiency, and emergency response (National Archives, 2022).

5.1.2 The European Union AI Initiatives and Policies

The EU Artificial Intelligence Act (AI Act) was passed by the European Union in 2024. This is the first comprehensive legal framework designed to regulate artificial intelligence within the European Union. AI regulatory sandboxes would enable cities to test new AI ideas in a controlled environment. The General Data Protection Regulation outlines how AI systems in smart cities collect and process personal data, including data from sensors, cameras, and apps. The regulation requires transparency, a legal foundation for data use, and protection of individual rights. It acknowledges that trust in AI is critical for urban mobility, smart policing, healthcare, and other applications. It encourages the reuse of public sector data, including real-time traffic, energy, and environmental data from cities. It also helps AI developers and businesses create data-driven smart city services and encourages cities to share high-value datasets with open licenses. The Act creates EU-wide cybersecurity certification frameworks and applies them to important AI systems in smart cities, such as grid management, emergency communication, and linked transportation to boost trust in urban AI infrastructure.

5.1.3 The Chinese National Policies and Strategic Plans

China has aggressively sought AI integration into smart city construction as part of its national technical leadership agenda. The Chinese government is scaling AI in urban administration, infrastructure, and services through a top-down, state-driven model that combines policy, investment, and regulation. The State Council's New Generation Artificial Intelligence Development Plan (2017) aimed to make China the global leader in AI by 2030. It promotes AI applications for urban planning, transportation, public safety, and government. To advance AI in smart healthcare, energy, environmental protection, and logistics. The China State Government's Smart City Development Plan (2014–2020) combines IoT, big data, and AI to improve urban services. It intends to expedite the digital transformation of cities using AI, cloud computing, and 5G, and supports national and local smart city infrastructure to promote digital governance.

5.2 International Standards and Frameworks

Many international standards and frameworks exist to facilitate the development and implementation of AI in smart cities. For example, the Institute of Electrical and Electronics Engineers (IEEE) Standards Association is actively engaged in standardizing smart cities, offering a range of standards and programs. Numerous frameworks and architectural standards for smart cities are among the initiatives they have highlighted. IEEE has been actively developing standards to guide the ethical and effective use of AI in smart cities. One of the most significant recent efforts is the IEEE P7803™ standard, which introduces a transformative framework for building Inclusive Sustainable Smart Cities (ISSC). Additionally, the International Organization for Standardization (ISO), in collaboration with the International Electrotechnical Commission (IEC) and the International Telecommunication Union (ITU), is playing a pivotal role in shaping AI policies for smart cities through a global initiative called the, 2025 International AI Standards Summit.

5.3 Public–Private Partnerships (PPPs)

Public–private partnerships (PPPs) are crucial for advancing and implementing AI in smart cities, as they combine the strengths, resources, and expertise of public sector organizations, such as governments and municipalities, with those of the private sector (Kang et al., 2019). This partnership is crucial for revolutionizing urban areas through technology, enhancing services, and addressing complex issues (Adel, 2023). Private partners supply essential capital, alleviating the financial strain on the public sector and facilitating project advancement (Gracias et al., 2023; Javed et al., 2022), thereby distributing risks among public and private actors, rendering large-scale, ambitious AI-driven initiatives more feasible and sustainable (Van Den Hurk & Verhoest, 2016).

For example, under the "Project Green Light" initiative, Boston, U.S. partnered with Google to utilize AI and Google Maps data for traffic flow analysis and intersection improvement. This cooperation aims to enhance traffic control and protect the city against potential operational hazards and cyberattacks. Working with T-Mobile, Georgia Tech, and other private sponsors, Peachtree Corners, U.S. created the 5G-enabled smart city technology park, Curiosity Lab. Emphasizing traffic control and road safety, the facility provides a trial environment for driverless vehicles, robotics, and other smart technologies. Working with Alibaba, Hangzhou, China adopted the City Brain system, which utilizes artificial intelligence and data from multiple government departments to manage urban traffic. Adopted in many cities around Asia, the platform maximizes traffic signal control, emergency response, and other municipal services (Caprotti & Liu, 2022). For example, in 2016, Kansas City, U.S., launched a $15 million smart city corridor using AI, IoT sensors, and Wi-Fi. The project faced financial challenges; the city funded $3.7 million, while the $12 million came from private sector partners (Sarma & Sunny, 2017).

6 Conclusion

Over the last seven decades, technological advances in AI have contributed to a wide range of transformative developments across society. AI has revolutionized industries by automating repetitive and complex tasks in robotics and process automation (Mitchell, 2019). It has been used in finance with algorithmic trading and fraud detection (Ojha, 2023). Customer service professionals have turned to AI-powered chatbots and virtual assistants to provide top-notch service to clients (Aoki, 2020). Healthcare professionals have reported gains in diagnostic tools and personalized treatment plans using AI tools (Negi, January 16, 2025).

This chapter discussed AI's transformative potential in smart cities. It discussed the evolution of AI technology, key milestones in AI and smart city integration, and shows that over the last several decades, AI technology has undergone significant improvements, enhancing its utility in smart cities. The chapter also discussed how AI-assisted smart tools contribute to smart governance, smart mobility, a smart economy, a smart environment, smart living, and a smart society. Recognizing that the use of advanced technologies, such as AI, raises ethical and legal concerns, the chapter discussed government efforts to regulate and develop ethical codes for their use.

6.1 AI and the Future of Smart Cities

The future of AI and smart cities is poised to be transformative, blending cutting-edge technology with urban living to create more efficient, sustainable, and livable environments. Looking to the future, AI will enable cities to adapt in real-time to the needs of individuals. From personalized public transportation routes to tailored energy usage in smart homes, urban life will become more responsive and intuitive. AI and smart cities will not be associated with elitism and affluence, but will be perceived as necessary for the functional government unit.

With technological advances, smart cities will be able to more effectively leverage AI to monitor air quality, manage water resources, optimize energy consumption, and reduce waste, thereby improving people's quality of life and life expectancy. By enhancing predictive analytics, AI will help cities to prepare for and respond to climate-related events more effectively. Self-driving vehicles, drone deliveries, and automated public services (like waste collection or street cleaning) will become more common. The future is promising, as AI orchestrates these systems to reduce congestion and improve safety. Moreover, governments will utilize AI to analyze vast amounts of data for more informed decision-making. This encompasses a range of services, including traffic management, crime prevention, public health, and emergency response.

However, as cities become increasingly connected, concerns about surveillance, data ownership, and algorithmic bias will intensify. Transparent governance, ethical AI frameworks, and citizen engagement will be crucial. Notwithstanding these challenges, the future smart cities will address these concerns through regulation and acceptance of technological intrusion into personal spaces. The most successful smart cities will prioritize inclusivity, ensuring that technological advancements benefit all residents, not just the affluent or tech-savvy.

Beyond the established applications of machine learning, several emerging AI technologies are set to redefine the capabilities of future smart cities:

Generative AI: This category, which includes Large Language Models (LLMs) and other AI systems capable of creating novel content (text, images, code, etc.), holds significant promise in powering advanced conversational AI for citizen services, assist in drafting policies or urban planning documents, generate diverse urban design scenarios for evaluation, or create synthetic datasets for training other AI models while enhancing data privacy.

Explainable AI (XAI): XAI encompasses techniques designed to make the decision-making processes of AI models understandable to humans (IBM, 2023, March 29). This fosters trust, allows for identifying and mitigating biases, facilitates error analysis, and supports regulatory compliance. For instance, if an AI system suggests increased patrols in a specific neighborhood, XAI can reveal whether the decision was based on historical crime data, socioeconomic factors, or biased inputs.

Federated Learning: This privacy-preserving machine learning technique enables AI models to be trained on decentralized datasets without requiring the raw data to be moved to a central location. Data can remain on local devices (e.g., citizens' smartphones) or within specific municipal departments. This is particularly valuable for smart city applications that involve sensitive personal or proprietary data, allowing for collaborative model building while upholding privacy principles.

AI-powered Digital Twins: Digital twins are dynamic virtual replicas of physical assets, processes, or entire city systems. Infused with AI, these models can run complex simulations to predict the outcomes of urban development projects, optimize city operations in real-time (e.g., traffic flow management and emergency response coordination), test policy interventions in a risk-free environment, and improve long-term strategic planning.

Edge AI: This refers to deploying AI algorithms directly on local hardware devices, such as sensors, cameras, or autonomous vehicles, rather than relying exclusively on centralized cloud-based processing. Edge AI reduces latency, conserves bandwidth, improves reliability (by enabling offline operation), and can enhance data privacy by processing information locally. It is critical for real-time applications, such as autonomous navigation, immediate anomaly detection in surveillance systems, or responsive smart infrastructure.

6.2 Practical Recommendations for Policymaking

Given the transformative potential of AI and smart cities, a strong call to action is essential for stakeholders to ensure that these technologies are developed, deployed, and utilized in a responsible, inclusive, and sustainable manner.

First, governments and policymakers should consider establishing ethical frameworks for AI deployment in urban settings. These officials should also consider investing in digital infrastructure that supports equitable access to smart city services, creating regulatory sandboxes to safely test and scale innovative technologies, and engaging citizens in decision-making through participatory platforms and digital town halls.

Second, as a matter of priority, urban planners and public managers should integrate AI into urban planning to optimize traffic, zoning, and resource management. They should consider adopting digital twins to simulate and improve city operations and prioritize green and resilient infrastructure using predictive analytics.

Third, tech companies and innovators should invest in designing inclusive AI systems that avoid bias and serve diverse populations. To be successful, they could collaborate with the public sector to co-develop solutions that address real urban challenges (Nukpezah et al., 2025). These companies should ensure algorithms and data usage transparency to allay privacy concerns.

Fourth, acknowledging the role of academia and research institutions in technology development, advanced interdisciplinary research on AI, urban studies, and ethics should be championed with generous funding from the government and the nongovernmental sectors. A commitment to developing open-source tools and datasets for smart city innovation would go a long way in enhancing the quality of the products as they educate the next generation of urban technologists and civic leaders.

Fifth, civil society and citizens should be encouraged to play an active role in AI and smart city development by staying informed and engaged in how AI is shaping their cities. They should advocate for and invest in digital rights, privacy, and equitable access to smart services, and participate in pilot programs and feedback loops to shape better outcomes.

References

Abduljabbar, R. L., Liyanage, S., & Dia, H. (2021). The role of micro-mobility in shaping sustainable cities: A systematic literature review. *Transportation Research Part d: Transport and Environment, 92*, Article 102734.

Abutabenjeh, S., Dimand, A. M., Brunjes, B. M., Azhar, A., & Nukpezah, J. (2024). Collaboration, organizational capacity, and sustainability: The cross-sector governance of smart cities. *Public Administration Quarterly, 48*(4), 239–262.

Abutabenjeh, S., Nukpezah, J. A., & Azhar, A. (2022). Do smart cities technologies contribute to local economic development? *Economic Development Quarterly, 36*(1), 3–16.

Adel, A. (2023). Unlocking the future: fostering human–machine collaboration and driving intelligent automation through industry 5.0 in smart cities. *Smart Cities, 6*(5), 2742–2782.

Agarwal, P. K., Gurjar, J., Agarwal, A. K., & Birla, R. (2015). Application of artificial intelligence for development of intelligent transport system in smart cities. *Journal of Traffic and Transportation Engineering, 1*(1), 20–30.

Ahmad, K., Maabreh, M., Ghaly, M., Khan, K., Qadir, J., & Al-Fuqaha, A. (2022). Developing future human-centered smart cities: Critical analysis of smart city security, data management, and ethical challenges. *Computer Science Review, 43*, Article 100452.

Alam, M., & Khan, I. R. (2022). Application of AI in smart cities. In *Industrial transformation* (pp. 61–86). CRC Press.

Aoki, N. (2020). An experimental study of public trust in AI chatbots in the public sector. *Government Information Quarterly, 37*(4), Article 101490. https://doi.org/10.1016/j.giq.2020.101490

Bagloee, S. A., Sarvi, M., & Patriksson, M. (2017). A hybrid branch-and-bound and benders decomposition algorithm for the network design problem. *Computer-Aided Civil and Infrastructure Engineering, 32*(4), 319–343.

Bagloee, S. A., Tavana, M., Asadi, M., & Oliver, T. (2016). Autonomous vehicles: Challenges, opportunities, and future implications for transportation policies. *Journal of Modern Transportation, 24*, 284–303.

Barabino, B., Di Francesco, M., & Mozzoni, S. (2015). Rethinking bus punctuality by integrating automatic vehicle location data and passenger patterns. *Transportation Research Part a: Policy and Practice, 75*, 84–95.

Batty, M. (2018). Digital twins. *Environment and Planning b: Urban Analytics and City Science, 45*(5), 817–820.

BBC. Durham police AI to help with custody decisions. http://www.bbc.com/news/technology-39857645. Accessed on January 31, 2020.

Bibri, S. E., Alexandre, A., Sharifi, A., & Krogstie, J. (2023). Environmentally sustainable smart cities and their converging AI, IoT, and big data technologies and solutions: An integrated approach to an extensive literature review. *Energy Informatics, 6*(1), 9.

Birhane, A. (2021). Algorithmic injustice: a relational ethics approach. *Patterns, 2*(2).

Blanco, H., Alberti, M., Olshansky, R., Chang, S., Wheeler, S. M., Randolph, J., London, J. B., Hollander, J. B., Pallagst, K. M., Schwarz, T., Popper, F. J., Parnell, S., Pieterse, E., & Watson, V. (2009). Shaken, shrinking, hot, impoverished and informal: Emerging research agendas in planning. *Progress in Planning, 72*(4), 195–250.

Bongo-Awah, E. (2024, December 30). A journey of GenAI with AWS Bedrock based sample Images. *DEV Community*. https://dev.to/bongoe/a-journey-of-genai-with-aws-bedrock-based-sample-images-24i5

Booth, H., & Pillay, T. (November 4, 2024). How AI is being used to respond to natural disasters in cities. https://time.com/7171445/ai-natural-disaster-cities/

Braun, T., Fung, B. C., Iqbal, F., & Shah, B. (2018). Security and privacy challenges in smart cities. *Sustainable Cities and Society, 39*, 499–507.

Brauneis, R., & Goodman, E. P. (2018). Algorithmic transparency for the smart city. *Yale Journal of Law & Technology, 20*, 103.

Caprotti, F., & Liu, D. (2022). Platform urbanism and the Chinese smart city: The co-production and territorialisation of Hangzhou City Brain. *GeoJournal, 87*(3), 1559–1573.

Chang, V. (2021). An ethical framework for big data and smart cities. *Technological Forecasting and Social Change, 165*, Article 120559.

Cortès, U., Sànchez-Marrè, M., Ceccaroni, L., R-Roda, I., & Poch, M. (2000). Artificial intelligence and environmental decision support systems. *Applied Intelligence, 13*, 77–91.

Cowls, J., Tsamados, A., Taddeo, M., & Floridi, L. (2023). The AI gambit: Leveraging artificial intelligence to combat climate change—Opportunities, challenges, and recommendations. *AI & Society*, 1–25.

Criado, J. I., & Gil-Garcia, J. R. (2019). Creating public value through smart technologies and strategies: From digital services to artificial intelligence and beyond. *International Journal of Public Sector Management, 32*(5), 438–450.

Das, D. K. (2025). Digital technology and AI for smart sustainable cities in the global south: A critical review of literature and case studies. *Urban Science, 9*(3), 72.

De Almeida, P. G. R., dos Santos, C. D., & Farias, J. S. (2021). Artificial intelligence regulation: A framework for governance. *Ethics and Information Technology, 23*(3), 505–525.

De Hert, P., & Gutwirth, S. (2006). Privacy, data protection and law enforcement. Opacity of the individual and transparency of power. *Privacy and the criminal law*, 61–104.

Dennedy, M. F., Fox, J., & Finneran, T. R. (2014). *The privacy engineer's manifesto: Getting from policy to code to QA to value* (p. 400). Springer Nature.

Desouza, K. C., & Bhagwatwar, A. (2012). Citizen apps to solve complex urban problems. *Journal of Urban Technology, 19*(3), 107–136.

Díaz-Rodríguez, N., Del Ser, J., Coeckelbergh, M., de Prado, M. L., Herrera-Viedma, E., & Herrera, F. (2023). Connecting the dots in trustworthy Artificial Intelligence: From AI principles, ethics, and key requirements to responsible AI systems and regulation. *Information Fusion, 99*, Article 101896.

Dibaei, M., Zheng, X., Xia, Y., Xu, X., Jolfaei, A., Bashir, A. K., Tariq, U., Yu, D., & Vasilakos, A. V. (2021). Investigating the prospect of leveraging blockchain and machine learning to secure vehicular networks: A survey. *IEEE Transactions on Intelligent Transportation Systems, 23*(2), 683–700.

Doğan, E., & Akgüngör, A. P. (2013). Forecasting highway casualties under the effect of railway development policy in Turkey using artificial neural networks. *Neural Computing and Applications, 22*, 869–877.

Dos Santos, S. C., Vilela, J. F., Carvalho, T. H., Rocha, T. C., Candido, T. B., Bezerra, V. S., & Silva, D. J. (2024). Artificial Intelligence in sustainable smart cities: A systematic study on applications, benefits, challenges, and solutions.

Eckhoff, D., & Wagner, I. (2017). Privacy in the smart city—Applications, technologies, challenges, and solutions. *IEEE Communications Surveys & Tutorials, 20*(1), 489–516.

Elmaghraby, A. S., & Losavio, M. M. (2014). Cyber security challenges in Smart Cities: Safety, security and privacy. *Journal of Advanced Research, 5*(4), 491–497.

Engin, Z., & Treleaven, P. (2019). Algorithmic government: Automating public services and supporting civil servants in using data science technologies. *The Computer Journal, 62*(3), 448–460.

Ergasheva, S. T., Kulueva, C. R., Maksytova, B. T., & Abdyrov, T. S. (2025). Creating green jobs and making environmental decisions using Big Data and AI. In *Big Data and Artificial Intelligence for decision-making in the smart economy* (pp. 305–313). Springer Nature Switzerland.

e-estonia. (2018, April 9) We have built a digital society and so can you. Retrieved April 2018, from e-estonia: https://e-estonia.com

Falco, G. (2019). Participatory AI: Reducing AI bias and developing socially responsible AI in smart cities. In *2019 IEEE international conference on computational science and engineering (CSE) and IEEE international conference on embedded and ubiquitous computing (EUC)* (pp. 154–158). IEEE.

Flynn, M. (March 12, 2025). Be prepared: How cities are using AI to tackle urban challenges. *Forbes*. https://www.forbes.com/sites/deloitte/2025/03/12/be-prepared-how-cities-are-helping-ai-tackle-urban-challenges/

Gadwal, V. (September 23, 2024). AI-enabled cities are the key to sustainability. *Forbes*. https://www.forbes.com/sites/delltechnologies/2024/09/23/ai-enabled-cities-are-the-key-to-sustainability/

Gharaibeh, A., Salahuddin, M. A., Hussini, S. J., Khreishah, A., Khalil, I., Guizani, M., & Al-Fuqaha, A. (2017). Smart cities: A survey on data management, security, and enabling technologies. *IEEE Communications Surveys & Tutorials, 19*(4), 2456–2501.

Gracias, J. S., Parnell, G. S., Specking, E., Pohl, E. A., & Buchanan, R. (2023). Smart cities—A structured literature review. *Smart Cities, 6*(4), 1719–1743.

Green, B. (2019). The smart enough city: Putting technology in its place to reclaim our urban future. MIT Press.

Gupta, M., Parra, C. M., & Dennehy, D. (2022). Questioning racial and gender bias in AI-based recommendations: Do espoused national cultural values matter? *Information Systems Frontiers, 24*(5), 1465–1481.

Halegoua, G. (2020). *Smart cities*. MIT Press.

Ham, Y. G., Kim, J. H., & Luo, J. J. (2019). Deep learning for multi-year ENSO forecasts. *Nature, 573*, 568–572. https://doi.org/10.1038/s41586-019-1559-7

He, W., & Chen, M. (2024). Advancing urban life: A systematic review of emerging technologies and artificial intelligence in urban design and planning. *Buildings, 14*(3), 835.

Herath, H. M. K. K. M. B., & Mittal, M. (2022). Adoption of artificial intelligence in smart cities: A comprehensive review. *International Journal of Information Management Data Insights, 2*(1), Article 100076.

Hjaltalin, I. T., & Sigurdarson, H. T. (2024). The strategic use of AI in the public sector: A public values analysis of national AI strategies. *Government Information Quarterly, 41*(1), Article 101914. https://doi.org/10.1016/j.giq.2024.101914

IBM. (2023, March 29). What is Explainable AI (XAI)? | *IBM* [Corporate]. https://www.ibm.com/think/topics/explainable-ai

Iqbal, R., Maniak, T., & Karyotis, C. (2019). Intelligent remote monitoring of parking spaces using licensed and unlicensed wireless technologies. *IEEE Network, 33*(4), 23–29.

Jagatheesaperumal, S. K., Bibri, S. E., Huang, J., Rajapandian, J., & Parthiban, B. (2024). Artificial intelligence of things for smart cities: Advanced solutions for enhancing transportation safety. *Computational Urban Science, 4*(1), 10.

Javed, A. R., Shahzad, F., ur Rehman, S., Zikria, Y. B., Razzak, I., Jalil, Z., & Xu, G. (2022). Future smart cities: Requirements, emerging technologies, applications, challenges, and future aspects. *Cities, 129*, 103794.

Jedličková, A. (2024). Ethical considerations in risk management of autonomous and intelligent systems. *Ethics & Bioethics, 14*(1–2), 80–95.

Kamrowska-Załuska, D. (2021). Impact of AI-based tools and urban Big Data analytics on the design and planning of cities. *Land, 10*(11), 1209. https://doi.org/10.3390/land10111209

Kang, S., Mulaphong, D., Hwang, E., & Chang, C. K. (2019). Public-private partnerships in developing countries: Factors for successful adoption and implementation. *International Journal of Public Sector Management, 32*(4), 334–351.

Kankanhalli, A., Charalabidis, Y., & Mellouli, S. (2019). IoT and AI for smart government: A research agenda. *Government Information Quarterly, 36*(2), 304–309. https://doi.org/10.1016/j.giq.2019.02.003

Kibriya, H., Khan, W. Z., Siddiqa, A., & Khan, M. K. (2024). Privacy issues in large language models: A survey. *Computers and Electrical Engineering, 120*, Article 109698.

Kitchin, R., & Dodge, M. (2020). The (in) security of smart cities: Vulnerabilities, risks, mitigation, and prevention. In *Smart cities and innovative urban technologies* (pp. 47–65). Routledge.

Kontokosta, C. E., & Hong, B. (2021). Bias in smart city governance: How socio-spatial disparities in 311 complaint behavior impact the fairness of data-driven decisions. *Sustainable Cities and Society, 64*, Article 102503.

Kshetri, N. (2014). Big data's impact on privacy, security and consumer welfare. *Telecommunications Policy, 38*(11), 1134–1145.

Lakhouit, A. (2025). Revolutionizing Urban Solid Waste Management with AI and IoT: A review of smart solutions for waste collection, sorting, and recycling. *Results in Engineering*, 104018.

Lazarus, J., Pourquier, J. C., Feng, F., Hammel, H., & Shaheen, S. (2020). Micromobility evolution and expansion: Understanding how docked and dockless bikesharing models complement and compete–A case study of San Francisco. *Journal of Transport Geography, 84*, Article 102620.

LeCun, Y., & Bengio, Y. (1995). Convolutional networks for images, speech, and time series. *The Handbook of Brain Theory and Neural Networks, 3361*(10), 1995.

LeCun, Y., Boser, B., Denker, J. S., Henderson, D., Howard, R. E., Hubbard, W., & Jackel, L. D. (1989). Backpropagation applied to handwritten zip code recognition. *Neural Computation, 1*(4), 541–551.

Lim, H. S. M., & Taeihagh, A. (2019). Algorithmic decision-making in AVs: Understanding ethical and technical concerns for smart cities. *Sustainability, 11*(20), 5791.

Lufkin, B. (2017, October 19) Could Estonia be the First 'Digital' Country? *BBC Future*. http://www.bbc.com/future/story/20171019-could-estonia-be-the-first-digitalcountry

Luusua, A., Ylipulli, J., Foth, M., & Aurigi, A. (2023). Urban AI: Understanding the emerging role of artificial intelligence in smart cities. *AI & Society, 38*(3), 1039–1044.

Mahamuni, A. (2018). Internet of Things, machine learning, and artificial intelligence in the modern supply chain and transportation. *Defense Transportation Journal*.

Maraveas, C., Loukatos, D., Bartzanas, T., & Arvanitis, K. G. (2021). Applications of artificial intelligence in fire safety of agricultural structures. *Applied Sciences, 11*(16), 7716.

Mashhadi, N., Shahrour, I., Attoue, N., El Khattabi, J., & Aljer, A. (2021). Use of machine learning for leak detection and localization in water distribution systems. *Smart Cities, 4*(4), 1293–1315.

McCray, T. (2024, April 1). Even Artificial Intelligence thinks public safety in San Francisco needs Artificial Intelligence | San Francisco Police Officers Association. San Francisco Police Association. https://sfpoa.org/node/1638

Mikhaylov, S. J., Esteve, M., & Campion, A. (2018). Artificial intelligence for the public sector: Opportunities and challenges of cross-sector collaboration. *Philosophical Transactions of the Royal Society a: Mathematical, Physical and Engineering Sciences, 376*(2128), 20170357.

Minoli, D., & Occhiogrosso, B. (2018). Internet of things applications for smart cities. In *Internet of Things A to Z: Technologies and applications* (pp. 319–358).

Minsky, M., & Papert, S. (1969). An introduction to computational geometry. *Cambridge Tiass., HIT, 479*(480), 104.

Mitchell, M. (2019). *Artificial Intelligence: A guide for thinking humans*. Farrar, Straus and Giroux.

Morrow, B. (2012). BYOD security challenges: Control and protect your most sensitive data. *Network Security, 2012*(12), 5–8.

Mycielski, J. (1972). Marvin minsky and seymour papert, perceptrons, an introduction to computational geometry.

Negi, S. (January 16, 2025). Top 10 smart cities leading the way in 2025. https://www.citiesabc.com/resources/top-10-smart-cities-leading-the-way-in-2025/

Nilsson, N. J. (1998). Artificial intelligence: A new synthesis. Elsevier.

Nissenbaum, H. (2020). Protecting privacy in an information age: The problem of privacy in public. In *The ethics of information technologies* (pp. 141–178). Routledge.

Nobel Prize Outreach. (2025, May 16). Geoffrey Hinton—Facts—2024. *NobelPrize.Org*. https://www.nobelprize.org/prizes/physics/2024/hinton/facts/

North, M. (July 24, 2024). These 5 cities are making innovative use of generative AI. Urban Transformation.

Ntoutsi, E., Fafalios, P., Gadiraju, U., Iosifidis, V., Nejdl, W., Vidal, M. E., Ruggieri, S., Turini, F., Papadopoulos, S., Krasanakis, E., Kompatsiaris, I., Kinder-Kurlanda, K., Wagner, C., Karimi, F., Fernandez, M., Alani, H., Berendt, B., Kruegel, T., Heinze, C., Broelemann, K., …, Staab, S. (2020). Bias in data-driven artificial intelligence systems—An introductory survey. *Wiley Interdisciplinary Reviews: Data Mining and Knowledge Discovery, 10*(3), e1356.

Nukpezah, J. A., Apalowo, J. T., & Abutabenjeh, S. (2025). Why do cities go smart? Investigating the determinants of local engagement with smart cities technologies. *Cities, 163*, Article 106036. https://doi.org/10.1016/j.cities.2025.106036

Nukpezah, J., Abutabenjeh, S., & Azhar, A. (2022). Do smart cities technologies contribute to revenue performance? Evidence from US local governments. *Public Performance & Management Review, 45*(5), 1155–1180.

OECD. (n.d.). Boti, the City's WhatsApp! Observatory of public sector innovation. Retrieved May 22, 2025, from https://oecd-opsi.org/innovations/boti-the-citys-whatsapp/

Ojha, S. (2023). Unified payments interface: Why made-in-India UPI is becoming a global favourite? https://www.livemint.com/money/personal-finance/unified-payments-interface-why-made-in-india-upi-is-becoming-a-global-favourite-11698047714911.html. Accessed on September 20, 2024.

Overstreet, K. (2021, June 11). Building a city from scratch: The story of Songdo, Korea | *ArchDaily*. https://www.archdaily.com/962924/building-a-city-from-scratch-the-story-of-songdo-korea

Pandey, A., & Caliskan, A. (2021, July). Disparate impact of artificial intelligence bias in ride-hailing economy's price discrimination algorithms. In *Proceedings of the 2021 AAAI/ACM conference on AI, ethics, and society* (pp. 822–833).

Petrov, V., Lema, M. A., Gapeyenko, M., Antonakoglou, K., Moltchanov, D., Sardis, F., Samuylov, A., Andreev, S., Koucheryavy, Y., & Dohler, M. (2018). Achieving end-to-end reliability of mission-critical traffic in softwarized 5G networks. *IEEE Journal on Selected Areas in Communications, 36*(3), 485–501.

Pramanik, M. I., Lau, R. Y., Demirkan, H., & Azad, M. A. K. (2017). Smart health: Big data enabled health paradigm within smart cities. *Expert Systems with Applications, 87*, 370–383.

Prem, E. (2023). From ethical AI frameworks to tools: A review of approaches. *AI and Ethics, 3*(3), 699–716.

Radu, R. (2021). Steering the governance of artificial intelligence: National strategies in perspective. *Policy and Society, 40*(2), 178–193.

Rjab, A. B., Mellouli, S., & Corbett, J. (2023). Barriers to artificial intelligence adoption in smart cities: A systematic literature review and research agenda. *Government Information Quarterly, 40*(3), Article 101814. https://doi.org/10.1016/j.giq.2023.101814

Rolnick, D., Donti, P. L., Kaack, L. H., Kochanski, K., Lacoste, A., Sankaran, K., et al. (2022). Tackling climate change with machine learning. *ACM Computing Surveys (CSUR), 55*(2), 1–96.

Rumelhart, D. E., Hinton, G. E., & Williams, R. J. (1985). Learning internal representations by error propagation.

Ruschemeier, H., & Hondrich, L. J. (2024). Automation bias in public administration—An interdisciplinary perspective from law and psychology. *Government Information Quarterly, 41*(3), Article 101953. https://doi.org/10.1016/j.giq.2024.101953

Salierno, G., Leonardi, L., & Cabri, G. (2025). Generative AI and large language models in Industry 5.0: Shaping smarter sustainable cities. *Encyclopedia, 5*(1), 30. https://doi.org/10.3390/encyclopedia5010030

Samala, A. D., Rawas, S., Wang, T., Reed, J. M., Kim, J., Howard, N. J., & Ertz, M. (2025). Unveiling the landscape of generative artificial intelligence in education: A comprehensive taxonomy of applications, challenges, and future prospects. *Education and Information Technologies, 30*(3), 3239–3278.

Sarma, S., & Sunny, S. A. (2017). Civic entrepreneurial ecosystems: Smart city emergence in Kansas City. *Business Horizons, 60*(6), 843–853.

Schwartz, R., Schwartz, R., Vassilev, A., Greene, K., Perine, L., Burt, A., & Hall, P. (2022). *Towards a standard for identifying and managing bias in artificial intelligence* (Vol. 3, p. 00). US Department of Commerce, National Institute of Standards and Technology.

Sharma, N., & Safa, M. (2022). Legal and ethical concerns of adopting digital solution for smart metropolises. *Journal of Legal Affairs and Dispute Resolution in Engineering and Construction, 14*(4), 04522020.

Silva, B. N., Khan, M., & Han, K. (2018). Towards sustainable smart cities: A review of trends, architectures, components, and open challenges in smart cities. *Sustainable Cities and Society, 38*, 697–713.

Singh, R., & Manoharan, G. (2025). AI integration to strengthen disaster resilience in smart cities. In *AI and emerging technologies for emergency response and smart cities* (pp. 1–30). IGI Global Scientific Publishing.

Smith, S. S. (2010). Race and trust. *Annual Review of Sociology, 36*(1), 453–475.

Snow, J. (2017, July 20). This AI traffic system in Pittsburgh has reduced travel time by 25% | Smart Cities Dive. *Smartcitiesdive.* https://www.smartcitiesdive.com/news/this-ai-traffic-system-in-pittsburgh-has-reduced-travel-time-by-25/447494/

Su, L. C., Wu, X., Zhang, X., & Huang, X. (2021). Smart performance-based design for building fire safety: Prediction of smoke motion via AI. *Journal of Building Engineering, 43*, Article 102529.

Szpilko, D., Naharro, F. J., Lăzăroiu, G., Nica, E., & de la Torre Gallegos, A. (2023). Artificial intelligence in the smart city—A literature review.

Talari, S., Shafie-Khah, M., Siano, P., Loia, V., Tommasetti, A., & Catalão, J. P. (2017). A review of smart cities based on the internet of concepts of things. *Energies, 10*(4), 421.

The Financial. (2025, May 16). The world's first operating system for smart cities. *FINCHANNEL.* https://finchannel.com/the-worlds-first-operating-system-for-smart-cities/125793/tech-2/2025/05/

Tilocca, P., Farris, S., Angius, S., Argiolas, R., Obino, A., Secchi, S., Mozzoni, S., & Barabino, B. (2017). Managing data and rethinking applications in an innovative managing data and rethinking applications in an innovative mid-sized bus fleet bus fleet. *Transportation Research Procedia, 25*, 1899–1919.

Townsend, A. M. (2013). *Smart cities: Big data, civic hackers, and the quest for a new Utopia.* WW Norton & Company.

Turing, A. M. (2009). *Computing machinery and intelligence.* Springer.

Turner Lee, N. (2018). Detecting racial bias in algorithms and machine learning. *Journal of Information, Communication and Ethics in Society, 16*(3), 252–260.

Valle-Cruz, D., Fernandez-Cortez, V., & Gil-Garcia, J. R. (2022). From E-budgeting to smart budgeting: Exploring the potential of artificial intelligence in government decision-making for resource allocation. *Government Information Quarterly, 39*(2), Article 101644. https://doi.org/10.1016/j.giq.2021.101644

Van Den Hurk, M., & Verhoest, K. (2016). The challenge of using standard contracts in public–private partnerships. *Public Management Review, 18*(2), 278–299.

Von Neumann, J. (1956). Probabilistic logics and the synthesis of reliable organisms from unreliable components. *Automata Studies, 34*(34), 43–98.

Wang, K., Zhao, Y., Gangadhari, R. K., & Li, Z. (2021). Analyzing the adoption challenges of the Internet of things (IoT) and artificial intelligence (AI) for smart cities in china. *Sustainability, 13*(19), 10983.

Williamson, S. M., & Prybutok, V. (2024). Balancing privacy and progress: A review of privacy challenges, systemic oversight, and patient perceptions in AI-driven healthcare. *Applied Sciences, 14*(2), 675.

Wirtz, B. W., Müller, W. M., & Schmidt, F. (2020). Public smart service provision in smart cities: A case-study-based approach. *International Journal of Public Administration, 43*(6), 499–516.

Wolniak, R., & Stecuła, K. (2024). Artificial Intelligence in smart cities—Applications, barriers, and future directions: A review. *Smart Cities, 7*(3), 1346–1389. https://doi.org/10.3390/smartcities7030057

Yigitcanlar, T., & Cugurullo, F. (2020). The sustainability of artificial intelligence: An urbanistic viewpoint from the lens of smart and sustainable cities. *Sustainability, 12*(20), 8548.

Yigitcanlar, T., Desouza, K. C., Butler, L., & Roozkhosh, F. (2020). Contributions and risks of artificial intelligence (AI) in building smarter cities: Insights from a systematic review of the literature. *Energies, 13*(6), 1473.

Zhang, K., Ni, J., Yang, K., Liang, X., Ren, J., & Shen, X. S. (2017). Security and privacy in smart city applications: Challenges and solutions. *IEEE Communications Magazine, 55*(1), 122–129.

Zhou, T. (2011). The impact of privacy concern on user adoption of location-based services. *Industrial Management & Data Systems, 111*(2), 212–226.

Zhou, Y., & Kankanhalli, A. (2021). AI regulation for smart cities: Challenges and principles. *Smart cities and smart governance: Towards the 22nd century sustainable city* (pp. 101–118). Springer International Publishing.

Part III

Challenges, Considerations, and Future Trends

How Government and AI Cannot Be Allied: The Contradiction Between Bureaucracy and Technology

13

Ringo Ossewaarde

1 Introduction

In this chapter it is argued that the discourse that public bureaucracies ought to digitally transform their operations (in decision-making, public service delivery, administrative processes, etc.) rests on a misconception of the nature of the administrative bureaucracy. The expectation that government operations will be automatically enhanced through their incorporation of artificial intelligence technologies is based on the flawed assumption that public bureaucracies are procedure-governed machines, in which democratic values, human decisions, quality of the mind, and power constellations do not matter. It is noteworthy that, in contemporary discourses on bureaucracy and AI, bureaucracies are typically considered as so-called "Weberian bureaucracies" (Cetina Presuel & Martinez Sierra, 2024; Newman et al., 2022; Suzuki & Hur, 2020). Bureaucracies are typically understood through the lens of Max Weber's highly popular and much-taught ideal type of bureaucracy. Also, Weber's famous machine metaphors (like the "bureaucratic machine" or bureaucracy as a "factory") are widely used. Thanks to this Weberian imagination and well-established vocabulary, bureaucracies are widely conceived to operate in a similar mechanical, rule-governed fashion as AI-technologies. From this perspective, the implementation of AI tools in the public sector—such as Open AI's ChatGPT, Microsoft Copilot or Google's Gemini, automated decision-making, metaverse tools, conversational chatbots, transcript tools, data analytics tools, automated monitoring tools, cybersecurity tools, or facial recognition tools—to enhance bureaucratic performance only seems a logical step (Giest & Klievink, 2022; Newman et al., 2022; Roehl & Crompvoets, 2023).

R. Ossewaarde (✉)
Department of Public Administration, University of Twente, Enschede, The Netherlands
e-mail: m.r.r.ossewaarde@utwente.nl

S. K. Aikins and T. Dimitrijevska-Markoski (eds.), *Artificial Intelligence and Government*, https://doi.org/10.1007/978-3-032-12344-2_13

In this chapter, the notion of "Weberian bureaucracy" is contested. Weber, the argument goes, studied corrupted forms of bureaucracy in which bureaucracy is out of touch with civilizational, cultural or democratic aspirations. As Waldo (1952, p. 100) puts it, "it can be plausibly argued that, for all his erudition, Weber was a child of his time in spite of himself and that he accepted without criticism some of the values of his undemocratic environment. Is bureaucracy technically "superior" sub specie aeternitatis or simply from the viewpoint of Max Weber writing in Imperial Germany?" In Weber's time and context of imperial Germany, German bureaucracies reflected a politics informed by the instrumental rationality geared to totalitarian domination, resulting in a Kafkaesque nightmare of oppression, absurdity and irresponsibility (Clegg et al., 2016; Ossewaarde, 2019a, 2019b). In a strong sense, this tendency has continued today in the contemporary context of de-democratization and the rise of the Big Tech oligarchs of Silicon Valley that sell the AI tools. In such circumstances of political and cultural decline, AI becomes further enmeshed in, irrationalities, lusts, ideologies, misunderstandings, self-interests, oligarchical power concentrations, and abuses of such concentrated power (Crawford, 2021).

That said, there is room for AI-technology within public bureaucracies as long as both bureaucracies and AI are rightly understood. This is one of the ideas that will be further developed in the rest of this chapter. This chapter does not deny that prudent use of certain AI tools in public bureaucracies may have potential benefits for certain designated administrative tasks. If used prudently by administrators, AI applications may well serve administrators, for instance, in infrastructure monitoring, traffic flow analysis, cyberattack prevention, or flood control. Yet, this chapter develops a cautionary message. It argues that the idea that AI technologies will solve the challenges inherent to bureaucracies misconceives the nature of these challenges. Such misconception is informed by the mechanistic worldview characterized by behaviorist assumptions, technocratic aspirations, fraudulent techno-utopian myths, misplaced machine metaphors, and oligarchical power relations that tend to distort and degenerate bureaucracy. In this chapter it is argued that to ensure that AI genuinely supports a prudent exercise of executive power, we need to overcome both "Weberian bureaucracy" and the corresponding flawed vision that AI-technology can be simply plugged in a bureaucracy. It means resisting the flawed idea that AI technology—and even worse, "AI" as such—will magically unburden civil servants from complex decision-making processes and dilemmas.

This chapter first discusses Weberian bureaucracy and AI. Secondly, it proceeds with an examination of bureaucracy as a cultural and political phenomenon that is manifested in the quality of mind and cultural and democratic vitality of the administrator who is charged with the task of exercising executive power responsibly, in the service of higher political ideals (like democracy, rule of law, justice, or common good). A political and cultural understanding of bureaucracy, as contrasted with a mechanistic understanding of bureaucracy, has implications for the bureaucratic possibilities of embedding AI tools in public administrations. The administrator carries ultimate (moral) responsibility for any decision made. This means that administration can be *supported* by AI tools but never equated with the working of these AI tools. In other words, any automatization of bureaucratic processes cannot be deemed to replace complex decision-making processes, which necessitate particular habits of the heart and mind. And thirdly, the case of the Dutch childcare benefits scandal (2013–2019) and its aftermath (2019–2025) is presented, as a cautionary example of how a Kafkaesque bureaucratic nightmare is created when an AI tool is mindlessly integrated in an already corrupted bureaucracy (the Dutch Tax Office) in a context of a process of democratic backsliding (Arts & Van den Berg, 2025; Hummel et al., 2023; Ossewaarde, 2023; Van den Berge & Gaakeer, 2025). A mindful integration of AI-systems in bureaucracies, it is concluded, will therefore involve a critical analysis of the rampant corruptions of particular bureaucracies as well as AI infrastructure that integrates the accountability of administrators. Cultural corruptions such as tyranny and bullying will obviously not be solved by the integration of AI-tools. Regulations to prevent AI-overreliance and complacency could possibly revive a democratic administrative culture by compelling regular collegial consultations and deliberations during which administrators are forced to explain their decisions informed by AI-tools.

2 "Weberian Bureaucracy" and AI: A Portrait of a Flawed View

Every historical era can be characterized by a particular "worldview" that informs both our interpretation of realities and our creative activities. It is not surprising that many leading scholars have conceived modern, industrial existence to be supported by a "mechanistic worldview". In this particular worldview, every aspect of human existence (natural, political, administrative, economic, etc.) is conceptualized or imagined as a kind of machine that operates according to mechanical rules, mechanisms or machine-like operations. Every aspect of human existence is, accordingly, computable, calculable and formalizable (Capra & Luisi, 2014; Pörksen, 2023). Mumford (1963) discovers the origin of the mechanistic worldview in the moment the mechanical clock was invented in around 996 CE. He attributes this technological innovation to Gerbert of Aurillac (Pope Sylvester II), one of the greatest mathematicians of his time, who had learned his trade from the mathematicians of Al-Andalus. The mechanistic worldview, Mumford explains, rose to predominance when the Church authorities decided to install the mechanical clock in the towers of churches, in the thirteenth century. From that time onwards, the mechanistic worldview became enforced in society. Human existence became increasingly mechanized, made calculable and formalizable, organized around the mechanical logic of the clockwork. Orderly routine, discipline and control, monastic regularity, the habit of abstraction, calculus, technique, mathematical precision, clarity, time consciousness (and concern with tempo and speed), and regulation of time-sequences thereby became normalized. "The clock, not the steam-engine, is the key-machine of the modern industrial age," Mumford (1963: 14) explains. It is the key-machine by which the mechanistic worldview became institutionalized in the regulation of everyday life.

Artificial intelligence—originally called "machine intelligence"— can be considered as an embodiment of this mechanistic worldview. Artificial intelligence was invented when the industrial mathematicians of the British Empire tried to make mathematics economically useful. In the late nineteenth century, Charles Babbage invented the first automated, programmable calculation machine to make the British factories operate more efficiently. The so-called "Babbage machine" is widely recognized as the precursor to the computer that would eventually be invented in 1948 (the 'Manchester Baby'). In the 1930s, the "dream of mechanizing people by way of anthropizing machines" (Midgley, 2018, 119) captured the imagination of Alan Turing who believed that he had created a machine with superhuman thinking powers. Turing stood in the strong scientistic tradition of behaviorism according to which behavior, including choices and decisions, is caused by physical causes. As Mary Midgley (2018, 172, 202) explains, according to behaviorist theory, which became an official creed in the social sciences in the 1950s, "only actions were real, which meant that psychologists were forbidden ever to mention motives, ideals or other background features of the inner life because these were unscientific." Turing presumed a mechanical brain marked by "mindless intelligence" (Proudfoot, 2011, p. 963), which could be surpassed by a machine. But such "intelligence" has never been human since it is devoid of the intellectual culture, sense of wonder or awe, worry and commitment that characterizes the intelligence of humans embedded in real worlds. But since Turing necessarily abstracted from such complex inner life and focused on the simple administrate tasks performed by lower ranking clerks, he concluded that these could be performed much more efficiently by a machine (Proudfoot, 2011; Sprevak, 2017; Watson, 2019).

Herbert Simon, one of the leading founders of artificial intelligence as a scientific discipline in 1956, has established the behaviorist commitments of Public Administration in his much-cited *Administrative Behavior* (1947). Simon's aim is ultimately to make the US government more efficient in its public expenditures (which had increased dramatically with the implementation of Roosevelt's New Deal policies). Like Turing, Simon recognizes no contradiction between bureaucracy and machine intelligence. In fact, Simon, like Turing, endorses the mechanistic worldview and presents bureaucracy as a machine or "a computerized organization" (Baber, 1988, p. 336). As Heyck (2008, p. 59) emphasizes, "as Simon saw it, the computer was the perfect bureaucracy." For Simon, bureaucracy is a "decision making machine" (Heyck, 2008, p. 47), which can be designed like a computer. For Simon, every aspect of bureaucracy or decision-making is, in principle, computable, calculable and formalizable. Defined as a decision-making machine, administration—which Simon conceives of as rule-following behavior—can be automated. Administrators, being office holders, Simon's argument goes, employ their bureaucratic minds as decision-making tools; hence AI can replace bureaucrats and improve administrative behavior (decision-making) (Baber, 1988; Schwarz et al., 2022). Like Turing, Simon identified administration as a machine.

He did not have a high opinion of administrators and their human intelligence: they were slow and/or had too little time to process large amounts of information in an efficient way (Heyck, 2008). Machine intelligence or what Simon calls "artificial intelligence" was the evident solution to this efficiency problem of administration.

The alliance of bureaucracy and technology that Simon envisions has become the near-unquestioned premise of Public Administration. This close alliance is based on the premise that bureaucracy is a machine—a vision of bureaucracy that has been largely popularized via the works of Max Weber. A bureaucracy, for Weber, is characterized by clear rules, unambiguous procedures, hierarchy of authority, managerial control, impersonality, and the slavish conformism of administrators (Cetina Presuel & Martinez Sierra, 2024). In such "Weberian bureaucracy"—implicitly or explicitly taken for granted by many Public Administration scholars (Cetina Presuel & Martinez Sierra, 2024; Newman et al., 2022; Suzuki & Hur, 2020)—AI technologies are deemed to reinforce rather than alter bureaucratic patterns. Weber himself seems to have had ambivalent evaluations of bureaucracies. On the one hand, he tends to applaud the efficiency of bureaucratically organized operations. On the other hand, he, like Rathenau, he criticizes the mechanization of everyday life. Weber sees the mechanization of administration as fostering bureaucratic mindlessness and hence cultural decline that was the breeding ground for the rise of totalitarianism. The apparent contradiction in Weber's thinking on bureaucracy stems from his generalization of historical forms of German bureaucracy and hence from the lack of differentiation between an "ideal" bureaucracy (as manifested in administrative history) and its corrupted or situated forms. For Weber, the bureaucratic ethos is an authoritarian ethos of conformism, command and obedience that the German *Reich* demanded: administrators are drilled to suspend personal convictions to obey imperial orders. For Hannah Arendt, Adolf Eichmann is the personification of such a machine-like, conformist, obedient, mindless bureaucrat. Bureaucrats like Eichmann can send millions to their death without a bad conscience not because they are exceptionally evil but rather because of their "thoughtlessness" (Arendt, 2006, 288).

In sum, the vision of bureaucracy as a rule-governed machinery of clerks, cogs, mindless and impersonal bureaucrats—a manifestation of the mechanistic worldview—is highly influential. In this vision, government and AI technologies can be married up, precisely because the administrator is portrayed as a machine, an Eichmannian, dehumanized, humorless, slavish, faceless figure, without mind, without creativity, and without will-power, drilled to obey orders in a most disciplined fashion. Government and AI can be married up, because it is supposed that the administrator can be programmed or formalized like a Turing machine or any mindless algorithm. Or, to put it differently, AI technologies can operate like a bureaucrat precisely because both AI and bureaucracy are mindless. Can we imagine and create a bureaucracy that does not become a mindless machine? Contrarily to Public Administration scholars like Simon who assume that the dichotomy between politics and bureaucracy can be maintained without serious effects for democratic culture, the argument here is that such a contradiction between politics and administration cannot be upheld: the exercise of executive power—and, correspondingly, the embedding AI tools in public bureaucracies—is thoroughly political. To exercise executive power in a responsible (for instance, democratic or constitutional) manner requires a very high degree of cultivation of administrators. To exercise executive power responsibly is not merely an issue of AI regulation and AI ethics but requires the construction of the mindful bureaucrat beyond the mechanistic worldview and beyond behaviorism, which is the topic of the next section.

3 The Construction of the Mindful Bureaucrat

The image of bureaucracy as a rule-governed machine can be blamed on the particular contexts of the mechanization of society of the British Empire, the German Reich, Nazi Germany or capitalist America. Even the term "bureaucracy" reflects a particular understanding of society and the particular manner in which executive power is exercised. The word "bureaucracy" was invented in the eighteenth century by Vincent de Gournay. He combined the words "bureau" (desk or office) and "cracy" (rule by), to show how, some decades before the events of the French Revolution, France had become governed irresponsibly from the office, by mindless officials, clerks, functionaries, and inspectors, who failed to serve the French common interest (Mathur, 2017). The exercise of executive power is, of course, much older than Gournay's newly invented word; and what is now understood as "bureaucracy" or "bureaucratic administration" is not merely desk rule, but the government's exercise of executive power to "run the constitution" (for instance, to run the state by administering justice). Bureaucracy *avant la lettre*, originally emerged some 8000 years ago in Mesopotamia, in the context of the so-called Agrarian or Neolithic Revolution (Farazmand, 2010). Bureaucracies were originally developed in the kingly city-states of Mesopotamia and in the Egyptian kingdom, for purposes of administering food storage, the running of irrigation programs, the organizing of postal systems, or the state construction of ziggurats and pyramids.

Farazmand (1998) notes that the Achaemenids were the first rulers who managed to develop highly sophisticated bureaucracies that enabled its administrators to govern a very large empire. The very success of the Achaemenid state, including its cultural flourishing, depended on its administrative capacity to prudently govern vast territories, peoples, diversities of cultures, traditions, religions, languages, states, and races (Farazmand, 1998). Likewise, the Romans could only flourish thanks to its sophisticated administration; and hence, as Cicero amongst other ancient Roman scholars pointed out, states collapse when bureaucracies come to fail in administering the state prudently (Ajdini, 2014). The political and cultural nature of bureaucracies that make states flourish are typically similar: ethos of statecraft, strategic elites and councils, full-time professional staff, paths of promotion, relative security, civility, moral zeal, and highly skillful administrators, who are educated to help, assist, serve, manage, direct, govern, run a constitution, carry out, implement, or execute (Ajdini, 2014; Farazmand, 1998). In Rome, for instance, administrators typically received a humanist education for developing the mind, with a focus on the study of Latin grammar, law, classical authors (including poets), eloquence, rhetoric and mythology (Ajdini, 2014; Veyne, 1987). In ancient China, the Sui dynasty introduced an examination system for administrators—later professionalized by the Song dynasty—to draw cultured men with literary education into the government to counter the dominance of the feudal lords and their military ethos. Exam success and the position of the educated administrator or "scholar-officials" (mandarins) in the Song dynasty carried enormous prestige, given that erudition, learning, scholarship, classical literacy, wisdom and mindful administration was invested with massive cultural, political and administrative importance (Dalby & Werthman, 1971; Elman, 1991).

Also, modern bureaucracies need high degrees of cultivation to exercise executive power responsibly, as Peters (2019) emphasizes. Foreign policy bureaucrats (like ambassadors and diplomats) in particular are often required to express humanist-literary culture, to represent highly developed inter-cultural knowledges and poetic refinement in communicating with other states. Hence, poets and novelists, including Paul Claudel, Pablo Neruda, Ivo Andric, Czeslaw Milosz, George Seferis and Octavio Paz, have often been diplomats and ambassadors. In today's bureaucracies, administrators are typically university graduates, often with a master's degree or doctorate degree in the humanities or social sciences, educated in prudent, empathic, creative, critical, reflexive and analytical thinking. Michael Lipsky points out that when it comes to the delivery of public services, so-called "street-level bureaucrats" —administrators who work on the frontlines of government and interact directly with people (including citizens, denizens, children, etc.)—have substantial bureaucratic discretion. Bureaucratic discretion requires from administrators that they have the reflexive capacity to articulate moral judgement, cope with political-administrative and moral dilemmas, mediate diverse interests, correct policy failures, initiate policy initiatives, settle value conflicts, and so forth (Chang & Brewer, 2023; Kjaerulff, 2020).

Just as the administrators of the great ancient states were often the guardians of a humanist, literary culture, today in the Western world administrators are the guardians of democratic culture (the politico-cultural manifestations of humanism). When democratic culture is at risk, when politics and political language brutalizes, and bureaucracies risk being corrupted so that de-democratized politicians or parties can advance illegitimate political objectives, mindful bureaucrats may well be the only civilized force that could be powerful enough to safeguard democracy (Bauer, 2023; Peters & Pierre, 2019). Yesilkagit et al (2024) make an argument for the so-called "guardian state", which is a bureaucracy in which administrators fortify against democratic backsliding and brutalized politics. In the guardian state, bureaucracy becomes the defender of democratic culture against non-democratic, anti-democratic and anti-constitutional politics. Thus understood, mindful bureaucrats are the representatives of democratic culture. Mindful bureaucrats assume a pro-active and creative role in personifying, cultivating and defending the style of democratic life, marked by empathic understanding of others, respect for minorities, reflective and critical re-examination of opinions, a certain academic skepticism (or absence of dogmatism), practices of compromise, and so forth.

More than any other Public Administration scholar, Waldo makes the argument that bureaucracies, at least in modern or contemporary Western societies, must be understood as a democratic and cultural phenomenon. Waldo (1955, p. 11) emphasizes that "the concept of culture—plus knowledge about the actual culture—enables us to see administration in any particular society in relation to all factors which surround and condition it." In a democratic state, bureaucracy, in his view, means "democratic administration" (Waldo, 1952), which means that bureaucracy is instilled with democratic culture and that that democracy is realized in administration. Administrators, in Waldo's view, practice the art of democratic statecraft. In Waldo's vision, administrative statecraft implies that administrators possess political knowledge, understanding, practical wisdom (phronesis), administrative skill, manner, speech and rhetoric needed to be able to safeguard democracy. In what is perhaps the most famous debate in the scientific field of Public Administration (the Simon/Waldo Debate), Simon famously criticized Waldo for his loose, literary, metaphorical style. Yet, from Waldo's classicist scientific point of view, this is precisely the academic style needed to understand bureaucracy as a democratic-literary-administrative complex. Waldo thereby freed Public Administration from the mechanistic worldview and restraints of behaviorism to which Simon conformed and even contributed.

Waldo asserts that not only bureaucracies, but technologies as well must be understood as political and cultural phenomena. Waldo (1955) points at the political character of technology when he explains that the making of the nuclear bomb is not primarily a technical accomplishment or an achievement of nuclear physics, but the result of skillful administration. The Manhattan Project is in the very first place a political-administrative project, characterized by political decisions, bureaucratic coordination, and the administrative mobilization of resources and administrative capacity. Along this line of reasoning, today's AI-technologies must be understood as deeply political, administrative and cultural phenomena. AI is a politically and administratively steered phenomenon. Almost all governments in the world have developed their own AI strategies. They have bureaucratically coordinated all sorts of AI partnerships (involving all sorts of stakeholder interests (tech firms, consultancy firms, investors, universities, AI regulators, AI supervisory authorities, etc.). And their politics of AI is invested with all sorts of myths, historical trajectories, ideologies, and collective identity constructions (Köstler & Ossewaarde, 2022; Ossewaarde & Gülenç, 2020; Von Essen & Ossewaarde, 2024). Some technologies may be allied with the humanist culture of bureaucracies and facilitate democratic administration. Technologies like the alphabet, script, the pen, book-printing, typewriter, and potentially also the Internet (as a textual phenomenon, including digital libraries, open access to texts and archives, etc.) are examples of artefacts that, if not abused but instead embedded and used prudently, may well be of help in making democracy work (Reinecke & Wrona, 2021). Perhaps AI technologies may also strengthen democratic administration, but this would only be possible on the condition that such tools do not dominate but facilitate administration; in other words, that AI is carefully put in place (like a pen or typewriter), in support of the humanist culture bureaucracy.

In democratic administration, AI tools cannot play a dominant role without corrupting bureaucracy or pushing bureaucracy into a state of machine-like mindlessness. The reason is that AI technologies, as advanced as they may be, are, like all machines, mindless, uncreative, unacademic and illiterate. In contrast with the "intelligence" democratic administration demands from its bureaucrats, AI is thoughtless. The risk of embedding AI tools (and with it, the interests of tech firms, technologists, and other AI-related stakeholders and AI propagandists) in democratic administration is that bureaucracy's cultural nature is denied or crushed. It is the risk that the executive power needed for running the constitution is made dependent on mindless machines. It is the risk that administrators are forced to adapt to the requirements and language of technologies and come to administer in a non-democratic bureaucratic environment of machines. It is the risk that the literary knowledge of administrators, needed to make democracy work as a culture of governing, becomes replaced by the technical knowledge in order to make AI assemblages work. It is the risk that bureaucracies are devalued into machines. Thereby bureaucracies would be destined to degenerate because the particular nature of bureaucracies would thereby be crushed by technical (like algorithmic) requirements, mathematical language, and technocratic aspirations (Ellul, 1990; Ossewaarde, 2019a, 2019b). Ellul (1990, p. 300) calls this false belief that machines can be compared with cultivated minds, so common among AI enthusiasts or techno-optimists, "technical madness". For in truth, AI has no mind and is not intelligent: it has no intellect, no imagination, no reflection, no spontaneity, it has no grasp of a situation, relation, or problem, no moral judgement, no academic culture, it cannot cope with ambiguity, and so forth (Ellul, 1990; Pörksen, 2023; Proudfoot, 2011; Watson, 2019).

To conclude this section, historically speaking, the view of bureaucracy as a political and cultural complex is deeply rooted. It is endorsed by what may be a minority yet highly influential scholars like Waldo, Ellul and Guy Peters. In the idealized view of bureaucracy, the administrator is presented as a political and literary or humanist figure, a highly cultivated and humanized person like the great administrators of antiquity (like Cineas, the prudent administrator of Pyrrhus). Such administrators are marked by a certain quality of mind, creativity, prudence, will-power, cultivated to exercise executive power in a mindful and, in modern contexts, in a democratic manner. In the idealized vision of bureaucracy, government and AI technologies can be married up if AI tools are prudently put in their place by administrators, subjected to the mindful bureaucrat, in the full awareness that bureaucracy and technology radically contradict in terms of premises, assumptions, worldviews, interests, intelligence, and concern. The cultivated administrator, that is, the mindful bureaucrat charged with the responsibility to run the constitution, cannot be legitimately compelled to adjust to technical requirements of Big Tech's products that have zero cultural or democratic significance and typically come with Big Tech perversities that are typical for oligarchical powers (Crawford, 2021).

The question arises whether this idealized view of bureaucracy, and hence the portrait of mindful administrators, is a realistic prospect in our contemporary age. In this chapter, the answer is that AI technologies confront bureaucracies with an existential threat and tend to pervert bureaucracies into Kafkaesque bureaucratic nightmares. In the next section, a Dutch AI scandal is discussed as an illustrative example of how such an AI-induced nightmare is constructed.

4 The AI Enhancement of Administrative Perversity: The Illuminous Case of a Dutch Scandal

In the Netherlands, Boston Consulting Group has, in March 2025, issued a report for the Dutch government in which it claims that the Dutch government may still become twenty percent more efficient (or less wasteful of public resources) via the use of AI tools, particularly via the reduction of paperwork (Boston Consulting Group, 2025). In response to the report, in April 2025, the Dutch cabinet made public statements and new agreements with governmental organizations to expand the use of AI tools in administrative processes. In the Netherlands, there are many AI success stories of AI products that have been prudently integrated into public bureaucracies. For instance, the Dutch Ministry of Infrastructure and Water Management, partnered by major Dutch construction companies like the Royal Bam Group, widely uses drone AI tools to inspect bridges, roads and locks (water navigation) and assess maintenance requirements. Similarly, Dutch regional governments widely collaborate with the Dutch company Spheer.ai in the AI-based monitoring of nature preserves. Dutch hospitals widely use AI tools that appear to provide more precision in the detection of breast cancer than a team of eleven pathologists. In the Netherlands, such AI success stories are manifestations of a successful subjection of technologies and tech firms to administration (rather than the other way around), well-adjusted to the political and cultural requirements of public bureaucracy, strictly limiting the impact of private interests in public organizations, without much dependence on tech firms. Dutch civil servants are not permitted to use ChatGPT, DeepSeek, Gemini and Midjourney products, given the risk of propaganda and data breaches. Dutch ministries, regional governments and local governments, for instance, have typically developed their own, tailor-made Dutch alternatives to ChatGPT that are available only for internal use, by administrators, for specific administrative tasks for which administrators are responsible.

AI technologies do not automatically or by themselves generate such public benefits. AI regulation and AI ethics do not ensure that AI technologies generate such benefits; that requires mindful administrators. Without cultivated, prudent administrators, AI may not strengthen but, on the contrary, weaken democratic administration and generate perversities. In today's despotic regimes, like Iran or Saudi Arabia, this is obvious: AI tools help in automating despotism (Crawford, 2021; Liyanage, 2024). In the current Western context of democratic backsliding, it is a risk that AI tools come to facilitate democratic backsliding.

Particularly when AI tools (or their designers, producers, and sellers, tech firms) come to dominate, serve private or corporate or oligarchical interests, and reduce the exercise of executive power to a technical performance, such technologies may well come to facilitate the degeneration of democratic administration into a Kafkaesque bureaucratic nightmare in which AI disasters are produced. Today there are many examples of how the push for further mechanization of administration generates Kafkaesque nightmares and AI disasters. Many well-known examples of technology-induced bureaucratic degeneration and administrative perversity include chatbots, AI monitoring, and AI detection tools. Such products frequently appear to give false information, advise citizens to break the law, provide false content in provided texts, or appear propagandistic or discriminatory (ageist, racist, classist, male dominant).

One of the most illustrative cases of an AI disaster that was produced in a corrupted bureaucracy in a context of democratic backsliding is the Dutch childcare benefits scandal (2013–2019) that was revealed by the Dutch press in 2017 (Giest & Klievink, 2022). In this cautionary case, the Dutch Tax Office used an automated fraud detection tool (based on machine learning techniques) to detect and punish fraudsters who allegedly had wrongly received allowances from the Tax Office to finance childcare for their children (Fenger & Simonse, 2024). In the Dutch administrative state, parents who reside in the Netherlands are legally entitled to childcare allowances for their childcare so that they themselves can join the Dutch labor force. This welfare system, however, may be abused. In 2007–2013, the Dutch Tax Office had found itself confronted with a large-scale fraud of Bulgarians, who, as Bulgaria had joined the European Union in January 2007, were free to move and settle in other EU member states such as the Netherlands. The case of the Bulgarian fraud scandal (Bulgarians residing in the Netherlands had illegally claimed welfare allowances) was uncovered by the Dutch press in 2013. It appeared that 805 Bulgarians had wrongly received four million euros in benefits. In some cases, this was because of negligence of alleged fraudsters in wrongly or incompletely filling in applications for childcare benefits; in other cases because of deliberate fraud. Because the Tax Office controlled fraud afterwards, the fraud was typically detected when the fraudsters had already returned to Bulgaria. To be better able to detect such fraud in a timely manner, the Tax Office implemented an automated fraud detection tool in 2013 (Amnesty International, 2021; Rutten, 2021; Stokmans & Vermeulen, 2023).

In 2013, the Tax Office was confronted with budget cuts, in a context of neoliberal austerity politics in the wake of the financial crisis (2007–2013). The fraud detection tool was believed to help the Tax Office to operate more efficiently (with less people) and hence to enable it to cope with its budget cuts (Kleinnijenhuis, 2021). The Tax Office invited a consulting firm (Deloitte) to design a fraud detection tool—a predictive and self-learning algorithm—marked by a risk (of fraud) classification model. Low income, single motherhood and parents with a migrant background were constructed as high-risk categories. In addition, the fraud detection tool was designed to categorize people who had made minor mistakes in their application for allowance as gross negligence, which resulted in no allowance

(Arts & Van den Berg, 2025; Giest & Klievink, 2022; Hummel et al., 2023). It soon appeared that the tool was marked by algorithmic bias. Not only was the fraud detection tool discriminatory in its constructed risk categories, but it was also biased in its assumption that the probability of fraudulent behavior for those listed in the risk categories would be eighty percent (Ossewaarde, 2023).

The implementation of the fraud detection tool by the Dutch Tax Office can be understood as a specific endeavor to further mechanize administrative processes. This push for further mechanization of administration makes it possible for the Tax Office to process very large numbers of potentially fraudulent allowance applications for which the Tax Office has no sufficient civil service personnel (Rutten, 2021). The awareness that any slight bias would have disastrous consequences for the common good, the welfare of vulnerable groups, and would greatly undermine the trust in government simply did not play a role in Deloitte's design or in the implementation of the tool. Instead, bureaucratic mindlessness and remoteness from the lived realities of welfare recipients penetrated an already degenerated bureaucracy (Fenger & Simonse, 2024). Almost 38,000 parents—mostly low income single parents with a non-Dutch or migrant background—were ordered by the Tax Office's fraud detection tool to repay tens of thousands of euro's that they had received in childcare allowances, even though it appeared afterwards that they had been legally entitled to their allowances (Hadwick & Lan, 2021). Parents thereby ended up severely indebted.

In July 2020 the Dutch Parliament commissioned an enquiry to find out to what extent politicians and (top level) administrators had been aware of the AI disaster produced by the Tax Office, and why administrative malpractices (continuing to rely on an erroneous fraud detection tool) continued until 2019, while the scandal had been revealed by the press two years earlier. Politicians and administrators, the parliamentary enquiry revealed in its report "Unprecedented Injustice" (*Ongekend Onrecht*) in December 2020, had failed to intervene even when it was known that Deloitte's product, the AI-enhanced fraud detection, produced unprecedented injustices; and thereby had failed to exercise their executive power responsibly (Hummel et al., 2023). The conclusion of the parliamentary enquiry was that the executive branch of government had violated the fundamental principles of the Dutch constitutional state, and that the judiciary had failed to protect the legal rights of Dutch residents. The ruling Dutch government—that is, Prime Minister Mark Rutte and his cabinet (ministers and secretaries of state)—offered its apologies, acknowledged institutional racism in the Tax Office, and decided to resign on 15 January 2021. Yet, the childcare benefits scandal has not come to an end yet, as compensation for the victims has not been settled yet. The scandal is an ongoing Kafkaesque nightmare that continues today, with victims being left in bureaucratic labyrinths and in administrative limbo (Arts & Van den Berg, 2025; Van den Berge & Gaakeer, 2025).

The fraud detection tool had become the core of the Tax Office, facilitating the (further) degeneration of bureaucracy. The administrative perversity of the Tax Office is most clearly manifested in its false beliefs of its own bureaucracy and its AI tool. The Tax Office wrongly understood itself as a decision-making machine without much administrator involvement in the decision-making process, while it falsely believed that its fraud detection tool, its latest gadget, was something iconic, something really special and groundbreaking. It adopted Deloitte's product on the basis of a false belief. Finn (2017, p. 6) describes such false belief in AI tools as the workings of what he calls the "myth of the algorithm". In the myth of the algorithm, AI technologies are depicted as mythical phenomena, that is, as signs of "progress" or "civilization" or "materialized Enlightenment", or as real "problem solvers". In its false belief, triggered by the myth of the algorithm, the Tax Office mindlessly identified Deloitte's tool as a solution to its own administrative problems in fraud detection. Herein lies the mythical meaning that the Tax Office attributes to the fraud detection tool: in a degenerated bureaucracy AI technologies are seen as hopeful signs of improvement. It can be said that the Tax Office embraced the fraud detection tool as a totem, believing that it would erase the most awkward realities of the Tax Office's administrative malfunctioning in fraud detection. Finn (2017, p. 17) describes such tool-based masking of awkward administrative realities as a construction of the "façade of the algorithm". Behind what Finn (2017, p. 49) calls the "façade of computer perfection" that the Tax Office's fraud detection tool signifies lies in fact a messy, biased and flawed technology, and a chaotic and brutal bureaucracy of a dominating Tax Office and its business partner.

The fraud detection tool is enmeshed in the myth of the algorithm. In this myth, administration is misunderstood and thought of as a technological or algorithmic phenomenon. The Tax Office identifies itself as a data-fed decision-making machine, in which the fraud detection tool is a celebrated machine whose supreme bureaucratic capacities in detecting fraud cannot be questioned. Indeed, the revealed Dutch childcare benefits scandal exposes the Kafkaesque nature of a corrupted bureaucracy in which AI is fetishized by administrators (and its automated decision-making is not questioned), at least in this specific context of the tax authorities' eagerness to detect fraud. In the hands of the Tax Office, the fraud detection tool degenerates into a "fetish". By "fetish" here is meant an exciting or enchanting object to which some supernatural or mysterious power is attributed. In the Tax Office, the fraud detection tool had become an object of idolatry (until that moment of disenchantment in 2019 when the Dutch press uncovered the totem as a racist tool). It could be said that such superstition is characteristic of degenerate bureaucracies that are captured by mindlessness, fraudulent myths and fetishisms. Seen in this light, the Dutch childcare benefits scandal is above all the result of baffling beliefs about bureaucracy and technology.

But the scandal is not all about the baffling beliefs of undemocratic or non-democratic or thoughtless administrators. In the context of democratic backsliding, marked by the decline of the humanist culture or democratic ethos of bureaucracy, brutal, unrefined lusts come into play to further corrupt and irrationalize or barbarize bureaucracy. The Tax Office's fraud detection tool was not only a totem or a fetish, but also a weapon in the quest for revenge after the earlier failures of the Tax Office to catch the Bulgarian fraudsters in 2007–2013. Implicitly, the Tax Office had reinvented itself as a hunter for fraudsters and it appeared indifferent to its prey. For the alleged fraudsters, the entire bureaucratic process from detecting fraud to punishment (repayment of allowance, confiscation of property, etc.) is arbitrary and obscure. Frequently, alleged fraudsters would never know what they had done wrongly or why they were being punished. True, there are rules, procedures and the fraud detection tool. Yet, all administrative behavior here is in reality governed by the base appetite to catch and punish fraudsters. The fraud detection tool comes with a perverse compulsion to dominate. This bureaucratic domination reveals itself inhumanely at the heart of the perverse administrative processes of the Tax Office, as a kind of automated human sacrifice, in which "algorithmic violence"—how algorithmic assemblages like the fraud detection tool feed and justify violence (Bellanova et al., 2021)—gives a perverse, deeply undemocratic meaning to administration in which humans play no role in deciding who has fraudulently claimed childcare benefits.

The algorithmic violence of the automated fraud detection tool—as an example of how executive power is exercised irresponsibly and how such administrative irresponsibility is facilitated by AI technologies—is real enough in the Dutch childcare scandal case. Some 270,000 parents were blacklisted as potential fraudsters, without valid proof and often without their knowledge. Most did not at all know that they were blacklisted or did not have a clue why they were blacklisted (Kleinnijenhuis, 2021). The automated punishment of the AI tool algorithmically violated tens of thousands of parents and children (of which seventy-one percent had a migrant background). After a screening it appeared that at least 39,000 allegations of fraud were unjustified (in late 2024 the number still increased by week). As (mostly single) parents were unjustly ordered to repay often tens of thousands of euros of claimed allowances, these algorithmically violated people typically ended up indebted. Approximately 70,000 children of such parents were raised in poverty. In 2015–2019, 2090 children were taken from their parents and placed in youth care (in 2022, 645 children had not yet returned to their parents). While in the Netherlands indebtedness is not a legitimate ground for the administrative removal of children from their parents, the automated punishment ruined parents' lives to the point that their children could no longer be cared for properly. The sudden indebtedness of the algorithmically violated generated massive stress, health issues, loss of jobs, loss of home, confiscation of property, divorce, mental problems, addictions (one person committed suicide) –these were the typical reasons for out-of-home placement of children. Deloitte's fraud detection tool had failed to take children rights—as laid down in the UN Convention on the Rights of the Child (CRC), as ratified in 1990—into account.

After it was publicly acknowledged by the Dutch government that the fraud detection tool—or rather, how fraud detection tool had been designed and, particularly, used by civil servants—had been unlawful and the algorithmically violated had to be compensated, tens of thousands of victims became entangled in the Kafkaesque maze of the so-called "compensation scheme" (Rutten, 2021). In June 2020, an administrative committee was established to settle the compensations, which, as a Dutch consultancy firm (Berenschot) reports in April 2024, radically failed in its democratic or constitutional exercise of executive power.

Berenschot reports that the compensation committee is suspicious of parents and cynical towards the workings of the compensation scheme. The committee performs only four to five assessments of compensations per week, while thousands of parents are waiting for a response. More than ten thousand parents received an unjustifiable rejection for compensation and have filed objections and find themselves in a state of administrative limbo (once again). In October 2021, the Dutch Ombudsman—a constitutionally anchored administrator who is appointed to look into citizens' complaints against the Dutch government—complained about the committee's extremely slow processing. Legal deadlines were grossly exceeded. Given that gathering all relevant information from each victim appears highly time consuming, algorithmically violated parents had to wait two years on average for some clarity about their compensation, and thousands of them will have to wait for years for final compensation. The political ambition of the Dutch government is to complete the compensation scheme by the end of 2027 at the latest, but this is impossible to achieve in the current Kafkaesque labyrinth.

In sum, the case of the Dutch childcare benefits scandal reveals the Kafkaesque alliance of democratic backsliding, corrupted bureaucracy, administrative perversity, and AI technology, made possible by four main undemocratic conditions that are illustrative for contemporary democratic backsliding. First, the fraud detection tool designed by Deloitte turns out to be opaque and xenophobic (racist, misogynistic, etc.) (Amnesty International, 2021). Second, the Tax Office was predisposed and hence receptive to such biased AI-tool. In other words, its administrative culture was already undemocratic, and the AI tool further institutionalized racism (as was publicly acknowledged in retrospect by the Dutch government) and normalized the hunt for the precariat, especially single women with a low income and a migrant background. Third, the absence of a democratic ethos in the minds of the administrators of the Tax Office enabled superstitions and fetishism to take hold of bureaucrats, thereby clouding their judgement and conscience. And finally, related to the previous two conditions, the commitment to democracy, justice and human dignity is absent, as a mark of administrative perversity that is further facilitated by AI technologies. Hence, the benefits scandal manifests a profound cultural decline. In its Kafkaesque guise, the Tax Office itself is characterized by a depraved bullying culture, mismanagement, and intimidation of its own civil servants, particularly of whistleblowers. In such a degenerated bureaucracy, marked by bureaucratic mindlessness, corporate interests, lusts, fraudulent myths, and fetishism, most civil servants do not dare to act responsibly, resist, or expose the masquerade of legitimate executive power (Essen & Straathof, 2017; Ossewaarde, 2023; Rutten, 2021; Stokmans & Vermeulen, 2023).

In the Netherlands, which has many AI success stories whenever administrators manage to subject AI tools (and their designers (like Deloitte), producers and implementers) to political and cultural requirements of public bureaucracy, the childcare benefits scandal is certainly not the only example of an AI disaster. Another major AI disaster is the Labor Capacity Act benefits scandal of the Netherlands Employees Insurance Agency (UWV) (2020–) in which ten thousands of benefits were wrongly calculated. It is another AI disaster that was produced by the implementation of a different kind of AI tool (designed to reduce paperwork, with an algorithm selecting files that are allegedly not correctly completed; and then the algorithm automatically decides which files need to be re-assessed). Yet, it is another cautionary case that has many similarities with childcare benefits scandal, in terms of Kafkaesque bureaucratic perversities and fetishisms, certainly in terms of its perverse consequences: livelihood and social protection destroyed by erroneous algorithm, recipients physically and mentally destroyed by erroneous algorithms. And such consequences create yet another breeding ground for further distrust of government or public institutions, which typically comes with a further democratic backsliding. In other words, while AI success stories may well strengthen trust in government, AI disasters like the Dutch childcare benefits scandal and the Labor Capacity Act benefits scandal seriously weaken democracy further.

5 Concluding Remarks

This chapter has made the argument that the use of AI tools in public bureaucracies can generate important public benefits, yet, such benefits can only be generated by mindful bureaucrats. This chapter has made the claim that the mechanistic worldview and its machine metaphors, so widely endorsed by Public Administration scholars, presents bureaucrats as mindless. Such a popular worldview fails to provide direction for the cultivation of great, mindful administrators. And it is precisely such administrators that are needed for making AI support a responsible exercise of executive power, ultimately for strengthening democracy, or at least for negating contemporary democratic backsliding or for resisting the rise of despotism and oligarchy. When regulating AI for public interests, worldviews matter. Wiliam Isaac Thomas noted that "if men define situations as real, they are real in their consequences." His famous dictum applies to both bureaucracy and AI. If bureaucracies and administrators are defined as machines and interpreted via misplaced metaphors like "digital government" or "algorithmic bureaucracy" (Ossewaarde, 2019a; Watson, 2019), then government and AI cannot be allied without generating a Kafkaesque nightmare like the Dutch childcare benefits scandal.

The Kafkaesque nightmare means that corrupted bureaucracies, like the Dutch Tax Office, maintain the masquerade of legitimate administration, but are ultimately characterized by the kind of nihilist absurdity, false beliefs, and lust for domination that Kafka recounts in his satires (Clegg et al., 2016; Ossewaarde, 2019b; Van den Berge & Gaakeer, 2025). In the Dutch childcare benefits scandal, the perversity of the Tax Office, facilitated by the fraud detection tool, is manifested in the form of mindlessness, unjustified accusations, bizarre misunderstandings, bureaucratic whims, possible perjury by officials, bureaucratic labyrinths, improper conduct, and the fetishizing of digital technology. On the outside, the Tax Office seemed to operate mechanically, procedurally, or algorithmically, but those who are inside, as the Dutch parliamentary enquiry revealed, always realized that this was only a pretense. But given that the Tax Office had already become a degenerate bureaucracy in a wider context of democratic backsliding, civil servants appeared too impotent to resist their political and administrative chief executives. Ultimately, it is always mindlessness that paves the way for the degeneration of bureaucracy, political and administrative failure, and the idolatry of AI tools.

The Dutch childcare benefits scandal, despite all its uniqueness and extraordinary administrative perversity, illustrates the disastrous consequences of the mechanistic misconception of both bureaucracy and AI technology. This misconception is closely connected to practice: the mechanistic conception of the Dutch Tax Office could only be possible in the context of weak democracies (or de-democratization) and an already corrupted bureaucracy. Deceptive ideologies (neoliberalism, nationalism), corporate interests, cynical mistrust, and nihilistic disbelief in democratic administration were perfect allies for a biased fraud detection tool. "The dark side" of digital transformation (Trittin-Ulbrich et al., 2021) might not even capture the complexity of the problem or challenge of embedding AI tools in corrupted or Kafkaesque bureaucracies. Current AI regulation, such as the European Union's AI Act or the United States' Blueprint for an AI Bill of Rights, marked by ethical notions like "transparent AI", "accountable AI", "trustworthy AI", or "human-centric AI", is highly insufficient. The proper design and embedding of AI-tools in democratic administration (as contrasted with Kafkaesque bureaucracies) is a necessary but not sufficient precondition for the democratic integration of AI-technology in bureaucracies. It is crucial, for the very survival of democracy and rule of law, that highly cultivated, mindful administrators remain responsible for the outcomes of well-designed and unbiased AI-tools, and that they do not give up the responsibility of judging and deciding in their exercise of executive power (Ossewaarde, 2019a, 2019b).

A responsible AI regulation implies that AI infrastructure in bureaucracies must formally and juridically integrate administrators' accountability. It means that however accurate and "ethical" AI might become, it can never be given priority in administrative decision-making regarding important matters that affect human lives or the political values of a humanist culture (democracy, rule of law) (Lalumera, 2025). This also means that AI-regulations must reinforce the consciousness that the fate of people's lives—and the fate of democracy and rule of law in a context of democratic backsliding—, lies in mindful administrators' hands. Practically, AI can be regulated through the organization of regular, mandatory collegial consultations and deliberations of highly cultivated administrators who are tasked to explain their administrative decisions informed by AI-tools. Such dialogical sessions are also necessary to improve AI-tools and expose biases, epistemic injustices, fraudulent myths, misplaced metaphors, oligarchical power structures, and private (or Big Tech) interests in public bureaucracies. Moreover, training sessions to get acquainted with AI-tools will have to include the complexity and ambiguity involved in administrative decision-making in human-AI interactions. An AI ethics module in such training cannot simply consist of procedural box-ticking, but will require the administrator's mindful engagement with the conflicts and dilemmas that arise from the interaction between algorithmic thinking and political and humanist thinking. In an ironical manner, AI regulations to prevent overreliance and complacency could therefore possibly revive a democratic administrative culture. But only if the integration of AI infrastructures in bureaucracies includes a simultaneous critical analysis of the rampant corruptions of particular bureaucracies in the current context of democratic backsliding. Cultural corruptions including despotic leadership, tech oligarchs, bullying, and fetishizing will obviously not be solved by the integration of AI-tools. On the contrary, these AI-tools will be lethal, highly efficient, weapons in the hands of dejected administrators in pursuit of illegitimate ends.

References

Ajdini, S. (2014). Public administration in ancient Rome and Egypt. *Academic Journal of Interdisciplinary Studies, 3*(6), 385–390. https://doi.org/10.5901/ajis.2014.v3n6p385

Amnesty International. (2021). *Xenofobe machines: Discriminatie door ongereguleerd gebruik* van *algoritmes* in de *toeslagenaffaire*. https://www.amnesty.org/en/documents/eur35/4686/2021/nl/

Arendt, H. (2006). *Eichmann in Jerusalem: A report on the banality of evil*. Penguin Books.

Arts, J., & Van den Berg, M. (2025). What the Dutch benefits scandal and policy's focus on 'fraud' can teach us about the endurance of empire. *Critical Social Policy, 45*(1), 177–187. https://doi.org/10.1177/02610183241281346

Baber, W. F. (1988). The arts of the natural: Herbert Simon and artificial intelligence. *Public Administration Quarterly, 12*(3), 329–347.

Bauer, M. W. (2023). Public administration under populist rule: Standing up against democratic backsliding. *International Journal of Public Administration, 47*(15), 1019–1031. https://doi.org/10.1080/01900692.2023.2243400

Bellanova, R., Irion, K. L., Jacobsen, K., Ragazzi, F., Saugmann, R., & Suchman, L. (2021). Toward a critique of algorithmic violence. *International Political Sociology, 15*(1), 121–150. https://doi.org/10.1093/ips/olab003

Boston Consulting Group. (2025). *GenAI: The path to a more productive, future-proof public sector in the Netherlands*. https://web-assets.bcg.com/e2/82/a76496d642989827b6cdb6023a40/genai-the-path-to-a-more-productive-future-proof-public-sector-in-the-netherlands.pdf

Capra, F., & Luisi, P. L. (2014). *The systems view of life: A unifying vision*. Cambridge University Press.

Cetina Presuel, R., & Martinez Sierra, J. M. (2024). The adoption of artificial intelligence in bureaucratic decision-making: A Weberian perspective. *Digital Government: Research and Practice, 5*(1), 1–20. https://doi.org/10.1145/3609861

Chang, A., & Brewer, G. A. (2023). Street-level bureaucracy in public administration: A systematic literature review. *Public Management Review, 25*(11), 2191–2211. https://doi.org/10.1080/14719037.2022.2065517

Clegg, S., Pina e Cunha, M., Munro, I., Rego, A., & Oom de Sousa, M. (2016). Kafkaesque power and bureaucracy. *Journal of Political Power, 9*(2), 157–181. https://doi.org/10.1080/2158379X.2016.1191161

Crawford, K. (2021). *Atlas of AI: Power, politics, and the planetary costs of artificial intelligence*. Yale University Press.

Dalby, M. T., & Werthman, M. S. (Eds.). (1971). *Bureaucracy in historical perspective*. Scott, Foresman and Company.

Ellul, J. (1990). *The technological bluff*. Eerdmans.

Elman, B. A. (1991). Political, social, and cultural reproduction via civil service examinations in late imperial China. *The Journal of Asian Studies, 50*(1), 7–28. https://doi.org/10.2307/2057472

Essen, E., & Straathof, A. (2017). Gebrekkige culturele blending: Problemen bij de belastingdienst bezien vanuit cultuurperspectief. *Goed Bestuur En Toezicht, 2*, 54–61.

Farazmand, A. (1998). Administrative legacies of the Persian world-state empire: Implications for modern public administration. *International Journal of Public Administration, 21*(1), 25–86. https://doi.org/10.1080/01900699808525297

Farazmand, A. (2010). Bureaucracy and democracy: A theoretical analysis. *Public Organization Review, 10*, 245–258. https://doi.org/10.1007/s11115-010-0137-0

Fenger, M., & Simonse, R. (2024). The implosion of the Dutch surveillance welfare state. *Social Policy & Administration, 58*(2), 264–276.

Finn, E. (2017). *What algorithms want: Imagination in the age of computing*. The MIT Press.

Giest, S. N., & Klievink, B. (2022). More than a digital system: How AI is changing the role of bureaucrats in different organizational contexts. *Public Management Review, 26*(2), 379–398. https://doi.org/10.1080/14719037.2022.2095001

Hadwick, D., & Lan, S. (2021). Lessons to be learned from the Dutch childcare allowance scandal: A comparative review of algorithmic governance by tax administrations in the Netherlands, France and Germany. *World Tax Journal, 13*(4), 609–645. https://ssrn.com/abstract=4282704

Heyck, H. (2008). Defining the computer: Herbert Simon and the bureaucratic mind. *IEEE Annals of the History of Computing, 30*(2), 42–62. https://doi.org/10.1109/MAHC.2008.18

Hummel, B., Yerkes, M. A., & Bal, M. (2023). "Unprecedented injustice": Digitalisation and the perceived accessibility of childcare benefits. *Journal of Social Policy, 2023*, 1–20. https://doi.org/10.1017/S0047279423000521

Kjaerulff, J. (2020). Discretion and the values of fractal man. An anthropologist's perspective on 'street-level bureaucracy'. *European Journal of Social Work, 23*(4), 634–644. https://doi.org/10.1080/13691457.2018.1553150

Kleinnijenhuis, J. (2021). Hoe de belastingdienst lage-inkomens profileerde in de jacht op fraude. *Trouw*, November 21, 2021.

Köstler, L., & Ossewaarde, R. (2022). The making of AI society: AI futures frames in German political and media discourses. *AI and Society, 37*(1), 249–263. https://doi.org/10.1007/s00146-021-01161-9

Lalumera, E. (2025). Ameliorating epistemic injustice with digital health technologies. In L. Bortolotti (Ed.), *Epistemic justice in mental healthcare*. Palgrave Macmillan. https://doi.org/10.1007/978-3-031-68881-2_8

Liyanage, C. (2024). Tyranny of city brain: How China implements artificial intelligence to upgrade its repressive surveillance regime. *Journal of Illiberalism Studies, 4*(3), 73–97. https://doi.org/10.53483/XCQW3581

Mathur, N. (2017). Bureaucracy. In *The open encyclopedia of anthropology*. https://doi.org/10.29164/17bureaucracy

Midgley, M. (2018). *What is philosophy for?* Bloomsbury Academic.

Mumford, L. (1963). *Technics and civilization*. Harcourt.

Newman, J., Mintrom, M., & O'Neill, D. (2022). Digital technologies, artificial intelligence, and bureaucratic transformation. *Futures, 136*, Article 102886. https://doi.org/10.1016/j.futures.2021.102886

Ossewaarde, M. (2019a). Digital transformation and the renewal of social theory: Unpacking the new fraudulent myths and misplaced metaphors. *Technological Forecasting and Social Change, 146*, 24–30. https://doi.org/10.1016/j.techfore.2019.05.007

Ossewaarde, M. (2019b). Kafka on gender, organization and technology: The role of 'bureaucratic eros' in administering change. *Gender, Work and Organization, 26*(7), 1000–1016. https://doi.org/10.1111/gwao.12278

Ossewaarde, M., & Gülenç, E. (2020). National varieties of AI discourses: Myth, utopianism and solutionism in West European policy expectations. *Computer, 53*(11), 53–61. https://doi.org/10.1109/MC.2020.2992290

Ossewaarde, R. (2023). Kafkaësk algoritmisch bestuur: Het toeslagenschandaal en de rol van irrationaliteit in de gemechaniseerde fraudejacht. *Tijdschrift over Cultuur & Criminaliteit, 13*(1), 69–76. https://doi.org/10.5553/TCC/221195072023013001005

Peters, B. G. (2019). The *politics of bureaucracy* after 40 Years. *The British Journal of Politics and International Relations, 21*(3), 468–479. https://doi.org/10.1177/1369148119866220

Peters, B. G., & Pierre, J. (2019). Populism and public administration: Confronting the administrative state. *Administration and Society, 51*(10), 1521–1545. https://doi.org/10.1177/0095399719874749

Pörksen, B. (2023). The image of man in artificial intelligence: A conversation with Joseph Weizenbaum. *Weizenbaum Journal of the Digital Society, 3*(3), 1–15. https://doi.org/10.34669/WI.WJDS/3.3.4

Proudfoot, D. (2011). Anthropomorphism and AI: Turing's much misunderstood imitation game. *Artificial Intelligence, 175*, 950–957. https://doi.org/10.1016/j.artint.2011.01.006

Reinecke, P. C., & Wrona, T. (2021). Meaning dynamics of emerging technologies: How technologies come into being in contested discourses. *Academy of Management Proceedings, 1*, 14565. https://doi.org/10.5465/AMBPP.2021.14565

Roehl, U., & Crompvoets, J. (2023). Inside algorithmic bureaucracy: Disentangling automated decision-making and good administration. *Public Policy and Administration.* https://doi.org/10.1177/09520767231197801

Rutten, R. (2021). Komt het ooit nog goed met de Toeslagenaffaire? *NRC Handelsblad*, 15 Octobre 2021.

Schwarz, G., Christensen, T., & Zhu, X. (2022). Bounded rationality, satisficing, artificial intelligence, and decision-making in public organizations: The contributions of Herbert Simon. *Public Administration Review, 32*(5), 902–904. https://doi.org/10.1111/puar.13540

Sprevak, M. (2017). Turing's model of the mind. In J. Copeland, J. Bowen, M. Sprevak, & R. Wilson (Eds.), *The Turing guide: Life, work, legacy* (pp. 277–285). Oxford University Press.

Suzuki, K., & Hur, H. (2020). Bureaucratic structures and organizational commitment: Findings from a comparative study of 20 European countries. *Public Management Review, 22*(6), 877–907. https://doi.org/10.1080/14719037.2019.1619813

Stokmans, D., & Vermeulen, S. (2023). Herstel slachtoffers toeslagenaffaire vastgelopen door ambtelijke chaos. *NRC Handelsblad*, 2 February 2023.

Trittin-Ulbrich, H., Scherer, A. G., Munro, I., & Whelan, G. (2021). Exploring the dark and unexpected sides of digitalization: Toward a critical agenda. *Organization, 28*(1), 8–25. https://doi.org/10.1177/1350508420968184

Veyne, P. (Ed.) (1987). *A history of private life: From pagan Rome to Byzantium.* Harvard University Press.

Van den Berge, L., & Gaakeer, J. (2025). Rereading Kafka's *The Trial*: Responsibility, reflection, and the case of the Dutch childcare allowance scandal. *Law and Humanities.* https://doi.org/10.1080/17521483.2025.2477931

Von Essen, L., & Ossewaarde, M. (2024). Artificial intelligence and European identity: The European Commission's struggle for reconciliation. *European Politics and Society, 25*(2), 375–402. https://doi.org/10.1080/23745118.2023.2244385

Waldo, D. (1952). Development of theory of democratic administration. *American Political Science Review, 46*(1), 81–103. https://doi.org/10.2307/1950764

Waldo, D. (1955). *The study of public administration.* Random House.

Watson, D. (2019). The rhetoric and reality of anthropomorphism in artificial intelligence. *Minds & Machines, 29*, 417–440. https://doi.org/10.1007/s11023-019-09506-6

Yesilkagit, K., Bauer, M., Peters, B. G., & Pierre, J. (2024). The guardian state: Strengthening the public service against democratic backsliding. *Public Administration Review, 84*(3), 414–425. https://doi.org/10.1111/puar.13808

Between AI-Laissez-Faireism and AI-Mercantilism: Day-Watchman and Regulating Artificial Intelligence in a Balanced Way

14

Maciej M. Sokołowski

1 Introduction

The state represents the public sector, while the market stands for private property. This division is obviously quite basic but made more complicated by various problems that may come to light in the course of the discussion of the state-market relationship (Sokołowski, 2016, 51). The current development of artificial intelligence (AI) prompts a revisit of this crucial relationship once more. What measures should be taken by the state within the emerging market of new technologies and solutions driven by AI like chatbots, robots, or cybernetic avatars (see Shimpo, 2018; Shimpo et al., 2025; Sokołowski, 2024)? What kinds of social interaction should be protected within this market? Under what circumstances and how should the state participate in this market? What are the proper functions of the state and the market? Where should the state-market boundary be established (Sokołowski, 2016, 51)? These are just a few questions that may arise when one thinks about development and regulation of AI-related businesses.

Depending on the socio-economic structure adopted, the degree of public participation in the economy inevitably varies; however, two extreme points can be differentiated on the axis of this impact: total subordination and complete release (see Sokołowski, 2016, 51–53). To address them, the chapter highlights the pro-market and pro-public approaches, both rooted in the market-based and state-based approaches and grounded in liberal and interventionist views. The differences between these extremes make it possible to demonstrate an intervening space filled by public law regulation, *a regulatory zone.* In order to analyse this

M. M. Sokołowski (✉)
Faculty of Policy Management, Keio University Shonan Fujisawa Campus, Fujisawa, Japan
e-mail: maciej@sfc.keio.ac.jp

Carey Law School, University of Pennsylvania, Philadelphia, USA

S. K. Aikins and T. Dimitrijevska-Markoski (eds.), *Artificial Intelligence and Government*, https://doi.org/10.1007/978-3-032-12344-2_14

space, occupied by a mixed economy, I refer to the concept of *a day-watchman* (Sokołowski, 2013, 309).[1] In general, this concept addresses mixed (balanced) regimes in which the regulator is a cautious observer who, under the powers of the state, creates the rules of the market game, provides information to market participants, and enforces the rules through sanctions. This way the regulator becomes the day-watchman.

Seen in this light, the goal of this chapter is to provide a theoretical framework for a regulatory model that could be applied to the needs of the development and future utilisation of AI (the day-watchman model). Behind a seemingly simple "regulation" stands a lot of different meanings: one may find a very general explanation, as well as complex and specific—among them regulation may also be defined by referring to the actions of the regulatory authorities—here, the regulation itself is the regulator, representing the state's actions of establishing, monitoring, and enforcing legal rules, yet it may also have adverse side-effects (see Macrory, 2008, 155; Kirkpatrick, 2006, 232; Morgan & Yeung, 2007, 3–4).

A reference to the Railway Fire Protection Association's (RFPA) 1925 Handbook—which contains the *recommendations on watchman* made by the National Fire Protection Association (NFPA)[2]—offers an intriguing and unconventional viewpoint on this issue from an unexpected angle. Albeit written with different needs in mind, the 1925 Handbook makes a clear division between the night and day watches, and, when interpreted with the help of literature on public law and regulation, the Handbook sheds a different light on the definition of the regulator-watchman. As a result, the text can provide a different perspective on some emerging consensus regarding what constitutes "best regulatory practice" in AI, as seen in a variety of regulatory systems, with best-practice policies, regulatory strategies, and enforcement (see Haines & Gurney, 2003, 356).

As the notion of the day-watchman is related to the idea of a night-watchman based on liberal theory, the chapter begins the discussion on liberalism with *laissez-faire* as its element analysed in the context on AI (Sect. 2), later juxtaposed (to illustrate another perspective of a public–private dichotomy) with the deliberation on the state-based approach in AI (Sect. 3). After delimiting the boundaries of these two regimes, where either the market or the state prevails, the chapter addresses the regulator in the role of the day-watchman as under the NFPA's guidelines (Sect. 4) in regulating AI. The final part of this study brings a conclusion (Sect. 5).

---

[1] One should note that although Cooperman and Walter (1962, 403) refer briefly to the day-watchman state, they discuss it in the context of a relation of individual freedom and public intervention that appeared in the liberal political tradition.

[2] National Fire Protection Association (1925). The Watchman—a Position of Trust (Suggestions of the National Fire Protection Association for Guidance in his Selection, Instruction and Duties). In: Railway Fire Protection Association, *Hand Book of Recommendations and Suggestions for the Protection of Railroad Property and Prevention of Fire Losses Therein: for the Use of Railroad Officials, Railroad Fire Inspectors and Fire Marshalls [and Others]*. Baltimore, MD: RFPA.

2 AI in the Hands of the Night-Watchman

In the discourse surrounding the regulation of AI, let us begin by examining the liberal approach. While liberalism, in popular thinking, is very often related only to the economy and economic analysis, it has its broader, legal dimension related to such essential legal topics as the state, the government, and the law. Thus, I refer to the night-watchman state (in original wording), a term that is strongly linked with the history of liberalism. Although this notion is very clearly identified with liberalism, it was used as an argument to criticise it (see Sokołowski, 2016, 53), where the personification of the state as the night-watchman limits its duties to "preventing burglary and theft" (Brandes, 1911, 125–126). Irrespective of the initial attempt to mock liberalism (see von Mises, 1985), history has shown that the popular recognition of night-watchman state as a term conveying the sense of liberal theory demonstrates that an everlasting connection between the night-watchman state and liberalism has been established (see Sokołowski, 2016, 53). Let us retain this term for further exploration in the context of AI.

The previously ridiculed limits of the night-watchman's duties have evolved into a concept of minimal state with reduced functions, restricted to the protection of citizens from violence, theft, fraud, and enforcement of contracts (Nozick, 2006, 26; see also Mitjashin, 2007, 97–98; Drury, 1982). From the perspective of AI development, this concept holds great promise, particularly for the AI business sector. The key function of such a state is to shield private property and private contract relations that people willingly enter (see Tomasi, 2001, xiii). The night-watchman, who stands guard, would not interfere unless he/she is likely to have a reason to believe that a malfunction is taking place (Hayashi, 2014, 144). The proponents of the night-watchman state advocate minimal government interference in the activities of individuals, particularly their economic activities. Additionally, the same proponents consider the legitimate role of the government to be limited to maintaining the rule of law internally and protecting the sovereignty of the state externally (Flikschuh, 2007, 63). To portray the night-watchman state Immanuel Wallerstein uses the following figure: night-watchman "sits in relative darkness, ... occasionally twirling ... baton or revolver when not asleep, and waiting; [night-watchman's] function is to ward off intruders who intend to pilfer property ... [night-watchman] does this primarily just by being there" (Wallerstein, 1999, 23–24). Just as the night-watchman state protects citizens' property rights, the liberal approach to regulating AI regulation would prioritise safeguarding intellectual property, data, and contracts. AI businesses rely on algorithms, datasets, and trade secrets (see Meyers, 2019). A minimal state approach would be focused on ensuring that these assets remain secure, encouraging investment and growth of this business.

The relative invisibility of the day-watchman interacts with another notion profoundly ingrained in liberalism: *laissez-faire* (see Einaudi et al., 2006, 80–84; Foucault, 2008, 25 n16, see also Cannan, 1964, 25). Despite the French origin of the expression, there is a consensus that Great Britain should be identified as the catalyst of its use (Hill, 2002, 287; cf. Daunton, 2008, 80). There, even before *laissez-faire* crystallised, the liberal-based current based on individualism developed under the influence of the works of Adam Smith, including his notorious "An Inquiry into the Nature and Causes of the Wealth of Nations" (see Buchan, 2006, 2; MacDonald et al., 2000, 30, Tanzi, 2011, 49; Viner, 1927, 231–232; see also Naggar, 1977; Pack, 1991). In popularising the individual approach, one should note the role of John Stuart Mill. His work "On Liberty" (1859) was an affirmation of *laissez-faire*, since it enhanced individual growth and development (Pressman, 2014, 61). In this work Mill addressed the limits of state entering individuals' liberty: the state and society had the right to restrict individual freedom only to prevent an individual from harming another person (see Brown, 1972, 134–135). Mill (1865) reasoned:

> the sole end for which mankind are warranted, individually or collectively, in interfering with the liberty of action of their number, is self-protection. That the only purpose for which power can be rightfully exercised over any member of a civilized community, against his will, is to prevent harm to others.

For his famous harm principle, Mill gave a variety of separate points, but one of his most significant remarks is that individuals are in the best position to know what is good for them—while the issue with outsiders, including government officials, is that they lack the information needed (see Sunstein, 2016, 10). Furthermore, as individuals act to maximise their well-being, and their yearning for actions and results reflects this awareness, they behave in a manner consistent with these preferences, in a desire to improve their well-being (Kopp et al., 1997, 4). The only valid limits on actions are best illustrated by the saying: "your freedom stops where mine begins" (see Ripstein, 2006, 229).

The limits—if implemented—in a democratic state governed by the rule of law must have a legal dimension. The same applies to liberalism, *laissez-faire*, and the night-watchman state introduced in the past as systems of rules (Clarence-Smith, 1999, 121; Sokołowski, 2016, 58, see Balogh, 1962, 14, see Lee Holroyd, 2002, 40; Art, 2004, 113) where the nineteenth-century state—especially from the mid-nineteenth century through the late nineteenth (and, in some respects, into the very early twentieth)—was limited in scope[3], in particular to defence, economic, and judicial affairs (Grady et al., 1995, 3). Apart from enacted legislation, it was courts' activity that paved the way for governmental neutrality or antiregulatory activism (Ryan, 2011, 81–82), as happened in the USA at the turn of the nineteenth and twentieth centuries, when the "Lochner era" (1897–1937)[4] affected the US Constitution by the doctrine of *laissez-faire* (see Benedict, 1985, 294–296; Gillman, 1993).

The examples of the implementation of liberal currents and *laissez-faire* indicate that, despite the common liberty-based core, individual cases of application have

---

[3] some scholars argue that in general the nineteenth century state was mainly a *laissez-faire* one– see Braithwaite, 2008, 15.

[4] Lochner v New York, 198 US 45 (1905).

varied in detail from one another. This also extends to governance models on AI, especially in the initial phase of recent rapid development of this business. In general, this phase is covered by a *laissez-faire* model with a structure based on private property institutions, free enterprise, competition, markets, meaningful private choice, and a presumption against the government activism where markets control the allocation of resources (see Samuels, 2011a, 2011b). This has been rather a market without state intervention, built on the premise that self-interest in a free society will lead to growth and development, and therefore individuals should be left free to pursue and advance their own ideas (see MacDonald et al., 2000, 30).

If referred to a system of rules, one may place a very pure version of liberalism on the boundary between the regulatory regimes, marking it as one of their extreme points. This would be a complete release—a state defined by the degree of market competition, lack of entry barriers, and freedom of market activity where private property and individual rights dominate (see Hazard & Orts, 2001, 80–82; Sokołowski, 2013, 310). To some extent, it reflects that version of liberalism where *laissez-faire* entirely prevails in the relationship between an individual and the state, and where the state's action is limited to certain functions like the protection of individuals (against violence, theft, and fraud), and enforcement of contracts (Nozick, 2006, 26)—a true night-watchman's approach.

In this context, AI left in the hand of the night-watchman, represents the regulatory minimalism where the state enforces a regulatory framework for AI that is as narrow as possible, focusing on preventing harm to individuals and ensuring the integrity of contracts. The introduced rules are aimed at protecting the rights of AI users and the intellectual property of AI developers, while respecting the autonomy of AI systems within legal boundaries. These AI users and developers have the liberty to explore and expand AI capabilities, as long as they operate within the bounds of the law and do not infringe upon the rights of others. The state encourages a competitive AI market, free from unnecessary regulatory barriers, allowing the AI sector to thrive through market mechanisms. The evolution and application of AI technologies and solutions are largely driven by own dynamics, with the state refraining from interfering in the progress of AI advancements. The government's role is limited to facilitating an environment for AI development, rather than actively steering it, and the state's involvement is reduced to what is necessary to protect individual rights and uphold the basic rule of law.

An example for night-watchman dealing with AI may be soon Argentina under the Milei's administration. A libertarian President Javier Milei is pitching to make Argentina "the world's fourth AI hub", promising hands-off regulation to lure US tech bosses to invest thee. In May 2024, during a meeting with top representatives of leading US AI companies, the Argentinian government presented the concept of a business-friendly legal framework (Nugent, 2024). According to Demian Reidel, then head of Council of Economic Advisors to the President of Argentina, the country "is actually putting forth the ideas of freedom, low regulation, free enterprise, and [President Milei] has captured the imagination of the tech world", while "extremely restrictive [regulations] killed AI in Europe" (Nugent, 2024).

3 AI Under the Power of the Leviathan

In contrast, the distinction for a state-based, public approach arises from the dominant government intervention (Sokołowski, 2016, 59). However, examples of liberalisation conducted in sectors of public interest such as aviation, rail, telecommunications, or energy industries, raise certain questions. One of them is to what degree the two models, the liberal, market-based, and the public, state-based are distinct from one another. Another relevant question, particularly in the context of AI, is whether there exists any convergence between these models, and if so, could it serve as a point of contact (see Sokołowski, 2016, 59–60).

From this perspective, what comes first when discussing the state-based approach is a much more intense degree of public control over the economy and the state's involvement through direct actions on the market, that can be easily contrasted with the market-based approach (Sokołowski, 2016, 63). As in the case of liberal-approach, it has various versions. One of them is the extreme "command economy" where the state determines, primarily or almost exclusively, the allocation of resources (Thomas, 1992, 5). Here, one can find the authoritarian approach with substantial government control when it comes to the allocation of economic resources (see Clarke, 2004; Robison et al., 2002), called by Grossman (1990, 58) a "centrally planned economy" (see Davis & Charemza, 1989), a "Soviet-type economy" (see Dunmore, 1980, 53), or a "bureaucratic economy" (see Šik, 1972).

In case of AI, a state-based approach would involve a higher degree of government control and oversight. This could manifest in several ways. For instance, like a command economy, the state could have the sole authority to determine the direction and priorities of AI development, potentially deciding in a central way which AI projects receive funding and which applications are prioritised. In this manner, the government would play a major role in allocating resources for AI research and development, potentially influencing which areas of AI are explored and which are abandoned. This also concerns stringent regulations that dictate how AI can be developed and used, with the aim of controlling the potential impacts on society and the economy.

In extreme cases, the state would exert substantial supervision over AI, similar to an authoritarian approach in economic systems. North Korea can be an example of this. Over the past decade, cyber tools have become crucial for the Democratic People's Republic of Korea in exploiting vulnerabilities of foreign militaries, businesses, and individuals (Harold et al., 2022). North Korea's approach to AI may follow a similar trajectory, prioritizing advancements that enhance its foreign-targeted operations, especially if it devotes sufficient time, resources, and prioritizes development through policy, similar to how it has been trying to make progress in tightly controlled fields like nuclear technology (Harold et al., 2022).

In other systems, this could limit the freedom of private entities to develop AI independently. For example, in a state-based regulatory model, the government might require all AI algorithms to be assessed and approved before deployment, ensuring they align with national interests and values. Here, China can be an example. In 2021, it rapidly expanded its AI governance with regulations. These mandated content intervention by companies for recommendation algorithms and required watermarking and safeguards for AI-generated content to protect such values as the "nation's image" (Sheehan, 2024). These regulations also established and expanded China's algorithm registry, a key element of its evolving AI control framework (Sheehan, 2024). In July 2023, China further strengthened its AI governance by issuing the Interim Measures for the Management of Generative Artificial Intelligence Services. The 2023 Measures require generative AI services to comply with relevant laws and respect social morality. For instance, Article 4 of the 2023 Measures prohibits generating content that deviates from core socialist values, incites the overthrow of the socialist system, harms national security, or undermines social stability.

Just like with the market-based approach, it is very difficult to find a homogeneous, pure situation that represents it in a very direct way (see Sokołowski, 2016, 64). Leaving the extremes of the command economy aside, in order to discuss the state-based approach, let us search for the concepts conflicting with *laissez-faire*. Among them is "mercantilism" (see Allen, 1991, 440; see Coleman, 1969, 37; see also de Deugd & Hoen, 2010, 20; Peterson, 1991, 83)—a trend preceding and contrasting *laissez-faire* (Viner, 1968, 435), an elitist policy in the service of aristocracy, an aid to absolutism, holding that the state had a responsibility to impose its order (Rich, 2002, 529). Although, this explanation is virtually universal—originating long before the advent of mercantilism, and going as far back as antiquity (see Bell, 1967, 81)—one may find some other state-based approaches following mercantilism. One was its systemic adaptation to the consolidation of power and the monopolisation of allegiance by nation-states—which, in their relations with other states, was driven by the Machiavellian code (Loyal, 2006, 123)—along with a greater regard for economic matters, a change in the basic nature of the economic goals of political authorities and a new administrative pattern (Viner, 1968).

Therefore, mercantilism was a kind of "economic nationalism" aimed at contributing to the growth of a wealthy, powerful state (LaHaye, 2008; Nettels, 1952, 105). This policy of high degree protectionism for achieving self-sufficiency, especially with regard to food supplies or raw materials required for critical industries and the military (Nettels, 1952, 105), sought to restrict competition faced by domestic producers. It was to be done through granting monopoly rights, controlling prices and market practices and, in particular, imposing restrictions, tariffs, and subsidies on the conduct of foreign trade—all aimed at contributing to the growth of a wealthy, powerful state (LaHaye, 2008). This was thus characterised by a labyrinth of rules, laws and standards explicitly involving the government in industry, labour, and consumer affairs (Peterson, 1991, 84). Apart from these measures, in the search for the sources of supply, mercantilism favoured colonial dependency over independent foreign partners; if this dependency was missing or insufficient mercantilism attempted, as far as possible, to control the trade in the country's own interests.

Just as mercantilism sought self-sufficiency through protectionist policies, AI mercantilism would involve safeguarding national interests with respect to AI solutions and technologies, with nations prioritising developing their own AI capabilities and ensuring self-reliance in critical areas such as AI research, development, and deployment. Moreover, mercantilism granted monopoly rights to certain industries—similarly, AI mercantilism would involve strategic control over AI-related sectors (cf. Farrand & Carrapico, 2022). This may include AI patents, data access, and proprietary algorithms to be supervised in a strict way by the state to maintain dominance in the global AI landscape—naturally, if the given state has this position. This could translate to policies governing cross-border data flows, technology transfer, as well as AI exports, supply chains, and technology partnerships as mercantilism imposed restrictions and tariffs on foreign trade. Finally, subsidies could be among other tools used by the government driven by AI-mercantilism to incentivise domestic AI research and startups, aimed at fostering a competitive advantage. However, it is a matter of scale that influences this assessment: AI-mercantilism entails government deep and wide intervention in industry.

While the state-based approaches may not be monolithic and their policy consequences experience some variations, what is evident is that the state is the central player who could initiate policies and rules and, most importantly, requires the money to control and steer (de Deugd & Hoen, 2010, 21). Thus—in contrast to liberalism, at the other end of the axis of public impact, one may find total subordination. In this model, under strong centralisation, the state takes on the role of Leviathan, shaping every type of behaviour by strict interventions (direct influence—commands, orders, etc.), adopting and exclusively executing laws, and managing the economy via subordinate entities like state monopolies (Hazard & Orts, 2001, 80–82; Sokołowski, 2016, 52). This involves an intensive level of state influence which, in a radical version, would be "a command economy" where the state primarily or almost exclusively determines the allocation of resources, like in communism (Sokołowski, 2016, 63–64; Thomas, 1992, 5). As previously discussed, one may find mercantilism among other examples of state-based approach. It is often presented as a doctrine in sharp contrast to *laissez-faire* (Viner, 1968), a general recipe for political-economic management based on the assumption that "whatever enhanced the state was right" (Landes, 1999, 443).

4 Big Government, *Laissez-Faire*, and Regulation

History is full of revolutionary changes, gradual evolutions, retreats and comebacks. In the first half of the nineteenth century, state-directed policies began to wane, gradually giving way to liberalism and freer trade (see Kiely, 2010, 31). Only a few decades later, protectionism resurfaced (Taylor, 1994, 155; Trentmann, 2008, 6). It was also a reaction against the radical *laissez-faire* ideology, motivated by the spread of socialism among the new industrial class, and a conviction that many more roles should be better assigned to the state (Horrocks, 1925, 199). The state's engagement in the economy continued to develop in the twentieth century. Among the reasons, one may find the effects of two world wars, the Great Depression of the interwar years, the rising power of socialism and labour parties, as well as the economic-thinking movement identified with John Maynard Keynes or Michał Kalecki (see Thomas, 1992, 6; King, 2002, 35–55; Feiwel, 1989, 45–80). Moreover, under Roosevelt's administration, these policies took on an unparalleled form of a "big government", influenced by the Keynesian spirit. Thus, Roosevelt's New Deal aimed to solve the economic downturn not just by massive public deficit expenditure and big government services, but also by intervention in the price system, and rigorous bureaucracy of business (Haberler, 1981, 7). On the one hand, after 1945, the approach of active public involvement in the economy continued and kept reappearing during tough times when it seemed to be the last resort. It happened at the time of the energy crisis of the 1970s, the global financial crisis of 2007–2008, during the COVID-19 pandemic, the 2022 energy crunch, and future crises that are yet to come (see Sokołowski, 2012, 2020a). On the other hand, alternatively, and sometimes in parallel, in different parts of the world, actions aimed at limiting the importance of government and establishing the minimal state were observed (see Randma-Liiv, 2008).

In this light, one may find that the state can be active, neutral, or rather passive with respect to AI—as reflected in the presented extreme models rooted either in the state-based (Leviathan) or the market-based (*laissez-faire*) approach (Sikor et al., 2008, 4). Hence, the scale (along with the answer on whether the previously mentioned justification exists or not) depends on the adopted socio-economic system and the regulatory regime or regimes applied (Sokołowski, 2016, 52). In their various forms, they range from public ownership regimes (with public monopolies and governments holding powers of making and setting exclusive rules) to private competition ones where the suppliers are private entities and regulation is aimed at ensuring that market competition is fair and efficient (see Thatcher, 2002, 869–870).

The opposing characteristics of these extremes make it possible to identify a space between them (Sokołowski, 2020b, 175). I find it filled with a mixed economy, where "both private and public enterprise have a role in economic activity and both market forces and the government determine the distribution of rewards" (Thomas, 1992, 6). This way the mixed economy is a dynamic web of private and public institutions and policies that tend to be the most capable of moving the country forward at any given time (see Petr, 1987, 1449). As Dani Rodrik (2000, 85) summarises:

> [t]he idea of a mixed economy is possibly the most valuable heritage that the 20th century bequeathed to the 21st in the realm of economic policy... The simple idea that markets and the state are complements—recognized in practice if not always in principle—made possible the unprecedented prosperity.

"[T]he role of the government in a mixed economy is not a question of the degree but of the nature of [the] intervention" find Harcourt and Kerr (2001, 83). The mixed economy relies on regulation. Christensen (2011, 96) writes: "[r]egulation defines the border between state and society, government and market". Pagallo et al., (2019, 3) underline that legal regulation is a way in which a balance between these systems may be struck. Among elements of regulation, one will find regulator (Sokołowski, 2018, 598). In mixed, balanced regimes, the regulator performs a role different to the one played in totally subordinated or completely released structures, he/she is a vigilant observer who, under the states' power (cf. Black, 2001, 112), creates the rules of the market game, provides information to market players, and enforces the rules through sanctions (see Sokołowski, 2013, 318; 2016, 89). In this way the regulator becomes the day-watchman.

The idea behind the notion of the day-watchman derives from the addressed middle approach, which balances both total subordination and complete release (Sokołowski, 2018, 598). In the same vein as the middle approach, which can be contrasted with the extremes, the regulation (or the position of regulatory authority) can exist in various forms under the Leviathan, minimal, and balanced government. For instance, Marsden (2011) identified at least twelve states of regulation, ranging from standard setting self-regulation to strong independent regulation.

If one could create an allegory of enforcement provided under the two previously discussed types of state, the Leviathan and the minimal government, it would be the story of two sheriffs (Sokołowski, 2020a, b, 174). The first, the "overzealous sheriff" (under the Leviathan-state) breaks into an office and looks for proof of illegal business practices, although no search warrant has been issued (Vago, 2000, 185; Hamilton & Spiro, 2015, 138); the other one—the "night-watchman" (under the minimal government-state), waits in relative darkness, and sometimes twirls a baton or a revolver to fend off possible intruders (Wallerstein, 1999, 23–24). In contrast, the regulator—the day watchman—the active detector, operates both in the daytime and at night-time, holds the baton or the revolver in readiness, is awake and observes (Sokołowski, 2020b, 174, 181). The day-watchman represents neither an active state's participation in the market nor a complete resignation from participation. It acts under the state's command (the rules in principle are established by the state) but serves the needs of both the state and the market (Sokołowski, 2020a, 3).

Drawing on the NFPA's recommendations, as outlined in the Railway Fire Protection Association's 1925 Handbook, some further comments on the day-watchman model can be provided. Despite seemingly different points of reference, the 1925 Handbook makes a noteworthy distinction between the night and the day watch. Although the remarks provided by the NFPA refer mainly to technical issues related to monitoring a property or a time-schedule, the NFPA's division into a *night-* and *day-watchman*, when anchored in literature on public law, sheds a different light on the concept of a regulator-watchman.

Given the middle-ground position, the day-watchman model—if appropriately introduced—can build a bridge between the extremes of total subordination and complete release in regulating AI (see Sokołowski, 2018, 598; 2020a, b, 175). In this context, Barton (2006), by presenting eight core elements of regulation, offers a useful frame. These pillars enable a better understanding of the role of the day-watchman (see Sokołowski, 2016, 77–81; see also Black, 2001, 134–135). On Barton's list one finds: (i) objectives, (ii) rules and standards, (iii) authorisation and permits, (iv) procedure, (v) monitoring and surveillance, (vi) enforcement, (vii) accountability, and (viii) institution. These elements are discussed in the following section.

5 AI Under the Day-Watchman's Custody

The regulator—watchman is an important factor in the protection of consumers and the regulated area against crises, misconduct, frauds, and systemic failures — "regulatory fires" (*objectives*). Crises and serious irregularities are least likely to occur—or are quickly contained—where the regulator-watchman remains vigilant and acts promptly (*enforcement*). Also, it must be recognised that those kinds of "regulatory fires" are prevented from being started (*monitoring and surveillance*) by the wakeful, loyal, and conscientious regulator-watchman (*accountability*) (NFPA, 1925, 291).

The state, the regulator's employer, must have implicit confidence in regulator's abilities. The watchman's responsibility is great, as they are often the sole authority figure overseeing the regulated area—AI in this case. To meet these needs, the state should get the right person, instruct fully, and offer complete support. This especially concerns these fields: *power to make rules and standards*, *authorisation and permits*, *procedure*, and *institution*. No one can do their " best without the whole-hearted support of ... superiors" (NFPA, 1925, 292). Cooperation, even under the legal regime granting independence to regulatory authorities, is always welcomed. "It should be a process of co-ordinating, steering, influencing, and balancing interactions between actors/systems" as advocated by regulatory strategies (see Black, 2001, 111). In this light, when the regulator finds "unsatisfactory conditions these should invariably be followed up and corrected" (NFPA, 1925, 292). Reports provided by the regulator to superior authorities (e.g. relevant minister) on budget limitations or staff shortages are a way of eliminating such insufficiencies.

This brings *accountability* that extends not only to the links between the regulator and regulated entities (AI industry and AI users) but also to the government and its authorised representatives like ministers, secretaries, etc. (Sokołowski, 2020a). This pillar also provides answers to the question of what power regarding independence should the regulators have, i.e. whether the regulator should be supervised or controlled by other authorities, whether the regulator should have a judge-like independence (see Böhme & Bartholl, 2020, 59), or be a minister-regulator (see Welfens & Jasiński, 1994, 57) with dual accountability, both legal and political (Sokołowski, 2016, 79–80).

This also highlights another listed pillar—*procedure*. It reveals the legal nature of public regulation where the regulators' decisions fall under concrete legal standards (Sokołowski, 2018, 594), including those provided by the supreme law, such as the constitution. Additionally, the procedure covers not only issuing decisions but also challenging them in an appeal (Sokołowski, 2013, 77). For these reasons, the regulator-watchman must be fully aware of the responsibilities of the role. Therefore, the regulator should be instructed to "anticipate, so far as possible, emergencies... [b]etter judgment will result even though the actual emergency could not have been anticipated" (NFPA, 1925, 292). However, the instructions under the standard of independent regulatory authorities are not orders. They are guidelines generally deriving from legislation (see Kelstrup & Toftemark, 2009).

Moreover, the law on the regulator's position is an instruction itself. The law creates the space in which the regulator can move. It imposes duties and introduces the means and the power. In this way, "[i]t must be impressed thoroughly upon the watchman that while [being] on duty [the regulator] is … custodian of the [regulated area] and will be held responsible for any occurrence within... control" (NFPA 1925, 293). Furthermore, the regulator-watchman should know the regulated area "from end to end" with its "every nook and corner" (NFPA, 1925, 292). Reports, surveys, questionnaires, audits, compliance filings, incident notifications, and risk assessments provided (or submitted) by regulated entities and other actors—including private consultants and governmental agencies—are among the measures increasing the regulator's awareness of the regulated area.

This leads us to the regulator's tasks. The first of these, as listed by Barton, includes an objective or objectives, a set of goals. They may be of a general nature—for instance, to act in a public interest (Barton, 2006, 19–20), to ensure reasonableness, non-discrimination, and reliable service (see Kearney & Merrill, 1998, 1334) or of a specific character like to protect privacy, safety, and security, or minimise impacts on the environment (see Chawla et al., 2022). In this respect, the regulator's role resembles that of the NFPA's watchman. In this light, these obligations may include:

> [t]o discover fire and extinguish it at the very start, while it is smouldering and before the blaze breaks out... [t]o give the alarm at once... [t]o find leakage … [and notify it] to those in authority … [t]o prevent … theft... [t]o note evidence of infractions... and report them. (NFPA, 1925, 294–295)

Just as the watchman must detect the first signs of fire while it is still smouldering, identify leakage before it causes serious loss, sound the alarm immediately, and report any infractions, the regulator is obliged to identify emerging risks and instances of non-compliance at the earliest possible stage, issue timely warnings and enforcement measures, ensure that breaches ("leakage") are promptly notified to the appropriate authorities, prevent unauthorised or harmful conduct, and document violations and secure appropriate remedial action. The same logic applies to *monitoring and surveillance*. Along with *enforcement*, they are used to detect and prevent misconduct regarding those binding elements of the regulator's activities like *rules or standards* (if the latter are binding), as well as *authorisations and permits* (guidance and recommendations do not usually cause enforceable effects) (see Yeom, 2017, 393). Monitoring and surveillance concern the identification of any wrongdoing by the regulated parties and the exercise of control powers. It involves the collection and screening of data in order to recognise potential violations, carried out to achieve the desired objectives (Ogus, 1994, 2; Sokołowski,

2016, 80). Furthermore, *enforcement*—through a potential, tailor-made sanction (see Bernatt, 2016)—allows or forces the regulated parties to act in accordance with set rules, standards, or guidance, granted authorisation, issued permits, or the law in general (Sokołowski, 2018, 2020a, 584).

The NFPA also raises the issue of the number of watchmen required. Leaving the traditional in-plant reference of the NFPA's suggestions that the day-watchman's task in "[t]he majority ... can satisfactorily be covered by one man ..., [w]here two or more men are employed one should be appointed Head Watchman" (NFPA, 1925, 296) let us follow its broader context, the one (public) used for the purposes of this work. This involves the last pillar, the institution performing the duties of the day-watchman. Regardless of its name (board, commission, council, etc.), the regulatory institution (in a regulatory state)—equipped with the power to create rules and standards, authorization and permits, acting according to the procedure, possessing the monitoring, and enforcement powers, and determining accountability—is necessary to provide effective public regulation (Sokołowski, 2016, 81).

The key elements of the day-watchman framework discussed, are summarised in Table 1. This Table outlines they day-watchman's approach in reference to eight core elements of regulation, as proposed by Barton (2006), commencing with the institution.

Table 1 Day-watchman regulatory framework

Core elements or regulation	Day-watchman's approach
Institution	• Board, commission, council, agency, or similar body established in accordance with this framework
Objectives	• Protecting consumers • Mitigating market failures • Maintaining a fair and competitive marketplace • Promoting market integrity • Enhancing consumer confidence
Rules and standards	• Power to issue and enforce those binding
Authorisation and permits	• Power to issue and enforce
Procedure	• Law-based actions • Defined process • Appeal and review
Monitoring and surveillance	• Proactive risk identification • Preventative measures • Early intervention
Enforcement	• Prompt intervention • Effective action • Maintaining vigilance
Accountability	• Wakeful and conscientious oversight • Loyalty to public interest • Transparency

Since the establishment of the European Artificial Intelligence Office (AI Office) in 2024 by the European Commission's (2024) and the enhanced by AI Act (2024), the framework can be applied to a concrete example. The AI Office incorporates the day-watchman framework for AI regulation, based on its roles and responsibilities, aligning with core elements like objectives, enforcement, and monitoring, with some aspects that vary due to the AI Office's specific focus. Table 2 juxtaposes the core elements with the legal position of the AI Office.

Grounded in the AI Act (2024) and the decision of the European Commission (2024), as outlined in Table 2, the AI Office incorporates all eight core elements of the day-watchman regulatory framework. Its roles and responsibilities align closely with the day-watchman's approach, encompassing proactive monitoring, enforcement, accountability, and institutional structure. Whilst the day-watchman framework is broader and more general in scope, the AI Office's duties are specifically tailored to AI regulation, positioning it as a specialised "day-watchman" for the AI domain. However, its role is weakened by its limited permitting powers and its subordination to the European Commission, a limitation stemming from the model of AI regulation established in the EU, which centralises authority with the Commission, delegates specific tasks to national competent authorities, and balances competences between Member States and the EU in accordance with the Treaties.

Table 2 AI Office and day-watchman regulatory framework

Core elements or regulation	European artificial intelligence office
Institution	• Established within the commission as part of the administrative structure of the directorate-general for communication networks, content and technology
Objectives	• Performs the European commission's function of contributing to the implementation, monitoring and supervision of AI systems and general-purpose AI models, and AI governance • Investigates possible infringements of rules on general-purpose AI models and systems, including by collecting complaints and alerts, assisting in the preparation of decisions of the commission and conducting evaluations pursuant to the AI Act (2024) • Supports the implementation of rules on prohibited AI practices and high-risk AI systems in coordination with relevant bodies responsible under sectoral legislation, including facilitating information exchange and collaboration between national authorities, collecting notifications and establishing information platforms and databases, in particular when a general-purpose AI model or system is integrated into a high-risk AI system
Rules and standards	• Assists the European Commission in the preparation of guidance and guidelines to support the practical implementation of the AI Act (2024) • Develops supportive tools, such as standardised protocols and best practices, in consultation with relevant Commission services and bodies, offices and agencies of the EU • Assist the Commission in the preparation of standardisation requests, evaluation of existing standards and the preparation of common specifications for the implementation of the AI Act (2024) • May invite all providers of general-purpose AI models to adhere to the codes of practice
Authorisation and permits	• Develops tools, methodologies and benchmarks for evaluating capabilities of general-purpose AI models, in particular for very large general purpose AI models with systemic risks • May develop and recommend voluntary model terms for contracts between providers of high-risk AI systems and third parties that supply tools, services, components or processes that are used for or integrated into high-risk AI systems
Procedure	• Acts on the basis of the AI Act (2024) and the decision of European Commission (2024) • By 2 August 2028, the European Commission shall evaluate the functioning of the AI Office, whether the AI Office has been given sufficient powers and competences to fulfil its tasks, and whether it would be relevant and needed for the proper implementation and enforcement of the AI Act (2024) to upgrade the AI Office and its enforcement competences and to increase its resources

(continued)

Table 2 (continued)

Core elements or regulation	European artificial intelligence office
Monitoring and surveillance	• Monitors the implementation and application of rules on general-purpose AI models and systems, in particular where the model and the system are developed by the same provider • Monitors the emergence of unforeseen risks stemming from general-purpose AI models, including by responding to alerts from the scientific panel • May take the necessary actions to monitor the effective implementation and compliance with the AI Act (2024) • May initiate a structured dialogue with the provider of the general-purpose AI model
Enforcement	• Ensures that when an AI system falls within the scope of relevant EU legislation for which the Commission has powers of supervision and enforcement, the supervision and enforcement of that legislation is fully coordinated with the supervision and enforcement of the AI Act • Although the Commission have exclusive powers to supervise and enforce Chapter V of the AI Act (2024), it entrusts the implementation of these tasks to the AI Office
Accountability	• May invite all providers of general-purpose AI models, as well as relevant national competent authorities, to participate in the drawing-up of codes of practice (civil society organisations, industry, academia and other relevant stakeholders, such as downstream providers and independent experts, may support the process) • Make publicly available a list of planned and existing sandboxes and keep it up to date in order to encourage more interaction in the AI regulatory sandboxes and cross-border cooperation • Provide standardised templates for areas covered by the AI Act (2024) • Develop and maintain a single information platform providing easy to use information in relation to the AI Act (2024) for all operators across the EU • Organise appropriate communication campaigns to raise awareness about the obligations arising from the AI Act (2024) • Evaluate and promote the convergence of best practices in public procurement procedures in relation to AI systems

6 Conclusion

In the reality of the twenty-first century, it is hard to find "pure" Smithian type or centrally planned regimes, as the liberal and state-based systems interpenetrate each other; the developed world consists rather of "mixed" systems, which vary as to the nature of the mix (see Petr, 1987, 1448). Although public opinion still attributes value to traditional public-sector roles—such as in the environmental regulation or providing social programmes—and generally accepts that the state bears responsibility for the economy, confidence has waned in public authorities' capacity or inclination to foster broader prosperity, particularly when this requires taking on novel responsibilities (Hacker & Pierson, 2016, 89).

Hence, to create a functioning system for the modern world, a significant number of citizens must regain trust in the government's ability to address their most pressing concerns (Hacker & Pierson, 2016, 89). With respect to AI, this requires building a position of trust—the "third sheriff", the active observer, operating both during the day and at night, being awakened in readiness, representing neither an active state's involvement in the AI-industry nor a full withdrawal from it, acting under the command of the state while serving both the states' and the business' needs. "[The] shift... implies a different role for the state, one of mediator, facilitator, enabler, and for the skills of diplomats rather than bureaucrats", writes Black (2001, 145). Such a regulator—the day-watchman can make it happen. This way, the reliance on the regulator's expertise may help to avoid the excesses of *laissez-faire* and the Leviathan the field of AI.

Nevertheless, nothing will be done without getting the right people for the job. At the same time, one should also pay attention to AI and robotics, as many current and future advances have significant implications for public administration, which could use new technologies to foster improved and lower-cost service delivery (see Kenneth, 2014). Accordingly, finding the right people involves making the right choices. In this case, too, the NFPA's guidelines prove useful. First, "character, habits and reliability must be unquestionable", combined with intelligence, good decision-making skills, sound judgment, courage and a temperament which "should be such that he [or she] will not be likely to become confused or 'rattled' in an emergency" (NFPA, 1925, 291). Second, as the NFPA recommends—"[p]hysical condition should be satisfactory" (NFPA, 1925, 291). While meeting the postulate of passing a special physical examination is hardly a common standard (even though determining fitness for work falls within the remit of occupational health service), the age criterion is widely applied. "A very young, or an extremely aged, watchman should not be employed. A very young ... ordinarily has not acquired judgment and a sense of responsibility. An extremely aged ... is not likely to be alert or to have the requisite physical strength and endurance" (NFPA, 1925, 291). By applying the NFPA's recommendations to the regulator one will notice their suitability and the fact that, in many ways, such criteria are also applied to the members of administration appointing the regulators.

This approach highlights one more important feature. At the end of *today*, the regulator is only human, and I am aware that in reality, the day-watchman model, as any other (Ellis et al., 2010; Short, 2013), may prove to be ineffective: "the wrong person matched to the wrong position introduces the wrong regulation" (Sokołowski, 2020b, 182). At the end of *tomorrow*, the regulator will be enhanced by AI—I am more than sure of that. What the day after tomorrow would bring? Would AI regulate itself? Is AI a better regulator than human? But why not to enhance them now with AI bringing the tomorrow closer to today? Why not to appoint AI-driven commissioner (a bureaunoid) among the human-based regulatory commission (see Sokołowski, 2025)?

The posed questions need further research and deliberations. What is certain now is that every good system, including the regulatory, needs safeguards (Pagallo, 2016, 387; Malgieri, 2019)—collegiate bodies such as commissions—which may, to some degree, rule out the errors of a single-man decision (Sokołowski, 2010).

No one should, of course, exclude any number of "wrong people" named as commissioners of a regulatory body, as seen before (Sokołowski, 2020b, 182). History has demonstrated more than once how the best solutions were crushed by the wrong people. That is not to suggest that we should not try to find the best solutions and models. "Seven falls, eight getting up", as the Japanese proverb says.

Acknowledgements I am very grateful to Professor David M. Driesen of Syracuse University College of Law and Professor Ugo Pagallo of the University of Turin for serving as the "daywatchmen" of this text and dedicating their valuable time to reading and commenting on the initial manuscript. The insightful and friendly remarks they provided not only sparked inspiration but also helped extinguish some fires in the original draft. My thanks also go to Piotr Mikusek and Iwo Buller for their comments on the revised version.

This work was supported by JST Moonshot R&D Grant Number JPMJMS2215.

References

Allen, W. R. (1991). Mercantilism. In J. Eatwell, M. Murray, & P. Newman (Eds.), *The New Palgrave: The world of economics* (pp. 440–448). Palgrave Macmillan.

Art, J. (2004). Social control in Belgium: The Catholic factor. In C. Emsley, E. A. Johnson, & P. Spierenburg (Eds.), *1800–2000 of Social control in Europe* (Vol. 2, pp. 112–124). Ohio State University.

Artificial Intelligence Act (2024). Regulation (EU) 2024/1689 of the European Parliament and of the Council of 13 June 2024 laying down harmonised rules on artificial intelligence and amending Regulations (EC) No 300/2008, (EU) No 167/2013, (EU) No 168/2013, (EU) 2018/858, (EU) 2018/1139 and (EU) 2019/2144 and Directives 2014/90/EU, (EU) 2016/797 and (EU) 2020/1828, OJ L 2024/1689, 12.7.2024.

Balogh, T. (1962). *Some aspects of economic growth of under-developed areas.* National Council of Applied Economic Research.

Barton, B. (2006). The theoretical context of regulation. In B. Barton, A. Lucas, L. Barrera-Hernández, & A. Rønne (Eds.), *Regulating energy and natural resources* (pp. 11–33). Oxford Univ. Press.

Bell, J. F. (1953, 1967). *A history of economic thought*. Ronald Press.

Benedict, M. L. (1985). Laissez-faire and liberty: A re-evaluation of the meaning and origins of laissez-faire constitutionalism. *Law and History Review, 3*(2), 293–331.

Bernatt, M. (2016). Administrative sanctions: Between efficiency and procedural fairness. *Review of European Administrative Law, 9*(1), 5–32.

Black, J. (2001). Decentring regulation: Understanding the role of regulation and self-regulation in a 'post-regulatory' world. *Current Legal Problems, 54*(1), 103–146.

Böhme, M., & Bartholl, C. (2020). Germany. In K. B. Wong (Ed.), *The renewable energy law review* (pp. 52–66). Law Business Research.

Braithwaite, J. (2008). *Regulatory capitalism: How it works, ideas for making it work better*. Edward Elgar.

Brandes, G. (1911). *Ferdinand Lassalle.* William Heinemann.

Brown, D. G. (1972). Mill on liberty and morality. *The Philosophical Review, 81*(2), 133–158.

Buchan, J. (2006). *The authentic Adam Smith: His life and ideas.* W.W. Norton & Co.

Cannan, E. (1964, 1929). *A review of economic theory.* Cass.

Chawla, Y., Shimpo, F., & Sokołowski, M. M. (2022). Artificial intelligence and information management in the energy transition of India: Lessons from the global IT heart. *Digital Policy, Regulation and Governance, 24*(1), 17–29.

Christensen, J. G. (2011). Competing theories of regulatory governance: Reconsidering public interest theory of regulation. In D. Levi-Faur (Ed.), *Handbook on the politics of regulation* (pp. 96–110). Edward Elgar.

Clarence-Smith, W. G. (1999). The modern colonial state and global economic integration 1815–1945. In D. A. Smith, D. J. Solinger, & S. C. Topik (Eds.), *States and sovereignty in the global economy* (pp. 120–137). Routledge.

Clarke, S. (2004). A very Soviet form of capitalism? The management of holding companies in Russia. *Post-Communist Economies, 16*(4), 405–422.

Coleman, D. C. (1969). *Revisions in mercantilism.* Methuen.

Cooperman, D., & Walter, E. V. (1962). *Power and civilization: Political thought in the twentieth century.* Crowell.

Daunton, M. (2008). *State and market in Victorian Britain: War, welfare and capitalism.* Boydell & Brewer.

Davis, C., & Charemza, W. (Eds.). (1989). *Models of disequilibrium and shortage in centrally planned economies.* Chapman and Hall.

Deugd de, N., & Hoen, H.W. (2010). *Dovetailing economics and political science: A paradigmatic introduction to international political economy.* Van Gorcum.

Drury, S. B. (1982). Locke and Nozick on property. *Political Studies, 30*(1), 28–41.

Dunmore, T. (1980). *The Stalinist command economy: The Soviet State apparatus and economic policy 1945–53.* Palgrave Macmillan.

Einaudi, L., Faucci, R., & Marchionatti, R. (2006). The end of 'laissez-faire'? In L. Einaudi, R. Faucci, & R. Marchionatti (Eds.), *Luigi Einaudi, selected economic essays* (pp. 80–84). Palgrave Macmillan.

Ellis, N. S., Fairchild, L. M., & Fletcher, H. D. (2010). The NYSE response to specialist misconduct: An example of the failure of self-regulation. *Berkeley Business Law Journal, 7*(1), 102–149.

European Commission. (2024). Commission Decision of 24 January 2024 establishing the European Artificial Intelligence Office. C/2024/390 OJ C C/2024/1459, 14.2.2024.

Farrand, B., & Carrapico, H. (2022). Digital sovereignty and taking back control: From regulatory capitalism to regulatory mercantilism in EU cybersecurity. *European Security, 31*(3), 435–453.

Feiwel, G. R. (1989). The legacies of Kalecki and Keynes. In M. Sebastiani (Ed.), *Kalecki's relevance today* (pp. 45–80). Palgrave Macmillan.

Flikschuh, K. (2007). *Freedom: Contemporary liberal perspectives.* Polity Press.

Foucault, M. (2008). 10 January 1979. In A. I. Davidson (Ed.), G. Burchell (transl.) *The birth of biopolitics: Lectures at the Collège de France, 1978–1979* (pp. 1–25). Palgrave Macmillan.

Gillman, H. (1993). *The constitution besieged: The rise and demise of Lochner era. Police Powers Jurisprudence.* Duke University Press.

Grady, P., Howse, R., & Maxwell, J. (1995). *Redefining social security.* Queen's University School of Policy Studies.

Grossman, G. (1990). Command economy. In J. Eatwell, M. Milgate, & P. Newman (Eds.), *The New Palgrave: Problems of the planned economy* (pp. 58–62). Palgrave Macmillan.

Haberler, G. (1981). *The great depression of the 1930s: Can it happen again?* American Enterprise Institute for Public Policy Research.

Hacker, J. S., & Pierson, P. (2016). Making America great again: The case for the mixed economy. *Foreign Affairs, 95*(3), 69–90.

Haines, F., & Gurney, D. (2003). The shadows of the law: Contemporary approaches to regulation and the problem of regulatory conflict. *Law & Policy, 25*(4), 353–380.

Hamilton, M. S., & Spiro, G. W. (2015, 2008). *The dynamics of law.* Routledge.

Harcourt, G. C., & Kerr, P. (2001, 1979). The mixed economy. In G. C. Harcourt (Ed.), *Selected essays on economic policy* (pp. 81–95). Palgrave Macmillan.

Harold, S. W., Beauchamp-Mustafaga, N., Jun, J., Myers, D. Y., & Grossman, D. (2022). Will artificial intelligence hone North Korea's cyber 'all-purpose sword'? *Korea Economic Institute. Special Report*, 7.

Hayashi, S. K. (2014). *The freedom of peaceful action: On the origin of individual rights*. Lexington Books.
Hazard, Jr G. C., & Orts, E. W. (2001). Environmental contracts in the United States. In E. W. Orts & K. Deketelaere (Eds.), *Environmental contracts: Comparative approaches to regulatory innovation in the United States and Europe* (pp. 71–91). Kluwer Law International.
Hill, C. (2002, 1961). *The century of revolution: 1603–1714*. Routledge.
Holroyd, C. L. (2002). *Government, international trade, and Laissez-Faire capitalism: Canada, Australia, and New Zealand's Relations With Japan*. McGill-Queen's Univ.
Horrocks, J. W. (1925). *A short history of mercantilism*. Methuen & Co.
Kearney, J. D., & Merrill, T. W. (1998). The great transformation of regulated industries law. *Columbia Law Review, 98*(6), 1323–1409.
Kelstrup, A., & Toftemark, K. (2009). Danes get new valuation and documentation guidelines. *International Tax Review, 20*(9), 48–51.
Kenneth, K. (2014). The rights and wrongs of robotics: Ethics and robots in public organizations. *Canadian Public Administration, 57*(4), 485–506.
Kiely, R. (2010). *Rethinking imperialism*. Palgrave Macmillan.
King, J. E. (2002). An economist from Poland. *A history of Post Keynesian Economics Since 1936* (pp. 35–55). Edward Elgar.
Kirkpatrick, C. (2006). Regulatory impact assessment. In M. A. Crew & D. Parker (Eds.), *International handbook on economic regulation* (pp. 232–254). Edward Elgar.
Kopp, R. J., Krupnick, A. J., & Toman, M. (1997). Cost-benefit analysis and regulatory reform: An assessment of the science and the art. Available at https://ageconsearch.umn.edu/record/10851/. Accessed March 3, 2025.
LaHaye, L. (2008, 1987). s.v. Mercantilism. In: S. N. Durlauf & L. E. Blume (Eds.), *The new Palgrave dictionary of economics*. Palgrave Macmillan.
Landes, D. S. (1999). *The wealth and poverty of nations: Why some are so rich and some so poor*. W.W. Norton & Co.
Loyal, S. (2006). On empire and its instantiations. *Journal of Sociology, 15*(1), 106–124.
MacDonald, S. B., Hughes, J. E., & Crum, D. L. (2000). *New tigers & old elephants: The development game in the 21st century*. Transaction Publishers.
Macrory, R. (2008). *Regulation, enforcement and governance of environmental law*. Cameron May.
Malgieri, G. (2019). Automated decision-making in the EU Member States: The right to explanation and other 'suitable safeguards' in the national legislations. *Computer Law & Security Review, 35*(5), Article 105327.
Marsden, C. T. (2011) Internet co-regulation and constitutionalism: towards a more nuanced view. Retrieved from: https://ssrn.com/abstract=1973328
Meyers, J. M. (2019). Artificial intelligence and trade secrets. *Landslide, 11*(3), 17–21.
Mill, J. S. (1865). *On liberty*. Longmans, Green, and Co.
Mises von, L. (1985, 1927). *Liberalism in the classical tradition*. Cobden Press.
Mitjashin, A. (2007). *Liberalism and skepticism*. Cambridge Scholars Publishing.
Morgan, B., & Yeung, K. (2007). *An introduction to law and regulation: Text and materials*. Cambridge Univ. Press.
Naggar, T. (1977). Adam Smith's laissez faire. *The American Economist, 21*(2), 35–39.
Nettels, C. P. (1952). British mercantilism and the economic development of the thirteen colonies. *The Journal of Economic History, 12*(2), 105–114.
Nozick, R. (2006, 1974). *Anarchy, state, and Utopia*. Blackwell.
Nugent C. (2024). Javier Milei pitches Argentina as low-regulation AI hub. *Financial Times*. Retrieved from: https://www.ft.com/content/90090232-7a68-4ef5-9f53-27a6bc1260cc
Ogus, A. (1994). *Regulation: Legal form and economic theory*. Oxford Univ. Press.
Pack, S. J. (1991). *Capitalism as a moral system: Adam Smith's critique of the free market economy*. Edward Elgar.
Pagallo, U. (2016). The impact of domestic robots on privacy and data protection, and the troubles with legal regulation by design. In S. Gutwirth, R. Leenes, & P. de Hert (Eds.), *Data protection on the move: Current developments in ICT and privacy/data protection* (pp. 387–410). Springer.

Pagallo, U., Casanovas, P., & Madelin, R. (2019). The middle-out approach: Assessing models of legal governance in data protection, artificial intelligence, and the Web of Data. *The Theory and Practice of Legislation, 7*(1), 1–25.

Peterson, R. D. (1991). *Political economy and American capitalism*. Springer.

Petr, J. L. (1987). The nature and necessity of the mixed economy. *Journal of Economic Issues, 21*(4), 1445–1468.

Pressman, S. (2014, 1999). *Fifty major economists*. Routledge.

Randma-Liiv, T. (2008). New public management versus the neo-Weberian state in Central and Eastern Europe. *The NISPAcee Journal of Public Administration and Policy, 1*(2), 69–81.

Rich, P. (2002). Policy studies and history. *Policy Studies Journal, 30*(4), 528–531.

Ripstein, A. (2006). Beyond the harm principle. *Philosophy & Public Affairs, 34*(3), 215–245.

Robison, R., Rodan, G., & Hewison, K. (2002). Transplanting the regulatory state in Southeast Asia: A pathology of rejection. *Southeast Asia Research Centre Working Papers, 33*.

Rodrik, D. (2000). Development strategies for the 21st Century. In B. Pleskovic & N. Stern (Eds.), *Annual World Bank Conference on Development Economics 2000* (pp. 85–108). World Bank.

Ryan, E. (2011). *Federalism and the tug of war within*. Oxford University Press.

Samuels, W. (2011). s.v. Laissez faire. In J. Beckert & M. Zafirovski (Eds.), *International encyclopedia of economic sociology*. Routledge.

Samuels, W. J. (2011). *Erasing the invisible hand: Essays on an elusive and misused concept in economics*. Cambridge University Press.

Sheehan, M. (2024). Tracing the roots of China's AI regulations. *The Carnegie endowment for international peace*. https://carnegieendowment.org/research/2024/02/tracing-the-roots-of-chinas-ai-regulations?lang=en. Accessed March 6, 2025.

Shimpo, F. (2018). The principal Japanese AI and robot law: Strategy and research toward establishing basic principles. *Journal of Law and Information System, 3*, 44–65.

Shimpo, F., Sokołowski, M. M., Mikusek, P., Chawla, Y., & Figueroa Jr., R. B. (2025). Cybernetic avatars for energy transformation: regulating the digital revolution for enhancing sustainable attitudes of energy consumers. *Digital Policy, Regulation and Governance*.

Short, J. L. (2013). Self-regulation in the regulatory void: 'blue moon' or 'bad moon'? *The ANNALS of the American Academy of Political and Social Science, 649*(1), 22–34.

Šik, O. (1972). *Czechoslovakia: The bureaucratic economy*. International Arts and Sciences Press.

Sikor, T., Barlösius, E., & Scheumann, W. (2008). Introduction: Public-private relations and key policy issues in natural resource governance. In T. Sikor (Ed.), *Public and private in natural resource governance: A false dichotomy?* (pp. 1–18). Earthscan.

Sokołowski, M. M. (2010). Kolegialny model ustrojowy organu jako droga do pełnej niezależności polskiego regulatora sektora energetycznego [Collective system model of the administrative body as a way to full independence of the Polish energy sector's regulator]. *Polityka Energetyczna [energy Policy], 13*, 99–109.

Sokołowski, M. M. (2012). Energy as a conflict trigger. Comparative analysis of international disputes in the middle east with energy relations in the background. In A Garnuszek, A. Surma, & L. Mazur (Eds.), *International disputes – a challenge for the contemporary world* (pp. 107–145). Faculty of Law and Administration of the University of Warsaw.

Sokołowski, M. M. (2013). Rozważania o istocie współczesnej regulacji [Considerations on the essence of modern regulation]. In A Walaszek-Pyzioł (Ed.), *Regulacja: Innowacja w sektorze energetycznym* [*Regulation: Innovation in the energy sector*] (pp. 309–329). C.H. Beck.

Sokołowski, M. M. (2016). *Regulation in the European electricity sector*. Routledge.

Sokołowski, M. M. (2018). Regulatory dilemma: Between deregulation and overregulation. In J. Jagielski, D. Kijowski & M. Grzywacz (Eds.), *Prawo administracyjne wobec współczesnych wyzwań. Księga jubileuszowa dedykowana profesorowi Markowi Wierzbowskiemu* [*Administrative law facing contemporary challenges: Jubilee anniversary publication dedicated to Professor Marek Wierzbowski*]. C.H. Beck.

Sokołowski, M. M. (2020a). Regulation in the COVID-19 pandemic and post-pandemic times: Day-watchman tackling the novel coronavirus. *Transforming Government: People, Process and Policy, 15*(2), 206–218.

Sokołowski, M. M. (2020b). Balancing energy regulation: A day-watchman approach. In R. Grzeszczak (Ed.), *Economic freedom and market regulation: In search of proper balance* (pp. 167–186). Nomos.

Sokołowski, M. M. (2024). Cybernetic avatars, robots, and sustanbility. *ICRES 2024: 9th International Conference on Robot Ethics and Standards*, Yokohama, Japan, 29–31 July 2024, https://doi.org/10.13180/icres.2024.29-31.07.017

Sokołowski, M. M. (2025). Robo-clerks and cyber-clerks as forms of bureaunoids: Applying robotics and cybernetic avatars in AI-driven public administration. In M. F. Silva et al. (Eds.),*Crisis or redemption with AI and robotics? The dawn of a new era: Proceedings of the ICRES 2025 conference* (pp. 161–168). Springer.

Sunstein, C. R. (2016). *Choosing not to choose: Understanding the value of choice*. Oxford University Press.

Tanzi, V. (2011). *Government versus markets: The changing economic role of the state*. Cambridge University Press.

Taylor, P. J. (1994). The state as container: Territoriality in the modern world-system. *Progress in Human Geography, 18*(2), 151–162.

Thatcher, M. (2002). Analysing regulatory reform in Europe. *Journal of European Public Policy, 9*(6), 859–872.

Thomas, G. P. (1992). *Government and the economy today*. Manchester University Press.

Tomasi, J. (2001). *Liberalism beyond justice: Citizens, society, and the boundaries of political theory*. Princeton Univ. Press.

Trentmann, F. (2008). *Free trade nation: Commerce, consumption, and civil society in modern Britain*. Oxford University Press.

Vago, S. (2000, 1981). *Law and society*. Prentice Hall.

Viner, J. (1927). Adam Smith and laissez faire. *Journal of Political Economy, 35*(2), 198–232.

Viner, J. (1968). Mercantilist thought. In D. L. Sills (Ed.), *International encyclopedia of the social sciences*. Macmillan Co.

Wallerstein, I. (1999). States? Sovereignty? The dilemmas of capitalists in an age of transition. In D. A. Smith, D. J. Solinger, & S. C. Topik (Eds.), *States and sovereignty in the global economy* (pp. 20–33). Routledge.

Welfens, P. J. J., & Jasiński, P. (1994). *Privatization and foreign direct investment in transforming economies*. Dartmouth.

Yeom, B. (2017). The legality of walking away from public service ombudsman reports: The United Kingdom's experience. *Monash University Law Review, 43*(2), 386–420.

Future Development of AI: AI-Driven Robotization and Automation of Public Services 15

Bernd W. Wirtz and Marcel Becker

1 Introduction

Due to the rapid development progress in the fields of artificial intelligence (AI) computing as well as semiconductor and chip production, the far-reaching potential of digital automation and the use of robot-assisted optimization approaches are penetrating ever further and deeper into various areas of life and work (Cascio & Montealegre, 2016; Pelau et al., 2021). AI-powered innovation is expected to have a profound impact on private and public sector activities as well as people and society (Batra et al., 2018; Madan & Ashok, 2023). The utilization of AI can, for instance, enhance (public) management by automating routine tasks and providing predictive analytics to optimize resource allocation. It also holds potential to help to streamline operations, reduce costs, and—in public management context—improve citizen services, making government agencies more efficient and responsive. Hence, the transfer of AI together with corresponding robot-assisted automation and tools offers an enormous opportunity to take organizational and public processes to a completely new level, also in terms of the quality of information, collaborative decision-making and work processes (Boyd & Wilson, 2017; Zheng et al., 2018).

A majority of pioneers and also users come from the private sector, so that in addition to well-known protagonists such as Google, IBM, and Microsoft, other companies from a wide range of sectors such as industry, retail, logistics and others are also streamlining their relevant processes with the help of AI-driven automation and robotization (Briggs & Kodnani, 2023; Wirtz & Müller, 2019). Whereas the origins of the first beginnings of utilization date back decades (Turing, 1950) and

B. W. Wirtz (✉) · M. Becker
Chair for Information and Communication Management, German University of Administrative Science Speyer, Speyer, Germany
e-mail: ls-wirtz@uni-speyer.de

S. K. Aikins and T. Dimitrijevska-Markoski (eds.), *Artificial Intelligence and Government*, https://doi.org/10.1007/978-3-032-12344-2_15

widespread use failed to materialize due to a lack of suitable methods and computing capacity, researchers and business leaders alike are now talking about AI as "one of the most important things that humanity is working on" (Pichai & Schwab, 2020). However, despite the acknowledged importance and potential, the necessary steps towards successful AI transition and robotization in the area of public administration and its respective services often remain unclear and lag behind the private sector to a certain extent (Wirtz et al., 2018). As Madan and Ashok (2023) state, despite the existence of various frameworks and guidelines, "public leaders are grappling with the tensions AI introduces in service design and delivery" (p. 18), especially with regard to the meso and micro level of public service offerings.

That is one of the reasons why planned investments in AI transition and the digital automation of public services offer substantial benefits, largely due to their inherently uniform design that enables wide-ranging applicability and facilitates replication across various domains. These advantages are further amplified by the rapidly increasing demand from citizens and other governmental stakeholders for enhanced digital interaction, spurred by the momentum of the open government data movement (Gao & Janssen, 2020).

Against this background, this chapter specifically aims to shed light on respective AI driven automation and robotization developments in the field of public services by categorizing dedicated types and manifestations of AI robotization/automation in the public sector context, thereby contributing to a better understanding and sustainable management of them. With the help of a proposed AI-specific strategic interaction model for public services, practitioners and researchers alike can leverage the interlinking and transmission of human–machine elements into a combined interaction environment including suitable automation and robotization approaches for further improvements in this field.

To this end, Sect. 2 first discusses the basic principles of AI and illustrates the extent to which a distinction can be made between different expansion stages of AI analysis methods before development and deployment can culminate in a self-sufficient robotization and automation approach. By extension, in Sect. 3 a strategic AI interaction model for the integration of processes of public institutions into AI-controlled robot and automation systems is introduced in order to later identify and demonstrate suitable strategic approaches to AI-based digitization in the public sector. Building on this, Sect. 4 examines the extent to which robotization and automation services differ in their underlying design and nature depending on the various fields of application in the public sector and which challenges can be overcome with the help of which strategies within the respective AI verticals. Section 5 provides a brief overview of various ethical and regulatory viewpoints related to AI using deeper insight into empirical data obtained from the European Union's AI law. To conclude, in Sect. 6, the key findings and structural guidelines derived are critically assessed and finally discussed against the backdrop of expected future developments.

2 Forms of Artificial Intelligence

Despite the fact that it is very difficult to define artificial intelligence (AI) in an all-encompassing and universally applicable way, due to its versatility in terms of potential areas of application, it is nevertheless valuable to synthetize existing concepts and knowledge (Russel & Norvig, 2021; Wirtz, 2024a). However, in order to be able to delineate self-sufficient systems for end-to-end digitization, robotization and automation of different processes in an application-oriented manner, which does not yet mean a comprehensive transfer to real fields of application, a basic understanding of the underlying structure and interdependence of AI is required.

To promote such a basic understanding, it is helpful to familiarize oneself with the Turing test, also known as "The Imitation Game" (Turing, 1950, ch. 4). In the Imitation Game, a human interviewer communicates with two unknown persons via a keyboard and a screen without any visual or auditory contact. Half of these participants is human; the other half is a machine. If the interviewer cannot determine which person is the machine after a detailed interaction, the Imitation Game is considered to have been passed. This result indicates that the machine is capable of thinking in a way that is comparable to humans. From this point of view, an AI must be able to perceive, reason, interact and learn, at least to a certain degree. Following on from this, AI can be defined as "the capability of a computer system to show human-like intelligent behavior characterized by certain core competencies, including perception, understanding, action, and learning, in order to support human and systemic behavior in the best possible way" (Wirtz, 2024a, p. 279), whose underlying technology "functions appropriately and with foresight in its environment" (Nilsson, 2009, p. 13).

In view of the fact that AI is still in its infancy and irrespective of its specific areas of application, it can already be seen when considering the term AI that a large number of potential classifications according to different criteria are possible. Due to the progressive development of AI and its respective analytical methods, an examination of the various stages of development and expansion can be of great benefit for better navigation. Prior to a dedicated derivation of suitable approaches and analytical methods for the use of AI, current statuses can be categorized into three consecutive development stages, namely Narrow AI, General AI and Super AI (Kaplan & Haenlein, 2019).

Narrow AI refers to advanced decision-making algorithms which are fielded by IT departments and offer restricted performance and independence. It is used in specific areas that require targeted decision-making. While these algorithms process large amounts of data and are often more powerful than traditional computers and humans at similar tasks, they are mainly used for repetitive tasks where humans could become biased or less reliable. Narrow AI can also support human labor. Unlike more sophisticated AI algorithms, it does not pose a significant threat to jobs and cannot fully take over tasks as it is lacking extensive self-improvement and skill enhancement capabilities.

General AI refers to a more autonomous technology with greater performance and independence than Narrow AI. It is used in various fields requiring automated decision-making and can perform intellectual tasks as effectively as humans, but more efficiently and reliably. General AI is superior to humans in combining intelligence factors and can reason, improve, and expand its abilities. As it outperforms humans in efficiency and reliability, General AI is expected to be able to take over certain tasks as a replacement for many traditional jobs.

Super AI is the most advanced form of artificial intelligence, capable of performing any task by analyzing huge amounts of data and autonomously learning in the process. It can operate in all areas and surpasses humans in every respect. The ability of super AI to constantly improve itself makes it capable of handling and revising entire process chains and, to a considerable extent, completing them without human intervention, which means that (human) work tasks are correspondingly substitutable. Figure 1 illustrates the various stages of development.

In addition to the differentiation of AI into three basic forms according to Kaplan and Haenlein (2019), five expansion stages can be distinguished with regard to derived AI analysis approaches and their respective automated type of analysis. According to Wirtz (2024b), the five AI analysis approaches can be categorized as follows: (1) Descriptive Analytics; (2) Diagnostic Analytics; (3) Predictive Analytics; (4) Prescriptive Analytics; and (5) Cognitive Analytics.

Understanding past events based on historical data constitutes the essence of analysis. While (1) descriptive analytics provides information about what happened, (2) diagnostic analytics can help to understand the reasons behind why it happened. In combination, descriptive and diagnostic analytics in AI not only represent data, but also interpret it to recognize correlations, thereby building the bridge to next stages where information can be used to guide future decisions and

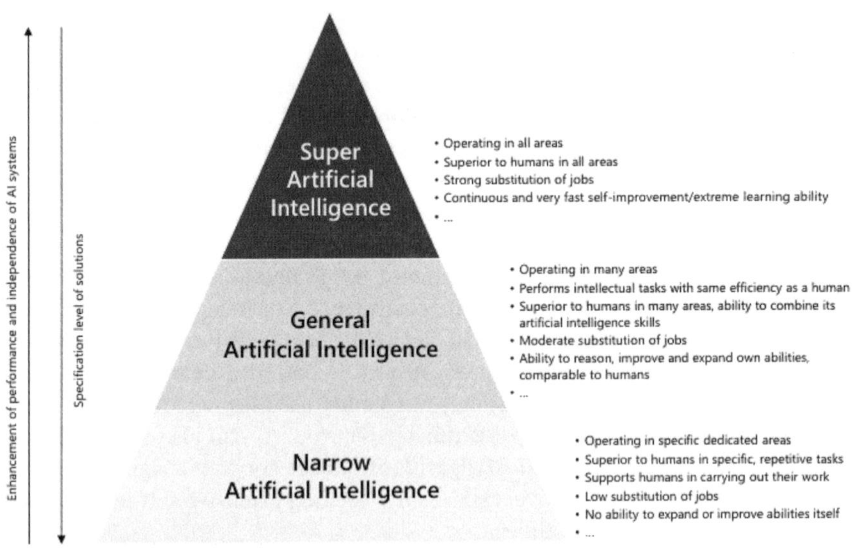

Fig. 1 Development stages of AI (Wirtz, 2024a, 2024b)

provide deeper insights. (3) Predictive analytics is the first stage to go further than only looking in the past. It uses past data to anticipate potential future trends by deriving mathematical models from historical events and applying them to recent data. While advances in big data and machine learning technologies are opening up new opportunities for future-oriented analytics, (4) prescriptive analytics, using and leveraging these data and technologies, goes even further by predicting future events and recommending actions that help improve the performance of (public) institutions and achieve specific goals. At the highest stage of development, (5) cognitive analytics aims to mimic human brain function by drawing conclusions from existing data and updating its knowledge base for future insights, leading to a self-learning feedback loop. Its key concept culminates in applying human-like intelligence to specific tasks and mimicking human reasoning in signal processing (see Fig. 2).

Consequently, in order to integrate suitable measures in terms of specific automation and robotization types using AI in the public management sector, an initial status quo assessment is necessary, which allows to delve deeper into detailed planning depending on the performance and maturity level of public AI efforts.

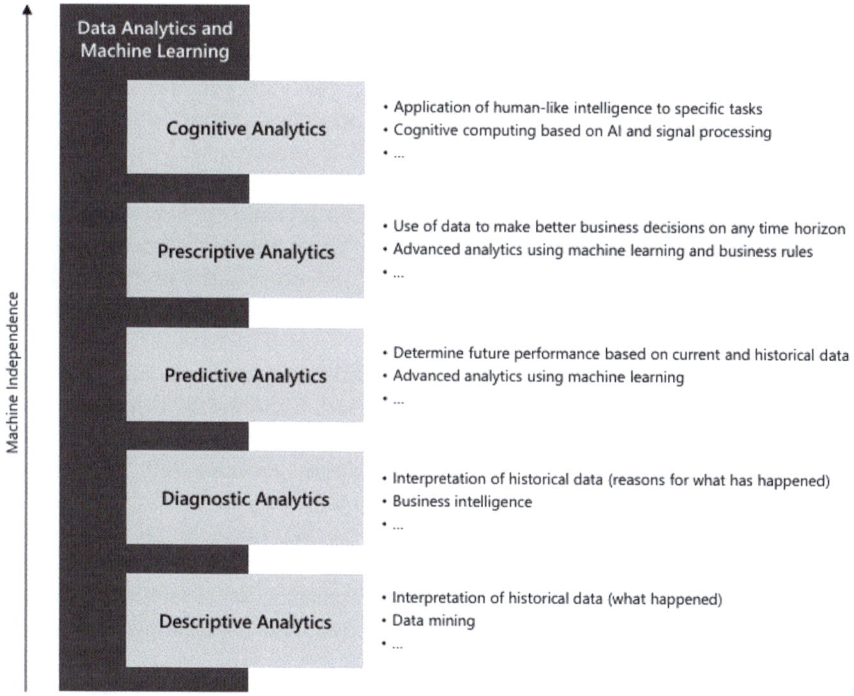

Fig. 2 AI analytics approaches (Wirtz, 2024a, 2024b)

3 Strategic Interaction Model of AI Driven Automation and Robotization

In order to identify and design suitable types and associated strategic approaches for AI-driven automation and robotization that promote overall success, a fundamental understanding of how stakeholders interact with AI respectively how humans and machines interact is required. This basic understanding about interaction logics is all the more important given that AI components "are inherently inconsistent due to poorly understood, probabilistic behaviors based on nuances of tasks and settings, and because they change via learning over time" (Amershi et al., 2019, p. 1f). Since key stakeholders of the state are people, regardless of whether they are employees, civil servants or citizens, with whom corresponding interaction ought to be as beneficial as possible, the three-level interaction structure proposed by Wirtz (2024a) can also be applied to public management sector as a basis for creating this essential understanding. Broadly defined, it can be said that three levels, namely (1) human, (2) AI and (3) the interaction itself, must be related and coordinated.

(1) Humans are characterized by their specific behaviors, experiences and social and emotional imprints and thus differ from rationally acting machines in particular by their individual uniqueness (Banerjee et al., 2018). Situational awareness is also an important element that has often not yet been sufficiently considered in the context of artificial intelligence. In addition, humans have exclusive normative value systems that are formed and manifested by influencing factors such as background, (political) education and individual experiences, feelings and also biases (Venkatesh, 2022). Individual abilities and skills of people, which are made up of a variety of dispositions, also have an indirect effect on the willingness and feasibility of interactions. The basic functional logic of human behavior in the context of interaction can be summarized as follows: People perceive their environment with their senses, whereupon the sensory signals are consciously or unconsciously processed cognitively, which leads to neuronal stimulation, which in turn triggers an individual action (Wirtz, 2024a).

The counterpart to interaction, (2) the AI, can be characterized quite differently in many areas, although not fundamentally opposed. In contrast to the human interaction partner, the essence of AI and the associated robotization and automation tools is largely fed by specific data, underlying algorithms along with technical and procedural links that are applied within the framework of dedicated AI programs (Sheikh et al., 2023). Moreover, the sensory perception and the interfaces of AI differ from those of humans in that they are, for the most practical cases, superior to human capabilities. This opens up, at least technically, the possibility of a much higher and more comprehensive information skimming, for example with regard to auditory, haptic or visual stimulus conversion.

However, this superiority comes at the cost of not facilitating the (complete) development and mimicking of normative value systems and emotional sensitivity that humans have, at least not without explicit manual system enhancement. Consequently, the behavior and action logic on which AI is based is quite different from that of humans and begins with the technical acquisition of sensory data, which his is followed by data processing through information technology, often involving database matching. Next, the control pulse is calculated based on the specified program heuristics and machine learning algorithms. The control pulse is then managed by suitable algorithms, which are dependent on the characteristics of the AI system. An electronic control signal is finally generated, which leads to an AI-controlled action (Xu et al., 2021).

The linking level, the (3) interaction itself, acts as the pivotal point of (1) human and (2) AI and, since it has no independent characteristics, is directly dependent on the expectations and behavior of the human as well as the AI or its specific method design, whereby interaction-specific influencing factors must be taken into account. For instance, the appearance of an AI-controlled robot is of great importance to humans, as it can have a positive influence on the relationship and therefore the interaction with the robot. This applies equally to the imitation of emotions on the part of the AI as well as the type and potential adaptability of the interaction interface with regard to visual, auditory or haptic stimulus transmissions (Pelau et al., 2021).

Besides the interaction-specific influencing factors, four central groups of success factors also have a general impact on the interaction between humans and AI, such as the service orientation of the AI developer or those responsible for AI. Comprehensive information provision in the form of service contact points or up-to-date service descriptions is just as conducive to interaction as technical and administrative support from those responsible for the software/tool in the context of (planned) use or integration into the user's operating environment. The same applies to the effects on success that are made possible by a potential—planned and unforeseen—system linkage of AI with other IT and automation tools, without necessarily creating or reinforcing lock-in effects.

The remaining groups of success factors, external range and grid performance as well as environmental support and pressure, have less of an impact on the AI component itself than on the basic willingness and opportunity of humans and their respective organizations to use it. This means that an AI tool as such can, in theory, be able to make positive contributions for a human being and yet, if network quality and stability are not sufficiently developed in certain adjacent application areas, for example, it cannot generate the level of sustainable communication that is actually needed for successful interaction, from human to AI and vice versa. Furthermore, elements of political and social discourse and the resulting legal norms can also influence the interaction between humans and AI, for example by declaring applications to be standard or restricting their use. The complete strategic interaction model is illustrated in Fig. 3.

An awareness of how the interaction between humans and AI is structured, which influencing factors need to be taken into account and which components need to be highlighted in such a scenario subsequently creates the basis on which dedicated AI tools can be developed and suitable strategies designed.

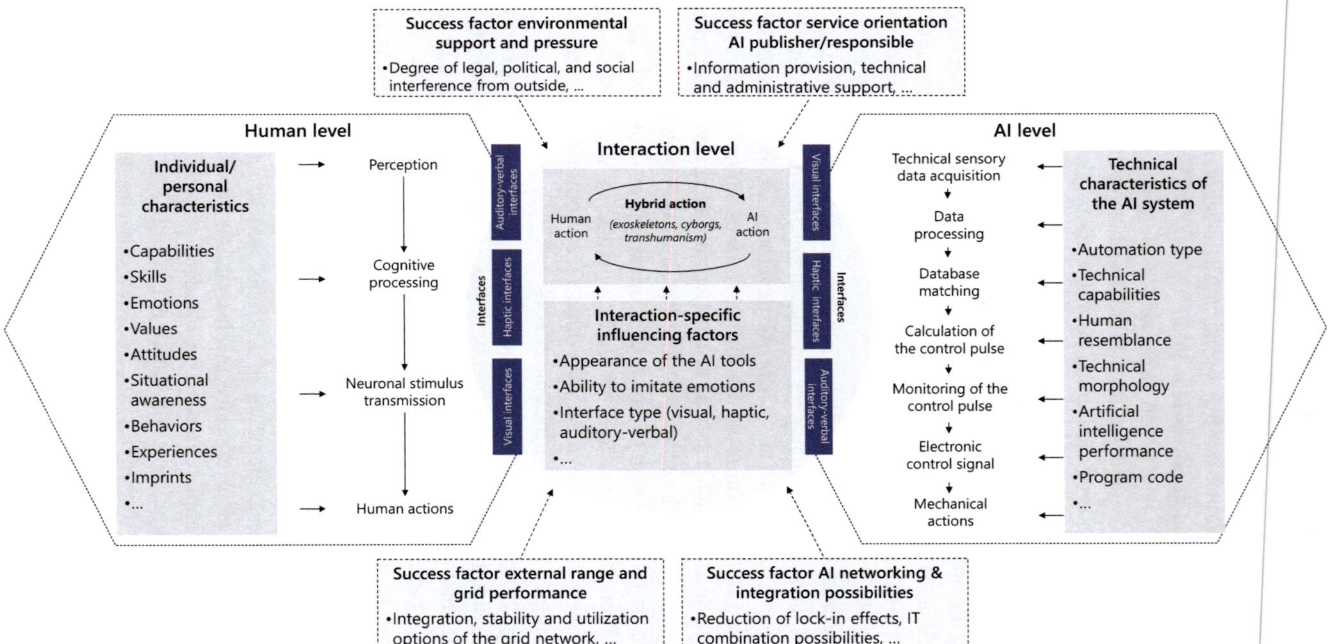

Fig. 3 Strategic human/AI interaction model. Adapted Wirtz (2024a, 2024b)

4 Automation and Robotization Types and Strategies for Public Services

Depending on the expansion level of the AI environment under consideration and the given structure of the interaction components together with their respective influencing factors, different automation and robotization approaches can be deployed. Although a wide variety of thematic and application areas continue to exist, digital software automation basically comprises three core areas: digital process automation (DPA), business process automation (BPA), and robotic process automation (RPA) (Rizk et al., 2020; Suri, 2022). Each of these areas uses AI algorithms to streamline and improve processes, with DPA focusing on the automation of generic, repetitive digital tasks and typically representing a higher-level combinatorial form of BPA and RPA. One example of this is Amazon's Alexa voice assistant, which improves automation by allowing users to control various devices and systems through natural voice commands. By enabling seamless human–machine interaction, Alexa simplifies tasks such as adjusting smart home settings and managing schedules—without further manual input or complex technical interfaces. This is an example of how BPA and RPA can be combined to automate the interaction between humans and AI while making everyday tasks more efficient and convenient (Pratt, 2021).

In this context, BPA targets broader business workflows, improving efficiency across multiple departments or functions, while RPA, on the other hand, uses software robots to replicate human actions in specific interaction tasks such as data entry or customer support. As described above, all of these AI automation functions are designed to learn, adapt and improve over time. However, since the entire discipline is still in its infancy, the field of software automation is set to remain very dynamic (Wirtz et al., 2018). Nevertheless, both software-based (mostly BPA) and robot-based (mostly RPA) applications are technically equally suitable for use in public management and can therefore be considered in combination.

In terms of BPA, in addition to basic components such as digitally controlled data and network infrastructures, differently oriented software tools such as content management systems (CMS), customer relationship systems or enterprise resource planning systems (ERP), application programming interfaces (API) are of key importance. An API is a set of rules that allows different software programs to communicate with each other. It defines how requests for data or actions should be made, and how responses are sent back. APIs allow one program to request information or services from another program without needing to know how it works internally. The fields of application are as diverse as they are technically and procedurally far-reaching.

For example, on one hand, a government website might use APIs to provide citizens with real-time traffic updates, retrieving data from traffic monitoring systems to inform users about road conditions and potential delays. On another hand, public health departments could use APIs to access and share real-time data on disease outbreaks, pulling information from hospitals and medical centers to provide the public with up-to-date statistics and health alerts. Due to the information and transaction complexity in the interplay between humans, existing and emerging IT architectures, it can be stated that BPA generally requires a comprehensive revision or restructuring of current system architecture and process environments, both in technical and organizational terms (Wirtz, 2024a).

In contrast, RPA typically represents very selective forms of software-based automation without requiring extensive changes to entire legacy systems (van der Aalst et al., 2018). Rather, RPA approaches can be embedded in existing process structures and, for example, take over the initial processing of incoming service requests from external parties relating to various governmental institutions before responsible officials take over the further management of pre-processed interaction and work packages. Figure 4 provides an overview of application fields and corresponding robot types for public services.

When looking at potential fields of application for RPA in public management, the versatility associated with the use of AI becomes apparent once again. The fields of application range, for example and not exhaustively, from healthcare and social work, traffic management, urban planning, public communication, combat and military purposes, and public safety to environmental monitoring. In these fields, a variety of different RPA measures can be deployed.

In terms of traffic management, for example, autonomous traffic guidance systems and robots are used in (smart) cities to control traffic flow, direct vehicles and monitor road conditions. Traffic robots and related AI tools can also predict and alleviate traffic jams, provide real-time traffic information and increase overall road safety. Autonomous environmental monitoring systems and corresponding robots are in turn used by public agencies to monitor air quality, water pollution and climate change. In this context, drones or robotic sensors can collect data on environmental conditions and help inform public policy or emergency response. In the field of public safety robots assist in respective operations by providing real-time information in disaster areas, such as earthquakes or fires with the help of rescue robots and police robots are used to facilitate surveillance, e.g., at major events, or to reduce crime in cities. This area can be supported by autonomous combat and military systems, which are usually deployed in public settings where defense capabilities overlap with civilian applications. While their primary purpose is and remains military, some of these robots can also serve civilian needs, especially in situations involving public safety, disaster relief, or security (Yunus & Doore, 2021).

The number of different types of robots is vast, with numerous subcategories depending on their specific application, function, or design and as technology advances, new types of robots continue to emerge. For instance, in the field of public healthcare and social work an array of different robot types can be used to provide support, such as telepresence robots, which enable doctors or specialists to consult patients remotely, reducing waiting times and improving access to public medical care. Robots equipped with UV light or other sterilization technologies are also used in hospitals and public healthcare facilities to disinfect rooms, equipment and high-touch surfaces as well as robotic surgery assistants to perform precision surgery, improve treatment outcomes and shorten recovery times.

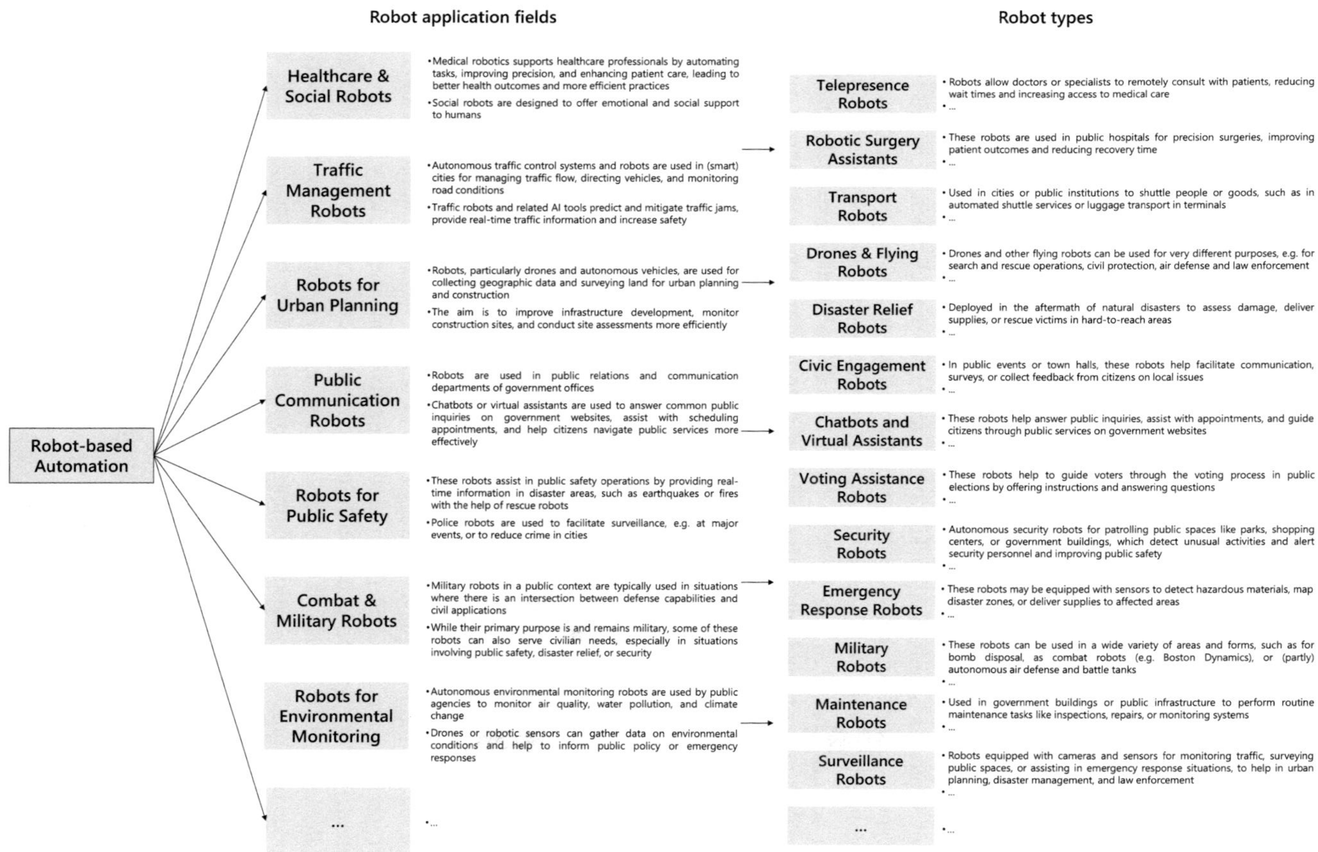

Fig. 4 Robot-based automation for public services

Comparing these deployment methods with related robot types from other areas, such as transport robots, security and surveillance robots, voting assistance robots or civic engagement robots, it becomes clear that dedicated strategies are needed to identify and successfully implement the most suitable software and robot-assisted systems for the respective agenda. In this context, strategic management in public administration will undergo significant changes as digital automation progresses. For example, new strategies focusing on the use of digital technologies and automation will emerge to improve public services and processes, which will be accompanied by a change in the way public organizations formulate and implement strategies. Traditional management models that focus on governance and policy, for example, can therefore increasingly be supplemented or modified by digitally focused approaches (Wirtz, 2024a). This applies regardless of whether DPA, BPA or RPA approaches are primarily pursued.

A key decision criterion for the selection and application of the right management strategies against the backdrop of increasing digitalization is to answer the question of what prior knowledge and capabilities are available in strategy work in connection with AI. Depending on the answer to this question, a classification can be made between five strategy types or role concepts for digital automation, namely being a partial automation adapter, automation process optimizer, automation layer player, automation leader and cross automation disruptor (Wirtz, 2024a). Figure 5 illustrates the strategy types accordingly.

The strategic approach of a partial automation adapter is the basic form in which digital automation supports the planning and implementation of operating and business models, as well as partially automating certain value creation activities. In this way, machines support human work and supplement the non-automated core business functions. Over the past two decades, this foundational strategic type, combined with the subsequent stage of strategic evolution, the automation process optimizer, has firmly established itself as a prominent strategic archetype. These two strategic approaches reflect a pattern of strategy development as organizations increasingly prioritize the automation and optimization of their processes. The automation layer player strategy type, in which (AI) automation is understood not just as one aspect, but rather as the decisive principle, is not yet widespread, although it "is expected to establish itself over the course of the current decade up to the year 2030" (Wirtz, 2024a, p. 424). The strategic concepts of an automation leader or a cross automation disruptor go even further by considering the ever-increasing opportunities arising from organizational automation and digitalization as a central maxim and striving for fully machine- or AI-automated value creation as a result. However, while helpful as a guiding framework, it may be some time before these comprehensive strategy types can be widely applied in public administration due to the early stage of AI in the organizational context and the limited opportunities for comprehensive linking.

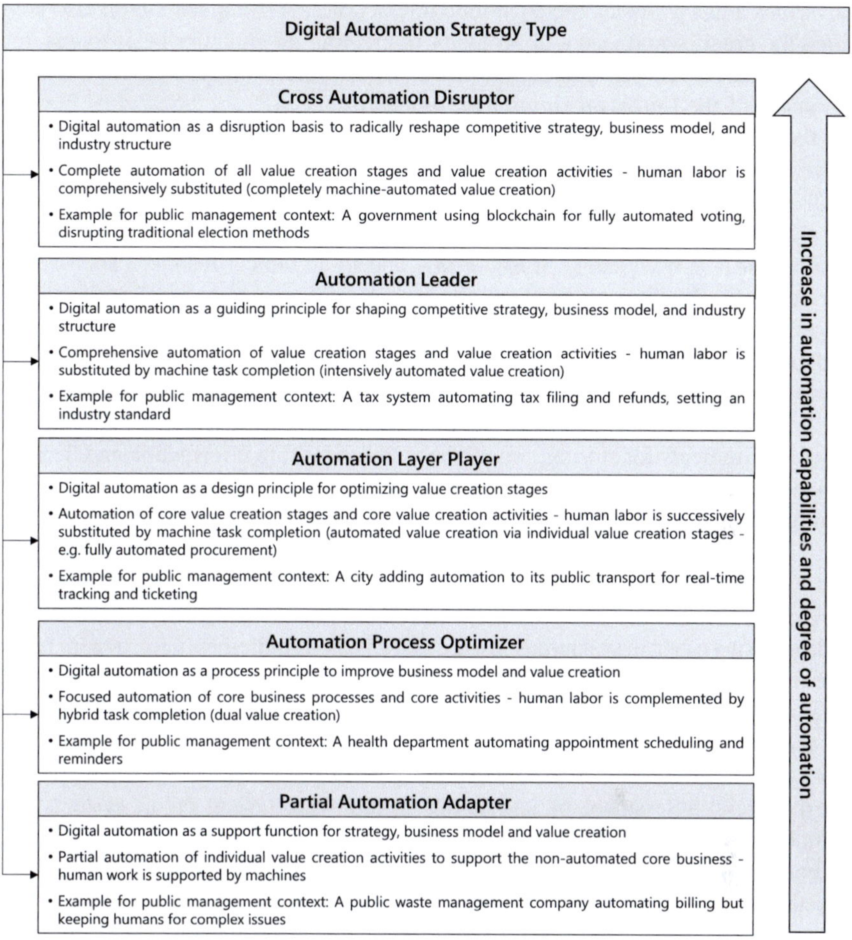

Fig. 5 Strategy types of digital automation (Wirtz, 2024a, 2024b)

5 Empirical Side View Towards AI Ethics and Regulation—EU AI Act

Sustainable efforts for risk minimization and ethically appropriate handling guidelines in terms of AI are all the more important as new fields of application are identified almost on a daily basis due to the extraordinarily comprehensive capabilities of AI (Coeckelbergh, 2020). Although still in its development phase overall, as described above, the initiatives of the European Union and its individual member states are examples of a strategic and planned implementation of AI approaches in the respective action and economic environments in the public sector. Overarching the logic of the interaction of AI and its dedicated tools as well as suitable strategies for the sustainable introduction and application of those AI approaches in various areas of social and economic interaction, the European Union also identified the great importance and necessity of creating a regulatory basis to ensure a proper balance between (AI) innovation and risk protection. As a result, the member states of the European Union have agreed on the AI Act, the world's first law for the comprehensive promotion, control and general regulation of AI (European Parliament & Council of the European Union, 2024).

The European Union's AI Act (Artificial Intelligence Regulation) has been developed over years and is designed to regulate the use of AI within the EU and ensure that it is used safely, trustworthily and in an ethical manner (Thelisson & Verma, 2024). It stipulates binding requirements with regard to transparency levels in general and documentation obligations for the long-term maintenance of these transparency levels in particular. In particular, AI-supported systems, which have a medium to high risk potential due to their sphere of influence, such as when people or large financial transactions are directly affected by decisions, are subject to strict requirements for storing, processing and forwarding information and deriving actions. Basically, the AI Act categorizes the potential risk of affected AI systems into four levels, depending on which regulation is more stringent or more moderate: (1) Minimum Risk Systems, such as AI-based games, receive little regulation and can be used largely without restrictions; (2) Little Risk Systems—organizations and publishers of AI systems that, for example, store extensive personal data and link it to other data sources must ensure basic requirements for transparency, traceability and retrievability; (3) High Risk Systems, e.g. in areas such as healthcare, transportation, police, justice or labor law are subject to strict regulations, so comprehensive requirements for transparency, security and ethical standards must be complied with; (4) Unacceptable Risk Systems, e.g. systems that are used for the social assessment of individuals by the state (social credit systems) are completely prohibited.

For a risk-minimizing and ethically sound implementation and application of AI, the Act provides fixed regulations with regard to information obligations (towards public authorities as well as users) and specifications concerning the monitoring and auditing of corresponding compliance with these obligations. For example, to ensure traceability and continuous proof of safety, providers must create comprehensive technical documentation for their AI systems, including the data sets used, the application processes and the AI development methodology. The higher the classification according to the AI risk level categorization, the more important constant monitoring is to ensure that the defined requirements are met over time. Providers must conduct regular audits to ensure that their AI systems are transparent, secure and ethically sound. To support this, the AI Act proposes the establishment of a central European authority responsible for monitoring compliance, providing support and developing best practice, which will also play a key role in the assessment of high-risk AI systems.

Given the entry into force in August 2024 and the relatively short grace periods granted, the member states of the European Union must transpose the AI Act into national law and the public administration apparatus, including its institutions and broad fields of application. Alongside the development of suitable support measures to increase AI innovation, this also includes the setting and enforcement of penalties and sanctions if actions are taken in contravention of the AI Act or the derived national regulations. In this context, it should not go unmentioned that, in addition to the state/legal perspective, there are other non-state stakeholders, for example from interest groups and business, who should also be integrated into these transfer processes (Tallberg et al., 2024). In Germany, for example, comprehensive action plans at ministry level (Federal Ministry of Education and Research, 2023) and specific initiatives at institutional level, such as the German Federal Employment Agency, have already been designed and partially implemented in order to comply with the requirements of the AI Act and at the same time strive to determine the optimal middle grounds between risk minimization and innovation promotion. However, the optimal degree of risk minimization on the one hand and an ethically correct approach to promoting innovation on the other still remains unclear and will be the subject of further efforts to expand understanding in research and practice (Laux et al., 2023).

6 Summary and Outlook

Artificial intelligence (AI) has become a major driving force for innovation in everyday life and thus also in terms of the development of public administration, with the primary aim of expanding opportunities to take organizational and public processes to a whole new level, for example in terms of the quality and efficiency of information, decision-making and work processes. This trend is widely recognized in both academic and practitioner circles, as evidenced by a growing number of collaborative research papers and initiatives looking at the role of AI in the public sector. However, while AI and public administration services have hitherto mostly been studied in isolation, a comprehensive understanding of how AI may be best used to optimize and innovate public administration remains unclear, at least in large part. As a result, one of the key challenges for public officials is identifying and integrating AI applications that can most effectively enhance the design and provision of automated public services. This study was motivated by the need to address this critical challenge and explore how AI can be strategically deployed to improve public administration services by means of software and robotic automation.

Against this background, the central components and the basic composition of AI, including its three principal stages of development, were first examined in general terms (see Fig. 1), before the extent to which AI analytics approaches differ in terms of their performance and also their increasing independence from human intervention over the course of development was shown (see Fig. 2). As an extension of this, a strategic interaction model was introduced to illustrate how human-AI interaction is structured (see Fig. 3), which factors it is influenced by and which key components come into play in such a scenario, which in turn serves as a basis for the designing of dedicated AI automation tools and the development of effective strategies. Consequently, the potential application fields of AI in a public management context were examined as well as the AI automation tools and robotization approaches that can be deployed within the respective verticals to generate innovative services (see Fig. 4). In addition, several fundamental strategic orientations regarding digital automation were presented and examined with regard to their respective basic principles and maturity levels (see Fig. 5). In order to create a better understanding of legally necessary regulations and to raise awareness of ethical requirements, a brief insight into the risk assessment of AI and the basic structure of the world's first law on the regulation of AI, issued by the European Union and its member states, was also provided. Consequently, the contents of the chapter can serve as a reference and orientation aid, be it for the initial development of suitable strategies, the identification and selection of suitable AI approaches or the transfer to specific public services.

Assistance in understanding and contextualizing AI is all the more important as the disruptive change potential associated with the application of AI in various areas of work and life is developing ever more rapidly and comprehensively over a relatively short period of time (see Fig. 6).

On the threshold of the hybrid augmentation automation phase and with regard to the subsequent phase of superior automation, in which AI will ultimately be able to act completely autonomously, it must not be overlooked: Although associated with great opportunities for value creation and prosperity, AI development is always accompanied by corresponding risks that need to be considered and calculated. Yet, it is all the more difficult to weigh up the value of opportunities and risks because "the body of knowledge on consequences of AI in terms of risks and governance implications is relatively small and fragmented, failing to provide a thorough understanding of AI risks and their specific implications for AI governance" (Wirtz et al., 2022, p. 16). Hence, this lack of understanding must be remedied in the future with the help of further research efforts and replaced by the most comprehensive possible development and provision of knowledge about the opportunities and risks of AI—in public administration and elsewhere.

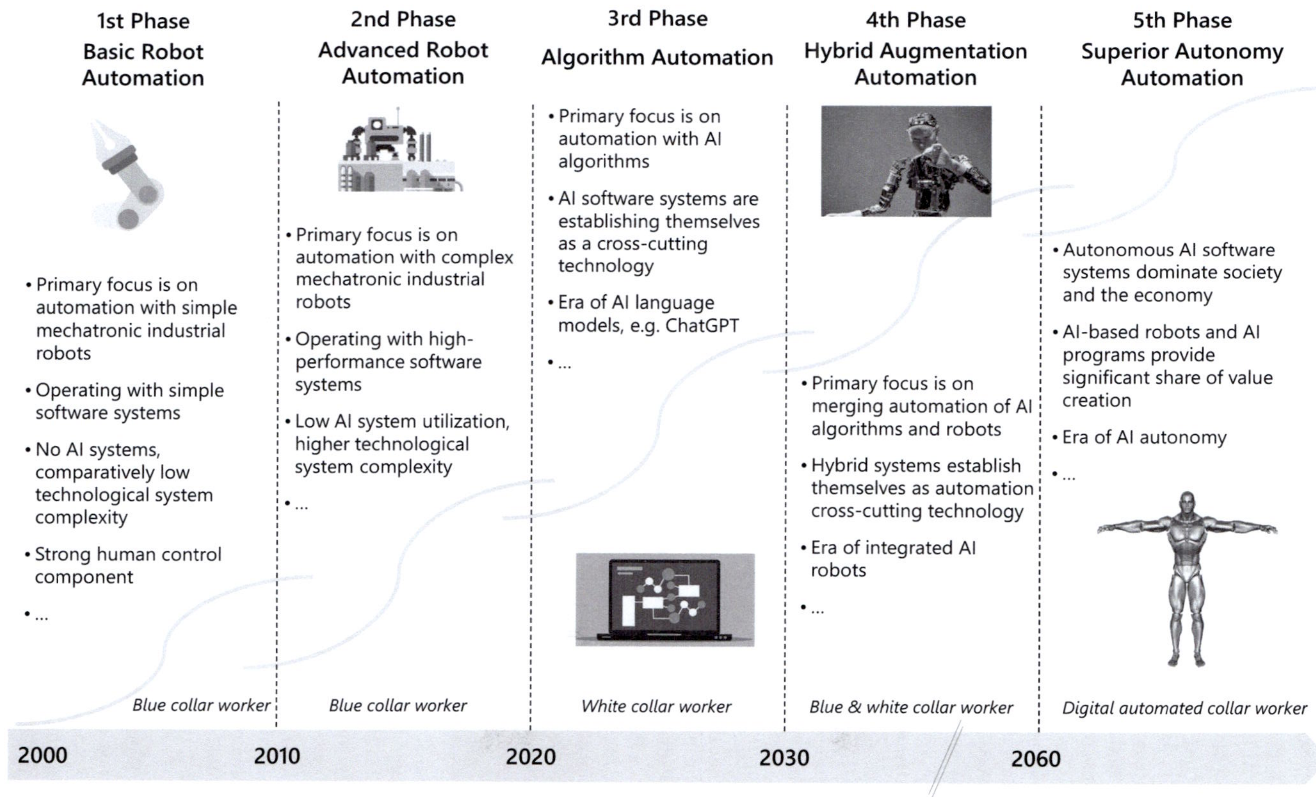

Fig. 6 5-phase model of digital automation (Wirtz, 2024a, 2024b)

References

Amershi, S., Weld, D., Vorvoreanu, M., Fourney, A., Nushi, B., Collisson, P., Suh, J., Iqbal, S., Bennett, P. N., Inkpen, K., Teevan, J., Kikin-Gil, R., & Horvitz, E. (2019). Guidelines for human-AI interaction. In *Proceedings of the 2019 CHI Conference on Human Factors in Computing Systems (CHI '19)* (pp. 1–13). Association for Computing Machinery, New York, NY, USA, Paper 3. https://doi.org/10.1145/3290605.3300233

Banerjee, S., Singh, P. K., & Bajpai, J. (2018). A comparative study on decision-making capability between human and artificial intelligence. In B. Panigrahi, M. Hoda, V. Sharma, & S. Goel (Eds.), *Nature inspired computing. Advances in intelligent systems and computing* (Vol. 652). https://doi.org/10.1007/978-981-10-6747-1_23

Batra, G., Queirolo, A., & Santhanam, N. (2018). *Artificial intelligence: The time to act is now*. McKinsey & Company. https://www.mckinsey.com/industries/advanced-electronics/our-insights/artificialintelligence-the-time-to-act-is-now

Boyd, M., & Wilson, N. (2017). Rapid developments in artificial intelligence: How might the New Zealand government respond? *Policy Quarterly, 13*(4), 36–44.

Briggs, J., & Kodnani, D. (2023). *The potentially large effects of artificial intelligence on economic growth (Global economics analyst)*. Goldman Sachs. https://www.gspublishing.com/content/research/en/reports/2023/03/27/d64e052b-0f6e-45d7-967bd7be35fabd16.html

Cascio, W. F., & Montealegre, R. (2016). How technology is changing work and organizations. *Annual Review of Organizational Psychology and Organizational Behavior, 3*(1), 349–375. https://doi.org/10.1146/annurev-orgpsych-041015-062352

Coeckelbergh, M. (2020). *AI ethics*. MIT Press.

Corley, K. G., & Gioia, D. A. (2011). Building theory about theory building: What constitutes a theoretical contribution? *Academy of Management Review, 36*(1), 12–32. https://doi.org/10.5465/amr.2009.0486

European Parliament & Council of the European Union. (2024). Regulation (EU) 2024/1689 of the European Parliament and of the Council of 13 June 2024 on Artificial Intelligence (AI Act). *Official Journal of the European Union*. https://eur-lex.europa.eu

Federal Ministry of Education and Research. (2023). *BMBF-Aktionsplan Künstliche Intelligenz—Neue Herausforderungen chancenorientiert angehen*. https://www.ki-strategie-deutschland.de/files/downloads/Aktionsplan_Kuenstliche_Intelligenz_2023.pdf

Gao, Y., & Janssen, M. (2020). Generating value from government data using AI: An exploratory study. In G. Viale Pereira, M. Janssen, H. Lee, et al. (Eds.), *Electronic government* (pp. 319–331).

Kaplan, A., & Haenlein, M. (2019). Siri, Siri, in my hand: Who's the fairest in the land? On the interpretations, illustrations, and implications of artificial intelligence. *Business Horizons, 62*(1), 15–25. https://doi.org/10.1016/j.bushor.2018.08.004

Laux, J., Wachter, S., & Mittelstadt, B. (2023). Trustworthy artificial intelligence and the European Union AI act: On the conflation of trustworthiness and acceptability of risk. *Regulation & Governance, 18*(1), 3–32. https://doi.org/10.1111/rego.12512

Madan, R., & Ashok, M. (2023). AI adoption and diffusion in public administration: A systematic literature review and future research agenda. *Government Information Quarterly, 40*(1), 1–18. https://doi.org/10.1016/j.giq.2022.101774

Nilsson, N. J. (2009). *The quest for artificial intelligence*. https://doi.org/10.1017/CBO9780511819346

Pelau, C., Dabija, D.-C., & Ene, I. (2021). What makes an AI device human-like? The role of interaction quality, empathy and perceived psychological anthropomorphic characteristics in the acceptance of artificial intelligence in the service industry. *Computers in Human Behavior, 122*. https://doi.org/10.1016/j.chb.2021.106855

Pichai, S., & Schwab, K. (2020). *An insight, an idea with Sundar Pichai*. World Economic Forum.

Pratt, M. K. (2021). *Technologien zur Prozessautomatisierung: RPA, BPA und DPA*. https://www.computerweekly.com/de/tipp/Technologien-zur-Prozessautomatisierung-RPA-BPA-und-DPA

Rizk, Y., Bhandwalder, A., Boag, S., Chakraborti, T., Isahagian, V., Khazaeni, Y., Pollock, F., & Unuvar, M. (2020). *A unified conversational assistant framework for business process automation.* https://doi.org/10.48550/arXiv.2001.03543

Russel, S., & Norvig, P. (2021). *Artificial intelligence: A modern approach* (4th ed., Global Edition). Pearson.

Sheikh, H., Prins, C., & Schrijvers, E. (2023). Artificial intelligence: Definition and background. In *Mission AI. Research for policy.* Cham. https://doi.org/10.1007/978-3-031-21448-6_2

Suri, V. K. (2022). *Functional automation and digital transformation.* Pittsburgh.

Tallberg, J., Lundgren, M., & Geith, J. (2024). AI regulation in the European Union: Examining non-state actorpreferences. *Business and Politics, 26*(2), 218–239. https://doi.org/10.1017/bap.2023.36

Thelisson, E., & Verma, H. (2024). Conformity assessment under the EU AI act general approach. *AI and Ethics, 4*, 113–121. https://doi.org/10.1007/s43681-023-00402-5

Turing, A. M. (1950). Computing machinery and intelligence. *Mind, 59*, 433–460. https://doi.org/10.1093/mind/LIX.236.433

van der Aalst, W. M. P., Bichler, M., & Heinzl, A. (2018). Robotic process automation. *Business & Information Systems Engineering, 60*(4), 269–272. https://doi.org/10.1007/s12599-018-0542-4

Venkatesh, V. (2022). Adoption and use of AI tools: A research agenda grounded in UTAUT. *Annals of Operations Research, 308*, 641–652. https://doi.org/10.1007/s10479-020-03918-9

Wirtz, B. W. (2024a). *Digital business and electronic commerce: Strategy, business models and technology* (2nd ed.). Cham.

Wirtz, B. W. (2024b). *Digital business, strategien, Geschäftsmodelle und technologien* (8th ed.). Cham.

Wirtz, B. W., & Müller, W. M. (2019). An integrated artificial intelligence framework for public management. *Public Management Review, 21*(7), 1076–1100. https://doi.org/10.1080/14719037.2018.1549268

Wirtz, B. W., Weyerer, J. C., & Geyer, C. (2018). Artificial intelligence and the public sector—Applications and challenges. *International Journal of Public Administration, 42*(7), 596–615. https://doi.org/10.1080/01900692.2018.1498103

Wirtz, B. W., Weyerer, J. C., & Kehl, I. (2022). Governance of artificial intelligence: A risk and guideline-based integrative framework. *Government Information Quarterly, 39*(4), 1–18. https://doi.org/10.1016/j.giq.2022.101685

Xu, Y.-J., Wang, Q., Wang, F., Zhang, L., Wu, Y., Dong, F., Qiu, C.-W., Liu, X., Qiu, J., Hua, K., Su, W., Xu, H., Han, Y., Cao, X., Liu, E., Fu, C., Yin, Z., Liu, M., & Zhang, J. (2021). Artificial intelligence: A powerful paradigm for scientific research. *The Innovation.* https://doi.org/10.1016/j.xinn.2021.100179

Yunus, A., & Doore, S. A. (2021). Responsible use of agile robots in public spaces. In *IEEE International Symposium on Ethics in Engineering, Science and Technology (ETHICS)* (pp. 1–5). https://doi.org/10.1109/ETHICS53270.2021.9632682

Zheng, Y., Yu, H., Cui, L., Miao, C., Leung, C., & Yang, Q. (2018). SmartHS: An AI platform for improving government service provision. In *Proceedings of the AAAI Conference on Artificial Intelligence* (Vol. 32, No. 1). https://doi.org/10.1609/aaai.v32i1.11382

AI in Government: Future Trends and Recommendations

16

Annus Azhar

1 Introduction

Artificial intelligence (AI) is no longer a futuristic concept; it is actively reshaping how governments function and interact with citizens worldwide. Driven by rapid advancements, especially in generative AI, governments increasingly turn to these technologies to boost efficiency, enhance decision-making, and foster more responsive public services (Dwivedi et al., 2021; Trajkovski, 2024). AI is redefining the relationship between citizens and the state, making governance more effective and citizen-centric than ever before. Here, effective governance implies improved efficiency in resource use, optimized processes, and enhanced policy outcomes (Ahn & Chen, 2022), while citizen-centric governance focuses on delivering public services that are more accessible, responsive, personalized, and equitable, ultimately strengthening the relationship and trust between the state and the public (Yigitcanlar et al., 2024).

However, this technological revolution brings a critical question: Will citizens trust it? As Israelsen (2017) points out, trust is the linchpin. Without public confidence in how the government applies AI, its transformative potential will be undermined. This is particularly crucial because AI systems are increasingly involved in decisions directly impacting individuals' lives, from social services to law enforcement. The inherent complexity and often opaque nature of AI systems ("black box" problem) pose a direct challenge to building this essential trust. The central tension, then, is how to leverage AI's power while ensuring it remains

A. Azhar (✉)
School of Public Affairs, Arizona State University, Phoenix, USA
e-mail: annus.azhar@asu.edu

S. K. Aikins and T. Dimitrijevska-Markoski (eds.), *Artificial Intelligence and Government*, https://doi.org/10.1007/978-3-032-12344-2_16

accountable and trustworthy in the eyes of the public. Several key trends characterize the evolution of AI in government, each carrying both opportunities and challenges:

- Hyper-personalized services: Tailoring government services and communication to individual citizen needs using AI (Saxena & Muneeb, 2024), raising questions of "filter bubbles" and equitable access.
- Predictive service delivery: Anticipating citizen needs and proactively delivering services using AI (Valle-Cruz et al., 2019), raising concerns about data privacy and algorithmic bias.
- Ethical AI Governance: Addressing central issues of fairness, transparency, and accountability in AI implementation (Sun & Medaglia, 2019), requiring careful consideration to ensure responsible use.

These trends reveal a fundamental dilemma: how to harness the benefits of increasingly sophisticated AI while mitigating the inherent ethical and societal risks. The practical implementation of AI in specific government services faces significant challenges. For instance, in healthcare, early AI deployments struggled with data quality and interoperability across departmental silos (Sun & Medaglia, 2019). In social welfare services, risk profiling algorithms have raised concerns about bias and transparency, as demonstrated by the Dutch childcare benefits scandal, where automated systems led to wrongful fraud accusations against thousands of families (Hadwick, & Lan, 2021). Law enforcement applications face similar challenges, with predictive policing tools like PredPol raising questions about potential bias in crime prediction (Lum & Isaac, 2016). These examples highlight the practical difficulties in achieving Explainable AI (XAI)—making algorithmic decision-making processes understandable to humans. XAI is crucial for addressing these challenges by providing transparency into algorithmic decision-making, allowing for the identification and correction of biases, and fostering public trust, particularly in high-stakes government applications where AI directly impacts citizens' lives and rights.

Furthermore, the globalized nature of AI intensifies these complexities. Roberts et al. (2024) emphasize that AI risks are not confined by national borders, requiring international cooperation in governance. This adds another layer of tension: balancing national innovation and autonomy with the need for global standards and collaborative governance to address shared risks associated with AI.

Looking ahead, AI will undoubtedly play an even more prominent role in government. Dosilović et al. (2018) highlight the urgent need for XAI to build trust, especially in critical sectors. Concerns about algorithmic bias and fairness (Barocas & Selbst, 2016; Bolukbasi et al., 2016) are not just technical problems but fundamental ethical and societal challenges that must be overcome. Ultimately, the future of AI in government hinges on navigating these tensions successfully.

This chapter will explore emerging trends, challenges, and critical recommendations concerning AI in government. It examines AI's predicted impact on services, organizations, governance, and democratic principles, aiming to provide a roadmap for harnessing its transformative power responsibly to serve the public good and strengthen democratic values. In essence, the chapter argues that the successful transition to an "algorithmic state" requires a holistic and ethically grounded approach that balances technological innovation with a commitment to democratic values, citizen trust, and the public good.

Designed to address these crucial elements systematically, the chapter begins by outlining the study's Methodological Framework (Sect. 2). It then proceeds to analyze the current landscape and future trajectory of the field in Sect. 3, covering emerging trends, the evolution of citizen engagement, and predictions for the state's algorithmic future. The core contribution of this work follows in Sect. 4, which details the Four-Pillar Framework for Responsible AI in Government. This comprehensive framework encompasses ethical guidelines, strategic implementation approaches, workforce preparation, and a future research agenda. The chapter concludes with final reflections in Sect. 5.

2 Methodological Framework

This study employs a comprehensive narrative literature review and thematic synthesis methodology to achieve the aims mentioned earlier. A structured search strategy was utilized to identify relevant literature across several major academic databases, including Google Scholar, Scopus, Web of Science, and JSTOR. The search focused primarily on publications between 2014 and 2024 and was limited to materials available in the English language. The search strategy employed combinations of the following keywords:

- Future AI AND government trends
- AI governance AND citizen engagement
- Future government AND AI transformation
- AI ethics AND government recommendations
- AI implementation AND government strategy
- Government workforce AND AI adaptation
- AI governance AND research priorities

Retrieved records were screened for relevance based on titles and abstracts, with full texts reviewed when necessary to determine inclusion eligibility based on their direct contribution to understanding AI's role and impact in government. The review prioritized peer-reviewed articles, significant conference proceedings, and influential governmental/organizational reports that offered conceptual insights, empirical findings, or policy-relevant recommendations. Works that were purely opinion-based without substantive grounding or clearly outside the scope of AI in government were excluded. The literature base identified through this process was further augmented by supplementary key reports and analyses identified through citation tracking and domain knowledge.

The emerging trends and predictions analyzed in Sect. 3, alongside the comprehensive recommendations presented in Sect. 4, are the direct outputs of this thematic synthesis. Specifically, the analysis derived the Four- Pillar Framework for Responsible AI in Government, which comprises Ethical Guidelines (Sect. 4.1), Strategic Approaches for Effective Implementation (Sect. 4.2), Workforce Preparation (Sect. 4.3), and Future Research Directions (Sect. 4.4). These findings represent the salient aspects derived from the rigorous analysis of literature gathered via the described search, screening, and inclusion protocol.

3 The Future of AI in Government

3.1 Emerging Trends in AI and Service Delivery: Reimagining the Public Service Paradigm

The following analysis of emerging trends and strategic imperatives is based on a thematic synthesis of the literature, as outlined in the 'Methodological Framework' section. It reflects convergent insights drawn from academic, policy, and technical sources to ensure the recommendations are grounded in both research and practice. Analysis of current literature and governmental practices suggests that the ongoing transformation in government is primarily driven by the application of core AI capabilities. These key capabilities can be categorized as: automation (e.g., robotics process automation, chatbots for routine tasks), cognition and decision-making support (including pattern recognition and prediction), and interaction (such as Natural Language Processing (NLP). According to Wirtz et al. (2021), these capabilities represent distinctive technological affordances that enable AI systems to transform public sector operations beyond mere efficiency improvements. As scholars like Dwivedi et al. (2021) argue, these technologies are not merely optimizing current processes but empowering governments to redefine their core functions and the nature of their engagement with citizens. These AI capabilities are being applied across a spectrum of government functions, which can be categorized into three main domains: (1) Internal Administrative Processes, (2) Citizen-Facing Service Delivery, and (3) Policy Implementation and Enforcement.

1. **Internal Administrative Processes**

This domain includes financial management, document processing, and resource allocation. Emerging prominently from the thematic synthesis of recent literature (e.g., Ahn & Chen, 2022; Dwivedi et al., 2021), one of the most immediate and visible trends is the rapid expansion of automated service delivery, encompassing various AI applications.

Governments can free up valuable human capital within public agencies by strategically offloading repetitive, high-volume tasks to AI. This allows human agents to focus their expertise and empathy on more complex, nuanced, and sensitive citizen needs requiring unique human skills and judgment. These AI applications range from automating internal back-office processes like financial administration and payslip management to validating applications using robotic process automation (Yigitcanlar et al., 2024). Estonia's 'KrattAI' system demonstrates this approach by facilitating the automation of numerous public services including tax declarations and pension applications (Medaglia et al., 2023), fundamentally changing the workflow of public agencies.

Automation of routine inquiries and transactions leads to significant gains in efficiency and substantial cost reductions for resource-constrained government agencies (Androutsopoulou et al., 2019; Chen & Gasco-Hernandez, 2024). However, achieving these efficiencies is often complicated by practical implementation challenges, notably the difficulty of integrating AI with entrenched legacy IT systems prevalent in many public agencies (Misra et al., 2023) and ensuring sufficient data quality and interoperability across departmental silos, issues highlighted in early AI deployments within public healthcare (Sun & Medaglia, 2019).

2. **Citizen-Facing Service Delivery**

This domain encompasses digital interfaces like chatbots and virtual assistants, and decision-support systems for benefit eligibility and service personalization. AI is transforming service delivery beyond simple automation, creating deeply customized user experiences.

'Intelligent Adaptive Forms' represent this evolution, using AI to automatically customize government interactions based on each citizen's specific profile. These systems modify their approach according to individual characteristics, including age, gender, literacy, and particular requirements (Dwivedi et al., 2021). These technologies promise 24/7 service availability, breaking down traditional time and access barriers and providing citizens unprecedented convenience in accessing government information and basic services.

This automation manifests concretely in initiatives like the California Department of Motor Vehicles' (DMV) use of NLP chatbots to manage citizen queries regarding license renewals (Ahn & Chen, 2020; Wang et al., 2023), both aiming to enhance efficiency and citizen convenience.

However, the pursuit of hyper-personalization is not without inherent risks. As Nguyen et al. (2014) highlights, personalization algorithms can inadvertently create 'filter bubbles,' potentially limiting citizens' access to a full spectrum of viewpoints or services and even reinforcing existing societal inequalities. This raises a critical ethical challenge: how can personalized government services be truly empowering and inclusive rather than inadvertently discriminatory or manipulative?

When adapting content for diverse audiences, governments must also ensure that the information's core meaning, and integrity are preserved across different presentations. Wirtz et al. (2020) caution that adapting complex government information for different literacy levels, cultural contexts, or accessibility needs must maintain factual accuracy and avoid oversimplification that could distort essential meaning or legal implications. This challenge is particularly significant in multilingual contexts or when technical information is translated into plain language formats.

3. **Policy Implementation and Enforcement**

This domain covers areas such as predictive maintenance of infrastructure, risk assessment in social services, and resource deployment optimization. Perhaps the most fundamentally transformative trend is the emergence of predictive service models. By harnessing the analytical power of AI to process vast datasets, governments are beginning to move from a reactive to a proactive service posture. As Sun and Medaglia (2019) illustrate, AI systems can analyze patterns in citizen data to anticipate future needs for specific services or benefits, ranging from unemployment support to healthcare interventions. Valle-Cruz et al. (2019) elaborate that this predictive capability enables a shift towards offering proactive assistance, delivering services and support directly to citizens before they even formally apply or request them.

Such predictive capabilities are being operationalized globally; examples include Japan's deployment of AI tools to forecast earthquakes and tsunamis, enabling timely public warnings (Ahn & Chen, 2022), while the European Space Agency uses AI to analyze satellite imagery for environmental monitoring, such as detecting deforestation and the city of Boston's application of predictive analytics to optimize snowplow deployment, reportedly yielding $5 million in annual operational savings (Yigitcanlar et al., 2023). In other contexts, Texas employs machine learning algorithms in its Medicaid program to detect potentially fraudulent claims, reportedly identifying over $200 million in suspect claims (Tangi et al., 2023).

The success of these predictive models hinges on the quality of data used, as data is the cornerstone of open government. Furthermore, the efficacy and societal acceptance of predictive systems, particularly in sensitive domains like law enforcement where the LAPD has used tools like PredPol for identifying potential crime hotspots (typically using supervised machine learning trained on historical crime data) (Lum & Isaac, 2016), remain subjects of intense debate concerning data bias, fairness, and the potential for discriminatory outcomes.

Overall, the emerging landscape of AI-driven government service delivery is characterized by a powerful triad of automation, personalization, and prediction. These trends promise to revolutionize public service, making it more efficient, accessible, and citizen-centric. However, realizing this promise responsibly requires a critical and ongoing engagement with the inherent tensions and ethical challenges they present. Navigating the path forward demands technological innovation and a parallel commitment to ethical design, robust governance, and a fundamental re-evaluation of the values and principles that should underpin the next generation of public service.

3.2 Evolution of Citizen Engagement and Communication in the AI Era: Towards Algorithmic Public Discourse

Beyond service delivery transformation, AI is positioned to radically reshape citizen engagement and communication with government. The increasing adoption of NLP technologies by public agencies signals a profound shift, a move towards potentially algorithmic forms of public discourse. These advancements promise to revolutionize citizen-government interactions, streamlining communication, offering unprecedented personalization, and expanding accessibility.

The proliferation of increasingly sophisticated NLP-powered chatbots and virtual assistants leads this evolution in government communication. According to Wirtz et al. (2019), government agencies rapidly integrate these AI-driven tools into their service infrastructure, offering immediate benefits through streamlined routine interactions. These systems handle high volumes of citizen inquiries with instant, personalized responses while providing 24/7 availability, dramatically enhancing government accessibility for citizens accustomed to on-demand digital services.

These efficiency gains, as Wirtz et al. (2019) emphasize, free human agents to focus on complex citizen needs requiring human judgment. Lewes and Eastbourne Council in the UK demonstrated this advantage by successfully redeploying full-time agents from live chat duties after implementing their 'ELLIS' chatbot. Similarly, Singapore's widely integrated 'Ask Jamie' virtual assistant has managed over 1.5 million inquiries across government websites while improving information access (Van Noordt & Misuraca, 2022).

Beyond merely streamlining one-way information flow, AI technologies have the potential to transform democratic dialogue between citizens and governments fundamentally. Recent research by Cortés-Cediela et al. (2023) examines how e-government chatbots are evolving to support information provision and active citizen participation in policy discussions. Their analysis of implementation patterns reveals technical and institutional barriers to dialogic communication. Similarly, Valle-Cruz et al. (2019) documents how NLP capabilities can systematically capture, analyze, and respond to citizen feedback at scale, creating feedback loops previously impossible due to resource constraints.

The drive for personalized responses, already evident in-service delivery, extends deeply into citizen engagement. Intelligent adaptive forms are a prime example, tailoring interactions based on individual characteristics (Janssen & van der Voort, 2016; Madan & Ashok, 2023). This personalization aims to make government communication more relevant and accessible to diverse populations, fostering greater equity, inclusivity and participation. By adapting to varying literacy levels or preferred communication styles, these AI-driven forms can lower barriers to civic engagement and ensure that a broader range of voices can be heard.

However, real-world experience reveals that fully automated interactions often struggle with complex or sensitive scenarios. This limitation has led to the development of hybrid models incorporating human oversight—a valuable lesson the

California DMV learned when addressing chatbot misinterpretations. Complementing this observation, Chen and Gasco-Hernandez (2024) found that successful AI chatbot implementations in US state governments depend on both technological sophistication and organizational readiness to respond substantively to citizen input, highlighting the importance of institutional adaptation alongside technological innovation.

The widespread adoption of these technologies also raises fundamental questions about the future of democratic dialogue and the role of human connection in the public sphere. Will algorithmic interactions, even if efficient, ultimately diminish the sense of human connection and empathy in citizen-government relations? Moreover, how can governments ensure these automated systems are truly "intelligent" and responsive to the full spectrum of human emotions and complex inquiries rather than simply providing pre-programmed responses?

Similarly, the promise of personalized engagement carries the risk of algorithmic manipulation or undue influence. If government communication becomes hyper-personalized, could it be used to subtly nudge or even manipulate citizen behavior? And how can we ensure that personalization empowers citizens with information, rather than simply tailoring messages to pre-determined profiles, potentially reinforcing echo chambers or filter bubbles even within the public sphere? Transparency and control over data used for personalization become paramount in this context.

More broadly, the rise of AI-driven citizen interaction systems signifies a transformative shift in the very nature of public discourse. These systems offer the potential for more dynamic, data-informed, and citizen-centric engagement, moving beyond traditional one-way communication channels. However, as Cortés-Cediela et al. (2023) wisely caution, maintaining a critical balance between automated assistance and essential human interaction is paramount. While AI promises efficiency and scale, the irreplaceable value of human-to-human dialogue in building trust, fostering mutual understanding, and ensuring that citizens feel genuinely heard in their interactions with government cannot be overlooked.

The trajectory of citizen-government communication is undeniably moving toward AI-augmented models. Driven by NLP and related technologies, these systems offer the potential for greater efficiency, personalization, and accessibility. However, this evolution is not without profound implications. As we move toward potentially algorithmic forms of public discourse, careful consideration must be given to preserving the human element in citizen engagement, safeguarding against manipulation, and ensuring that AI enhances rather than erodes the core principles of democratic communication, transparency, and trust. How effectively governments navigate these complex tensions will define the future of citizen engagement in the AI era.

3.3 Predictions for AI's Role in Government: Reconstituting the State in the Algorithmic Age

Looking beyond immediate service enhancements, AI integration signals a profound transformation: a potential reconstitution of the state in what might be termed the "algorithmic age." This transformation promises incremental improvements and a redefinition of government structure, function, and legitimacy in the twenty-first century.

Transformation of Service Delivery and Operations
AI is positioned to penetrate virtually every aspect of governmental activity, driving unprecedented efficiencies and reshaping internal processes. Dwivedi et al. (2021) envision AI bringing exceptional service personalization and efficiency levels, creating a future where government services are dynamically adapted and proactively delivered with previously unattainable operational agility. AI-based services can significantly improve government operations, particularly in e-government and public service delivery (Madan & Ashok, 2023). This represents a paradigm shift toward an "algorithmic state," where core governmental functions are increasingly mediated and optimized through intelligent systems.

Organizational and Workforce Evolution
As AI systems assume increasingly sophisticated roles in routine tasks, data analysis, and elements of decision-making, the public sector workforce will undergo a profound metamorphosis. Trajkovski (2024) emphasizes that successful AI adoption requires fundamental organizational reforms beyond technological upgrades, encompassing new skills development, organizational redesign, and novel governance frameworks for human-AI collaboration. The public sector will demand a workforce characterized by agility, adaptability, and deep understanding of both AI's potential and limitations. This evolution requires a strategic approach to cultivating dynamic capabilities, enabling public servants to critically evaluate, ethically guide, and effectively oversee increasingly autonomous systems. Wirtz et al. (2020) emphasize that successful AI integration demands concrete upskilling initiatives focused on data literacy, algorithmic awareness, and critical evaluation skills across all organizational levels. Yigitcanlar et al. (2024) argue that algorithmic legal literacy remains essential for navigating the dynamic regulatory landscape, while Trajkovski (2024) emphasizes the need for interdisciplinary communication given the cross-functional nature of complex AI projects.

Addressing Workforce Challenges
Recent reports highlight persistent recruitment challenges, with government departments struggling to fill specialist roles due to uncompetitive pay compared to the private sector (UK House of Commons Committee of Public Accounts, 2025). Rigley et al. (2024) identify several successful approaches to address these gaps,

including: establishing AI centers of excellence within public institutions, implementing diverse recruitment pathways such as apprenticeships, and developing public–private partnerships focused on technical and ethical training.

Job Transformation and Emerging Roles
This workforce evolution necessitates careful consideration of potential impacts on existing public sector jobs. Proactively addressing concerns about job displacement requires investing in reskilling initiatives, creating new roles leveraging human expertise in AI oversight and ethical governance, and supporting workers whose jobs may be affected by automation (Lane & Saint-Martin, 2021). New roles are emerging within the public sector, including dedicated 'AI Ethics Officers,' 'Public Algorithm Auditors' responsible for assessing bias, and specialists in 'Human-AI Teaming' (Berryhill et al., 2019).

Implications for Democratic Processes
Perhaps most significantly, AI's role extends into the heart of democratic processes and principles. Jungherr (2023) raises profound questions about how AI's inherent capacities for observation, prediction, and potential manipulation could fundamentally alter democratic governance dynamics. AI's capacity to enhance surveillance, shape information environments through personalized content, and potentially influence public opinion introduces new dimensions to challenges facing democratic societies. Concerns about transparency and accountability are paramount; slow progress in embedding transparency around algorithm-assisted decision making can jeopardize public trust, which is key to AI's successful and legitimate adoption. A 2025 UK report highlighted that few government bodies met algorithmic transparency standards, undermining public confidence. These capabilities necessitate rigorous re-examination of core democratic tenet and public values such as self-rule, equality, transparency, and accountability. Roberts et al. (2024) point to the global scale of these challenges, emphasizing that risks to democratic values transcend national borders and demand international cooperation.

The Tension: Enhancing Versus Eroding Democracy
The potential for AI to either enhance or erode democratic governance represents perhaps the most consequential tension in the algorithmic state. Recent scholarship offers contrasting perspectives on this relationship. AI-driven personalization can potentially enrich democratic discourse by making civic information more accessible to diverse citizens, potentially increasing engagement from previously marginalized communities. Complementing this view, Tangi et al. (2023) document how AI tools are enhancing participatory governance in European municipalities by identifying citizens with relevant expertise for specific policy questions and facilitating their meaningful contribution to decision-making processes. However, as Jungherr (2023) critically notes in his comprehensive framework, the same capabilities for observation, prediction, and targeting that enable personalized engagement also create unprecedented opportunities for manipulation of democratic processes. Analyzing this fundamental tension, Roberts et al.

(2024) emphasize that democratic AI governance must balance innovation with accountability through mechanisms that maintain human agency and oversight in algorithmic systems. This requires institutional designs that prioritize algorithmic transparency while ensuring that AI augments rather than replaces human deliberation in democratic processes. The fundamental question emerges: Can AI strengthen democratic participation and government responsiveness, or will its properties of data-driven optimization ultimately undermine citizen agency, erode transparency, and concentrate power in opaque systems? Navigating this tension is the defining challenge for governments embracing AI responsibly.

Monitoring and Assessment

Ensuring responsible and effective AI deployment necessitates robust mechanisms for ongoing monitoring. Yigitcanlar et al. (2024) emphasize that AI integration is not a one-time event but an evolving process requiring continuous evaluation to understand impacts, validate performance, and maintain public trust. This involves tracking key performance indicators, operational efficiencies, cost savings, and citizen satisfaction—to gauge whether AI systems meet their intended objectives. Monitoring must extend beyond technical performance to encompass ethical considerations and societal impacts, including processes for identifying potential biases post-deployment. Establishing feedback loops where input from citizens and frontline public servants informs system refinement is crucial. Systematic evaluation of pilot projects before scaling may help avoid widespread issues and ensures effective resource allocation.

The predicted role of AI in government is revolutionary. We stand at the cusp of a potential reconstitution of the state in the algorithmic age. While AI promises unprecedented efficiency and service delivery gains, it simultaneously presents profound challenges to organizational structures, workforce dynamics, and democratic governance foundations.

Successfully navigating this transformative landscape requires proactive, ethically grounded strategies. The future of government in the AI age will be defined not just by technological innovation but by our capacity to address inherent tensions, uphold democratic values, and ensure that AI enhances public values rather than diminishes just, equitable, and human-centered governance.

Before turning to the proposed ethical guidelines for AI governance, it is essential to highlight a foundational, cross-cutting consideration: the ongoing monitoring and assessment of AI systems throughout the entire policy and service delivery value chain. As discussed in earlier sections, the implementation of AI in government is not a one-time deployment but a continuous, iterative process that must be regularly evaluated in terms of technical performance, ethical and public value impact, and public perception. This imperative applies to all stakeholder groups, from frontline civil servants to end-users and broader communities, and provides a necessary accountability infrastructure that underpins each of the strategic and ethical recommendations that follow.

4 Recommendations and Guidelines

4.1 Ethical Guidelines for AI Governance: A Compass for Navigating the Algorithmic State

As AI increasingly permeates government, ethical guidelines are no longer merely aspirational, they become essential for navigating the emerging algorithmic state. Responsible AI integration into public sector decision-making requires a robust ethical foundation. Without clearly defined principles, AI's transformative potential risks being undermined by unintended harms, eroded public trust, and the potential for algorithmic governance to weaken rather than enhance societal public values. These guidelines aim to shape AI as a force for the public good proactively, ensuring alignment with fundamental democratic and public values. The following ethical guidelines are derived from the thematic synthesis described in the 'Methodological Framework' section. They reflect cross-cutting principles that emerged consistently across the literature. Through analysis of governmental reports and academic literature, several core ethical principles emerge as essential for AI governance frameworks:

Transparency and Explainability: Illuminating the Black Box
Transparency is fundamental to ethical AI governance, directly addressing the inherent opacity—the "black box" nature—of many advanced AI systems (Radanliev, 2025). In the public sector, where accountability is paramount, this algorithmic opacity is more than a technical challenge; it represents an ethical deficit. To foster trust and ensure legitimate governance, AI frameworks must prioritize both transparency and XAI techniques. Indeed, Madan and Ashok (2023) argue that interpretability is a prerequisite for stakeholders—from policymakers to citizens—to understand AI's rationale. In contrast to the often-opaque nature of machine learning systems, rule-based AI offers a different path to transparency. These systems, a subset of AI, operate on explicit 'if–then' rules defined by experts. Unlike machine learning, frequently criticized for its opacity, rule-based systems are inherently interpretable; their logic is visible and traceable to specific rules. This inherent explainability is a valuable asset for public governance (Wang et al., 2023).

However, even when employing machine learning, transparency remains crucial, particularly to address potential discriminatory or manipulative practices. Several techniques can enhance transparency. First, meticulous scrutiny of training data is essential to identify and mitigate inherent biases, recognizing that AI tools can inadvertently reinforce societal biases (Jain, 2023). Second, disparate impact testing can detect if an AI system produces significantly different outcomes across demographic groups. Third, detailed documentation of the data used and the model's logic is vital for transparency in algorithmic decision-making.

XAI techniques are key to making AI more understandable. Examples include LIME (Local Interpretable Model-agnostic Explanations), which explains individual predictions (Ribeiro et al., 2016), and SHAP (SHapley Additive exPlanations), which assigns importance values to input features (Lundberg & Lee, 2017). These techniques translate complex model behavior into human-understandable terms (Adadi & Berrada, 2018). Furthermore, operationalizing transparency requires concrete steps. For instance, governments could mandate the creation of public-facing 'explainability statements' for high-risk AI systems, detailing data sources, core logic (in simplified terms), and known limitations (Goodman & Flaxman, 2017). Internal review boards could also be established, tasked with evaluating and approving the use of specific XAI techniques based on the system's context and risk level before deployment (Leslie & Mazzarella, 2019). Developing standardized templates for Algorithmic Impact Assessments that include mandatory sections on data bias checks, fairness metric testing, and stakeholder consultation is another crucial action to embed transparency into practice (Yeung, 2018). Beyond building trust, XAI tools enable auditors and overseers to scrutinize AI logic for flaws, inappropriate proxies, or bias (Miller, 2019).

Moving beyond principles, concrete actions are essential Sweden has mandated 'explainability testing' for public service AI (Yigitcanlar et al., 2021). Proactive strategies also include bias detection tools within datasets and Algorithmic Impact Assessments before high-risk deployments, drawing from frameworks like the EU's Ethics Guidelines (Van Noordt & Misuraca, 2022).

Finally, it is important to consider the AI tasks involved. Personalized government services may employ supervised learning (e.g., eligibility decisions, trained on labeled data) and unsupervised learning (e.g., anomaly detection for fraud). A 'human-in-the-loop' approach, where AI supports but humans oversee decisions, is valuable in both scenarios to ensure accountability and mitigate bias.

Fairness and Bias Mitigation: Algorithmic Equity as a Societal Imperative
Ethical AI in government requires proactive commitment to fairness and mitigation of algorithmic bias. As Barocas and Selbst (2016) demonstrate, AI systems can inadvertently amplify existing societal biases encoded in training data. In public service, where equitable treatment is foundational, algorithmic bias directly threatens justice and social equity.

Ethical guidelines must mandate concrete measures:

- Using diverse and representative datasets
- Rigorously auditing algorithms for bias
- Conducting ongoing impact assessments to monitor discriminatory outcomes

This involves moving beyond general principles to concrete actions. Some jurisdictions, like Sweden, have mandated 'explainability testing' for public service AI models to increase transparency and accountability (Yigitcanlar et al., 2021). Proactive strategies should also include implementing bias detection tools directly within datasets before training and enforcing mandatory Algorithmic Impact Assessments prior to deploying high-risk, public-facing systems, drawing inspiration from established frameworks like the EU's Ethics Guidelines or Singapore's Model AI Governance Framework (Van Noordt & Misuraca, 2022).

Prioritizing fairness means embedding equity into the very design and deployment of AI systems, ensuring they promote equality rather than perpetuating existing inequities (Dwivedi et al., 2021). To track progress, policymakers should mandate pre-deployment and annual post-deployment bias audits for all high-risk systems, aiming for a measurable reduction in identified disparities across demographic groups over time. However, implementing robust bias audits requires significant investment in specialized tools and potentially personnel with data science expertise, or contracting with qualified external auditors (Mpofu, 2023). The imperative to mitigate bias is underscored by real-world controversies, such as the criticism directed at predictive policing tools like ShotSpotter in Chicago for potentially exacerbating racial disparities through biased targeting (Preeya, 2022). Such cases highlight the necessity for mandated algorithmic impact assessments, ongoing audits for discriminatory outcomes, and transparent governance structures involving community stakeholders.

Accountability and Responsibility: Mapping the Algorithmic Chain of Command

Robust ethical AI governance frameworks must establish clear lines of accountability for AI systems' actions and consequences. As Pasquale (2015) observes, AI systems' distributed and often opaque nature can obscure responsibility chains, making it challenging to trace decisions back to human agents or organizations. This opacity is unacceptable in government, where public trust depends on clear accountability.

Governance structures must prioritize clear allocation of responsibility for AI-driven decisions and establish effective redress mechanisms when AI systems err or cause harm. Effective redress mechanisms might include establishing dedicated algorithmic review boards or ombudsman offices, or leveraging legal frameworks like the EU's GDPR, which provides individuals with rights regarding automated decision-making, including the right to obtain human intervention and contest decisions (European Parliament and Council, 2016). Ensuring organizational accountability for the societal impacts of government AI is ethically imperative for maintaining public trust and the legitimacy of algorithmic governance (Bignami, 2022).

Human-Centric Design and Oversight: Centering Human Values in Algorithmic Governance

Ethical guidelines must ground AI development in a human-centric approach. This principle dictates that human well-being, values, and fundamental rights take priority over purely technical or efficiency-driven considerations. AI in government should augment human capabilities, enhance human flourishing, and serve humanity's broader aspirations, not supplant essential human values such as respect, dignity, and autonomy (Floridi et al., 2018).

Human rights principles should be central to AI systems' design and implementation, ensuring they respect fundamental freedoms and promote well-being (IEEE, 2017). This human-centric imperative means AI systems must prioritize safety, dignity, and autonomy of individuals, particularly vulnerable populations, while remaining subject to appropriate human oversight and ethical review (Rahwan, 2017).

A key strategy for operationalizing human oversight is adopting 'Human-in-the-Loop' (HITL) frameworks, where AI systems augment rather than replace human judgment in critical decision pathways. For example, consider implementing an AI tool for the initial screening of welfare applications. An effective HITL approach would ensure that while the AI flags potential eligibility or risks based on data patterns, a human caseworker always reviews complex cases or denials, has the authority to override the AI's suggestion with justification, and communicates the final decision directly to the applicant. Practical examples include the hybrid AI-human chatbot response model used by California's DMV for complex inquiries (Benedikt et al., 2020) and Japan's protocol of combining AI earthquake predictions with expert human verification prior to issuing public alerts (Benedikt et al., 2020). Designing effective HITL systems, however, requires careful consideration of interface design and training to mitigate risks like automation bias (humans overly trusting the AI) and ensure human reviewers retain final authority in high-stakes situations. Ensuring inclusivity might also involve specific design choices, such as Ohio adding voice-assisted applications to its AI job matching system for visually impaired users or Singapore providing multilingual chatbot services. Crucially, well-designed HITL systems maintain clear lines of responsibility by ensuring human reviewers retain final authority and accountability for decisions in sensitive situations, thereby providing a mechanism for meaningful oversight and potential redress.

Ethical AI governance in government requires a robust framework built upon these interconnected principles: transparency, fairness, accountability, and human-centric design. These guidelines are foundational pillars upon which trustworthy, responsible AI systems within government must be constructed and continuously evaluated. Navigating the algorithmic state requires not just technical expertise but a deep ethical commitment to ensuring AI serves humanity, upholds democratic values, and strengthens trust between governments and citizens.

4.2 Strategic Approaches for Effective AI Implementation: Building a Responsible Algorithmic State

While the ethical guidelines in the previous section articulate normative priorities, the strategic imperatives below translate those principles into institutional and operational pathways for implementation. Derived from the thematic synthesis described in the Methodological Framework, these imperatives are grounded in both academic research and case-based evidence. They aim to help governments navigate real-world barriers—such as regulatory gaps, procurement limitations, legacy IT systems, and workforce constraints, while drawing on comparative practices and reform models that have shown early promise. Together, these

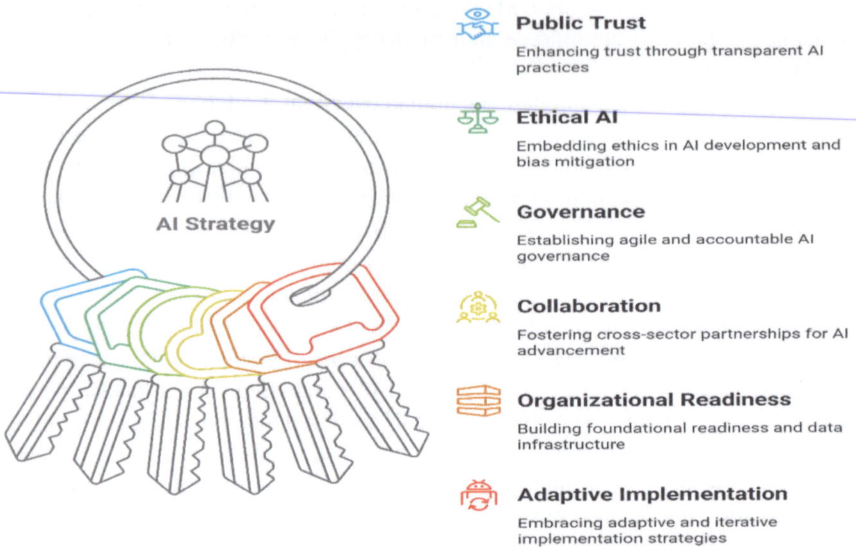

Fig. 1 Strategic approaches for effective AI implementation. *Source* Author's own illustration

imperatives offer a roadmap for building a responsive, accountable, and resilient algorithmic state.

Based on the comprehensive narrative literature review, thematic synthesis, and the groundwork laid in the preceding discussion, several indispensable strategic approaches emerge. Each address distinct but interwoven dimensions of successful and ethical AI deployment. These strategic approaches are shown in Fig. 1.

Strategic Imperative 1: Enhancing Public Trust Through XAI: Public trust is paramount in the algorithmic state, making XAI a strategic priority, not just a technical feature. XAI is a vital tool for building citizen confidence by creating demonstrably transparent, interpretable, and trustworthy AI systems (Birkstedt et al., 2023; Trajkovski, 2024). Strategic investment in XAI research, development, and implementation empowers citizens and stakeholders to understand and verify AI-driven decisions, fostering algorithmic accountability and positioning AI as a partner in government, not an opaque "black box." This focus is especially crucial in high-stakes sectors like healthcare, social services, and criminal justice. Balancing maximal explainability with AI complexity and performance is a key tension. Governments must strategically invest in XAI techniques that are both robust and meaningfully interpretable, tailoring "explainability" to specific contexts and audiences.

Strategic Imperative 2: Embedding Ethics Through Proactive AI Development and Bias Mitigation: A strategic approach necessitates proactively embedding ethics throughout AI development, moving beyond reactive review to ethical design from the outset (Birkstedt et al., 2023). This requires a multi-pronged strategy: using diverse data to combat algorithmic bias (Barocas & Selbst, 2016), integrating robust bias mitigation techniques (Bolukbasi et al., 2016), and establishing clear ethical guidelines to shape AI development in line with public values. This proactive stance is a strategic investment in inherently ethical AI, building trust and ensuring AI promotes equity (Dwivedi et al., 2021). However, ethical AI development is complex, with varying fairness definitions and value trade-offs. The challenge lies in creating technically sound ethical processes that reflect diverse public values and pluralistic ethics.

Strategic Imperative 3: Establishing Agile and Accountable AI Governance and Regulatory Frameworks: Effective AI implementation requires robust yet agile governance, moving beyond ad-hoc ethics to dynamic oversight (Birkstedt et al., 2023). Governance should structure responsible AI evolution, aligning with public values, norms, and laws, incorporating clear rules, transparent oversight (potentially external review boards). Static regulations are ill-suited to AI's rapid evolution. To achieve agility, governments can pilot 'regulatory sandboxes' for AI projects, allowing controlled testing and iteration. This structure can be enhanced by creating tiered governance requirements based on AI system risk levels (e.g., simple checklists for low-risk automation versus mandatory external audits and ethical reviews for high-risk predictive systems) (Truby et al., 2022). It must incorporate clear rules, transparent oversight mechanisms (like external review boards or dedicated bodies such as the UK's CDEI, and clear accountability. Crucially, defining clear roles and responsibilities for AI oversight—potentially establishing a Chief AI Ethics Officer or an AI Governance Council within government structures—is essential for accountability. 'Hybrid governance' blending public and private expertise can also be strategically valuable (Radu, 2021). However, a key tension lies in balancing robust governance with fostering innovation. Overly rigid frameworks risk stifling AI benefits, while insufficient governance invites unchecked risks. The challenge is to design enabling yet constraining frameworks, fostering responsible innovation with necessary safeguards. Developing such frameworks requires engaging with ongoing international efforts, such as the revised OECD AI Principles (2024), initiatives within the EU like Horizon Europe research programs, and observing diverse national strategies. For example, Japan's early 2025 policy direction indicated a preference for a lighter-touch, sector-specific regulatory approach, relying more on existing laws and voluntary industry measures alongside newly proposed legislation focused on promotion and cooperation, contrasting with the EU's comprehensive AI Act (Habuka, 2023). However, a critical gap remains: how to reconcile agile exceptions with the rigidity of traditional hierarchies. Existing tools fail to resolve the informational bottlenecks inherent in static governance. Future research must therefore investigate how oversight can be embedded directly into digital infrastructures, moving beyond temporary workarounds to achieve continuous, system-level adaptation.

Strategic Imperative 4: Cultivating Cross-Sector Collaboration and Ecosystem Partnerships: Recognizing government AI implementation is rarely solitary, strategically fostering cross-sector collaboration is crucial for building a dynamic ecosystem of responsible innovation. This involves proactive engagement with industry, academia, civil society, and international partners (Taeihagh, 2021). Such partnerships are invaluable for pooling expertise, sharing best practices, co-developing ethical standards, and ensuring technically sound and socially responsible AI. They also facilitate shared resources and accelerate innovation across government. However, challenges arise from differing cultures, conflicting priorities, and data/IP issues. The tension lies in creating equitable and mutually beneficial collaborative frameworks that effectively navigate conflicts of interest and prioritize public interests in cross-sector AI initiatives.

Strategic Imperative 5: Building Foundational Organizational Readiness and Data Infrastructure: Underpinning all AI strategy is building foundational organizational readiness and robust data infrastructure. Effective AI implementation requires transforming organizational culture, capabilities, and infrastructure, not just acquiring tools. Governments must strategically invest in fostering innovation, experimentation, and data-driven decision-making, including internal AI expertise, cross-functional teams, and continuous learning (Dwivedi et al., 2021). Simultaneously, strategic investment in data infrastructure is non-negotiable, encompassing data quality, security, ethics, and interoperable platforms (Akter et al., 2020). Organizational maturity, in human capital and data ecosystems, is prerequisite for realizing AI benefits. This readiness confronts tangible obstacles, including the technical debt associated with incompatible legacy IT systems (Misra et al., 2023), the significant financial investment required for AI acquisition and maintenance, and navigating complex, often slow public procurement processes unsuited for rapid technological iteration. Furthermore, the lack of adequate technical infrastructure, particularly high-performance computing resources or reliable internet access in some regions, can pose a fundamental barrier, while shortages of AI-literate staff within public agencies can directly hinder implementation, as initially experienced with Estonia's KrattAI initiative (Androniceanu & Colesca, 2025). Therefore, building this foundation is resource-intensive and long-term. The tension lies in balancing immediate AI adoption pressures with crucial long-term investments, ensuring sustainable implementation built on a solid organizational base, not rushed deployments.

Strategic Imperative 6: Embracing Adaptive and Iterative Implementation Strategies: In the rapidly evolving AI landscape, adaptive and iterative implementation is strategically essential. Rigid, static plans are ill-suited to AI's dynamism and evolving ethical challenges. Therefore, embrace adaptive governance, enabling continuous learning and strategy iteration in response to new technologies, risks, and societal expectations (Taeihagh, 2021). A core component of this is the systematic monitoring and assessment of deployed AI systems, focusing not only on technical performance but also on their actual impact and how they are perceived by citizens and government employees across the service delivery chain (Birkstedt et al., 2023; Wirtz et al., 2019). This requires ongoing stakeholder engagement, continuous impact monitoring, and iterative policy updates, ensuring agile and responsive AI initiatives (Radu, 2021). However, adaptive implementation presents accountability and predictability challenges. The tension lies in designing agile yet accountable frameworks, balancing necessary flexibility with stability and clear responsibility, while consistently applying ethical principles. Resolving this tension requires moving beyond ad-hoc adjustments. Future research must examine how feedback loops can be structurally embedded within digital systems, transforming adaptive implementation from a manual administrative task into a digitally integrated capability.

Effective AI implementation in government is not merely a technological challenge, but a complex strategic endeavor that demands a holistic and deeply integrated approach. Governments can proactively navigate the complexities of AI adoption by strategically prioritizing trust-building through XAI, embedding ethics into AI development, establishing robust and agile governance, fostering cross-sector partnerships, building organizational readiness, and embracing adaptive implementation. Implementation strategies should not only focus on technical feasibility but also on AI's social and ethical implications, ensuring that these technologies are deployed responsibly and beneficially (Wirtz et al., 2019). These six strategic imperatives, taken together, provide a roadmap for building a responsible algorithmic state—one that harnesses the transformative power of AI for public benefit while upholding fundamental ethical principles, fostering citizen trust, and strengthening the foundations of democratic governance in the twenty-first century.

4.3 Preparing the Workforce for an AI-Enhanced Public Sector: Investing in Human Capital for Algorithmic Governance

Beyond technological infrastructure and ethical frameworks, strategic workforce preparation is the linchpin of successful AI integration in building a responsible algorithmic state. Equipping public servants to use, evaluate, guide, and oversee AI is paramount, requiring multifaceted, future-oriented development for all roles to ensure human expertise remains central. This necessitates focusing on two overarching themes: building technical foundations for the algorithmic public sector and cultivating responsible algorithmic governance and adaptability.

A core aspect of workforce preparation involves building strong technical foundations. This begins with developing deep technical expertise in AI within the public sector itself, crucial for long-term autonomy and the ability to innovate and oversee AI effectively. While partnerships are valuable, internal capacity in areas like machine learning and data engineering must be strategically cultivated. Simultaneously, it's vital to broaden foundational algorithmic literacy across all public service roles. This multi-faceted effort encompasses STEM literacy, ensuring universal understanding of essential concepts (Rigley et al., 2024); core data skills, equipping all employees with data proficiency (Rigley et al., 2024); and inclusive algorithmic readiness, creating broad programs to reach all segments and citizens (Rigley et al., 2024). This approach promotes a broad understanding of

AI concepts and capabilities across all public service roles, not just those directly involved in AI development or implementation (Boyd & Wilson, 2017).

Beyond foundational technical skills, successful workforce preparation must prioritize cultivating essential competencies for responsible algorithmic governance and adaptability. This requires explicitly recognizing the need for a dual approach: developing broad AI literacy across the entire public sector workforce while simultaneously building deep specialized skills in key areas. Simply understanding basic AI concepts is insufficient; governments require personnel proficient in AI ethics auditing, legal expertise specific to AI regulation, human-AI interaction design, robust data governance practices, and effective change management capabilities to responsibly navigate the complexities of AI deployment (UK parliament, 2025).

However, acquiring and retaining such talent presents significant hurdles. Recent reports highlight persistent recruitment and retention difficulties, with government departments struggling to fill specialist roles (e.g., a 2025 UK report indicated 70% of departments faced such challenges), often due to uncompetitive pay compared to the private sector and needing more technical roles within digital professions. Addressing these gaps requires concrete strategies. Investing in targeted training programs for civil servants is crucial, as demonstrated by Estonia's response to initial AI implementation setbacks caused by staff proficiency issues. Other effective strategies include establishing AI centers of excellence within public institutions to centralize expertise and resources, utilizing diverse recruitment pathways such as apprenticeships and specialized fast streams, and fostering public–private partnerships specifically focused on delivering technical and ethical training. Furthermore, building internal AI expertise, particularly attracting and retaining specialists, may face challenges competing with private sector salaries and require creative recruitment strategies like dedicated fellowship programs or specialized public-sector pay scales for high-demand tech roles (UK parliament, 2025).

Furthermore, cultivating algorithmic legal literacy remains essential for navigating AI's dynamic legal landscape (Dosilović et al., 2018), enhancing interdisciplinary communication and collaboration skills vital for complex AI projects. Institutionalizing continuous learning and building dynamic capabilities (Dwivedi et al., 2021; Trajkovski, 2024) will ensure the public sector remains agile and adaptable in rapid AI evolution. These combined governance, adaptability, and specialist competencies ensure that AI is deployed responsibly, ethically, and effectively in alignment with public values.

4.4 Future Research Directions for Advancing AI in Government: A Research Agenda for Responsible Algorithmic Innovation

To fully realize the transformative potential of AI in government, while proactively mitigating its inherent risks and navigating its complex ethical dimensions,

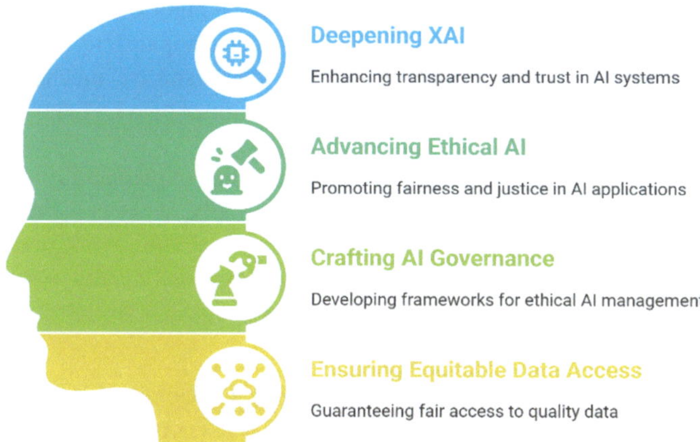

Fig. 2 Future research directions for advancing AI in government. *Source* Author's own illustration

concerted and strategically focused research efforts are not merely beneficial, but absolutely essential. Addressing critical gaps in our current understanding and expanding our practical capabilities in responsible AI deployment is not just an academic exercise; it is a foundational prerequisite for building a trustworthy and effective algorithmic state. Advancing AI for genuine public good necessitates a robust and forward-looking research agenda, squarely focused on three interconnected pillars: enhancing algorithmic effectiveness *and* accountability, deeply embedding ethical principles into AI systems and governance frameworks, and ensuring equitable access to the resources and expertise needed to drive responsible AI innovation across the public sector. Based on the comprehensive narrative literature review, thematic synthesis, and the groundwork laid in the preceding discussion, several key research priorities stand out as particularly crucial for charting a course for truly responsible algorithmic innovation in the government. These research priorities are shown in Fig. 2.

Research Imperative 1: Deepening XAI for Public Trust and Accountability: The opacity ("black box" nature) of many advanced AI systems is a fundamental barrier to public trust and accountability in algorithmic governance, as highlighted by Dosilović et al. (2018) and Pasquale (2015). Therefore, accelerating the development and refinement of XAI models and methodologies is a strategically important research imperative, especially for high-stakes public sector applications like healthcare, criminal justice, and social welfare.

Future research must prioritize enhancing the interpretability of AI decisions. This includes inventing novel XAI methodologies (moving beyond post-hoc explanations), developing standardized frameworks to evaluate the effectiveness of explanations in governmental contexts, and creating practical guidelines for deploying XAI techniques. The ultimate goal is to enable stakeholders, policymakers, oversight bodies, and citizens, to understand how AI systems reach outcomes, foster trust, ensure accountability, and mitigate opaque algorithms' risks (Dosilović et al., 2018). Yet, technical explainability alone cannot cure opacity. To fully pierce the 'black box,' research must also define the administrative mechanics of legibility, the specific instruments required to render distributed systems visible to continuous oversight.

However, this research faces tensions. Maximizing explainability might compromise predictive accuracy or efficiency. Additionally, what constitutes a satisfactory explanation varies by stakeholder and context. Future work must navigate these trade-offs, developing XAI techniques that are technically robust, practically meaningful, and strike a context-sensitive balance between explainability, accuracy, and efficiency.

Research Imperative 2: Advancing Ethical and Fair AI Deployment: From Bias Mitigation to Algorithmic Justice: Strategically critical research must advance ethical and fair AI, progressing from bias mitigation to proactive algorithmic justice. AI systems can perpetuate societal biases (Barocas & Selbst, 2016), posing a social justice threat. Future research must prioritize proactive bias detection, mitigation, and crucially, prevention methods. This ethically driven research agenda should develop novel detection, evaluate mitigation techniques, and explore justice-focused ethical frameworks (Dosilović et al., 2018). This is about justice-centered design (Roberts et al., 2024), not just technical correction. However, algorithmic justice is complex. Fairness is contested and context-dependent. Achieving equity needs both technical solutions and understanding of social/historical bias roots. Research must address fairness concepts, translate ethics into algorithms, and foster comparative and interdisciplinary dialogue.

Research Imperative 3: Crafting Agile and Ethical AI Governance and Policy Frameworks: Responsible AI advancement in government critically depends on effective, agile, and ethical governance frameworks, not just technology or ethics alone. Static regulation is insufficient given rapid AI evolution. Future research must prioritize comprehensive *yet adaptive* frameworks ensuring transparency, accountability, and oversight (Scherer, 2016). Key research areas include designing external oversight mechanisms, balancing innovation with regulatory guardrails, and defining public/private roles in AI governance (Cihon et al., 2020; Radu, 2021). Crucially, research must explore adaptive models that dynamically evolve. Crafting such frameworks is complex, facing tensions between innovation and control, effective oversight versus bureaucracy, and the need for international harmonization. Future research must address these tensions, seeking robust, ethical, and adaptable governance that fosters responsible AI innovation.

Research Imperative 4: Ensuring Equitable Access to High-Quality and Representative Data: From Data Scarcity to Data Justice: Ensuring equitable access to high-quality, representative data is a foundational research imperative for fair and effective government AI, crucial for advancing "data justice." AI's effectiveness and fairness depend directly on data quality and representativeness, as data is not neutral and shapes AI outcomes (Dwivedi et al., 2021). Future research must strategically prioritize innovative, ethical strategies to improve data access for public sector AI, while rigorously addressing privacy and security. This includes exploring responsible data sharing, data augmentation, and privacy-preserving AI techniques. This imperative is not just about technical data access but advancing data justice, ensuring equitable AI benefits for all (Dwivedi et al., 2021). However, achieving data justice presents ethical, logistical, and political challenges. Balancing data sharing with privacy, defining "representative" data, and building citizen trust in data use are key tensions for future research.

Responsible algorithmic innovation in government requires a strategic, ethical research agenda addressing interconnected imperatives: advancing XAI to ensure accountability; promoting ethical AI deployment beyond bias mitigation; developing agile governance frameworks; ensuring equitable data access; and preventing AI from widening existing inequalities. These research priorities are about shaping algorithmic governance's future, building transparency, fairness, accountability, and data justice while enabling collaborative navigation of AI complexities. The trajectory of governmental AI will be determined by today's research agenda, ensuring algorithms advance progress, equity, and public trust (Dwivedi et al., 2021; Jungherr, 2023; Trajkovski, 2024).

5 Conclusion

In conclusion, as explored throughout this chapter, the integration of AI in government represents not merely a technological upgrade but a paradigmatic shift, one that redefines governance, transforms public service delivery, and reshapes the relationship between citizens and the state. The algorithmic state is no longer a speculative construct but an emergent reality, powered by AI's growing capacity to automate, personalize, predict, and augment core governmental functions (Dwivedi et al., 2021; Trajkovski, 2024).

Yet, this transformative potential is inseparable from a host of ethical, institutional, and societal risks that must be addressed with equal urgency. To meet this challenge, this chapter advances the Four-Pillar Framework for Responsible AI in Government, a holistic model that integrates ethical, strategic, workforce, and research imperatives into a coherent structure for governance innovation. This framework explicitly provides future direction and guidelines, structured around AI in government: First, robust ethical guidelines (Sect. 10.1) serve as a normative compass to guide decision-making under uncertainty. Second, six interlocking Strategic Imperatives (Sect. 10.2) offer a roadmap for implementation: fostering public trust through XAI, embedding ethics throughout the lifecycle, constructing agile and anticipatory governance frameworks, cultivating cross-sector partnerships, building organizational readiness, and adopting adaptive, iterative deployment strategies. Third, responsible AI adoption requires sustained investment in public sector capacity and workforce development (Sect. 10.3), encompassing both broad algorithmic literacy and specialized technical expertise. Finally, a forward-looking research agenda (Sect. 10.4), organized around four

Research Imperatives—advancing explainability, promoting algorithmic fairness and justice, enabling adaptive regulation, and ensuring equitable data access, must inform and support policy design.

This chapter also contributes to bridging fragmented discourses across AI ethics, algorithmic governance, and public administration by providing an actionable framework tailored to the unique institutional realities of government. While prior research has addressed these dimensions in isolation, the Four-Pillar Framework emphasizes their interdependence and provides a structure for policy alignment and organizational readiness.

At the heart of this framework is the imperative to build and sustain public trust in algorithmic governance. Trust is the essential currency of legitimacy in the algorithmic state. This trust cannot be retrofitted, it must be designed from the outset, through commitments to transparency, accountability, fairness, and human-centered design. These values are not optional, they are foundational to democratic legitimacy and sustained public confidence.

Looking ahead, the success of AI in government will not be measured solely by gains in efficiency or technological sophistication. Rather, it will be defined by its contribution to a more just, transparent, equitable, accountable, and human-centered public sector. Building a responsible algorithmic state is not a technological inevitability, it is a governance choice. The Four-Pillar Framework presented in this chapter offers a roadmap for making that choice wisely and ethically.

References

Adadi, A., & Berrada, M. (2018). Peeking inside the black-box: A survey on explainable artificial intelligence (XAI). *IEEE Access, 6*, 52138–52160. https://doi.org/10.1109/ACCESS.2018.2870052

Ahn, M. J., & Chen, Y. C. (2020). Artificial intelligence in government: potentials, challenges, and the future. In *Proceedings of the 21st International Conference on Digital Government Research* (dg.o 2020) (pp. 243–252). https://doi.org/10.1145/3396956.3396967

Ahn, M. J., & Chen, Y. C. (2022). Digital transformation toward AI-augmented public administration: The perception of government employees and the willingness to use AI in government. *Government Information Quarterly, 39*(2), Article 101664.

Akter, S., Michael, K., Uddin, M. R., McCarthy, G., & Rahman, M. (2020). Transforming business with digital innovations: The application of AI, blockchain, cloud, and data analytics. *Annals of Operations Research, 308*(1–2), 7–39. https://doi.org/10.1007/s10479-020-03620-w

Androutsopoulou, A., Karacapilidis, N., Loukis, E., & Charalabidis, Y. (2019). Transforming the communication between citizens and government through AI-guided chatbots. *Government Information Quarterly, 36*(2), 358–367.

Barocas, S., & Selbst, A. D. (2016). Big data's disparate impact. *California Law Review, 104*(3), 671–732.

Bignami, F. (2022). Artificial intelligence accountability in public administration. *The American Journal of Comparative Law, 70*(Suppl 1), i312–i346. https://doi.org/10.1093/ajcl/avac012

Benedikt, L., Joshi, C., Nolan, L., Henstra-Hill, R., Shaw, L., & Hook, S. (2020). Human-in-the-loop AI in government: A case study. In *Proceedings of the 25th International Conference on Intelligent User Interfaces* (IUI 2020) (pp. 488–497). https://doi.org/10.1145/3377325.3377489

Birkstedt, T., Minkkinen, M., Tandon, A., & Mäntymäki, M. (2023). AI governance: Themes, knowledge gaps and future agendas. *Internet Research, 33*(7), 133–167.
Bolukbasi, T., Chang, K. W., Zou, J. Y., Saligrama, V., & Kalai, A. T. (2016). Man is to computer programmer as woman is to homemaker? Debiasing word embeddings. *Advances in Neural Information Processing Systems, 29*, 4349–4357.
Boyd, M., & Wilson, N. (2017). Rapid developments in artificial intelligence: How might the New Zealand government respond? *Policy Quarterly, 13*(4). https://doi.org/10.26686/pq.v13i4.4619
Berryhill, J., Heang, K. K., Clogher, R., & McBride, K. (2019). Hello, world: Artificial intelligence and its use in the public sector. *OECD Working Papers on Public Governance, 36*, 1–184.
Chen, T., & Gasco-Hernandez, M. (2024). Uncovering the results of AI chatbot use in the public sector: Evidence from US state governments. *Public Performance & Management Review.* https://doi.org/10.1080/15309576.2024.2389864
Cihon, P., Maas, M. M., & Kemp, L. (2020). Fragmentation and the future: Investigating architectures for international AI governance. *Global Policy, 11*(5), 545–556. https://doi.org/10.1111/1758-5899.12890
Cortés-Cediela, M. E., Pardo-Bosch, A., Velasco-Montero, C., & Piattini, M. (2023). Trends and challenges of e-government chatbots: Exploratory research on their application to open government data and citizen participation content. *Government Information Quarterly, 40*(4), Article 101877.
Dosilović, F. K., Brčić, M., & Hlupić, N. (2018). Explainable artificial intelligence: A survey. In *MIPRO 2018 Proceedings* (pp. 210–215).
Dwivedi, Y. K., Hughes, L., Coombs, C., Constantiou, I., Duan, Y., Edwards, J. S., & Wamba, S. F. (2021). Artificial intelligence (AI): Multidisciplinary perspectives on emerging challenges, opportunities, and agendas for research, practice, and policy. *International Journal of Information Management, 57*, Article 101994.
European Parliament and Council of the European Union (2016) Regulation (EU) 2016/679… General Data Protection Regulation. *Official Journal of the European Union* L 119/1.
Floridi, L., Cowls, J., Beltramelli, A., Balkin, J. M., Goebelbecker, C. J., Herrmann, M., et al. (2018). AI4People—An ethical framework for a good AI society: Opportunities, challenges, and recommendations. *Minds and Machines, 28*, 689–707.
Goodman, B., & Flaxman, S. (2017). European Union regulations on algorithmic decision-making and a "right to explanation." *AI and Society, 32*(3), 611–627.
Habuka, H. (2023). Japan's approach to AI regulation and its impact on the 2023 G7 presidency. *Center for Strategic & International Studies Report.*
Hadwick, D., & Lan, S. (2021). Lessons to be learned from the dutch childcare allowance scandal: A comparative review of algorithmic governance by tax administrations in the Netherlands, France and Germany. *World Tax J., 609.*
IEEE Global Initiative on Ethics of Autonomous and Intelligent Systems. (2017). *Ethically Aligned Design: A Vision for Prioritizing Human Well-being with Autonomous and Intelligent Systems*, Version 2. IEEE.
Israelsen, B. W. (2017). "I can assure you... that it's going to be all right"—A definition, case for, and survey of algorithmic assurances in human-autonomy trust relationships. *arXiv* 1708.00495.
Jain, L. R. (2023). A comprehensive study of algorithmic bias: Fairness in AI, ethical and social implications in real-world applications. PhD thesis, *University of Alabama in Huntsville.*
Janssen, M., & van der Voort, H. (2016). Adaptive governance: Towards a stable, accountable and responsive government. *Government Information Quarterly, 33*(1), 1–5.
Jungherr, A. (2023). Artificial intelligence and democracy: A conceptual framework. *Social Media + Society, 9*(3), 20563051231186353.
Lane, M., & Saint-Martin, A. (2021). The impact of artificial intelligence on the labour market: What do we know so far? *OECD Social, Employment and Migration Working Papers,* 256. https://doi.org/10.1787/7c895724-en

Leslie, D., & Mazzarella, E. (Eds.). (2019). *Understanding Artificial Intelligence Ethics and Safety: A Guide for the Responsible Design and Implementation of AI Systems in the Public Sector*. The Alan Turing Institute.

Lundberg, S. M., & Lee, S. I. (2017). A unified approach to interpreting model predictions. *Advances in Neural Information Processing Systems, 30*, 4765–4774.

Lum, K., & Isaac, W. (2016). To predict and serve?. *Significance, 13*Significance, 13(5), 14–19.

Medaglia, R., Gil-Garcia, J. R., & Pardo, T. A. (2023). Artificial intelligence in government: Taking stock and moving forward. *Social Science Computer Review, 41*(1), 123–140.

Miller, T. (2019). Explanation in artificial intelligence: Insights from the social sciences. *Artificial Intelligence, 267*, 1–38.

Misra, S. K., Sharma, S. K., Gupta, S., & Das, S. (2023). A framework to overcome challenges to the adoption of artificial intelligence in Indian government organizations. *Technological Forecasting and Social Change, 194*, Article 122721.

Mpofu, F. Y. (2023). The application of artificial intelligence in external auditing and its implications on audit quality: A review of the ongoing debates. *International Journal of Research in Business and Social Science, 12*(9), 496–512. https://doi.org/10.20525/ijrbs.v12i9.2737

Nguyen, T. T., Hui, P. M., Harper, F. M., Terveen, L., & Konstan, J. A. (2014, April). Exploring the filter bubble: the effect of using recommender systems on content diversity. In *Proceedings of the 23rd International Conference on World Wide Web* (pp. 677–686).

OECD. (2024). OECD AI Principles. https://www.oecd.org/en/topics/ai-principles.htm

Pasquale, F. (2015). *The black box society: The secret algorithms that control money and information*. Harvard University Press.

Preeya, P. (2022). *The costs of technology: An analysis of the community concerns about the use of shotspotter in Chicago*.

Radu, R. (2021). Steering the governance of artificial intelligence: National strategies in perspective. *Policy and Society, 40*(2), 178–193.

Rahwan, I. (2017). Society-in-the-loop: Programming the algorithmic social contract. *Ethics and Information Technology, 20*(1), 5–14. https://doi.org/10.1007/s10676-017-9430-8

Ribeiro, M. T., Singh, S., & Guestrin, C. (2016). Why should I trust you? Explaining the predictions of any classifier. In: *Proceedings of the 22nd ACM SIGKDD International Conference on Knowledge Discovery and Data Mining*. https://doi.org/10.1145/2939672.2939778

Rigley, E., Bentley, C., Krook, J., & Ramchurn, S. D. (2024). Evaluating international AI skills policy: A systematic review of AI skills policy in seven countries. *Global Policy, 15*(1), 204–217.

Roberts, H., Hine, E., Taddeo, M., & Floridi, L. (2024). Global AI governance: Barriers and pathways forward. *International Affairs, 100*(3), 1275–1286.

Saxena, A., & Muneeb, S. M. (2024) Transforming financial services through hyper-personalization: The role of artificial intelligence and data analytics in enhancing customer experience. In J. Truby et al. (eds.). *AI-driven decentralized finance and the future of finance* (pp. 19–47). IGI Global.

Scherer, M. U. (2016). Regulating artificial intelligence systems: Risks, challenges, competencies, and strategies. *Harvard Journal of Law & Technology, 29*(2), 353–400.

Sun, T. Q., & Medaglia, R. (2019). Mapping the challenges of artificial intelligence in the public sector: Evidence from public healthcare. *Government Information Quarterly, 36*(2), 368–383.

Taeihagh, A. (2021). Governance of artificial intelligence. *Policy and Society, 40*(2), 137–157.

Tangi, L., van Noordt, C., & Rodriguez Müller, A. P. (2023). The challenges of AI implementation in the public sector. An in-depth case studies analysis. In *Proceedings of the 24th Annual International Conference on Digital Government Research* (pp. 414–422).

Trajkovski, G. (2024). Bridging the public administration–AI divide: A skills perspective. *Public Administration and Development, 44*(5), 412–426.

Truby, J., Brown, R. D., Ibrahim, I. A., & Parellada, O. C. (2022). A sandbox approach to regulating high-risk artificial intelligence applications. *European Journal of Risk Regulation, 13*(2), 270–294.

UK Parliament, House of Commons Committee of Public Accounts. (2025). Use of AI in government. 18th Report of Session 2024–25, HC 356. *Parliamentary Papers.*

Van Noordt, C., & Misuraca, G. (2022). Artificial intelligence for the public sector: Results of landscaping the use of AI in government across the European Union. *Government Information Quarterly, 39*(3), Article 101714.

Valle-Cruz, D., Ruvalcaba-Gomez, E. A., Sandoval-Almazan, R., & Criado, J. I. (2019) A review of artificial intelligence in government and its potential from a public policy perspective. In: *Proceedings of the 20th Annual International Conference on Digital Government Research* (pp. 91–99).

Wang, G., Guo, Y., Zhang, W., Xie, S., & Chen, Q. (2023). What type of algorithm is perceived as fairer and more acceptable? A comparative analysis of rule-driven versus data-driven algorithmic decision-making in public affairs. *Government Information Quarterly, 40*(2), Article 101803.

Wirtz, B. W., Weyerer, J. C., & Geyer, C. (2019). Artificial intelligence and the public sector—Applications and challenges. *International Journal of Public Administration, 42*(7), 596–615.

Wirtz, B. W., Langer, P. F., & Fenner, C. (2021). Artificial intelligence in the public sector-a research agenda. *International Journal of Public Administration, 44*(13), 1103–1128.

Yeung, K. (2018). 'Algorithmic impact assessments': Towards accountable automation in public sector decision-making. *Information, Communication & Society, 21*(11), 1550–1566.

Yigitcanlar, T., Agdas, D., & Degirmenci, K. (2023). Artificial intelligence in local governments: Perceptions of city managers on prospects, constraints and choices. *AI & Society, 38*, 1135–1150.

Yigitcanlar, T., Senadheera, S., Marasinghe, R., Bibri, S. E., Sanchez, T., Cugurullo, F., & Sieber, R. (2024). Artificial intelligence and the local government: A five-decade scientometric analysis on the evolution, state-of-the-art, and emerging trends. *Cities, 152*, Article 105151.

MIX
Papier aus verantwortungsvollen Quellen
Paper from responsible sources
FSC® C105338

If you have any concerns about our products,
you can contact us on
ProductSafety@springernature.com

In case Publisher is established outside the EU,
the EU authorized representative is:
Springer Nature Customer Service Center GmbH
Europaplatz 3, 69115 Heidelberg, Germany

Printed by Libri Plureos GmbH
in Hamburg, Germany